Pr[illegible]
& the Côte d'Azur

Nicola Williams

LONELY PLANET PUBLICATIONS
Melbourne • Oakland • London • Paris

PROVENCE & THE CÔTE D'AZUR

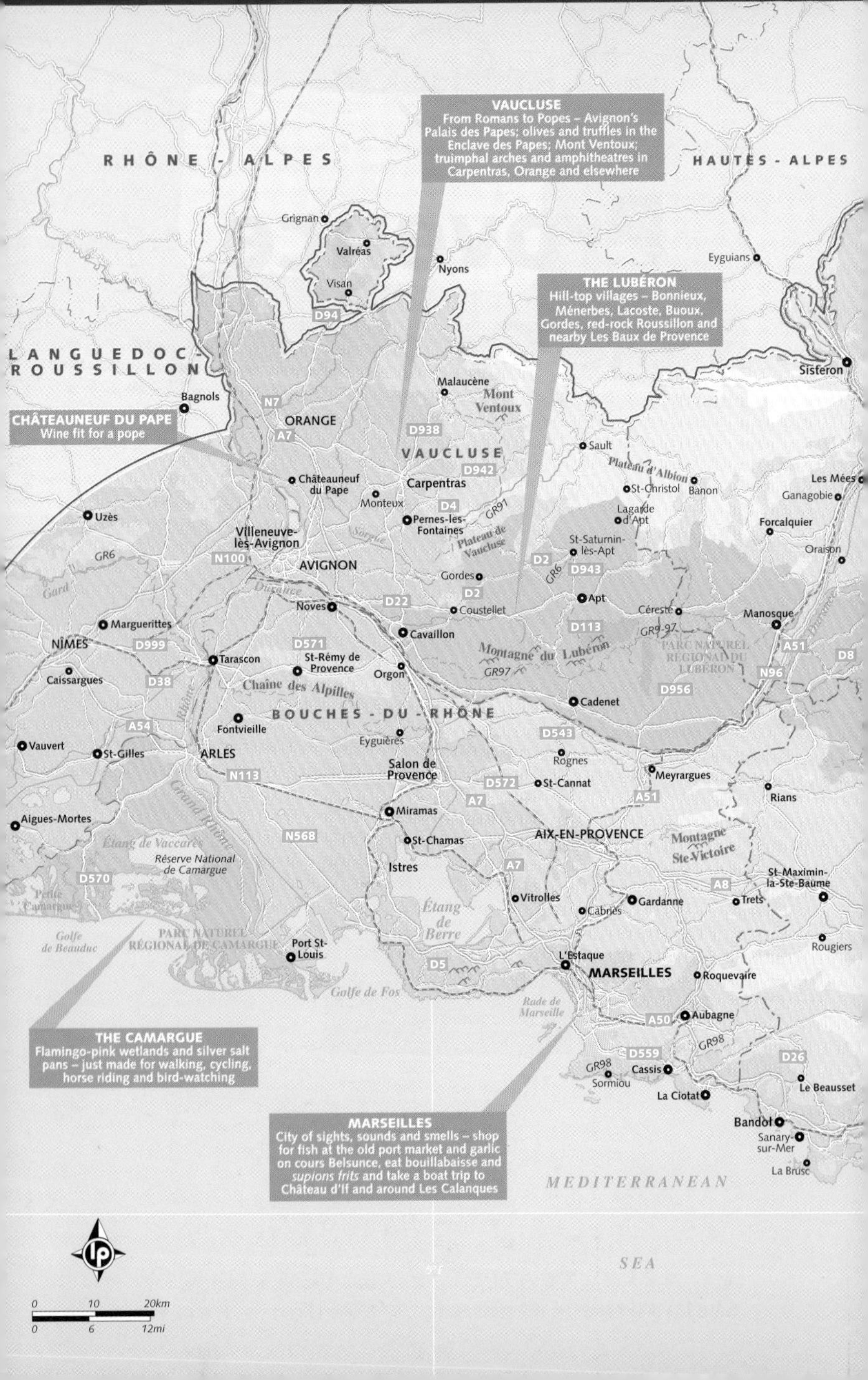

VAUCLUSE
From Romans to Popes – Avignon's Palais des Papes; olives and truffles in the Enclave des Papes; Mont Ventoux; truimphal arches and amphitheatres in Carpentras, Orange and elsewhere

THE LUBÉRON
Hill-top villages – Bonnieux, Ménerbes, Lacoste, Buoux, Gordes, red-rock Roussillon and nearby Les Baux de Provence

CHÂTEAUNEUF DU PAPE
Wine fit for a pope

THE CAMARGUE
Flamingo-pink wetlands and silver salt pans – just made for walking, cycling, horse riding and bird-watching

MARSEILLES
City of sights, sounds and smells – shop for fish at the old port market and garlic on cours Belsunce, eat bouillabaisse and *supions frits* and take a boat trip to Château d'If and around Les Calanques

RHÔNE - ALPES
HAUTES - ALPES
LANGUEDOC-ROUSSILLON
VAUCLUSE
BOUCHES - DU - RHÔNE
MEDITERRANEAN SEA

Grignan
Valréas
Visan
Nyons
Eyguians
Sisteron
D94
Malaucène
Mont Ventoux
Bagnols
N7
ORANGE
A7
D938
Sault
Plateau d'Albion
D942
St-Christol
Banon
Les Mées
Ganagobie
Châteauneuf du Pape
Carpentras
Monteux
D4
Pernes-les-Fontaines
GR91
Lagarde d'Apt
Forcalquier
Uzès
Villeneuve-lès-Avignon
Sorgue
Plateau de Vaucluse
St-Saturnin-lès-Apt
Oraison
GR6
N100
AVIGNON
D2
D943
Gard
Durance
Gordes
Apt
Noves
D22
Coustellet
Céreste
Manosque
Marguerittes
Cavaillon
D113
GR9-97
NÎMES
D999
D571
Montagne du Lubéron
Parc Naturel Régional du Lubéron
A51
D8
Tarascon
St-Rémy de Provence
Orgon
GR97
N96
Caissargues
D38
Chaîne des Alpilles
Cadenet
D956
Rhône
Fontvieille
A54
Eyguières
D543
Vauvert
St-Gilles
ARLES
Rognes
Salon de Provence
Meyrargues
N113
D572
St-Cannat
Rians
Grand Rhône
A7
A51
Aigues-Mortes
Miramas
AIX-EN-PROVENCE
N568
St-Chamas
Montagne Ste-Victoire
Étang de Vaccarès
Réserve National de Camargue
Istres
A7
St-Maximin-la-Ste-Baume
D570
A8
Petite Camargue
Vitrolles
Gardanne
Trets
Étang de Berre
Cabriès
Golfe de Beauduc
Parc Naturel Régional de Camargue
Port St-Louis
Rougiers
L'Estaque
D5
MARSEILLES
Roquevaire
Golfe de Fos
Rade de Marseille
A50
Aubagne
GR98
D559
D26
GR98
Cassis
Sormiou
Le Beausset
La Ciotat
Bandol
Sanary-sur-Mer
La Brusc

0 10 20km
0 6 12mi

PROVENCE & THE CÔTE D'AZUR

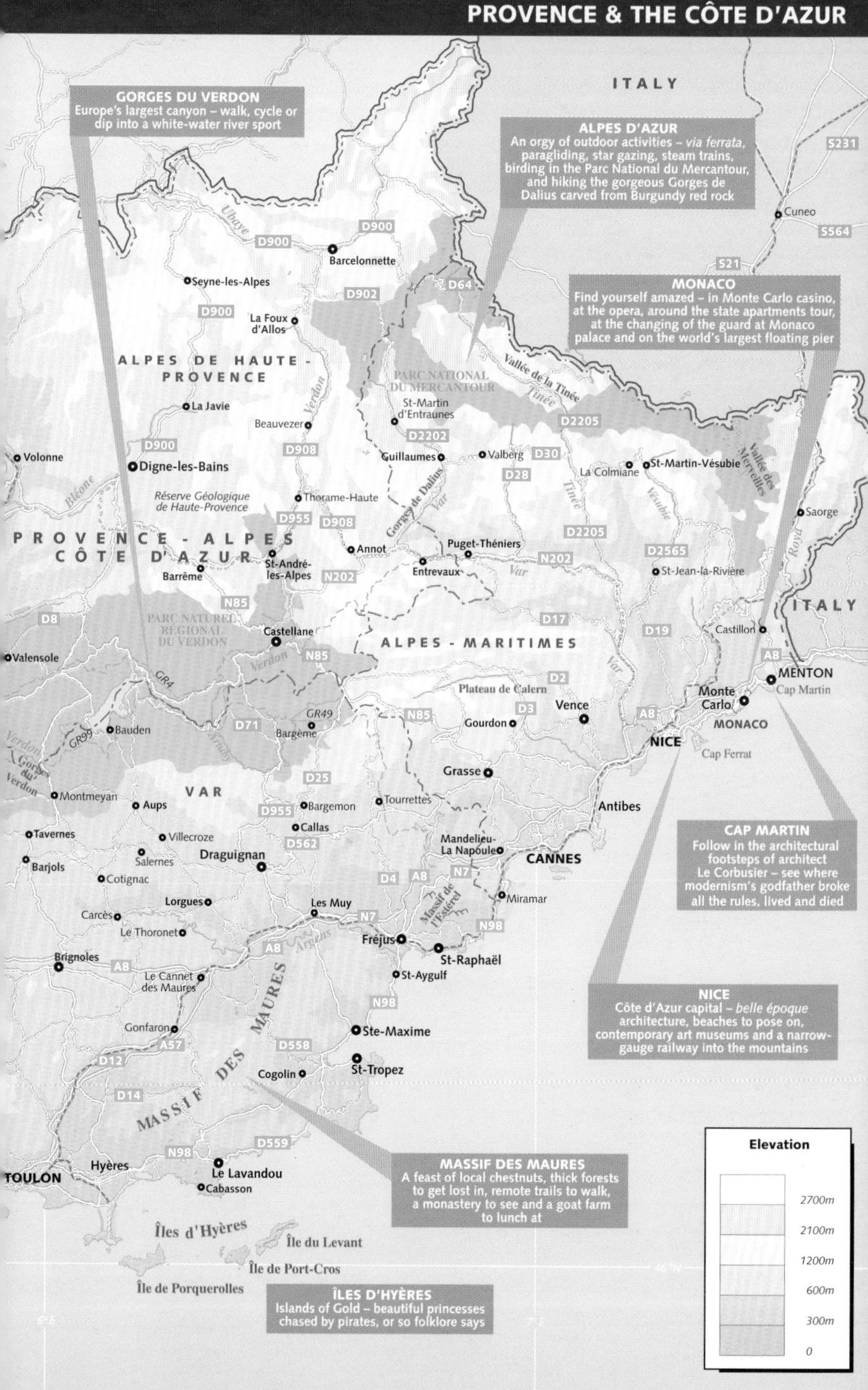

GORGES DU VERDON
Europe's largest canyon – walk, cycle or dip into a white-water river sport
ALPES D'AZUR
An orgy of outdoor activities – via ferrata, paragliding, star gazing, steam trains, birding in the Parc National du Mercantour, and hiking the gorgeous Gorges de Dalius carved from Burgundy red rock
MONACO
Find yourself amazed – in Monte Carlo casino, at the opera, around the state apartments tour, at the changing of the guard at Monaco palace and on the world's largest floating pier
CAP MARTIN
Follow in the architectural footsteps of architect Le Corbusier – see where modernism's godfather broke all the rules, lived and died
NICE
Côte d'Azur capital – belle époque architecture, beaches to pose on, contemporary art museums and a narrow-gauge railway into the mountains
MASSIF DES MAURES
A feast of local chestnuts, thick forests to get lost in, remote trails to walk, a monastery to see and a goat farm to lunch at
ÎLES D'HYÈRES
Islands of Gold – beautiful princesses chased by pirates, or so folklore says
ITALY
ALPES DE HAUTE-PROVENCE
PROVENCE-ALPES CÔTE D'AZUR
ALPES-MARITIMES
VAR
MONACO
PARC NATIONAL DU MERCANTOUR
PARC NATUREL RÉGIONAL DU VERDON
Réserve Géologique de Haute-Provence
MASSIF DES MAURES
Massif de l'Estérel
Plateau de Calern
Vallée de la Tinée
Vallée des Merveilles
Gorges de Dalius
Gorges du Verdon
Barcelonnette
Seyne-les-Alpes
La Foux d'Allos
La Javie
Beauvezer
St-Martin d'Entraunes
Guillaumes
Valberg
La Colmiane
St-Martin-Vésubie
Saorge
Volonne
Digne-les-Bains
Thorame-Haute
Annot
Puget-Théniers
Entrevaux
St-André-les-Alpes
Barrême
St-Jean-la-Rivière
Castillon
Castellane
Valensole
MENTON
Cap Martin
Monte Carlo
Vence
Gourdon
NICE
Cap Ferrat
Bauden
Bargème
Grasse
Montmeyan
Aups
Bargemon
Tourrettes
Antibes
Callas
Tavernes
Villecroze
Salernes
Draguignan
Mandelieu-La Napoule
CANNES
Barjols
Cotignac
Lorgues
Les Muy
Miramar
Carcès
Le Thoronet
Fréjus
St-Raphaël
Brignoles
Le Cannet des Maures
St-Aygulf
Gonfaron
Ste-Maxime
St-Tropez
Cogolin
Hyères
TOULON
Le Lavandou
Cabasson
Îles d'Hyères
Île du Levant
Île de Port-Cros
Île de Porquerolles
Cuneo
Elevation
2700m
2100m
1200m
600m
300m
0

Provence & the Côte d'Azur
3rd edition – April 2003
First published – June 1999

Published by
Lonely Planet Publications Pty Ltd ABN 36 005 607 983
90 Maribyrnong St, Footscray, Victoria 3011, Australia

Lonely Planet Offices
Australia Locked Bag 1, Footscray, Victoria 3011
USA 150 Linden St, Oakland, CA 94607
UK 10a Spring Place, London NW5 3BH
France 1 rue du Dahomey, 75011 Paris

Photographs
Many of the images in this guide are available for licensing from Lonely Planet Images.
w www.lonelyplanetimages.com

Front cover photograph
Meadow with flowers and stone hut, Vaucluse
(Michael Busselle,Taxi)

ISBN 1 74059 343 X

Printed by SNP SPrint (M) Sdn Bhd
Printed in Malaysia

Contents – Text

Contents – Maps

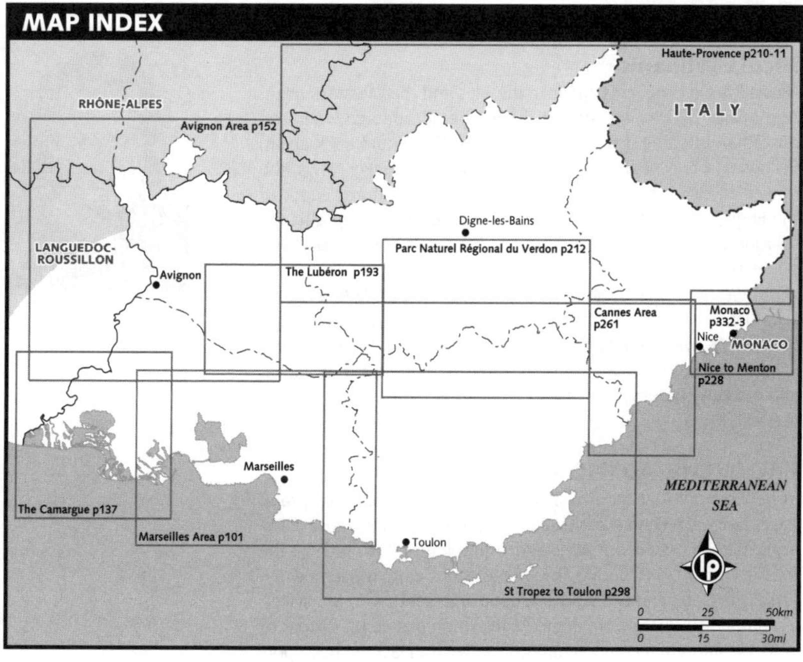
MAP INDEX
RHÔNE-ALPES
Avignon Area p152
Haute-Provence p210-11
ITALY
LANGUEDOC-ROUSSILLON
Digne-les-Bains
Parc Naturel Régional du Verdon p212
The Lubéron p193
Avignon
Cannes Area p261
Monaco p332-3
Nice
MONACO
Nice to Menton p228
Marseilles
The Camargue p137
Marseilles Area p101
Toulon
St Tropez to Toulon p298
MEDITERRANEAN SEA
0
25
50km
0
15
30mi

The Author

Nicola Williams

Nicola lives in Lyon, crossroads to the Alps and the Mediterranean. A journalist by training, she hit the road a decade ago when she bussed and boated it from Jakarta to East Timor and back again. Following a two-year stint at the *North Wales Weekly News*, she moved to Latvia to bus it round the Baltics as Features Editor of the English-language *Baltic Times* newspaper. Following a happy 12 months writing and editing prose for the *In Your Pocket* city guide series, she traded in Lithuanian *cepelinai* for Lyonnaise *andouillette*. Nicola graduated from Kent and did an MA in Islamic Societies & Cultures at London's School of Oriental & African Studies. As well as writing this guide, she has authored Lonely Planet's *The Loire*, *Milan, Turin & Genoa* and *Romania & Moldova*, and worked on numerous other European titles.

FROM THE AUTHOR

In between all that mouthwatering wining and dining, *un grand merci* to French chefs Alain Ducasse and Roger Vergé whose culinary expertise provided a basis and/or inspiration for much of the foodie stuff in this book. The *gîte* owners who welcomed me warmly in Goult and Grimaud also deserve a mention. In Marseilles, Christophe La Rocca from France 2 television passed on dozens of insider restaurant recommendations to me, not least the best spots on the coast to dance all night and eat *bouillabaisse* Toulon-style. At home, sweet *bisous* to my parents Ann and Paul Williams and my parents-in-law Christa and Karl-Otto Lüfkens for entertaining Niko while I worked, and to my husband Matthias for making life more fun.

This Book

The 1st edition of *Provence & the Côte d'Azur* was written by Nicola Williams in 1999. She also updated the 2nd edition.

From the Publisher

This 3rd edition of *Provence & the Côte d'Azur* was produced in Lonely Planet's Melbourne office. Editing was coordinated at various times during the production process by Kalya Ryan, Nina Rousseau and Simone Egger. Yvonne Byron coordinated the editing side of layout. They were assisted by Adrienne Costanzo, Melanie Dankel, Jocelyn Harewood, Louise McGregor and Sally Steward. Daniel Fennessy coordinated mapping, with assistance from Jacqueline Nguyen, Tessa Rottiers, Jacqui Saunders, Mandy Sierp, Chris Thomas and Chris Tsismetzis. Larisa Baird compiled the colour pages and coordinated layout. She was assisted by Birgit Jordan, Sally Morgan, John Shippick and Tamsin Wilson. Erin Corrigan saw the project through as commissioning editor after initial work by Sam Trafford. Csanád Csutoros prepared the climate charts and helped with mapping, Quentin Frayne compiled the Language chapter and Annika Roojun designed the cover. Thanks to LPI for the images, Pepi Bluck for coordinating illustrations, Kate McDonald for layout supervision and Ray Thomson who guided the project through the twists and turns of production. Mark Griffiths assisted with checking.

Thanks

Many thanks to the following travellers who use the last edition and wrote to us with helpful hints, useful advice and interesting anecdotes.

Esther Allen, Guillaume Allouard, Maria Campbell, C Cao, Pauline Chan, Signe Engkjaer Christensen, Mike Clark, Dave Cooke, Fabrice Corbiere, Mara Cosentino, Hans Engh, Rob Erickson, Gordon Fear, Tony Feeney, Robert Feldman, Gary Freedman, KL Fuchs, Christopher Gabel, Anne Gigney, Ian Harrison, Alyson & David Hilbourne, Kathleen Kimball, Richard Kimball, Kendrick Ling, Philip Littler, Bjorn Ljunghill, Jen Mair, Michael Moloff, Caroline Morissette, Scott & Julie Myers, Rory Murray, Jenny Pryce-Davies, John Pryce-Davies, Sophie Raniwala, Peter Rasmussen, Peter Rombach, Jon Sadler, Carlos Salamanca, Barb Satink, Sally Scott, Ritva Siikala, Jennifer Smith, Rob Spragg, Barry Thompson, Lillian Todorov, Clare Tomlinson, Gloria Torraca, Gordon Trousdale, Astrid van Dijk, Mary Viola, Anna Watson, Angel Wesley, Amanda Wilkinson, Jo Wort and Matt Wort

Foreword

ABOUT LONELY PLANET GUIDEBOOKS

The story begins with a classic travel adventure: Tony and Maureen Wheeler's 1972 journey across Europe and Asia to Australia. There was no useful information about the overland trail then, so Tony and Maureen published the first Lonely Planet guidebook to meet a growing need.

From a kitchen table, Lonely Planet has grown to become the largest independent travel publisher in the world, with offices in Melbourne (Australia), Oakland (USA), London (UK) and Paris (France).

Today Lonely Planet guidebooks cover the globe. There is an ever-growing list of books and information in a variety of media. Some things haven't changed. The main aim is still to make it possible for adventurous travellers to get out there – to explore and better understand the world.

At Lonely Planet we believe travellers can make a positive contribution to the countries they visit – if they respect their host communities and spend their money wisely. Since 1986 a percentage of the income from each book has been donated to aid projects and human rights campaigns, and, more recently, to wildlife conservation.

Although inclusion in a guidebook usually implies a recommendation we cannot list every good place. Exclusion does not necessarily imply criticism. In fact there are a number of reasons why we might exclude a place – sometimes it is simply inappropriate to encourage an influx of travellers.

UPDATES & READER FEEDBACK

Things change – prices go up, schedules change, good places go bad and bad places go bankrupt. Nothing stays the same. So, if you find things better or worse, recently opened or long-since closed, please tell us and help make the next edition even more accurate and useful.

Lonely Planet thoroughly updates each guidebook as often as possible – usually every two years, although for some destinations the gap can be longer. Between editions, up-to-date information is available in our free, monthly email bulletin *Comet* (w www.lonelyplanet.com/newsletters). You can also check out the *Thorn Tree* bulletin board and *Postcards* section of our website, which carry unverified, but fascinating, reports from travellers.

Tell us about it! We genuinely value your feedback. A well-travelled team at Lonely Planet reads and acknowledges every email and letter we receive and ensures that every morsel of information finds its way to the relevant authors, editors and cartographers.

Everyone who writes to us will find their name listed in the next edition of the appropriate guidebook. The very best contributions will be rewarded with a free guidebook.

We may edit, reproduce and incorporate your comments in Lonely Planet products such as guidebooks, websites and digital products, so let us know if you don't want your comments reproduced or your name acknowledged.

How to contact Lonely Planet:
Online: e talk2us@lonelyplanet.com.au, w www.lonelyplanet.com
Australia: Locked Bag 1, Footscray, Victoria 3011
UK: 10a Spring Place, London NW5 3BH
USA: 150 Linden St, Oakland, CA 94607

Introduction

There's much more to Provence than *pétanque*, pastis and medieval villages perched on hills.

Roughly sandwiched between rough-cut Marseilles with its raucous fish markets and streetwise music scene, and megalomaniacal Monte Carlo with its Hong Kong-style skyline and Europe's highest number of sports cars per capita, this sunny southern spot screams action, glamour and just a hint of the ridiculous.

The lively port city of Marseilles, settled by the Greeks on the shores of the Mediterranean Sea, is the capital of Provence. The region is named after Provincia Gallia Transalpina, a province created by the Romans. Travellers with a fascination for the ancient will be rewarded with more triumphal arches, aqueducts and amphitheatres than anywhere else in France.

The mighty River Rhône ends its 813km-course west of Marseilles in the Camargue delta, a wild waterland – as untamed as the Romans – where cowboys herd cattle and Roma people flock from across Europe to honour their patron saint and blaze a fiesta of flamenco and *Bamboleo* music in the streets. Visiting action-lovers can ride bareback with cowboys, cycle around salt pans, or simply look to the skies with a pair of binoculars to watch Europe's largest colony of pink flamingos at work and play.

East of Marseilles is the famously alluring Côte d'Azur or French Riviera. Immortalised on the silver screen by Grace Kelly, Brigitte Bardot et al, and on canvas by legions of celebrated artists, this strip of coast is a legend in its own time. Works by Renoir, Matisse and Picasso, displayed in museums in and around Nice, Cannes and St-Tropez, attract millions of tourists each year – as do the nearby Massif des Maures, Estérel, and Alpine foothills that plummet precipitously into the Mediterranean east of Nice. Cats on leads, dogs in handbags and prima donnas dusting sand from their toes with shaving brushes are among the madcap sights that await travellers at its

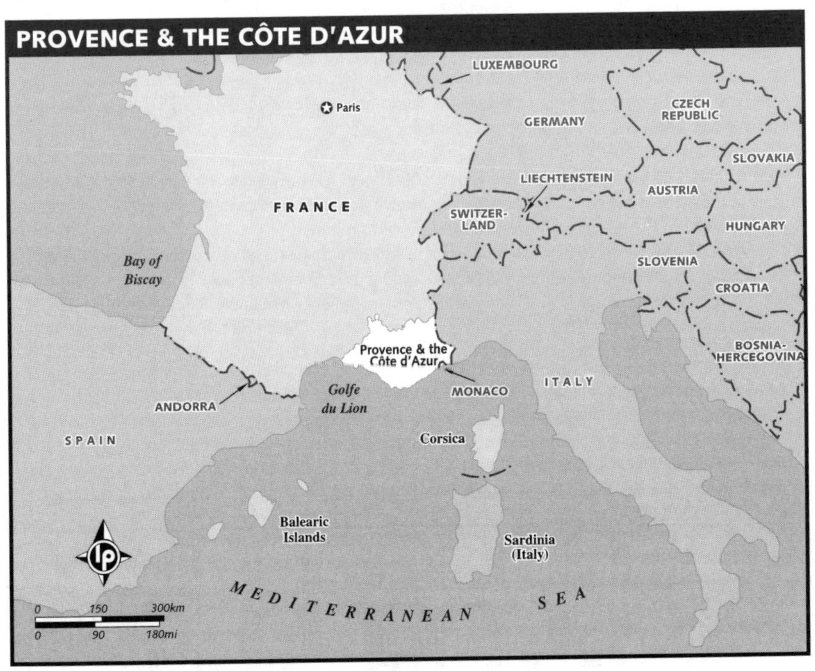

numerous coastal resorts. Offshore is a cluster of islands that offer rare peace and tranquillity.

Inland Provence is a far cry from all this pandemonium. Rome's popes, exiled to Avignon in the 14th century, left behind a resplendent palace and a wealth of vineyards that today produce one of France's most sought-after (and strongest) red wines, Châteauneuf du Pape. Eating, drinking and savouring the sensual orgy of hues and scents that this papal city and the Vaucluse region offers – springtime almond blossoms, asparagus, red cherries and strawberries, summer melons and pumpkins, fields of lavender in July and August, truffles all winter – are as good reasons as any to visit this pretty neck of the woods.

Paragliding, walking, white-water sports and mountain biking are just some of the unexpected thrills and spills guaranteed to set the heart racing in Haute-Provence, the region's 'great outdoors'. Dubbed the Alpes d'Azur, this is where you take your foot off the speed pedal and cruise for days without passing another tourist. Natural treasures awaiting motorists, cyclists and walkers include clear Alpine lakes, a national park with a rich archaeological heritage and Europe's largest canyon.

Then there is the great hulk of Mont Ventoux, the king of Provence who – with the sun and the mistral – commands his action-packed kingdom from the top of barren, sun-baked slopes in northwestern Provence. The mistral winds add a bitter bite to the air, while the sun bathes Provence in the most glorious southern sunshine, with a warmth and intensity of light absolutely unknown in any other part of Europe.

Facts about Provence

HISTORY

Early Inhabitants

Provence (Prouvènço in Provençal) was inhabited from an exceptionally early period. Prehistoric rock scratchings in the Grottes de l'Observatoire in Monaco, carved one million years ago, are among the world's oldest. Traces of fire discovered in the Grotte de l'Escale at St-Estève Janson show prehistoric people to have used fire from 600,000 BC. The Terra Amata site in Nice was inhabited as early as 400,000 BC.

During the Middle Palaeolithic period (about 90,000 to 40,000 BC), Neanderthal hunters occupied the coast. The precious Grotte de la Baume Bonne near Quinson, only uncovered in the 1960s, dates from this era. Modern man followed in 30,000 BC. The ornate wall paintings of bison, seals, ibex and other animals inside the decorated Grotte Cosquer (named after the Cassis diver who discovered it in 1991) in the Calanque de Sormiou, near Marseilles, are dated at 20,000 BC. Many more undiscovered examples of prehistoric art are believed to exist in the region in cave dwellings like this.

The Neolithic period (about 6000 to 4500 years ago), also known as the New Stone Age, witnessed the earliest domestication of sheep in Châteauneuf-lès-Martigues, followed by the cultivation of lands by the Ligurians. The first dwellings to be built (around 3500 BC) were *bories*, evident in Gordes. These one- or two-storey beehive-shaped huts, constructed without mortar using thin wedges of limestone, were inhabited until as late as the 18th century. The collection of 30,000 Bronze Age petroglyphs – drawings or carvings on rock – date between 1800 and 1500 BC. They are located at the foot of Mont Bégo in the Vallée des Merveilles and remain among the world's most spectacular.

Ancient Provence

The eastern part of the Mediterranean coast was colonised around 600 BC by Greeks, from Phocaea in Asia Minor, who settled in Massalia (Marseilles). The Greeks were the first to develop the region, establishing trading posts at other coastal points from the 4th century BC: at Antipolis (Antibes), Olbia (Hyères), Athenopolis (St-Tropez), Nikaia (Nice), Monoïkos (Monaco) and Glanum (near St-Rémy de Provence). The Greeks brought olives and grape vines with them.

At the same time as Hellenic civilisation was developing on the coast, the Celts were penetrating the northern part of the region. They mingled with ancient Ligurians to create a Celto-Ligurian stronghold around Entremont. Its influence extended as far south as Draguignan.

In 125 BC the Romans were called in by the Greeks to help defend Massalia against the threat of invasion by Celto-Ligurians from Entremont. The Romans were victorious, and this success marked the start of the Gallo-Roman era and the creation of Provincia Gallia Transalpina, the first Roman provincia (province), from which the name Provence is derived.

The Gallo-Roman Era

Provincia Gallia Transalpina, which quickly became Provincia Narbonensis, was much larger than modern-day Provence. It embraced all of southern France, from the Alps to the Mediterranean Sea and as far west as the Pyrenees. Narbonne was its capital. In 122 BC the Romans destroyed the Ligurian capital of Entremont and established the Roman stronghold of Aquae Sextiae Salluviorum (Aix-en-Provence) at its foot.

During this period the Romans started building roads to secure the route between Italy and Spain. The Via Aurelia linked Rome to Fréjus, Aix-en-Provence, Arles and Nîmes; the northbound Via Agrippa followed the River Rhône from Arles to Avignon, Orange and Lyons; and the Via Domitia linked the Alps with the Pyrenees by way of Sisteron, the Lubéron, Beaucaire and Nîmes. Vestiges of these roads, such as the Pont Julien (dating from 3 BC) near Bonnieux and an arch in Cavaillon, still remain.

The Roman influence on Provence was tremendous, though it was only after Julius Caesar's conquest of Gaul (58–51 BC) and its consequent integration into the Roman Empire that the region really began to flourish. Massalia, which had retained its independence following the creation of Provincia, was incorporated by Caesar in

49 BC. In 14 BC, the still-rebellious Ligurians were defeated by Augustus, who built a trophy monument at La Turbie (6 BC) to celebrate his victory. Arelate (Arles) became the chosen regional capital.

Under the emperor Augustus, grandiose amphitheatres seating 10,000 spectators were built to host gladiator combats at Arelate, Nemausus (Nîmes), Forum Julii (Fréjus) and Vasio Vocontiorum (Vaison-la-Romaine). Triumphal arches were raised at Arausio (Orange), Cabelio (Cavaillon), Carpentorate (Carpentras) and Glanum, and a series of aqueducts were constructed. The mammoth Pont du Gard – 275m in length – was part of a 50km-long system of canals built around 19 BC by Agrippa, Augustus' deputy, to bring water from Uzès to Nîmes. Most of these ancient public buildings remain exceptionally well preserved.

The end of the 3rd century saw the reorganisation of the Roman Empire. Provincia Narbonensis was split into two provinces in AD 284. The land on the right bank of the Rhône (Languedoc-Roussillon today) remained Narbonensis and the land on the left bank (today's Provence) became Provincia Viennoise. Christianity penetrated the region and was adopted by the Romans. Provençal legend says it was brought to the region by Mary Magdalene, Mary Jacob and Mary Salome who sailed into Stes-Maries de la Mer in AD 40. St Honorat founded the Lérins monastical order on the Îles de Lérins at this time.

Medieval Provence

After the collapse of the Roman Empire in AD 476, Provence suffered successive invasions by a clutch of Germanic tribes: the Visigoths (West Goths, from the Danube delta region in Transylvania), the Ostrogoths (East Goths, from the Black Sea region) and the Burgundians of Scandinavian origin. Provence was ceded to the Franks (also a Germanic tribe, from whom the word 'France' comes) at the start of the 6th century. Rebellions in Marseilles, Arles and Avignon (AD 732–9) against the Frankish rule were brutally squashed.

In the early 9th century the Saracens (an umbrella term adopted locally to describe Muslim invaders such as Turks, Moors and Arabs) emerged as a warrior force to be reckoned with. Attacks along the Maures coast, Niçois hinterland and more northern Alps, persuaded villagers to take refuge in the hills. Many of Provence's perched, hilltop villages date from this chaotic period. But the Saracens did teach the local population what could be done with the bark of cork oak – that is, use it to make cork bottle stoppers. In AD 974 the Saracen fortress at La Garde Freinet was defeated by William the Liberator (Guillaume Le Libérateur), count of Arles, who consequently extended his feudal control over the entire region, marking a return of peace and unity to Provence, which became a marquisate. In 1032 it joined the Holy Roman Empire.

At the start of the 12th century, the marquisate of Provence was split in two: the north fell into the hands of the counts of Toulouse from 1125 and retained the title of marquisate while the Catalan counts of Barcelona gained control of the southern part, which stretched from the Rhône to the Durance and from the Alps to the sea. This became the county of Provence (Comté de Provence). Raymond Bérenger V (1209–45) was the first Catalan count to reside permanently in Aix (the capital since 1186). In 1229 he conquered Nice to gain better control of eastern Provence and the southern Alps and, in 1232, he founded Barcelonnette. In 1246, after Bérenger's death, the county passed to the House of Anjou, under which it enjoyed great prosperity.

The Popes

In 1274 Comtat Venaissin, situated in Provence's northern realm (namely Carpentras and its Vaucluse hinterland), was ceded to Pope Gregory X in Rome. In 1309, French-born Clement V (1305–14) moved the papal headquarters from feud-riven Rome to Avignon, thus beginning the most resplendent period in that city's history.

Between 1309 and 1376, nine pontiffs headed the Roman Catholic church from Avignon. Under the reign of Avignon's third pope, Benoît XII (1334–42), work started on the resplendent Palais des Papes (Papal Palace), enlarged to monumental status during the reign of his successor Clement VI (1342–52) and admired at the time as the 'most handsome of houses and greatest of strongholds in the world'. In 1348 Pope Clement VI purchased the city of Avignon (not within the boundaries of Comtat

Venaissin) from the reigning countess of Provence, Queen Jeanne of Naples (1343–82). Accused of murdering her husband, she fled to Avignon where she sold the city for 80,000 florins – in exchange for a papal pardon. Clement VI had Avignon bridge built in 1350.

In 1376 the city was given a break when Pope Gregory XI left Avignon. But his death two years later led to the Great Schism (1378–1417), during which rival popes – up to three at one time, each with his own College of Cardinals – resided at Rome and Avignon and spent most of their energies denouncing and excommunicating each other. They also went to great effort to gain control of church revenues, including the sale of indulgences. Even after the schism was settled and a pope, Martin V – acceptable to all factions – established himself in Rome, Avignon and the Comtat Venaissin remained under papal rule until 1792.

Cultural life in Provence flourished inside and outside the papal sphere during the 14th century. A university was established in Avignon as early as 1303, followed by a university in Aix, Provence's capital, a century later. In 1327, the Italian poet Petrarch (1304–74), exiled in Avignon, first encountered his muse, Laura. In 1336 he became the first person to climb to the top of Mont Ventoux. The reign of good King René, king of Naples (1434–80), further enhanced this period of peace and prosperity. French became the courtly language and a castle was built at Tarascon.

French Provence

In 1481, René's successor, his nephew Charles III, died heirless and Provence was ceded to Louis XI of France. In 1486 the state of Aix ratified Provence's union with France and the centralist policies of the French kings saw the region's autonomy greatly reduced. Aix Parliament, a French administrative body, was created in 1501.

This new addition to the French kingdom did not include Nice, Barcelonnette, Puget-Théniers and the hinterlands of these towns which, in 1388, had become incorporated into the lands of the House of Savoy. The County of Nice (essentially today's Alpes-Maritimes department), with Nice as its capital, did not become part of French Provence until 1860.

A period of instability ensued. Jews living in Provençal France fled to ghettos in Carpentras, Pernes-les-Fontaines, L'Isle-sur-Sorgue, Cavaillon or Avignon – all were part of the pontifical enclave of Comtat Venaissin, where papal protection remained assured until 1570. Following the French conquest of Milan during the Italian wars during the 1520s, Charles V invaded Provence. This was followed by another attack and further bloodshed in 1536. The Villers-Cotterêts statute approved in 1539 made French, rather than Provençal, the official administrative language in Provence.

An early victim of the Reformation that swept Europe in the 1530s and the consequent Wars of Religion (1562–98) was the Lubéron. In April 1545, the population of 11 Vaudois villages in the Lubéron was massacred in six days. Numerous clashes followed between the staunchly Catholic stronghold of Comtat Venaissin and its Huguenot (Protestant) neighbours to the north around Orange. In 1580 the plague temporarily immobilised the otherwise volatile region. Treatments first used by the prophetic Nostradamus (1503–66) in St-Rémy de Provence were administered to plague victims. The Edict of Nantes in 1598, which recognised Protestant control of certain areas, including Lourmarin in the Lubéron, brought an uneasy peace to the region – until its revocation by Louis XIV in 1685. A full-scale persecution of Protestants in Provence ensued. Leading Huguenots were killed or imprisoned, many in the Tour de Constance in Aigues-Mortes and Château d'If near Marseilles.

The plague of 1720 killed half of Marseilles' population. The close of the century was marked by the French Revolution in 1789: As the National Guard from Marseilles marched north to defend the Revolution, a merry little tune composed in Strasbourg several months earlier for the war against Prussia – *Chant de Guerre de l'Armée du Rhin* (War Song of the Rhine Army) – sprung from their lips. France's stirring national anthem, *La Marseillaise*, was born.

La Route Napoléon

Provence was divided into three *départements* (departments) in 1790: Var, Bouches du Rhône and the Basse-Alpes (Lower Alps). Two years later papal Avignon and Comtat Venaissin were annexed by France, making way for the creation of a fourth department, Vaucluse.

In 1793 the Armée du Midi marched into Nice and declared it French territory on 31 January. France also captured Monaco, which until now had been a recognised independent state ruled by the Grimaldi family. When Toulon was besieged by the English, it was thanks to the efforts of a dashing young Corsican general named Napoleon Bonaparte (Napoleon I) that France recaptured it.

The Reign of Terror that swept through France between September 1793 and July 1794 saw religious freedoms revoked, churches desecrated and cathedrals turned into 'Temples of Reason'. In the secrecy of their homes, people hand-crafted thumbnail-sized, biblical figurines, hence the rather inglorious creation of the Provençal *santon* (see the boxed text 'Little Saints' in the Marseilles Area chapter).

In 1814 France lost the territories it had seized in 1793. The County of Nice was ceded to Victor Emmanuel I, king of Sardinia. It remained under Sardinian protectorship until 1860 when an agreement between Napoleon III and the House of Savoy helped drive the Austrians from northern Italy, prompting France to repossess Savoy and the area around Nice. In Monaco, meanwhile, the Treaty of Parisrestored the rights of the Grimaldi royal family; from 1817 until 1860 the principality also fell under the protection of the Sardinian king.

Meanwhile, the Allied restoration of the House of Bourbon to the French throne at the Congress of Vienna (1814–15), following Napoleon I's abdication and exile to Elba, was rudely interrupted by the return of the emperor. Following his escape from Elba in 1815, Napoleon landed at Golfe-Juan on 1 March with a 1200-strong army. He proceeded northwards, passing through Cannes, Grasse, Castellane, Digne-les-Bains and Sisteron en route to his triumphal return to Paris on 20 May. Unfortunately, Napoleon's glorious 'Hundred Days' back in power ended with the Battle of Waterloo and his return to exile. He died in 1821.

During the revolutions of 1848, French revolutionaries adopted as their own the red, white and blue tricolour of Martigues, a small town near Marseilles. This became France's national flag.

The Belle Époque

The Second Empire (1852–70) brought to the region a revival in all things Provençal, a movement spearheaded by poet Frédéric Mistral (see Literature later in this chapter). Rapid economic growth was the era's other hallmark: Nice, which had finally become part of France in 1860, was among Europe's first cities to have a purely tourist-based economy. Between 1860 and 1911 it was also Europe's fastest-growing city. The city became particularly popular with the English aristocracy in the Victorian period. They followed their queen's example of wintering in Nice to indulge in its mild winter. European royalty followed soon after. The train line reached Toulon in 1856, followed by Nice and Draguignan, and in 1864 work started on a coastal road from Nice to Monaco. The same year, exotic palm trees, mimosas and eucalyptus trees were imported from Australia. In fine Second Empire architectural style, Nice Opera House and the neoclassical Justice Palace were built.

In neighbouring Monaco, the Grimaldi family had given up its claim over its former territories of Menton and Roquebrune in 1861 (under Monégasque rule until 1848) in exchange for France's recognition of its status as an independent principality. When Monte Carlo casino opened four years later, Monaco leapt from being Europe's poorest state to one of its richest.

The Third Republic ushered in the glittering *belle époque* (literally 'beautiful age'), with Art Nouveau architecture, a whole field of artistic 'isms' including impressionism, and advances in science and engineering. Wealthy French, English, American and Russian tourists and tuberculosis sufferers (for whom the only cure was sunlight and sea air) discovered the coast, attracted by its beauty and temperate climate in winter. The intensity and clarity of the region's colours and light appealed to many painters including Cézanne, Van Gogh and Matisse. Writers and other celebrities were also attracted to the region and contributed to its fame. Little fishing ports such as St-Tropez became exclusive resorts with lavish, castle-like villas hugged by manicured gardens, tennis courts and golf courses. In 1887 the first guidebook to the French coast was published, following which the coast finally had a name it could call its own – the Côte d'Azur.

The Sky-Blue Coast

The Côte d'Azur (literally 'Azure Coast') first gained its name from an early, 19th-century guidebook.

La Côte d'Azur, published in 1887, was the work of Stéphane Liégeard (1830–1925), a lawyer-cum-aspiring poet from Burgundy who lived in Cannes. The guide covered the coast from Menton to Hyères and was an instant hit.

Its title, a reflection of the coast's clear blue cloudless skies, became the hottest buzz word to hit town. And it never tired. The Côte d'Azur is known as the French Riviera by most Anglophones.

WWI & the Interwar Period

No blood was spilled on southern French soil during WWI. Soldiers were conscripted from the region, however, and the human losses included two out of every 10 Frenchmen between 20 and 45 years of age. With its primarily tourist-based economy, the Côte d'Azur recovered quickly from the postwar financial crisis that lingered in France's more industrial north.

The Côte d'Azur sparkled as an avant-garde centre in the 1920s and 1930s, with artists pushing into the new fields of cubism and surrealism, Le Corbusier rewriting the architectural textbook and foreign writers attracted by the coast's liberal atmosphere: Ernest Hemingway, F Scott Fitzgerald, Aldous Huxley, Katherine Mansfield, DH Lawrence and Thomas Mann were among the scores to seek solace in the sun. Guests at Somerset Maugham's villa on Cap Ferrat included innumerable literary names, from TS Eliot and Arnold Bennett to Noël Coward, Evelyn Waugh and Ian Fleming.

Nightlife gained a reputation for being at the cutting edge, with everything from jazz clubs to striptease. Rail and road access to the south improved: the railway line between Digne-les-Bains and Nice was completed and in 1922 the luxurious *Train Bleu* (Blue Train) made its first run from Calais, via Paris, to the coast. The train only had 1st-class carriages and was quickly dubbed the 'train to paradise'.

The glorious 1920s hailed the start of the summer season on the Côte d'Azur. Outdoor swimming pools were built, seashores were cleared of seaweed to uncover lovely sandy beaches, and sunbathing sprang into fashion after a bronzed Coco Chanel appeared on the coast in 1923, draped over the arm of the duke of Westminster. France lifted its ban on gambling, prompting the first casino to open on the coast in the Palais de la Méditerranée on Nice's promenade des Anglais in 1927. The first Formula One Grand Prix took to the streets of Monaco in 1929, while the early 1930s saw wide pyjama-style beach trousers and the opening of a nudist colony on Île du Levant. With the advent of paid holidays for all French workers in 1936, even more tourists flocked to the region. Second- and 3rd-class seating was added to the *Train Bleu*, which had been running daily since 1929.

WWII

With the onset of war, the Côte d'Azur's glory days turned grey. Depression set in and on 3 September 1939 France and Britain declared war on Germany. But again, Provence and the Côte d'Azur remained relatively unscathed. Following the armistice treaty agreed with Hitler on 22 June 1940, southern France fell into the 'free' Vichy France zone, although Menton and its northern Vallée de Roya (around Sospel) were occupied by the Italians. The Côte d'Azur – particularly Nice – immediately became a safe haven from war-torn occupied France; by 1942 some 43,000 Jews had descended on the coast to seek refuge. Monaco remained neutral for the duration of the war.

On 11 November 1942 Nazi Germany invaded Vichy France. Provence was at war. At Toulon port, 73 ships, cruisers, destroyers and submarines – the major part of the French fleet and under the command of Admiral Jean-Baptiste Laborde – were scuttled by their crews to prevent the Germans seizing them. Almost immediately, Toulon was overcome by the Germans and Nice was occupied by the Italians. In January 1943 the Marseilles quarter of Le Panier was razed, its 40,000 inhabitants being given less than a day's notice to pack up and leave. Those who didn't were sent to Nazi concentration camps. The Resistance movement was particularly strong in Provence, where it became known as *maquis*, named after the Provençal scrub in which it hid.

Two months after D-Day, on 15 August 1944, Allied forces landed on the southern coast. They arrived at various beaches along the Côte d'Azur, including Le Dramont near St-Raphaël, Cavalaire, Pampelonne and the St-Tropez peninsula. St-Tropez and Provence's hinterland were almost immediately liberated, but it was only after five days of heavy fighting that Allied troops, led by the French Général de Montsabert, freed Marseilles on 28 August (three days after the liberation of Paris). Toulon was liberated on 26 August, one week after French troops under Général de Lattre de Tassigny first attacked the port.

The Italian-occupied areas in the Vallée de Roya were not returned to France until 1947.

Modern Provence

The first international film festival at Cannes in 1946 heralded the return to 'normal life' on the Côte d'Azur; party madness resumed. Noël Coward, Somerset Maugham and the rest of the coast's intellectual set returned to their abandoned seaside villas, while Picasso set up a studio in Golfe-Juan. The 1950s and '60s saw a staccato succession of glamorous society 'events': the fairytale marriage of a Grimaldi prince to Hollywood film legend Grace Kelly in 1956; Vadim's filming of *Et Dieu Créa la Femme* (And God Created Woman) with Brigitte Bardot in St-Tropez the same year; the emergence of the bikini and the Nice New Realists in the late 1950s; the advent of topless sunbathing (and consequent nipple-covering with bottle tops to prevent arrest for indecent exposure); and Miles Davis, Ella Fitzgerald and Ray Charles appearing at the 1961 Juan-les-Pins jazz festival.

In 1962 the troubled French colony of Algeria negotiated its independence with President Charles de Gaulle. During this time some 750,000 *pieds noirs* (literally 'black feet', as Algerian-born French people are known in France) flooded into France. A substantial number settled in Provence (particularly in the large urban centres of Marseilles, Nice and Toulon), as did immigrants from other French colonies and protectorates in North Africa.

Rapid industrialisation marked the 1960s. A string of five hydroelectric plants were constructed on the banks of the River Durance and in 1964 Électricité de France (EDF), the French electricity company, started digging a canal from north of Manosque south to the Étang de Berre, west of Marseilles. The following year construction work began on a 10,000-hectare petrochemical zone and an industrial port at Fos-sur-Mer, southern Europe's most important. Eyesore tanker terminals and oil refineries were raised at the site soon after. The first metro line opened in Marseilles in 1977 and TGV high-speed trains reached the city in 1981.

From the 1970s onwards, mainstream tourism, which had been almost exclusively limited to the Côte d'Azur until then, started making inroads into Provence's rural heart. While a concrete marina was being constructed at Villeneuve-Lourbet-Plage on the coast west of Nice, the region's first purpose-built ski resort popped up inland at Isola 2000.

The small flow of foreigners that trickled into Provence to buy crumbling old *mas* (Provençal farmhouses) at dirt-cheap prices in the late 1970s had become an uncontrollable torrent a decade on – as had the coachloads of tourists who flooded to the region to follow in the footsteps of British novelist Peter Mayle, whose bestseller, *A Year in Provence* (1989), captured the imagination of millions with its vivid description of life in Provence.

Corruption cast a shady cloud over France's hot south in the 1980s and early '90s. Nice's mayor, the corrupt right-wing Jacques Médecin (son of another former mayor, Jean Médecin, who ruled Nice for 38 years) was twice found guilty of income tax evasion during his 24-year mayorship (1966–90). In 1990, King Jacques – as the flamboyant mayor was dubbed – fled to Uruguay, following which he was convicted in absentia of the misuse of public funds (including accepting four million francs in bribes and stealing two million francs from the Nice opera). Médecin was extradited in 1994 and imprisoned in Grenoble where he served two years of a 3½-year sentence. Upon being released the ex-mayor, who died in 1998 aged 70, returned to Uruguay to sell hand-painted T-shirts.

During 1994 Yann Piat became the only member of France's National Assembly (parliament) since WWII to be assassinated while in office. Following her public denunciation of the Riviera Mafia, the French *député* (member of parliament) was shot in her Hyères constituency. Her assassins, dubbed the 'baby killers' by the press after their conviction in 1998, were local Mafia king-pins barely in their 20s.

On a tastier note, French chef Alain Ducasse scored a first in 1998 when his Monte Carlo restaurant, Louis XV, made him become the world's first chef to score six sparkling Michelin stars (split across Louis XV and his Paris restaurant).

Politics, Popular Culture & New-found Optimism

Blatant corruption, coupled with economic recession and growing unemployment, fuelled the rise of the extreme-right Front National (FN; National Front) in the mid-1990s. Nowhere else in France did the xenophobic party gain such a fierce stronghold as in Provence, where the FN stormed to victory in municipal elections in Toulon, Orange and Marignane in 1995, and in Vitrolles in 1997.

Despite such victories in local politics, the FN led by Jean Marie Le Pen failed to make any real headway in the national arena. Party support for the FN rose from 1% in 1981 to 15% in the 1995 presidential elections, yet the FN did not hold any seats in the National Assembly. And, despite gaining 15.5% of the nationwide vote in the last regional elections in 1998 (the next will be held in 2003), Le Pen failed in his bid to become chairman of the Provence-Alpes-Côte d'Azur *région* (administrative region).

A deathly blow for the FN came in December 1998 when second-in-command, Bruno Mégret, split from Le Pen to create his own breakaway faction. In the 1999 European parliamentary elections, Le Pen and the FN won just 5.7% of the national vote (enough to secure just five of the 87 French parliamentary seats), while Mégret's splinter group, the Mouvement National Républican (MNR) party trailed with just 3.28% (and no seats). This was in contrast to the Socialists, Rassemblement pour la République (RPR), communists and extreme-left who won the backing of 21.95%, 12.7%, 6.8% and 5.2% of the French electorate, respectively.

This trend was further reflected in the 2001 municipal-election results that saw the extreme-right lose the mayorship of Toulon, a FN stronghold since 1995. Extreme-right mayors Jacques Bompard (FN) and Daniel Simonpiéri (MNR) held onto Orange and Marignane respectively, but in Vitrolles – a mayorship held by no other than Bruno's wife, Catherine Mégret, since 1995 – the elections (which Mégret 'won') were later declared invalid because of defamatory pamphlets (against the RPR candidate) circulated during the election campaign. New elections in October 2002 saw the MNR incumbent mayor smashed to smithereens by the left-wing candidate Guy Obino who landed 54.05% of votes.

The national media immediately pounced on Mégret's defeat as the ruin of the 'house of Mégret'. Not only that, it portrayed the latter as ultimate proof that the extreme-right in France was no longer a force to be reckoned with. This came in light of the 2002 presidential elections, which saw thousands of protestors take to the streets after Le Pen of the FN stunned the nation by sweeping through to the second round after landing an unexpected 16.86% (4.8 million votes). 'I am ashamed to be French,' was most protestors' disgusted response. The second round (which saw 79.7% of the electorate actually vote compared to an apathetic 41.41% in the first round) saw Le Pen pitted against incumbent president Jacques Chirac. Chirac held onto his post by an overwhelming majority (82.21%).

The new millennium witnessed a new-found optimism in France. Nowhere was this upbeat turn more pronounced than in multicultural Marseilles, France's third-largest city that, since the victory by the French team in the 1998 football World Cup and Euro 2000, has been at the cutting edge of hip-hop, rap and football. In both 1998 and again in 2000 '*on est champions*' ('we are the champions') became the catch phrase of the moment – thanks, in no small part, to the champion of both tournaments, Zinedine Zidane. The midfielder from Marseilles is the world's most expensive player (he transferred to Real Madrid in 2001 for €75.1m) and is one of France's most popular heroes. His humble grin has been used across the country to sell everything from Adidas sports gear to Volvic mineral water and Christian Dior fashions.

France's sunny south sped into the 21st century with the opening of the high-speed TGV Méditerranée railway line linking Paris and Marseilles – just three hours by train – in 2001. In Marseilles, the Euroméditerranée project laid the foundations for a new station building as part of its 15-year project, which will see €3.05 billion invested in two central Marseillais quarters by 2010. In the Lubéron, the world-renowned French designer, Pierre Cardin, confirmed his commitment to promoting arts within the region by purchasing Lacoste's ruined chateau in the Lubéron in 2002 and transforming it into an enchanting opera stage. In the meanwhile, Spyland – the world's first espionage theme park set to open in Provence during mid-2005 – will see an estimated €124 million invested in the region. The park will feature a museum dedicated to the adventures and techniques of 007-style spies from antiquity to the present day, James Bond-type interactive games etc, and is expected to attract over one million visitors a year. In Monaco, international fanfare heralded the much-awaited arrival by sea of the world's largest floating dike.

Flash floods devastated the northwestern part of the region in September 2002, killing 26 and leaving more than 1000 people in the Gard, Vaucluse and neighbouring Herault departments homeless. The French government and the EU pledged €10 million and €500 million to help clean up after the disaster; total damage costs are estimated at €1.2 billion.

GEOGRAPHY

Provence and the Côte d'Azur cover 25,851 sq km in France's southeasternmost corner. Shaped like an elongated oval, the area is bordered by the southern Alps to the northeast, which form a natural frontier with Italy; and by the River Rhône to the west. The Grand Rhône (east) and Petit Rhône (west) form the delta of the Rhône, a triangular alluvial plain otherwise known as the Camargue.

Provence's southern boundary is washed by the Mediterranean. The 70km-long stretch of coastline from Marseilles (west) to Menton on the French-Italian border (east), is called the Côte d'Azur in French and the French Riviera by Anglophones. Off its shore, lie several islands: the Îles du Frioul (Marseilles), the Îles des Embiez (Toulon) and the Îles de Lérins (Cannes). The Îles d'Hyères, offshore from Hyères, are the most southern.

Three mountain ranges cut off this coastal strip from the region's vast interior. These are the Massif de l'Estérel, which are formed from red volcanic rock, the limestone Massif des Maures, and the foothills of the Alps that kiss the Arrière-Pays Niçois (Niçois hinterland) immediately north of Nice. Marseilles' coastline is formed from a chain of calcareous rocks, known as Les Calanques. France's highest cliff (406m) crowns Cap Canaille.

The interior of Provence is dominated by hills and mountains that peak with Mont Ventoux (1912m) in the northwest and the southern Alps in the northeast. Lower-lying ranges from west to east include the Alpilles, Montagne Ste-Victoire, the Ste-Baume and Vaucluse hills, and the Lubéron range. Farther east are the Gorges du Verdon, with Europe's largest most spectacular canyon.

Marseilles is Provence's largest city.

France's Point Zero

Be it Mont Ventoux (1912m) or Mont Blanc (4807m), the *point zéro* (point zero) from which the elevation of all French villages, towns and mountains are measured is the Marégraphe de Marseille, on the corniche Président John F Kennedy in Marseilles.

CLIMATE

If you like hot summers and mild winters, the Mediterranean climate is for you: frost is rare, spring and autumn downpours are sudden but brief and summer has virtually no rain. The region is blessed with 2500 to 2800 hours of sunshine per year, accounting for its extraordinary light.

The Côte d'Azur enjoys an annual average temperature of 15°C, dropping to 5°C in the higher-altitude northeast. Temperatures can reach 40°C on the coast in July and August. Sea-water temperature (surface) is 20°C to 25°C in summer and a toe-numbing 12°C to 13°C in winter. Annual precipitation is low: 250mm in the Marseilles region, 1100mm in the Alpes-Maritimes department and 1500mm in the southern Alps, which are usually snow-covered December to March.

Storms are most frequent in the mountains at the end of summer, but can start as early as August. Extreme bouts of cold can suddenly hit the region in early spring, winter and late autumn – blame the menacing mistral (see the boxed text 'The Mud-Eating Mistral' later).

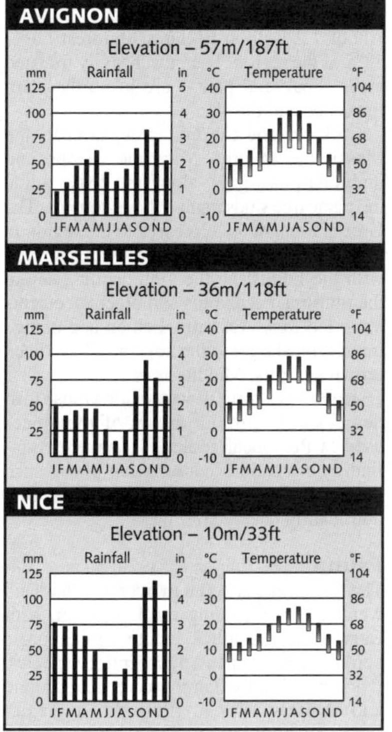

To get a weather forecast for the region (in French), telephone ☎ 08 36 68 02 followed by the two-digit departmental code (Alpes de Haute-Provence: 04, Alpes-Maritimes: 06, Bouches du Rhône: 13, Var: 83 and Vaucluse: 84), log on to W www.meteo.fr in English, or tune in to Riviera Radio (see under Radio & TV in the Facts for the Visitor chapter).

To access a national marine forecast, if you are planning to head out on a boat, call ☎ 08 36 68 08 08.

ECOLOGY & ENVIRONMENT

Ecology

Since the late 1980s, the state-owned electricity company, Électricité de France or EDF, has produced about three-quarters of France's electricity requirements using nuclear power. EDF also controls the country's hydroelectric programme, damming rivers to produce electricity and, in the process, creating a number of huge recreational lakes such as Lac de Ste-Croix, Lac de Castillon and Lac de Chaudanne around the Gorges du Verdon. This high level of activity has had the consequence of destroying habitats of many animals.

Environmental pressure groups continue to fight tooth and nail against the Boutre-Broc-Carros high-voltage line (400,000V), which will cross the protected Parc Naturel du Verdon. The 225,000V line currently linking Nice with power plants in the Rhône Valley is insufficient to meet the city's power demands in emergency situations. High voltage lines electrocute at least 1000 birds of prey each year.

The wind turbine (32V), which was erected at Port-St-Louis du Rhône in 2002, is the region's first.

Environment

Forest Fires Of Provence's 1.2 million hectares of forest, a mere 8.5% are protected. A concerted campaign to prevent summer forest fires is paying off. In 2000, forest fires fell by 45% (3000 hectares of forest compared to 6663 in 1999). Most fires are caused by careless day-trippers, although some are deliberately lit in the Maures and Estérel ranges to get licences to build on the damaged lands. Almost 85% of the 2000 fires affected forests in the Bouches du Rhône department (mainly around Marseilles and Les Calanques) and in Alpes-Maritimes (inland from Nice).

Tourism The nine million-odd tourists that descend on the region annually are an environmental hazard. The Côte d'Azur – already a concrete minefield – continues to be developed to cater for the increasing number of tourists. Port-Cros' fragile ecosystem is threatened not only by fire but by marine pollution, caused mainly by the boats that bring 120,000 tourists annually to the island.

Bathing Water The quality of bathing water is surprisingly good. In 2002 beaches that received the European blue flag – awarded annually to environmentally clean, safe and well-maintained beaches in Europe – included those in and around Cannes, Antibes, Cap d'Ail, Juan-les-Pins, Golfe-Juan, Mandelieu-La Napoule, Ste-Maxime, Menton, Port Gardian beach at Stes-Maries de la Mer and most beaches in Hyères, Le Lavandou, Grimaud, Port Grimaud and

The Mud-Eating Mistral

Folklore claims it drives people crazy. Its namesake, Provençal poet Frédéric Mistral, cursed it; while peasants in their dried-out fields dubbed the damaging wind *mange fange* (*manjo fango* in Provençal), meaning 'mud eater'.

The mistral is a cold, dry northwesterly wind that whips across Provence for several days at a time. Its furious gusts, reaching over 100km/h, destroy crops, rip off roofs, dry the land and drive tempers round the bend. It chills the bones for 100 days a year and is at its fiercest in winter and spring.

The mistral's intense and relentless rage is caused by high atmospheric pressure over central France, between the Alps and the Pyrenees, which is then blown southwards through the funnel of the narrow Rhône Valley to an area of low-pressure over the Mediterranean Sea. On the upside, skies are blue and clear of clouds when the mistral is in town. A soaking of rain in July, followed by a healthy dose of sun and mistral in August, followed by more showers and more mistral in early September works wonders for the grape harvest. The mistral has 31 siblings.

Fréjus. Of the 92 beaches in Bouches du Rhône, just 10 – in La Ciotat, Martigues, Port de Bouc and Fos-sur-Mer – scored a blue flag. Beaches in Marseilles, Nice and St-Tropez have not been flagged for several years.

Industrial Development Northwest of Marseilles, a large area of the Crau plain – France's last remaining steppe – has been devoured by the eyesore industrial complex and port at Fos, on the southwestern shores of the Étang de Berre. Numerous oil refineries dominate the southern and eastern shores of the lagoon. Fishing in its heavily polluted waters has been banned since 1957.

By 2013 a new highway tunnel will cut beneath the Parc National du Mercantour, linking the southern Alps with Italy, and creating a direct route from Barcelona to Milan.

FLORA & FAUNA

Provence is blessed with a rich variety of flora and fauna: around 2000 of the 4200 flora species known to France are found in the Parc National du Mercantour alone.

Flora

About 1.2 million hectares of forest cover 38% of the region. The most heavily forested areas – oak and pine – are in northeastern Provence and the Var.

Cork oak and chestnut trees dominate the Massif des Maures. Maritime, aleppo and umbrella pines grow along the coast; while the plane tree studs many village squares. The Greeks brought the olive tree to the region in the 4th century BC, and the palm tree arrived with the English in the 19th century, as did the mimosa, eucalyptus and other succulents imported from Australia. Lemon and orange trees, typical only to the hot coast, have been grown since the Middle Ages.

Maquis is a form of vegetation whose low, dense shrubs provide many of the spices used in Provençal cooking. *Garrigue*, typified by aromatic Mediterranean plants such as juniper, broom and fern, grows on predominantly chalky soil.

Fauna

The Camargue is home to over 400 land and water birds, including the kingfisher, bee-eater, stork, shelduck, white egret, purple heron and more than 160 migratory species. It is France's only flamingo breeding ground and shelters 10% of the world's greater flamingo population. The Camargue also has a large native white horse and bull population. Port-Cros is an important stopover for migratory birds in autumn; seabirds include the puffin, ash-grey shearwater and yelkouan shearwater.

Endangered Species

The Hermann tortoise, once indigenous to Mediterranean Europe, is now found only in the Massif des Maures (and Corsica).

Many birds, including vultures and storks, have all but disappeared from the skies; the Bonnelli eagle can occasionally be seen in Les Calanques. Some animals, such as the vulture, only remain in the wild thanks to reintroduction programmes instigated in protected areas such as the Gorges du Verdon or the Parc National du Mercantour; see the boxed text 'Vulture Culture' in the Haute-Provence chapter.

National & Regional Parks

There are two national parks, the largest is Parc National du Mercantour in northeastern

The Village des Tortues was set up to ensure survival of the endangered Hermann tortoise.

Provence. Created in 1979 to protect 68,500 hectares on the French-Italian border, the uninhabited park embraces seven valleys. In its heart lies the Vallée des Merveilles (Valley of Marvels), an archaeological zone at the foot of Mont Bégo (2873m), which protects Europe's most important collection of Bronze Age stone carvings. A 146,500-hectare inhabited peripheral zone surrounds the park. Within the park, Mont Gélas (3143m) is the highest peak and Col de Restefond la Bonette is the highest mountain pass – in the whole of Europe!

The Parc National de Port-Cros – France's smallest national park and Europe's first marine park when created in 1963 – protects the island of Port-Cros (650 hectares) and its surrounding waters (1800 hectares), plus a 300-hectare slither of land on Cap Lardier, on the southern tip of the St-Tropez peninsula. Île de Porquerolles is also protected.

Large areas of the Lubéron and the Camargue embrace *parcs naturel régionaux* (regional nature parks), including the Parc Naturel du Verdon (146,000 hectares) around the Gorges du Verdon. Provence also has two marine reserves – the Parc Marin de la Ciotat (60 hectares) near Marseilles; and the Parc Régional Marin de la Côte Bleue (70 hectares) around Cap Couronne, west of Carry-le-Rouet. The latter is managed by the Conservatoire du Littoral, an association that manages some 60 sites in the region and is forever acquiring new sites to restore, rejuvenate and protect. Numerous other areas, both inland (such as the Crau plain) and coastal (such as Les Calanques on the Marseilles coast) are preserved areas.

The largest protected area of its type in Europe is the Réserve Géologique de Haute-Provence (the Haute-Provence Geological Reserve); it protects some 190,000 hectares surrounding Digne-les-Bains. Its geological wonders include the fossilised skeleton of an ichthyosaur dating from 185 million years ago and fossils from the tropical forests of 300 million years ago.

The region's highest mountain, Mont Ventoux, has been protected by the Réserve de Biosphère du Mont Ventoux (Mont Ventoux Biosphere Reserve) since 1994.

GOVERNMENT & POLITICS

Provence-Alpes-Côte d'Azur is one of 22 French *régions* (administrative regions). It has an elected *conseil régional* (regional council) based in Marseilles.

The region is split into six *départements* (departments). This guidebook covers five of them: Alpes de Haute-Provence (04), Alpes-Maritimes (06), Bouches du Rhône (13), Var (83) and Vaucluse (84). The town of Nîmes on the western banks of the River Rhône falls into the Gard department in the neighbouring Languedoc-Roussillon region. Departments are known by their two-digit code (listed above), included in postcodes and on the number plates of cars registered there. France (including Corsica) has 96 departments.

Each of the departments has a *préfet* (prefect) – based in a *préfecture* (prefecture) – who represents the national government, and an elected *conseil général* (general council). There is a prefecture located in Digne-les-Bains (04), Nice (06), Marseilles (13), Toulon (83) and Avignon (84).

ECONOMY

Provence is among France's wealthiest regions, thanks to its Mediterranean coastline and mild climate, which generate its primary income: tourism. More than three-quarters of the region's workforce is employed in the service industry.

The region's secondary income is generated by its booming information technology sector, the stronghold of which is 'Europe's California', alias the Sophia Antipolis Science & Technology Park, near Cannes. The 2300-hectare techno-pole was established in 1969 by France Télécom as a launch pad for piloting advanced technology. In early 2002, the 1227 companies at the park employed over 24,550 people.

During 2002 the annual turnover of high-tech industries on the Côte d'Azur notched up almost €4 billion. Despite the region's

relatively high unemployment rate (12.9% in the region, 14.6% in Bouches du Rhône), continuing expansion at Sophia Antipolis places the region second only to Paris in job creation and business growth.

Exports overall for the Provence-Alpes-Côte-d'Azur region clocked up a record €14 billion in 1999 and annual imports rose by 35% to €18 billion. Italy is the region's most important trading partner. Between 1999 and 2000, the region's gross domestic product grew by 4.7% to €95.7 billion. Grasse's perfume industry (see the boxed text 'Follow Your Nose' in the Cannes Area chapter) represents 7% of world turnover in the industry.

Despite Provence's abundance of fruit and vegetables, agriculture only employs 3% of the region's workforce. Almost 70% of France's rice production comes from Bouches du Rhône, and the region produces 29.2% of France's tomatoes and 58.1% of its grapes. Almost 75% of French olive oil comes from Provence.

POPULATION & PEOPLE

The Provence-Alpes-Côte d'Azur region has a population of 4,534,000, 40% of whom live in Bouches du Rhône. About 15% of the region's population inhabits the three interior departments, the most rural and largest being Alpes de Haute-Provence (6925 sq km) where 3% of people live. Population density here remains low – 20 people per sq km (compared to 361 per sq km in Bouches du Rhône).

Approximately 7% of the Provence and Côte d'Azur region's population is not a French national, the exception being in the Alpes-Maritimes where foreigners account for about 8%. Of the foreign population, 31.4% are European, 19% are Algerian, 19% are Moroccan, 13.8% are Tunisian, and 1.7% are Turkish.

The south's Algerian community originates from the 1950s and early 1960s when, as the French colonial empire collapsed, over one million French settlers returned to metropolitan France from Algeria, other parts of Africa and Indochina. At the same time, millions of non-French immigrants from these places were welcomed as much-needed manpower. Large-scale immigration was stopped by a 1974 law banning all new foreign workers.

ARTS

Dance

The *farandole* is a Provençal dance, popular in and around Arles. Dating from the Middle Ages, it is danced at the close of a village festival. Young men and women take their partner by the hand or remain linked with a cord or handkerchief. The brisk jig is accompanied by a tambourine and a *galoubet* (shrill flute with three holes).

In classical ballet, France led the way until the 19th century when the centre for innovation shifted to Russia and its imperial ballet. France's leading talent, Marius Petipa (1818–1910), a native of Marseilles, moved to St Petersburg in 1847 where he created masterpieces such as *La Bayadère* (1877) and *Le Lac des Cygnes* (Swan Lake; 1895). Petipa mixed French dance tradition with Slavic sensibilities. He choreographed more than 50 full-length ballets.

Literature

Middle Ages Lyric poems of courtly love composed by troubadours dominated medieval Provençal literature. They were written solely in Occitan *langue d'oc*, from which Provençal evolved.

Provençal life featured in the works of Italian poet Petrarch (1304–74), who was exiled to Avignon in 1327. Here he met the beautiful Laura to whom he dedicated his life's works. Petrarch lived in Fontaine de Vaucluse from 1337 to 1353, where he composed his song book *Canzonière* and wrote poems and letters about local shepherds, fishermen he met on the banks of the Sorgue and his pioneering ascent up Mont Ventoux.

Renaissance A great landmark in Provençal literature is the work of Bellaud de la Bellaudière (1533–88), a native of Grasse who wrote *Œuvres et Rîmes* in Occitan, a book of 160 sonnets drawing on influences by Petrarch and the French epic writer, Rabelais. In 1555, the philosopher and visionary writer Nostradamus (1503–66), a native of St-Rémy de Provence, published (in Latin) his prophetic *Centuries* in Salon de Provence where he lived until his death (from gout, as he had predicted). The papal authorities immediately banned his work as blasphemous.

17th & 18th Centuries The 17th *grand siècle* (grand century) was the century of the French classical writers. In Provence it yielded the *Noëls Provençaux*, a series of poems encapsulating a nativity scene, by Nicolas Saboly. The pious tone, very occasionally humorous, was representative of the strait-laced fervour that dominated Baroque Provençal literature.

Utterly outrageous were the sexually explicit works of Marquis de Sade (1740–1814), a descendant of Petrarch's Laura, who grew up in Lacoste. The writer wrote his best-known works between 1780 and 1800, but no-one knew about them until after WWII when they were published without censor. See the boxed text 'Sadism' in the Lubéron chapter for all the gory details.

19th-Century Revival The 19th century witnessed a massive revival in Provençal literature, largely due to one man, Frédéric Mistral (1830–1914), the only minority-language writer to be awarded a Nobel Prize for Literature (1904). A native of Maillane, Mistral's passion for Provence, its culture, history and language, was awakened by his Avignon tutor Joseph Roumanille (1818–91), who published *Li Margarideto* in 1847. In 1851 Mistral started work on what would become his most momentous work, *Mirèio*. Three years later Le Félibrige was founded by seven young Provençal poets who pledged to revive the Provençal language and codify its orthography. They published *L'Armana Prouvençau* (1859), the first journal to appear in Provençal.

Mistral's epic poem *Mirèio* – which tells the story of a beautiful girl who flees to Stes-Maries de la Mer in the Camargue when her parents forbid her to marry her true love, only to die of a broken heart on the beach – was published in 1859. A succession of poems followed, all written in Provençal and depicting a facet of Provence. Between 1878 and 1886, Mistral's most influential work on Provençal culture was published, the monumental *Trésor du Félibrige*. This encyclopaedia-style work utilised parts of the first Provençal-French dictionary, which was published as early as 1840 in Digne-les-Bains. The 1890s saw Le Félibrige popularise his work with the opening of a museum in Arles (the Musée Arletan) devoted to all things Provençal, and the publication of the less academic *L'Aïoli* journal.

Another outstanding Provençal writer was Nîmes-born Alphonse Daudet (1840–97), who spent a considerable period with Mistral in Maillane. In Fontvieille, near Arles, he wrote *Lettres de Mon Moulin* (Letters from My Windmill, 1869). Daudet is best remembered for his comic novels that evoke the small Provençal town of Tarascon through the eyes of his anti-hero Tartarin. The *Tartarin de Tarascon* trilogy was published between 1872 and 1890.

Although he was not born in Provence, Parisian novelist Émile Zola (1840–1902) lived in Aix-en-Provence, where he befriended the young Cézanne, from the age of three to 18. The aim of Zola, who claimed literary peer Flaubert as a precursor of his school of naturalism, was to convert novel writing from an art to a science by the application of experimentation. His theory may seem naive, but his work (especially his *Les Rougon-Macquart* series) was powerful and innovative. Aix-en-Provence is evoked in *La Conquête de Plassans* (1874) and his friendship with Cézanne is the focus of *L'Œuvre* (The Masterpiece; 1886).

Edmond Rostand (1868–1918), author of the novel *Cyrano de Bergerac* (1897), was a native of Marseilles.

20th Century Early 20th-century Provençal literature is dominated by Provence's best-known writers who depicted their homeland. Jean Giono (1895–1970), a native of Manosque, blended myth with reality in novels that remain a celebration of the Provençal Alps and their people. The writer/film-maker Marcel Pagnol (1895–1974) spent his life in Aubagne, where he wrote novels and screen adaptations (including Giono's *La Femme du Boulanger* in 1938). His realistic portraits of characters in rural Provence won him international acclaim. *L'Eau des Collines* (The Water of the Hills, 1963), set in the interwar period and comprising *Jean de Florette* and *Manon des Sources*, is the best known.

The surrealism that played a vital force in French literature until WWII is evident in the works of Jean Cocteau (1889–1963), the French poet, dramatist and film-maker for whom the Côte d'Azur proved to be highly influential. Cocteau ran away from home to the coast at the age of 15, then returned to settle there from 1924 and is buried in Menton. His work, in his prose, on the cinematic set (including the allegorical *Orphée*, 1950) and in the chapels and other buildings that he decorated (see under Architecture later in this section), capture the spirit of the surrealist movement: the fascination with dreams, divination and all manifestations of 'the marvellous'. His best-known novel, *Les Enfants Terribles* (1955), portrays the intellectual rebellion of the postwar era.

During WWII Roussillon in the Vaucluse served as a refuge to playwright Samuel Beckett, who arrived in the village in 1942 after fleeing Paris. He stayed until April 1945 and wrote *Watt* (not published until after *Waiting for Godot* in 1953) while he was here. Colette (1873–1954), who thoroughly enjoyed tweaking the nose of conventional readers with titillating novels that detailed the amorous exploits of such heroines as the schoolgirl Claudine, lived in St-Tropez from 1927 until 1938. *La Naissance du Jour* evokes an unspoilt St-Tropez before tourism took over.

Following WWII existentialism, a literary movement developed that was based around Jean-Paul Sartre (1905–80), Simone de Beauvoir (1908–86) and Albert Camus (1913– 60). The latter moved to Lourmarin in the Lubéron (where he is buried) in 1957, and started his unfinished autobiographical novel *Le Premier Homme* (The First Man) there. The manuscript was found in the car wreckage when the Algerian-born writer – son of an illiterate mother – died in a car accident three years later.

The British novelist and travel writer Lawrence Durrell (1912–90) settled in Sommières, near Nîmes, and dedicated the last 33 years of his literary career to writing about Provençal life. Other notable figures who settled in the region in the latter part of their careers include Dirk Bogarde, James Baldwin and Anthony Burgess.

Architecture

Prehistoric The earliest monuments in France were stone megaliths erected during the Neolithic period from 4000 to 2400 BC. Remnants can be seen at Musée d'Archéologie Méditerranée in Marseilles; Monaco's Musée d'Anthropologie Préhistorique, from where it is possible to visit the Grottes de l'Observatoire; the Musée de Digne at Digne-les-Bains; and Quinson's Musée de la Préhistoire des Gorges du Verdon, which organises treks to the Grotte de la Baume Bonne. Numerous menhirs are evident in the Vallée des Merveilles and examples of the region's earliest habitats known as *bories* (beehive-shaped huts built from dry limestone) can be seen near Gordes.

Gallo-Roman The Romans constructed an incredible number of public works throughout Roman Provincia from the 1st century BC, including aqueducts, fortifications, marketplaces, temples, amphitheatres, triumphal arches and bathhouses. They also established regular street grids at many settlements.

Testimony to Roman architectural brilliance includes the Pont du Gard aqueduct between Nîmes and Avignon; the colossal amphitheatres at Nîmes and Arles; the theatres at Orange and Fréjus; the Maison Carrée in Nîmes; the public buildings in Vaison-la-Romaine; the excavated temples at Glanum; and the triumphal arches at Orange and Carpentras.

Dark Ages Quite a few churches were constructed in the Merovingian and Carolingian periods (5th to 10th century), but few remain. Fine traces of churches from this era are reflected in the octagonal, 5th-century baptistry at Fréjus. The earliest Christian relics, dating from the 2nd to 4th centuries, can be seen at the Musée du Pays Brignolais in Brignoles, Fréjus' Musée Archéologique and the Musée d'Archéologique d'Arles.

The region has numerous examples of *villages perchés* (hill-top villages) that took root in Provence from the 10th century. Villagers from the plains built new villages on top of rocky crags as a defence against Saracen attacks. Economics forced many to move back to the plains in the 19th and 20th centuries.

Romanesque A religious revival in the 11th century led to the construction of Romanesque churches, so-called because the architects adopted many of the architectural elements (eg, vaulting) from Gallo-Roman buildings. Romanesque buildings typically have round arches, heavy walls with few windows and a lack of ornamentation. The region's most famous examples of the style

Art Portfolio

With its designer chapels, cutting-edge architecture and avant-garde art museums, the region is practically a living art museum. Here's its portfolio.

18th- to 20th-Century Art Collections

Musée Granet with plenty of Cézannes (Aix-en-Provence); Musée Réattu (Arles); Musée Calvet (Avignon); Centre de la Vieille Charité (Marseilles); Musée des Arts Asiatiques, Musée International d'Art Naïf Anatole Jakovsky and Musée Masséna (Nice); Musée des Beaux-Arts (Nice, Menton & Marseilles); Musée de l'Annonciade (St-Tropez)

One-Man Shows

Musée National Message Biblique Marc Chagall (Nice); Musée Jean Cocteau (Menton); Musée Matisse (Nice); Musée National Fernand Léger (Biot); Musée Renoir (Cagnes-sur-Mer); Musée Picasso (Antibes); Musée National Picasso (Vallauris); Fondation Vasarely (Aix-en-Provence)

Designer Chapels

Chapelle de la Congrégation (Manosque) by Carzou; Chapelle Notre Dame de Jérusalem (Fréjus) and Chapelle de St-Pierre (Menton) by Cocteau; Chapelle du Rosaire (Vence) by Matisse; Chapelle La Guerre et La Paix (Vallauris) by Picasso

Contemporary Art & Installations

Musée d'Art Méditerranéen Moderne (Cagnes-sur-Mer); Crestet Centre d'Art (Crestet); Villa Noailles (Hyères); Musée d'Art Contemporain (Marseilles); Espace de l'Art Concret (Mouans-Sartoux); Fondation d'Art de la Napoule (Mandelieu-La Napoule); Grimaldi Forum (Monaco); Musée d'Art Moderne et d'Art Contemporain (Nice); Carré d'Art (Nîmes); Fondation Maeght and Galerie Guy Pieters (St-Paul de Vence)

are Cistercian abbeys at Sénanque (1148), Le Thoronet (1160) and Silvacane (1175).

The majestic but sober Chartreuse de la Verne (1170), the older monastery (1073) on Île St-Honorat and the church at Stes-Maries de la Mer are examples of the fortress-like sacred buildings that also characterised this era. Chateaux, like Château Grimaldi in Antibes, also tended to be sturdy, heavily fortified structures that afforded few luxuries to their inhabitants. The exceptional dimensions of Digne-les-Bains cathedral (1200–1330) are typical of the late Provençal-Romanesque style.

Gothic The structures of this period are characterised by ribbed vaults carved with great precision, pointed arches, slender verticals, chapels along the nave and chancel, refined decoration and large stained-glass windows. Provence's most important examples of Gothic architecture are Avignon's Palais des Papes, the Val de Bénédiction Charterhouse in Villeneuve-lès-Avignon and Carpentras' Cathédrale St-Siffrein.

Frescoes emerged at the end of the Gothic era as a means of interior decoration. Small churches, tucked in the Niçois hinterland, benefited most from these treasured adornments. The interior of the Chapelle Notre Dame des Fontaines in the Vallée de la Roya is a classic example.

Provence was scarcely touched by the French Renaissance period. The 16th century saw the emergence of citadel architect, Sébastien Le Prestre de Vauban (1633–1707), as a force to be reckoned with. His works in Provence include the Fort Carré in Antibes with his signature star-shaped walls, the fortification of the hill-top village of Entrevaux and constructions at Toulon port and Sisteron.

Baroque During the Baroque period, which lasted from the end of the 16th century to the late 18th century, painting, sculpture and classical architecture were integrated to create structures and interiors of great subtlety, refinement and elegance. Nice's Chapelle de la Miséricorde and Menton's Italianate Église St-Michel are grand Baroque churches. Marseilles' Centre de la Vielle Charité (1671–1749) is built around a beautiful Baroque-domed chapel designed by Pierre Puget (see Sculpture later in this section).

Neoclassical From about 1740, neoclassicism emerged from a renewed interest in classical forms; a search for order, reason and serenity through adoption of the forms and conventions of Graeco-Roman antiquity: columns, simple geometric forms and traditional ornamentation.

Neoclassicism came into its own under Napoleon III, who used it extensively for

Trailing Le Corbusier

Radical modernist Le Corbusier revolutionised architecture. His trail can be tracked in Marseilles (where he built the ground-breaking Unité d'Habitation), Cap Martin (where he had a seaside studio) and Roquebrune (where he is buried).

Swiss-born, it was the latter part of his life that saw Charles Édouard Jeanneret (1887–1965), alias Le Corbusier, turn to southern France for inspiration. Of all his architectural achievements, it was the mammoth concrete apartment block he designed in Marseilles that was the most influential – and controversial. Built between 1947 and 1952 as a low-costing housing project, the **Unité d'Habitation** saw 337 apartments arranged inside an elongated block on stilts. Apartments were built in 23 different configurations, and everything needed for functional living, including a school and gym, was on site.

Considered a coup by architects worldwide, the apartment block – or rather, its facade, communal corridors and roof-top terrace – has been classified as a historical monument since 1986. Apartments on the 7th and 8th floors function as a 22-room hotel (see Hótel Le Corbusier under Marseilles in the Marseilles Area chapter), and the rest are private apartments, home to 1400 people. Apartment tours (minimum three people, arranged through the hotel reception) cost €5.

Le Corbusier frequently visited the coast from the 1930s, often staying with his architect friends, Irish Eileen Gray and Romanian-born Jean Badovici, in their 1920s seaside villa on Cap Martin, **E-1027**. In 1938 Le Corbusier painted a trio of wall frescoes in E-1027, one of which featured three entangled women and offended Gray (a proclaimed lesbian) so much that she broke off her friendship with the architect and moved to Menton.

monumental architecture designed to embody the grandeur of imperial France. Nice's Justice Palace and Palais Masséna, and Toulon's Église St-Louis are examples. The true showcase of this era, though, are Monaco's Monte Carlo Casino (1878) and opera house (1879), both designed by French architect Charles Garnier (1825–98) and ranked as some of the Second Empire's finest achievements. Garnier, with Gustave Eiffel (1832–1923), who lived in Beaulieu-sur-Mer, also designed the Observatoire de Nice (1887).

Aix-en-Provence's public fountains and *hôtels particuliers* (private residences) also date from this period; as do Provence's intricate wrought-iron *campaniles*, originally a feature of rural Provençal architecture, that top most church bell towers in cities and towns.

Eclecticism Alongside neoclassicism, the *belle époque* heralded a fantastical eclecticism that lasted into the early 20th century. Trademarks included anything from decorative stucco friezes, trompe l'œil paintings and glittering wall mosaics, to brightly coloured Moorish minarets and Turkish towers. Anything went. Nice is exceptionally well endowed with these chocolate-box creations; see the boxed text 'Absolutely Fabulous' in the Nice to Menton chapter. In Barcelonnette, Mexican-inspired Château des Magnans is another buoyant reflection of this beautiful age.

The stark, concrete and glass Villa Noailles (1923) in Hyères is an expression of the cubist movement that gained momentum in the interwar period. Examples of surrealist interiors designed by Jean Cocteau (see Literature earlier), who lived in Menton at this time, include Menton's Salles des Mariages (1957), the Chapelle de St-Pierre (1959) in Villefranche-sur-Mer and Cap d'Ail's amphitheatre.

Post-WWII Architecture France's most celebrated 20th-century architect is Le Corbusier; for details see the boxed text 'Trailing Le Corbusier'.

The building of the Fondation Vasarely in Aix-en-Provence, designed by Victor Vasarely (1908–97), was an architectural coup when unveiled in 1976. Its 14 giant monumental hexagons reflected what he had already achieved in art: the creation of optical illusion and changing perspective through the juxtaposition of geometrical shapes and colours. Vasarely also designed the town hall in La Seyne-sur-Mer, near Toulon, and the stained-glass windows inside Port Grimaud's church. The single most influential period in Vasarely's career was spent in Gordes. He was dubbed 'the father of Op Art'.

Trailing Le Corbusier

After WWII Le Corbusier befriended Thomas Rebutato who ran neighbouring **L'Étoile de Mer**, a shack restaurant overlooking the sea. He bought a plot of land from Rebutato and in 1951 came up with the **Cabanon**, a one-room log-cabin containing everything needed for holiday living in 13 square metres. He gave this experiment in minimalist habitation to his wife, Monagésque model Yvonne Gallis (who he wed in 1930), as a birthday present. It remained their summer home until 1965 when Le Corbusier suffered a fatal heart attack while swimming in the sea.

Twice-weekly visits to the Cabanon are arranged by Cap Martin-Roquebrune tourist office (see that section in the Nice to Menton chapter). In the future, the site will be developed as a museum and architectural research centre, incorporating the Cabanon as well as L'Étoile de Mer (still owned by the Rebutato family) and E-1027 (inhabited by squatters from 1990 until 1999).

Promenade Le Corbusier, a coastal footpath leads to the site from Roquebrune-Cap Martin train station; exit the station and bear left along the *sentier littoral* (coastal path – signposted 'Plage de Carnolés').

Le Corbusier is buried with his wife, who died in 1957, in Roquebrune cemetery. The grave – designed by Corbusier before his death – is adorned by a cactus and the epitaph, *ici repose Charles Édouard Jeanneret (1887–1965)*, painted in Le Corbusier's cursive hand on a small yellow, red-and-blue ceramic tile. To get to the cemetery from central place des 2 Frères, walk eastwards to the end of rue Grimaldi, turn left onto rue d'Église, right onto rue de la Fontaine, then left onto chemin de Gorbio from where steps lead to Le Corbusier's grave (section J).

Steel meets glass at the modern Carrée d'Art (1993) in Nîmes. The reflective 'Square of Art' was designed by British architect Sir Norman Foster (born 1935), responsible for the seminal Hong Kong, the Shanghai Bank building in Hong Kong and, more recently, the Musée de la Préhistoire des Gorges du Verdon in Quinson. Nîmes also sports a bus stop on ave Carnot designed by Philippe Starck (born 1949), a contemporary French designer who also redesigned Nîmes' coat of arms and, more recently, worked with French chef Alain Ducasse to design the interior of the upmarket Monaco restaurant, Bar & Bœuf.

Other examples of modern architecture include Monaco's monumental glass-and-steel Grimaldi Forum (2000), two- thirds of which is beneath sea level; Nice's Musée d'Art Moderne et d'Art Contemporain (1990) and Bibliothèque Louis Nocera (2002); the Fondation Maeght (1964) in St-Paul de Vence and also Matisse's Chapelle du Rosaire (1943–51) in Vence, where the exterior reflects a traditional Provençal cottage. Port Grimaud (1969), which is a holiday village, was the conception of Francis Spoerry (1912–99) who later designed Port Liberty in New York.

Painting

To the 16th Century Sculpture and stained glass were the main adornments of the medieval Gothic churches, in part because the many windows left little wall space. The Sienese, French and Spanish artists working at the papal court in Avignon in the 14th century, however, created an influential style of mural painting, examples of which can be seen in the city's Palais des Papes.

While the rest of France found itself preoccupied with the Hundred Years' War, art flourished in Nice county, where the School of Nice emerged, led by Louis Bréa. Bréa, exalted as the 'Fra Angelico Provençal', created the burgundy colour known as *rouge bréa*. His works can be seen in Cimiez (Nice) and Menton's Palais Carnolès. This school of primitive painters worked notably for the Penitent Brotherhoods, which explains why their works are in rural chapels once used as a place of pilgrimage.

17th & 18th Centuries Blindman's bluff, stolen kisses and other courtly frivolities were the subject matter of the French school of artists that emerged in the late 17th and early 18th centuries during the Enlightenment. Avignon-born Joseph Vernet (1714–89) was among the most influential, leaving a series of 15 landscapes depicting French ports, including Toulon. Rococo influences played on the landscapes of Jean-Honoré Fragonard (1732–1806), whose playful scenes immortalised his native Grasse and captured the silliness of the rococo spirit. The elevated works of Nice-born Carle van Loo (1705–65) represented rococo's more serious 'grand style'. Works by these artists are on display in the Musée des Beaux-Arts Jules Chéret in Nice; the Musée des Beaux-Arts in Marseilles; Avignon's Musée Calvet; Musée Fragonard in Grasse; and the Musée Granet, Aix-en-Provence.

19th Century François Marius Granet (1775–1849), who was born and died in Aix-en-Provence, was a pupil of the influential artist Jacques Louis David. Granet displayed a strong empathy with nature in his watercolours, a trademark of Provençal painters at this time.

Landscape painting further evolved under the Barbizon School. Jean-François Millet took many of his subjects from peasant life and had a strong influence on Van Gogh. Millet anticipated the realist programme of Gustave Courbet (1819–77), a prominent member of the Paris Commune, who frequently visited southern France. Among his most fervent pupils was Provençal realist Paul Guigou (1834–71), a native of Villars in the Vaucluse, who painted numerous canvases of the Durance plains over-drenched in bright sunlight. *Deux Lavandières devant la Ste-Victoire* (Two Washing Women in front of Mont Ste-Victoire) painted by Guigou near Aix-en-Provence in 1986, is in the Musée Grobet-Labadié, Marseilles.

It was Provence's astonishing intensity of light that drew the impressionists to the region. Impressionism, initially a term of derision, was taken from the title of an experimental painting by Claude Monet in 1874, *Impression: Soleil Levant* (Impression: Sunrise). Monet was the leading figure of the school, which counted among its members Alfred Sisley, Camille Pissarro, Berthe Morisot and Pierre-Auguste Renoir (1841–1919). Renoir lived in Cagnes-sur-Mer on the Riviera from 1903 until his death. Many of his works are displayed in the Musée Renoir (his former home and studio) in Cagnes-sur-Mer.

Paul Cézanne (1839–1906) is Provence's best-known artist. He was born and died in Aix-en-Provence, and is celebrated for his still-life and landscape works. Cézanne painted numerous canvases in and around Aix, particularly of Mont St-Victoire. *Les Baigneuses* (The Bathers) is in Aix's Musée Granet. Southern France was also immortalised by Paul Gauguin (1848–1904), who spent much time during the late 19th century in Arles. Both he and Cézanne are usually referred to as post-impressionists, something of a catch-all word for the diverse styles that flowed from impressionism.

When in Arles, Gauguin worked for a time with Dutch artist Vincent van Gogh (1854–90), who spent most of his painting life in Paris and Arles. A brilliant and innovative artist, Van Gogh produced haunting selfortraits and landscapes, in which colour assumes an expressive and emotive quality. Unfortunately, Van Gogh's talent was largely unrecognised during his lifetime. He was confined to an asylum in St-Rémy de Provence and eventually committed suicide. He painted his most famous works, *Sunflowers* and *Van Gogh's Chair* (1888), in Arles. Van Gogh's later technique, exhibited in works dating from his St-Rémy period such as *Starry Night* and *Olive Trees* (1889), foreshadowed pointillism.

Pointillism was developed by Georges Seurat (1859–91), who applied paint in small dots or with uniform brush strokes of unmixed colour. His most devout pupil was Paul Signac (1863–1935), who settled in St-Tropez from 1892 onwards. Part of the Musée de l'Annonciade in St-Tropez is devoted to pointillist works and includes *Étude pour le Chenal de Gravelines* (Study for the Channel at Gravelines) painted by Seurat in 1890 as well as numerous works by Signac, most of which depict the coastal towns of St-Tropez or Marseilles.

20th Century French painting in the 20th century has a bewildering diversity of styles, including fauvism and cubism. Two of their leading exponents, Matisse (fauvism) and Picasso (cubism) spent their most creative years in Provence, where they contributed enormously to the development of these two movements.

Fauvism took its name from the slur of a critic who compared the exhibitors at the 1905 Salon d'Automme in Paris with *fauves* (wildcats) because of their radical use of intensely bright colours. Among these 'wild' painters was Henri Matisse who spent much time in the region, lapping up the sunlight and vivacity of the coast in and around Nice. While in St-Tropez with Signac, he started sketches that later produced *Luxe, Calme et Volupté* (Luxury, Calm and Tranquillity). The signature uniform brush strokes of pointillism were still evident, but were also intermingled with splashes of violent colour. Matisse's consequent painting, *La Gitane* (1906), displayed in St-Tropez's Musée de l'Annonciade, is considered the embodiment of fauvist principles.

Cubism was effectively launched in 1907 by Spanish prodigy Pablo Picasso (1881–1973), for whom Provence had a tremendous importance; he spent most of his creative life in the region. As demonstrated in his pioneering *Les Demoiselles d'Avignon*, cubism deconstructed the subject into a system of intersecting planes and presented various aspects of it simultaneously. The collage, incorporating bits of cloth, wood, string, newspaper and anything lying around, was a cubist speciality. Picasso went on to experiment (and succeed) with a number of other mediums and concepts, but his cubist works remain highly popular.

Provence continued to inspire the leading artists of various movements. After WWI, the School of Paris was formed by a group of expressionists, mostly foreign, such as Marc Chagall (1887–1985), who was born in Vitebsk (present-day Belarus) but lived in France from 1922. His pictures combine fantasy and folklore. Chagall spent the last few years of his life in St-Paul de Vence where he is buried. The largest collection of his works is in Nice. Many of Chagall's later works were influenced by the surrealists, most active in the interwar period. Surrealism attempted to reunite the conscious and unconscious realms, to permeate everyday life with fantasies and dreams.

With the onset of WWII many artists left France's sunny south, and although some returned after the war, the region never regained its old magnetism. Picasso moved permanently to the Côte d'Azur, settling first in Golfe-Juan, then Vallauris and finally Mougins, where he died. In 1946 he set up his studio in Antibes' Château Grimaldi, the works which he completed here being exhibited in the Musée Picasso inside the chateau. Among his other accomplishments was the interior decoration of the chapel in Vallauris.

The other great artist of this period was Henri Matisse (1869–1954), who lived in Nice from 1917 until his death – with the exception of the WWII period when he took refuge in nearby Vence. He also decorated a chapel after WWII. His bold and colourful works culminated in his familiar blue and white cut-out montages, which he completed in the early 1950s prior to his death. Works representing his whole career can be seen at Nice's Musée Matisse.

In the wake of Matisse came the 1960s new realists, well represented in the Musée d'Art Moderne et d'Art Contemporain, Nice. Led by Provençal artists such as Arman, Yves Klein and César (see Sculpture later in this section), these artists rejected the abstraction of the postwar years and turned to 'modern nature'. Suddenly, art was generated from recycled trash, dirty crockery, crushed cars and scrap metal. In 1960, Nice-born Klein (1928–1962) produced *Anthropométrie de l'Époque Bleue*, a series of blue imprints made by two naked women (covered from head to toe in blue paint) rolling around on a white canvas – in front of an orchestra of violins and an audience in evening dress. Arman, also born in Nice in 1928, became known for his trash-can portraits, made by framing the litter found in the subject's trash bin. Another influential realist from the School of Nice was Martial Rayasse, bornin Golfe-Juan in 1936, and renowned for pioneering the use of neon in contemporary art. Most notable is his 1964 portrait of *Nissa Bella* (Beautiful Nice), which incorporates a flashing blue heart on a human face.

Another influential artist was Hungarian-born Victor Vasarely (1908–97). In Gordes from 1948, the avant-gardist turned his attention to geometrical forms, juxtaposed in contrasting colours to create shifting perspectives. Forty-two works by Vasarely are displayed in the Fondation Vasarely – designed and funded by the artist himself (see Architecture earlier in this section) – in Aix-en-Provence.

The supports-surfaces movement that took root in the 1970s focused on deconstructing the traditional concept of a painting and transforming one of its structural components – such as the frame or canvas – into a work of art instead. The Groupe 70, specific to Nice, expressed an intellectual agitation, typical to Vivien Isnard's 1987 *Sans Titre* (Without Title) and Louis Chacallis' *Tension* (1978).

Sculpture

At the end of the 11th century, sculptors decorated the portals, capitals, altars and fonts of Romanesque churches, illustrating Bible stories and the lives of the saints for the illiterate. Two centuries later, when the cathedral became the centre of monumental building, sculpture spread from the central portal to the whole facade, whose brightly painted and carved surface offered a symbolic summary of Christian doctrine. In the 17th century, Marseilles-born sculptor, Pierre Puget (1620–94), made his mark in France. He introduced the idea of adorning ship sterns with elaborate ornamentation, and was among the first to experiment with atlantes – the use of figures of men instead of columns to support an entablature. The anguished figures that support the balcony of honour at the old city hall on quai Constradt in Toulon are a celebrated example. The Musée des Beaux-Arts in Marseilles has a large collection of his works.

Marseilles also produced César Baldaccini (known as César). He (1921–98) was greatly inspired by Michelangelo (a replica of his David stands in Marseilles today) and Picasso (one of the first to use scrap metal as a medium). Post-WWII he used wrought-iron and scrap metals to create a series of insects and animals. Later he graduated to pliable plastics. In 1960 he became the first artist to use motorised vehicles (crushed cars) as a medium. Between 1960 and 1989 he compressed 23 cars, some of which are displayed in the Musée d'Art Moderne et d'Art Contemporain, Nice. His work can be also seen in Marseilles. Arguably his best-known work is the little statue handed to actors at the Césars (named after him), the French cinema awards dating from 1976 and equivalent to Hollywood's Oscars.

Cinema

Beginnings to WWII With its spectacular light and subtle shadows, it is not surprising that Provence was as inspirational to cinema as it was to art. Cinematographic pioneers, the Lumière brothers – who invented 'moving pictures' – made their earliest films on the Côte d'Azur. The world's first motion picture – a series of two-minute reels – was shown for the first time in Château Lumière, a property owned by their father in La Ciotat, in September 1895. The film, entitled *L'Arrivée d'un Train en Gare de La Ciotat* (The Arrival of a Train at La Ciotat Station), made the audience jump out of their seats as the steam train rocketed towards them. It only made its debut in Paris three months later.

Nice was catapulted to stardom in the 1920s. The Victorine film studios, which Serge Sandberg had established in 1920, were sold for US$5 million to Hollywood director Rex Ingram in 1925. He transformed the studios overnight into the hub of European film-making, welcoming avant-garde directors such as the intensely productive Jean Renoir, son of the famous artist, to his studios. These were innovative times for film in France.

A big name at this time was Aubagne-born, Provençal writer Marcel Pagnol, whose film career kicked off in 1931 with *Marius*, the first part of his legendary *Fanny* trilogy starring Raimu (see Silver-Screen Heroes later in this section) and portraying prewar Marseilles. Pagnol filmed *La Femme du Boulanger* (The Baker's Wife, 1938) in the hill-top village of Castellet. Throughout his career, he stuck to depicting what he knew best – Provence and its ordinary people.

New Wave Nice's film industry stagnated after WWII until the 1950s, when *nouvelle vague* (new wave) burst onto the scene. With small budgets, sometimes self-financed, no extravagant sets or big-name stars, directors made films such as *Et Dieu Créa la Femme* (And God Created Woman, 1956), which brought sudden stardom to Brigitte Bardot, the little fishing village of St-Tropez and the young director Roger Vadim. The film, which examined the amorality of modern youth, received international acclaim. For a list of films shot in the region by foreign directors at this time, see Film in the Facts for the Visitor chapter.

The new wave lost its experimental edge in the mid-1970s: just two films were made at the Victorine studios in 1976, followed by a paltry three in 1977. The studios have since produced television commercials.

Silver-Screen Heroes Film stars congregate on the Côte d'Azur once a year for an orgy of glitz and glamour at the *Festival International du Film* (Cannes International Film Festival), the French film industry's main annual event (see the boxed text 'Starring at Cannes' in the Cannes Area chapter).

Provence produced one of France's earliest screen heroes – Raimu. The great comic actor was born in Toulon as Jules Auguste César Muraire (1883–1946) and is best remembered for his colourful portrayal of Provençal characters, notably in Pagnol's early *Fanny* trilogy, *La Femme du Boulanger* and later *La Fille du Puisatier* (1940). In the latter, Raimu starred with Fernandel (1903–71), France's other legendary comic, known as 'Horseface' because of his inimitable grin. Horseface was an honorary citizen of Carry-le-Rouet, where he spent summer most years. The indisputable star of the 1950s and 1960s was sexy Brigitte Bardot (see the boxed text 'BB' in the St-Tropez to Toulon chapter).

The beautiful, blonde-haired actor, Jean Marais (1914–98), lived in Vallauris near Cannes most of his life. He was best known for his lead role in Jean Cocteau's *La Belle et la Bête* (Beauty and the Beast, 1946), *Orphée* (Orpheus, 1950) and more recently as Prospero in the 1990s adaptation of *The Tempest* by Shakespeare. Marais and Cocteau (see Literature – 20th Century earlier in this section) met in 1937 and were lovers until Cocteau's death in 1963.

SOCIETY & CONDUCT

While Parisians systematically slam every city other than their own, so people in Provence perceive the cold north – anything north of Avignon, capital included – as far less attractive than their own sunlit region. Provence, for them, is bathed in a golden glow year round. Come the big chill of the mistral in autumn and winter, true Provençaux are barely bitten by the unbearable cold, unlike their foreign neighbours who shut the shutters tight, curl up by the fire – and still shiver in their sleep. Unless you're born and bred in Provence, you have little hope of ever adjusting to the mistral's menacing climes, as any true Provençaux will very proudly point out.

Provençaux are staunchly proud of their natural treasures and rich cultural heritage. Most have an equally staunch loyalty to the hamlet, village, town or city where they live. The rough and tumble Marseillais are famed throughout France for their blatant exaggerations and imaginative fancies – such as the tale about the sardine that blocked Marseilles port. The Niçois by contrast are more Latin in outlook and temperament, sharing a common zest for the good life with their Italian neighbours. Monagésques in Monaco tend to dress on the flashy side, while St-Tropez's colourful community is clearly split between bronzed-year-round glamour queens and reborn hippies. Wild gesticulations, passionate cheek kissing and fervent hand-shaking are an integral part of Provençal daily life, regardless of geographical location.

Food, a topic that miraculously wangles its way in to the most seemingly unrelated of conversations, is an extremely serious affair in this part of France. Offences warranting social ostracism include expressing even a mild dislike for a traditional culinary dish such as *pieds et paquets* (sheep tripe) or *testicules de mouton* (sheep testicles); or declining a *dégustation* (wine-tasting) session, regardless of time, day or circumstance.

Dining dos and don'ts include never asking for ice cubes to drop into warm wine, or tomato sauce (ketchup) and mayonnaise to douse over food. When tasting wine, be sure to perform the series of facial contortions required. If invited to lunch, don't bother making plans for the afternoon; lunch will last at least three hours and leave you feeling so blissfully full that it is doubtful you'll be able to move. Skipping lunch is the ultimate sin and a quick snack standing up is a no no.

Handy tricks to make friends quickly include saying 'Bonjour, monsieur/madame/mademoiselle' when you sail into a shop/café/restaurant, or saying it with flowers when visiting someone's home. Never offer chrysanthemums unless you intend laying them on a gravestone. Money, time and politics are all taboo subjects.

When travelling in Monaco, do not mention the revolution – or refer to Monaco as a part of France. Monagésques will explain that their principality is a distinctly separate country with its own strong history, culture and traditions. Listen to what they have to say and respect their patch of land. At many cultural events in Monaco, a jacket and tie is required. See Legal Matters in the Facts for the Visitor chapter for details on what you can and cannot wear when strolling the streets of Monaco and other towns.

RELIGION

Countrywide, 80% of people identify themselves as Catholic, although few attend mass. Catholicism is the official state religion in neighbouring Monaco, which marks a number of religious feasts with public holidays (see Public Holidays & Special Events in the Facts for the Visitor chapter). Protestants account for less than 2% of today's population.

Many of France's four to five million nominally Muslim residents live in the south of France, comprising the second-largest religious group. France's Jewish community numbers 650,000, Europe's largest. There are synagogues in Avignon, Marseilles, Cavaillon and Carpentras.

Facts for the Visitor

HIGHLIGHTS

Natural Wonders

Awe-inspiring natural wonders include Mont Ventoux's white summit; the burgundy-red Gorges de Dalius in Haute Vallée du Var and Europe's largest canyon, the Gorges du Verdon; the Pénitents des Mées, larger-than-life stone figurines in the Vallée de la Durance; the dramatic vivid-red ochre rock formations in the Lubéron; Marseilles' Les Calanques; and France's highest cliff on Cap Canaille near Cassis.

The chestnut-forested Massif des Maures, the rocky red Massif de l'Estérel and the Camargue's flamingo-pink wetlands rank among the region's most dramatic landscapes. The fragile beauty and isolation of the Parc National du Mercantour in northeastern Provence remains unrivalled. The pinprick island of Port-Cros – Europe's first marine national park – ranks second.

Gardens & Villages

Hill-top villages firmly placed along the tourist trail include Les Baux de Provence, Gordes, Bonnieux, Ménerbes, Lacoste, Èze and St-Paul de Vence. The quiet villages tucked in the Niçois hinterland, north of Nice, and also those west of Grasse in the northern Var, are comparatively bare of commercialism (so far).

The region's temperate climate nurtures some beautiful gardens, including those surrounding Cap Ferrat's Villa Rothschild, the Villa Grecque Kérylos in Beaulieu-sur-Mer, and the little known Jardin de la Villa Noailles in Grasse. The green-fingered should not miss Menton's gardens (see the boxed text 'Menton Gardens' in the Nice to Menton chapter).

Food & Wine

Culinary thrill-seekers should shop at a Provençal market – the best of Provence's markets are listed in Food & wine of Provence special section; watch a harvest (lavender in July, rice in August, grapes in September, olives from November to January); sniff out truffles (from November to March); sip red wine in Châteauneuf du Pape; sample *bouillabaisse* in Marseilles; dine à la Ducasse/Vergé in Monaco, La Celle, Moustiers Ste-Marie, Mougins and St-Tropez; and devote plenty of time to sampling regional dishes over long and lazy lunches in *fermes auberges* (farmhouse restaurants).

High Life

Savour the ritz and glitz and the rich and not-so-famous in Monaco's Monte Carlo Casino; in Marseilles' Musée de la Mode (Fashion Design Museum); on La Croisette in star-struck Cannes; or at St-Tropez's yacht-filled Vieux Port. Legendary places to eat, sleep and spend a small fortune include Hôtel de Paris, Louis XV and Bar & Bœuf (Monaco); La Colombe d'Or (St-Paul de Vence); Hôtel du Cap Eden Roc (Cap d'Antibes); the Carlton Inter-Continental and Hôtel Majestic Barrière (Cannes); Moulin de Mougins (Mougins); and Hôtel Byblos and Spoon (St Tropez). Bars and clubs so hot that even celebrities go there include Le Club 55, VIP Room and Bodega du Papagayo (St-Tropez); and Palm Square, Le Loft, Living Room and others in Cannes' so-called *carré magique* (magic square).

Art & Architecture

Precious architectural gems include the Roman relics at Pont du Gard, Orange, Arles, Nîmes and St-Rémy de Provence; the 12th-century Romanesque abbeys of Sénanque, Silvacane and Thoronet; the walled city of Aigues-Mortes; Avignon's Gothic Palais des Papes; Aix-en-Provence's fountains and *hôtels particuliers* (private mansions); Nice's *belle époque* follies; the Matisse chapel in Vence; Villa Grecque Kérylos in Beaulieu-sur-Mer; Le Corbusier's Cité Radieuse in Marseilles; and Nîmes' Carrée d'Art.

See the 'Art Portfolio' boxed text in the Facts about Provence chapter for a list of outstanding art museums.

Just Kidding

Acrobatic killer-whale shows at Marineland (Biot), giant waterslides at the Niagara Parc Nautique (near La Môle), and tortoises at the Village des Tortues in the Massif des Maures are but some of the ways to win the heart of a howling child. Museum-wise, try the Musée Océanographique in Monaco, the Grande Expo du Pont du Gard with its kid-friendly Ludo centre.

Horse riding on the beach in the Camargue, paddling in a canoe beneath the Pont du Gard, cycling around the island of Porquerolles (there are pedal-powered chariots for kids too small to pedal themselves), snorkelling off Port-Cros' shores, roller-blading in Nice or skiing in Haute-Provence are great, kid-friendly, outdoor highlights. The Parc National du Mercantour and Office National des Forêts (ONF) both organise nature walks for children.

SUGGESTED ITINERARIES

Depending on how long you plan to stay in the region, you may like to consider the following itineraries.

One Week

Spend three days in Avignon, with half-day trips to Châteauneuf du Pape and Pont du Gard, followed by two days in the Camargue or around Mont Ventoux in the Vaucluse, and two days in Marseilles and/or Aix-en-Provence. Alternatively, spend a week in Nice, with day trips along the three Corniches to Monaco, Menton, Cannes and Antibes, and inland to the remote Niçois hinterland.

Two Weeks

Combine the one-week itineraries, or spend a fortnight exploring one region in more depth: From the Camargue, add side trips to Arles and Nîmes; and take a couple of days touring the Lubéron by car, bike or foot after visiting the Mont Ventoux area; or head north to the Gorges du Verdon. From Nice, either enjoy a week of 'the great outdoors' in Haute-Provence or continue west along the coast to glitzy St-Tropez.

Three Weeks

Combine the other itineraries, or linger longer in one place to enjoy the fine walking, cycling and river activities on offer (Lubéron, Mont Ventoux and Gorges du Verdon) or immerse yourself in the glitz and glamour of Riviera high life.

One Month

The region's your oyster.

PLANNING

When to Go

In short, not in July and August. Summer is generally considered to be from June to mid-Spetember.

May and June are the best times to visit, followed by September and October. Spring in Provence is a cocktail of flowering poppy fields, blossoming almond trees and colourful wildflowers. In September, age-old vines sag with plump red grapes, pumpkin fields turn orange and the first olives turn black in Van Gogh's silver-branched olive groves. The vendange (grape harvest) starts around 15 September, followed by the cueillette des olives (olive harvest) from 15 November through to early January.

Stone-capped Mont Ventoux – Provence's highest point – stays snow-capped until as late as the middle of May. The southern Alps in Haute-Provence are snow-covered from late November until early April; the ski season starts just before Christmas and lasts until March.

On the coast, sun worshippers lay their bodies out to bake from April to early October. July and August are notoriously hot and unbearable for those not within dipping distance of a pool or the sea. Discomfort brought on by the sweltering heat is further exacerbated by the hordes of tourists and French holiday-makers who descend on the region, clogging up the roads, hotels and camp sites and generally making life hell for anyone visiting the region to 'get away from it all'. Dream on.

Inland, lavender fields blaze purple for just a few weeks from late June to late July, when the flowers are harvested. In August and September the days shorten and sudden storms and rain showers are frequent.

The region's rich pageant of festivals can also be a deciding factor when you are considering when to visit – see Public Holidays & Special Events later in this chapter.

World Heritage Sites

The region's most precious sights, included on Unesco's list of 'cultural and natural world treasures', are Orange's Roman theatre and triumphal arch (1981), Arles' Roman and Romanesque monuments (1981), the Pont du Gard (1985) and Avignon's historic centre with its Papal palace and nursery rhyme bridge (1995).

Maps

Quality regional maps are widely available outside France. **Michelin** (W *www.viamichelin.com)* and **IGN** (W *www.ign.fr)* both have Internet boutiques where you can purchase maps. Michelin's yellow-jacketed map *Provence and the Côte d'Azur* No 245 covers the area included in this guide at a scale of 1: 200,000.

Within the region, you can find city maps at newsagencies *(maisons de la presse)* in most towns and cities, at stationery shops *(papeteries)*, tourist offices, travel bookshops, and also many of the mainstream bookshops. Kümmerly + Frey, with its orange-jacketed *Blay-Foldex Plans-Guides* series, and Éditions Grafocarte with its blue-jacketed *Plan Guide Bleu & Orange*, are the main city-map publishers. A city map typically costs around €4. The free street maps *(plans)* distributed by tourist offices range from the superb to the useless.

Michelin's *Guide Rouge* includes maps for larger cities, towns and resorts that show one-way streets and have numbered town entry points coordinated with its yellow-jacketed 1: 200,000 scale road maps.

What to Bring

As little as possible: forgotten items can be picked up practically anywhere in the region.

Hostellers have to provide their own towel and soap; bedding can be hired. Bring a padlock to secure your backpack by day and your storage locker (provided by most hostels) at night.

Other handy little numbers include a torch (flashlight), an adapter plug for electrical appliances, a universal bath/sink plug (a plastic film canister or squash ball usually does the trick) and some clothes pegs. Essentials for surviving July and August include a water bottle, premoistened towelettes or a large cotton handkerchief (to soak in fountains and mop your face with), sunglasses, a sun hat, and plenty of sunscreen and after-sun lotion.

A warm sweater is useful on early and late summer evenings. If you're venturing into the mountains, bring a light, waterproof garment. Those heading into the Camargue need a pair of binoculars and an excess of mosquito repellent.

RESPONSIBLE TOURISM

The summertime tourist invasion of southern France brings environmental and social stress. Coastal and narrow inland roads are clogged with horn-honking cars and coaches, car parks built at the foot of pretty villages overflow, and locals go into hibernation as tourists overrun markets and festivals.

Reduce your own impact on the region by ditching the car and travelling by train, bike or on foot. You can do even better – and keep your own stress level down – by lingering longer in fewer places, and visiting during the low or mid-season. Camping on farms or staying in *chambres d'hôtes* (B&Bs) rather than mainstream hotels and eating at *fermes auberges* gives locals a bigger share of the money you spend, as does buying *produits du terroir* (local, homemade produce) straight from the farm or market stall, rather than from the supermarket or tourist shop.

Respect signs telling you not to walk on the grass *(pelouse interdite)*, picnic *(pique nique interdit)* or enter private property *(propriété privée)*. Likewise, adhere to the rules of the forest: don't smoke, don't light fires or barbecues (forbidden on beaches too), stick to marked trails, and don't block cleared forest tracks – be it with your bike, car, hammock or picnic rug. When venturing into the mountains, ensure you are properly equipped and know where you're going.

TOURIST OFFICES

Local Tourist Offices

Almost every city, town and village has an *office du tourisme* (tourist office run by some unit of local government) or a *syndicat d'initiative* (tourist office run by an organisation of local merchants). Both are excellent resources and can always provide a local map and information on accommodation possibilities. Many make local hotel reservations.

Regional tourist information is handled by five *comités départementaux du tourisme* (departmental tourist offices):

Alpes de Haute-Provence (☎ 04 92 31 57 29, fax 04 92 32 24 94, W www.alpes-haute-provence.com) Maison des Alpes de Haute-Provence, 19 rue du Docteur Honnorat, F-04000 Digne-les-Bains

Alpes-Maritimes (☎ 04 93 21 80 95, fax 04 93 86 01 06, W www.guideriviera.com) 55 promenade des Anglais, F-06011 Nice

Bouches du Rhône (☎ 04 91 13 84 13, fax 04 91 33 01 82, W www.visitprovence.com) Le Montesquieu, 13 rue Roux de Brignoles, F-13006 Marseilles

Var (☎ 04 94 50 55 65, fax 04 94 50 55 51) 1 blvd Maréchal Foch, BP 99, F-83003 Draguignan

Vaucluse (☎ 04 90 80 47 00, fax 04 90 86 86 08, W www.provenceguide.com) 12 rue Collège de la Croix, BP 147, F-84008 Avignon

For tourist information on the principality of Monaco, contact its national tourist office in Monte Carlo (see the Monaco chapter).

French Tourist Offices Abroad

French tourist offices abroad (Ⓦ www.franceguide.com), otherwise called *maisons de la France*, include:

Australia (☎ 02-9231 5244, fax 9221 8682, Ⓔ france@bigpond.net.au) Level 20, 25 Bligh St, Sydney, NSW 2000
Belgium (☎ 0902 88 025, fax 02-505 38 29, Ⓔ info@france-tourisme.be) 21 ave de la Toison d'Or, B-1050 Brussels
Canada (☎ 514-876 9881, fax 845 4868, Ⓔ mfrance@attcanada.net) Suite 490, 1981 ave McGill College, Que H3A 2W9 Montreal
Germany (☎ 0190-57 00 25, fax 59 90 61, Ⓔ franceinfo@mdlf.de) Westendstrasse 47, D-60325 Frankfurt
Ireland (☎ 01-560 235 235, fax 679 0814, Ⓔ frenchtouristoffice@eircom.net) 30 Herrion St Upper, Dublin 2
Italy (☎ 166 116 216, fax 02 584 86 221, Ⓔ info@turismofrancese.it) Via Larga 7, I-20122 Milan
Netherlands (☎ 0900 112 2332, fax 020-620 3339, Ⓔ informatie@fransverkeersbureau.nl) Prinsengracht 670, NL-1017 KX Amsterdam
Spain (☎ 906 34 36 38, fax 91 541 24 12, Ⓔ info.francia@mdlfr.com) Plaza de Espana 18, Torre de Madrid 8, E-28008 Madrid; (☎ 906 34 36 38, fax 93 317 29 71, Ⓔ info.francia@mdlfr.com) Fontanella 21-23, E-08010 Barcelona
Switzerland (☎ 0900 900 699, fax 022-901 00 04, Ⓔ mdlfgva@bluewin.ch) 2 rue Thalberg, CH-1201 Geneva; (☎ 0900 900 699, fax 217 46 17, Ⓔ info.zrh@mdlfr.com) Rennweg 42 Postfach 7226, CH-8023 Zürich
UK (☎ 09086 244 123, 020, fax 7493 6594, Ⓔ info@mdlf.co.uk) 178 Piccadilly, London W1J 9AL
USA (☎ 410-286 8310, fax 838 7855, Ⓦ www.francetourism.com) 16th Floor, 444 Madison Ave, New York, NY 10022; (☎ 312-751 7800, fax 337 6339) 676 North Michigan Avenue, 60611 Illinios, Chicago. Offices also in Miami and Beverley Hills.

Monégasque Tourist Offices Abroad

Monaco has its own string of tourist offices; check out the information on the website at Ⓦ www.monaco-tourisme.com.

France (☎ 01 42 96 12 23, fax 01 42 61 31 52) 9 rue de la Paix, F-75002 Paris
Germany (☎ 211-323 7843, fax 323 7846) WZ Center, Königsallee 27-31, D-40212 Düsseldorf
Italy (☎ 02 8645 8480, fax 02 8645 8469) Via Dante 12, I-20121 Milan
UK (☎ 0500 006 114, 020-7352 9962, fax 020-7352 2103, Ⓔ monaco@monaco.co.uk) The Chambers, Chelsea Harbour, London SW10 0XF
USA (☎ 800 753 9696, 212-286 3330, fax 286 9890, Ⓦ www.monaco.mc/usa) 565 5th Ave, 23rd floor, New York NY 10017

VISAS & DOCUMENTS

A visa for France is good for Monaco too. Despite having its own diplomatic missions abroad, the principality of Monaco does not issue a visa of its own; rather it directs visa applicants to the nearest French consulate.

By law, everyone in France and Monaco, including tourists, must carry ID on them at all times. For foreign visitors, this means a passport or national ID card.

Visas

Tourist France is one of the 15 countries that have signed the Schengen Convention, an agreement whereby many European Union (EU) member countries plus Iceland and Norway have abolished checks at common borders. The other EU countries involved are Austria, Belgium, Denmark, Finland, Germany, Greece, Italy, Luxembourg, the Netherlands, Portugal, Spain and Sweden. Legal residents of one Schengen country do not require a visa for another Schengen country. Citizens of the UK and Ireland are also exempt from visa requirements for Schengen countries. In addition, nationals of several other countries, including the USA, Canada, Japan, Australia, New Zealand and Switzerland, don't require visas for tourist visits of up to 90 days to any Schengen country.

In practice, however, it is not recommended to travel without a passport. Individual Schengen countries may also impose additional restrictions on certain nationalities, so check visa regulations with the consulate of each country you plan to visit.

The standard tourist visa issued by French consulates is the Schengen visa. To obtain a visa you must present your passport, air or other tickets in and out of France, proof of finances and possibly accommodation, two passport-size photos and the visa fee in cash. A 30-day tourist visa generally costs around

€25; a three-month single-/multiple-entry visa is €30/35. Visas are usually issued on the spot. Schengen visas can only be applied for in your country of residence and are not renewable inside France.

Tourist visas cannot be extended except in emergencies (such as medical problems). If you have an urgent problem, contact your own nearest consular office in France for guidance or call the nearest *préfecture* (see Carte de Séjour following).

Carte de Séjour If you intend staying in France longer than three months, you must apply for a *carte de séjour* (residence permit) within eight days of arrival in France. For details, inquire at your place of study or the local prefecture (*préfecture*), subprefecture (*sous-préfecture*), city hall (*hôtel de ville*), town hall (*mairie*) or police station (*commissariat de police*). Prefectures in **Nice** *(☎ 04 93 72 29 99; 147 route de Grenoble)* and **Marseilles** *(☎ 04 91 15 60 00; place Félix Baret)* have special visa sections that tackle *cartes de séjour*.

Long-Stay, Student & Au Pair If you'd like to work or study in France or stay for over three months, apply to the French embassy or consulate for a *visa de long séjour* (long-stay visa) costing €99. Unless you are an EU citizen, it is difficult to get a visa allowing you to work in France. People with student visas can apply for permission to work part-time (inquire at your place of study). Au pair visas likewise have to be arranged before leaving home (unless you're an EU citizen).

Travel Insurance

Travel insurance usually covers you for medical expenses (EU citizens holding an E111 form do not need to pay for medical insurance; see Health Insurance later in this chapter for details) and luggage theft or loss, as well as for cancellation or delays in your travel arrangements. Level of cover depends on your insurance and sometimes on your type of airline ticket, so be sure to ask your insurer and ticket-issuing agency about the details.

Driving Licence & Permits

A driving licence from an EU country is valid in France. Most non-EU driving licences are likewise valid, although it's still a good idea to bring along an International Driving Permit (IDP; a multilingual translation of the vehicle class and personal details noted on your local driving licence). The latter is not valid unless accompanied by your original. An IDP can be obtained for a small fee from your local motoring association.

Hostel Card

A Hostelling International (HI) card is necessary at official youth hostels *(auberges de jeunesse)*. If you aren't a member of your own national **Youth Hostelling Association** *(YHA; W www.iyhf.org)*, you can buy a card costing €10.70/15.25 for those under/over 26 at many HI-affiliated hostels. Some sell one-night membership (€1.50) and family cards (€16).

Student, Youth, Teacher & Press Cards

An International Student Identity Card (ISIC; W www.carteisic.com) costs €10 and can easily pay for itself through half-price admissions, discounted air and ferry tickets, and cheap meals in student cafeterias. Many stockists stipulate a maximum age, usually 24 or 25. If you're under 26 but not a student you can apply for an International Youth Travel Card (IYTC; €10) instead which entitles you to much the same discounts as an ISIC. Both cards are administered by the International Student Travel Confederation (W www.istc.org) and issued by student travel agencies. Within the region try branches of **OTU Voyages** *(W www.otu.fr)* in **Aix-en-Provence** *(☎ 04 42 27 76 85; ave Jules Ferry)* or **Nice** *(☎ 04 93 96 85 43; 80 blvd Éduard Herriot)*.

A Carte Jeunes (€10) is available to anyone under 26 who has been in France for six months. It gets you discounted air tickets, car rental, sports events, concerts and so on.

Teachers, professional artists, museum conservators, journalists and certain categories of students are admitted to somemuseums free. Bring along proof of affiliation, for example, an International Teacher Identity Card (ITIC) or official press card.

Seniors Card

Reductions are often available for people over 60 or 65; see under Senior Travellers later for more details. The Société Nationale des Chemins de Fer (SNCF) sells an annual Carte Senior (€46) for those aged 60 and over, yielding reductions of 25% or 50% on train tickets.

Camping Card International

The Camping Card International (CCI) is an ID, valid for one year, that can be used instead of a passport when checking into a camp site and includes third-party insurance for damage you may cause. As a result, many camp sites offer a small discount if you sign in with one. CCIs are issued by automobile associations, camping federations and, sometimes, on the spot at camp sites. In the UK, the **AA** *(W www.theaa.com)* and **RAC** *(W www.rac.co.uk)* both issue them to their members for UK£6.50. Members of the Cyclists' Touring Club (see Cycling Organisations under Bicycle in the Getting Around chapter) can buy a card for UK £4.50.

Carte Musées Côte d'Azur

The French Riviera Museum Pass (W www.cmca.net) gives card-holders unlimited admission to 62 museums along the coast. A one-/three-day pass costs €5.50/13 (no reduced rate); and a seven-day pass valid for seven days within a 15-day period costs €24. Passes are sold at participating museums, tourist offices and FNAC stores.

Billets Jumelés

Several museums and monuments sell *billets jumelés* (combination tickets), which include admission to more than one sight and can offer a considerable saving. Some cities – including Arles, Marseilles and Nice – have museum passes that cut the cost of visiting city sights. Details are listed in the respective chapters.

Copies

All important documents (passport data page and visa page, credit cards, travel insurance policy, air/bus/train tickets, driving licence etc) should be photocopied before you leave home. Leave one copy with someone at home and keep another with you, separate from the originals.

Alternatively, store your vital travel documents in Lonely Planet's online travel vault (W www.ekno.lonelyplanet.com).

EMBASSIES & CONSULATES

French Embassies & Consulates

France has representation in the following countries.

Australia (☎ 02-6216 0100, fax 6216 0127, W www.ambafrance-au.org) 6 Perth Ave, Yarralumla, ACT 2600
Consulate: (☎ 02-9262 5779, fax 02-9283 1210, e consulat@consulfrance-sydney.org) 31 Market St, St Martin Tower, Level 26, Sydney NSW 2000

Belgium (☎ 02-548 8711, fax 513 6871, W www.ambafrance-be.org) 65 rue Ducale, B-1000 Brussels
Consulate: (☎ 02-229 8500, fax 02-229 8510, W www.consulfrance-bruxelles.be) 12a place de Louvain, BP 82, B-1000 Brussels

Canada (☎ 613-789 1795, fax 562 3704, W www.ambafrance-ca.org) 42 Sussex Drive, Ottawa, Ont K1M 2C9

Germany (☎ 030-206 39000, fax 206 39010, W www.amb-allemagne.de) Kochstrasse 6-7, D-10969 Berlin
Consulate: (☎ 030-885 90243, fax 030-885 5295, e consulat-berlin@diplomatie.gouv.fr) Kurfürstendamm 211, D-10719 Berlin

Ireland (☎ 01-260 1666, fax 283 0178, W www.ambafrance.ie) 36 Ailesbury Rd, Ballsbridge, Dublin 4

Italy (☎ 06 68 60 11, fax 06 68 60 13 60, W www.france-italia.it) Piazza Farnese 67, I-00186 Rome
Consulate: (☎ 06 68 60 11, fax 06 68 60 13 60) Via Giulia 251, I-00186 Rome

Netherlands (☎ 070-312 5800, fax 312 5824, W www.ambafrance-nl.org) Smidsplein 1, NL-2514 BT The Hague
Consulate: (☎ 020-530 6969, fax 530 6988, W www.consulfrance-amsterdam.org) Eerste Weteringdwarsstraat 107, 1000 HA Amsterdam

New Zealand (☎ 04-384 2525, fax 384 2579, W www.ambafrance-nz.org) 34–42 Manners St, PO Box 11-343, Wellington

Spain (☎ 91 423 8900, fax 91 423 8901, W www.ambafrance.es) Calle de Salustiano Olòzaga 9, ES-28001 Madrid
Consulate: (☎ 91 7000 7800, fax 91 7000 7801) Calle Marqués de la Enseñada 10-3, ES-28004 Madrid

Switzerland (☎ 031-359 2111, fax 359 2191, W www.ambafrance-ch.org) Schosshaldenstrasse 46, CH-3006 Bern

UK (☎ 020-7073 1000, fax 7073 1004, W www.ambafrance.org.uk) 58 Knightsbridge, London SW1X 7JT
Consulate: (☎ 020-7073 1200, fax 7073 1201) 21 Cromwell Rd, London SW7 2EN

USA (☎ 202-944 6000, fax 944 6166, W http://ambafrance-us.org) 4101 Reservoir Rd NW, Washington, DC 20007

Consulate: (☎ 212-606 3600, fax 212-606 3620, W www.consulfrance-newyork.org) 934 Fifth Ave, New York, NY 10021

Monégasque Embassies

Monaco has the following diplomatic missions abroad:

Belgium (☎ 02-347 4987, fax 343 4920, e ambassade.monaco@skynet.be) 17 place Guy d'Arezzo, B-1180 Brussels
France (☎ 01 45 04 74 54, fax 01 45 04 45 16, e ambassade.de.Monaco@wanadoo.fr) 22 blvd Suchet, F-75016 Paris
Germany (☎ 0228-23 20 07/08, fax 23 62 82, e gouvmonaco@aol.com) Zitelmannstrasse 16, D-53113 Bonn
Italy (☎ 06 84 14 357, fax 06 88 40 349) Largo Spinelli 5, I-00184 Rome
Spain (☎ 91 578 2048, fax 91 435 7132) Calle Villanueva 12, ES-28001 Madrid
Switzerland (☎ 031-356 2858, fax 356 2855, e monaco@swissonline.ch) 34 Hallwylstrasse, CH-3005 Bern
USA (☎ 212-286 05000, fax 286 1574, W www.monaco-consulate.com) 565 Fifth Ave, 23rd Floor, New York NY 10017

Consulates in Provence & Monaco

Foreign embassies are in Paris but most countries have a consulate in Nice, Marseilles and/or Monaco:

Belgium (☎ 04 96 10 11 16) 75 cours Pierre Puget, F-13006 Marseilles
(☎ 04 93 87 79 56) 5 rue Gabriel Fauré, F-06406 Nice
(☎ 377-93 50 59 89) 13 ave des Castelans, Monaco
Canada (☎ 04 93 92 93 22) 64 ave Jean Médecin, F-06000 Nice
(☎ 377-97 70 62 42) 1 ave Henri Dunant, Monaco
France (☎ 377-92 16 54 60) 1 chemin du Ténao, Monaco
Germany (☎ 04 91 16 75 20) 338 ave du Prado, F-13125 Marseilles
(☎ 04 93 83 55 25) Le Minotaure, 34 ave Henri Matisse, F-06200 Nice
(☎ 377-97 97 49 65) 27 blvd Princesse Charlotte, Monaco
Italy (☎ 04 91 18 49 18) 56 rue d'Alger, F-13005 Marseilles
(☎ 04 93 14 41 06, 04 93 14 40 96, e consultatditalie@wandoo.fr) 72 blvd Gambetta, F-06048 Nice
(☎ 377-93 50 22 71) 17 ave de l'Annonciade, Monaco
Monaco (☎ 04 91 33 30 21) 3 place aux Huiles, F-13001 Marseilles
(☎ 04 93 80 00 22) Villa Printemps, 12 montée Désambrois, F-06000 Nice
Netherlands (☎ 04 91 25 66 64) 137 ave de Toulon, F-13005 Marseilles
(☎ 04 93 87 52 94) 14 rue Rossini, F-06000 Nice
(☎ 377-92 05 15 02) 24 ave de Fontvieille, Monaco
Switzerland (☎ 04 91 10 14 10) 7 rue d'Arcole, F-13006 Marseilles
(☎ 04 93 88 85 09) 13 rue Alphonse Karr, BP 1279, F-06005 Nice
UK (☎ 04 91 15 72 10) 24 ave du Prado, F-13006 Marseilles
(☎ 04 93 62 13 56) 26 ave Notre Dame, F-06000 Nice
(☎ 377-93 50 99 54) 33 blvd Princesse Charlotte, Monaco
USA (☎ 04 91 54 92 00, W www.amb-usa.fr) place Varian Fry, F-13006 Marseilles
(☎ 04 93 88 89 55) 7 ave Gustave V, 06000 Nice)

CUSTOMS

The usual allowances apply to duty-free goods purchased at airports or on ferries outside the EU: tobacco (200 cigarettes, 50 cigars or 250g of loose tobacco), alcohol (1L of strong spirits or 2L of less than 22% alcohol by volume; and 2L of wine), coffee (500g or 200g of extracts) and perfume (50g of perfume and 0.25L of toilet water).

Do not confuse these with duty-paid items (including alcohol and tobacco) bought at normal shops and supermarkets in another EU country and brought into France, where certain goods might be more expensive. In that case, the allowances are more than generous: 800 cigarettes, 200 cigars or 1kg of loose tobacco; and 10L of spirits (more than 22% alcohol by volume), 20L of fortified wine or aperitif, 90L of wine or 110L of beer.

MONEY

Currency

The euro (€) – Europe's common currency in circulation in 12 Euroland countries since 1 January 2002 – is the only legal tender in France and Monaco.

One euro is divided into 100 cents, also called centimes in France (see the boxed text '500 or 5 Cents?'). Coins come in one, two, five, 10, 20 and 50 cents and €1 and €2; the latter has a brass centre and silvery edges and €1 has the reverse (silvery centre and brass edges). Euro banknotes, adorned with

500 or 5 Cents?

If a *vendeur* (shopkeeper) asks you for *cinq cent/s*, does he mean 5 cents or 500? Good question. Which is why France's Conseil National de la Consommation (CNO; National Consumer Committee), in consultation with the minister of economy, ditched the word 'cent' (meaning 100 in French) in favour of the less-confusing centime.

fictitious bridges (which bear a striking resemblance to the Pont du Gard) are issued in denominations of €5, €10, €20, €50, €100, €200 and the severely frowned-at-in-shops €500.

France's former national currency – the French franc (FF) – has been out of circulation since February 2002: 10FF was traded in for €1.52.

Exchange Rates

The Universal Currency Converter gives the latest currency exchange rates online at **W** www.xe.net/ucc. Exchange rates at the time of publication included:

country	unit	euros
Australia	A$1	€0.55
Canada	C$1	€0.61
Japan	¥100	€0.80
New Zealand	NZ$1	€0.51
UK	UK£1	€1.52
USA	US$1	€0.94

Exchanging Money

Rates vary, so it pays to compare. France's central bank, Banque de France, can offer the best rate, but branches only exchange foreign currency for two or three hours weekday mornings, making it a pain in the neck to catch them open. Commercial banks and post offices open longer weekday hours (some even open Saturday) and can charge up to €10 per foreign currency transaction. Exchange offices *(bureaux de change)*, however, are generally quickest, easiest, open the longest hours and they give the best exchange rate.

Most banks cash travellers cheques issued by American Express (Amex; in US dollars or euros) and by Visa (in euros) for a charge of €4 to €6 per transaction or a percentage fee. Within the region, Amex offices in **Aix-en-Provence** *(☎ 04 42 26 84 77; 15 cours Mirabeau)*, **Cannes** *(☎ 04 93 38 15 87; 8 rue des Belges)*, **Marseilles** *(☎ 04 91 13 71 26; 39 La Canebière)*, **Nice** *(☎ 04 93 16 53 53; 11 promenade des Anglais)* and **Monaco** *(☎ 377-97 70 77 59; 35 blvd Princesse Charlotte, Monaco)* cash Amex cheques.

For many travellers, automated teller machines or ATMs – known as *distributeurs automatiques de billets* or *points d'argent* in France – provide the easiest means of getting cash. Most spit out euro banknotes at a superior exchange rate through Visa or MasterCard and there are plenty of ATMs in the region linked to the international Cirrus and Maestro networks. If you remember your PIN code as a string of letters, translate it into numbers; French keyboards don't show letters.

Credit Cards This is the cheapest way to pay for things and to get cash advances. Visa (Carte Bleue) is the most widely accepted, followed by MasterCard (Access or Eurocard). Amex cards are not very useful except at upmarket establishments, but they do allow you to get cash at certain ATMs and at Amex offices (see Exchanging Money earlier). Travelling with two different credit cards (stashed in different wallets) is safer than taking one.

If your Visa card is lost or stolen, call **Carte Bleue** *(☎ 02 54 42 12 12)*. To report a lost or stolen MasterCard, Access or Eurocard call **Eurocard France** *(☎ 01 45 67 53 53)* and, if you can, call your credit-card issuer back home. For cards from the USA, call ☎ 001-314 275 6690. To replace any card, you must deal with the issuer.

Costs

Provence and the Côte d'Azur are among France's most expensive spots, and never more so than in July or August when prices soar sky high. If you stay in a camp site, a hostel or showerless/toiletless room in a budget hotel and dine on picnics rather gourmet dinners, it's possible to travel around Provence and the Côte d'Azur for about €40 per person per day (€50 in July/August).

Travelling with someone else immediately cuts costs; few hotels in the region offer single rooms. Those that do charge almost the same price for singles and doubles. Triples and quads (usually with two double beds) are the cheapest per person. On the Côte d'Azur, consider staying in Nice where accommodation is cheaper, and from where day trips can easily be made along the coast.

As far as dining, carrying a water bottle instead of forking out an outrageous €3-odd for a poxy canned drink is an immediate money-saver. In restaurants, opt for a *menu* – guaranteed to leave you stuffed and offering far better value than dining à la carte. However cheeky it might seem (it's not in France), always ask for *une carafe d'eau* (jug of tap water) instead of bottled water, and order a carafe or *pichet* (jug) of house wine rather than beer or bottled AOC wine.

Discounts Museums, cinemas, the SNCF, ferry companies and other institutions offer all sorts of price breaks to people aged under 25 or 26, students with ISIC cards, and people over 60 or 65. Look for the words *demi-tarif* or *tarif réduit* (half-price tariff or reduced rate) on admission-price lists and ask if you qualify. Many museums offer special tariffs to families and free admission to those aged under 18.

Look for freebies too – admission to Nice museums is free on the first Sunday of the month, for example. Throughout the region, numerous galleries, museums, palaces, gardens and other historic or cultural places that usually demand an admission fee are free for two days in mid-September during France's *Journées du Patrimoine* (Days of Patrimony).

For information on discount-yielding cards valid in the region see Visas & Documents earlier in this chapter.

Tipping & Bargaining

French law requires that restaurant, café and hotel bills include a service charge (usually 10 to 15%), so a tip is neither necessary nor expected. However, most people – dire service apart – usually leave a euro or two in restaurants.

Little bargaining goes on at Provençal markets.

Taxes & Refunds

France's Value Added Tax (VAT; TVA in French) is 20.6% on most goods except food, medicine and books, for which it's 5.5%; it goes as high as 33% on such items as watches, cameras and video cassettes. Prices are rarely given without VAT.

If you are not an EU resident, you can get a refund of most of the VAT provided that you're aged over 15, you'll be spending less than six months in France, you purchase goods (not more than 10 of the same item) worth at least €175 (tax included) at a single shop and that the shop offers duty-free sales.

Present your passport at the time of purchase and ask for an export sales invoice. Some shops refund 14% of the purchase price rather than the full 17.1% you are entitled to in order to cover the time and expense involved in the refund procedure. When you leave France or another EU country, ensure that the country's customs officials validate all three pages of the invoice; the green sheet is your receipt. You will receive a transfer of funds in your home country.

If you are flying out of Nice-Côte d'Azur, Marseille-Provence or Toulon-Hyères airports, certain stores can arrange for you to receive your refund as you're leaving the country. At the airport, validate your invoice at the customs office where you will be told which customs refund window or exchange bureau to go to for your VAT refund.

POST & COMMUNICATIONS

Post

Postal services in France are fast (next-day delivery for most domestic letters), reliable and expensive. Post offices are signposted 'La Poste'. For a pretty postage stamp *(un timbre)* rather than the uninspiring blue sticker *(une vignette)* that comes out of post office coin-operated machines, go to a window marked *toutes opérations* (all services). Most tobacconists and shops that sell postcards sell stamps too. French stamps can be used in Monaco, but Monégasque stamps are only valid in Monaco.

From France and Monaco, domestic letters up to 20g cost €0.46. Postcards and letters up to 20g cost €0.46 within the EU, €0.58 to most of the rest of Europe and Africa, €0.67 to the USA, Canada and the Middle East and €0.79 to Australasia. Sending a 62g parcel to Estonia? Calculate how much it will cost at W www.laposte.fr.

Telephone

France has one of the world's most modern and sophisticated telecommunications systems in the world. Monaco has a separate telephone system. Most public telephones require a *télécarte* (phonecard), sold at post offices, tobacconists, supermarket checkout counters and SNCF ticket windows.

French telephone numbers have 10 digits and need no area code. Telephone numbers starting with the digits 06 are mobile-phone numbers. To call anywhere in Provence and the Côte d'Azur from Monaco and abroad, dial your country's international access code, followed by 33 (France's country code) and the 10-digit number, dropping the initial 0. To call abroad from France, dial 00 (France's international access code), followed by the country code, area code (dropping the initial 0 if necessary) and local number.

Telephone numbers in Monaco only have eight digits and likewise need no area code. To call Monaco from France and abroad, dial the international access code, followed by 377 (Monaco's country code) and then the eight-digit number. To call abroad (including France) from Monaco, dial 00, followed by the country code, area code (dropping the initial zero if necessary) and local number.

Mobile-wise, France uses GSM 900/1800 – compatible with the rest of Europe and Australia but not with the North American GSM 1900 or the totally different system in Japan. Mobile phones are impossible to rent in the region, but assuming your phone is GSM 900/1800-compatible you can buy a SIM card package from mobile-phone providers Bouygues, Orange (France Télécom's mobile arm) or SFR. Card packages, sold at phone shops and branches of FNAC in Avignon, Nice, Nîmes and Marseilles, enable you to have your own French mobile telephone number and make/receive calls at local rates (see Domestic Tariffs later).

Collect Calls & Inquiries To make an international reverse-charge (collect) call *(en PCV)*, dial 00-33, then the country code of the place you're calling (dial 11 instead of 1 for the USA and Canada). If you're using a public phone, you must insert a phonecard to place operator-assisted calls through the international operator.

To find out a country code *(indicatif du pays)* or a subscriber's telephone number in France, call directory inquiries (☎ 12); it costs €0.37 to €0.45 from a public, €0.67 from a private phone. (Bizarrely, costs from a public phone vary, depending on what type of phonecard you are using; a 120-unit card yields the lowest rate.)

Yellow Pages

France's electronic *Pages Jaunes* (Yellow Pages) at **W** www.pagesjanes.fr is an online telephone directory. Click on the miniature Union Jack in the right-hand corner of the page to access the English version. Search here for telephone numbers, fax numbers, street and email addresses.

To find out a subscriber's telephone number abroad, call the international directory inquiries service (☎ 00-3312 plus relevant country code – dial ☎ 11 instead of 1 for the USA and Canada). This service costs €1.86 to €2.24 per inquiry from a public, €2.26 from a private phone.

International Rates The cheapest time to call home is during reduced-tariff periods – weekdays from 7pm to 8am (until 1pm to the USA and Canada), weekends and public holidays. Updated tariffs are published on France Télécom's website at **W** www.francetelecom.com.

A phone call to most of Europe, the USA and Canada costs €0.11 for the first 15 seconds, then €0.23 per minute; reduced tariffs are €0.12 per minute. To telephone Australia, New Zealand or Japan costs €0.11 for the first 10 seconds then around €0.70 per minute (reduced tariff €0.55 per minute). International calls to Europe/USA and Canada made from an Orange mobile phone typically cost €0.70/0.80.

France Télécom's Ticket de Téléphone (a cheap telephone card available from tobacconists) is handy for those on the move. The Ticket de Téléphone International costs €15.24 and, if used exclusively during reduced-tariff periods, covers 100 minutes of calls to Europe, the USA and Canada. Cards can be used from private and public phones; to use one, dial ☎ 3089 followed by the code written on the reverse side of your card, '#' and the subscriber's number.

Domestic Tariffs For local calls, the first three minutes costs €0.11, followed by €0.034 per minute during peak periods (weekdays 8am to 7pm) and €0.018 per minute at off-peak times (weekdays 7pm to 8am and at any time over the weekend). National calls cost €0.11 for the initial 20 seconds, then €0.091 per minute (€0.061 in reduced-rate periods).

Calls from a fixed phone to Orange or SFR mobiles clock in at €0.30 per minute during peak times (8am to 9.30am weekdays and 8am to noon Saturday) and €0.15 during off-peak periods (9.30pm to 8am weekdays, noon to 8am Saturday, and all day Sunday and public holidays). Calls to Bouygues phones cost €0.35 per minute at peak times (8am to 9.30pm weekdays) and €0.17 during reduced-rate periods (9.30pm to 8am weekdays, weekends and holidays).

Mobile-phone calls made within France from France Télécom's Orange network with its pay-as-you-go Mobicarte cards (sold at FNAC for €15, €25 and €35) cost €0.41 per minute.

ekno Communication Service

Lonely Planet's ekno global communication service provides low-cost international calls – for local calls you're usually better off with a local phonecard. Ekno also offers free messaging services, email, travel information and an online travel vault, where you can securely store all your important documents. You can join online at W www.ekno.lonelyplanet.com, where you will find the local-access numbers for the 24-hour customer-service centre. Once you have joined, always check the ekno website for the latest access numbers for each country and updates on new features.

Email & Internet Access

France's postal service, La Poste, operates Internet stations known as Cyberposte at many post offices across the region. A Carte Cyberposte – a rechargeable chip card – costs an initial €7, including one hour's online access, then €7 per hour. Private mail boxes that can receive email messages can be set up at any Cyberposte station. Alternatively, simply set up your own Web-based email account for free with Hotmail, Yahoo or ekno. French accents in email addresses can safely be ignored. Addresses in France are sometimes preceded by *mél*, short for *message électronique*. Commercial Internet cafés in Aix-en-Provence, Apt, Arles, Avignon, Cannes, Carpentras, Marseilles, Monaco, Nice, Nîmes, St-Tropez and Toulon charge about €4 an hour.

If you plan to take along your laptop or palmtop computer, note that the power-supply voltage in France may vary from that at home. Invest in a universal AC adapter for your appliance. You'll also need an adapter between your telephone plug and the standard T-shaped French receptacle.

Most mid-range hotels in France are quite savvy about the Internet, although telephones hard-wired into the wall remain a common problem; if this is the case, ask the receptionist if you can plug directly into the hotel's fax line. On newer SNCF trains an 'office space' next to the luggage compartments between carriages – complete with desk and plug to hook your laptop into the electricity supply – is provided for passengers. At Marseilles-Provence international airport there are Internet hook-up stations (for which you can pay by credit card) in hall 4 of domestic departures.

DIGITAL RESOURCES

There's no better place to start your Web explorations than at W www.lonelyplanet.com, where you'll find succinct summaries on travelling to France, postcards from other travellers and the Thorn Tree bulletin board, where you can ask questions before you go or dispense advice when you get back.

Provence-specific websites are plentiful. Nearly every tourist office has an English-French site (listed in the regional chapters), loaded with practical information. English-language sites worth a click include:

AngloINFO (W www.angloinfo.com) Comprehensive site depicting life on the Côte d'Azur in English; features some 2000 entries and oodles of links to other informative and practical sites

Avignon & Provence (W www.avignon-et-provence.com) Selective and discerning hotel, *chambre d'hôte* and restaurant online guide, highly respected within the region; make it your first stop when seeking mid-range to top-end accommodation

France Holiday Store (W www.fr-holidaystore.co.uk) One-stop holiday shop for trips to France from the UK; everything from the latest Eurostar deals to package breaks, property searches and online bookings

Lubéron News (W www.luberon-news.fr) Events and entertainment listings, last-minute accommodation deals, weather reports, news and everything else imaginable for the Lubéron-bound traveller

Provence Beyond (W www.beyond.fr) Comprehensive site with information on everything from gastronomy and astronomy to hotel/restaurant/museum/hilltop-village listings

BOOKS

Lonely Planet

Lonely Planet guides to *France*, *Western Europe*, *Mediterranean Europe* and *Europe on a shoestring* include sections on Provence and the Côte d'Azur. You might also want to check *Paris*, *The Loire*, *Corsica*, *Southwest France* and *World Food France*. It also publishes a handy French phrasebook and, for those who want even more action, *Walking in France* and *Cycling in France*.

General

To get the feel of the region before you leave, delve into the following:

Gardens of the French Riviera (2002) by Louisa Jones. A 200-page book that captures the region's stunning, wild and fantastical horticultural masterpieces in words and images.

Luminous Debris: Reflecting on Vestige in Provence and Languedoc (1999) by Gustaf Sobin. In part philosophical, this series of essays reflects on Provence's prehistoric past.

The Man Behind the Iron Mask (1988) by John Noone. An academic study on the identity of the enigmatic man behind the iron mask, immortalised by Dumas in his Three Musketeers trilogy (see the boxed text 'The Man in the Iron Mask' in the Cannes Area chapter).

Queen Victoria and the Discovery of the Riviera (2001) by Michael Nelson. A colourful account of Queen Victoria's nine visits to the Côte d'Azur from 1882.

Wine & War (2002) by Don & Petie Kladstrup. This is the cliff-hanger story of France's winemakers and how they saved their country's greatest treasure – its vineyards – from destruction during WWII.

Riviera High Life

If you want to know where and how to rub shoulders with the rich and famous, these books might help.

Côte d'Azur: Inventing the French Riviera (1992) by Mary Blume looks at the glamorous rise and fall of the Côte d'Azur.

Everybody was So Young (1998) by Amanda Vaill. Beautiful evocation of American couple Gerald and Sara Murphy on the Riviera, their glamorous set of literary friends (F Scott Fitzgerald, Hemingway, Cole Porter, Picasso, etc) and the jazzy 1920s era in which they lived.

The Grimaldis of Monaco (1992) by Anne Edwards. This detailed biography of Monaco's royal family covers 'centuries of scandal, years of Grace' from 1215 through to 1990.

Hollywood on the Riviera: The Inside Story of the Cannes Film Festival (1992) by Cari Beauchamp & Henri Béhar. This history of the festival and its stars is laced with celebrity names.

King of Cannes: Madness, Mayhem & the Movies (2000) by Stephen Walker. The true story of a British filmmaker who goes to Cannes to make a movie.

Two Weeks in the Midday Sun – A Cannes Notebook (1987) by Roger Ebert. 'Disneyland for adults' (Cannes' International Film Festival) as seen through the back door by a festival hack.

Art & Literature

Provence and the Côte d'Azur has been immortalised in foreign literature since the 18th century when the first European writers ventured here. By the early 20th century it had blossomed into a bohemia for artists seeking sunlight and social freedom. Works by Provençal writers are included under Literature in the Facts about Provence chapter.

Art-wise, try *Artists and their Museums on the Riviera* (1998) by Barbara Freed; and *Lartigue's Riviera* (essay by Mary Blume, picture selection by Martine d'Astier), with a stunning collection of black-and-white photographs of the coast taken by Jacques Lartigue between the 1920s and 1960s.

Other works worth reading include:

The Avignon Quintet (1992) by Lawrence Durrell. A one-volume, awesome 1367-page edition of five Durrell novels, written 1974–85 and opening on an Avignon-bound train.

Bits of Paradise (1976) by F Scott & Zelda Fitzgerald. Collection of 21 short stories by one of the Riviera's most notorious couples.

Collected Short Stories (1990) by Somerset Maugham. Includes 'The Facts of Life' about a tennis player taking to the gambling tables at Monte Carlo, and 'Three Fat Women from Antibes' inspired by the years Maugham lived on Cap Ferrat.

The Count of Monte Cristo (1845) and *The Three Musketeers* (1844) by French novelist Alexandre Dumas (1802–70). Two classics partly set in 19th-century Marseilles.

The Doves' Nest & Other Stories (1923) by Katherine Mansfield. The title story dissects the lives of lonely women living in a villa on the Riviera.

The Fly-Truffler (2000) by Gustaf Sobin. Philosophical novel centred around a professor of the

Provençal language and his insatiable appetite for truffles.

Garden of Eden (1987) by Ernest Hemingway. Posthumously published novel set in 1920s Le Grau du Roi, near Aigues-Mortes in the Camargue. Two honeymooners pursue a hedonistic life in the sun.

The Hairdressers of St-Tropez (1995) by Rupert Everett. Comedy of hairdressers and talking dogs that kicks off on St-Tropez's Pampelonne beach in 2042.

Hallucinating Foucault (1996) by Patricia Duncker. Thrilling post-modern novel that sees a heterosexual Cambridge postgraduate get entwined in a passionate affair with schizophrenic, homosexual French writer Paul Michel; the novel climaxes in Nice.

Jericho (1992) by Dirk Bogarde. A sleuth novel set in rural Provence where Bogarde lived for more than 20 years. Its sequel *A Period of Adjustment* (1994) is likewise set in Provence.

The Long Afternoon (2001) by Giles Waterfield. Tells the tale of the Williamsons and their quest for a quiet life, following husband Henry premature retirement from the Indian Civil Service, on the French Riviera.

Loser Takes All (1955) by Grahame Greene. Short novel written in 1955 in which a young couple are manipulated into honeymooning at Monte Carlo's Hôtel de Paris.

The Mystery of the Blue Train (republished 2000) by Agatha Christie. Hercule Poirot investigates a mysterious murder aboard the Train Bleu to the Riviera.

An Orderly Man (1983) and *A Short Walk from Harrods* (1996) by Dirk Bogarde. The British film icon describes his renovation of a Provençal farmhouse and his subsequent retirement in Provence in the third and sixth volumes of his seven-volume autobiography.

Perfume (1985) by Patrick Süskind. Evocation of the horrors of the 18th-century perfume industry. Much of the action – a quest to create the perfect perfume from the scent of murdered virgins – takes place in Grasse.

Provença (1910) and *Cantos* (1919) by imagist poet Ezra Pound. Two collections of poems based around modern adaptations of traditional Provençal songs and troubadour ballads.

The Rover (1923) by Joseph Conrad. Set in and around Toulon.

Tender is the Night (1934) by F Scott Fitzgerald. Vivid account of life during the decadent 1920s Jazz Age; set on Cap d'Antibes with day trips to Cannes.

Travelogues

Provence has inspired travellers to write about their experiences for centuries.

Cesar's Vast Ghosts: Aspects of Provence (1990) by Lawrence Durrell. Philosophical reflections on Provençal history and culture, published just a few days before the author's death in Somières, near Nîmes.

A Little Tour in France (1885) by Henry James vividly portrays Van Gogh's 19th-century Arles, first visited by James in 1882.

The Luberon Garden (2002) by Alex Dingwall-Main tells the tale of an English garden designer who uproots his family from London to landscape a secret garden in Ménerbes.

A Motor-Flight through France (1908) by Edith Wharton. Amusing account of the author's motor trip from Paris to Provence in 1906 and 1907.

A Spell in Wild France (1992) by Bill & Laurel Cooper. A vivid portrait of the highs and lows of life on a boat moored near Aigues-Mortes in Camargue cowboy land.

Travels through France & Italy (1766) by Tobias Smollett. The Scottish author's ruthless candour caused outrage amongst local Niçois when this book was published in the late 18th century.

Two Towns in Provence (1964) by MFK Fisher. A street-by-street, fountain-by-fountain celebration of Aix-en-Provence and Marseilles.

A Year in Provence (1989) by Peter Mayle. First of a clutch of best-selling accounts of life in the Lubéron that take a witty look at the Provençal through English eyes.

Cuisine

There are dozens of cookery books dedicated to the region's legendary cuisine. Those written by chefs from within the region are the most authentic, and tasty to boot.

Flavours of France (1998) by Alain Ducasse. Olive oil reigns supreme in Ducasse's kitchen, as this gorgeous recipe book reveals.

New Entertaining in the French Style (2002) by Roger Vergé. Celebrated for his *cuisine du soleil* (cooking of the sun) in the 1970s, the king of Provençal cuisine reveals some of his secrets on food shopping, choosing cheese, picking wines, setting the table, and so on. Over 50 recipes are included in this lavish entertaining guide.

Patricia Wells: At Home in Provence (1999) by Patricia Wells. Some 175 recipes from the Vaison-la-Romaine farmhouse kitchen of this American, recognised as one of the few foreign cooks to have embraced the soul of Provençal cooking.

Provence of Alain Ducasse (2000) by Alain Ducasse. A beautifully illustrated book in which the world's only chef since the 1930s to scoop six Michelin stars, spread between his gastronomic temples in Monaco and Paris, reveals his own favourite gastronomic haunts in Provence.

FILMS

Several 1950s classics were filmed in the region, among them François Truffaut's *Les Mistons* (1958) filmed exclusively in Nîmes; Jacques Démy's *La Baie des Anges* (The Bay of Angels, 1962); Henri Decoin's *Masque de Fer* (Iron Mask, 1962), parts of which were filmed in Sospel; Rohmer's *La Collectionneuse* (The Collectors, 1966), filmed in St-Tropez; and the first in the series of Jean Girault's celebrated *Gendarme de St-Tropez* (1964). In 1972 François Truffaut filmed part of *La Nuit Américaine* (The American Night, 1972) in the Victorine studios, the Niçois hinterland and the Vésubie Valley.

The region also featured in foreign films, most notably Hitchcock's suspense thriller, *La Main au Collet* (To Catch a Thief, 1956), starring Cary Grant and Grace Kelly; John Frankenheimer's *French Connection 2*; and Disney's lovable *Herbie goes to Monte Carlo* (1977) starring Herbie the Volkswagen Beetle.

Modern French cinema has seen a renewed interest in Pagnol's great classics of Provence. In 1986 Claude Berri came up with *Jean de Florette* followed by *Manon des Sources*, modern versions of Pagnol's original works, which proved enormously popular both in France and abroad. Parts of the films were shot in the Plan-d'Aups-Ste-Baume. In 1990 Yves Robert directed *La Gloire de Mon Père* (My Father's Glory) and *Le Château de Ma Mère* (My Mother's Castle), Pagnol's autobiographical novels.

The 1998 Hollywood box office hit *The Man in the Iron Mask* – a modern adaptation of the 'iron mask' mystery that occurred on the Île Ste-Marguerite near Cannes in the late 17th century – starred Gérard Depardieu, Leonardo DiCaprio and Jeremy Irons.

The first novel in the Dumas trilogy, *Le Comte de Monte Cristo* (The Count of Monte Cristo) – which opens with the lead character's dramatic escape from the Château d'If near Marseilles – has been adapted for cinema or television 29 times since 1907. The most recent version was Josée Dayan's TV-series adaptation (1998) starring Gérard Depardieu as the revengeful Dantès.

Other big hit films to be filmed in the region include James Ivory's portrait of Picasso and his relationship with Francoise Gilot in *Surviving Picasso* (1996), starring Anthony Hopkins and shot in Hyères; *Sword Fish* (2001) starring John Travolta; and Neil Jordan's *The Honest Thief* (2002), which sees Nick Nolte try his hand in a casino on the Riviera. For films by Provence-born directors, see Film in the Facts about Provence chapter.

NEWSPAPERS & MAGAZINES

The leading regional, daily newspapers are *Nice Matin* (W www.nicematin.fr), which has a separate Toulon-based Var edition called *Var-Matin*; and *La Provence* (W www.laprovence-presse.fr), which is the result of a merger between *Le Provençal* and the right-wing *Le Méridional*.

The free *Riviera Reporter* (W www.riviera-reporter.com) is an A4-sized magazine, published every two months. It runs job and property listings, local gossip and various other titbits and can be picked up in most English-language bookshops. Similar, but paid-for, is the *Riviera Gazette* (€3; W www.TheRivieraGazette.com), which markets itself as 'the Côte d'Azur's English-language newspaper'. The third in the trio, the *Riviera Times* (€2.50; W www.rivieratimes.com) has a marginally stronger news bias.

In Marseilles, the daily edition of the freebie *Metro*, doled out as you enter/exit metro stations, runs one page of local and international news in English.

The two glossy magazines for Riviera socialites – both bilingual French-English – are the quarterly, 250-plus-page *Nice Riviera-Magazine* (€6), a mainly fashion-driven magazine with hotel and restaurant reviews, a strong arts section, social diary and plenty of gossip; and *Côte Magazine* (€2.30), which is great for uncovering the hottest dining and partying spots of the season. *Nice Riviera-Magazine* runs separate Cannes, St-Tropez and Monaco editions; while *Côte Magazine* puts out a Marseille-Provence edition.

English-language newspapers of the day – *International Herald Tribune*, *Washington Post*, *USA Today*, and the *Guardian* or *The Times* – are easy to pick up in Nice, Marseilles and most coastal resorts – but practically impossible to find in Haute-Provence and other rural spots.

RADIO & TV

Monte Carlo-based Riviera Radio (106.3MHz FM in Monaco, 106.5MHz FM along the rest of the Côte d'Azur) is an English-language radio station that broadcasts 24 hours a day and includes BBC World Service news in English every hour; it has Internet relay at W www.rivieraradio.mc.

Radio International (100.5MHz FM and 100.9MHz FM) also has BBW World Service slots (6am to 8.45am and 6pm to 7pm Monday to Friday, 6pm to 7pm Saturday and Sunday). Otherwise, fiddle with your shortwave knob to pick up the BBC World Service in English on 6195kHz, 9410kHz, 11955kHz, 12095kHz (a good daytime frequency) and 15575kHz. BBC Radio 4 broadcasts at 198kHz.

Indispensable for motorists, particularly in high season, is Traffic FM (107.7MHz FM), which broadcasts regular traffic reports in English, French and Italian.

Local French-language radio stations include Radio Provence (103.6MHz and 102.9MHz FM), Radio Vaucluse (100.4MHz FM), Radio Lubéron (88.6MHz FM) and Cannes Radio (91.5MHz FM). Popular music channels include Nostalgie (98.3MHz FM) for golden oldies and Chérie FM (100.1MHz FM) for the latest hits.

You can tune in to TV programmes in English via cable in many mid-range and all top-end hotels; news channels BBC Prime, CNN, Sky and Euronews are typically available. *Qui veut gagner des millions* (Who wants to win millions?), with its million-euro questions popping up on screen in written form, is a great TV show to watch for French learners wanting to improve their language skills. TF1 – France's most popular private station – broadcasts it early evening.

PHOTOGRAPHY & VIDEO

Colour-print and slide film is widely available in supermarkets, photo shops and FNAC stores, as are replacement video cartridges for your camcorder.

Photography is rarely forbidden, except in museums, art galleries and some churches (such as Matisse's Chapelle du Rosaire in Vence).

TIME

French and Monégasque time is GMT/UTC plus one hour, except during daylight- saving time (from the last Sunday in March to the last Sunday in October) when it is GMT/UTC plus two hours. The UK and France are always one hour apart – when it's 6pm in London, it's 7pm in Nice. New York is six hours behind Nice.

France uses the 24-hour clock and writes time like this: 15h30 (ie, 3.30pm). Time has no meaning for many people in Provence.

ELECTRICITY

France and Monaco run on 220V at 50Hz AC. Sockets have two round prongs and a protruding earth (ground) prong.

WEIGHTS & MEASURES

France uses the metric system. When writing numbers with four or more digits, the French use full stops (periods) or spaces (as opposed to commas): one million is 1.000.000 or 1 000 000. Decimals, on the other hand, are written with commas, so 1.75 becomes 1,75.

LAUNDRY

In most towns there is an unstaffed, self-service laundrette, open from about 7am to 7pm or 8pm. It generally costs €3/5 to wash a 5/10kg load, plus €0.50 per five minutes to tumble-dry it.

TOILETS

Public Toilets

Public toilets, signposted *toilettes* or WC, are surprisingly few and far between, which means you can be left feeling really rather desperate. Towns that have public toilets generally tout them near the *mairie* (town hall) or in the port area. Many have coin-operated, self-flushing toilet booths – highly disconcerting should the automatic mechanism fail with you inside. They can usually be found in car parks and public squares; they cost €0.20 to enter. Some places sport flushless, kerbside *urinoirs* (urinals) reeking with generations of urine. Failing that, there's always McDonald's.

Restaurants, cafés and bars are often woefully underequipped with such amenities, so start queuing ahead of time. Bashful males be warned: some toilets are almost unisex; the urinals and washbasins are in a common area through which all and sundry pass to get to the toilet stalls. Older establishments often sport Turkish-style *toilettes à la turque* – a squat toilet with a high-pressure flushing mechanism that can soak your feet if you don't step back in time.

Bidets

A bidet is a porcelain fixture that looks like a shallow toilet with a pop-up stopper in the base. Originally conceived to improve the personal hygiene of aristocratic women, its primary purpose is for washing the genitals and anal area, though its uses have expanded to include everything from hand-washing laundry to soaking your feet.

Bidets are to be found in many hotel rooms. Cheap hotels often offer rooms with a bidet and/or washbasin *(lavabo)*.

HEALTH

The Provence region is a healthy place. Your main risks are sunburn, foot blisters, insect bites and an upset stomach from eating and drinking too much.

Predeparture Planning

Immunisations No jabs are required to travel to France. However, there are a few routine vaccinations that are recommended whether you're travelling or not: polio (usually administered during childhood), tetanus and diphtheria (usually administered together during childhood and updated every 10 years) and sometimes measles. All vaccinations should be recorded on an International Health Certificate. These are available from your doctor or the government health department.

Health Insurance Ensure you have adequate health insurance if you are not a citizen of an EU country; see Travel Insurance under Visas & Documents earlier. Citizens of EU countries are covered for emergency treatment throughout the EU on presentation of an E111 certificate, though charges are likely for medication, dental work and secondary examinations, including X-rays and laboratory tests. Ask about the E111 at your national health service or travel agency at least a few weeks before you depart. In the UK, you can get the forms at post offices. Claims must be submitted to a local sickness insurance office *(caisse primaire d'assurance maladie)* before you leave France.

Other Preparations Ensure that you are healthy before you start travelling. If you are going on a long trip, make sure your teeth are OK. If you wear glasses take a spare pair and your prescription.

If you require a particular medication take an adequate supply, as it may not be available locally. Take part of the packaging showing the generic name, rather than the brand, which will make getting replacements easier. It's a good idea to have a legible prescription or letter from your doctor to show that you legally use the medication to avoid any problems.

Medical Treatment

Major hospitals are indicated on the maps in this book, and their addresses and phone numbers are mentioned in the text. Tourist offices and hotels can put you on to a doctor or dentist, and your embassy or consulate will probably know one who speaks your language. For emergency phone numbers, see the boxed text 'Help' later in this chapter.

Anyone (including foreigners) who is sick can receive treatment in the casualty ward or emergency room of any public hospital. Hospitals try to have people who speak English in the casualty wards, but this is not done systematically.

Pharmacies French pharmacies are marked by a green cross, the neon components of which are lit when it's open. Pharmacists can often suggest treatments for minor ailments.

Pharmacies coordinate their closure so that a town isn't left without a place to buy medication. Details of the nearest weekend or night-duty pharmacy *(pharmacie de garde)* are posted on most pharmacy doors. There are 24-hour pharmacies in Nice and Marseilles.

SAMU When you ring ☎ 15, the 24-hour dispatchers of the Service d'Aide Médicale d'Urgence (Emergency Medical Aid Service) take down details of your problem and send out a private ambulance with a driver or, if necessary, a mobile intensive-care unit. For less serious problems, SAMU can dispatch a doctor for a house call. If you prefer to be taken to a particular hospital, mention this to the ambulance crew, as the usual procedure is to take you to the nearest one. In emergency cases (those requiring intensive-care units), billing will be taken care of later. Otherwise, you need to pay in cash at the time.

[Continued on page 55]

Food & Wine of Provence

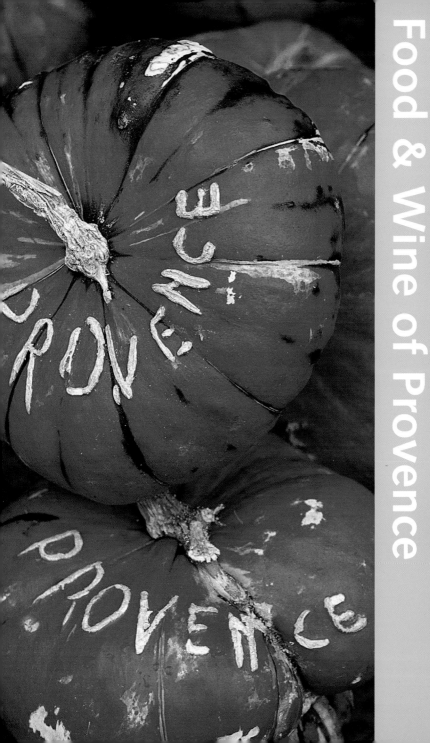

FOOD HIGHLIGHTS & WINE REGIONS

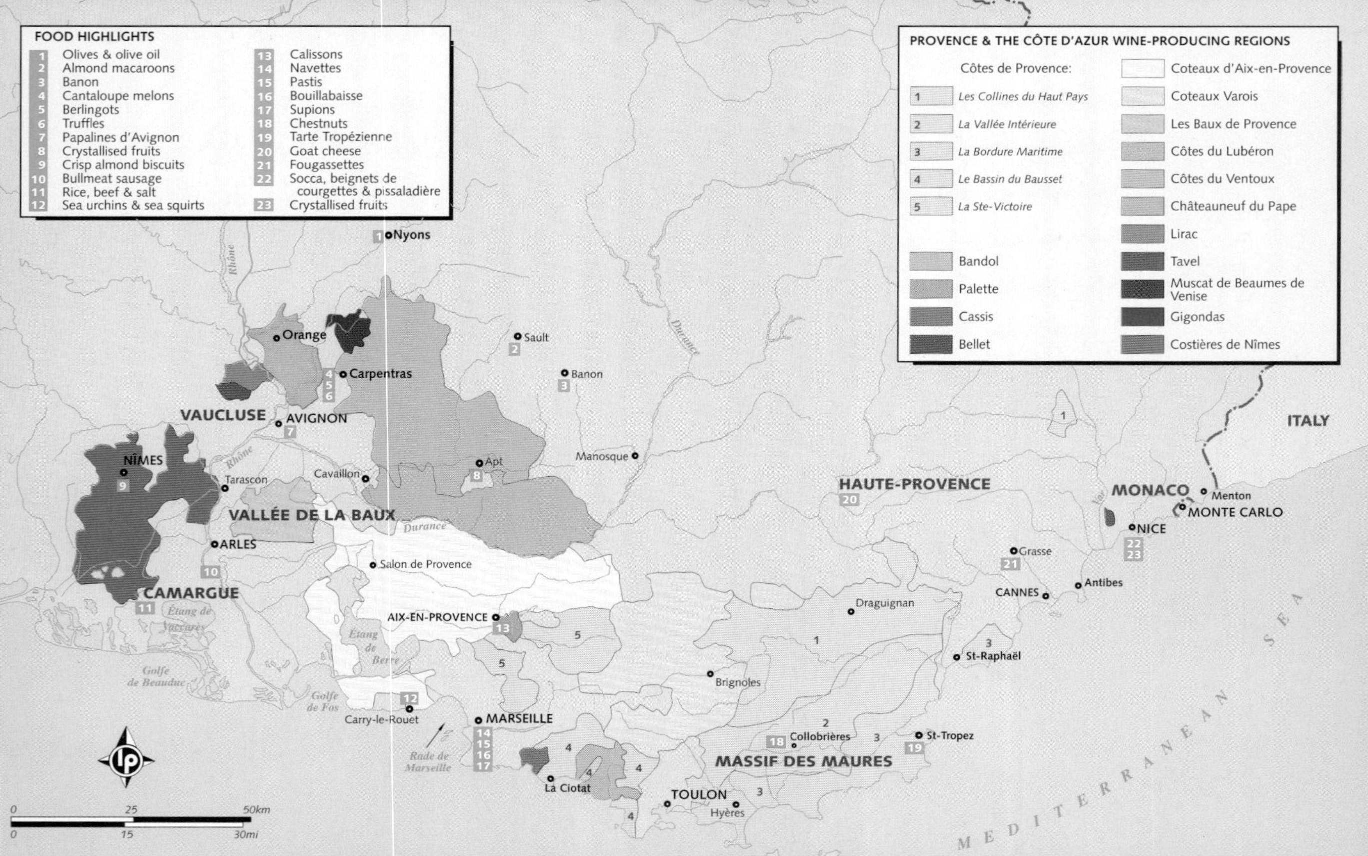

FOOD HIGHLIGHTS
1 Olives & olive oil
2 Almond macaroons
3 Banon
4 Cantaloupe melons
5 Berlingots
6 Truffles
7 Papalines d'Avignon
8 Crystallised fruits
9 Crisp almond biscuits
10 Bullmeat sausage
11 Rice, beef & salt
12 Sea urchins & sea squirts
13 Calissons
14 Navettes
15 Pastis
16 Bouillabaisse
17 Supions
18 Chestnuts
19 Tarte Tropézienne
20 Goat cheese
21 Fougassettes
22 Socca, beignets de courgettes & pissaladière
23 Crystallised fruits
PROVENCE & THE CÔTE D'AZUR WINE-PRODUCING REGIONS
Côtes de Provence:
1 Les Collines du Haut Pays
2 La Vallée Intérieure
3 La Bordure Maritime
4 Le Bassin du Bausset
5 La Ste-Victoire
Bandol
Palette
Cassis
Bellet
Coteaux d'Aix-en-Provence
Coteaux Varois
Les Baux de Provence
Côtes du Lubéron
Côtes du Ventoux
Châteauneuf du Pape
Lirac
Tavel
Muscat de Beaumes de Venise
Gigondas
Costières de Nîmes
Nyons
Rhône
Orange
Carpentras
Sault
Banon
Durance
VAUCLUSE
AVIGNON
NÎMES
Tarascon
Cavaillon
Apt
Manosque
ITALY
HAUTE-PROVENCE
MONACO
Menton
MONTE CARLO
Var
NICE
VALLÉE DE LA BAUX
ARLES
Salon de Provence
Grasse
Antibes
CANNES
CAMARGUE
Étang de Vaccarès
AIX-EN-PROVENCE
Draguignan
Étang de Berre
St-Raphaël
Golfe de Beauduc
Brignoles
Golfe de Fos
Carry-le-Rouet
MARSEILLE
Collobrières
St-Tropez
Rade de Marseille
MASSIF DES MAURES
La Ciotat
TOULON
Hyères
MEDITERRANEAN SEA
0 25 50km
0 15 30mi

FOOD

The secret of Provençal cuisine lies not in elaborate preparation techniques or state-of-the-art presentation, but in the use of fresh ingredients produced locally. Despite regional differences, some traditions are upheld everywhere – oodles of olive oil and garlic. Tomatoes are another common ingredient; any dish described as *à la Provençale* is guaranteed to involve garlic-seasoned tomatoes.

Common vegetables include onions, aubergines (eggplant) and courgettes (summer squash or zucchini). Tomatoes, aubergines and courgettes, stewed with green peppers, garlic and various aromatic herbs, produce that perennial Provençal favourite, *ratatouille*. Artichokes, another typical vegetable, are eaten very young and can be stuffed with a salted pork, onion and herb mix, then baked, to become *petits légumes farcis* (little stuffed vegetables). Stuffed courgette flowers are an enchanting variation of this dish. Tomatoes and black olives star in many dishes, including *tian* (vegetable and rice gratin).

Another favourite way to eat vegetables is as *crudités*, served raw as an aperitif with *anchoïade*, a strong, anchovy paste laced with garlic and olive oil; and *tapenade*, a sharp, black olive-based dip seasoned with garlic, capers, anchovies and olive oil. *Brandade de morue* is a mix of crushed salt cod, olive oil and garlic.

Strong-tasting sauces complement soups and fish dishes. *Soupe au pistou* is a hearty vegetable, three- or four-bean and basil soup, always served with *pistou*, a spicy basil, garlic and olive oil sauce that you stir into the soup to spice it up, or spread onto small pieces of toast. *Soupe de poisson* (fish soup) also comes with crisp toast, as well as a pot of pink *rouille* and a garlic clove. *Rouille* is mayonnaise combined with garlic, breadcrumbs and crushed red chilli peppers. Rub the garlic over the toast, then douse the latter with the already-very-garlicky *rouille*.

Specialist Food Markets

Fish Monkfish, conger eels, sea urchins and other catches of the day – Quai des Belges, Marseilles' Vieux Port, mornings, year round; place St-François, Nice, mornings Tuesday to Sunday, year round; place aux Herbes, St-Tropez, Tuesday to Sunday, winter only

Garlic Loose or in plaits woven before your eyes – Cours Belsunce in Marseilles, daily, June and July; Èze, 24 June

Melons Mountains of sweet-fleshed cantaloupes – Cavaillon, mornings, May to September

Truffles Bring a plastic bag – Aups on Thursday, Carpentras on Friday, Richerenches and Apt on Saturday, all November to March

Title page: Decorated Provençal pumpkins at Carpentras Market

Inset: *Bouillabaisse* on the balcony, overlooking Marseilles harbour (Photos by Greg Elms).

Regional Savouries In seafaring Marseilles, *rouille* is a condiment for *bouillabaisse*. *Bourride* is a variation of *bouillabaisse*. The many other fish dishes that characterise Marseillais cooking are almost always accompanied by *aïoli*, a garlicky sauce similar to *rouille*, but lacking the chilli peppers and thus yellow in colour. *Aïoli* is smeared over everything from fish to vegetables: *aïoli Provençal complet* is a plate of vegetables (including artichokes), boiled potatoes, a boiled egg and *coquillages* (small shellfish) to dunk in the pot of *aïoli* that comes with it. Many restaurants only serve *aïoli Provençal complet* on Friday.

One quintessential Marseillais dish not accompanied by *aïoli*, but rather pan fried with fresh garlic and parsley, is *supions frits* (squid). In fishing ports west of Marseilles two specialities are: *oursins* (sea urchins), with the orange roe scooped out with a spoon like a soft-boiled egg; and clam-like *violets* (sea squirts), whose iodine-infused yellow flesh tastes of the sea itself.

Niçois cooking is Italianate in flavour, while the cuisine of the Camargue is the region's meatiest. *Guardianne de taureau* is a bullish (literally) Camarguaise equivalent of a traditional *daube Provençale*. Arles is known for its air-dried sausages, and lamb features on many menus in the Alpilles. *Pieds et paquets* (literally 'feet and packages') are sheep's feet wrapped in tripe and cooked with wine and tomatoes.

Cheese is typical of the region's rural hinterland. *Banon* is a type of *chèvre* (goat cheese) or *brebis* (sheep cheese), wrapped in a chestnut leaf.

And finally, there are *truffes* (truffles), black fungi uncovered in modest amounts in the Vaucluse and as precious as gold dust to truffle aficionados.

Regional Pastries & Desserts Lavender and thyme flavour milk-based dishes such as *crème brûlée* as well as jams and honey. Anis and orange blossom, among other things, give *navettes* (canoe-shape biscuits from Marseilles) and *fougassettes* (sweet bread) their distinctive flavours. A secret 60 different Mont Ventoux herbs are used to make the liqueur which laces *papalines d'Avignon* (pink liqueur-laced chocolate balls). Almonds are turned into *gâteaux secs aux amandes* (crisp and snappy almond biscuits) around Nîmes; into *calissons* (sweets, frosted with icing sugar) in Aix-en-Provence; and into black honey nougat throughout the region.

Nice and Apt excel at *fruits confits* (crystallised or glazed fruits); see them made at the Confiserie Florian in Pont du Loup (see the Cannes Area chapter). *Berlingots* are hard caramels originating in Carpentras, and *tarte Tropézienne* is a cream-filled sandwich cake from St-Tropez. Massif des Maures desserts star *glace aux marrons glacés* (chestnut ice cream) or *crème de marrons* (chestnut cream). A popular dessert in the Vaucluse is cantaloupe melon from Carpentras doused in Muscat de Beaumes de Venise, a sweet dessert wine.

The Essentials

Herbs The titillating array of aromatic herbs and plants used in Provençal cooking is a legacy of the heavily scented *garrigue* (herbal scrub) covering much of the region. Its classic herbal mix of dried basil, thyme and rosemary is used to season dishes throughout Europe. In Provençal cooking, fresh basil lends its pea-green colour and strong fragrance to *pistou* and is used dried to flavour *soupe de pistou*. Sage, traditionally an antiseptic, is another *pistou* ingredient. Aromatic rosemary, a common Mediterranean shrub, is used fresh or dried to flavour most meat dishes. In medieval Provence it was said to possess magical powers which, if eaten regularly, ensured eternal youth.

Chervil leaves are used in omelettes and meat dishes, while tarragon's tender young shoots lightly flavour sauces accompanying seafood. The sensual aniseed scent of the bulbous fennel is rife in the region. Its leaves (picked in spring) are finely chopped and used in fish dishes and marinades, while its potent seeds (plucked at summer's end) form the basis of several herbal liqueurs, including pastis and the 50% alcohol by volume Lérina liqueur made by monks on Île St-Honorat. Equally distinctive to Provençal cuisine is the use of lavender; only its green leaves are used in the kitchen.

Olive Oil Succulent, sun-baked black olives – born from clusters of white flowers that blossom on knotty trees from May to June – are harvested from 15 November to January, during the *cueillette des olives* (olive harvest). Olives destined for the oil press are not picked until December; 5kg of olives produce one litre of oil. Olive oils from northern Vaucluse around Nyons, the Vallée de la Baux and the Alpilles have their own AOC *(appellation d'origine contrôlée)*. *Oléiculteurs* (olive growers) in these regions have to comply to a rigid set of rules in order to have their bottles of oil stamped with the quality-guaranteed AOC mark.

Olive oil can be tasted in the same way one samples wine. It can have various degrees of sweetness or acidity, and can be clear or slightly murky (which means the oil has not been filtered). A bottle of olive oil should be kept out of direct sunlight and consumed within six months of opening. Don't use it to cook – it loses some of its taste when heated above 80°C.

Olive trees only grow at altitudes between 300m and 800m. They live for an absolute age. For information on places to buy olive oil see the boxed text 'Shopping for Olive Oil' in the Facts for the Visitor chapter.

Bouillabaisse This dish was brewed up by the seafaring Marseillais. It is essentially a fish stew made with at least four kinds of fresh fish, cooked in a rockfish stock (broth) with onions, tomatoes, garlic, saffron (hence its pungent yellow-orange colour) and herbs such as parsley, bay leaves and thyme. Its name is derived from the French *bouillir* (to boil) and *baisser* (to lower, as in a flame), which reflects the cooking method required: a true *bouillabaisse* is rapidly brought to the boil, bubbled ferociously for some 15 minutes, and then is ready to serve!

No two cooks serve up an identical *bouillabaisse*. There are endless debates about exactly which fresh fish constitutes the true dish, although a general consensus insists it is *rascasse* (scorpion fish). A *bouillabaisse royale* touts shell fish, including *langouste* (crayfish) or *langoustine* (small saltwater lobster), while the Toulonnais throw potatoes in their *bouillabaisse*. *Bourride* is a cheap variation of *bouillabaisse*; it contains no saffron, features cheaper white-fleshed fish, and is served with *aïoli* instead of *rouille*.

Bouillabaisse is an entire meal. The *bouillon* (broth) is served as a soup entree, accompanied by bite-sized toasts and spicy *rouille*. The fish flesh is then served on a platter as a main course. The pot of bouillon remains on the table, allowing you to spoon it over the fish as desired.

See the boxed text 'Tasty Tip' in the Marseilles chapter for authentic *bouillabaisse* restaurants.

Truffles Provence's blackest gastronomic treat is the truffle – a type of mushroom *(Tuber melanosporum)* that takes root underground at the foot of a tree, usually in symbiosis with the roots of an elm or oak tree. These black diamonds, as they are known, are harvested in Vaucluse, around Carpentras, Vaison-la-Romaine and in the Enclave des Papes. The region's leading wholesale market is held in Richerenches and the precious fungi are canned in Puymeras. For more truffle trivia, see the boxed text 'Black Diamonds' in the Avignon Area chapter.

Food Fests

Foodie festivals in gastronomic Provence include:

January

Messe de la Truffe Truffle Mass, Richerenches, Sunday nearest to 17 January

Journée de la Truffe d'Aups 'Day of the Truffle' with truffle market, truffle dog competitions and demonstrations of how pigs snout out truffles, Aups, 4th Sunday in January

February

Fête des Citrons Lemon festival with street sculptures constructed from lemons, Menton

June

Fête de la Cerise Cherry Festival, Apt, Pentecost weekend

July

Fête du Fromage Cheese fair in Banon, Haute-Provence

Fête du Melon Three-day melon festival to honour the town's prized fruit, Cavaillon, mid-July; another in Pernes-les Fontaines

September

Fête des Prémices du Riz Week-long festival to celebrate the start of the rice harvest with crowning of a rice ambassadress, Arles, mid-September

October

Fête de la Châtaigne Chestnut Festival, Collobrières, last three Sundays in October

December

Fête de l'Huile d'Olive Nouvelle et de la Truffe Olive Oil & Truffle Festival, Aix-en-Provence

Bonnes Tables

A *bonne table* (quite literally, a 'good table') is a restaurant or bistro known for its delicious and enticing cuisine. *Bonnes tables* range from state-of-the-art, designer joints (such as Ducasse's Spoon in St-Tropez or Bar & Bœuf in Monaco) to simple bistros (Les Girandoles in Tourtour, Chez Fuchs in St-Tropez), village inns (Beau Séjour in Gorbio) and isolated farmhouses (Chèvrerie du Peigros in the Massif des Maures, Domaine d'Aiguines near the Gorges du Verdon, Auberge Perry near Céreste).

Many meals' worth of *bonnes tables* are listed in Michelin's red-jacketed *Guide Rouge* to France (€21.30; downloadable for a PDA for €39.99 at W www.viamichelin.com); and the annual *Guide Gault Millau France* (€29; W www.gaultmillau.fr). Farmhouse kitchens feature in the annual, French-English *Guide Gantié Provence & Côte d'Azur* (€23; W www.guidegantie.com).

WINE

Provençal wines are by no means France's most sought after, but their making and tasting is an art and a tradition which bears their own unique and tasty trademark. Each AOC is stamped by one common trait – an exceptionally cold mistral wind and an equally exceptional, hot ripening sun.

A crisp, Côtes de Provence rosé is Provence's classical summer drink. Wine is drunk with most meals: house wine is served in a *carafe* (glass jug), *pichet* (pottery jug) or *bouteille* (bottle).

For wine-related terms see the Glossary at the back of the book.

Tasting, Buying & Celebrating Wine

Wine can be bought direct from the *domaine* (wine-growing estate) of the *producteur* (wine producer) or *vigneron* (wine grower) – at a lower price than in the shops. Most places offer *dégustation* (wine tasting), which allows you to sample two or three vintages, with no obligation to buy. Purchasing one or two bottles or one to 20 boxes (six or 12 bottles per box) is equally acceptable.

Tasting and buying more sought-after wines, such as Châteauneuf du Pape, where the annual production is bought years in advance, is trickier. Few producers have bottles to sell and those who do require you to make an appointment and buy a substantial amount. Complete lists of *caves* (wine cellars) open to travellers are available from the Comité Interprofessionnel des Vins Côtes de Provence in Les Arcs sur Argens and the Comité Interprofessionnel des Vins Côtes du Rhône in Avignon.

Most wine-producing villages or areas have a local cooperative that sells wine produced by local chateaux and cheaper-than-cheap *vin de table* (table wine). To reduce the cost still further, take your own container with you.

Wine Festivals The best wines of the last *millésime* (vintage) are cracked open in Châteauneuf du Pape during the **Fête de la St-Marc** (around 25 April). Hot on its heels are the **Fêtes de la Vigne et du Vin**, May-time wine-tasting festivals celebrated in Beaumes de Venise and Sablet.

The start of the grape harvest brings the **Féria des Vendanges** – a three-day bullfighting festival held in Nîmes' Roman amphitheatre during the third weekend in September – to town. Harvest celebrations continue farther north with Apt's **Fête de la Vendange et du Vin**, held the third Sunday in October.

The region's best known appellation is honoured with the **Fête des Côtes du Rhône Primeurs**, a celebration of the first Côtes du Rhône wines of that year, in Avignon in mid-November.

Wine Regions

Côtes du Rhône Provence's most renowned vintage is Châteauneuf du Pape, a full-bodied red wine grown 10km south of Orange. It is one of the many diverse wines in the respected Côtes du Rhône appellation, dating from 1937.

Châteauneuf du Pape vineyards were bequeathed to Provence by the Avignon popes. Its strong, well-structured reds are considered masters in their field. White wine, traditionally only made by *vignerons* for private use, now accounts for 7% of total annual production. Both whites and reds can be drunk young (two to three years) or old (seven years or more). Irrespective of age, whites should be served at 12°C; reds at 16 to 18°C.

Châteauneuf du Pape has a relatively high alcohol content of at least 12.5%. It was the first wine in France to be granted its own AOC in 1929, one rule being that grapes must be harvested by hand. Some *vignerons* claim it is the *galets* (large smooth, yellowish stones) covering their vineyards that distinguish Châteauneuf du Pape from other vineyards. Exceptional Châteauneuf du Pape vintages across the board are 1988–90, 1995 and 1997.

The Tavel rosé is another popular Rhône Valley *grand cru* (literally 'great growth') in Provence. The vineyards around the Dentelles de Montmirail, some 15km east of Orange, produce notable red and rosé Gigondas, and the sweet wine, Muscat de Beaumes de Venise.

Côtes de Provence The 18 hectares of vineyards sandwiched between Nice and Aix-en-Provence produce red, rosé and white Côtes de Provence, France's sixth largest appellation dating from 1977. The *terroir* (land) ranges from sandy coastal soils around St-Tropez to chalky soils of the subalpine slopes around Les Arcs.

The appellation is the largest in Provence with an annual production of 100 million bottles; 75% are rosé. Côte de Provence rosé is always drunk young and served at a crisp 8 to 10°C. Reds drunk young should be served at 14 to 16°C, while older red *vins de garde* – a traditional accompaniment to game, sauced meats and cheese – are best drunk at 16 to 18°C. Côte de Provence whites, a golden friend to fish, should be chilled to 8°C.

Others Six other pocket-sized appellations are dotted in the Côtes de Provence wine-growing area: Bandol, Cassis, Coteaux Varois, Coteaux d'Aix-en-Provence, Bellet and Palette. Of these, Bandol is the most respected, known for its deep-flavoured reds produced from the dark-berried *mourvèdre* grape, which needs oodles of sun to ripen (hence its rarity). In neighbouring Cassis, crisp whites (75% of its production) are drunk with gusto.

Those who like a dry rosé should try Coteaux d'Aix-en-Provence. Palette, east of Aix, is just 20 hectares. It dates from 1948, and produces well-structured reds from its old vines. Four of every five Palette bottles are Château Simone. Wines from the Bellet AOC are rare outside Nice.

The centre of Provence is carpeted with vineyards of the Côtes du Ventoux appellation (6900 hectares established in 1973) and Côtes du Lubéron (3500 hectares dating from 1988).

[Continued from page 48]

24-Hour Doctor Service If your problem is not sufficiently serious to call SAMU, but you still need to consult a doctor at night, call the **24-hour doctor service** *(in Nice ☎ 04 93 52 42 42; in Aix-en-Provence ☎ 04 42 26 24 00; in Avignon ☎ 04 90 87 75 00, 04 90 87 76 00)*, operational in most towns in the region. The hospitals in all three cities also operate a 24-hour emergency service.

In the Alpes-Maritimes department, a group of local English-speaking doctors form the **Riviera Medical Services** *(☎ 04 93 26 12 70)*; call it to get English-speaking medical assistance.

Basic Rules

Water Tap water all over France is safe to drink. Despite Provence's sheer abundance of fountains, the water spouting out of them is not always drinkable: *eau non potable* means 'undrinkable water'. Most fountains are signposted accordingly.

It's very easy to not drink enough liquids, particularly in summer, on hot days or at high altitude. Don't rely on thirst to indicate when you should drink. Not needing to urinate or very dark-yellow urine is a danger sign. Carrying a water bottle is a good idea.

Environmental Hazards

Fungal Infections Most fungal infections occur more often in hot weather and are usually found on the scalp, between the toes or fingers, in the groin and on the body (ringworm). You get ringworm (which is a fungal infection, not a worm) from infected animals or other people. Moisture encourages these infections.

To prevent fungal infections wear loose, comfortable clothes, avoid artificial fibres, wash frequently and dry carefully. If you do get an infection, wash the infected area at least daily with a disinfectant or medicated soap and water, then rinse and dry well. Apply an antifungal cream or powder like tolnifate (Tinaderm). Try to expose the infected area to air or sunlight as much as possible and wash all towels and underwear in hot water, change them often and let them dry in the sun.

Hay Fever Those who suffer from hay fever can look forward to sneezing their way around rural Provence in May and June when the pollen count is at its highest.

Heat Exhaustion Dehydration and salt deficiency can cause heat exhaustion. Take time to acclimatise to high temperatures, drink sufficient liquids and do not do anything too physically demanding.

Salt deficiency is characterised by fatigue, lethargy, headaches, giddiness and muscle cramps; salt tablets may help, but adding extra salt to your food is better.

Motion Sickness Eating lightly before and during a trip will reduce the chances of motion sickness. If you are prone to motion sickness try to find a place that minimises movement – near the wing on aircraft, close to midship on boats, near the centre on buses. Fresh air usually helps; reading and cigarette smoke don't. Commercial motion sickness preparations, which can cause drowsiness, have to be taken before the trip commences. Ginger (available as capsules) and peppermint (including mint-flavoured sweets) are natural preventatives.

Prickly Heat This is an itchy rash caused by excessive perspiration trapped under the skin. It usually strikes people who have just arrived in a hot climate. Keeping cool, bathing often, drying the skin and using a mild talcum or prickly heat powder, or resorting to air-conditioning may help.

Sunburn You can get sunburnt surprisingly quickly, even through cloud. Use a sunscreen, hat, and barrier cream for your nose and lips. Both Calamine lotion and Stingose are good for mild sunburn. Protect your eyes with good quality sunglasses, particularly if you will be near water, sand or snow.

Infectious Diseases

Diarrhoea Simple things such as a change of water, food or climate can all cause a mild bout of diarrhoea, but a few rushed toilet trips with no other symptoms are not indicative of a major problem.

Dehydration is the main danger with any diarrhoea, particularly in children or the elderly, as it can occur quickly. Fluid replacement (at least equal to the volume being lost) is most important. Weak black tea with a little sugar, soda water, or soft drinks allowed to go flat and diluted 50% with clean water are all good. Keep drinking small amounts often. Stick to a bland diet as you recover.

AIDS & HIV The Human Immunodeficiency Virus (VIH in French), develops into AIDS, Acquired Immune Deficiency Syndrome (SIDA in French), which is a fatal disease. Any exposure to blood, blood products or body fluids may put an individual at risk. The disease is often transmitted through sexual contact or dirty needles – vaccinations, acupuncture, tattooing and body piercing can be potentially as dangerous as intravenous drug use. HIV/AIDS can also be spread through infected blood transfusions; some developing countries cannot afford to screen blood used for transfusions. Fear of HIV infection should never preclude treatment for serious medical conditions.

For information on free and anonymous HIV-testing centres *(centres de dépistage)*, ring the **SIDA Info Service** *(☎ 08 00 84 08 00)* toll-free, 24 hours a day. Information is available in Nice at the **Centre de Dépistage du VIH** *(☎ 04 93 85 12 62; 2 rue Édouard Béri)* in Hôpital St-Roch; and in Marseilles at the **Centre de Dépistage** *(☎ 04 91 78 43 43; 10 rue St-Adrien)*.

CRIPS *(Centres Régionaux d'Information et Prévention sur le SIDA; in Marseilles ☎ 04 91 13 03 40; in Nice ☎ 04 92 14 41 20)* is a national chain of information centres offering practical help and guidance. **AIDES** *(☎ 08 20 16 01 20; e aidesprovence@pacman.fr; w www.aides.org; 1 rue Gilbert Dru, F-13011 Marseilles)* is a national organisation that works for the prevention of AIDS and assists AIDS sufferers.

Sexually Transmitted Diseases Gonorrhoea, herpes and syphilis are among these diseases; sores, blisters or rashes around the genitals, discharges, or pain when urinating are common symptoms. In some STDs, such as wart virus or chlamydia, symptoms may be less marked or not observed at all, especially in women. The symptoms of syphillis eventually disappear completely but the disease continues and can cause severe problems in later years. While abstinence from sexual contact is the only 100% effective prevention, using condoms is also efective. The treatment of gonorrhoea and syphilis is with antibiotics. The different sexually transmitted diseases each require specific antibiotics. There is no cure for herpes or AIDS.

All pharmacies carry condoms *(préservatifs)* and many have 24-hour automatic condom dispensers outside the door. Some brasseries, discotheques, metro stations and WCs in cafés and petrol stations are also equipped with condom machines. Condoms that conform to French government standards are marked with the letters NF *(norme française)* in black on a white oval inside a red and blue rectangle.

Bites & Stings

Bee and wasp stings are usually painful rather than dangerous. However, in people who are allergic to them severe breathing difficulties may occur and they may require urgent medical care. Calamine lotion or Stingose spray will give relief, and ice packs will reduce the pain and swelling.

Jellyfish Local advice will help prevent your coming into contact with jellyfish *(méduses)* and their stinging tentacles, often found along the Mediterranean. Dousing the wound in vinegar will deactivate any stingers that have not 'fired'. Calamine lotion, antihistamines and analgesics may reduce the reaction and relieve the pain. The sting of the Portuguese man-of-war, which has a sail-like float and long tentacles, is painful but rarely fatal.

Ticks Check all over your body if you have been walking through a potentially tick-infested area, as ticks can cause bad skin infections and other more serious diseases. If a tick is found attached, press down around the tick's head with tweezers, grab the head and gently pull upwards. Avoid pulling the rear of the body as this may squeeze the tick's gut contents through the attached mouth parts into the skin, increasing the risk of infection and disease. Smearing chemicals on the tick will not make it let go and is not recommended.

Women's Health

Antibiotic use, synthetic underwear, sweating and contraceptive pills can lead to fungal vaginal infections when travelling in hot climates. Maintaining good personal hygiene, and wearing loose-fitting clothes and cotton underwear will help to prevent them. Fungal infections, characterised by a rash, itch and discharge, can be treated with a vinegar or lemon-juice douche, or with yogurt. Nystatin, miconazole or clotrimazole pessaries or vaginal cream are the usual treatment.

WOMEN TRAVELLERS

French men have clearly given little thought to the concept of *harcèlement sexuel* (sexual harassment). Most still believe that staring suavely at a passing woman is paying her a compliment. Women need not walk around the region in fear, however. Suave stares are about as adventurous as most French men get, with women rarely being physically assaulted on the street or touched up in bars at night.

Unfortunately, it's not French men that women travellers have to concern themselves with. While women attract little unwanted attention in rural Provence, on the coast it's a different ball game. In the dizzying heat of the high season, the Côte d'Azur is rampant with men (and women) of *all* nationalities out on the pull. Apply the usual 'women traveller' rules and the chances are you'll emerge from the circus unscathed. Remain conscious of your surroundings, avoid going to bars and clubs alone at night and be aware of potentially dangerous situations: deserted streets, lonely beaches, dark corners of large train stations, and on night buses in certain districts of Marseilles and Nice.

Topless sunbathing is not generally interpreted as deliberately provocative.

Organisations

SOS Viol is a voluntary women's group that staffs the national **rape-crisis hotline** *(☎ 08 00 05 95 95)*. Its centre in Marseilles is spearheaded by **SOS Femmes** *(☎ 04 91 24 61 50, fax 04 91 24 61 58; ⓔ sosfemmes@free.fr; 14 blvd Théodore Thurner)* and in Nice by **Femmes Battues** *(☎/fax 04 93 52 17 81; 44 blvd Auguste Raynaud)*.

GAY & LESBIAN TRAVELLERS

France is one of Europe's most liberal countries when it comes to homosexuality, in part because of the long French tradition of public tolerance towards groups of people who have chosen not to live by conventional social codes. There are large gay and lesbian communities in Aix-en-Provence, Nice, Cannes and Marseilles, the latter being host to the colourful **Gay Pride march** *(ⓦ www.marseillepride.org)* in late June or early July and the week-long Universités Euroméditerranéennes des Homosexualités, which is a Euro-Mediterranean gay and lesbian summer school, which brings gays and lesbians from across Europe to Marseilles each year in July. Smaller gay groups along the Riviera join forces for the annual **Gay Pride Côte d'Azur** *(☎ 04 93 36 32 30; ⓦ www.gaypride.fr.st; BP 51047, F-06331 Grasse Cedex)*, held most years in Cannes.

The lesbian scene is less public than its gay counterpart. The region's most active gay and lesbian groups are in Marseilles: they include **Act Up Marseilles** *(☎ 04 91 42 89 29; ⓔ actupp@compuserve.com; 19 rue du Loisir)*; **Arc-en-Ciel** *(☎ 04 91 91 01 17; 20 rue Colbert, BP 2081)*; and lesbian group, **Centre Évolutif Lilith** *(CEL; ☎ 04 91 05 81 41; ⓦ http://celmrs.free.fr; 17 allées Léon Gambetta)*.

Entertainment-wise, the region's leading gay bars and nightclubs are in Cannes and Nice, and there are also large gay nightclubs in Juan-les-Pins and Toulon. See Entertainment under the relevant city sections of the regional chapters for listings.

DISABLED TRAVELLERS

The region is not user-friendly for *handicapés* (people with disabilities): kerb ramps are few and far between, older public facilities and budget hotels lack lifts, and the cobblestone streets typical of Provence's numerous hill-top villages are a nightmare to navigate in a wheelchair.

But all is not lost. Many two- or three-star hotels are equipped with lifts; Michelin's *Guide Rouge* indicates hotels with lifts and facilities for those with disabilities. On the coast, there are beaches with wheelchair access in Cannes, Marseilles, Nice, Hyères and Ste-Maxime. For information about Monaco's *handiplage* (handi-beach), open from July to September on Larvotto beach, contact the **Club Soroptimiste de Monaco** *(☎ 377-95 02 62 62)*.

The region's international airports offer assistance to travellers with disabilities. At Aéroport International Nice-Côte d'Azur, contact the **Service Handicapés GIS** *(☎ 04 93 21 44 58)*; and at Aéroport International Marseille-Provence, telephone **Assistance Midi-Provence** *(☎ 04 42 14 27 42)*. Both TGV and regular trains are also accessible for passengers in wheelchairs *(fauteuil rouant)*, provided they reserve by phone or at a train station at least 48 hours before departure; call the SNCF's **Accessibilité Service** *(☎ 08 00 15 47 53)* for information. Wheelchair users and their travelling companion can travel in 1st class for the prices of a 2nd-class fare.Details are available in SNCF's booklet *Le Mémento du Voyageur à Mobilité Réduite* (one page in English). Alternatively, contact SNCF Accessibilité Service.

SENIOR TRAVELLERS

Senior travellers are often entitled to discounts on public transport, museum admission fees etc, provided they can show proof of their age (either over 60 or 65, depending on the establishment). At large main-line train stations such as Marseilles, **SOS Voyageurs** *(☎ 04 91 62 12 80; open 7am-7pm Mon-Sat)* – a voluntary group usually run by retirees – offers help to elderly train travellers.

TRAVEL WITH CHILDREN

Many places along the coast offer special children's activities – see Highlights at the start of this chapter for some specific 'just kidding' ideas on what to do with the kids.

Most car-rental firms hire children's car seats for around €30 per rental. Highchairs and cots are standard in most restaurants and hotels, although you often have to ask. The choice of baby food, infant formulas, soy and cow's milk, disposable nappies (diapers) and the like is as great in French supermarkets as it is back home.

Tourist offices generally maintain lists of baby-sitting services and creches. A further information source is Lonely Planet's *Travel with Children*.

DANGERS & ANNOYANCES

Theft

Theft – from backpacks, pockets, cars, trains, laundrettes, beaches – is a problem, particularly along the Côte d'Azur. Keep an eagle eye on your bags, especially at train and bus stations, on overnight train rides, in tourist offices, in fast-food restaurants and on beaches.

Always keep your money, credit cards, tickets, passport, driving licence and other important documents in a money belt worn inside your trousers or skirt. Keep enough money for the day in a separate wallet. Theft from hotel rooms is less common but it's still not a great idea to leave your life's belongings in your room. In hostels, lock your nonvaluables in a locker provided and cart your valuables along. Upmarket hotels have safes *(coffres)*.

When swimming at the beach or taking a dip in the pool, have members of your party take turns sitting with packs and clothes.

At the train station, if you leave your bags at a left-luggage office or in a luggage locker, treat your claim chit (or locker code) like cash. Daypack snatchers have taken stolen chits to the train station and taken possession of the rest of their victims' belongings.

Forest Fires

Forest fires are common in heavily forested areas in July and August when the sun is hot and the land is dry. Such fires spread incredibly quickly – between 20m and 30m per minute. Between 1 July and the second Sunday in September, the forest authorities close high-risk areas. Never walk in a closed zone. Tourist offices in the region can tell you if a walking path is closed. If you come across a fire, call the fire brigade immediately (see the boxed text 'Help' later).

All forested areas are crisscrossed with road tracks enabling fire crews to penetrate the forest quickly. These roads – signposted DFCI *(défense forestière contre l'incendie)* – are closed to private vehicles but you can follow them on foot.

Lighting a camp fire or barbecue anywhere in the region is forbidden.

Rivers & Lakes

Major rivers in Provence are connected to hydroelectric power stations operated by the national electricity company, Electricité de France (EDF). Water levels rise dramatically if the EDF opens a dam. White-water sports on the Verdon River downstream of the Chaudanne Dam *(barrage)* are forbidden when the water flow is less than 5 cu metres/sec. For information on water levels and dam releases, call ☎ 04 92 83 62 68.

Swimming is prohibited in lakes that are artificial and have steep, unstable banks (ie, Lac de Ste-Croix, southwest of the Gorges du Verdon; and Lac de Castillon and the adjoining Lac de Chaudanne, northeast of the gorges). Sailing, windsurfing and canoeing are restricted to flagged areas.

Beaches

Most larger beaches on the Côte d'Azur have a *poste de secours* (safety post) during the beach season, staffed by lifeguards. In water-sport areas, a section of the sea is always sectioned off for swimmers. Always note the colour of the flag flying before diving in: a green flag means that it is safe to swim; yellow means bathing is risky but allowed; red means that swimming is forbidden; and purple means the sea water is polluted.

It is not unheard of for beaches to be closed.

Poisonous Mushrooms

Wild-mushroom picking is a national pastime in Provence. Pick by all means but don't eat anything until it has been positively identified as safe by a pharmacist. Most pharmacies in the region offer a mushroom-identification service.

The Mistral

During the balmy days of June and the steamy days of July and August, it is hard to believe that the region can be freezing cold when the mistral strikes (see the boxed text 'The Mud-Eating Mistral' in the Facts about Provence chapter).

Thunderstorms in the mountains and hot southern plains can be extremely sudden, violent and dangerous. Check the weather report before you set out on a long walk; even then, be prepared for a sudden weather change. Storms are very common in August and September.

LEGAL MATTERS

The police are allowed to search anyone at any time, regardless of whether there is an obvious reason to do so or not. As elsewhere in the EU, laws are tough when it comes to drinking and driving. The acceptable blood-alcohol limit is 0.05%. Licences can be immediately suspended fro infringements. Importing or exporting drugs can lead to a jail sentence of up to 30 years. The fine for possession of drugs for personal use can be as high as €75,000.

Nude bathing is forbidden on St-Tropez's municipal beaches (but bathers still strip off). Since 1994 fines have been imposed in St-Raphaël, Ste-Maxime and Monaco on tourists who walk in town bare-chested or bikini-clad. St-Tropez has banned bikinis and topless men on its streets since 2002.

Help

Dial the following emergency telephone numbers (toll-free) in times of trouble:

SAMU medical treatment/ambulance	☎ 15
Police	☎ 17
Fire brigade	☎ 18
Rape crisis hotline	☎ 08 00 05 95 95

BUSINESS HOURS

Museums and shops (but not cinemas, restaurants or bakeries) are closed on public holidays. On Sunday, a bakery is usually about all that opens (morning only) and public transport services are less frequent. In villages, shops (including bakeries) close for a long lunch between 2pm and 4pm. In Provence, hotels, restaurants, cinemas, cultural institutions and shops close for their *congé annuel* (annual closure) in winter. Commercial banks generally open 8am or 9am to 11.30am or 1pm and 1.30pm or 2pm to 4.30pm or 5pm weekdays.

Some hotels, museums and *chambres d'hôtes* only open *Pâques à la Tous-saint*; this means Easter to All Saints' Day (1 November). Many places to eat and/or drink in Nice and Marseilles brandish 'open nonstop' signs. Far from meaning they open 24 hours, it actually means that the place opens nonstop – without breaking for that all-essential lunch – between the morning or evening opening hours advertised.

PUBLIC HOLIDAYS & SPECIAL EVENTS

In Provence, festivals *(fêtes)* and fairs *(foires)* are a crucial part of community life, with every city, town, village and hamlet throwing a street party at least once a year (usually more often) to celebrate everything from a good lavender or olive crop to the feast of their patron saint. An abundance of wonderful food (colossal *aïolis*, paellas and the like), a *pétanque* (Provençal boules) championship and dancing late into the night are guaranteed to stir the soul of any traveller lucky enough to be on hand to witness such a joyous occasion.

Festivals: Famous Five or Otherwise

The Cannes Film Festival, Avignon theatre festival and the Roma pilgrimages to Stes-Maries de la Mer in the Camargue rank among Provence's most famous five festivals, those are covered in the regional chapters. Lesser known but equally colourful festivals capturing the true spirit of Provence include:

Fête de la Transhumance The region's age-old pastoral traditions come to life in this fabulous festival, celebrated in Salin de Provence and St-Rémy de Provence in June. Each year at this time, more than 100,000 sheep move from the arid Crau plain to the greener mountainside to graze. With the onset of winter, they return to the irrigated plain. Until the 1970s, shepherds drove their flocks into the mountain on foot, accompanied by donkeys and goats. Up to 30 days could be on spent the road to reach the southern Alps' lush pastures. Today, the task is done by lorry and at night (to reduce traffic chaos). Before hitting higher altitudes, the thousands of sheep stroll the festival streets of Salin and St-Rémy.

Fête de la Tarasque The terrible Tarasque is the indisputable star of this five-day fiesta of bonfires, fireworks, street processions and carnivals, held each year in Tarascon around 24 June to celebrate the region's most legendary beast. Celebrated by King René as early as 1474, the festival re-enacts the story of St Martha who tamed Tarasque, a terrifying dragon-like creature who lived in the Rhône and gobbled up humans. The giant Chinese-style dragon that parades through the streets today is a substantially bigger and better version of the devilish, fire-spouting monster that later villagers captured and killed.

St-Tropez's Bravades Macho military parades mark St-Tropez's trio of *bravades* ('bravery' in Provençal). Several dozen 'soldiers' wear 18th-century military uniforms as they march through the streets to the noisy din of musket fire. The parades are led by the *capitaine de ville* (town captain), an evocation of the captains who ruled the autonomous town between 1481 and 1672. *Bravades* take place on 15 June to mark St-Tropez's victory over a fleet of Spanish galleons in 1637; and on 16, 17 and 18 May to mark the town's patron saint's day. *Bravades* have been celebrated since 1558.

Festo Vierginenco Otherwise known as the Fête des Vièrges (Festival of Virgins), this festival is one of Provence's oldest. Held each year in July, it was created by Provençal poet Mistral in 1904 to honour young girls from Arles who don traditional Arlésienne dress for the first time. The festival opens with the blessing of the girls, after which a bull is let loose into the arena. Later, the costumed girls proceed through the streets accompanied by Camargue cowboys on horseback. Unlike the Arlésienne *mireille* which can be worn every day, the traditional dress donned at this festival can only be worn on Sunday.

French National Holidays

National public holidays *(jours fériés)* are often a cue for festivities to spill into the streets.

New Year's Day (Jour de l'An) 1 January
Easter Sunday (Pâques) & **Easter Monday** (lundi de Pâques) Late March/April
May Day (Fête du Travail) 1 May – buy a *muguet* (lily of the valley) from a street vendor for good luck
Victoire 1945 8 May – Celebrates the Allied victory in Europe that ended WWII
Ascension Thursday (L'Ascension) May to early June – celebrated on the 40th day after Easter
Pentecost/Whit Sunday & **Whit Monday** (Pentecôte & lundi de Pentecôte) – celebrated on the 7th Sunday after Easter
Bastille Day/National Day (Fête Nationale) 14 July
Assumption Day (L'Assomption) 15 August
All Saints' Day (La Toussaint) 1 November
Remembrance Day (Le onze novembre) 11 November – celebrates the armistice of WWI
Christmas (Noël) 25 December

While not official public holidays, many Provençal festivals fall on Shrove Tuesday (Mardi Gras), Maundy (Holy) Thursday and Good Friday, or Boxing Day (26 December).

Monégasque National Holidays

Monaco shares the same holidays with France *except* those on 8 May, 14 July and 11 November. Additional public holidays are:

Feast of Ste-Dévote 27 January – patron saint of Monaco
Corpus Christi June – three weeks after Ascension
Fête Nationale (National Day) 19 November
Immaculate Conception 8 December

Feasts & Festivals

Provence has a spicy cultural calendar. Most festivals celebrate a historical or folklore tradition, or a performing art. Festivals the celebrate the region's most beloved pastimes – food and wine – are listed in the Food & Wine of Provence special section.

Only key festivals are listed below. For a complete listing, pick up *Terre de Festivals* – a meaty 200-page festival-listing guide – for free at most tourist offices or read it online (in English) at Ⓦ www.viafrance.com/paca.

February

Féria Primavera Three-day bullfighting Spring Festival, Nîmes

Carnaval de Nice The region's most celebrated two-week carnival with floats, masks, fireworks and flower battles, Nice, Mardi Gras

May

Fête des Gardians The day of the Camargue cowboys, Arles, 1 May

Cannes International Film Festival Ten-day International Film Festival, Cannes

Bravade St-Tropez honours its patron saint with a traditional *bravade*, 15–17 May

Pélerinage des Gitans Three-day international gypsy pilgrimage, Stes-Maries de la Mer, 24–26 May

June

Féria de la Pentecôte Five-day Pentecost Festival, marked in Nîmes with bullfights

Fête de la Transhumance Traditional pastoral festival when shepherds lead their flocks (some 3000 sheep) to pastures new, St-Rémy de Provence, Pentecost Monday

Bravades des Espagnols St-Tropez celebrates its victory over a fleet of Spanish galleons, 15 June

Les Nuits du Théâtre Antique In June (and again in August), Orange's ancient Théâtre Antique is lit up with concerts, cinema screenings and other musical events

Fête de la Tarasque Five days of bonfires, fireworks, street processions and carnival starring the folkloric Tarasque dragon, Tarascon, around 24 June

July

Festival International d'Art Lyrique Prestigious month-long lyrical art festival in Aix-en-Provence

Fête de la Mer et des Pêcheurs Two days honouring St Peter, patron saint of fishermen. In La Ciotat, there's a Provençal Mass, folk music, and benediction of fishing boats; in St-Raphaël local fishermen don traditional dress and joust Provençal-style from boats.

Nice Jazz Festival One-week jazz festival with main venue being a lovely old olive grove in Cimiez, Nice

Jazz à Juan Celebrated jazz festival in and around Juan-les-Pins, from mid-July

Festival d'Avignon Among Europe's best-known theatre festivals, dating from 1947; Avignon, July. Festival Off is its funkier, fringe side.

Les Nuits Musicales de Nice Three weeks of open-air, classical music concerts around Cimiez Monastery and the Musée d'Art Moderne et d'Art Contemporain, Nice, from mid-July

Les Chorégies d'Orange Two-week classical and choral music festival held in Orange's Roman amphitheatre

Éstivales de Carpentras A two-week music, dance and theatre festival, Carpentras

Festival Mosaïque Gitane Gypsy culture celebrations, Arles and Marseilles' Plage du Prado in Marseilles, mid-July

Festo Vierginenco Festival created by Provençal poet Mistral in 1904 to honour young girls from Arles who don traditional Arlésienne costume for the first time, Arles, mid-July

Festival des Chœurs Lauréats Polyphonic festival in the Théâtre Antique (Roman theatre) in Vaison-la-Romaine, last week of July

Festival de Lacoste Music with open-air concerts around Pierre Cardin's restored castle, mid-July to mid-August, Lacoste

August

Choralies Choral Festival Two-week choral concert, the largest of its kind in Europe, every three years in Vaison-la-Romaine's Roman theatre

Corso de La Lavande Five-day festival to celebrate the lavender harvest, Digne-les-Bains, first weekend in August

September & October

Fête Mistralienne The birthday of literary hero Frédéric Mistral is celebrated 12–13 September throughout the entire Provençal region

Pélerinage des Gitans Gypsy pilgrimage, Stes-Maries de la Mer, 22 October

November & December

Fête de St-Siffrein Huge market and fair to mark the feast day of Carpentras' patron saint, Carpentras, 27 November

Noël Most villages celebrate Christmas with midnight Mass, traditional chants in Provençal and a ceremony in which shepherds offer a newborn lamb. Séguret is one of the few places to still celebrate Christmas with Mass and a living creche; see the boxed text 'A Village Christmas' in the Avignon Area chapter.

ACTIVITIES

The Provence and Côte d'Azur region lives up to its reputation as being a land of sea and mountains, offering a wealth of outdoor pursuits that are guaranteed to thrill even the most adventurous – as well as the lazy – travellers.

Cycling

Pedalling Provence is tremendously popular. Bar the barren slopes of Mont Ventoux in the Vaucluse, the region has few killing hills to climb, making it an ideal area to two-wheel. The country roads in the Lubéron, which saunter through vineyards and fruit orchards, are popular with cyclists (see the boxed text 'Lubéron by Bike' in that chapter), as are the quiet roads traversing the Massif des Maures. Bicycles are forbidden in the Mercantour and Port-Cros national parks, but allowed on the protected island of Porquerolles, where they are the only means of transport.

Cycling is less tranquil on the coast where the noisy motorway is never far away. Two-wheelers on a budget often base themselves in Nice, from where they take a train along the coast each morning with their bicycles, to avoid the trauma of cycling out of the city. Some GR trails (see the Walking section following) are open to mountain bikes. Between Hyères and Toulon, there is a smooth-as-silk, two-lane cycling path *(piste cyclable)* that runs for 18.5km along the coast.

Lonely Planet's *Cycling France* details six cycling itineraries in the region. It is the only Provence-specific cycling guide in English. If you read French, Didier-Richard publishes *Les Guides VTT*, a series of cyclists' topoguides and the Conseil Général des Alpes-Maritimes (see Walking following) publishes the excellent *Rando VTT* cycling guide in its *Guides RandOxygène* series. Many tourist offices sell cycling itineraries compiled by local cycling clubs.

See the Getting Around chapter for information on bicycle rental, local cycling clubs and organisations, and cycling tours in the region.

Walking

The region is crisscrossed by a maze of *sentiers balisés* (marked walking paths) and *sentiers de grande randonnée* (long-distance paths with alphanumeric names beginning 'GR'). Some of the latter are many hundreds of kilometres long, including the GR5 which goes from the Netherlands through Belgium, Luxembourg and the spectacular Alpine scenery of eastern France, before ending up in Nice. The GR4, GR6 and GR9 (and their various diversions the GR99, GR98 etc) all traverse the region too.

No permits are needed but there are restrictions on where you can camp, especially in the Parc National de Mercantour. Between 1 July and 15 September paths in heavily forested areas – such as the section of the GR98 that follows the Calanques between Cap Croisette (immediately south of Marseilles) and Cassis – are closed due to the high risk of forest fire. The GR51 crossing the Massif des Maures, paths in the Montagne de Ste-Victoire east of Aix-en-Provence and numerous trails in Haute-Provence are likewise closed.

Many walking guides – predominantly in French – cover the region. English-language guides include Lonely Planet's *Walking in France*; *Walking in Provence* (2000) by Janette Norton; and the excellent *Walks in Provence: Lubéron Regional Nature Park*, a topoguide written by the Fédération Française de Randonnée Pédestre (FFRP; French Ramblers' Association).

If you read French, the *Guides Rand-Oxygène* walking guides published by the Conseil Général des Alpes-Maritimes (Alpes-Maritimes General Council) are outstanding. The guides detail 60 walks of varying lengths – for seaside amblers to serious walkers – in the Alpes-Maritimes department: *Rando Haut-Pays* covers the Mercantour national park, *Rando Moyen-Pays* tackles the hill-top villages north of Nice and *Rando Pays Côtier* features 60 invigorating coastal walks. Incredibly, the glossy 80-page guides are free at tourist offices. Their contents – minus the maps – are also posted online at **W** www.cg06.fr; follow the link under 'Sortir-Les guides randoxygène'.

Many tourist offices take bookings for short two- to three-hour guided nature walks in their areas; many are organised by the local branch of the Office National des Forêts. From Digne-les-Bains, guides organise walks into the mountains with a donkey (to lug your luggage); see the Haute-Provence chapter. See also Organised Tours in the Getting Around chapter for walking tours.

Rafting, Canoeing & Canyoning

Haute-Provence is exquisite white-water rafting, canoeing, kayaking and canyoning terrain. The Rivers Verdon, Vésubie, Roya and Ubaye are the region's most dramatic waters. Leading centres where you can sign up for expeditions include Castellane (for the

Gorges du Verdon), St-Martin-Vésubie (for the Vésubie descent), Breil-sur-Roya (for the Vallée de la Roya) and Barcelonnette (for the Vallée de l'Ubaye). Details are listed in the Haute-Provence chapter.

The less intrepid can try paddling in circles beneath the Pond du Gard or 8km along the River Sorgue from Fontaine de Vaucluse to L'Isle-sur-la-Sorgue (see the Avignon Area chapter for details).

AET Nature in Breil-sur-Roya organises white-water expeditions of several days in the Roya Valley; see Organised Tours in the Getting Around chapter.

Water Sports

Sailing is big business on the French Riviera. Antibes, Cannes, Mandelieu-La Napoule and St-Raphaël are among the largest water-sports centres where non-boat owners can hire a set of sails. Tourist offices have a list of sailing centres *(stations violes)* that rent gear and run courses. Count on paying at least €20 per hour to rent a catamaran.

Other water sports readily available on the beach include windsurfing (€20 per hour to rent a board, plus €15 for one hour's tuition), water-skiing (€22 per hour), jet-skiing (around €50 for 30 minutes) and rides from the back of a boat in a parachute (€40/55 for one/two people for a 10-minute ride) or hair-raising rubber ring (€20 per person for a 10-minute ride).

Diving & Snorkelling

The coastline and its offshore islands – Porquerolles and Embiez particularly – offer enticing diving opportunities. Experienced divers enjoy the waters around Hyères, where the sea beds are graced with numerous shipwrecks. Military WWII wrecks can be explored from St-Raphaël.

The region's most spectacular dives are around Marseilles' Calanques. Henri Cosquer, known for his discovery of prehistoric paintings in a cave around the Calanques, has his own diving school in Cassis (see the Marseilles Area chapter). There are underwater nature trails designed for amateur snorkellers at the Domain du Rayol on the Corniche des Maures and on the island of Port-Cros (see the St-Tropez to Toulon chapter).

Diving shops and clubs where you can hire equipment and learn how to dive are listed in the relevant regional chapters.

Bird-Watching

The spectacular Camargue delta – where clouds of pink flamingos are a common sight – and the Parc National du Mercantour lure ornithologists. The **Provence-Alpes-Côte d'Azur branch** *(☎ 04 94 12 79 52; ⓔ paca @lpo-birdlife.asoo.fr; rond point Beauregard, F-834000 Hyères)* of the national **Ligue pour la Protection des Oiseaux** *(LPO: League for the Protection of Birds; ⓦ www.lpo-birdlife .asso.fr)* can tell you where to spot what, and put you in touch with LPO-affiliated bird-watching groups in the region.

Ballooning

Hot-air ballooning is a fabulous but expensive means of viewing the region. Flights (1½ hours) generally cost €230 per person, including breakfast or a champagne picnic. Operators include **La Provence en Ballon** *(☎ 04 90 95 53 28; ⓔ jmassemin@net-up.com; Traverse Castel Mouisson, Barbentane)* near Avignon; **Hot-Air Ballooning Provence** *(☎ 04 90 05 79 21; ⓔ hot-air@avignon-et-provence .com; Le Mas Fourniquière, Joucas)*, just outside Gordes; and **Les Montgolfières du Sud** *(☎ 04 66 37 28 02; ⓦ www.sudmontgolfiere .com; 64 rue Sigalon, Uzès)*, which floats around the Pont du Gard from its base in neighbouring Languedoc.

Golf

Golf hit the Riviera in the 1890s. Among France's oldest golf courses – dubbed *béton vert* (green concrete) – is **Golf Club de Cannes-Mandelieu** *(☎ 04 92 97 32 00; route du Golf)*, an 18-hole course established in Mandelieu-La Napoule by Grand Duke Michael of Russia in 1891. Green fees are €48/55 per day/weekend. The Monte Carlo Golf Club dating back to 1911 is another prestigious place to play – see the Nice to Menton chapter for details. Information on the Riviera's 20-odd other greens are listed in the free *Golf Destination: Côte d'Azur French Riviera* guide, available at tourist offices abroad.

Horse Riding

With its famous cowboys and cream-coloured horses, the Camargue is the obvious spot to saddle up – see that chapter for details. Elsewhere, tourist offices have lists of stables and riding centres where you can ride.

Ferme Équestre des Tilleuls *(☎ 04 94 67 50 38; Ⓦ www.cheval-rando83.com; ferme route d'Entrecasteaux, F-83690 Salernes)*, in the Haut-Var west of Draguignan, is the regional representative for the Féderation Française des Relais d'Etape de Tourisme Équestre – an association that arranges riding itineraries and accommodation. Ferme Équestre des Tilleuls organises short day rides as well as rides of several days around Lac de Ste-Croix du Verdon and through the Massif des Maures.

Skiing & Snowboarding

Haute-Provence's few ski resorts are low-key, with little of the glitz and the glamour attached to the Alps' better-known resorts. They are best suited to beginners and intermediates and are marginally cheaper than their northern neighbours.

Resorts include the larger Pra Loup (1500m) and La Foux d'Allos (1800m), which share 230km of downhill pistes and 110km of cross-country trails; the pinprick sister resorts of Le Sauze (1400m) and Super-Sauze (1700m) in the Vallée de l'Ubaye, which tend to attract domestic tourists; and Barcelonnette (1300m), a small town surrounded by a sprinkling of tiny hill-side villages. Isola 2000 (2450m) is the largest of the resorts – and the ugliest.

These resorts – all in the Parc National du Mercantour – open for the ski season from December to March/April/May (depending on the snow conditions), and for a short period in July and August for summer walkers. Buying a package is the cheapest way to ski. For online information, try Ⓦ www.skifrance.com.

Mont Ventoux offers limited downhill and cross-country skiing; the Chalet Reynard in Bedoin (listed under Mont Ventoux in the Avignon Area chapter) has details.

Rock Climbing & Via Ferrata

The Gorges du Verdon, the Calanques around Marseilles, the lacy Dentelles de Montmirail in the Vaucluse, Buoux in the Lubéron and the Vallée des Merveilles in the Parc National du Mercantour are but a handful of the region's climbing sites *(sites d'escalade)*. Most tourist offices and branches of Club Alpin Français (CAF; listed in the regional chapters) stock lists of spots to climb.

There are some heart-thumping *via ferrata* (a type of rock climbing using preattached cables) courses in Haute-Provence – see the boxed text 'Via Ferrata' in that chapter.

Spas

Wallowing in lavender or algae baths, shiatsu massages, Mediterranean mudpacks and a rash of other self-pampering pleasures can be found at a handful of spas. A super soak in a bubbling thermal bath laced with essential lavender oil at **Les Thermes de Digne-les-Bains** *(☎ 04 92 32 32 92, fax 04 92 32 38 15; Ⓔ thermes.digne@eurothermes.com; 29 ave des Thermes)* in Digne-les-Bains costs €18.

Thermes Sextius (see the Marseilles Area chapter), a Roman spa in Aix-en-Provence, offers Zen massages (€40 for 30 minutes), Camargue-salt skin scrubs (€40) and dozens more soothing treatments and packages.

The region's most exclusive and luxurious spa is Les Thermes Marins in Monte Carlo (see the Monaco chapter). Six-day slimming, stress, well-being and cellulite-attack packages start at €2955/1125 with/without accommodation.

Paragliding

St-André-les-Alpes, 20km north of Castellane in Haute-Provence, is the French capital of paragliding *(parapente)*. If the thermals are good – as in St-André – you can stay up for hours, peacefully circling the area and enjoying breathtaking aerial views. There is a paragliding school here and in St-Dalmas-Valdeblore and Digne-les-Bains. See the Haute-Provence chapter for details.

Rollerblading

Rollerblading (inline skating) is a tiptop way to cruise around town – and be seen. A set can be hired in any of the larger cities as well as most resorts on the Côte d'Azur for around €5 per day. Nice's promenade des Anglais, La Croisette in Cannes and La Canebière in Marseilles are the most chic spots to blade.

Hundreds of rollerbladers meet each week for a police-escorted evening blade around town in Avignon, Marseilles and Nice; see Activities in those city sections for details. In Hyères, **Hyères Roller Attitude** *(☎ 04 94 00 68 74; Ⓔ hyeres-roller-attitude@wanadoo.fr; 3579 route de l'Almanare)* runs rollerblading courses, costing upwards of €24/16 for one-hour private/group tuition.

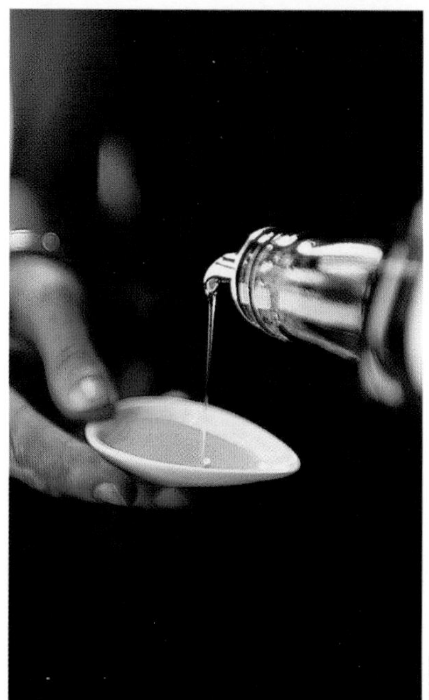
GREG ELMS

Tasting olive oil in St-Rémy de Provence

GREG ELMS

Fresh baguettes at a road-side stall in Provence

ROCCO FASANO

Fresh garlic by the ton in Marseilles

JEAN-BERNARD CARILLET

Bars and cafés along the Vieux Port in Marseilles

GREG ELMS

Beignets de fleur in Nice

RICHARD NEBESKY

Breakfast alfresco in Orange, north of Avignon

JEAN-BERNARD CARILLET

A small snack shop in Les Baux de Provence

GREG ELMS

Provençal olive bread at Carpentras Market

JEAN-BERNARD CARILLET

Restaurant menu board in Les Baux de Provence

GREG ELMS

Short black coffee and *eau de vie* in Nice

Spelunking

Pockets of the region are riddled with *grottes* (caves) and *avens* (pot holes and sink holes), just waiting to be discovered. Those already uncovered can generally only be visited with a professional guide.

The Plateau d'Albion – a harsh and spooky plain in the Vaucluse's easternmost corner – is prime spelunking territory. See the boxed text 'Plateau d'Albion' in the Avignon Area for details.

The Musée de la Préhistoire des Gorges du Verdon in Quinson organises visits on foot to the Grotte de la Baume Bonne, an incredible prehistoric cave. See the Lacs du Verdon section in the Haute-Provence chapter for details.

Bungee Jumping

The brave and daring can leap off bridges in Guillaumes, in the Vallée de la Tinée, and from Europe's highest bridge in the Gorges du Verdon. See the Haute-Provence chapter for details.

Astronomy

With its fine, clear nights, Provence is an obvious place to watch stars in the dardk skies. Observatories welcoming stargazers include Observatoire de Haute-Provence in St-Michel l'Observatoire, west of Manosque; Observatoire de Nice, in La Trinité, east of Nice; and Observatoire de la Côte d'Azur, north of Grasse on the Plateau de Calern. See the regional chapters for visiting details.

Naturism

Nudist spots – an *aire naturiste*, not to be confused with an *aire naturelle* which is a primitive farm camp site – range from small rural camp sites to large chalet villages with cinemas, tennis courts and shops. Most open April to October; visitors need an International Naturist Federation (INF) *passeport naturiste*, available at naturist centres.

The coastline between Le Lavandou and the St-Tropez peninsula is well endowed with nudist beaches. Héliopolis on Île du Levant – an oddball island off the coast between Le Lavandou and Hyères, 90% of which is occupied by the French military – is the region's only genuine nudist colony. It dates from the 1930s and can be easily visited on a day trip by boat.

The **Fédération Française de Naturisme** *(☎ 01 47 64 32 82; W www.ffn-naturisme.com; 65 rue de Tocqueville, F-75017 Paris)* can tell you exactly where you can roam in the buff in Provence.

COURSES

French Language

There are dozens more language schools than those listed below. Tourist offices have lists. Online, see W www.worldwide.edu/ci/france.

Alliance Française (☎ 04 93 62 67 66, W www.alliance-francaise.com) 2 rue de Paris, F-06000 Nice. Extensive/intensive (two/four hours' tuition per day), evening classes (two hours), private lessons and speciality courses (literature, business etc). Sister school in Marseilles.

Association de Langue Française d'Avignon (ALFA; ☎ 04 90 85 86 24, W www.alfavignon.com) 4 impasse Romagnoli, F-84000 Avignon. Courses from €460 for a two-week course, with 15 hours' group tuition per week and B&B accommodation costing €107 a week.

Centre Méditerranéen d'Études Françaises (☎ 04 93 78 21 59, W www.monte-carlo.mc/centremed) chemin des Oliviers, F-06320 Cap-Ail. School dating to 1952 with an open-air amphitheatre designed by Cocteau

Crea Langues (☎ 04 92 77 74 58, W www.crealangues.com) Monastère de Segres, F-04360 Moustiers-Ste-Marie. Intensive two-week courses in a lovely cloistered monastery, from €840 plus €560 for full-board accommodation

Institut Euro'Provence (☎ 04 91 33 90 60, e euro-provence@infonie.fr) 69 rue de Rome, F-13001 Marseilles. One-/three-month courses with 20 hours' group tuition a week costs €270/850; equivalent courses with just four hours' tuition per week costs €70/215

International House (☎ 04 93 62 60 62, W www.ih-nice.com) 62 rue Gioffredo, F-06000 Nice. Two-week course with 50 lessons (45 minutes) for €566, plus €61 enrolment fee

Université d'Aix Marseille III (☎ 04 42 21 70 90, W www.univ.u-3mrs.fr) 23 rue Gaston de Saporta, F-13625 Aix-en-Provence. One-/two-term courses (€1100/1700) and four-week intensive course (€450) at the university's Institute of French Studies for Foreign Students

Provençal Cooking

Most culinary courses for globe-trotting gourmets revolve around markets, vineyards, olive groves – and the kitchen table. The *Guide to Cooking Schools*, published annually by **Shaw Guides** *(W http://cookingcareer.shawguides.com)*, has an exhaustive listing.

At Home with Patricia Wells (fax 919-845 9031, ⓦ www.patriciawells.com) c/o Judith Jones, 708 Sandown Place, Raleigh, NC 27615, USA. Four-day truffle and five-day wine, food and fitness workshops with Patricia Wells, the only wholly foreign cook considered to have truly embraced the soul of Provençal cooking. Courses cost US$3000 (excluding accommodation) and take place in Wells' 18th-century farmhouse kitchen (where she cooked up the 175 recipes for her cookbook *Patricia Wells: At Home in Provence*) near Vaison-la-Romaine.

Hostellerie de Crillon le Brave (☎ 04 90 65 61 61, ⓦ www.crillonlebrave.com) place de l'Église, F-84410 Crillon le Brave. Five-day courses with the hotel's French chef Philippe Monti; US$2800 per person per week, including accommodation in a double room. Wine workshops too.

La Cuisine du Soleil (☎ 04 93 75 35 70, ⓔ info@moulin-mougins.com) Restaurant L'Amandier, place du Commandant Lamy, F-06250 Mougins. Morning or afternoon sessions (2½ hours) in the kitchen of top Provençal chef Roger Vergé cost €51/230 for one/five sessions. Reserve at least 72 hours in advance.

Le Marmiton (☎ 04 90 85 93 93, ⓦ www.la-mirande.fr) Hôtel de la Mirande, 4 place de la Mirande, F-84000 Avignon. Hotel cookery school with morning/afternoon/evening class costing €95/75/115, including a taste of the class' culinary creation with coffee or wine depending on the time of day.

Mas de Cornud (☎ 04 90 92 39 32, ⓦ www.mascornud.com) route de Mas Blanc, F-31210 St-Rémy de Provence. Week-long cookery classes in a four-star, 18th-century farmhouse near St-Rémy, costing US$3000, including eight night's accommodation.

Arts & Crafts

Few courses are conducted in English.

Ateliers de l'Image (☎ 04 90 92 51 50, ⓔ ateliers-images@pacwan.fr, ⓦ www.hotelphoto.com) 5 ave Pasteur, 13210 St-Rémy de Provence. Bilingual English-French photography workshops.

Maison de la Céramique (☎ 04 90 72 32 61, ⓦ www.ceramique.com/Luberon-Ceramique) place de la Gare, F-84220 Les Beaumettes. Five-day pottery, ceramics and faïence courses (in French only), run by the House of Ceramics in the Lubéron. Introductory courses from €61 per day.

Usine Mathieu Okhra (☎ 04 90 05 66 69, ⓔ info@okhra.com) F-84220 Roussillon. Imaginative paper dying, wall-mural painting and wood-craft workshops using traditional techniques and natural dyes and pigments, extracted from thevillage's ochre earth (€100/85/70 for the 1st/2nd/3rd day).

WORK

To work legally you need a *carte de séjour* (see Visas & Documents earlier in this chapter). Work 'in the black', without documents, is possible in the Côte d'Azur's tourist industry and during Provence's grape harvest. A useful book for those lucky enough to land a job in France is *Living & Working in France* (2002) by David Hampshire.

Agricultural Work

To pick up a job in a field, ask around in areas where harvesting is taking place; Provence sees a succession of apple, strawberry, cherry, peach, pear and pumpkin harvests from mid-May to September.

The annual grape harvest happens from about mid-September to mid- or late October. The sun-soaked fruits of the Côtes de Provence vineyards are ready for harvest before those of the more northern, Châteauneuf du Pape vineyards. Harvesting is being increasingly done by machine, although mechanical picking is forbidden in some places (such as Châteauneuf du Pape). Once the harvest starts, it lasts just a couple of weeks. The start date is announced up to one week in advance.

Food for grape pickers *(vendangeurs)* is usually supplied but accommodation is often not (that is why most pickers live locally). Tourist offices in the region have a list of producers in the region who might need an extra pair of hands, as do the different Maisons des Vins (wine houses).

Environmental

Each summer, the Village des Tortues (Tortoise Village), 20km north of Collobrières in the Massif des Maures, offers a limited number of placements to students aged 17 and over. The centre allows its students to spend 15 days to a month working at the village, March to November. Free board and lodging is included: to apply, contact **Village des Tortues** *(☎ 04 94 78 26 41; ⓔ soptom@soptom.com; BP 24, F-83590 Gonfaron)*.

Au Pair

Under the au pair system, single young people (aged 18 to about 27) who are studying in France live with a French family and receive lodging, full board and a bit of pocket money in exchange for taking care of the kids, babysitting, doing light housework and perhaps teaching English to the children.

Many families want au pairs who are native English speakers, but knowing at least some French may be a prerequisite. **Association Familles & Jeunesse** *(☎ 04 93 82 28 22; W www.afj-aupair.org/apfrance.htm; 4 rue Masséna, F-06000 Nice)* is one of dozens of au pair agencies on the Côte d'Azur that arrange placements. There's an online directory of agencies at W www.europa-pages.com/au_pair.

Ski Resorts

The region's ski resorts – Isola 2000, Pra-Loup and La Foux d'Allos among them – are fairly small and offer few work opportunities. If you contact the ski resort months in advance you might be able to pick up some hospitality work in a hotel or restaurant.

Crewing on a Yacht

Working on a yacht looks glamorous but the reality is far from cushy. Cannes, Antibes or any other yacht-filled port on the Côte d'Azur are the places to look. In Antibes, **International Crew Recruitment** *(☎ 04 93 34 27 71; W www.intl-crewrecruitment.com; 16B rue du 24 Août)* might be able to assist.

Yacht owners often take on newcomers for a trial period of day crewing before hiring them for the full charter season. By late September, long-haul crews are in demand for winter voyages to the West Indies.

Beach Hawkers & Street Performers

Selling goods and services on the beach is one way to make a few francs, though you've got to sell an awful lot of *beignets* (doughnuts) or wrap a lot of hair with coloured beads to make a living.

One good place street musicians, actors and jugglers might try to busk is in Avignon during its July theatre festival.

ACCOMMODATION

Accommodation in the region is notorious for being France's most expensive. But it is not unaffordable. With a bit of planning and consideration of all the options, you can stay here cheaply.

In July and August, don't even contemplate the coast unless you have a reservation or are prepared to pay a fortune for the few rooms still available. The exception is rock-bottom budget accommodation, especially in Nice, which rarely gets booked up weeks in advance – but is full most days by noon. So get there early! The tourist office can usually tell you where rooms are available, but not necessarily make the booking for you. Some mid-range hotels will only accept a reservation accompanied by a credit card number or confirmation of your plans by letter or fax.

Local authorities impose a tourist tax *(taxe de séjour)* on each visitor in their jurisdiction, usually only enforced in the high season (Easter to September). At this time, prices charged at camp sites, hotels etc will be €0.75 to €1 per person higher than the posted rates.

Camping

The region has hundreds of camp sites, generally open March or April to September.

Stars reflect facilities and amenities. Separate tariffs are charged for people, tents or caravans, and vehicles. Many places have *forfaits* (fixed-price deals) for two people with tent and car. Camp-site receptions are often closed during the day; the best time to call is early morning or evening.

Camping à la ferme (camping on the farm) is coordinated by Gîtes de France (see Self-Catering Accommodation later) which publishes the annual *Campings & Campings à la Ferme* guide (€9).

Wild camping *(camping sauvage)* is illegal although it is tolerated in some places. Some hostels (like the Relais International de la Jeunesse on Cap d'Antibes) allow travellers to pitch in the back garden.

Refuges & Gîtes d'Étape

Refuges (simple mountain shelters) and *gîtes d'étapes* (basic dorm rooms) are options in rural Provence – the Parc National de Mercantour and Haute-Provence – where undeveloped areas still exist.

Gîtes d'étapes tend to be in towns or villages popular with walkers and mountain climbers – like Sospel, Castellane, Digne-les-Bains etc – which serve as gateways to these areas. *Refuges* are in isolated wildernesses, often accessible only on foot and marked on most walking maps.

Both are basic, usually equipped with bunks, mattresses and blankets, but not sheets. Nightly rates start at €8 to €10 per person per night. Meals, prepared by an attendant, are sometimes available. Most *refuges* open June to September; some have a telephone, so you can call ahead to book.

To reserve a *refuge* bed in the Alpes-Maritimes department, contact **Club Alpin Français des Alpes-Maritimes** *(☎ 04 93 62 59 99, fax 04 93 92 09 55; W http://cafnice.free.fr; 14 ave Mirabeau; open 4pm-8pm Mon-Fri)* in Nice. Haute-Provence *refuges* and *gîtes d'étapes* are handled by the **Centre d'Information Montagne et Sentiers** *(CIMES; ☎ 04 76 42 45 90; 14 rue de la République, F-38019 Grenoble)*.

Self-Catering Accommodation

Tourist offices have lists of self-catering studios, apartments and seaside villas to rent on a short- (one week) or long-term (several months) basis. The most sought-after properties are booked a year in advance.

Some of Provence's most charming self-catering accommodation – a century-old *mas* (Provençal farmhouse) in an olive grove or cherry tree orchard, say, or converted farm stables surrounded by a menagerie of farmyard animals – are represented by Gîtes de France, an organisation that liaises between owners and renters.

These idyllic little nests, known as *gîtes ruraux*, can be rented on a weekly basis. Amenities range from basic bathroom facilities and a simple kitchenette (with oven, hot plates and fridge) to a bathroom, fully equipped kitchen, washing machine, colour TV, telephone, private garden and pool. Linen is never provided, but sheets can be rented. *Gîtes panda* are *gîtes ruraux* in protected regional and national parks.

Bookings can be made online (W www.gites-de-france.com) or through a Gîtes de France office, each of which publishes an annual catalogue (€6.50 to €8.50) listing – with photo – the *gîtes ruraux* in their respective departments. They all sell Gîtes de France's national guide listing *gîtes panda* (€9).

Alpes de Haute-Provence (☎ 04 92 31 52 39, fax 04 92 32 32 63, W www.gites-de-france-04.fr) rond point du 11 Novembre, F-04001 Digne-les-Bains

Alpes-Maritimes (☎ 04 92 15 21 30, fax 04 93 37 48 00, W www.crt-riviera.fr/gites06) 55 promenade des Anglais, BP 1602, F-06011 Nice

Bouches du Rhône (☎ 04 90 59 49 39, fax 04 90 59 16 75, e gitesdefrance@visitprovence.com) Domaine du Vergon, F-13370 Mallemort

Var (☎ 04 94 50 93 93, fax 04 94 50 93 90, e gites.de.france.var@wanadoo.fr) rond point du 4 Decembre 1974, BP 215, F-83006 Draguignan

Vaucluse (☎ 04 90 85 45 00, fax 04 90 85 88 49) place Campana, BP 164, F-84008 Avignon

Chambres d'Hôtes

A *chambre d'hôte* is a French B&B. Breakfast is always included in the price, and some places provide dinner for an extra fee (usually €15 to €25). Many are in beautiful *châteaux* (castles), farmhouses or *moulins* (mills) and are a highly sought-after option. A night's stay for two people in a double room can cost anything from 180FF to 750FF per night.

Tourist offices have lists of *chambres d'hôtes*. Some are also listed in the annual catalogues published by Gîtes de France (see Self-Catering Accommodation earlier) and there are many more in *Chambres d'Hôtes Provence & Côte d'Azur* (€4.50), specific to the region, and *Chambres d'Hôtes de Charme* (€19), a national guide listing the region's most upmarket B&Bs. Bookings are made directly through the owner.

Hostels

There are hostels located along the coast at Cap d'Antibes, Cap d'Ail, Cassis, Cannes, Fréjus-St-Raphaël, Le Trayas, Marseilles, Menton, Monaco, Nice, Saignon (near Apt) and Stes-Maries de la Mer; in the mountains at La Foux d'Allos, La Palud-sur-Verdon and Manosque; and towards the west in Aix-en-Provence, near Saignon 6km from Apt, Avignon, Arles, Nîmes, Tarascon and Fontaine de Vaucluse.

Expect to pay around €10 per night, plus €3/3/8 for sheets/breakfast/an evening meal. Not all hostels have kitchen facilities. Most do not accept telephone reservations so turn up early, especially in July and August, if you want to ensure you get a bed for the night.

Affiliates of the **Fédération Unie des Auberges de Jeunesse** *(FUAJ; W www.fuaj.org)* and the **Ligue Française pour les Auberges de Jeunesse** *(LFAJ; W www.auberges-de-jeunesse.com)* need HI or similar cards (see Visas & Documents earlier). Private hostels charge more than those affiliated to either of the latter.

Hotels

Hotels generally have one to four stars. Breakfast *(petit déjeuner)* is almost never included in the room price and costs anything from €5 to €20 per person extra. Rooms with bathtubs are always more expensive than rooms with showers. Most beds tout neck-aching, hot-dog-shaped bolsters *(traversins)* – regular pillows *(oreillers)* are usually hidden in a cupboard.

Many hotels close for at least a couple of weeks in winter for their *congé annuel* (annual closure). Some remain closed between September/October and March/April. In Haute- Provence's ski resorts, hotels only open for the winter ski season and a couple of months in summer for walkers. Across the board, many hotels only operate – deplorably so – on a half-board basis in July and August, meaning you are obliged to fork out the hefty prices they set for breakfast and an evening meal in a stuffy, cramped hotel restaurant (invariably inside).

In a budget joint, expect to pay about €25 a night for a double with washbasin in your room, and a shared toilet and shower in the corridor. Doubles with shower start at €30. Single rooms in most budget establishments don't exist – rather a double-bed room is flogged as a single. Triples and quads normally have two double beds.

Move into the mid-range price bracket and you're confronted with three sets of seasonally adjusted prices – low-season (October/ November to February/March), mid-season (March to May and September/ October) and high season (June to September). Count on paying upwards of €35/40 low/high season for a double with shower and toilet. Usually a reliable bet in this price bracket are the 350-odd family-run places in the region affiliated to **Logis de France** (W *www.logisdefrance.com)*, an organisation that demands strict standards of service and amenities. Affiliated hotels are listed on its website.

Most of the region's top-end, four-star hotels and restaurants are housed in traditional properties: farmhouses, monasteries *(monastères)*, oil mills *(moulins à huile)*, priories *(prieurés)* or restored Cistercian abbeys *(abbayes)*. Lakes, rose gardens and olive groves pepper the vast grounds typical of these exclusive estates. A night's sleep at one of these places can cost anything upwards of €150. **Châteaux & Hotels de France** *(W www.chateauxhotels.com)* and **Relais & Châteaux** *(W www.relaischateaux.fr)*, owned by world-renowned Provençal chef Alain Ducasse, are two umbrella organisations under which these exclusive and expensive hotels often fall. Catalogues with listings for both can be ordered online.

Welcome to the Farm

Bienvenue à la Ferme – literally 'Welcome to the Farm' – is a string of 4000-odd chartered farms across France offering an invigorating taste of rural life for tourists, be it *ferme de séjour* (farm accommodation), *ferme auberge* (farm restaurant), *ferme de découverte* (small-group farm tours) or – tastier still – *gouter à la ferme* (sampling farm produce). Feasting on farm-made *foie gras* (a rich duck-liver pâté), seeing how *chèvre* (goat's cheese) is ripened or galloping through open fields on horseback are just some of the joys of farm life.

Participating farms are listed in *Bienvenue à la Ferme*, the departmental guide (free) published by the local Chamber of Agriculture. Provençal farms also feature in the national *Bienvenue à la Ferme* guide, sold in FNAC and bookshops or available by mail order from the **Assemblée Permanente des Chambres d'Agriculture** *(APCA; ☎ 01 53 57 11 44; W www.bienvenue-a-la-ferme.com; 9 ave George V, F-75008 Paris)*.

Many *agriculteurs* (farmers) in the programme speak little or no English.

Chateaux

There are several wine-growing estates *(domaines)* – invariably arranged around a gorgeous chateau – in the Côtes de Provence wine region where you can stay. In addition to a comfortable bed, hearty breakfast and, upon request, an evening meal of fabulous proportions, many offer guests the opportunity to taste wine and tour their vineyards. The Maison des Vins in Les Arcs-sur-Argens (see the St-Tropez to Toulon chapter) has a list of such places.

Should you wish to buy a chateau, *domaines viticoles* (estates with vineyards, olive groves and woods) are the speciality of **Le Bureau Viticole** *(☎ 04 90 92 48 74; W www.bureauviticole.fr; 10 blvd Mirabeau, 13210*

St-Rémy de Provence), run by upmarket real-estate agent **Émile Garcin** (w *www.emilegarcin.fr)* with offices in St-Rémy de Provence, Mougins and Ménerbes.

The Riveria's *belle époque* follies, celebrity real estate and various other properties of dreamy proportions are handled by **John Taylor** (w *www.john-taylor.fr)*.

FOOD

People in Provence generally think, dream and live food; most people's working day is completely geared around satisfying their insatiable appetite for dining well.

Consumer warning: Provençal cuisine oozes garlic. After consumption, munch on a sprig of parsley to avoid reeking breath.

Meals of the Day

Breakfast One of the most delightful (and coolest) times of day in Provence is *petit déjeuner*, best spent on a terrace watching the world go by or gazing out across a sea of vineyards and fruit orchards. Breakfast comprises a croissant and a piece of crusty baguette (usually with butter and jam), accompanied by a strong black coffee or *café au lait* (coffee with lots of hot milk).

Lunch & Dinner For most Provençaux, *déjeuner* (lunch) is the main meal of the day. It starts at noon on the dot, continues well into the afternoon, and entails eating (and of course drinking) a delightfully excessive amount that will leave you vowing never to eat that much again – until tomorrow.

If you turn up at a popular restaurant without a reservation later than 1pm, the chances are you will be turned away. Most places stop serving at 2.30pm and open again for *dîner* (dinner) from 7pm or 7.30pm to sometime around 10pm. There is *nowhere* open to eat between 3pm and 7pm.

Most places have a *plat du jour* (dish of the day) or *formule* (fixed main course plus starter or dessert) at lunchtime as well as the *menus* available in the evening. A *menu* offers better value than ordering à la carte (hand-picking a dish for each course); it usually includes an entree, *plat principal* (main course) and *fromage* (cheese) or dessert, with drinks and coffee costing extra. An increasing number of restaurants tout a *menu enfant* (children's *menu*). Vegetarian *menus* remain scarce.

The order of courses for à la carte dining is as follows:

apéritif – predinner drink, often with olives or tapenade (an olive-based dip seasoned with garlic, capers, anchovies and olive oil)
amuse-bouche – complimentary morsel to whet the appetite (only in top restaurants)
entrée – first course/starter
plat principal – main course
fromage – cheese
dessert – delicious of course
café – coffee
digestif – after-dinner drink such as La Farigoule or a *marc* (a type of brandy made from grape pressings)

Types of Eateries

Restaurants Dining à la Provençale can mean spending anything from €10 (in a village bistro) to €75 or more (in one of the region's multistar, gastronomic temples). Regardless of price, most places have a *carte* (menu) pinned up outside, allowing for a quick price and dish check for those not wanting to end up washing the dishes or dining on *pieds et paquets* (literally 'feet and packets', in reality sheep tripe).

The most authentic Provençal places to eat are in tiny hamlets off the beaten track – living proof that the locals will drive any distance for a good meal. These places tout just one *menu* with *vin compris* (wine included). The *patron* (owner) of the place is often the chef who, at the end of your meal or during it, comes to your table – clad in kitchen whites – to ask about your food. Dogs snoozing under tables are a common sight.

No restaurant can call itself truly Provençal unless it serves you a continual flow of chunky cut bread from the start to the very end of your meal (if it runs out, just ask for more – it's free). Except in the most expensive places, side plates are not provided. Don't attempt to balance your bread chunk on your main-course plate – sprinkling the table with crumbs is perfectly acceptable.

In cheaper restaurants, you might be expected to use the one set of eating utensils for the duration of your meal. Upon finishing your entree, replace your knife and fork (a subtle wipe clean with bread is allowed; licking – less cool) on the table either side of your dirty plate. If you don't, the waiter will do it for you. The waiter is also likely to add up the *addition* (bill) on your paper tablecloth.

Châteaux & Fermes Auberges The main house or building on a wine-producing estate is called a *château*, and a *ferme auberge* or *auberge de Provence* is a small, family-run inn attached to a working farm or chateau. They are two of the most delightful places to dine à la Provençale.

Typical Provençal cuisine is guaranteed at both. Dining is around shared tables with wooden benches. Portions are sufficiently hearty for those with the largest of appetites to leave in a merry state of stuffed bliss. A *menu*, comprising four courses and often wine too, usually costs around €20. Prime examples of a *ferme auberge* include the Domaine d'Aiguines, a duck farm near the Lacs du Verdon (see that section in the Haute-Provence chapter); the Domaine de la Maurette in La Motte, 5km east of Les Arcs, and the Chèvrerie du Peigros, a goat farm on a mountain pass near Collobrières (both listed in the St-Tropez to Toulon chapter).

The Maison des Vins in Les Arcs has a list of Côtes de Provence chateaux where you can eat. Many *fermes auberges* belong to the Bienvenue à la Ferme (Welcome to the Farm) association; see the 'Welcome to the Farm' boxed text earlier in this chapter).

Cafés The café is an integral part of French society, and nowhere more so than in the sun-filled south where it is the hub of village life and a highly respected institution. Many double as the village bar and bistro too. Most serve simple baguettes filled with cheese (around €3) or *charcuterie* (cold meats). Others have select terraces hidden out the back where you can dine in the shade of overhead vines.

In towns, a café on a grand boulevard (or any other chic place to be seen such as the Vieux Port in St-Tropez) charges far more than a place fronting a quiet side street.

Les Deux Garçons in Aix-en-Provence is the region's most famous café. It sits on the shady side of cours Mirabeau – a street considered to be the finest in southern France. In fine café tradition, prices are hiked up after 10pm.

Salons de Thé & Creperies *Salons de thé* (tearooms) are trendy and expensive establishments that offer quiches, salads, cakes, tarts, pies and pastries in addition to tea and coffee.

Creperies serve ultra-thin pancakes with a variety of sweet or savoury fillings, except in Nice where *socca* – a hearty Niçois pancake comprising chickpea flour and lashings of olive oil – is served.

Self-Catering

Provence's premier culinary delight is to stock up on breads, pastries, fruit, vegetables and prepared dishes and sit down for a gourmet *pique nique* (picnic).

When shopping, do as the locals do: spurn the supermarket and buy fresh local products from the market, followed by a stroll to the local *boulangerie* (bakery) for a baked-that-hour baguette or some *pain aux noix* (walnut bread); then on to the *pâtisserie* (pastry shop) for a *tarte Tropézienne*, *tarte aux fruits* (fruit tart) or other yummy cake or pastry. Margarine-based croissants can be identified by their almost touching tips; buttery ones have their tips facing outwards.

Purchase cheese in the *fromagerie*, and ask how best to preserve the cheeses you buy, which wines are best served with them and so on. If you don't know a cheese type, ask to *goûter* (taste) it. Prewrapped cheese sold in supermarkets is unripe and utterly tasteless by comparison. Shop for slices of cold meats, seafood salads, tapenade or sweet peppers marinated in olive oil at a *charcuterie* (delicatessen) – an equally colourful experience. The catch of the day is sold at a *poissonnerie* (fishmongers), general meat can be bought from a *boucherie* (butcher) and poultry from a *marchand de volaille* (poultry seller).

Any titbits you still need are probably sold at the local *épicerie* (literally 'spice shop' but actually a grocery store) or *alimentation générale*. Self-caterers who are keen to stock up on shedloads of beer, bottled water and the like will – of course – find it cheaper to shop at a supermarket (Casino, Monoprix etc) in town or at one of the giant *hypermarchés* (Leclerc, Intermarché etc) on the outskirts of most Provençal towns.

Markets Every village, town and city in Provence has a weekly or daily morning market that sprawls across the central square and a neighbouring patchwork of streets. Farmers flock into town from the outlying farms and villages to sell their fresh produce and chat with friends. Bargaining is not really allowed.

Shopping for Olive Oil

The best place to buy Provence's most cherished nectar is from its source – the *moulin* (mill). Many, such as the one in Maussane-les-Alpilles, near Fontvieille, date from the 17th century. Mills are not museums however. Travellers wanting to buy are warmly welcomed by the region's busy mill owners; voyeurs are not.

Huile d'olive (olive oil) is sold by the litre, either in pretty glass bottles or in larger, plastic containers (cheaper). Expect to pay anything from €10.50 to €17.50 per litre. *Dégustation* (tasting) is an integral part of selecting the right oil for your needs. Most millers will pour a tiny drop of the oil onto a spoon for you to taste; the taste is unique and incomparable to bottled oil sold in supermarkets.

Mills or olive-oil cooperatives *(coopératives oléicoles)* usually open 9am to noon and 3pm to 5pm or 6pm weekdays. The best time to visit is after the olive harvest, from January through to Easter. Depending on the year's crop, mills can sell out of the year's production as early as August. Some mills are listed in the regional chapters; most tourist offices stock lists of mills in their areas.

Other places to shop for oil include markets and the exclusive chains of olive-oil shops that have cropped up in recent years to pander to tourist tastes: Oliviers & Co (Cannes, St-Tropez and Valbonne), Le Comptoir des Oliviers (Aix-en-Provence) and Olive: Les Huiles du Monde (St-Rémy de Provence and Les Baux de Provence). All stock dozens of Provençal and Mediterranean olive oils to taste and buy, as well as tapenades and oily delights.

The staple ingredients are fresh fruit and vegetables, olives, locally milled olive oil (see the boxed text 'Shopping for Olive Oil' later), herbs and spices. Garlic *(aïl)* is always sold in a bunch or woven plait. A wealth of green and black olives, marinated in every imaginable concoction, are displayed in plastic tubs or buckets. Herbs are dried, mixed, and displayed in stubby coarse sacks; the classic cocktail is *herbes de Provence*, a mix of *basilic* (basil), *romarin* (rosemary), *thym* (thyme), *origan* (oregano), *sarriette* (savory) and *marjolaine* (marjoram). If you are in the Vaucluse between November and March you might also come across *truffes* (truffles) or, if in the Massif des Maures, *marrons* (chestnuts).

Everything from bread, cheese, cold meats, *miel* (honey), marmalade and *confiture* (homemade jam) to enticing nonedibles (art and crafts, wicker baskets, clothing etc) are sold in most markets too.

Specialist food markets are listed in the Food & Wine of Provence special section; morning markets are listed under the relevant town and village sections in the regional chapters.

DRINKS

Alcoholic Drinks

Indulging in an aperitif on a shaded terrace is among the region's great sensual delights. Pastis (see the boxed text 'The Milk of Provence') is the quintessential Provençal drink, closely followed by a crisp, cold Côtes de Provence rosé (see the special Food & Wine of Provence special section). Both are wonderfully refreshing on hot and sunny days. Beaumes de Venise, a sweet muscat wine, is a popular aperitif in northern Vaucluse. Amandine (an almond liqueur) and Rinquinquin de Pêche (peach liqueur mixed with chilled white wine) – both from Distillerie Domaine de Haute-Provence, Forcalquier – feature on plenty of drinks menus in the Lubéron and neighbouring part of Haute-Provence. Liqueur de Châtaignes (chestnut liqueur) from Collobrières in the Massif des Maures can also be mixed with white wine to create a pleasant aperitif.

To ensure that appropriately 'plump and contented' feeling following a deliciously long and lazy meal, a digestif such as *marc* or *eau de vie* (literally 'water of life') can be taken. *Marc* is a fiery spirit (similar to Italian *grappa*), distilled from grape skins and pulp left over from the wine-making process. Eaux de vie is the generic name for brandies distilled from the region's many fruits.

Ending a meal with a sweeter liqueur is considered more 'womanly'. Try Reverend Father Gaucher's Elixir, a yellow chartreuse from Tarascon elaborately blended from 30 different aromatic herbs, or La Farigoule, a thyme liqueur also distilled in Forcalquier.

Beer is not a Provençal drink and is priced accordingly; wine is, however, and likewise priced accordingly.

Nonalcoholic Drinks

Tap water is safe to drink. Don't drink water spouting from fountains that tout a sign reading *eau non potable* (nondrinking water). In restaurants, it is acceptable to order *une carafe d'eau* (carafe of tap water) instead of a pricier wine, soft drink or *eau de source – plate* or *gazeuse* (mineral water – still or carbonated). Soft drinks cost about €2.50 to €3 per glass (wine can be cheaper).

The dazzling, pea-green drink you see people sipping through straws in cafés is *sirop de menthe* (mint syrup) diluted with water. Other cordials include *cassis* (blackberry), *grenadine* (pomegranate) and *citron* (lemon). The most expensive soft drink is a *citron*, *orange* or *pamplemousse pressé* – freshly squeezed lemon, orange or grapefruit mixed with iced water and sugar.

Coffee costs from €1 to €2.50 a cup. Unless you specify otherwise, you get a small, strong, black espresso. For a bigger caffeine fix ask for *un grand café* (a double espresso). Milky versions include *un café crème* (espresso with steamed milk or cream) and *un café au lait* (hot milk with a dash of coffee). Coffee is never served with cold milk.

Thé (tea) and *chocolat chaud* (hot chocolate) are widely available. Most *salons de thé* serve a choice of *infusions* (herbal teas).

ENTERTAINMENT

Local tourist offices are the best source of information on what's on where. In addition, there is a plethora of regional entertainment journals and newspapers – many are free and in English – that contain comprehensive cinema, theatre and festival listings. *L'Officiel des Loisirs* (€0.80) and *Semaine des Spectacle* (€1) are two such listings mags that cover the week's events on the Côte d'Azur, Wednesday to Tuesday. Tobacconists on the coast sell both.

FNAC *(☎ 08 36 68 93 39; W www.fnac.fr)* is the leading hub for tickets and reservations for everything from theatre, opera and exhibitions to rock concerts, football matches and festivals. Most stores have a *billetterie* (ticket desk) where a calendar of upcoming events is posted, advance bookings are made and tickets are sold. There is a FNAC in Avignon, Nice, Nîmes and Marseilles. The latter also has a Virgin Megastore with a ticket desk.

Pubs & Bars

Lively pubs and bars abound in coastal hot spots and university towns such as Marseilles, Nice, Avignon and Aix-en-Provence where the keenest of drinkers can find plenty of places to entertain themselves, drink in hand. English- and Irish-style pubs offering a wealth of happy hours, beach parties, live bands at weekends and punters dancing on tables, are particularly rife in Marseilles and Nice. In summer, many places stay open until well into the wee hours. Come winter, last orders are called well before midnight.

The Milk of Provence

When in Provence, do as the Provençaux do: drink pastis. The aniseed-flavoured alcoholic drink is a classic aperitif in the region, although it can be drunk at any time of day.

Amber-coloured in the bottle, it turns a milky white when mixed with water. Bars and cafés serve it straight, allowing you to decide how much water to add (roughly five-parts water to one-part pastis). It's best drunk in the sun and on the rocks.

A dash of mint cordial *(sirop de menthe)* transforms a regular pastis into a *perroquet* (literally 'parrot'). A *tomate* (tomato) is tarted up with one part grenadine, while the sweet Mauresque is dressed with *orgeat*, a smooth orange and almond syrup.

Pastis was invented in 1932 in Marseilles by industrialist Paul Ricard (1909–97). The earliest aniseed liqueur to hit the market was absinthe, a dangerous and potent liqueur distilled with wormwood oil that, from the early 1800s, was manufactured in France by Henri-Louis Pernod. The drink – which boasted an astonishing 72% alcohol content – was banned in 1915, paving the way for Ricard's 45%-alcohol pastis and other harmless (except for the alcohol) aniseed and liquorice liqueurs, such as the modern-day Pernod. Leading pastis brands are Pastis 51 (Pastis de Marseille) and Ricard, both owned by the Ricard empire (in addition to Pernod, taken over by Ricard in 1974).

PASTIS DE MARSEILLE

JANE SMITH

Head inland into Haute-Provence and you'll be hard pushed to find anything more adventurous than a village café-cum-bar.

Discos & Clubs

Discos (*discothèque* or *boîte* in French) and clubs are few and far between once you escape the coast and enter rural Provence. Anything goes on the Côte d'Azur however – it's engulfed in party madness from mid-June until mid-September. Nice's party season sees discos on the beach and wild dancing on tables in many of its Anglophone music bars. Music (live or recorded) ranges from jazz and rai to Latino and techno. The crowd can be gay, lesbian, straight or mixed.

Tenue correcte exigée means 'appropriate dress required'. The action doesn't hot up in most places until at least midnight. Bouncers are invariably big and paid to indulge their megalomaniacal animalistic tendencies by keeping out 'undesirables', which, depending on the place, ranges from unaccompanied men who aren't dressed right to members of certain minority groups.

Gay & Lesbian Venues

Marseilles, Nice and Cannes have the most active gay and lesbian scenes, with a handful of homosexual venues to prove it. See the Entertainment section in the chapter listings for details. There are also well-known gay clubs in Toulon and Juan-les-Pins.

Music & Theatre

Provence is a land of music and theatre, playing host to some of the country's major festivals (see Feasts & Festivals under Public Holidays & Special Events, earlier in this chapter) – including the much celebrated performing-arts Festival d'Avignon and concurrent Festival Off (fringe). The Fête de la Musique brings live music to every corner of the region on 21 June.

Cinema

You can see films in their original language (with French subtitles) in selected cinemas in Marseilles, Nice and Aix-en-Provence. Look for the letters 'VO' *(version originale)* on the cinema billboards. Some of the spots along the coast (such as Villefranche-sur-Mer and Monaco) have outside screenings during the summer that are a joy to attend, regardless of language.

SPECTATOR SPORTS

Football

Marseilles has long been considered the heart of French football and never more so than since France's stunning victory in the 1998 World Cup and subsequent victory in Euro 2000. The clear champion in both of the matches was Marseilles-born Zinedine Zidane, a midfielder of North African origin whose goal-scoring headers and extraordinary footwork has made him the world's most expensive footballer – his transfer fee from Juventus (Italy) to Real Madrid (Spain) in 2001–02 was worth a breathtaking €75.1 million – the highest in football history. 'Zizou' Zidane, who won the titles of World Player of the Year in 1998 and 2000, best player of the Euro 2000 tournament and took Real Madrid to a 2-1 victory in the 2002 Champions League final, has an official website at W www.zidane.fr.

At club level, in 1991 Olympique de Marseilles (OM) became the first French team to win the European Champions League. The team was national champion for four consecutive years between 1989 and 1992, but has won no major titles since. This is, in part, due to the 1995 Bosman decision to allow European clubs to field as many European players as they wish – resulting in a great exodus of French players to better-paid clubs abroad (including Zidane, who kicked off with Cannes, but went on to play for Italian club Juventus then Spain's Real Madrid). See the boxed text 'OM' in the Marseilles Area chapter for information on visiting OM's home ground, the Stade Vélodrome, and buying tickets for matches.

The region's other strong football club is AS Monaco (ASM), whose goalkeeper Fabian Barthez (transferred to Manchester United since 2000), stole the heart of a nation with his goal-saving heroics in France 1998. Arsenal manager Arsène Wenger and star striker Thierry Henry also began their careers at ASM.

Motor Racing

The annual Monaco Grand Prix is the most glamorous race in the Formula One calendar. It is also the only race that sees F1 mean machines tear around regular town streets rather than a track solely for motor sports. The Grand Prix takes place in May and attracts some 150,000 spectators. For more details see the boxed text 'The Formula One Grand Prix' in the Monaco chapter.

Known among motorcycle enthusiasts is the Circuit du Castellet near Le Castellet, owned by French industrialist Paul Ricard since the 1970s and sold to F1 tycoon Bernie Ecclestone in 1999. See the St-Tropez to Toulon chapter for further details.

Bullfighting

Many consider it downright cruel. Others see it as a sport or theatre, and never more so than in southwestern Provence where bullfighting is regarded as a passionate celebration of Provençal tradition. Many bullfights do end with a dead bull, though the *course Camarguaise* (Camargue-style bullfight) is bloodless (see the Camargue chapter for details).

The season generally runs from Easter to September. Fights can be seen in Aigues-Mortes (mid-October), Arles (Easter weekend, last Sunday in April and 1 May), Nîmes (February, June and mid-September), Pernes-les-Fontaines and Stes-Maries de la Mer. See the relevant city listings for details.

Cycling

The three-week Tour de France, which hits the road every year in July, rarely visits Provence and the Côte d'Azur (intense heat and horrendous traffic are big deterrents). But the early season, Paris–Nice race – dubbed the 'race to the sun' and considered the official start to the professional cycling season – always does, as does the four-day Mediterranean Tour in early February.

Out of the 12 times since 1951 that the Tour de France has crossed Provence (the last was in 2000), it is 1967 that is remembered most: British cyclist Tommy Simpson suffered a fatal heart attack on the climb up Mont Ventoux during the 211km Marseilles to Carpentras stage. The 1965 world cycling champion, who had won the Paris–Nice stage that same year, was considered one of the greats of the sport at the time.

Numerous cyclist-pilgrims continue to follow in Simpson's tracks up Ventoux's barren slopes today. A road, such as the one up Ventoux, that is sealed immaculately and graffitied with large slogans starting with *'allez'* is a sure sign that a cycling race has recently passed by.

Pétanque

Provençal boules *(pétanque)* Provence's national pastime. Despite the game's humble appearance – a bunch of village men in work

Polish Your Boules

The rules of *pétanque* are precise and inviolable.

Two to six people, split into two teams, can play. Each player has three solid metal boules (two if there are six players), weighing 650g to 800g and stamped with the hallmark of a licensed boule maker. Personal initials, a name or a family coat of arms can be crafted on to made-to-measure boules. The earliest boules, scrapped in 1930, comprised a wooden ball studded with hundreds of hammered-in steel nails. Antique shops sell them.

Pétanque revolves around the *cochonnet* (jack), a small wooden ball 25mm to 35mm in diameter. Each team takes it in turn to aim a boule at this marker, the idea being to land the boule as close as possible to it. The team with the closest boule wins the round; points are allocated by totting up how many boules the winner's team has closest to the marker (one point for each boule). The first to notch up 13 wins the match.

The team throwing the cochonnet (initially decided by a coin toss) has to throw it from a small circle, 30cm to 50cm in diameter, scratched in the gravel. It must be hurled 6m to 10m away. Each player aiming a boule must likewise stand in this circle, with both feet planted firmly on the ground. At the end of a round, a new circle is drawn around the cochonnet, determining the spot where the next round will start.

Underarm throwing is compulsory. Beyond that, players can opt between rolling the boule in a dribble along the ground (known as *pointer*, literally 'to point') or hurling it high in the air in the hope of it landing smack-bang on top of an opponent's boule, sending it flying out of position. This flamboyant tactic can turn an entire game around in a matter of seconds and is called *tirer* (literally 'to shoot').

Throughout matches, boules are lovingly polished with a soft white cloth. Players unable to stoop to pick up their boules can lift them up with a magnet attached to a piece of string.

clothes throwing dusty balls on a gravel pitch scratched out wherever there's shade – it is a serious sport.

Pétanque was invented in La Ciotat, near Marseilles, in 1910, when arthritis-crippled Jules Le Noir could no longer take the running strides prior to aiming that were demanded by the *longue* boule game. The local champion opted to stand with his feet firmly on the ground instead – a style that became known as *pieds tanques* (Provençal for 'tied feet'). Pétanque is a slurred version of pieds tanques. *Jeu Provençal* – which uses heavier balls and requires a hop before throwing – is still played in parts of Provence. See the boxed text 'Polish Your Boules' for details.

Nautical Jousting

Joutes nautiques or *joutes Provençales* (Provençal jousting) is typical only in the south of France. Spurred on by bands and a captive audience, the participants (usually male and traditionally dressed in white) try to knock each other into the water from rival boats with 2.60m-long lances. The jouster always stands balanced at the tip of a *tintaine*, a wooden gangplank protruding from the wooden boat where the rest of his team members spur him on.

The sport is particularly strong in St-Raphaël where the annual Provençal jousting championships are invariably held. Contact the **Société des Joutes Raphaëloises** *(☎ 04 94 82 39 74, 06 09 77 89 67; 47 allée des Bruyères, Boulouris, F-83700 St-Raphaël)* for details. In the Vaucluse, river jousters set L'Isle-sur-la-Sorgue ablaze with colour on 14 and 26 July.

SHOPPING

Those intent on sampling a different culinary item every day should follow the Food Highlights & Wine-Producing Regions map in the Food & Wine of Provence special section. Olive oil-shopping tips and tricks are included in the special Food & Wine section.

Many edible products that are typical of Provence – such as *marrons au sirop* (chestnuts in syrup) from the Massif des Maures, *calissons* from Aix-en-Provence and rice from the Camargue – are easy to transport home. But most glass-jar products sold at markets are homemade and rarely contain preservatives. Lavender marmalade from Carpentras market, for example, lasts one month after being opened, while onion chutney from the Lubéron – mind-blowingly delicious as it is – will not survive outside a fridge. The same goes for bread, cheese and fresh truffles. But not for wine.

Less-tasty treats worth a shopping spree include perfumes from Grasse; leathersandals from St-Tropez; colourful wicker baskets and carnations from Antibes; glassware from Biot; Picasso-inspired ceramics from Vallauris; faïence from Moustiers-Ste-Marie; pipes and carpets from Cogolin; soap and *santons* (ornamental figures) from Marseilles or Salon de Provence; *courgourdons* (traditional ornaments made from dyed and hollowed marrows/squash) from Nice; lavender oil, pottery, sundials and wrought-iron pieces from the Lubéron; colourful Provençal fabrics from practically anywhere in Provence; antiques from L'Isle-sur-la-Sorgue; terracotta and ceramic tiles from Salernes; gallery art from St-Paul de Vence and Mougins; or the latest haute-couture designs from Monaco.

Getting There & Away

AIR

Airports & Airlines

France's national carrier, Air France, and scores of other airlines link **Marseilles-Provence airport** *(Aéroport International Marseille-Provence; W www.marseille.aeroport.fr)* and **Nice-Côte d'Azur airport** *(Aéroport International Nice-Côte d'Azur; W www.nice.aeroport.fr)* – the region's leading airports – with most European cities, as well as with far-flung spots around the globe. Major airlines have an office at both airports. Despite both airports being fiercely marketed as major international transport hubs, most long-haul destinations still require you to change plane in Paris, London or some other European capital. Only direct flights are mentioned in this chapter.

The odd international flight also uses **Nîmes-Arles-Camargue airport** (Aéroport de Nîmes-Arles-Camargue), also called Aéroport Nîmes-Garons; **St-Tropez–La Môle airport** *(Aéroport-International St-Tropez–La Môle; W www.st-tropez-airport.com)*, 20km west of St-Tropez in La Môle; and nearby **Toulon-Hyères airport** (Aéroport de Toulon-Hyères).

Within Europe, cheap 'no-frills' flights service Marseilles, Nice, Nîmes and Toulon (see The UK & Ireland later in this section for details).

Domestic routes are also served by small **Avignon airport** *(Aéroport d'Avignon; W www.avignon.aeroport.fr)*. Charters and private planes use **Cannes airport** *(W www.cannes.aeroport.fr)*.

For details on travelling between the airport and city centres, see the Getting Around section in the relevant chapters.

Buying Tickets

Generally, there is nothing to be gained by buying a ticket direct from the airline. Discounted tickets are released to selected travel agencies and specialist discount agencies, and these are usually the cheapest deals going. One exception to this rule is the expanding number of 'no-frills' carriers, which only sell direct to travellers. Unlike the 'full-service' airlines, no-frills carriers often make one-way tickets available at around half the return fare, meaning that it is easy to put together an open-jaw ticket when you fly to one place but leave from another. The other exception is booking on the Internet. Many airlines offer some excellent fares to Web surfers. They may sell seats by auction or simply cut prices to reflect the reduced cost of electronic selling.

Student and Youth Fares

Full-time students and people aged under 26 have access to better deals than other travellers – not always cheaper fares, but certainly more flexibility with changing flights and/or routes. You have to show a document proving your date of birth, or a valid International Student Identity Card (see Student Cards under Visas & Documents in the Facts for the Visitor chapter) when buying your ticket.

Travellers with Special Needs

If they're warned early enough, airlines can often make special arrangements for travellers, such as wheelchair assistance at airports or vegetarian meals on the flight. Children under two travel for 10% of the standard fare (or free on some airlines) as long as they don't occupy a seat. They don't get a baggage allowance. Children aged two to 12 can usually occupy a seat for half to two-thirds of the full fare.

The disability-friendly website W www.everybody.co.uk has an airline directory that provides information on the facilities offered by various airlines.

Other Parts of France

Air France is the leading carrier on domestic routes between Paris and Provence. Smaller domestic carriers Air Littoral and Air Lib Express, the 'no-frills' arm of Air Lib, likewise run several flights daily from Paris to/from Nice and Marseilles. At peak times, between the three airlines, there are arrivals/departures every half-hour. In Paris flights generally use Paris Orly airport, although a small number fly in and out of Roissy Charles de Gaulle airport. From Paris there are also daily flights to/from Toulon, Nîmes and Avignon.

To other parts of France, there are daily flights from Marseilles and Nice to most airports, including Bordeaux, Clermont-Ferrand,

Lille, Lyons, Metz-Nancy, Mulhouse, Nantes, Strasbourg, Toulouse, and Corsican airports at Ajaccio, Bastia, Calvi and Figari. From Toulon, there are weekly flights to Bordeaux, Brest, Clermont-Ferrand, Lille, Nantes and Strasbourg. From Avignon, Air France has two daily flights to/from Clermont-Ferrand. Corsica is served by regular flights from Nice and Marseilles to/from Ajaccio and Bastia (with Corse Méditerranée), Calvi and Figari (with Air Littoral).

In 2002 Air France operated five daily return flights between Nice and St-Tropez–La Môle airport, and twice-weekly flights to/from the latter and Lyon. Flight schedules at St-Tropez–La Môle airport appear to change dramatically each year though, meaning St-Tropez could well have air links to different cities in the future.

Fares With Air France and Air Littoral, unless you qualify for a reduced youth or student fare, it is usually cheaper to train or motor it south from Paris or other cities in France to Provence

In contrast, **Air Lib Express** *(☎ 08 25 09 09 09; Ⓦ www.airlibexpress.com)*, the low-cost service of domestic carrier **Air Lib** *(☎ 08 25 80 58 05; Ⓦ www.air-liberte.fr)*, offers some incredibly cheap fares on its ticketless Paris–Nice, Paris–Marseilles and Paris–Toulon routings. France's only 'no-frills' airline operates on a first-come-first-served basis, meaning the earlier you book your ticket, the cheaper the fare is. There are also four fare options, ranging from a non-refundable, non-changeable 'best-offer' fare (€29 one-way on all three routes) to a more-expensive, fully flexible, refundable fare (€140). Airlib Express flies up to 11/four/five flights daily from Paris Orly to Nice/Marseilles/Toulon.

UK-based budget airline **easyJet** (see The UK & Ireland later) also flies year round between Nice and Paris Roissy Charles de Gaulle. There are up to four return flights daily and a single fare booked on the Internet costs from €50, including airport tax, for departures from either city.

Both **Air Littoral** *(☎ 08 25 83 48 34; Ⓦ www.air-littoral.fr)* and **Air France** *(☎ 08 02 80 28 02; Ⓦ www.airfrance.fr)* operate in the traditional manner. Air France give discounts to travellers aged over 60, families and couples who are married or have proof of cohabitation. Cheaper youth/student fares (with no restrictions or advance booking requirements) are available to those aged under 25 and student-card holders aged 26 or under. The cheapest Paris–Nice return with Air France cost around €100 in late 2002 (booked 14 days in advance, with a Saturday night stay in Nice), while a one-way/return Nice–St-Tropez airfare in 2002 was €124/210.

France has a network of student travel agencies that can supply discount tickets to travellers of all ages, including **OTU Voyages** *(☎ 08 25 00 10 21; Ⓦ www.otu.fr)*, **Voyages Wasteels** *(☎ 08 25 88 70 70; Ⓦ www.voyages-wasteels.fr)* and **Nouvelles Frontières** *(☎ 08 25 00 08 25; Ⓦ www.nouvelles-frontieres.fr)*. Some branches are listed in the regional chapters.

Continental Europe

There are flights two or three times daily between Nice/Marseilles and most other European cities, the cheapest are in early spring and late autumn. Air France's youth fares are only marginally more than charters.

There are also a handful of interesting no-frills routes, kicking off with easyJet's (see the next section The UK & Ireland) daily flights year round from Geneva and Amsterdam to/from Nice. Lead-in one-way fares on these routes at the time of research were Sfr61 and €50 respectively. **Virgin Express** *(in UK ☎ 0207 744 0004; in France ☎ 08 00 52 85 28; Ⓦ www.virgin-express.com)* meanwhile flies between Nice-Côte d'Azur airport and Brussels, from where onward connections abound. Virgin has several fare levels: promotional, discounted and economy tickets can't be changed or refunded, but pricier flexible ones can. From Nice, Virgin flies up to four times daily to/from Brussels, with promotional/fully flexible, one-way fares clocking in at a dramatically different €32.50/198.

During 2002 the since-defunct Swissair flew twice weekly between Geneva and St-Tropez–La Môle airport, and up to three times a week to/from Zürich, May to September. These seasonal flights are expected to be taken over by another airline in 2003. Contact St-Tropez tourist office for details; see the St-Tropez to Toulon regional chapter.

Across Continental Europe, there are many agencies with ties to **STA Travel** *(Ⓦ www*

.statravel.com) where cheap tickets can be purchased and STA-issued tickets altered.

The UK & Ireland

No-frills airlines have slashed fares between the UK and southern France considerably. As with Air Lib Express (see Other Parts of France earlier), they operate on a first-come-first-served basis and offer some great deals. Sporadic ticket sales yield even greater bargains. Internet bookings are the norm with these airlines; telephone bookings cost marginally more.

In late 2002, **easyJet** *(in UK ☎ 0870 600 000, in France ☎ 08 25 08 25 08; Ⓦ www.easyjet.com)* flew from Nice-Côte d'Azur airport to London Gatwick, London Stansted, Luton, Liverpool and Bristol. The one-way fares, booked on the Internet, on this no-tickets-issued airline from any British airport to Nice were advertised for as little as UK£44.85, including airport taxes (UK£63/64 from Bristol/London Stansted). Telephone bookings (available up to one month before departure) cost UK£5 or €10 more; bookings can be changed for UK£10 or €10. EasyJet currently operates one return flight daily between Nice and both Bristol and London Stansted, one to three daily to/from Liverpool and London Gatwick, and three to five daily to Luton.

Buzz *(in UK ☎ 0870 240 7070, in France ☎ 01 55 17 42 42; Ⓦ www.buzzaway.com)* flies from London Stansted to Toulon-Hyères and Marseilles-Provence airports up to three times daily. The lead-in fare on its London Stansted–Marseilles fare was advertised in late 2002 for UK£40, although promotional fares available at various times saw this dip to UK£21. The Marseilles–London Stansted fare kicked off at €38. Telephone customers pay UK£3 or €6 more per single flight.

Dublin-based **Ryanair** *(in Ireland ☎ 0818-30 30 30, in UK ☎ 0871 246 0000, in France ☎ 08 92 55 56 66; Ⓦ www.ryanair.com)* operates one daily, low-fare flight between Nîmes-Arles-Camargue airport and London Stansted. The lead-in one-way fares from Stansted/Nîmes are UK£9.99/€0.99, excluding airport taxes. Tickets can't be refunded, but they can be changed subject to flight availability for a UK£15 or €25 fee.

Both Nice and Marseilles are served by regular, daily British Airways and Air France flights to/from London. The cheapest fare from London to Nice/Marseilles return with British Airways in late 2002 was UK£96.70/99.30. Tickets are valid for one month and are also nonrefundable, nonchangeable and require a minimum Saturday night stay.

The USA & Canada

Any journey to Provence from the North American continent entails a flight to Paris, London or another European transport hub, from where there are train/ferry/plane connections to the region. A New York-Paris round trip can cost anything from US$400/800 in low/high season with Air France or British Airways.

Council Travel *(☎ 800 226 8624; Ⓦ www.counciltravel.com)*, America's largest student travel organisation, has 60-odd offices in the USA. **STA Travel** *(☎ 800 777 0112; Ⓦ www.statravel.com)* is another large agency with offices in Boston, Chicago, New York, Philadelphia, San Francisco and other major cities.

In Canada, try **Travel CUTS** *(☎ 800 667 2887; Ⓦ www.travelcuts.com)*.

Australia & New Zealand

Airlines such as Thai Airways International, Malaysia Airlines, Qantas Airways and Singapore Airlines have frequent promotional fares. Low/high-season return fares to Paris start at around A$1700/2200 from Melbourne or Sydney, and NZ$2000/3000 from Auckland. A round-the-world ticket from Australia/New Zealand that takes in Paris will cost about A$2300/NZ$2500.

Two well-known agencies for cheap fares are **STA Travel** *(☎ 03-9349 2411, Australia-wide ☎ 131 776; Ⓦ www.statravel.com.au; 224 Faraday St, Carlton, Melbourne)*, with offices in major cities and on many university campuses; and **Flight Centre** *(Australiawide ☎ 133 133; Ⓦ www.flightcentre.com.au; 82 Elizabeth St, Sydney)*, with dozens of offices throughout Australia. Both also have branches across New Zealand.

North Africa

Marseilles is a hub for flights to/from North Africa. **Air Algérie** *(in Marseilles ☎ 04 95 09 31 10, 04 42 14 22 72, in Nice ☎ 04 93 21 48 20; Ⓦ www.airalgerie.dz)* operates up to five flights daily to Algiers, Annaba and Constantine in Algeria. It also has weekly flights from Marseilles to Batna, Bejaia, Oran and

Tlemcen; and a once-weekly flight between Nice and Constantine. The cheapest Marseilles to Algiers return is €290.

Royal Air Maroc *(in Marseilles ☎ 04 42 14 24 79, 04 91 95 04 01, in Nice ☎ 04 93 21 48 80; W www.royalairmaroc.com)* and Air France code-share on daily flights between Casablanca in Morocco and Nice and Marseilles. A return fare costs upwards of €320. Royal Air Maroc also runs direct Marseilles–Oujda flights four times weekly.

The cheapest return from Nice or Marseilles to Tunis or Monastir with **Tunis Air** *(nationwide ☎ 08 20 04 40 44, in Marseilles ☎ 04 91 32 84 32, 42 14 21 75, in Nice ☎ 04 93 21 35 05; W www.tunisair.com.tn)* is €220. From both Nice and Marseilles, flights arrive/depart up to three times daily to/from Tunis and weekly to Monastir. Air France also flies to both cities.

In-House Movies

Those travelling by train to/from Marseilles, Avignon or Aix-en-Provence TGV station and another big-city station in France (eg, Lyons, Paris, Bordeaux or Montpellier), can enjoy an in-house movie. At these train stations, you can rent a portable DVD player, headphones and one of 400 films – some in their original language with French subtitles – to take on board. Upon arrival, you drop the whole lot off at the **Cinétrain kiosk** *(☎ 04 72 33 51 87; W www.cinetrain.fr)* in the station.

One/two films cost €9.95/19.95, a second set of headphones is €3, payable only by credit card. Proof of your onward journey and identity are also required; flash your train ticket and passport. View latest releases and reserve online at the website.

LAND

Other Parts of France

Bus French transport policy is completely biased in favour of its state-owned rail system making inter-regional bus services extremely limited. Take a train.

Train France's efficient rail network, run by the state-owned SNCF (Société Nationale des Chemins de Fer), reaches almost every part of the country. The network is very Paris-centric, with key lines radiating from the capital like the spokes of a wheel. While travel between towns on different 'spokes' can be tricky and tedious, rail links between Provence and the rest of France warrant few complaints.

SNCF's pride and joy is the TGV (pronounced 'teh-sheh-veh'; W www.tgv.com), short for *train à grande vitesse* (high-speed train). The TGV Sud-Est service links Paris with Dijon and Lyons, from where the TGV Rhône-Alpes continues southeast to Valence. Here, the TGV Méditerranée continues south at a breathtaking 310km/h to Avignon where the superfast track splits – east to Marseilles and west to Nîmes and Montpellier in neighbouring Languedoc.

In Avignon and Aix-en-Provence TGV trains use out-of-town TGV train stations, separate from the town-centre stations used by regional trains. France's super-speedy rail service places Paris a startling three hours by train from Marseilles, 782km south of the capital. A 1st-/2nd-class single fare costs €112.70/66.

In addition to TGV trains, the SNCF operates less-speedy rail services, which are often cheaper – ideal for budget travellers with time on their hands. Both *grande ligne* (main line) trains and those operated by **TER** *(Transport Express Régional; W www.ter-sncf.com)* link smaller cities and towns with the TGV network. Many towns not on the SNCF network are linked with nearby railheads by SNCF or TER buses (see the Getting Around chapter for details). For schedules and fares for main-line trains call ☎ 08 36 67 68 69.

Sample TGV fares between Paris and Provence destinations include: Orange (€74.60, 3¼ hours), Avignon (€60.80, 3½ to four hours), Marseilles (€66.60, three hours) and Nice (€79.40, 5½ hours).

From Lille in northern France, there are two direct trains daily to Nice (€109.30, nine to 13½ hours); one runs overnight. Other northern destinations such as Roissy Charles de Gaulle airport require a change of train in Lyons or Paris, as do destinations in western France. From eastern France, there are direct Strasbourg–Nice trains (€94.10, 12¼ to 13 hours). To/from cities such as Bordeaux in southwestern France, change trains in Narbonne, Toulouse or Montpellier.

Reservations & Tickets Most trains, including TGVs, have 1st- and 2nd-class sections.

In this book we quote fares for 2nd-class travel, which works out at about €8 to €10 per 100km for longer cross-country trips, or €10 to €15 per 100km for shorter hops. A return ticket is twice the price of a one-way ticket. Travel in 1st class costs 50% more than 2nd class. Children under four travel free; those aged four to 11 travel half-price.

A €1.50/3 reservation fee on national/international journeys is obligatory for TGV travellers (automatically included in the ticket price) and for non-TGV passengers on some trains during holiday periods – such as July and August on jam-packed coastal-bound trains. Most overnight trains are equipped with *couchettes* (sleeping berths), which must be reserved. A couchette costs €14.50 or €17, depending on the train; 2nd-class couchettes have six berths and 1st-class have four bunks.

Reservations can be made by telephone, via SNCF's website (see the boxed text 'SNCF Hotlines'), at any SNCF ticketing office, or by using a ticket-vending machine (see the Getting Around chapter for further information) at any SNCF train station. Tickets issued via machines are valid for two months. Reservations can be changed by telephone; or up to one hour before the scheduled departure time if you are actually at your departure station.

Tickets bought with cash can be reimbursed for cash (by you or a thief); keep them in a safe place. Alternatively, you can pay with a credit card at the ticket counter, at one of the touch-screen, ticket-vending machines, or online at the SNCF website. Prohibitive tariffs apply for tickets bought directly from the conductor on board trains.

Validating Your Ticket You risk an on-the-spot fine if you fail to validate your train ticket before boarding: time-stamp it in a *composteur*, a bizarre-looking orange post situated at the platform entrance. If you forget, find the conductor on board so he/she can punch it for you. Tickets are usually checked and punched by the conductor midway through a journey.

Tickets are valid for 24 hours after they have been time-stamped, meaning you can break your journey briefly providing you are not on a line (such as a TGV) requiring a reservation. Time-stamp your ticket when you reboard.

SNCF Hotlines

SNCF information lines accept advance ticket reservations, dole out updated train schedules and can update you on fares and everything else you might need to know about trains within the region. Lines are open 7am to 10pm daily.

To call from abroad dial 33 and drop the initial zero. Domestic calls are charged at €0.34 per minute. Call ☎ 08 36 35 35 39 to contact the English-speaking information service, or ☎ 08 36 35 35 35 for information in French.

Within France, reservations can be made through the SNCF website at W www.sncf.com. SNCF don't post tickets outside France.

Unused tickets *without a reservation* can be exchanged for another or – for tickets costing €4.50 or more – reimbursed (90% of the original ticket price) up to two months after the date of issue. Refunds are available from any train station ticket window.

Unused tickets (over €4.50) *with a reservation* can be exchanged for another up to one hour before the departure of the train you were originally ticketed for. Only 50% of the original ticket price (for tickets over €4.50) can be reimbursed, either before the original reservation expires or up to 60 days after.

Auto Train Under Motorail's Auto Train scheme you can travel with your car on a train. Cars are loaded on the train one hour before departure and unloaded 30 minutes after arrival. This service is available at Avignon, St-Raphaël, Marseilles and Nice train stations.

Information in the UK is available from Rail Europe (see the boxed text 'Rail Passes & Discount Fares' later in this chapter). In France, ticketing is handled by SNCF.

Transporting a Bicycle On main-line and TGV trains, bicycles can be transported free of charge as hand luggage, *if* they are packed, with the front wheel removed, in a special cover measuring no more than 120cm by 90cm (available from bike shops).

Some main-line trains – flagged with a bicycle symbol on timetables – have a luggage van or bicycle compartment in which bikes

On the Road

Motorist-friendly radio station Autoroute FM broadcasts traffic reports on 107.7MHz in English, French and Italian every 30 minutes at peak times. It also gives motorists traffic forecasts for the next few days: *rouge* (red) means 'traffic conditions are hell – avoid!'; *orange* translates as 'roads are busy, but tolerable'; and *vert* (green) is for 'go – little traffic on the roads'.

For general information on tolls, itineraries and travelling conditions call ☎ 01 47 05 90 01; for a traffic update call ☎ 08 92 68 10 77 or 08 92 70 70 01 (both €0.34 per minute). Alternatively, log onto France's fabulous *autoroute* website (in English) at W www.autoroutes.fr where you can tune into Autoroute FM, view toll-station web cams, check weather conditions, plan your itinerary, calculate journey distances (in miles or kilometres) and petrol costs (in your chosen currency), and see how much you will fork out in tolls.

can be transported (for free) without being dismantled or folded up. Tandems can only be transported in luggage vans. Cyclists are responsible for loading and unloading them.

On night trains and select high-speed trains on the TGV Sud-Est and TGV Méditerranée routes, bikes can only be transported in a four- to six-bicycle wagon which must be reserved in advance; reservations cost €10.

Boxed bicycles can be sent as baggage between two stations in France for €29.73, or door to door for €44.90. Both services operate weekdays only. Delivery can take up to three or four days. For information call ☎ 08 25 84 58 45. Further details are included in the multilingual SNCF brochure *Guide Train & Vélo* (free), available at any train station.

Car & Motorcycle Number one rule when motoring to Provence: avoid July and August. If this is impossible, be prepared to sit and wait in some mighty long *bouchons* (traffic jams), both on and off the *autoroute* (motorway).

The main southbound route from Paris is along the A6 and its continuation from Lyons, the A7 Autoroute du Soleil (literally the 'Road of the Sun'), which continues south through Orange and Avignon to Marseilles. From Marseilles, the A8 (called La Provençale) bears east to Nice and beyond into Italy where it becomes the A10. The A9 bears west from just south of Orange to Nîmes, Montpellier, and farther south to Spain. The A51 is the main road into the interior of Provence, leading northeast from Aix-en-Provence to Sisteron from where Alpes de Haute Provence can be accessed. Approaching Sisteron from the north, the N85 (Route Napoléon) follows the Napoléon Bonaparte trail from Grenoble, through Gap to Sisteron, Digne-les-Bains, Castellane and farther south to Grasse and Cannes along the coast.

Road tolls are imposed on most stretches of *autoroute*, the exception being around major cities such as Nice or Cannes. Count on paying between €4 and €5 per 100km (see the Road Distances & Road Tolls table later in this chapter). Some parts of the *autoroute* have toll plazas every few dozen kilometres; most have a machine that issues a little ticket you hand over at a *péage* (toll booth) when you exit. You can pay in euro or by credit card.

Autoroutes in southern France are managed by the **Autoroutes du Sud de la France** (*☎ 04 90 32 90 05; W www.asf.fr*) and the **Société des Autoroutes Estérel Côte d'Azur-Provence-Alpes** (*information ☎ 08 36 69 36 36; W www.escota.com*). The national *autoroute* **Association des Sociétés Françaises d'Autoroutes** (*W www.autoroutes.fr*) has an excellent website with masses of traffic-related information.

Hitching The student-inspired **Ecotrajet** (*☎ 06 73 88 35 54; W www.ecotrajet.com*) puts people looking for rides in touch with drivers going to the same destination: There are no cover charges; you simply split the cost of the trip with the driver and other passengers.

Continental Europe

Bus Generally, buses are slower and less comfortable than trains but they are cheaper, especially if you qualify for the often well-worthwhile discounts that most companies offer to seniors, students, youths and children. Several of the major companies include Provence and the Côte d'Azur in their European routes.

Bis

You will often see road signs at *autoroute* exits marked *bis* on an orange panel. This stands for *bison futé* and indicates alternative routes – generally well away from the *autoroute*, along the national and departmental roads – which avoid areas prone to peak-period congestion.

For information on *bis* routes and bottlenecks to avoid telephone ☎ 08 36 68 20 00. An annually updated, free map of *bis* routes is published by the French government (in collaboration with mapmaker IGN); contact your local automobile association or Maison de la France (see Tourist Offices in the Facts for the Visitor chapter) for a copy.

Eurolines Linking cities in Provence such as Nice, Marseilles and Avignon with points all over Western and Central Europe, Scandinavia and Morocco, **Eurolines** *(☎ 08 36 69 52 42, fax 01 49 72 51 61; Ⓦ www.eurolines.fr)* is an association of companies that together form Europe's largest international bus network.

Eurolines' main offices in the region are at the respective bus stations in **Avignon** *(☎ 04 90 85 27 60)*, **Marseilles** *(☎ 04 91 50 57 55)* and **Nîmes** *(☎ 04 66 29 49 02)*; in Aix-en-Provence and Toulon, Voyages Wasteels (see Fares under Air – Other Parts of France, earlier in this chapter) sells tickets and makes reservations for Eurolines buses; in Nice, contact Intercars (see the next section).

Buses are slower and less comfortable than trains, but they are cheaper, especially if you qualify for the 10 to 20% discount available to people who are aged under 26 or over 60. Children aged four to 12 also get discounts (up to 80% of the adult fare). In summer, book tickets well in advance. Return tickets cost substantially less than two one-way tickets. In addition to the standard fare, Eurolines offers cancellation/baggage and health insurance (€3/5) and a change-date option (€4), which enables you to change the date on which you intend travelling, after the ticket has been issued. Passengers are allowed to transport two pieces of luggage per person; a €7.60 fee is charged for each additional bag.

Travelling from Nice, Cannes or Toulon, sample single/return fares include Amsterdam (€84/147), Brussels (€77/132), Rome (€46/84) and Florence (€35/64). A one-way/return Nîmes–Barcelona trip costs €43/80, Orange–Frankfurt is €60/109 and Avignon–Berlin costs €93/167. Sample fares for journeys originating in Marseilles going to neighbouring countries include Barcelona (€46/69) and Budapest (€127/218).

Eurolines-affiliated companies across Europe include those in **Amsterdam** *(☎ 020-560 8788; Ⓦ www.eurolines.nl)*, **Frankfurt** *(☎ 069-79 03 50; Ⓦ www.deutsche-touring.com)*, **Brussels** *(☎ 02-203 0707)*; Madrid *(☎ 91 528 1105)*, **Prague** *(☎ 02-2421 3420; Ⓦ www.eurolines.cz)*, **Rome** *(☎ 06 44 23 39 28; Ⓦ www.eurolines.it)* and **Vienna** *(☎ 01-712 04 35; Ⓦ www.eurolines.at)*.

Intercars Bus services to cities in southern and Central Europe are operated by **Intercars** *(Ⓦ www.intercars.fr)*. In Provence, it has offices at the respective bus stations in **Nice** *(☎ 04 93 80 08 70; Ⓔ nice@intercars.fr)*, **Aix-en-Provence** *(☎ 04 91 50 57 55)*, **Marseilles** *(☎ 04 91 50 08 66; Ⓔ marseille@intercars.fr)* and **Nîmes** *(☎ 04 66 29 84 22; Ⓔ nimes@intercars.fr)*.

Those aged under 26 and over 60, and children aged two to 12 years are entitled to discounted fares (approximately 5% and 10% respectively off a full adult fare). Passengers are allowed to transport a suitcase and one piece of hand luggage.

Sample one-way adult fares from Nice include those to Bratislava (€75), Budapest (€94) and Warsaw (€107).

Linebùs The cities of Avignon and Nîmes are linked with Barcelona (7½ hours), Lisbon (24 hours) and other cities in Spain and Portugal by **Linebùs** *(in Avignon ☎ 04 90 86 88 67, in Nîmes ☎ 04 66 29 50 62, in Barcelona ☎ 932 650 700, in Lisbon ☎ 021-357 17 45)*. Buses to/from Barcelona/Lisbon depart five/three times weekly; a single fare costs €109/35 (€177/60 return). On both routes passengers aged under 26 or over 60 pay about €4 less one way. Linebùs has an office at the bus station in all four cities.

Busabout A UK-based company, **Eurolines** *(☎ 020-7950 1661, fax 7950 1662; Ⓦ www.busabout.com; 258 Vauxhall Bridge Rd, London SW1V 1BS)* runs coaches on several loops covering a variety of destinations in

Road Distances (km) & Road Tolls (euro)

Key: km (€)

	Aix/Marseilles	Avignon	Cannes	Nice	Nîmes	Menton	Monaco	Orange	Toulon
Aix/Marseilles	- (-)								
Avignon	98 (4.20)	- (-)							
Cannes	166 (11)	226 (15.20)	- (-)						
Nice	205 (13.40)	262 (18.70)	34 (2.40)	- (-)					
Nîmes	123 (4.60)	50 (1.40)	250 (15.50)	279 (18)	- (-)				
Menton	236 (16.30)	240 (20.80)	66 (5.30)	30 (1)	315 (20.90)	- (-)			
Monaco	228 (16.50)	285 (20.70)	58 (5.50)	20 (2)	310 (21.40)	12 (-)	- (-)		
Orange	115 (5.60)	29 (1)	243 (16.60)	274 (19)	56 (2.50)	304 (21.90)	302 (22.10)	- (-)	
Toulon	65 (3.20)	160 (7.40)	120 (5.10)	143 (7.50)	185 (7.30)	180 (10.40)	170 (10.60)	177 (8.80)	- (-)
Bordeaux	648 (35.50)	573 (35.70)	775 (19.90)	804 (52.30)	532 (33.70)	836 (55.20)	834 (55.40)	584 (37.20)	712 (42.10)
Calais	1071 (61.50)	482 (51.30)	1204 (72.50)	1232 (76)	1011 (58.80)	1259 (77.80)	1255 (78)	955 (55.80)	1133 (64.70)
Lyons	328 (18.50)	279 (14.30)	448 (29.50)	429 (33)	253 (15.90)	504 (34.30)	502 (35)	202 (12.80)	380 (21.70)
Paris	781 (44.30)	692 (40.10)	911 (55.30)	941 (55.80)	720 (41.60)	966 (60)	965 (60.50)	615 (38.40)	842 (47.50)
Toulouse	407 (20.70)	331 (20.10)	534 (35.10)	562 (37.60)	291 (18.10)	595 (40.40)	543 (40.60)	342 (22.40)	470 (27.30)

Western and Central Europe, Scandinavia and Morocco. Two loops that include France go to northern Europe and to Spain and Portugal. A Busabout Pass – valid for 15 consecutive days, 10 days in two months, or 30 days in four months – lets you get on and off whenever you choose, at designated pick-up points. These pick-up points – in France, Avignon, Nice, Bordeaux, Paris and Tours – are often convenient for hostels and camp sites. Busabout operates year round, with services every two or three days at pick-up points.

Passes are sold through major youth-travel agencies throughout Europe. A two-week consecutive-day pass costs €299 (€269 for under 26s) and a flexible pass valid for 10/25 days over two/four months costs €439/929 (€389/839 for under 26s). 'Early-bird' equivalents – €30 to €60 cheaper depending on the length of pass – are available for those travelling between January and mid-May.

Train Paris abounds with connections from all over Europe. Other major border stations in France are in Lille, Metz, Strasbourg, Bordeaux, Mulhouse and Lyons. Within the region, Nice is the major hub, sitting on the Barcelona–Rome train line – a service that gets packed out (and heavily booked well in advance) by backpackers during the summer. Day and overnight trains run in both directions. In late 2002, a single Rome fare from Nice cost €54.10 (plus €14.50 for a couchette) for the 10-hour journey. Nice is also served by direct train services to/from Milan (€32.70, 4½ hours). Marseilles touts direct daily trains to/from Brussels (€121.20, seven to 8½ hours), one of which continues to Nice.

You can book tickets and get information from Rail Europe up to two months ahead (see the boxed text 'Rail Passes & Discount Fares' later). Direct bookings through **SNCF** *(in French ☎ 08 36 35 35 35, in English 08 36 35 35 39)* are possible, but SNCF won't post tickets outside France. For more on SNCF see Train under Other Parts of France earlier in this Land section.

If you intend to do a lot of train travel, consider purchasing the *Thomas Cook European Timetable*, a trainophile's bible with a complete listing of train schedules, supplements and reservations information. It is updated monthly and available from Thomas Cook outlets. In the USA, call ☎ 800-367 7984.

Auto Train This arrangement (see Train under Other Parts of France earlier in this chapter) allows you to transport your car by passenger train to Avignon and St-Raphaël. In France, the SNCF offices have information; contact any Rail Europe office in other European countries. Advance bookings of at least two months are generally required.

The UK

The Channel Tunnel, inaugurated in 1994, is the first dry-land link between England and France since the Ice Age.

Bus Eurolines (see Bus under Continental Europe earlier) operates direct bus services, up to four times weekly, from London's Victoria Coach station via the Dover–Calais Channel crossing. The single fares from London/Nice include Avignon (UK£60/(82) and Aix-en-Provence/Marseilles/Toulon/Nice (UK£64/(90). Bookings can be made with **Eurolines UK** *(☎ 0870 5143 219; W www.eurolines.co.uk)* or at any National Express office.

For Busabout services from London, see Continental Europe earlier in the chapter. If you're beginning your journey in London, Busabout charges an extra UK£30/40 one way/return for the Channel crossing.

Train The direct high-speed passenger service through the Channel Tunnel, **Eurostar** *(in UK ☎ 0870 5186 186, in France ☎ 08 92 35 35 39; W www.eurostar.com)*, takes three hours from London (Waterloo) to Paris and 6¼ hours to warm and sunny Avignon.

The Eurostar to/from Avignon – a new service inaugurated in 2002 – currently runs once weekly, July to September, but more direct services from London to southern France are expected following the completion of the first phase of the Channel Tunnel rail link in 2003. The latter – a UK£5.2 billion project linking London (St-Pancras) and the Channel Tunnel (109km) with high-speed rail track by 2007 – will slash travelling time between London (Waterloo) and the tunnel from an embarrassingly slow 75 minutes to a more respectable 35 minutes. Completion of the first phase will reduce the painfully slow journey through the Kent countryside by an initial 20 minutes.

Otherwise, you can take a Eurostar to Lille or Paris, from where there are numerous southbound trains (see Train in Other Parts of France earlier in the Land section).

Full fares can be more than twice those for rail-sea-rail, but certain nonrefundable, nonexchangeable European rail tickets, which include a Eurostar Channel crossing, are competitive: a 2nd-class return ticket from London to Avignon, Marseilles, Nice, Toulon or St-Raphaël costs UK£145 (nonrefundable, nonreimbursable, includes a Saturday-night stay in Provence, and must be booked a week ahead). The fare for those aged 26 or under costs the same but carries no restrictions. From Avignon, Marseilles, Aix-en-Provence TGV or Cannes, a weekend/fully flexible return fare to London costs €187.50/375.

In the UK, Eurostar and non-Eurostar tickets are sold at travel agents, main-line train stations and SNCF-owned Rail Europe (see the boxed text 'Rail Passes & Discount Fares' following).

Car & Motorcycle High-speed shuttle trains operated by **Eurotunnel** *(in UK ☎ 0870 535 3535, in France ☎ 03 21 00 61 00; W www.eurotunnel.com)* whisk cars, motorcycles, bicycles and coaches from Folkestone via the Channel Tunnel to Coquelles, 5km southwest of Calais, in air-conditioned and soundproofed comfort. Journey time is 35 minutes. Trains run three to four times an hour (one or two per hour between midnight and 6am).

A fully flexible return (valid for a year) for a car and its passengers costs UK£319, compared to a five-day return which costs UK£199. Numerous promotional fares – including special 'overnight' fares, weekend and day-trip deals are available, so check the fine print carefully before submitting your credit card number. Tickets booked by telephone cost UK£2 more.

When calculating costs, include road tolls from Calais to Provence (see the 'Road Distances & Road Tolls' table earlier in this chapter).

Bicycle The organisation **European Bike Express** *(☎ 01642-251 440, fax 01642-232 209; W www.bike-express.co.uk)* transports

Rail Passes & Discount Fares

The following passes are sold at student travel agencies, major train stations within Europe, and the SNCF subsidiary **Rail Europe** *(☎ 0870 5848 848; Ⓦ www.raileurope.com; 178 Piccadilly, London W1V 0BA).* In the USA, contact Rail Europe on ☎ 800 438 7245; in Canada on ☎ 800 361 7245.

SNCF Discount Fares & Passes

Children aged under four travel free of charge; those aged four to 11 travel for half-price. Discounted fares (25% reduction) automatically apply to travellers aged 12 to 25, seniors aged over 60, one to four adults travelling with a child aged four to 11, two people on a return journey together or anyone taking a return journey of at least 200km and spending a Saturday night away.

Purchasing a one-year travel pass can yield a 50% discount (25% if the cheapest seats are sold out): a **Carte 12-25**, aimed at travellers aged 12 to 25 costs €44; the **Carte Enfant Plus** for one to four adults travelling with a child aged four to 11 costs €55; and seniors aged over 60 qualify for a €45 **Carte Sénior**.

The **France Railpass** entitles nonresidents of France to unlimited travel on SNCF trains for four to 10 days over a one-month period. A four-day pass in 1st/2nd class costs US$210/240; each additional day of travel costs US$30. A cheaper youth version exists.

European Rail Passes for European Residents

The **Euro Domino Pass**, available to those who have been resident in Europe for at least six months, can be used in France for three to eight consecutive days, or non-consecutive days over a one-month period, of 2nd-class travel. The adult versions cost UK£115/136/176/217 for three/four/six/eight days, and for those aged under 26 they are UK£85/101/134/166. The pass covers supplements on TGV trains, but does not include seat or couchette reservations.

cyclists and their bikes by bus and trailer from the UK to places all over Europe, including southern France. Route details and further information can be found on its website. Return fares start at UK£159 (UK£10 less for CTC members; see under Bicycle in the Getting Around chapter).

SEA

Provence has ferry links with Corsica, Italy and North Africa; boats sail to/from Nice, Toulon and Marseilles.

The UK & Ireland

There are no direct ferries, but you can take a ferry year round from Dover to Calais or from Folkestone to Boulogne – the shortest crossings and the most competitive fares between the UK and France – and motor it south. Longer channel crossings include Newhaven–Dieppe, Poole–Cherbourg, and Portsmouth–Cherbourg/Le Havre/Ouistreham/St-Malo. Services to St-Malo and Roscoff in Brittany run less frequently than those across the Straits of Dover, particularly in winter.

Fares are wildly seasonal. Winter tickets can cost less than half as much as in the high season (each company has its own complex definition of high season). Three- or five-day excursion return fares cost about the same as regular one-way tickets. Return fares are generally less than two one-way tickets. Children aged four to 14 or 15 travel for half to two-thirds of an adult fare. Most crossings also have higher fares for lounge seats and cabins. For a list of ferry companies and ports served, see the boxed text 'Ferry 'cross the Channel' later in the chapter.

Corsica

SNCM Nearly all ferries between Provence (Nice, Marseilles and Toulon) and Corsica (Ajaccio, Bastia, Calvi, Île-Rousse, Porto Vechio and Propriano) are handled by **SNCM** *(Société Nationale Maritime Corse Méditerranée; ☎ 0891 701 801; Ⓦ www.sncm.fr).* Schedules and fares are listed on the website and in its pocket timetable, free from tourist offices, some hotels and SNCM offices. In peak season, there are up to five ferries daily to/from Nice, up to three daily to/from Marseilles and up to five times weekly to/from Toulon. In winter there are as few as one per day to/from Nice and Marseilles. Corsica–Toulon ferries run April to October.

Rail Passes & Discount Fares

With the **InterRail Pass** (W *www.inter-rail.co.uk*) you can travel in 29 European countries organised into eight zones; France is in Zone E, grouped with the Netherlands, Belgium and Luxembourg. For 12 days of unlimited 2nd-class travel in one zone, the cost is UK£119/169 for those aged under/over 26; and a 22-day pass is UK£139/209. You also get 50% off travel from your home country to your zone(s) and between nonadjacent zones, as well as a considerable discount on Eurostar tickets.

European Rail Passes for Non-European Residents

If you are not a resident of Europe but are aged under 26 on your first day of travel and anticipate clocking up more than 2400km around Provence, the rest of France and Europe, consider buying a **Eurail Pass** (W *www.eurail.on.ca*), which entitles you to unlimited train travel for 15/21 days or one/two/three months. One/two/three months of unlimited travel in 1st class costs around US$918/1298/1606. Youth equivalents in 2nd class cost US$644/910/1126.

Eurail Youth Flexipass covers 10/15 non-consecutive days of travel in a two-month period, costing around US$473/622. Adult equivalents cost US$674/888.

In the USA and Canada, you can purchase Eurail passes online or by telephone (☎ 1888 667 9734); tickets are mailed to your home by courier.

The **Euro Pass** allows you to travel in five European countries for between five and 15 nonconsecutive days over a two-month period. The adult pass, good for 1st-class train travel within France, Germany, Italy, Spain and Switzerland, ranges from US$360 for five days to US$710 for 15 days (20% less for two adults travelling together with a saver pass). Cheaper **Youth Pass** equivalents, available for those aged under 26, are only good for 2nd-class travel and cost US$293/497 for five/15 days.

A one-way passage in a *fauteuil* (literally 'armchair' but actually meaning a hard, bum-numbing, straight-backed chair in a small cabin), costs €35/45 in low/high season on sailings to/from Nice, and €40/57 for sailings to/from Marseilles or Toulon. Daytime crossings take about 6½ hours. For overnight trips, the cheapest/dearest cabin costs an extra €3/68 per person.

Fauteuil passengers aged 12 to 25, students under 27, seniors aged over 60 and parents travelling with three children aged under 18 pay €27/37 in low/high season for all sailings to/from Nice and €31/45 from Marseilles and Toulon. Children aged four to 12 pay €17/21 from Nice and €25/31 from the other two ports; under-4s travel for free. Taking a small car costs between €40 and €107, depending on the season and port you depart from. Motorcycles under 100cc cost €26/59 to transport in low/high season and a €14 fee is imposed for bicycles.

The above fares do not include port tax – an additional €7.61 to €10.56 per passenger, plus €6.23 to €9.27 per vehicle, depending on which port you depart from and sail into.

SNCM also operates a 70km/h express NGV (Navire à Grande Vitesse) to Calvi (2¾ hours) and Bastia (3½ hours) from Nice, and to Ajaccio (6½ hours) from Toulon. Fares on these zippy NGVs, which carry up to 500 passengers and 148 vehicles, command a €5 supplement in addition to the basic fares listed above for regular ferries. NGVs cannot sail in bad weather; last-minute cancellations are not unknown.

In July and August, ferries get fully booked; reservations for both vehicles and couchettes should be made well in advance. Tickets in Corsica are sold from the SNCM office in **Ajaccio** (*☎ 04 95 29 66 69, 04 95 29 66 63; 3 quai l'Herminier*); **Bastia** (*☎ 04 95 54 66 99, 04 95 54 66 60; New Port*); and **Calvi** (*☎ 04 95 65 01 38, 04 95 65 17 77; quai Landry*). In France, contact the SNCM office in Nice, Marseilles or Toulon (see relevant chapters for details).

Corsica Ferries The company **Corsica Ferries** (*nationwide ☎ 08 25 09 50 95;* W *www.corsicaferries.com*) sails from Nice to Bastia, Calvi and Ajaccio; and from Toulon to Ajaccio and Bastia.

In late 2002 the basic single fare for an armchair seat from Nice or Toulon to Corsica cost €28/44 in low/high season (children

Ferry 'cross the Channel

Ferrying it across the channel tosses up a merry assortment of routes, vessels and fares. The following sample prices are for a high-season single fare for a car plus driver and one passenger (with two reclining seats aboard).

Brittany Ferries (in UK ☎ 08703 665 333, in Ireland ☎ 021-4277 801, in France 08 25 82 88 28, W www.brittany-ferries.com). Poole–Cherbourg (UK£230, 4½ hours), Portsmouth–Caen (UK£240, 5¾ hours) and Portsmouth–St-Malo (UK£304, 10½ hours), all up to three daily; Plymouth–Roscoff (UK£161, six hours, one or two daily March to November, once weekly November to March); Plymouth–Cherbourg (UK£155, twice weekly November to March); Plymouth–St-Malo (UK£153, once weekly November to March); Cork–Roscoff (€530, 14 hours, once weekly April to September)

Condor Ferries (in UK ☎ 0845 345 2000, in St-Malo ☎ 02 99 20 03 00, W www.condorferries.co.uk). Weymouth/Poole–St-Malo with change of vessel in Guernsey (UK£208, 5½ hours, daily March to September)

Hoverspeed (in France ☎ 08 20 00 35 55, in UK ☎ 0870 240 8070, W www.hoverspeed.co.uk). Nippy SeaCat catamarans, Dover–Calais (UK£133, one hour, hourly); Newhaven–Dieppe SuperSeaCats (UK£159, two hours, three daily)

Irish Ferries (in Cherbourg ☎ 02 33 23 44 44, in Roscoff ☎ 02 98 61 17 17, in UK ☎ 0990 171 717, in Ireland ☎ 053-33158, 24-hour information in Ireland ☎ 01-661 0715, W www.irishferries.ie). Rosslare–Roscoff (€209, 15 hours, summer); Rosslare–Cherbourg (€209, 17 hours, two or four times weekly)

P&O Portsmouth (in France 08 25 01 30 13, in UK ☎ 0870 520 20 20, W www.poportsmouth.com). Portsmouth–Le Havre ferries (UK£130, six to 8¼ hours, three daily); Portsmouth–Cherbourg (UK£223, 5½ to 7½ hours, six daily)

P&O Stena Line (in France ☎ 08 20 010 020, in UK reservations ☎ 0870 600 0600, info ☎ 0870 600 0611, W www.posl.com). Daily Dover–Calais ferries (1½ hours), slightly more expensive, faster and more frequent than SeaFrance. Portsmouth–Le Havre, Portsmouth–Cherbourg ferries too

SeaFrance (in Calais ☎ 08 03 04 40 45 office hours, ☎ 03 21 46 80 00 weekends and evenings, in UK ☎ 0870 5711 711, W www.seafrance.com). Daily Dover–Calais ferries (UK£79.50 daily)

from 4 to 12 €10.50/20.50). Those under 25, seniors over 60, students under 27 and parents travelling with children were eligible for a reduced fare of €5/17. Cabin supplements started at €20 for a day cabin and €17/23 in low/high season for a bed in a four-bunk cabin during night crossings. Transporting a small car cost €40/105 in low/high season and a bicycle could be transported for a flat year-round fee of €3. For port taxes levied, see the SNCM section above.

Corsica Ferries has ticket offices at the ports in **Nice** *(☎ 04 92 00 42 93)* and **Toulon** *(☎ 04 94 41 11 89)*, as well as the **Corsican ports** *(in Bastia ☎ 04 95 32 95 95, in Calvi ☎ 04 95 65 43 21, in Ajaccio ☎ 04 95 50 78 82)* it serves.

Italy

SNCM (see the Corsica section earlier) operates two or three car ferries weekly from Marseilles or Toulon to Porto Torres on the Italian island of Sardinia (Sardaigne in French). Sailing time is 15½ hours and boats depart in the afternoon or early evening.

A one-way passage in an armchair seat costs €63/72 in low/high season (those aged 4 to 12 €36/40). A reduced fare of €46/55 in low/high season for passengers aged 12 to 25, InterRail Pass holders (see the boxed text 'Rail Passes & Discount Fares' earlier in this chapter) and seniors aged over 60 is only valid on return fares. A place in a two- or four-berth cabin costs an additional €9/11 in low/high season, and transporting a car costs an extra €56/104. Fares quoted do not include port tax – an additional €2.78/2 per passenger departing from Marseilles/Toulon, plus €2.82/4.09 per vehicle.

Tickets and information are available from any SNCM office in Provence. In Sardinia, tickets are sold by SNCF agent, **Paglietti Petertours** *(☎ 079-51 44 77; Corso Vittorio Emanuele 19)* in Porto Torres.

Tunisia

SNCM (see the Corsica section earlier) and **CTN** *(Compagnie Tunisienne de Navigation; ☎ 216-135 33 31; 122 rue de Yougoslavie)* in Tunis together operate two weekly car ferries (almost daily services mid-June to mid-September) between Marseilles and Tunis (20-22 hours). Over the same period, SNCM also operates a weekly ferry between Toulon and Tunis. A single/return fare for an armchair seat from either port costs €144/262 (€72/130 for those aged 2 to 16), plus from either port it costs €9/18 each way for a bunk in a four-berth cabin in low/high season. If you're taking a vehicle (€320/512 single/return), it is vital to book ahead, especially in summer. Port taxes levied in 2002 were €8/7 for passengers departing from Marseilles/Toulon, plus €5 per vehicle leaving from either French port.

Algeria

Ferries from Marseilles to the Algerian port cities of Algiers, Bejaia, Annaba, Skikda and Oran are aimed at the local North African community. Political troubles have prompted a state of emergency in Algeria since 1992 and travel is considered dangerous for foreign tourists.

Algérie Ferries *(W www.algerieferries.com)* operates three ferries weekly between Marseilles and Algiers, an overnight sailing of 24 hours. Ferries to/from Bejaia, Annaba, Skikda and Oran set sail up to four times monthly. A single/return fare on any of these routes costs €169/314 for an armchair seat, and €259/468 in a four-bunk cabin. Children aged two to 12 and students get discounts. Transporting a car one-way/return costs a hefty €480/770. Add another €5/7/9 each way per armchair passenger/cabin passenger/vehicle in port taxes.

Ticketing is handled in Marseilles by the **Algérie Ferries** *(☎ 04 91 90 64 70; 29 blvd des Dames)* office near the port. In Algeria, there are ticketing offices at the port in **Algiers** *(☎ 021-74 78 28; quai d'Ajaccio)*, **Bejaia** *(☎ 034-20 27 66)* and **Annaba** *(☎ 021-42 30 50)*.

RIVER

Canal Boat

Provence is well-connected with waterways thanks to the Rhône. Cruising along its sun-flooded channels on a canal boat can be one of the most relaxing and romantic ways of getting to Provence – providing time is not of the essence.

The most popular canal route to Provence is via the Canal du Midi, a 240km waterway that runs from Toulouse to the Bassin de Thau between Agde and Sète, from where you continue northeast past Sète to Aigues-Mortes in the Camargue. From Toulouse, the Canal du Midi is connected with the Gardonne River leading west to the Atlantic Ocean at Bordeaux. The Midi affords great views over the sun-dried Languedoc plain and passes through more than 100 *écluses* (locks) – sometimes nine in a row, as is the case near Béziers. See under Boat in the Getting Around chapter for details on self-cruising boat rental agencies abroad and within the region.

Cruises

Many agencies offer luxury river cruises to Provence, departing primarily from Lyons. Year round, **Alsace Croisières CroisiEurope** *(☎ 03 88 76 44 44, fax 03 88 32 49 96; W www.croisiere.com; 12 rue de la Division Leclerc, F-67000 Strasbourg)* offers three- to seven-day cruises from Lyons to the Camargue, taking in Avignon and Martigues. Cruises follow a theme (the 'Wild Rhone', 'Escape to Provence', 'Provençal Christmas', 'Mimosa magic' and so on) and cost from €334/609 for five/seven days.

A dreamy seven-night river cruise from Lyons to Arles and back again aboard the luxurious four-star MV *Princesse de Provence* is from US$1900/1320/1100 based on single/double/triple cabin occupancy with American cruise operator **Peter Deilmann Cruises** *(☎ 800-348 8287, 703-549 1741; W www.deilmann-cruises.com; 1800 Diagonal Rd, Suite 170, Alexandria VA 22314, USA)*. In Europe, it has an agent in **France** *(☎ 04 78 39 13 06; 5 rue Gentil, F-69002 Lyons)*, **UK** *(☎ 020-7436 2931; e gv13@dial.pipex.com; Albany House, Suite 404, 324-326 Regent St, London W1R 5AA)* and **Germany** *(☎ 045-613 960, fax 045-619 157; Am Hafensteig 17-19, D-23730 Neustadt/H)*.

In the UK, **VFB Holidays** *(☎ 01242-240 338, fax 570 340; W www.vfbholidays.co.uk; Normandy House, High St, Cheltenham, Glos GL50 3FB, UK)* sails from Dijon to Avignon and the Camargue during a seven-day 'Burgundy & Provence' river cruise (which costs from UK£715, including airfare and full-board accommodation on board); and from Châteauneuf du Pape to the Camargue in a luxurious seven-day Camargue cruise (from UK£1789, including airfare, full board, and unlimited drinks from the bar).

ORGANISED TOURS

In Australia, **French Travel Connection** *(☎ 02-9966 8600, fax 9966 5888; W www.frenchtravel.com.au; Suite 601, 83 Mount St, North Sydney NSW 2060)* and **Tempo Holidays** *(☎ 03-9646 0277, fax 03-9646 6722; W www.tempoholidays.com; 1st Floor, Beach St, Port Melbourne, Victoria 3207)* are leading French travel specialists.

Food & Wine

Arblaster & Clarke (☎ 01730-893 344, fax 892 888, W www.arblasterandclarke.com) Farnham Rd, West Liss, Hants GU33 6JQ, UK. A five-night 'south of France' wine tour, with winery visits and lots of fine dining (UK£999 per person, including airfare), and a four-night 'Gourmet Provence' tour with accommodation in a four-star chateau (UK£1699, with flights and two cookery demonstrations), were on this wine-tour specialists' 2003 repertoire.

Wine Trails (☎ 01306-712 111, fax 713 504, W www.winetrails.co.uk) Vann Lake, Ockley, Dorking RH5 5NT, UK. Walking tours of Provence around the Alpilles with a strong focus on wine and gourmet cuisine; six-night independent walking/cycling tours, with half-board accommodation in one- and two-star hotels, costing UK£385/399. It also runs escorted 10-night group walks, with two- or three-star hotel accommodation, for UK£995.

Art & Architecture

Martin Randall Travel (☎ 020-8742 3355, fax 020-8742 7766, W www.martinrandall.com) 10 Barley Mow Passage, London W4 4PH. A fabulous wealth of art and architecture tours led by art historians or experts in their field. Tours in 2002-03 included a seven-day 'modern art on the Cote d'Azur' trip costing UK£1380/1560 without/with flights from the UK.

Cycling & Walking

Most cycling tour operators lighten the load by taking charge of transporting cyclists' baggage by minibus between hotels. Many tours take in chateaux and other sights en route.

ATG Oxford (☎ 01865-315 678, fax 315 697, W www.atg-oxford.co.uk) 69–71 Banbury Rd, Oxford OX2 6PJ, UK. Independent walking holidays. The eight-day 'footloose' itinerary in the Vaucluse costs UK£410 excluding flights.

Belle France (☎ 01797-223 777, fax 223 666, W www.bellefrance.co.uk) 15 East St, Rye, East Sussex TN31 7JY, UK. A seven-day walking holiday through the Alpilles, averaging 10 miles a day and costing UK£470/560/580 per person based on self-drive/rail/air.

Europeds (☎ 800 321 9552, 831-646 4920, fax 831-655 44501, e europeds@aol.com) 761 Lighthouse Ave, Monterey, CA 93940, USA. Cycling, walking and hiking tours by this California-based Europe specialist.

Explore Worldwide (☎ 01252-760 000, fax 760 001, W www.explore.co.uk) 1 Frederick St, Aldershot, Hants GU11 1LQ, UK. Eight-day walking tour around the Gorges du Verdon by the adventure specialists costs UK£370/380 in low/high season.

Headwater (☎ 01606-720 033, fax 720 034, W www.headwater-holidays.co.uk) The Old School House, Chester Rd, Castle, Northwich, Cheshire CW8 1LE, UK. Seven- to 11-day walking, cycling and gastronomic tours in the Lubéron, northern Var and on the coast; nine-day gastronomic cycling adventures, starting at UK£667 (UK£457 self-drive).

Inn Travel (☎ 01653-629 001, fax 628 741, W www.inntravel.co.uk) Hovingham, York YO62 4JZ, UK. Gastronomy weekends (two nights from UK£389), weekends of indulgence (three nights from UK£568, including airfare) and other short breaks, as well as riding holidays, six-day or more discovery journeys and cycling tours (seven nights from UK£537/739 self-drive/by air); accommodation in family-run hotels, inns and chateaux.

Susi Madron's Cycling for Softies (☎ 0161-248 8282, fax 248 5140, W www.cycling-for-softies.co.uk) 2 & 4 Birch Polygon, Rusholme Manchester M14 5HX, UK. Seven- to 14-day tours of the Camargue or Lubéron start at UK£836, excluding travel to/from Provence; all cycling abilities.

Self-Drive Camping

Canvas Holidays (☎ 01383-629 000, fax 620 070, W www.canvas.co.uk) East Port House, Dunfermline KY12 7PG, UK. Canvas and mobile-home accommodation at camp sites in St-Tropez, St-Raphaël, Fréjus, Cannes, St-Aygulf and Port Grimaud; 12 nights' tent accommodation (two adults and children) from UK£264/559/899 in low/mid/high season, including ferry crossing to/from Calais.

Eurocamp (☎ 08703-667 599, W www.eurocamp.co.uk) Hartford Manor, Greenbank Lane, Northwich, Cheshire CF8 1HW, UK. Has numerous sites the length of the Côte d'Azur. Based at the same address is **Out There Birdwatching** (W www.outtherebirdwatching.com), Eurocamp's ornithological arm, which organises some specialist bird-watching tours in Provence, costing from UK£495 per person for seven nights.

Getting Around

AIR

There are no scheduled, inter-regional plane flights within Provence but increasing numbers of high-flyers are taking to the air by helicopter.

Year round, **Héli Air Monaco** *(☎ 377-92 05 00 50; Ⓦ www.heliairmonaco.com)* at **Héliport de Monaco** *(☎ 92 05 00 10; ave des Ligures)* operates scheduled helicopter flights between Nice and Monaco – Europe's busiest helicopter route – (approximately every 30 minutes between 7.15am and 8pm or 9pm April to October, twice hourly November to March). A single/return fare costs €75/135 (two to 12 yrs €38/76). Charters start at €430/980 one-way for up to five/10 people. Tickets in Monaco are sold at **Héli-Air Voyages** *(☎ 377-97 70 80 20, fax 377-97 70 80 21; 11 blvd du Jardin Exotique)* and in Nice at the **Héli-Air Monaco desk** *(☎ 04 93 21 34 32)* in Terminal 1 at the Nice-Côte d'Azur airport (Aéroport International Nice-Côte d'Azur).

Héli-Inter Riviera *(in Nice ☎ 04 93 21 46 46; in Monaco ☎ 377-97 77 84 84)*, based at Nice-Côte d'Azur airport, also flies between Nice and Monaco, March to October, and charges similar fares.

Cannes-based **Nice Hélicoptères** *(in Cannes ☎ 04 93 43 42 42; in Nice ☎ 04 93 21 34 32; Ⓔ nicehelicopteres@wanadoo.fr)*, with its base at **Héliport du Palm Beach** *(☎ 04 93 43 42 42; blvd de la Croisette)* in Cannes and a desk in both terminals at Nice-Côte d'Azur airport, operates scheduled flights between Cannes and Nice (single/return €76/131), March to September, and charter flights the rest of the year (up to €395 per person in a five-seat helicopter).

A clutch of other helicopter operators run charter flights within the region. **MonacAir** *(☎ 377-97 97 39 00; Ⓦ www.monacair.mc)*, runs charters from its Monaco-heliport base to practically anywhere you wish to go in France, and offers its privilege-card-holders discounts of up to 25% on Héli-Inter Riviera's scheduled Monaco-Nice flights (see above). St-Tropez-based **Hélisecurité** *(in Grimaud, St-Tropez ☎ 04 94 55 59 99; in Nice ☎ 04 93 21 45 85; Ⓦ www.helicopter-saint-tropez.com)*, with desks at the Hélistation St-Tropez-Grimaud in Grimaud and in terminal 1 at Nice-Côte d'Azur airport, charges €750/800/650 for a charter flight for up to five passengers from its Grimaud base to Nice/Monaco/Cannes or €1190 to Toulon/Marseilles. **Mont Blanc Hélicoptères Azur** *(in La Môle ☎ 06 21 01 20 42; Ⓦ www.montblanchelicopteres.fr)* maintains a base at St-Tropez–La Môle airport (Aéroport International de St-Tropez–La Môle) near La Môle.

Farther west, **Global Héli-Services** *(☎ 04 91 44 18 87)* operates chartered flights from the Cuers airfield (Aérodrome de Cuers), which is 20km north of Toulon, to Giens (€125 one way) and the island of Porquerolles (€125 one way).

For helicopter jet setters, a handy source of information on the Web is **Héli Riviera** *(Ⓦ www.heliriviera.com)*.

BUS

Buses are used for short-distance travel within departments, especially in rural areas such as Haute-Provence where there are relatively few train lines. However, services and routes are extremely limiting for any traveller hoping to pack in as many hill-top villages as possible. No more than one or two daily buses trundle their way from the coast to the handful of villages in the Niçois hinterland, for example. Bus services are more efficient between towns that are served by just a few trains (or no train at all). There are several daily trains between Marseilles and Aix-en-Provence, but buses speed between the two towns approximately every 30 minutes.

Autocars (regional buses) are operated by a muddling host of different bus companies, most of whom usually have an office at the bus station *(gare routière)* in the cities they serve. One company usually sells tickets for all the bus companies operating from the same station.

Some uneconomical SNCF train lines have been replaced by SNCF buses in recent years. Routes covered by buses (known as Autocars LER) include Marseilles to Digne-les-Bains, Manosque and Sisteron; Nice, Toulon and Avignon to Aix-en-Provence; Arles to Avignon; and Carpentras to Aix and Marseilles via Cavaillon.

Few bus stations in the region have left-luggage facilities.

TRAIN

The SNCF's regional rail network in Provence, served by *trains express régionaux* (TER; regional express trains), is efficient – like its national network. It comprises two routes – one that follows the coast and another that traverses the interior.

The Côte d'Azur between St-Raphaël and Ventimiglia (Vintimille in French), past the Italian border, is served by numerous daily TER trains that shuttle back and forth along the coast. From St-Raphaël the train line cuts inland to Les Arcs-sur-Argens, then plunges back on to the coast at Toulon, from where it continues its journey westwards along the coast to Marseilles and a little beyond. At Miramas, the tracks bear inland to Arles and Avignon.

Inland, the Briançon–Marseilles train line slices through the western fringe of Alpes de Haute-Provence, linking the coast with the Provençal interior. Train stations *(gares)* from the north to the south include Sisteron, Château-Arnoux St-Auban, Manosque and Aix-en-Provence.

In addition to SNCF routes, there is a narrow-gauge railway linking Nice with Digne-les-Bains in Haute-Provence. Details are listed in the Haute-Provence chapter.

Information

Most train stations have separate *guichets* (ticket windows) and information or reservation offices.

Indispensable for anyone doing a lot of train travel, the *Guide Régional des Transports* is a free booklet of inter-regional rail and SNCF bus schedules available at larger train stations.

Left-Luggage

Nice, Marseilles and other larger stations either have a *consigne manuelle* (left-luggage office) where you pay about €5/6 per bag/bicycle for 24 hours, or *consignes automatiques*, computerised luggage lockers that issue you with a lock code in exchange for €3/4.50/6.10 for a small/medium/large locker per 72 hours. Most left-luggage lockers/offices can be accessed from around 7am to 10.30pm.

Schedules

SNCF issues two sets of timetables *(horaires)* per year: a winter schedule valid from the end

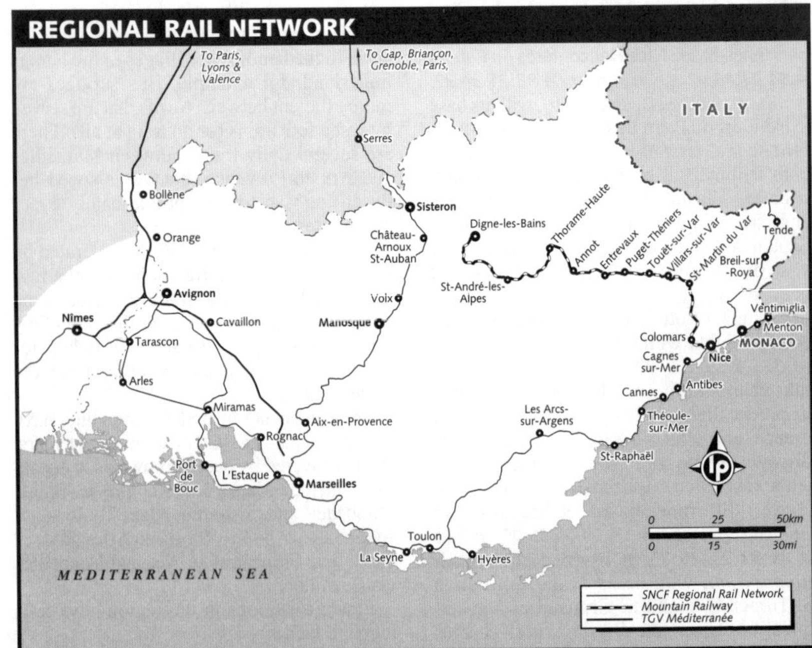

of September (or November on some routes) to the end of May; and a summer schedule that runs from the end of May to the end of September (occasionally November).

There are separate pocket-sized timetables (free at train stations) for regional TER trains and the *grandes lignes* (big lines) covering TGV (*train à grande vitesse;* high-speed train) and other main-line services. The footnotes at the bottom of both explain whether trains run *(circule)* Monday to Friday; until *(jusqu'au)* a certain date; or every *(tous les jours)*/except *(sauf)* Saturday, Sunday and/or holidays *(fêtes)*. Ticket attendants at Nice station speak English, as do most of the information-desk operators at stations along the coast.

Updated schedules are posted on the TER website at W www.ter-sncf.com/paca; click on the Union Jack in the left-hand corner for English.

Rail Passes

Two regional passes are available to travellers of all ages, from July to September.

The Carte Isabelle costs €10 and is a one-day pass allowing unlimited train travel along the coast between Théoule-sur-Mer and Ventimiglia. Inland, it covers the Nice–Tende train line and local buses in Cagnes-sur-Mer. The pass cannot be used on TGVs and is only cost-cutting if you intend making an inland trip, in addition to visiting several coastal resorts before returning to your original destination. It also allows you to sit in 1st class for no extra supplement – a distinct advantage in July and August when the coastal trains are packed.

The one-day Carte Bermuda (€5), only valid Saturday or Sunday, gives unlimited travel in 2nd class between Marseilles and Miramas on La Côte Bleue (The Blue Coast).

SNCF Information

Ligne Direct (general information)
☎ 08 92 35 35 35 (€0.34 per minute)
Info Trafic (traffic information)
☎ 08 91 67 68 69 (€0.22 per minute)
TER Provence & Côte d'Azur (regional services)
W www.ter-sncf.com/paca
SNCF (national services) W www.sncf.com

Other countrywide SNCF discounts and rail passes (such as the Carte 12-25, Carte Enfant Plus and Carte Sénior) are all available on regional trains. See the 'Rail Passes & Discount Fares' boxed text under Land – Other Parts of France in the Getting There & Away chapter.

Tickets

In most stations, you can buy your ticket at a ticket window or from an automatic, touch screen vending machine *(billetterie automatique)*.

Return tickets *(aller-retour)* are always double the price of their one-way *(aller-simple)* counterparts. Count on paying between €15 and €20 per 100km for short hops with 2nd-class travel. Train fares for specific routes in Provence are included in the relevant regional listings.

Reservations are neither mandatory nor necessary on most regional trains. If you intend travelling on a straight-through train however, say, from Marseilles to Avignon, it is advisable in summer to buy your ticket well in advance. Tickets are valid for two months from the date of purchase; advance reservations are also possible for many trains, meaning you will be assured a seat for the duration of the journey.

Tickets can be purchased on board but cost marginally more. Moreover, unless the ticket window where you boarded was closed (quite often the case in smaller stations in Provence) *and* the station had no ticket machine (rarely the case), pricier prohibitive tariffs apply. Finally, remember to time-stamp your ticket before boarding (see Validating Your Ticket in the Getting There & Away chapter) or you risk a stiff fine.

CAR & MOTORCYCLE

Having your own wheels is the secret to discovering the region's least touched backwaters. Numerous treasures tucked in Haute-Provence's nooks and crannies are impossible to uncover by public transport. Moreover, a car or motorcycle allows you to avail yourself of a wider range of places to stay on city outskirts and in the countryside.

If you're planning to drive along the coast in July or August, be prepared to take hours to move a few kilometres. Inland, mountain roads – with torturous hairpin bends *(lacets)* and dimly lit tunnels – are quiet all year.

In forested areas such as the Massif des Maures, Massif de l'Estérel and Haute-Provence, unpaved roads wend off the main roads into the forest. These tracks are signposted DFCI *(défense forestière contre l'incendie)* and are for fire crews to gain quick entry to the forest when there is a fire: they are strictly off-limits to private vehicles.

Except for the traffic-plagued high season, the Côte d'Azur is easy to navigate by road. Fastest is the A8 *autoroute* which, travelling west to east, from near Aix-en-Provence, approaches the coast at Fréjus, skirts the Estérel range and runs parallel to the coast from Cannes to Ventimiglia. In addition to the *autoroute*, there are three other types of road: *routes nationales* are wide, well signposted highways; *routes départmentales* are local roads; and *chemins communaux* are narrow rural roads.

For distances between towns and cities in the region, and other motoring tips, see Car & Motorcycle in the Getting There & Away chapter.

Documents

Car drivers are required by French law to carry a national ID card or passport; a valid driving permit or licence *(permis de conduire)*; car ownership papers, known as a *carte grise* (grey card); and proof of insurance, called a *carte verte* (green card). If you're stopped by the police and don't have one or more of these documents, you risk a hefty on-the-spot fine. Never leave your car ownership or insurance papers in the vehicle.

Equipment

A reflective warning triangle, to be used in the event of breakdown, must be carried in your car. Recommended accessories – not mandatory in France but recommended in the interests of safety – are a first-aid kit, a spare bulb kit and a fire extinguisher. In the UK, contact the **RAC** *(☎ 0906 470 1470; Ⓦ www.rac.co.uk)* or the **AA** *(☎ 0870 600 0371; Ⓦ www.theaa.com)* for more advice. In other countries, contact the appropriate automobile association.

Road Rules

In France, as throughout continental Europe, people drive on the right side of the road and overtake on the left. Unless otherwise indicated, you must give way to cars coming from the right. North American drivers should remember that turning right on a red light is illegal in France.

Speed Limits Unless otherwise posted, a speed limit of 50km/h applies in all areas designated as built up, no matter how rural they may appear. On intercity roads, you must slow to 50km/h the moment you pass a white sign with red borders on which a place name is written in black or blue letters. This remains in force until you pass an identical sign – but with a red diagonal bar across the name – the other side of town.

Outside built-up areas, speed limits are 90km/h (80km/h if it's raining) on undivided N and D highways, and 110km/h (100km/h in the rain) on dual carriageways (divided highways) or short sections of highway with a divider strip. Speed limits are generally not posted unless they deviate from those mentioned above.

Alcohol French law is tough on drunk drivers and the police do conduct random breathalyser tests to weed out drivers whose blood-alcohol concentration (BAC) is over 0.05% (0.50g per litre of blood). Licences can be suspended.

Road Signs

Common road signs include *sens unique* (one way) and *voie unique* (one-lane road) – prevalent in Haute-Provence where there are numerous narrow bridges. Another handy one to know if you intend motoring along the famous, tunnel-linked corniches is *allumez vos feux* (switch your headlights on) and *fin d'allumage* (switch your headlights off). A sign reading *8 lacets* means there are eight consecutive hairpin bends coming up – a sign that is particularly favoured in the Niçois hinterland and the Roya and Vésubie Valleys.

If you come to a *route barrée* (a closed road), you'll usually also find a yellow panel with instructions for a *déviation* (detour). Signs for *poids lourds* (heavyweights) are meant for lorries (trucks), not cars. The words *sauf riverains* on a no-entry sign mean 'except residents' – common at the foot of most hill-top villages. Road signs with the word *rappel* (remember) featured mean you should already know what the sign is telling you (eg, the speed limit).

Petrol

Petrol *(essence)*, also known as *carburant* (fuel), is expensive in France, incredibly so if you're used to Australian or North American prices. In mid-2002, *sans plomb* (unleaded) petrol (95/98 octane) cost around €1.08/1.10 per litre. *Faire le plein* (filling up) is cheapest at petrol stations on city outskirts and at supermarkets, and most expensive at garages on the *autoroute*.

Parking

Finding a place to park in Nice, Marseilles or any fairly large town or touristy village, is likely to be the single greatest hassle you'll face. Public parking facilities are marked by a white letter 'P' on a blue background. *Payant*, written on the asphalt or on a nearby sign, means you have to pay. Hungry parking meters on the street or in street-level car parks generally swallow around €1.50 per hour. Subterranean, multistorey car parks demand about €2/15 per hour/24 hours. Motorists staying in one city for more than a few days should consider buying a short-stay parking card *(forfait courte durée)*, available at most underground car parks and costing about €50/70 for 5/10 days.

The most touristy hill-top villages have large, purpose-built car parks at their foot where the charge is at least €3 per day (no hourly fee is available), paid to an attendant. On the coast, purpose-built beachside car parks, a waddle away from the sea, cost between €4 and €6.50 a day (again, there's no hourly fee).

Défense de stationner means 'No Parking'.

Accidents

If you're involved in a minor accident with no injuries, the easiest way for drivers to sort things out with their insurance companies is to fill out a Constat Aimable d'Accident Automobile (jointly agreed accident report), known in English as a European Accident Statement. This form is automatically included in documents you get with a rental car (see Car Rental following). Make sure the report includes any details that will help you prove that the accident was not your fault. If problems arise, alert the police (☎ 17).

Car Rental

Although multinational rental agencies such as Avis, Budget, Hertz (which also rents camping cars), Europcar (Europe's largest) or National Citer can be expensive for on-the-spot rental, their prepaid promotional rates are usually reasonable. Fly-drive deals offered by Avis and Europcar are also worth looking into. For quick, walk-in car rental, domestic firms such as Rent-a-Système, Century or ADA usually offer the best rates. In Cannes a handful of firms rent Ferraris, Porsches and other luxury cars, while beach resorts such as Fréjus have electric car hire outlets. Companies are noted in the Getting There & Away sections for individual cities; major firms also have desks at Nice and Marseilles airports.

Most rental companies require the driver to be over 21 years and have had a driving licence for at least one year. The packet of documents you are given should include a 24-hour number to call in case of a breakdown and a European Accident Statement (see under Accidents earlier in this chapter). Check how many 'free' kilometres are in the deal you're offered; *kilométrage illimité* (unlimited mileage) means you can drive to your heart's content.

Insurance *Assurance* (insurance) for damage or injury you cause to other people is mandatory, but things such as collision damage waivers vary greatly from company to company. The policies offered by some small, discount companies may leave you liable for up to €1000 – when comparing rates, the most important thing to check is the *franchise* (excess/deductible). If you're in an accident where you are at fault, or the car is damaged and the party at fault is unknown (eg, someone dents your car while it's parked), or the car is stolen, this is the amount you are liable for before the policy kicks in. In many cases you can pay an extra daily fee (anything from to €15 to €50 per day) and reduce the excess to either zero or a minimal amount.

Rates The big advantage of booking a hire car before leaving home is that you can generally scoop a deal with unlimited mileage for the same (or a cheaper) cost as hiring a vehicle with limited kilometres (about 1500km per week) upon arrival in France.

At the time of writing, a three-door Opel Corsa booked through **Avis** *(☎ 0870 60 60 100; Ⓦ www.avis.co.uk)* in the UK, including unlimited mileage, costs UK£122 per week. **Budget** *(☎ 01442-280 181; W www.budget.co.uk)* was offering a similar deal for about UK£136, while **Europcar** *(☎ 0870 607 5000; W www.europcar.co.uk)* quoted UK£137. The company **Autos Abroad** *(☎ 0870 066 7788; W www.autosabroad.co.uk)* charged a standard rate of UK£139/149 per week October to June/July to September for a three-door Citroën Saxo, but guarantees to beat its competitors' rates.

Within the region, the cost for an equivalent small car for a day/week (including 250/1750km) rented from National Citer in St-Tropez was €75/268. For exactly the same deal, Budget charged €71/256.

All major rental companies accept payment by credit card. They also require a *caution* (deposit); most ask you to leave a signed credit card slip without a sum written on it as a deposit. If you don't like this arrangement, ask them to make out two credit card slips: one for the sum of the rental; the other for the sum of the excess. Make sure to have the latter destroyed when you return the car.

Motorcycle

Provence is superb country for motorcycle touring. Make sure your wet-weather gear is up to scratch in spring and autumn. Easy riders caught bareheaded can be fined and have their bike confiscated. Bikes of more than 125cc must have their headlights on during the day. No special licence is required to ride a scooter with an engine capacity of 50cc or less.

To rent a scooter or *moto* (motorcycle) you have to leave a deposit of several hundred euro, which you forfeit (up to the value of the damage) if you're in an accident and it's your fault. Since insurance companies won't cover theft, you'll also lose the deposit if the bike is stolen. Most places accept deposits made by credit card, travellers cheques or Eurocheques. Expect to pay about €25/50 per day for a 50/125cc scooter and €50/95/120 per day for a 125/600/1100cc motorcycle. Rental rates usually include hire of the helmet *(casque)*.

Provence Moto Évasion *(☎/fax 04 93 58 77 58; W www.provencemotoevasion.com; 846 chemin de la Sine, F-06140 Vence)* organises motorcycle tours of Provence. The weekend/five-day tours typically cost in the region of €396/1051 per person. Fees include bikes, helmets, luggage assistance, two-star hotel accommodation and a motorcycle guide.

In 2002, the **Service Loisirs Accueil Bouches du Rhône** *(☎ 04 90 59 49 36, fax 04 90 59 16 75; W www.visitprovence.com; 13 rue Roux de Brignoles, F-13006 Marseilles)* was offering a three-/six-day discovery tour around Provence on a two-person 125cc scooter costing €185/409 per person (€113/273 single room supplement), plus €765 deposit. Rates include half-board accommodation (breakfast and dinner included), scooter hire and petrol.

BICYCLE

Provence – particularly the Lubéron – is an eminently cyclable region, thanks to its extensive network of inland secondary and tertiary roads, which carry relatively light traffic (compared to the coast). These back roads, a good number of which date from the 19th century or earlier, are an ideal vantage point from which to view Provence's celebrated rural landscapes, be it lavender fields, vineyards or olive groves. Cycling in national parks in Provence (Mercantour and Port-Cros) is forbidden.

By law, your bicycle must have two functioning brakes, a bell, a red reflector on the back and yellow reflectors on the pedals. After sunset and when visibility is poor, cyclists must turn on a white light in front and a red one in the rear.

Bicycles are not allowed on most local and intercity buses, but you can take them on local TER trains in the Provence-Alpes-Côte d'Azur region, except in peak times – 7am to 9am and 4.30pm to 6.30pm wekdays.

For information on transporting bicycles by train on the national network, see the Train section under Land in the Getting There & Away chapter.

Cycling Organisations

The volunteer-run **Fédération Française de Cyclotourisme** *(FFTC; ☎ 01 44 16 88 88; 8 rue Jean-Marie Jégo, F-75013 Paris)* liaises between 3100-odd cycling clubs in France, and can send you a free packet of general information in English. It also sells touring itineraries, cycling maps and topoguides for cyclists, and organises bicycle trips and tours that are open to nonmembers.

For members, the **Cyclists' Touring Club** *(CTC; ☎ 0870 873 0060, fax 0870 873 0064;*

www.ctc.org.uk; Cotterell House, 69 Meadrow, Godalming, Surrey GU7 3HS, UK) has a free information sheet on cycling in France, as well as touring notes and itineraries for some 70 routes around the country, including several in Provence. The CTC also offers tips on bikes, spares and insurance; it sells maps and topoguides by mail order.

See the Activities section in the Facts for the Visitor chapter for more two-wheeling information. The Organised Tours section in the Getting There & Away chapter contains information on cycling tours.

Rental

You can hire a mountain bike *(vélo tout-terrain; VTT)* in most towns and resorts for about €15 per day. Most places have children's bikes and some – particularly in the Lubéron and in coastal areas – have tandems and *remorques* (covered buggies which energetic parents can pedal their little kids along in). A deposit of €150 to €300 is usuallyrequired, which you forfeit if the bike is damaged or stolen. In general, deposits can be made in cash, with signed travellers cheques or by credit card (a passport often suffices). Rental shops are listed in the Getting Around sections of individual city and town listings.

Never leave your bicycle locked up outside overnight if you want to see it or most of its parts again.

HITCHING

Hitching is never entirely safe in any country in the world, and we don't recommend it. Travellers who decide to hitch should understand that they are taking a small but potentially serious risk. People who do choose to hitch will be safer if they travel in pairs and let someone know where they are planning to go.

The student-inspired **Ecotrajet** *(☎ 06 73 88 35 54; www.ecotrajet.com)* puts people looking for rides in touch with drivers going to the same destination: There are no cover charges; you simply split the cost of the trip with the driver and other passengers.

BOAT

Yacht

Among the Côte d'Azur's largest pleasure ports *(ports de plaisance)* are Port Vauban in Antibes and Port Camargue in La Grau du Roi which, with 4350 moorings, claims to be Europe's biggest.

Yachts can be hired at most marinas along the coast, including the less-pompous sailing centres at Ste-Maxime and Le Lavandou. In Antibes and Juan-les-Pins, there are some 20-odd outlets where yachts can be hired with/without a crew. A complete list of yacht rental places is included in the free booklet *Nautisme: Côte d'Azur Riviera* published by the Comité Régional du Tourisme Riviera Côte d'Azur, available from tourist offices.

For up-to-date marina or harbour master information, contact the **Fédération Française des Ports de Plaisance** *(FFPP; ☎ 01 43 35 26 26; www.ffports-plaisance.com; 9 rue Léopold Robert, F-75001 Paris)*. Follow the links on its website to get a full listing of ports in the Provence and Côte d'Azur region (in French only).

Ferry

A plethora of boats ply the waters from the shores of the Côte d'Azur to its various off-shore islands. Daily ferries sail to the Îles de Lérins from Cannes (year round), from Juan-les-Pins (May to October) and Vallauris-Golfe Juan (May to October).

To get to Port-Cros, the national park in the Îles d'Hyères archipelago, you can take a boat from Le Lavandou or Hyères (year round); Toulon, Ste-Maxime or St-Tropez (June to September); and Port Miramar, La Croix-Valmer or Cavalaire-sur-Mer (July and August).

Its bare little sister, Île du Levant, is accessible by boat from Le Lavandou and Hyères (year round), or Port Miramar, La Croix-Valmer and Cavalaire-sur-Mer (July and August). Porquerolles, the last in the Hyères trio, is served by a regular passenger ferry from Le Lavandou and Hyères (year round); Toulon, Ste-Maxime or St-Tropez (June to September); and Port Miramar, La Croix Valmer and Cavalaire (July and August).

The Paul Ricard islands near Bandol and Toulon are equally well served by ferry. Boats to Île de Bendor depart year round from Bandol, while ferries to the larger Île des Embiez depart from Le Brusc (year round) and Sanary-sur-Mer (June to September). From Marseilles, there are plenty of boats to the Îles du Frioul.

From St-Tropez there are additional boat services to/from St-Raphaël (April to July),

Port Grimaud (June to mid-September) and Ste-Maxime (April to November).

In season, soulless boat excursions aimed solely at tourists, often with blaring music and always with loud recorded commentaries, service most hot spots along the Côte d'Azur.

Canal Boat

One of the most relaxing ways to see the region's most southeastern corner is to rent a houseboat for a leisurely cruise along the Camargue's canals and navigable rivers. Boats usually accommodate two to 12 passengers and can be rented on a weekly basis. Anyone over 18 can pilot a river boat without a licence, and learning the ropes takes about half an hour. The speed limit is 6km/h on canals and 10km/h on rivers. The tourist cruising season runs March to November.

To get a boat in July and August, reservations must be made several months ahead. In the region, boats can be rented through **Rive de France** *(☎ 04 66 53 81 21, fax 04 66 51 02 61; Ⓦ www.rive-de-france.tm.fr; Péniche St-Louis, route de Grau de Roi, F-30220 Aigues-Mortes)*. Rates start at €1022 (€1715 in July and August) per week or €511 (March to June and September to November only) per weekend for a six-berth boat.

Route Marine *(☎ 04 78 39 13 06, fax 04 78 29 94 85; Ⓔ info@route-marine.fr; Ⓦ www.route-marine.fr; 5 rue Gentil, F-69002 Lyon)* is another French boat specialist. It runs eight-day cruises, March to November, departing from Avignon aboard the 71-cabin *Princesse de Provence* or 50-cabin *MS Cézanne*.

Self-cruising boats can also be hired through **Crown Blue Line Camargue** *(☎ 04 66 87 22 66, fax 04 66 87 15 20; Ⓦ www.crownblueline.com; 2 quai du Canal, F-30800 St-Gilles)*. You board at St-Gilles, 19km south of Nîmes, from where you cruise along the Canal du Rhône to Aigues-Mortes and farther west to the Toulouse area. Eastbound, you can cruise in three or four hours as far as Beaucaire and Tarascon, south of Avignon.

Boats can be booked in the UK through **Crown Travel** *(☎ 01603-630 513, fax 01603-664 298; Ⓔ boating@crownblueline.co.uk; 8 Ber Street, Norwich NR1 3EJ)*. The weekly rates for a boat that will cater for six people start at €1520/2034/2338 during low/mid/high season.

UK-based self-cruising boating specialists abroad operating in the region include the following.

French Country Cruises (☎ 01572-821 330, fax 01571-821 072, Ⓔ abrock3650@aol.com) Andrew Brock Travel, 29A Main Street, Lyddington, Oakham, Rutland LE15 9LR, UK. Brock Travel, an agent for French Country Cruises, offers one-/two-week and 10-day holidays in the Camargue aboard a *pénichette* (glass-fibre canal cruiser). Boat hire starts at UK£441 per week for a two-person *pénichette*, not including running costs (an additional UK£90 to UK£160 per week).

Hoseasons (☎ 01502-502 588, fax 01502-514 298, Ⓦ www.hoseasons.co.uk) Sunway House, Lowestoft, Suffolk NR32 2LW, UK. The company has boats moored in Beaucaire, from where a southbound voyage to Aigues-Mortes (137km) takes one week.

From Avignon, Beaucaire, Tarascon, Aigues-Mortes and Arles, there are plenty of river excursions organised along the Rhône (see the Organised Tours sections in regional chapters).

LOCAL TRANSPORT

Getting around cities and towns in Provence is a straightforward affair, thanks to excellent public transport systems. Marseilles is the only city in the region to have a metro; tramways are planned for Nice and Toulon. Details of routes, fares, tourist passes and so on are available at tourist offices and local bus company information counters; see Getting Around at the end of each city and town listing.

Taxis are generally expensive. Most towns have a taxi rank in front of the train station. Count on paying between €0.50 and €1.50 per kilometre depending on the time of day and distance you are travelling. Rates to/from the city centre and any airport are criminally expensive.

ORGANISED TOURS

Most organised tours home in on the region's most frequented resorts and sights, many of which are well served by public transport. Tourist offices and reception desks in bigger hotels in larger towns and cities – such as Avignon, Aix-en-Provence, Nice and Marseilles – take bookings for a wealth of half- and full-day excursions which, though more expensive might be of interest to travellers with limited time.

Longer tours focusing on the great outdoors include the following.

AET Nature (☎/fax 04 93 04 47 64, W www.aetcanyoning.com) Le Foussa, 392 chemin de Foussa, F-06540 Breil-sur-Roya. An outdoor-activity specialist in Haute-Provence, operated by experienced mountain guides. Offers two-/four-day canyoning and other white-water sporting expeditions with *gîte d'étape* accommodation, costing €118/265 in low/high season.

Destination Merveilles (☎/fax 04 93 73 09 07, W www.destinations-merveilles.com) 10 rue des Mesures, F-06270 Villeneuve-Loubet. Imaginative, six-day walks from the mountains to the sea through the Alpes d'Azur and plenty of hill-top villages. A six-day lake-to-lake tour in the Mercantour national park, for example, costs €434 per person, including 'full board' in mountain huts.

Provence Grandeur Nature (☎ 04 90 76 68 27, fax 04 90 76 65 13, W www.provence-gr-nature.com) 203 rue Oscar Roulet, F-84440 Robion. This nature specialist organises fascinating, imaginative and alternative tours of Provence's lavender fields, truffle 'fields', vineyards, private and hidden gardens and other 'green' nuggets (from €400 for four days). It also runs walking and cycling tours (from €222/476 for four/seven days).

Service Loisirs Accueil Bouches du Rhône (☎ 04 90 59 49 36, fax 04 90 59 16 75, W www.visitprovence.com) 13 rue Roux de Brignoles, F-13006 Marseilles. Two-day impressionist-painting courses (€247), three-day explorations of Marseilles' *calanques* and islands in a sea kayak (€358) and four-day courses in Provençal quilting and natural dyeing (€150 to €379) are but some of the imaginative packages offered by the Bouches du Rhône tourist board.

Rando Lavande (☎ 04 92 32 27 44, 06 12 73 43 70, e bietrix@free.fr) 7 rue de Provence, D-04000 Digne-les-Bains. A small mountaineering and walking outfit led by experienced mountain guide Jean-Louis Bietrix. A seven-day hike in the Mercantour mountains, with mountain hut accommodation, costs €472; backpacks are carried by four-wheel vehicle.

Var Tours (☎ 04 94 54 78 91, fax 04 94 54 03 80) ave Georges Clémenceau, Cogolin. Runs numerous coach tours, with several coastal pick-up points including ones in Toulon, Hyères, Le Lavandou, Ste-Maxime and Fréjus. Sample itineraries include the Gorges du Verdon (€21/39 without/with lunch), Cassis' *calanques* (€28/44 without/with lunch), an evening in St-Tropez (€12/32 without/with lunch) and France's largest prehistory museum in Quinson (€38/56 without/with lunch). Most tourist offices in the Var take bookings for these coach tours.

Marseilles Area

The urban geography and rough-and-tumble atmosphere of Marseilles, utterly atypical of Provence, are a function of the diversity of its inhabitants, many of whom are immigrants (or their children and grandchildren) from Greece, Italy, Armenia, Spain, North Africa, West Africa and Indochina.

Cynics reckon the port city's 'centre' lies 15km-odd north in graceful Aix-en-Provence (pronounced like the letter 'x') where Marseilles' rich and wealthy live in luxurious mansions alongside a harmonious fusion of majestic public squares, shaded avenues and mossy, century-old fountains. Aix's eastern edge is flanked by the Montagne Ste-Victoire, immortalised on canvas by Cézanne in the 19th century.

Marseilles' southern tip is kissed by some of France's most dramatic coastline. From Callelongue on the true city outskirts, a series of sharp-ridged, overhanging rocks known as Les Calanques (literally 'rocky inlets') plunge south to sweet Cassis, known for its wine, and La Ciotat, known for its shipyards.

West is something of an eyesore. Rapid industrialisation has polluted the water and fast encroached upon the land surrounding the Étang de Berre, a salty, 6m-deep pool which – with a surface area of 15,530 hectares and volume of 900 million cubic metres – is Europe's largest brine lake.

Salon de Provence, 10km north of the Étang de Berre and 37km west of Aix-en-Provence, marks the boundary between the soft green and purple hues of Pays d'Aix (literally 'Aix Country') and the savage cut of the barren Crau plains in the lower Rhône Valley.

Highlights

- Eye up the catch of the day at Marseilles' portside fish market and discover the city's revitalised docklands
- Walk, dive or take a boat trip around Les Calanques; lunch between rocks at La Baie des Singes and dance beneath stars at La Maronaise, both on Cap Croisette
- Tour Aix-en-Provence's fountains, museums and *hôtels particuliers* followed by a pastis at Les Deux Garçons
- See what inspired Cézanne in Aix-en-Provence and neighbouring Montagne Ste-Victoire
- Explore Cap Canaille and the panoramic route des Crètes

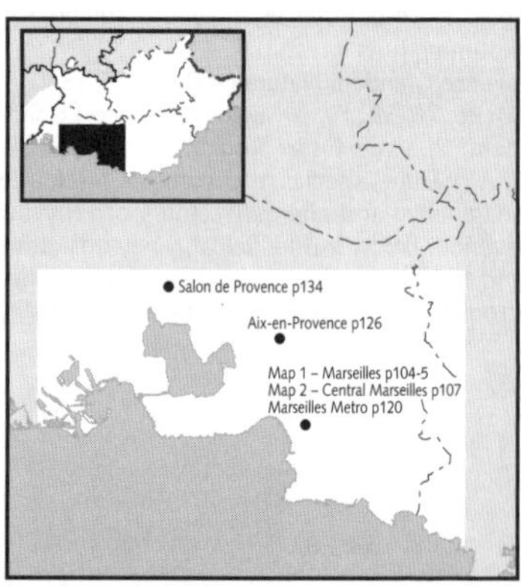

Food Highlights

supions frits – pan-fried squid with garlic and parsley at Marseilles' Pizzaria Étienne
bouillabaisse – a traditional Provençal fish stew
calissons – Aixois almond-paste sweets
pastis – an aniseed-flavoured spirit drunk as an aperitif

Marseilles

postcode 13001 (poste restante)
• pop 798,430

The cosmopolitan port of Marseilles (Marseille in French; Marsihès in Provençal) is Provence's largest city (and France's second). Notorious in the 1980s and 1990s for organised crime and racial tensions, the city has since gained a new dynamism. Far from being seen as the hellhole it once was, modern Marseilles – with its rejuvenated old quarters, warehouses-turned-nightclubs, cutting-edge music scene, cultural centres and clutch of art museums – is a happening place to be. Tell anyone in France you're off to La Canebière and they'll know instantly which city you mean.

Visitors who enjoy exploring on foot will be rewarded with more sights, sounds, smells

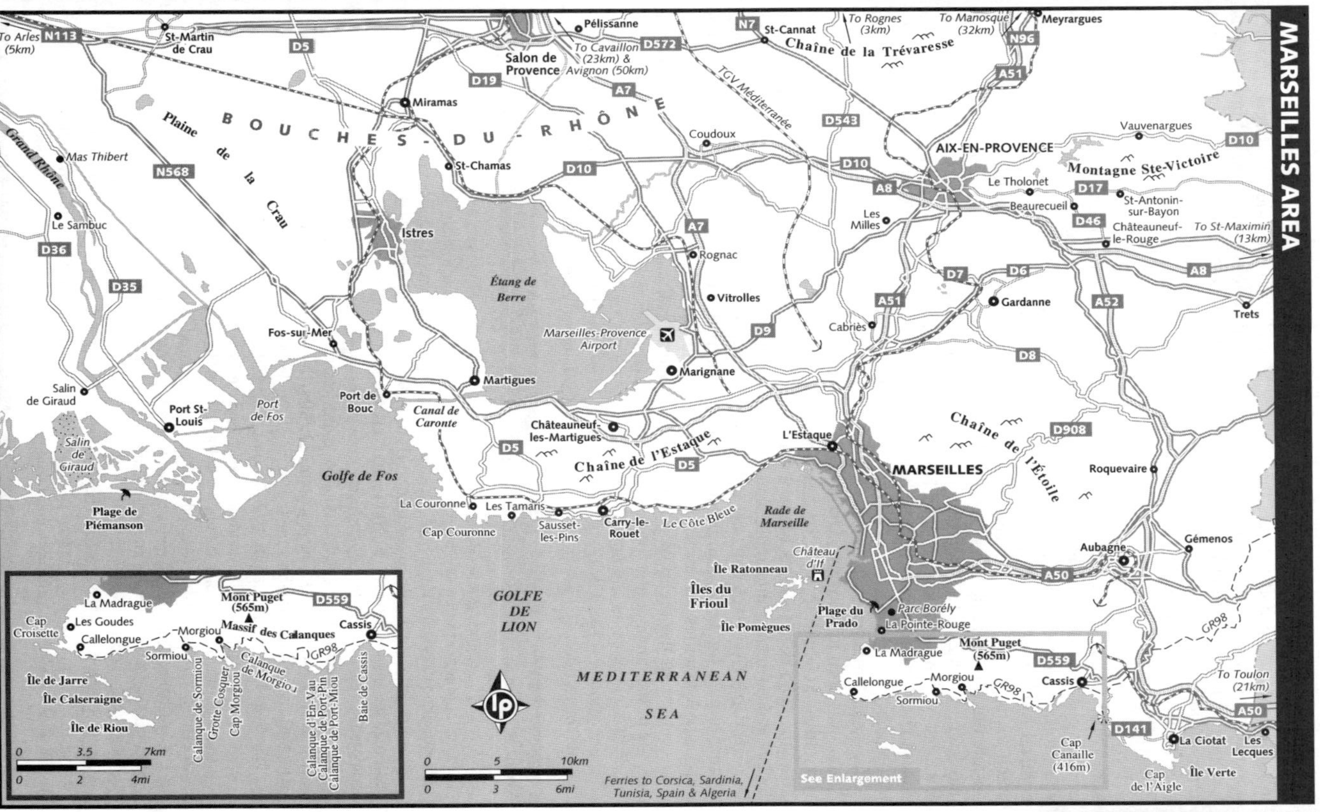
MARSEILLES AREA
AIX-EN-PROVENCE
MARSEILLES
Montagne Ste-Victoire
Chaîne de la Trévaresse
Chaîne de l'Étoile
Chaîne de l'Estaque
Vauvenargues
Meyrargues
To Manosque (32km)
To Rognes (3km)
To St-Maximin (13km)
St-Antonin-sur-Bayon
Châteauneuf-le-Rouge
Beaurecueil
Le Tholonet
Trets
Gardanne
Roquevaire
Gémenos
Aubagne
To Toulon (21km)
Les Lecques
La Ciotat
Île Verte
Cap de l'Aigle
Cap Canaille (416m)
Cassis
Mont Puget (565m)
Morgiou
Sormiou
La Madrague
Callelongue
Parc Borély
La Pointe-Rouge
Plage du Prado
Château d'If
See Enlargement
Les Milles
Cabriès
L'Estaque
Rade de Marseille
Île Ratonneau
Îles du Frioul
Île Pomègues
St-Cannat
TGV Méditerranée
Vitrolles
Coudoux
Rognac
Marignane
Marseilles-Provence Airport
Le Côte Bleue
MEDITERRANEAN SEA
Ferries to Corsica, Sardinia, Tunisia, Spain & Algeria
Pélissanne
To Cavaillon (23km) & Avignon (50km)
Salon de Provence
BOUCHES-DU-RHÔNE
Châteauneuf-les-Martigues
Carry-le-Rouet
Sausset-les-Pins
Les Tamaris
Étang de Berre
Martigues
St-Chamas
Miramas
Istres
Canal de Caronte
La Couronne
Cap Couronne
GOLFE DE LION
Port de Bouc
Golfe de Fos
Fos-sur-Mer
Port de Fos
Plaine de la Crau
St-Martin de Crau
Port St-Louis
Plage de Piémanson
Mas Thibert
Le Sambuc
Salin de Giraud
Grand Rhône
To Arles (5km)
Baie de Cassis
Calanque de Port-Miou
Calanque de Port-Pin
Calanque d'En-Vau
Calanque de Morgiou
Massif des Calanques
Cap Morgiou
Grotte Cosquer
Calanque de Sormiou
Les Goudes
Cap Croisette
Île de Jarre
Île Calseraigne
Île de Riou
0 5 10km
0 3 6mi
0 3.5 7km
0 2 4mi

and big-city commotion than anywhere else in the region. Its seaport remains the most important in France and the third-largest in Europe (after Antwerp and Rotterdam), and super-speed rail tracks place Marseilles just three hours from Paris and four hours from Brussels by train.

Despite this level of development, Marseilles' high unemployment rate (up to 30% in some quarters) is impossible to ignore as you stroll the city's streets, as is its dubious political leaning, which for years was very much to the right. Neighbouring Vitrolles ousted out its extreme-right xenophobic mayor in late 2002, but a member of the fascist Front National (National Front; FN) continues to hold the mayoralty in neighbouring Marignane.

Provençal writer and film maker Marcel Pagnol was born in Aubagne, 16km east of Marseilles. Senegalese novelist Sembène Ousmane, who portrayed his life as a black docker and African ghetto inhabitant in *Le Docker Noir* (The Black Docker, 1956), is another literary figure who turned to rough-and-ready Marseilles for inspiration in the 20th century. In the realm of popular culture, the best-known contemporary product 'made in Marseilles' is champion footballer Zinedine Zidane – the world's most expensive player to boot.

HISTORY

Massalia was founded by Greek mariners from Phocaea (a city in Asia Minor) around 600 BC. The city backed Pompey the Great in the 1st century BC, prompting Caesar's forces to capture the city in 49 BC and exact revenge by confiscating its fleet and directing Roman trade elsewhere. Massalia retained its status as a free port and was, for a while, the last western centre of Greek learning. But the city soon declined. It was revived in the 10th century by the counts of Provence.

Marseilles was pillaged by the Aragonese in 1423, but the greatest calamity in its history was in 1720, when the plague – carried by a merchant vessel from Syria – killed some 50,000 of the city's 90,000 inhabitants. Under French rule, the Marseillais quickly gained a rebellious reputation. It is after them that France's national anthem is named (see the Facts about Provence chapter).

In the 19th century, Marseilles grew prosperous from colonial trade. Commerce with North Africa grew rapidly after the French occupation of Algeria in 1830, and maritime opportunities expanded further when the Suez Canal opened in 1869. During WWII, Marseilles was bombed by the Germans and Italians in 1940 and by the Allies between 1943 and 1944 following Nazi Germany's invasion of Vichy France in 1942. The city was

Docklands

Nowhere is the sparkling rejuvenation of the city's notoriously tatty squats and districts more explicit than in Euroméditerranée, a 15-year project which will see €3.05 billion poured into Marseilles' downtrodden docklands (La Joliette Quarter) and train station area (St-Charles Quarter).

Unemployment in these two central districts (population 28,000) currently stands at 30%. By 2010, Euroméditerranée will create 15,000 to 20,000 new jobs, 4000 homes and 800,000 sq metres of commercial real estate. The two districts' green recreational areas will have doubled in size.

At the docklands, offices and a couple of trendy restaurants have already moved into Les Docks, a former warehouse on place de la Joliette. By 2004, the old grain stores on quai d'Arenc will house a theatre and restaurant with stunning views of the Îles du Frioul, and a tramway will link place de la Joliette and place Sadi Carnot. In 2008 lumbering Fort St-Jean will house a new Musée des Civilisations de l'Europe et de la Méditerranée (to replace, much to many people's horror, the National Museum of Arts and Popular Traditions, in Paris since 1937); and a Centre de la Mer (Sea Centre), with exhibitions of seafaring Marseilles, is being considered for the waterside quarter.

The St-Charles Quarter of town is to be the site of a new Grand Halle (Grand Hall) at the train station (by 2004); the country's first national Internet school (by 2005); and an alternative and fabulous cultural centre, known as La Friche la Belle de Mai, in an old tobacco factory and sugar-refining plant at 23 rue Guibal and 41 rue Jobin. The cultural centre will house theatrical and artists' workshops, dance and film studios, and a couple of radio stations (Radio Grenouille on 88.8FM and Radio Galère on 88.4FM). Multimedia and exhibition halls are among the innovative spaces that are housed here.

freed by Allied troops, led by French Général de Lattre de Tassigny on 28 August 1944.

ORIENTATION

The city's main thoroughfare, the famed wide boulevard La Canebière, stretches east from the Vieux Port (old port). The train station is north of La Canebière at the northern end of blvd d'Athènes. A few blocks south of La Canebière is cours Julien, a pedestrian square dominated by a water garden and palm trees, and lined with cafés, restaurants and theatres. Marseilles' commercial heart is around rue Paradis. The ferry terminal is west of place de la Joliette, a few minutes' walk north from the Nouvelle Cathédrale de la Major.

Marseilles is divided into 16 *arrondissements* (districts); most travellers mingle in the first (1er), second (2e), sixth (6e) and seventh (7e). Places mentioned have the district, together with the metro stop, listed after the street address. Locally, everything north of the old port is known as the Quartier Nord (northern quarter) and everything south, the Quartier Sud (southern quarter).

Items referred to on the maps are cross-referenced in the text. Map 1 refers you to the Marseilles map, Map 2 to the Central Marseilles map.

INFORMATION

Tourist Offices

The **tourist office** *(Map 2; ☎ 04 91 13 89 00, fax 04 91 13 89 20; W www.marseille-tourisme.com; 4 La Canebière, 1er; metro Vieux Port; open 9am-7.30pm Mon-Sat, 10am-6pm Sun July-Sept, 9am-7pm Mon-Sat, 10am-5pm Sun Oct-June)* distributes free maps and organises fascinating guided tours (see Organised Tours later). Its annexes at the train station and on place des Pistoles in Le Panier open shorter hours.

For tourist information about Bouches-du-Rhône *département* (department), head to the **Comité Départemental du Tourisme** *(Map 1; ☎ 04 91 13 84 13, fax 04 91 33 01 82; W www.visitprovence.com; Le Montesquieu bldg, 13 rue Roux de Brignoles, 6e; metro Estrangin-Préfecture)*.

Money

There are several banks and exchange bureaus west of the old port (metro Vieux Port) on La Canebière, 1er, including American Express agent, **Canebière Change** *(Map 2; ☎ 04 91 13 71 26; 39 La Canebière, 1er; metro Vieux Port)* inside Canebière Voyages.

Post & Communications

Marseilles' postcode is 130 plus the arrondissement number (for example, postcode 13001 for addresses in the 1st arrondissement, 1er). The central **post office** *(Map 2; 1 place de l'Hôtel des Postes, 1er; metro Colbert; open 8am-7pm Mon-Wed & Fri, 8.30am-7pm Thur, 8am-noon Sat)* has Cyberposte.

At the port, **Info Café** *(Map 2; ☎ 04 91 33 74 98; W www info-cafe.com; 1 quai de Rive Neuve, 1er; metro Vieux Port; open 9am-10pm Mon-Sat, 2.30pm-7.30pm Sun)* charges €1.50/2/3.80 for up to 17/30/60 minutes.

Along cours Julien, try **Le Rézo** *(Map 1; ☎ 04 91 42 70 02; e lerezo@lerezo.com; 68 cours Julien, 6e; metro Notre Dame du Mont-Cours Julien; open 10am-8pm Mon-Thur, 10am-midnight Fri & Sat)*, which charges €1.50/4.60 per 10/60 minutes, or the neighbouring **Bug's Café** *(Map 1; ☎ 04 96 12 53 43; 80 cours Julien; open 10am-11pm Mon-Sat, 2pm-7pm Sun)*.

Travel Agencies

Voyages Wasteels *(Map 2; ☎ 08 25 88 70 46; e marseille@wasteels.fr; 67 La Canebière, 1er; metro Noailles; open 9.15am-12.15pm & 2pm-6pm Mon-Fri, 9.30am-12.30pm Sat)* also caters to ISIC holders.

Bookshops

Librairie Lamy *(Map 2; ☎ 04 91 33 57 07; 26 rue Paradis, 1er; metro Vieux Port; open 9.30am-7pm Mon-Sat)* stocks an excellent selection of English-language novels.

Seafaring books, maps and guides are sold at **Librairie Maritime et Outremer** *(Map 2; ☎ 04 91 54 79 26; 26 quai de Rive Neuve, 1er; metro Vieux Port)*, founded in 1838. Closer to the metro stop, the **Maison de la Presse** *(Map 2; 29 quai des Belges, 1er; metro Vieux Port)* is unbeatable for English-language newspapers, magazines and local guides.

Laundry

It costs €3.50/5 to wash a 7/10kg load at **La Savonnerie** *(Map 2; 5 rue Breteuil, 1er; metro Vieux Port; open 6.30am-8pm daily)*.

Medical Services & Emergency

The **Anglo-American pharmacy** *(Map 2; 37 La Canebière; metro Vieux Port; open 8am-8pm*

MAP 1 – MARSEILLES (MARSEILLE)

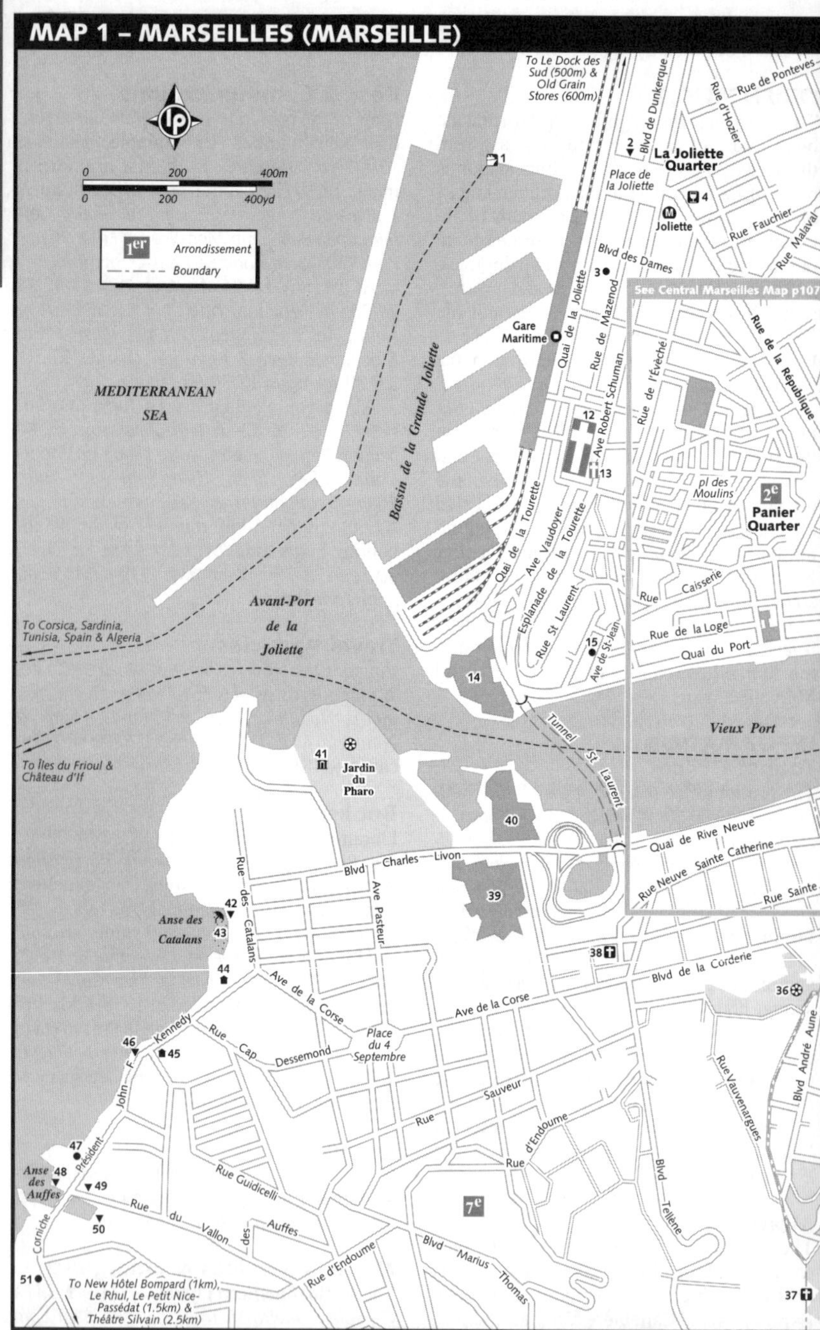

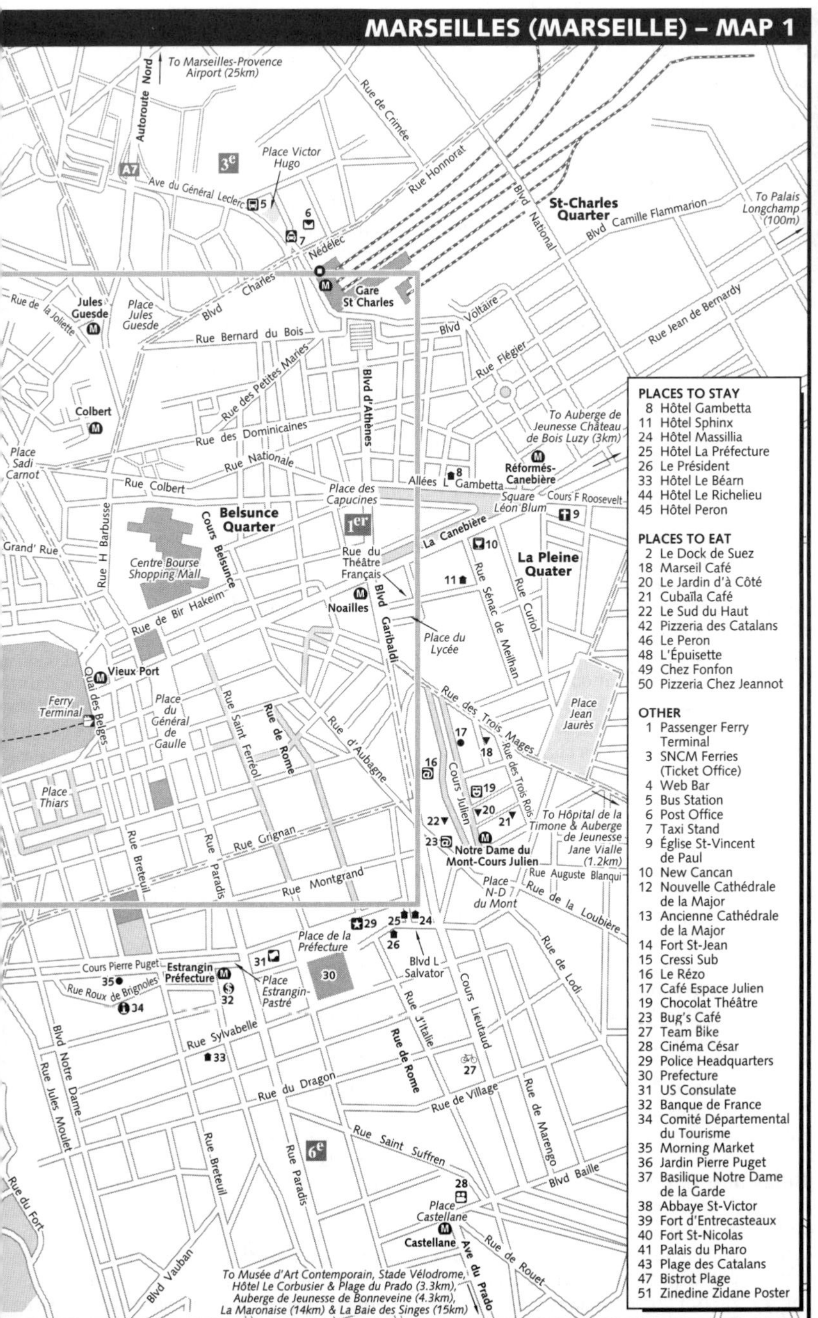
MARSEILLES (MARSEILLE) – MAP 1
To Marseilles-Provence Airport (25km)
Autoroute Nord
A7
3e
Place Victor Hugo
Ave du Général Leclerc
Rue de Crimée
Rue Honnorat
Nédélec
Blvd Charles
Blvd National
St-Charles Quarter
Blvd Camille Flammarion
To Palais Longchamp (100m)
Gare St Charles
Rue de la Joliette
Jules Guesde
Place Jules Guesde
Rue Bernard du Bois
Blvd Voltaire
Rue Jean de Bernardy
Rue des Petites Maries
Blvd d'Athènes
Rue Flégier
Colbert
Rue des Dominicaines
To Auberge de Jeunesse Château de Bois Luzy (3km)
Place Sadi Carnot
Rue Nationale
Réformés-Canebière
Rue Colbert
Place des Capucines
Allées L Gambetta
Square Léon Blum
Cours F Roosevelt
Belsunce Quarter
1er
Cours Belsunce
La Canebière
Grand' Rue
Rue H Barbusse
Centre Bourse Shopping Mall
Rue du Théâtre Français
La Pleine Quater
Rue Sénac de Meilhan
Rue Curiol
Rue de Bir Hakeim
Noailles
Blvd Garibaldi
Place du Lycée
Vieux Port
Quai des Belges
Ferry Terminal
Place du Général de Gaulle
Rue Saint Ferréol
Rue de Rome
Rue d'Aubagne
Rue des Trois Mages
Place Jean Jaurès
Rue des Trois Rois
Cours Julien
Place Thiars
Rue Grignan
To Hôpital de la Timone & Auberge de Jeunesse Jane Vialle (1.2km)
Notre Dame du Mont-Cours Julien
Rue Breteuil
Rue Paradis
Rue Montgrand
Rue Auguste Blanqui
Place N-D du Mont
Rue de la Loubière
Place de la Préfecture
Blvd L Salvator
Rue de Lodi
Cours Pierre Puget
Estrangin-Préfecture
Rue Roux de Brignoles
Place Estrangin-Pastré
Rue d'Italie
Cours Lieutaud
Rue Sylvabelle
Blvd Notre Dame
Rue Jules Moulet
Rue du Dragon
Rue de Village
Rue de Marengo
Rue Saint Suffren
6e
Blvd Baille
Rue du Fort
Place Castellane
Castellane
Ave du Prado
Rue de Rouet
Blvd Vauban
To Musée d'Art Contemporain, Stade Vélodrome, Hôtel Le Corbusier & Plage du Prado (3.3km), Auberge de Jeunesse de Bonneveine (4.3km), La Maronaise (14km) & La Baie des Singes (15km)
PLACES TO STAY
8 Hôtel Gambetta
11 Hôtel Sphinx
24 Hôtel Massillia
25 Hôtel La Préfecture
26 Le Président
33 Hôtel Le Béarn
44 Hôtel Le Richelieu
45 Hôtel Peron
PLACES TO EAT
2 Le Dock de Suez
18 Marseil Café
20 Le Jardin d'à Côté
21 Cubaïla Café
22 Le Sud du Haut
42 Pizzeria des Catalans
46 Le Peron
48 L'Épuisette
49 Chez Fonfon
50 Pizzeria Chez Jeannot
OTHER
1 Passenger Ferry Terminal
3 SNCM Ferries (Ticket Office)
4 Web Bar
5 Bus Station
6 Post Office
7 Taxi Stand
9 Église St-Vincent de Paul
10 New Cancan
12 Nouvelle Cathédrale de la Major
13 Ancienne Cathédrale de la Major
14 Fort St-Jean
15 Cressi Sub
16 Le Rézo
17 Café Espace Julien
19 Chocolat Théâtre
23 Bug's Café
27 Team Bike
28 Cinéma César
29 Police Headquarters
30 Prefecture
31 US Consulate
32 Banque de France
34 Comité Départemental du Tourisme
35 Morning Market
36 Jardin Pierre Puget
37 Basilique Notre Dame de la Garde
38 Abbaye St-Victor
39 Fort d'Entrecasteaux
40 Fort St-Nicolas
41 Palais du Pharo
43 Plage des Catalans
47 Bistrot Plage
51 Zinedine Zidane Poster

daily) has long opening hours. A list of others that open late and on Sunday is pinned outside the tourist office.

Hôpital de la Timone *(off Map 1; ☎ 04 91 38 60 00; 264 rue St-Pierre, 5e; metro La Timone)* is 1.2km southwest of place Jean Jaurès.

The **police headquarters** *(Préfecture de Police; Map 1; ☎ 04 91 39 80 00; place de la Préfecture, 1er; metro Estrangin-Préfecture)* is open 24 hours.

AROUND THE VIEUX PORT

Vieux Port & Le Panier

Marseilles grew around the Vieux Port, where ships have docked for at least 26 centuries. The main commercial docks were transferred to the Joliette area on the coast north of here in the 1840s, but the old port remains active as a harbour for fishing boats, pleasure yachts and ferries to Château d'If. The harbour entrance is guarded by **Fort St-Nicolas** (on the southern side) and, across the water, **Fort St-Jean**, founded in the 13th century by the Knights Hospitaller of St John of Jerusalem. In 2008 a national **Musée des Civilisations de l'Europe et de la Méditerranée** (Museum of European & Mediterranean Civilisations) will open inside the lumbering **Fort St-Jean** as part of the Euroméditeranée project (see the boxed text 'Docklands' earlier in this chapter).

Marseilles' 17th-century **town hall** dominates quai du Port, the port's northern quay. The Musée des Docks Romains and Musée du Vieux Marseille are a two-minute walk from here, as is the increasingly trendy quarter of Le Panier (literally 'the basket') which slinks uphill from the quayside. This neighbourhood – a now seedy area that once had a strong Resistance presence – was dynamited by the Germans in 1943, and rebuilt after the war. Several windmills used to stand on pretty **Place des Moulins**, which lies at the heart of this so-called 'Montmartre of Marseilles'. Atop the hill sits the impressive Centre de la Vieille Charité and its museums.

Belsunce & La Pleine

La Canebière – derived from the Provençal word *canebe*, meaning 'hemp', after Marseilles' rope industry – stretches northeast from the old port to Square Léon Blum (metro Vieux Port or Noailles). The tourist office at the port end of La Canebière is inside the former **Café Turc**, a stopover for eastbound travellers in the 1950s.

The area bounded by La Canebière, cours Belsunce and rue d'Aix, rue Bernard du Bois and blvd d'Athènes is Belsunce, a poorer immigrant neighbourhood that's slowly being rehabilitated. The neighbourhood's glass-fronted public library on cours Belsunce stands on the spot where Marseilles' legendary Alcazar music hall hosted stars from 1857 until 1964.

North of here lies the train station area and, beyond that, **La Friche la Belle de Mai**, well worth a visit for a glimpse into Marseilles' underground arts scene (see the boxed text 'Docklands' earlier in this chapter). Aubagne-born Marcel Pagnol (1895–1974) grew up in La Pleine, east of Belsunce around place Jean Jaurès. He lived at 52 rue Terrusse; ask at the tourist office for information on Pagnol city tours.

ALONG THE COAST

A fine place for a stroll is along **corniche Président John F Kennedy**, 7e, which follows the coast for 4.5km. It begins 200m southwest of **Jardin du Pharo**, a park with breathtaking views of the old port and new ferry terminal, and home to the **Palais du Pharo** *(Map 1; 58 blvd Charles Livon)*, built by Napoleon III. The road continues south past the small and busy **Plage des Catalans** – which resembles a scene from *Baywatch* with its bronzed, bikini-clad volleyball players – to **Anse des Auffes**. The cove, harbour and village is presided over by a WWI memorial statue of a 'mother of liberty', framed by a giant archway. A narrow staircase leads from corniche Président John F Kennedy to the harbour around which the village nestles.

Farther south, you will pass the face of Adidas – local hero **Zinedine Zidane** – peering out in gigantic form from the side of a building at 82B corniche Président John F Kennedy. At No 271 is the fabulous **Villa Valmer** (1868) and its luxuriant gardens, a potent cocktail of pistachio, palm and pine trees. At No 281 **Château Berger** is another fine example of the beautiful architecture that sprang up along the coast under the Second Empire. The **propeller**, sculpted in bronze by local artist César in 1971 to honour those who returned from North Africa, is a short walk farther south along the coast. After passing the small **Plage du Prophète**, you eventually

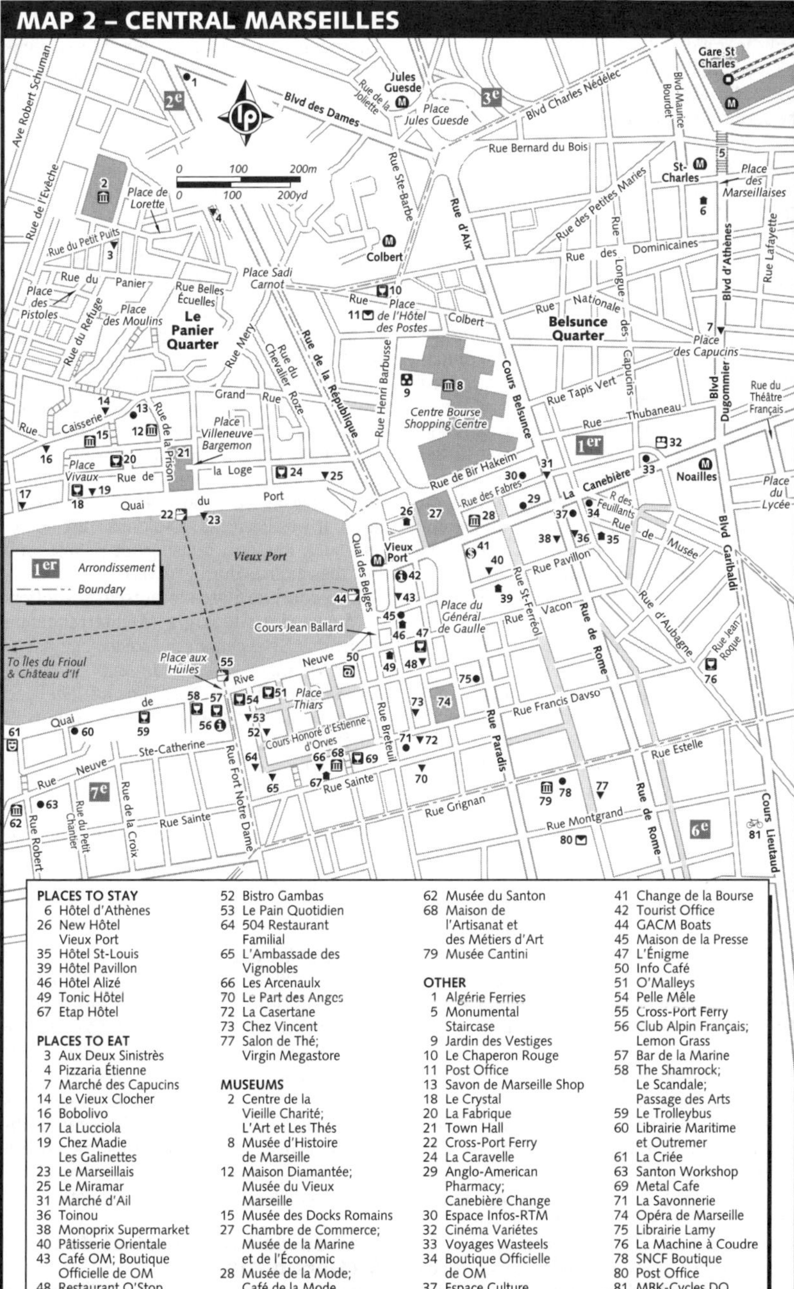
MAP 2 – CENTRAL MARSEILLES
0 100 200m
0 100 200yd
Blvd des Dames
Jules Guesde
Place Jules Guesde
Rue de la Joliette
Blvd Charles Nédélec
Gare St Charles
Blvd Maurice Bourdet
Rue Bernard du Bois
St-Charles
Place des Marseillaises
Ave Robert Schuman
Rue de l'Evêche
Place de Lorette
Rue du Petit Puits
Rue Ste-Barbe
Rue d'Aix
Rue des Petites Maries
Rue des Dominicaines
Rue Longue des Capucins
Blvd d'Athènes
Rue Lafayette
Colbert
Rue du Panier
Place des Pistoles
Rue du Refuge
Place des Moulins
Rue Belles Écuelles
Le Panier Quarter
Place Sadi Carnot
Rue Colbert
Place de l'Hôtel des Postes
Rue Nationale
Belsunce Quarter
Place des Capucins
Rue Mery
Rue du Chevalier Roze
Rue de la République
Rue Henri Barbusse
Centre Bourse Shopping Centre
Cours Belsunce
Rue Tapis Vert
Blvd Dugommier
Rue du Théâtre Français
Grand Rue
Rue Caisserie
Rue de la Prison
Place Villeneuve Bargemon
Rue Thubaneau
1er
Place Vivaux
Rue de la Loge
Rue de Bir Hakeim
Rue des Fabres
La Canebière
Noailles
Place du Lycée
Quai du Port
R des Feuillants
Rue de Musée
Blvd Garibaldi
Vieux Port
Quai des Belges
Rue Pavillon
Arrondissement
Boundary
Place du Général de Gaulle
Rue St-Ferréol
Rue Vacon
Rue de Rome
Rue d'Aubagne
Cours Jean Ballard
Rue Jean Roque
To Îles du Frioul & Château d'If
Place aux Huiles
Rive Neuve
Place Thiars
Rue Francis Davso
Quai de Rive Neuve
Cours Honoré d'Estienne d'Orves
Rue Breteuil
Rue Paradis
Rue Ste-Catherine
Rue Neuve
Rue Estelle
7e
Rue Sainte
Rue Fort Notre Dame
Rue Grignan
Rue Montgrand
6e
Cours Lieutaud
Rue Robert
Rue du Petit Chantier
Rue de la Croix
2e
3e

PLACES TO STAY
6 Hôtel d'Athènes
26 New Hôtel Vieux Port
35 Hôtel St-Louis
39 Hôtel Pavillon
46 Hôtel Alizé
49 Tonic Hôtel
67 Etap Hôtel

PLACES TO EAT
3 Aux Deux Sinistrès
4 Pizzaria Étienne
7 Marché des Capucins
14 Le Vieux Clocher
16 Bobolivo
17 La Lucciola
19 Chez Madie Les Galinettes
23 Le Marseillais
25 Le Miramar
31 Marché d'Ail
36 Toinou
38 Monoprix Supermarket
40 Pâtisserie Orientale
43 Café OM; Boutique Officielle de OM
48 Restaurant O'Stop
52 Bistro Gambas
53 Le Pain Quotidien
64 504 Restaurant Familial
65 L'Ambassade des Vignobles
66 Les Arcenaulx
70 Le Part des Anges
72 La Casertane
73 Chez Vincent
77 Salon de Thé; Virgin Megastore

MUSEUMS
2 Centre de la Vieille Charité; L'Art et Les Thés
8 Musée d'Histoire de Marseille
12 Maison Diamantée; Musée du Vieux Marseille
15 Musée des Docks Romains
27 Chambre de Commerce; Musée de la Marine et de l'Économic
28 Musée de la Mode; Café de la Mode
62 Musée du Santon
68 Maison de l'Artisanat et des Métiers d'Art
79 Musée Cantini

OTHER
1 Algérie Ferries
5 Monumental Staircase
9 Jardin des Vestiges
10 Le Chaperon Rouge
11 Post Office
13 Savon de Marseille Shop
18 Le Crystal
20 La Fabrique
21 Town Hall
22 Cross-Port Ferry
24 La Caravelle
29 Anglo-American Pharmacy; Canebière Change
30 Espace Infos-RTM
32 Cinéma Variétes
33 Voyages Wasteels
34 Boutique Officielle de OM
37 Espace Culture
41 Change de la Bourse
42 Tourist Office
44 GACM Boats
45 Maison de la Presse
47 L'Énigme
50 Info Café
51 O'Malleys
54 Pelle Mêle
55 Cross-Port Ferry
56 Club Alpin Français; Lemon Grass
57 Bar de la Marine
58 The Shamrock; Le Scandale; Passage des Arts
59 Le Trolleybus
60 Librairie Maritime et Outremer
61 La Criée
63 Santon Workshop
69 Metal Cafe
71 La Savonnerie
74 Opéra de Marseille
75 Librairie Lamy
76 La Machine à Coudre
78 SNCF Boutique
80 Post Office
81 MBK-Cycles DO

come to **Plage du Prado**, Marseilles' heavily built-up, modern beach resort.

Overlooking this sandy, body-packed beach is **Parc Borély**, a vast park that encompasses the **Jardin Botanique** *(botanical garden; ☎ 04 91 55 24 96; allée du Parc Borely; adult/under 12 €1.52/free; open 1pm-5pm daily Oct-Apr, 2pm-7pm daily May-Sept)* and 18th-century **Château Borély** *(☎ 04 91 25 26 34; 134 ave Clot Bey)*, hosts temporary art exhibitions. Admission prices and opening hours vary, depending on the exhibition. Take bus No 19 to ave du Prado or bus No 44 to ave Clot Bey.

Along almost its entire length corniche Président John F Kennedy, and its continuation promenade Georges Pompidou, is served by bus No 83, which goes to the old port (quai des Belges) and the rond-point du Prado metro stop on ave du Prado. To get to the beach from here, bear west along ave du Prado to the monumental statue of **David** – an impressive 1903 marble mimic of Michelangelo's masterpiece by Jules Cantini – on the busy intersection of ave du Prado and promenade Georges Pompidou. The well-endowed nude is a well-known landmark among local Marseillais.

Parc Chanot sits on the southeastern corner of the rond-point du Prado (Prado roundabout). From here, blvd Michelet leads south to the **stade vélodrome**, home ground since 1937 of the Olympique de Marseille football club (see the boxed text 'OM' later in this chapter).

Continuing south past the stadium is Le Corbusier's **Cité Radieuse**, a 337-apartment housing block on stilts, which was hugely innovative when designed (1947–52); see the boxed text 'Trailing Le Corbusier' under Architecture in the Facts about Provence chapter. The estate straddles the corner of blvd Michelet and ave Guy de Maupassant. West of here is Marseilles' Musée d'Art Contemporain.

From **Plage du Prado**, promenade Georges Pompidou continues south along the coast to **La Pointe-Rouge**, **La Madrague** and **Callelongue**, a tiny harbour village lying on Cap Croisette from where breathtaking **calanques** (see Les Calanques later in this chapter) can be accessed on foot. Bus No 19 from the rond-point du Prado metro stop runs along promenade Georges Pompidou to La Madrague; from La Madrague bus No 20 continues to Callelongue.

MUSEUMS

Those intent on visiting several museums might want to invest in a Carte Marseille Privilèges, which is sold at the tourist office. The city card costs €15.25/22.87/30.49 for one/two/three consecutive days and covers admission to all city museums, unlimited use of public transport, free guided city tours and a boat trip to Île d'If.

Centre de la Vieille Charité

The Old Charity Cultural Centre *(Map 2; ☎ 04 91 14 58 80; 2 rue de la Charité, 2e; metro Joliette)* is built around Provence's most impressive Baroque church, designed by Marseilles-born architect Pierre Puget. Its stone dome is the centrepiece of Le Panier, Marseilles' oldest district. There are superb permanent exhibits and imaginative temporary exhibitions in a workhouse and hospice built between 1671 and 1745. Before restoration, it was barracks, a soldiers' rest-home, and later, low-cost housing for people who lost their homes during WWII.

The courtyard arcade presently shelters a **Musée d'Archéologie Méditerranéenne** *(Museum of Mediterranean Archaeology; adult/10-18 yrs €2/1; open 11am-6pm Tues-Sun July-Sept, 10am-5pm Tues-Sun Oct-June)* and a **Musée des Arts Africains, Océaniens & Amérindiens** *(Museum of African, Oceanic & American-Indian Art; adult/10-18 yrs €2/1; open 11am-6pm Tues-Sun July-Sept, 10am-5pm Tues-Sun Oct-June)*. Admission to the temporary exhibitions on the ground floor typically costs €3/1.50. Complete your visit with lunch at L'Art et les Thés (see Places to Eat later in this section).

Musée Cantini

Inside a 17th-century *hôtel particulier* (private mansion), the Musée Cantini *(Cantini Museum; Map 2; ☎ 04 91 54 77 75; 19 rue Grignan, 6e; metro Estrangin-Préfecture; adult/10-16 yrs €2/1; open 10am-5pm Tues-Sun Oct-May, 11am-6pm Tues-Sun June-Sept)* has a permanent exhibition of 17th- and 18th-century Provençal ceramics, rotating modern and contemporary art exhibitions, and also a centre dedicated to 21st-century works.

Maison de l'Artisanat et des Métiers d'Art

Contemporary photography, sculpture and calligraphy exhibitions – among others – are hosted at this Maison de l'Artisanat et des Métiers d'Art *(House of Arts & Crafts; Map 2; ☎ 04 91 54 80 54; 21 cours Honoré d'Estienne d'Orves, 1er; metro Vieux Port; admission free; open 1pm-6pm Tues-Sat)*.

Musée d'Histoire de Marseille

Roman history buffs should visit Marseilles' History Museum *(Map 2; ☎ 04 91 90 42 22; metro Vieux Port, 1er; adult/10-16 yrs €2/1; open noon-7pm Mon-Sat)*, just north of La Canebière on the ground floor of the Centre Bourse shopping centre, 1er. Exhibits include the remains of a merchant vessel – discovered by chance in the old port in 1974 – that plied the waters of the Mediterranean in the early 3rd century. The 19m-long timbers, which include five different kinds of wood, show evidence of having been repaired repeatedly. To preserve the soaked and decaying wood, the whole thing was freeze-dried right where it now sits – hidden behind glass in a very dimly lit room.

Roman buildings, uncovered during the construction of the Centre Bourse, can be seen just outside the museum in the **Jardin des Vestiges** (Garden of Ruins), which fronts rue Henri Barbusse, 1er.

Musée des Docks Romains

At the Roman Docks Museum *(Map 2; ☎ 04 91 91 24 62; place Vivaux, 2e; metro Vieux Port; adult/10-16 yrs €2/1; open 10am-5pm Tues-Sun Oct-May, 11am-6pm Tues-Sun June-Sept)*, 1st-century Roman structures, discovered in 1947 during postwar reconstruction, are displayed. The huge jars on display could hold up to 2000L of wine or oil.

Musée du Vieux Marseille

All things traditional to old Marseilles – *santons*, Marseillais tarot cards etc – can be seen in the Museum of Old Marseilles *(Map 2; ☎ 04 91 55 28 68; 2 rue de la Prison, 2e; metro Vieux Port; adult/10-16 yrs €2/1; open 10am-5pm Tues-Sun Oct-May, 11am-6pm Tues-Sun June-Sept)*, inside the Maison Diamantée. The facade of the 16th-century townhouse, built in 1570 for a wealthy trader, is covered in diamond-shaped cut stones, hence its name.

At the time of writing, the museum was closed for renovation. Contact the tourist office for an update and information on guided tours of its interior.

Musée de la Mode

Glitz and glamour is the name of the game at Marseilles' Fashion Design Museum *(Map 2; ☎ 04 91 56 59 57; 11 La Canebière, 1er; metro Vieux Port; adult/10-16 yrs €3/1.50; open 11am-6pm Tues-Sun)*. Housed in the city's **Espace Mode Méditerranée** *(Mediterranean Fashion Centre; ☎ 04 91 14 92 00; ⓔ imm@wanadoo.fr)*, the museum traces all the fashion trends from 1930 to the present day and

Little Saints

The custom of creating a *crèche* (Christmas crib) with figurines of Mary, Joseph, shepherds, kings, oxen, a donkey and so on, dates from the Avignon papacy of John XII (1319–34). But it was only after the 1789 revolution and consequent Reign of Terror that these figures were cut down to size, marking the birth of the *santon* and the Provençal *crèche*.

Santons (from *santoùn* in Provençal, meaning 'little saint') stand no higher than 2.5cm to 15cm. The first colourfully painted figures were created by Marseillais artisan Jean-Louis Lagnel (1764–1822), who came up with the idea of crafting clay miniatures in a plaster mould and allowing them to dry before firing the figures at 950°C. *Santonniers* (santon makers) still stick to Lagnel's method today.

In a traditional Provençal crib there are 55 *santons* ranging from the tambourine man, fishwife and miller, to the tinsmith, scissors grinder, woman carrying garlic and a trumpet-blowing angel. Since 1806 *santonniers* have flocked to Marseilles each December to take part in the Foire aux Santonniers, which sees the length of La Canebière transformed into one great big *santon* fair.

Santons dating from the 18th and 19th centuries are displayed in Marseilles' magical **Musée du Santon** *(Map 2; ☎ 04 91 13 61 36; ⓔ carbonel@carbonel.com; 49 rue Neuve Ste-Catherine, 7e; metro Vieux Port; admission free; open 9.30am-12.30pm & 2pm-6.30pm or 7pm Mon-Sat)*. The museum houses the private collection of *santonnier* Marcel Carbonnel, who crafts *santons* in the adjoining **workshop** *(admission free; open 8.30am-1pm & 2pm-5.30pm Mon-Thur, 8.30am-1pm Fri)*.

displays some 2000 items of clothing and accessories. Several original Chanel designs (many worn by Madame herself) are on display, along with more contemporary pieces by Gaultier, Dior, Yves St-Laurent and funky British designer Alexander McQueen. Taking photos with/without a flash costs an outrageous €8/2. Free guided tours (only in French) start at 4pm at the weekends.

Musée de la Marine et de l'Économie

A few doors from the Musée de la Mode is the colonnaded Chambre du Commerce (Chamber of Commerce, also known as the Palais de la Bourse), built from 1854 to 1860. It houses the Musée de la Marine et de l'Économie *(Naval & Economic Museum; Map 2; 9 La Canebiére; ☎ 04 91 39 33 33; metro Vieux Port, 1er; adult/10-16 yrs €2/1; open 10am-6pm Tues-Sun)*.

Palais Longchamp

Constructed in the 1860s, the colonnaded Longchamp Palace (off Map 1) was designed in part to disguise a water tower built at the terminus of an aqueduct from the Durance River. The palace's two wings house the **Musée des Beaux-Arts** *(☎ 04 91 14 59 30; blvd Philippon, 4e; metro Cinq Avenues Longchamp; adult/10-16 yrs €2/1; open 10am-5pm Tues-Sun Oct-May, 11am-6pm Tues-Sun June-Sept)*, Marseilles' oldest museum, whose speciality is 15th- to 19th-century paintings. A **Musée d'Histoire Naturelle** *(Natural History Museum; ☎ 04 91 14 59 90; adult/10-16 yrs €2/1; open 10am-5pm Tues-Sun Oct-May, 11am-6pm Tues-Sun June-Sept)* captures prehistoric Provence.

Musée d'Art Contemporain

Marseilles' Museum of Contemporary Art *(MAC; off Map 1; ☎ 04 91 25 01 07; 69 blvd de Haïfa, 8e; adult/10-16 yrs €2/1; open 10am-5pm Tues-Sun Oct-May, 11am-6pm Tues-Sun June-Sept)* is north of the Prado beach area and Parc Borély. On display are works by Christo, Nice new realists Ben and Klein, pop artist Andy Warhol and Marseilles' very own César, who designed the statue handed to stars at the Césars (the French cinema awards that bear his name).

Take bus No 44 from the rond-point du Prado metro stop to the place Bonnefons stop, from where it is a short walk along ave de Hambourg to rond-point Pierre Guerre – easily recognisable by a giant metal thumb (César's doing) that proudly sticks up from the middle of the roundabout.

CHURCHES & CATHEDRALS

Basilique Notre Dame de la Garde

This basilica *(Map 1; place Colonel Edon, 6e)* is not to be missed, especially if you like overwrought 19th-century architecture or great panoramas, but count on a stiff walk up to the enormous Roman-Byzantine structure, 1km south of the old port. It stands on a hilltop (162m) – the highest point in the city – and provides staggering views of sprawling Marseilles.

The domed basilica, ornamented with all manner of coloured marble, intricate mosaics, murals and gilded objects, was erected between 1853 and 1864. The bell tower is topped by a 9.7m-tall gilded statue of the Virgin Mary – traditional protector of the city – on a 12m-high pedestal. The great bell inside is 2.5m high and weighs a hefty 8.3 tonnes (the clapper alone weighs 387kg). Bullet marks from Marseilles' Battle of Liberation (15–25 August 1944) scar the cathedral's northern wall.

Bus No 60 links the port (from cours Jean Ballard) with the basilica. Count on 30 minutes each way by foot.

Nouvelle Cathédrale de la Major

Marseilles' Roman-Byzantine Nouvelle Cathédrale de la Major *(New Cathedral of the Major; Map 1; place de la Major, 2e; metro Joliette)*, just off quai de la Tourette, is topped with cupolas, towers and turrets of all shapes and sizes. Built between 1852 and 1893 (a period not known for decorative or architectural understatement), the structure is enormous: 140m long and 60m high. It dwarfs the nearby old cathedral, **Ancienne Cathédrale de la Major** *(Map 1 place de la Major; ☎ 04 91 90 53 57; admission free; visits by appointment)*, a mid-11th-century Provençal Romanesque building that stands on the site of what was once a temple to the goddess Diana.

Abbaye St-Victor

The twin tombs of 4th-century martyrs and a 3rd-century sarcophagus are among the sacred objects that reside in the imposing

Romanesque 12th-century Abbaye St-Victor *(Map 1; 3 rue de l'Abbaye, 7e; metro Vieux Port)*, set on a hill (162m) above the old port. Each year on 2 February the statue of the Black Virgin inside the abbey is carried through the streets in a candle-lit procession during the annual Pèlerinage de la Chandeleur. Marseilles' annual sacred music festival is also held here. (See Special Events later in this section.)

CHÂTEAU D'IF

Château d'If *(Map 1; ☎ 04 91 55 50 09; adult/10-16 yrs €4/2, admission free 1st Sun of month; open 9am-7pm daily Apr-Sept, 9am-5.30pm Tues-Sun Oct-Mar)*, the 16th-century fortress-turned-prison, built between 1524 and 1528 and made famous by Dumas' classic work, *Le Comte de Monte Cristo*, is on a 3-hectare island (Île d'If) 3.5km west of the entrance to the old port. Among the people incarcerated here were political prisoners; hundreds of Protestants; the revolutionary hero Mirabeau, who served a stint here in 1774 for failing to pay debts, some 1848 revolutionaries; and the Communards of 1871.

Boats run by **GACM** *(☎ 04 91 55 50 09; 1 quai des Belges, 1er; metro Vieux Port)* leave for Île d'If from outside the GACM office at the old port. Hourly boats run between 9am and 7pm or 8.30pm during busy periods. Sailing time is 20 minutes and a return fare costs €8.

ÎLES DU FRIOUL

The islands of Ratonneau and Pomègues, each about 2.5km long, are a few hundred metres west of Île d'If. They were linked by a dike in the 1820s. From the 17th to the 19th centuries the islands were used as a place of quarantine for those suspected of being infected with plague or cholera. Today the rather barren islands (with a total area of about 200 hectares) shelter sea birds, rare plants and bathers, and are dotted with fortifications (used by German troops during WWII), the ruins of the old quarantine hospital, **Hôpital Caroline**, and **Fort Ratonneau**.

GACM boats to Château d'If (see that section earlier) also serve Îles du Frioul. A return fare is €8 (€13 with a stop on Île d'If too).

AUBAGNE

Marcel Pagnol's home town lies on this vast port city's easternmost fringe, 14km from the coast. Although the writer moved to Marseilles proper at the age of two, he evoked 19th-century Aubagne's brick-and-tile factories in many of his works. See Literature, 20th Century in the Facts about Provence chapter.

The primary reason to visit this otherwise unmomentous place today is for its Biennale de l'Art Santonnier in early December. During the two-day *santon* festival, *santonniers* set up street stalls on central cours Maréchal Foch, traditional Provençal musicians perform on nearby cours Foch, Christmas carols are sung and *santon* workshops held. The **tourist office** *(☎ 04 42 03 49 98, fax 04 42 03 83 62; ⓔ ot.aubagne@visitprovence.com; ave Antide Boyur; open 9am-noon & 2pm-6pm Mon-Sat)* has a complete list of *santon* workshops to visit.

ACTIVITIES

Scout out walks in the area with outdoor enthusiasts at the **Club Alpin Français** *(CAF; Map 2; ☎ 04 91 54 36 94; 12 rue Fort Notre Dame, 1er; metro Vieux Port)*.

Beaches

Marseilles' main beach, 1km-long **Plage du Prado** is about 5km south of the city centre. Take bus No 19 or 72 from the rond-point du Prado metro stop or bus No 83 (No 583 at night) from the old port (quai des Belges) and get off at either the Plage David or La Plage stop. On foot, follow corniche Président John F Kennedy, which runs along the coast, past the short **Plage des Catalans** *(admission €4.50; open 7am-7pm)*. For the latter, walk down the steps signposted 'Bains des Catalans'.

If you don't like sand between your toes, spread yourself out on one of the wooden sundecks built atop the rocky seafront near **Anse des Auffes**, from where bathers climb down short ladders to take a dip in the sea. **Bistrot Plage** *(☎ 04 91 31 80 32; 60 corniche Président John F Kennedy)* has a waterside bistro and plush mattresses (€10/5 for a full/half-day, plus beach admission €4) on which to sprawl. By bus, get off at the Vallon des Auffes stop.

Diving & Snorkelling

Les Calanques (see that section later) and the offshore islands and wrecks offer spectacular diving. Equipment can be hired at **Cressi Sub**

(Map 1; ☎ 04 91 90 95 74; 11 ave de St-Jean, 1er; metro Vieux Port), a diving school near the Vieux Port. A baptism dive typically costs €30; equipment hire is €18.50.

Rollerblading

If blading's your thing, scoot down to Marseille's stadium, the **Stade Vélodrome** *(off Map 1; 3 blvd Michelet, 8e; metro rond-point du Prado)*, where 500-odd rollerbladers meet each week at 9.15pm on Friday for a police-escorted, 12km-long blade around town. It is run by **Marseille en Roller** *(MER; w www.marseilleenroller.org – French only)*. At the stadium, look for the guys in the orange bibs.

ORGANISED TOURS

The tourist office (see Information earlier) prints a list of the guided tours it runs each month. Many are thematic and include everything from 'in the footsteps of novelist Alexandre Dumas' to the forts of the Vieux Port and Marseille's Art Deco architecture. From 1 July to mid-September, it runs nocturnal port tours at 9.30pm on Friday. Stadium tours (see the boxed text 'OM' later in this chapter) only run in July and August. Tours cost €6.50 (€14 for those by bus) and must be booked in advance.

The tourist office also sells tickets for Marseilles' **Histobus** *(☎ 04 91 10 54 71)*, a three-hour city tour run by local bus company RTM. Tours depart daily at 2.30pm, July to September, from the old port and tickets cost €11/4.60 per adult/child.

From Easter to September, GACM (see Château d'If earlier in this chapter) runs an equivalent Histoboat two-hour boat trip around the port for €13. Four-hour return boat trips costing €20 also depart twice daily from quai des Belges for Cassis. Boats pass by the stunning Les Calanques – see that section later in this chapter. It also runs separate boat trips around Les Calanques for €20 in a glass-bottomed boat.

SPECIAL EVENTS

The **Pèlerinage de la Chandeleur** (Candlemas Pilgrimage) held on 2 February at Abbaye St-Victor (see that section earlier in this chapter) kicks off the year's busy cultural calendar, followed by the **Carnaval de Marseille** – a street carnival with decorated floats – in March. Plage du Prado hosts the beach volleyball world championships in July.

The **Festival de Marseille** in July brings three weeks of contemporary dance, theatre, music and art to various venues around town. October's month-long **Festival des Chants Sacrés en Méditerranée** sees the Abbaye St-Victor and other churches play host to some beautiful sacred music concerts. The **Fête de l'Assomption** (Assumption) on 15 August honours the city's traditional protector, the Virgin Mary, with a mass in the Nouvelle Cathédrale de la Major and a solemn procession through Le Panier.

October's month-long **Fiesta des Suds**, held at the Dock des Suds each October, is a massive celebration of world music.

PLACES TO STAY – BUDGET

Marseilles has some of France's cheapest hotels although many are filthy dives in dodgy areas whose main business is renting out rooms by the hour. Those we list here appeared, at the time, to be relatively clean and reputable.

Hostels

Auberge de Jeunesse de Bonneveine *(off Map 1; ☎ 04 91 17 63 30, fax 04 91 73 97 23; e marseille-bonneveine@fuaj.org; impasse du Docteur Bonfils, 8e; dorm bed with breakfast 1st/subsequent night €12.80/11.10, doubles with breakfast 1st/subsequent night per person €15.40/13.70; open Feb–mid-Dec)* is about 4.5km south of the town centre. An HI card is obligatory. Bikes are rented for €10/13 per four hours/day. Take bus No 44 from the rond-point du Prado metro stop and get off at the place Bonnefons stop. Alternatively, take bus No 19 from the Castellane metro stop or bus No 47 from the Ste-Marguerite Dromel metro stop.

Auberge de Jeunesse Château de Bois Luzy *(off Map 1; ☎/fax 04 91 49 06 18; allées des Primevères, 12e; B&B €10.60; reception open 7.30am-noon & 5pm-10.30pm daily)* is 4.5km east of the centre, in a restored chateau in the Montolivet neighbourhood. An evening meal costs €7.70, a hostelling card is mandatory and the push-button showers are highly irritating according to several readers. Take bus No 6 from near the Réformés-Canebière metro stop or bus No 8 from La Canebière.

Auberge de Jeunesse Jane Vialle *(☎ 04 96 12 43 98, fax 04 96 12 43 99; 9 blvd Fabrici, 5e single/double studios with kitchenette*

€24/30, per week €160/200), near La Timone metro stop, is a LFAJ-affiliated hostel with self-catering studios.

Hotels

Train Station Area Generally, most the rock-bottom hotels around the train station are unsavoury dumps.

Hôtel d'Athènes *(Map 2; ☎ 04 91 90 03 83, fax 04 91 90 72 03; 37 blvd d'Athènes, 1er; metro Gare St-Charles; singles/doubles with shower €25/31, with shower & toilet €36/40) is an exception*. At the foot of the monumental staircase leading from the station to town, this two-star place has well-kept TV-clad rooms.

Around La Canebière A sound budget choice north of Marseilles' main thoroughfare is **Hôtel Gambetta** *(Map 1; ☎/fax 04 91 62 07 88; 49 allées Léon Gambetta, 1er; metro Réformés-Canebière; singles/doubles with shower & toilet €23.50/36.30)*.

South of La Canebière, there's a liberal sprinkling of sleazy rock-bottom hotels on rue Sénac de Meilhan, rue Mazagran, rue du Théâtre Français and around place du Lycée (all near metro Réformés-Canebière, 1er). Slightly to the west, rue des Feuillants (metro Noailles) has several one-star hotels.

Hôtel Pavillon *(Map 2; ☎ 04 91 33 76 90; 27 rue Pavillon, 1er; metro Vieux Port; singles/doubles/triples with washbasin €20/26/33, singles/doubles/triples/quads with shower €27/32/44/49)* touts rock-bottom rooms with no perks. Use of the hall shower costs an overpriced €3.05, but breakfast is cheap at €3.80.

Prefecture Area Blvd Louis Salvator, in a decent neighbourhood, has several two-star hotels with bright rooms and modern decor.

Hôtel Massilia *(Map 1; ☎ 04 91 51 79 28; 25 blvd Louis Salvator, 6e; metro Estrangin-Préfecture; doubles with shower €22, with shower & toilet €25)*, a one-star place at the top of the hill, is dirt cheap. Guests punch in a *code confidentiel* to enter. Rooms can also be rented on a weekly/monthly basis.

Hôtel de la Préfecture *(Map 1; ☎ 04 91 54 31 60, fax 04 91 54 24 95; 9 blvd Louis Salvator, 6e; metro Estrangin-Préfecture; doubles with shower, toilet & TV €32)*, the best of the bunch, is a friendly place with beautifully clean and modern rooms.

Le Président *(Map 1; ☎ 04 91 48 67 29, fax 04 91 94 24 44; 12 blvd Louis Salvator, 6e; metro Estrangin-Préfecture; doubles with shower & toilet €32)*, directly opposite Hôtel de la Préfecture, comes a very close second.

Hôtel Le Béarn *(Map 1; ☎ 04 91 37 75 83, fax 04 91 81 54 98; 63 rue Sylvabelle, 6e; metro Estrangin-Préfecture; singles/doubles with shower €17/22, with shower & toilet €32/40)* is a quiet one-star place with colourfully decorated rooms. Guests can watch TV in the common room. Reception closes at 11pm or midnight.

PLACES TO STAY – MID-RANGE

Two atmospheric mid-range choices look straight out to sea.

Hôtel Le Richelieu *(Map 1; ☎ 04 91 31 01 92, fax 04 91 59 38 09; 52 corniche Président John F Kennedy, 7e; doubles/triples from €38/59)*, near Plage des Catalans, is a two-star place built into the rocks to offer idyllic sea and beach views. Breakfast on the terrace is a treat. **Hôtel Péron** *(Map 1; ☎ 04 91 31 01 41; 119 corniche Président John F Kennedy, 7e; doubles €53)*, despite its weathered appearance, touts decent two-star rooms; take bus No 83 from quai des Belges (Vieux Port).

Right in the hub of things, try the following places:

Hôtel St-Louis *(Map 2; ☎ 04 91 54 02 74, fax 04 91 33 78 59; 2 rue des Récollettes; doubles from €40)*, pretty-in-pink, is an elegant old pile overlooking rue de Rome in the hub of Marseilles' shopping district. The wrought-iron balconies add an ornate touch.

New Hôtel Vieux Port *(Map 2; ☎ 04 91 99 23 23, fax 04 91 90 76 24; ⓔ marseillevieuxport@new-hotel.com; 3 bis rue Reine Elisabeth, 1er; metro Vieux Port; doubles €65)*, overlooking the bustling old port, is a renovated complex with 47 modern, rooms with air-conditioning.

Etap Hôtel *(Map 2; ☎ 04 91 54 73 73, fax 04 91 54 95 75; 46 rue Sainte; singles/doubles/triples €42.50/46.50/50.50)* might be part of a chain, but its quiet location in an old building overlooking cours Honoré d'Estienne d'Orves makes its rooms a real steal.

Hôtel Alizé *(Map 2; ☎ 04 91 33 66 97, fax 04 91 54 80 06; ⓦ www.alize-hotel.com; 35 quai des Belges, 1er; metro Vieux Port; singles/doubles €53/58, with port view €66/71)*, at the port, is an atmospheric, elegant pile wedged between cafés.

Tonic Hôtel *(Map 2; ☎ 04 91 55 67 46, fax 04 91 55 67 56; W www.tonichotel.com; 43 quai des Belges 1er; metro Vieux Port; singles/doubles/triples €88/104/120, with port view €107/123/135)*, in another well-restored old building, is a three-star portside pad.

A short ride out of town by metro or bus No 83 from the old port to rond-point du Prado, or bus No 21 from the old port to the 'Le Corbusier' stop, is a memorable choice – if you're into Le Corbusier.

Hôtel Le Corbusier *(off Map 1; ☎ 04 91 16 78 00, fax 04 91 16 78 28; e hotelcorbusier@wanadoo.fr; 280 blvd Michelet; doubles with shower €40, singles/doubles/triples with shower & toilet €60/60/80)*, frequented mainly by architects or architecture fiends, is a 1950s concrete block built by no other than Le Corbusier (see the boxed text 'Trailing Le Corbusier' in the Facts about Provence chapter). Showers are shared by two rooms.

PLACES TO STAY – TOP END

New Hôtel Bompard *(off Map 1; ☎ 04 91 99 22 22, fax 04 91 31 02 14; e marseillebompard@new-hotel.com; 2 rue des Flots Bleues, 7e; singles/doubles with street view €78/90, with garden view €87/103)*, just off corniche Président John F Kennedy, has good sea breezes, a swimming pool, extensive grounds and three-star rooms with all the gadgets.

Le Rhul *(off Map 1; ☎ 04 91 52 01 77, fax 04 91 52 49 82; 269 corniche Président John F Kennedy, 7e; doubles from €80)* is known as much for its legendary *bouillabaisse* (see the boxed text 'Tasty Tip' later in this chapter) as for its lovely three-star rooms overlooking the sea.

Le Petit Nice-Passédat *(off Map 1; ☎ 04 91 59 25 92, fax 04 91 59 28 08; W www.petitnice-passedat.com; Anse de Maldormé, 7e; doubles from €168)*, built atop rocks above a little cove, is part of the prestigious Relais & Châteaux chain. Marseilles' most sought-after hotel sports 12 rooms, a stunning location and the city's most prestigious restaurant (lunch/dinner *menus* from €59/76).

PLACES TO EAT

This lively port offers an incredible variety of restaurants, although fish predominates, be it *huîtres* (oysters), *moules* (mussels), *violets* (sea squirts) or *bouillabaisse* – the city's most quintessential dish (see the boxed text 'Tasty Tip' later in this chapter).

Restaurants

Vieux Port The quays around the Old Port are plastered with cafés and touristy restaurants. Those on northern quai du Port and the overspill into Le Panier (see that section later) are markedly more original than those on the southern quai de Rive Neuve.

La Lucciola *(Map 2; ☎ 04 91 91 84 56; 184 quai du Port, 1er; metro Vieux Port; mains €10-15)*, worth the short walk west along the quay, is a casual yet chic Italian-inspired place where you can eat pasta, meal-sized *assiettes* (salad platters) and *gambas* (king prawns) in various guises.

Chez Madie Les Galinettes *(Map 2; ☎ 04 91 90 40 87; 138 quai du Port, 1er; metro Vieux Port; mains €10-15)* must be the best place without a doubt to sample *pieds et paquets* (sheep tripe, literally 'feet and packages'), *rougets au pistou* (mullet in basil sauce) and other hearty regional specialities.

Le Marseillais *(Map 2; ☎ 04 91 90 72 52; e pierre@latruffenoire.com; quai du Port, 1er; metro Vieux Port; starters/mains from €8/15)*, a galleon moored in the water opposite the town hall, dishes up traditional cuisine with cooling sea breezes.

From southern quai de Rive Neuve, lively place Thiars and cours Honoré d'Estienne d'Orves, with their late-night restaurants and cafés, stretch south. The neighbouring place aux Huiles offers several places worth a pit stop.

Bistro Gambas *(Map 2; ☎ 04 91 33 26 44; 29 place aux Huiles, 1er; metro Vieux Port; menus €20 & €28.90)* cooks up *gambas* with a wild choice of sauces. Those with a fetish for lip-smacking, finger-licking dishes should opt for the *menu crevettes à volonté* (€15.50) – a bottomless *menu* allowing you to eat as many prawns as your tummy will allow.

504 Restaurant Familial *(Map 2; ☎ 04 91 33 57 74; 34 place aux Huiles, 1er; metro Vieux Port; tajines/couscous from €13/11.50)* is a change from the norm in terms of its colourful and exotically furnished interior. Tajines and couscous star here.

L'Ambassade des Vignobles *(Map 2; ☎ 04 91 33 00 25; 42 place aux Huiles, 1er; metro Vieux Port; menus with wine from €30)* is Marseilles' self-professed Ambassador of Vineyards. Diners can sample a different selected vintage with each course.

Les Arcenaulx *(Map 2; ☎ 04 91 59 80 30; 25 cours Honoré d'Estienne d'Orves, 1er; metro*

Vieux Port; menus €23.50, €24.50 & €44.97), a restaurant-cum-*salon de thé* wrapped around an interior courtyard, is a fine spot for dining amid historic splendour. One of its three *menus* is vegetarian.

Around cours Honoré d'Estienne d'Orves are many more tasty choices. **La Casertane** *(Map 2; ☎ 04 91 54 98 51; 71 rue Francis Davso, 1er; metro Vieux Port)* has traded in on its well-earned reputation as one of Marseilles' best Italian *épiceries* (groceries) and now serves tasty morsels to eat in, too.

Chez Vincent *(Map 2; ☎ 04 91 33 96 78; 25 rue des Glandèves, 1er; metro Vieux Port; mains around €10)* is a pizzeria like no other. It is small, simple and ruled with a heart of gold by roughly 75-year-old Rose – chef, patron and legendary grandmother of this Marseillais establishment.

Restaurant O'Stop *(Map 2; ☎ 04 91 33 85 34; place de l'Opéra, 1er; metro Vieux Port)*, opposite the opera, is a simple bar-cum-bistro that welcomes diners any time of day or night – it opens 24 hours.

Toinou *(Map 2; ☎ 04 91 33 1494; 3 cours St-Louis, 1er; metro Noailles)* is famed for its *coquillages* (shellfish). It runs a stall where you can taste on the move, and a restaurant where you can sit down and feast (in season) on *oursins* (sea urchins; €9.70 a dozen), *violets* (sea squirts; €1.10 a piece), oysters (from €9.80 a dozen), bowlfuls of *bulots* (whelks) and magnificent two-person seafood platters (€40).

Le Part des Anges *(Map 2; ☎ 04 91 33 55 70; 33 rue Sainte, 1er; metro Vieux Port)* is a well-stocked wine shop run by knowledgable staff where you can also drink regional wine and dine on Provençal bistro dishes until 2am.

Lemon Grass *(Map 2; ☎ 04 91 33 97 65; 10 rue Fort Notre Dame, 7e; metro Vieux Port; 2/3 courses €23/28)* is a refined, very modern and delicious Thai choice. Its fresh tuna rolls with mint and coriander are well worth wrapping your tongue around. *Bouillabaisse de Bangkok*, featuring lots of coconut milk and lemongrass, costs an extra €4.

Le Panier On, or just off, rue de la République – the busy street on the quarter's eastern fringe – are several Vietnamese and Chinese restaurants worth a nibble.

Pizzaria Étienne *(Map 2; 43 rue de Lorette, 2e; metro Colbert; pizza for 1/2/3/4 people €7/11/14/18.50, meat dishes from €11.50)*, evocative of the real Marseilles, has been run by the same family since the 1940s and is renowned for its *supions frits* (see Highlights at the start of the chapter) and juicy *pavé de bœuf* (beef steaks). From rue de la République, cut down passage de Lorette and walk up the staircase.

Aux Deux Sinistrès *(Map 2; ☎ 04 91 91 72 77; place de Lorette, 2e; metro Vieux Port; menus around €11)*, up the hill from Pizzaria Étienne, at the end of rue du Petit Puits, is a small and friendly bistro, frequented by a local clientele who clearly know each other.

Bobolivo *(Map 2; ☎ 04 91 90 20 68; 29 rue Caisserie, 2e; metro Vieux Port; mains €10-15)* is known around town as an unpretentious, good-value spot. Its summertime terrace is delightful.

Le Vieux Clocher *(Map 2; ☎ 04 91 90 52 95; 12 place des Augustines, 2e; metro Vieux Port; pizza €10-14, menus €10-18.30)*, a pizzeria with shady terrace under a whopping plane tree, makes for a quick and easy lunch.

L'Art et les Thés *(Map 2; ☎ 04 91 14 58 71; 2 rue de la Charité, 2e; metro Joliette; mains €8-12/desserts €5)*, nestled in the courtyard of the Centre de la Vieille Charité, serves tasty savoury tarts, salads and sweet things to follow – perfect for lunch.

Le Panier's western fringe flows into the commercial port area where grand old warehouses are being turned into smart, London docks–feel complexes with offices, hip bistros and restaurants.

Le Dock de Suez *(Map 1; ☎ 04 91 56 07 56; 10 place de la Joliette, 2e; metro Joliette; 2-course menu €18, plat du jour €12.20)* exudes an industrial feel with its voluminous interior and bistro-style menu. As you face No 10 on the square, the entrance is on the right side of the building.

Cours Julien Marseilles' bohemian patch of town, in the 6e *arrondissement*, is lined with restaurants offering a tantalising variety of French and ethnic cuisines. Rue des Trois Mages cooks up Greek, Indian, Lebanese and Spanish. By day, the elongated tree-studded square buzzes with family activity. Come dusk, the tone is less jolly. Stand-out Provençal choices include the following two places.

Le Sud du Haut *(Map 1; ☎ 04 91 92 66 64; 80 cours Julien, 6e; metro Notre Dame du*

Tasty Tip

No trip to Marseilles is complete without trying *bouillabaisse*, a traditional fish stew, pronounced 'bwee-ya-bess'. Although many touristy restaurants around the port advertise Provence's signature dish for as little as €15, a truly authentic *bouillabaisse* – evident from the manner in which it is served and its fresh fish content – will cost you around €50 per person.

Kosher *bouillabaisse* restaurants generally don't dish up the stew to solo diners (minimum two people). Most also demand that you order the dish at least 24 hours in advance – a sure sign of freshness. Among the 16-odd places to have signed the Charte de la Bouillabaisse Marseillaise – a charter aimed at safeguarding the century-old culinary creation – are Marseilles' best-known *bouillabaisse* restaurants: **L'Épuisette** *(Map 1; ☎ 04 91 52 17 82; rue du Vallon des Auffes, 7e; menus €35.50, €46.50 & €63.50)*, a concrete-and-glass edifice perched on a rock looking out to sea; **Chez Fonfon** *(Map 1; ☎ 04 91 52 14 38; 140 rue du Vallon des Auffes; menus €29.73 & €47.26)*, overlooking a quaint harbour, where non-*bouillabaisse* diners can opt for a fish flambéed in pastis; portside **Le Miramar** *(Map 2; ☎ 04 91 91 10 40; W www.bouillabaisse.com; 12 quai du Port, 1er; metro Vieux Port)*; and hotel-restaurant **Le Rhul** *(Map 1; ☎ 04 91 52 54 54; 269 corniche Président John F Kennedy, 7e)*. Advance reservations are essential at all four places.

More details about *bouillabaisse* are in the special Food & Wine of Provence section earlier in the book.

Mont-Cours Julien; mains around €10) is a brightly painted place with an eclectic interior and a colourful, sky-topped terrace.

Le Jardin d'à Côté *(Map 1; ☎ 04 91 94 15 51; 65 cours Julien, 6e; metro Notre Dame du Mont-Cours Julien; mains around €10)* cooks up fish dishes and a variety of traditional Marseillais platters.

By the Beach Three of Marseilles' best-known *bouillabaisse* restaurants – as renowned for their other fish and seafood dishes as for their fishy stew – overlook the sea. See the boxed text 'Tasty Tip' for details.

Pizzeria Chez Jeannot *(Map 1; ☎ 04 91 52 11 28; 129 rue du Vallon des Auffes, 7e; pizza/pasta from €5.50/8.50)* is not pricey and always packed, thanks to its great location. Jeannot serves fresh salads, pasta, oysters and shellfish as well as pizza. Her terrace restaurant is a great boat-watching spot.

Le Péron *(Map 1; ☎ 04 91 52 15 22; 56 corniche Président John F Kennedy, 7e; menus €39 & €54, starters/mains/desserts €14/25/8)*, the hottest thing since sliced bread at the time of writing, is a chic London-feel place with a *très moderne* interior and inventive menu to match.

Other seaside spots include **Pizzeria des Catalans** *(Map 1; ☎ 04 91 52 37 82; 3 rue Catalans, 7e)*, which boasts an enviable terrace next to the beach-volley courts on Plage des Catalans; and **Bistrot Plage** (see Beaches earlier in this chapter), adjoining a private beach farther south along the corniche. Both offer unbeatable coastal views.

If you don't mind a short moonlight stroll between rocks, the Baie des Singes (Bay of Monkeys) is for you.

La Baie des Singes *(☎ 04 91 93 68 89; Anse Croisettes)*, by no means a gastronomic temple, is still worth the trip for its stunning location amid rocks on Cap Croisette, 15km south of the centre on the city's southern limits. *Bouillabaisse* costs €40.

Cafés

Cafés crowd quai du Port, quai de Rive Neuve and cours Honoré d'Estienne d'Orves, 1er. There is a less touristy cluster overlooking the fountain on place de la Préfecture, at the southern end of pedestrianised rue St-Ferréol, 1er.

Le Pain Quotidien *(Map 2; 18 place aux Huiles)*, not open at the time of writing, will be well worth lunching at if it is anything like its counterpart in Nice (see the Nice to Menton chapter for details).

Salon de Thé *(Map 2; ☎ 04 91 55 55 00; 75 rue St-Ferréol, 6e; metro Estrangin-Prefécture; open 9.30am-9pm Mon-Fri, 9.30am-midnight Sat)*, inside the Virgin Megastore, is trendy with a young crowd.

Café de la Mode *(Map 2; ☎ 04 96 11 54 16; 11 La Canebière, 1er; metro Vieux Port)*, inside the Musée de la Mode, is minimalist and cool, both figuratively and literally. Salami, pastrami, roast beef and prawns dress its well-filled sandwiches, and there's free (French) newspapers to read.

Marseil Café *(Map 1; rue des Trois Mages, 6e; metro Notre Dame du Mont-Cours Julien)* is a bohemian café-cum-bar inside La Passerelle, a comic-strip bookshop, where you can read, giggle and glug.

Self-Catering

Marseilles' most aromatic market is its daily **fresh fish market** *(Map 1; quai des Belges, 1er; metro Vieux Port; open 8am-noon daily)* at the old port. Equally aromatic is the **Marché d'Ail** (garlic market) held in season on cours Belsunce. Fruit, vegetables, fish and dried products are sold at the **Marché des Capucins** *(Map 2; place des Capucins, 1er; metro Noailles; open 8am-7pm daily)*.

Monoprix *(Map 2; 36 La Canebière, 1er; metro Noailles; open 8.30am-8.30pm Mon-Sat)*, Marseilles' most central supermarket, has an in-house bakery. For baklava and other calorie-loaded pastries, try the **Pâtisserie Orientale** *(Map 2; ☎ 04 91 33 65 20; 28 rue Pavillon, 1er; metro Noailles)*, a busy Middle Eastern bakery.

ENTERTAINMENT

Sporting and cultural events are listed in *Agenda*, a free monthly listing magazine published by the **Espace Culture** *(Map 2; ☎ 04 96 11 04 60; W www.espaceculture.net – French only; 42 La Canebière, 1er; metro Vieux Port)* or the tourist office. The latter sells tickets for most events, as does the *billetterie* (ticket desk) in **FNAC** *(Map 2 ☎ 04 91 39 94 00; Centre Bourse, 1er; metro Vieux Port)* and the **Virgin Megastore** *(Map 2; ☎ 04 91 55 84 11; 75 rue St-Ferréol, 6e; metro Estrangin-Préfecture)*.

Café Espace Julien *(Map 1; ☎ 04 91 24 34 10; 39 cours Julien, 6e; metro Notre Dame du Mont-Cours Julien)* is a leading venue for rock concerts, opérock, alternative theatre, reggae festivals, hip hop, Afro-groove and other cutting-edge entertainment. Admission costs nothing to €15 depending on what's on.

Le Dock des Suds *(☎ 04 91 99 00 00; W www.dock-des-suds-org – French only; 12 rue Urbain V; 2e)*, near the commercial port, is Marseilles' other music venue.

Pelle Mêle *(Map 2; ☎ 04 91 54 85 26; 8 place aux Huiles, 1er; metro Vieux Port)* is a jazz bistro.

Bars & Pubs

Quai de Rive Neuve *(Map 2; 7e & 1er; metro Vieux Port)* is lined with places to drink and be merry: **O'Malleys** *(9 quai de Rive Neuve)* and **The Shamrock** *(17 quai de Rive Neuve)* are Irish watering holes. Pagnol drank at **Bar de la Marine** *(quai de Rive Neuve 15)*, while **Le Scandale** *(17 quai de Rive Neuve 17)* lures a young and bolshy crowd with its 5am weekend closing. More refined options across the water include the following.

Le Crystal *(Map 2; ☎ 04 91 91 57 96; 148 quai du Port, 2e; metro Vieux Port)*, decked out 1950s style, is a lovely place to lounge away an hour or two.

La Caravelle *(Map 2; ☎ 04 91 90 36 64; 34 quai du Port, 2e; metro Vieux Port)* is a trendy boat-inspired bar, tucked on the 1st floor of the Hôtel Bellevue. It hosts live jazz concerts and cooks up an awesome Sunday-morning brunch (€15).

La Fabrique *(Map 2; ☎ 04 91 91 40 48; 3 place Jules Verne, 2e; metro Vieux Port; open 7pm-2am Thur-Sun)*, behind Marseilles' quayside town hall, is a fabulously authentic and very hip bar-cum-restaurant with sofa seating just made for lounging on, lots of board games to lose track of time and Sunday brunch (from 1pm).

Web Bar *(Map 1; ☎ 04 91 11 65 11; W www.webbar.fr – French only; 114 rue de la République, 2e; metro Joliette; open 10am-2am daily)* is much more than its name suggests. Yes, it has Internet access (€5/hour) but its startling industrial decor, contemporary art exhibitions, urban feel and DJs are the main reasons to come here.

Discos & Clubs

Le Trolleybus *(Map 2; ☎ 04 91 54 30 45; 24 quai de Rive Neuve, 7e; metro Vieux Port; open 11pm-6am Thur-Sat)*, inside an 18th-century warehouse, is a Marseillais institution. DJs play soul, groove, house and tech-house, and early evening drinkers can play *pétanque* over an aperitif.

Metal Café *(Map 2; ☎ 04 91 54 03 03; 20 rue Fortia, 1er; metro Vieux Port)*, the other 'in' choice, sits at the foot of the staircase linking cours Honoré d'Estienne d'Orves with rue Sainte. Look for the steely grey door.

Cubaïla Café *(Map 1; ☎ 04 91 48 97 48; 40 rue des Trois Rois, 6e; metro Notre Dame du Mont-Cours Julien)* is a Tex-Mex restaurant that, at midnight, turns into a pulsating

OM

Olympique de Marseille (OM) is not just another football team. It's an institution backed by a city full of fans who sing *'Nous sommes les Marseillais! Et nous allons gagner!'* ('We are the Marseillais! And we will win!') both inside and outside the stadium.

Guided tours of OM's home ground, the **Stade Vélodrome** *(Map 1; 3 blvd Michelet, 8e; metro rond-point du Prado)* kick off from the stadium six times daily Monday to Saturday, mid-June to 31 August. One-hour tours cost €6.50; reserve in advance at the tourist office.

Built in 1930, the stadium can seat up to 60,000 screaming spectators. Within the stadium complex is the **Musée-Boutique de l'OM** *(☎ 04 91 71 46 00; admission free; open 2.30pm-7pm Mon-Sat)*, a museum-shop that unravels the history of the club from its creation in 1899 and sells the club's pale-blue-and-white colours. If the latter is closed, try **Virage Sud** *(☎ 04 91 77 15 28; 46 blvd Michelet; open 9.30am-noon & 2pm-6.30pm Mon-Sat)*, opposite the stadium.

In town, match tickets (€20 to €40), shirts, scarves and other OM paraphernalia are sold at OM's **Boutique Officielle** *(official OM shop; Map 2; ☎ 04 91 33 52 28; 44 La Canebière, open 2.30pm-7pm Mon, 10am-7pm Tues-Sat • Map 2; ☎/fax 04 91 33 96 75; 3 quai des Belges; open 10.30am-7pm daily)*. The latter branch adjoins **Café OM** *(Map 2; ☎ 04 91 33 80 33; 3 quai des Belges, 1er)*, the club café-cum-bar where supporters who fail to score a ticket can be found during matches staring agog at the TV screen.

OM has an official website with online boutique at Ⓦ www.olympiquedemarseille.com (in French only) and is the second club in the world (after Manchester United's MUTV) to have its own TV channel that fans pay to watch. OMTV broadcasts four hours a day (5pm to 9pm) on Canal Satellite.

nightclub where salsa, Latino and other hot jives rule.

La Machine à Coudre *(Map 2; ☎ 04 91 55 62 65; 6 rue Jean Roque, 1er; metro Noailles)*, in a small street off the southern end of blvd Garibaldi, plays funk, punk, blues and rap.

La Maronaise *(☎ 04 91 73 98 58; route de la Marronnaise, 8e)*, in the seaside quarter of Les Goudes on Cap Croisette, 10km south of Plage du Prado, is an outdoor disco where you can dance beneath the stars to hip beats. Anyone in the know has heard of this place before even setting foot in Marseilles.

Gay & Lesbian Venues

Popular gay spots include **L'Énigme** *(Map 2; ☎ 04 91 33 79 20; 22 rue Beauvau, 1er; metro Vieux Port)*, a busy bar, and **New Cancan** *(Map 1; ☎ 04 91 48 59 76; 3 rue Sénac de Meilhan, 1er; metro Noailles or Réformés-Canebière; open until 6am)*, Marseilles' best-known gay nightclub, said to be camper than a row of tents and full of fun.

Opera & Ballet

Opéra de Marseille *(Map 2; ☎ 04 91 55 11 10; 2 rue Molière, 1er; metro Vieux Port; tickets €8-22)* is housed in an Art Deco building dating from 1921. Tickets for performances can be bought from the box office inside the opera house (the entrance to the building is on place Ernest Reyer).

Théâtre Silvain *(Map 1; corniche Président John F Kennedy, 7e)* is an open-air amphitheatre midway between plage des Catalans and plage du Prophète. Performances are staged here in June and July.

Theatre

Marseilles has an active alternative theatre scene. Performance venues include comedy theatre-restaurant **Chocolat Théâtre** *(Map 1; ☎ 04 91 42 19 29; 59 cours Julien, 6e; metro Notre Dame du Mont-Cours Julien)* and three pocket-sized places in **Passage des Arts** *(Map 2; 16 quai de Rive Neuve, 7e; metro Vieux Port)*: **Théâtre Off** *(☎ 04 91 33 12 92)*; café-theatre **Le Quai du Rire** *(☎ 04 91 54 95 00)*, where you can be entertained while you dine; and **Théâtre Badaboum** *(☎ 04 91 54 40 71)*.

Mainstream dramas are hosted at Marseille's National Theatre, otherwise known as **La Criée** *(Map 2; ☎ 04 96 17 80 00; 30 quai de Rive Neuve, 7e; metro Vieux Port; tickets €20)*, inside Marseilles' old fish auction house built in 1909.

Cinema

Cinéma Variétés *(Map 2; ☎ 04 96 11 61 61; ⓔ cesarvarietes@wanadoo.fr; 37 rue Vincent*

Scotto, 1er; metro Noailles; tickets €6.50) and **Cinéma César** *(Map 1; ☎ 04 91 37 12 80; 4 place Castellane, 6e; metro Castellane; tickets €6.50)* show foreign films in their original language with French subtitles.

In July and August, during the Ciné Plein Air festival, films (in French) are screened outside at various venues; look for posters around town or ask at the tourist office. Admission is free.

SHOPPING

Marseilles' premier market, which has to be seen to be believed is the fabulous Sunday morning **Marché aux Puces** *(ave du Cap Pinède, 15e; open 9am-7pm Sun)*. Live chickens killed to order and African carved animals are among the colourful sights you can enjoy as you stroll the indoor and outdoor stalls. Take bus No 35 or No 70 from rue des Fabres (in front of Espace Infos RTM). The market is north of the centre, near the docks.

Cours Julien *(Map 1; metro Notre Dame du Mont-Cours Julien, 6e)* hosts various morning markets: fresh flowers on Wednesday and Saturday, fruit and veg on Friday, antique books every second Saturday, and stamps or antique books on Sunday. Stalls laden with everything from second-hand clothing to pots and pans fill the nearby place Jean Jaurès from 8am to 1pm Saturday.

The best place to shop for traditional Provençal *santons* is the boutique inside the Musée du Santon (see the boxed text 'Little Saints' earlier in this chapter). Marseillais soaps can be bought at **Savon de Marseille** *(Map 2; ☎ 04 91 56 20 94; 1 rue Caisserie, 2e; metro Colbert or Vieux Port)*, which specialises in self-pampering products made from Provençal herbs, plants and ochre. You can fill your water bottle with table wine costing €1.30 per litre at **Le Part des Anges** (see Restaurants – Vieux Port under Places to Eat earlier in this chapter.)

GETTING THERE & AWAY

Air

The **Marseilles-Provence airport** *(Aéroport Marseille-Provence; ☎ 04 42 14 14 14; W www.marseille.aeroport.fr – French only)* is 25km northwest of Marseilles in Marignane.

Bus

The **bus station** *(Map 1; ☎ 04 91 08 16 40; place Victor Hugo, 3e; metro Gare St-Charles)* will remain 150m to your right as you exit the train station until 2004, when it will be incorporated within the train station complex, behind the new Grande Halle (see Train later). Bus drivers sell tickets. Some buses to/from Bandol, La Ciotat and Cassis use place Castellane (metro Castellane, 6e), south of the centre.

There are buses to/from Aix-en-Provence (€4.10, 35 minutes via the A51 *autoroute*/one hour via the N8, every 15 minutes). Nice-based **Phocéens Cars** *(☎ 04 93 85 66 61)* operates regular services between Marseilles and Nice (€22.50, 2¾ hours, up to three daily) via Cannes (€21, 2¼ hours) and Nice-Côte d'Azur airport (€22.50, 2½ hours); and one or two daily to/from Manosque (€8.30, 1½ hours) and Sisteron (€13.10, 2½ hours).

Year-round services going to/from Digne-les-Bains (€13.50, 2¼ hours) and ski-season buses to/from Pra-Loup (€24.10, 4½ hours) via Barcelonnette (€21.60, four hours) are operated by the Gap-based **Société des Cars Alpes Littoral** *(SCAL; ☎ 04 92 51 06 05)*.

Other services include two to four buses daily to/from Cassis (€3.10, 1¼ hours), La Ciotat (€3.90, one hour to 1½ hours), Carpentras (€12.40, two hours), Cavaillon (€11.70, one hour) and Avignon (€15.20, two hours). Buses to/from Arles (€14.60, two hours, five daily except Sunday) stop in Salon de Provence (€8.50, 1¾ hours), Les Baux de Provence (€11.40 1½ hours) and Fontvieille (€12.80 1¾ hours).

For international routes and fares run by **Eurolines** *(☎ 04 91 50 57 55)* and **Intercars** *(☎ 04 91 50 08 66)*, both at the bus station, see the Getting There & Away chapter.

Train

Marseilles' passenger train station, served by both metro lines and under renovation until 2004 (when the Grande Halle, complete with shops and underground parking, will open), is called Gare St-Charles (metro Gare St-Charles). The luggage lockers, next to the tracks on platform A, are accessible 24 hours (€3.20 for a medium-sized locker per 72 hours). In town, train tickets can be bought at the **SNCF Boutique** *(Map 2; 17 rue Grignan, 1er; open 9.30am-6pm Mon-Fri, 10am-5.30pm Sat)*.

There are direct trains to Aix-en-Provence (€5.80, 30 minutes, 16 to 24 daily), Nîmes (€15.70, 1¼ hours, 12 daily) via Arles

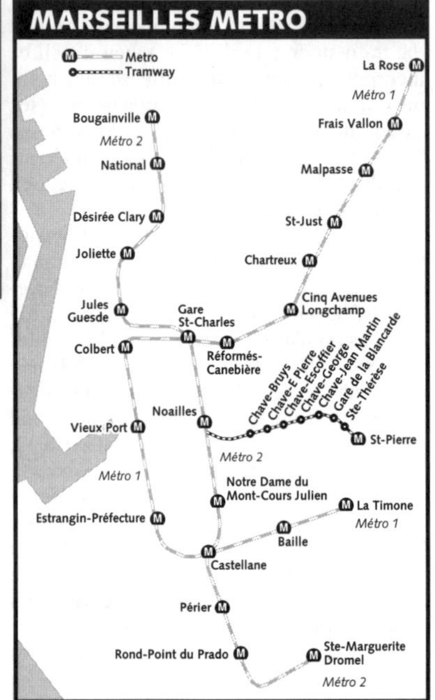

(€11.40, 50 minutes), Orange (€17.70, 1½ hours, 10 daily), Avignon (€23.90, one hour, hourly) and other destinations. Heading east along the coast, over two dozen trains per day chug on the Marseilles–Ventimiglia (Vintimille in French) line, linking Marseilles with Toulon (€9.30, 45 minutes to one hour), Les Arcs-sur-Argens (€18.10, 1¼ hours), St-Raphaël (€20.40, 1½ hours), Cannes (€23.30, two hours), Antibes (€24.20, 2¼ hours), Nice (€25.90, 2½ hours), Monaco (€27.30, three hours) and Menton (€27.50, 3¼ hours). The Marseilles to Hyères train (€12.70, 1¼ hours, four daily) stops at Cassis, La Ciotat, Bandol, Ollioules, Sanary-sur-Mer and Toulon.

For trains to other parts of France and Europe see the Getting There & Away chapter.

Car & Motorcycle

Avis *(☎ 04 91 64 71 00)* has a desk at the train station. **Europcar** *(☎ 04 91 99 09 32; 7 blvd Maurice Bourdet)* is nearby.

Boat

From Marseilles' **passenger ferry terminal** *(Map 1; Gare Maritime; ☎ 04 91 56 38 63; quai de la Joliette, 2e; metro Joliette)*, **SNCM** *(Map 1; ☎ 08 91 70 18 01; 61 blvd des Dames, 2e; metro Joliette)* operates ferries to/from Corsica, Sardinia, Tunisia, Spain and Algeria. It also handles ticketing and reservations for the Tunisian ferry company, Compagnie Tunisienne de Navigation (CTN). **Algérie Ferries** *(Map 2; ☎ 04 91 90 64 70; 29 blvd des Dames, 2e; metro Joliette)* operates boats to/from Algeria.

In town, **Change de la Bourse** *(Map 2; ☎ 04 91 13 09 00; 3 place du Général de Gaulle, 1er)* sells SNCM tickets up to 24 hours before departure.

For more information see Sea in the Getting There & Away chapter.

GETTING AROUND

To/From the Airport

Shuttle buses (in Marseilles ☎ 04 91 50 59 34; at airport ☎ 04 42 14 31 27) link the Marseilles-Provence airport with Marseilles train station (adult/six to 10 years €8/4.60). Buses to the airport leave from in front of the train station's main entrance approximately every 20 minutes between 5.30am and 9.50pm. Journey time is 25 minutes.

Bus & Metro

Marseilles' two metro lines (Métro 1 and Métro 2), tramline and extensive bus network are operated by Régie des Transports de Marseille (RTM). Services start to run about 5am and continue to about 9pm. Between 9.25pm and 12.30am, metro and tram routes are covered every 15 minutes by surface bus Nos M1 and M2, and tramway No 68; the stops are clearly marked with fluor escent green signs reading *métro en bus* (metro by bus). Most of the 'Fluobus' night buses begin their runs in front of the **Espace Infos-RTM** *(Map 2; ☎ 04 91 91 92 10; 6 rue des Fabres, 1er; metro Vieux Port; open 6am-6pm Mon-Fri, 9am-12.30pm & 2pm-5.15pm Sat)*. You can also buy tickets for the entire transport network here.

A ticket for a solo trip on bus, tram or metro costs €1.40, a six-/10-journey card is available for €6.50/13 and a one-day/week pass allowing unlimited travel is €3.80/7.90. Tickets can be used on any combination of metro, bus and tram for one hour after they've been time-stamped (aboard buses or in blue ticket distributors at tram stops and metro stations).

Taxi

There's a taxi rank in front of the train station. **Marseille Taxi** *(☎ 04 91 02 20 20)*, **Radio Taxi France** *(☎ 04 91 85 80 00)* and **Taxi Blanc Bleu** *(☎ 04 91 51 50 00)* dispatch taxis 24 hours a day.

Bicycle

MBK-Cycles DO *(Map 2; ☎ 04 91 54 33 14; 68-76 cours Lieutaud)* and **Team Bike** *(Map 1; ☎ 04 91 92 76 73; 122 cours Lieutaud)* both rent mountain bikes and scooters. **Tandem** *(☎ 04 91 22 64 80; 6 ave du Parc Borély)* is a rental outlet near Plage du Prado.

Boat

Hot and bothered visitors who can't face walking another step can indulge in the shortest boat ride on the Riviera, a trip immortalised by Marcel Pagnol in his writing. A small ferry yo-yos between the town hall on quai du Port and place aux Huiles on quai de Rive Neuve 8am to 6.30pm daily. A one-way fare costs €0.50/free for adults/under-7s and sailing time is about three minutes.

Les Calanques

Since 1975, this 20km strip of coast, and the inland Massif des Calanques covering 5000 hectares, has been protected as a natural monument. Despite its barren landscape, the massif shelters an extraordinary wealth of flora and fauna – including 900 plant species, of which 15 are protected, such as the dwarf red behen, Marseilles astragalus and tartonraire sparrow wort. Myrtle and wild olive trees grow in the warmer valleys. The Bonnelli eagle is a frequent visitor to Les Calanques, which also shelters Europe's largest lizard and longest snake – the eyed lizard (60cm) and the Montpellier snake (2m) – in their darker cracks and crevices.

Les Calanques offers ample walking opportunities, including the coastal **GR98**, which leads south from the Marseilles suburb of **La Madrague** to Callelongue on **Cap Croisette**, and then east along the coast to Cassis. Count on 11 to 12 hours at least to walk this 28km stretch. See Along the Coast earlier in this chapter for bus information from Marseilles to Callelongue.

Boat excursions in Les Calanques set sail from Marseilles, Cassis and La Ciotat, as well as Bandol, Sanary-sur-Mer and Le Brusc (see the St-Tropez to Toulon chapter).

No Entry

The threat of forest fire to the semi-arid flora skirting Marseilles' limestone coastline prompts the Office National des Forêts (National Forestry Office) to close Les Calanques each year from 1 July until the second Saturday in September.

The entire massif interior is off-limits when winds blow 80km/h or more. At other times, walkers can only access footpaths between 6am and 11am. Anyone found ignoring these strict 'No Entry' rules is fined €135 on the spot.

SORMIOU & MORGIOU

There are plenty of shorter, marked trails (inaccessible from late June to mid-September), the most popular being those that lead to Calanque de Sormiou and neighbouring Calanque de Morgiou.

Sormiou, the largest *calanque*, hit the headlines in October 1991 when Henri Cosquer, a diver from Cassis (see Diving in that section later in this chapter) discovered an underwater cave. Its interior was adorned with prehistoric wall paintings from around 20,000 BC. The only access was a narrow, 150m-long passage, 36m underwater. Named the Grotte Cosquer, the cave is protected as a historical monument and closed to the public. Many more are believed to exist.

To get here by car from place Louis Bonnefon (next to Château Borély) in Marseilles, follow the southbound ave de Hambourg past César's thumb on rond-point Pierre Guerre to chemin de Sormiou. From the end of this road, the route du Feu forest track (a 45-minute walk) leads to Sormiou's small fishing port and beach in the Calanque. By bus, take No 23 from the rond-point du Prado metro stop to La Cayolle stop, from where it is a 3km walk to Sormiou.

Sormiou and Morgiou are separated by the headland Cap Morgiou. **Calanque de Morgiou** nestles on the eastern side of the cape. During the 17th century, Louis XIII came to Marseilles to fish for tuna in the bay. From ave de Hambourg, follow the Morgiou road signs past Marseilles' infamous prison in Les Beaumettes. Morgiou beach is one hour's

Naturally Wonderful Cassis

One of Europe's highest maritime cliffs – the imposing 416m-high **Cap Canaille** – dominates the southwestern side of Baie de Cassis. The hollow peak of the rocky limestone cape hides **Grotte des Espagnols** (Spaniards' Cave), a fantastic cave filled with a magical assortment of stalactites and stalagmites. It cannot be visited. From the cliff there are magnificent views of Cassis and Mont Puget (565m), the highest peak in the Massif des Calanques.

An equally awesome panorama unfolds as you drive along the well-maintained but very wiggly **route des Crêtes** (literally 'road of crests') that leads 16km from Cassis, along the top of its cliff-caked coastline, to La Ciotat.

walk from the car park. By bus, take No 23 and continue past La Cayolle. Get off at the Morgiou-Beauvallon bus stop.

EN-VAU, PORT-PIN & PORT-MIOU

Continuing east along the stone sculptured coast you come to Calanque d'En-Vau which, with its emerald waters encased by cliffs occasionally studded with dangling rope-clad climbers, is the most photographed calanque. Its entrance is guarded by the **Doigt de Dieu** (literally 'God's Finger), a giant rock pinnacle, and its beach is pebbly. En-Vau is accessible by foot. There is a three-hour marked trail starting from the car park on the Col de la Gardiole (south off the D559), 5km west from Cassis on a wiggly dirt road into Forêt de la Gardiole. Approaching from the east, it is a good 1½-hour walk on the GR98 from Port-Miou. En route you pass the neighbouring Calanque de Port-Pin, a 30-minute walk from Port-Miou.

In summer, boats sail from Cassis to En-Vau. Calanque de Port-Miou, immediately west of Cassis, is one of the few inlets accessible by car; the tourist office in Cassis distributes free maps featuring the three Calanques plus the various walking trails that lead to them.

CASSIS

postcode 13260 • pop 8070

Sweet little Cassis is best known for its white wines, of which Provençal poet Frédéric Mistral wrote 'the bee does not have a sweeter honey, it shines like an untroubled diamond.' Quality aside, the neat picture-postcard appearance of Cassis' terraced vineyards, which climb up the slopes in little steps against a magnificent backdrop of sea and cliffs, can hardly be disputed.

Unfortunately, the fishing port – complete with a 14th-century chateau, views of Baie de Cassis and France's highest cliff – is a hub for summer boat trips along Les Calanques and gets overrun with camcorder-wielding tourists. An open-air market fills place du Marché on Wednesday and Friday morning. Stalls to look out for include one that sells the sweetest, moistest, freshest raisin bread in Provence, and another that displays a rainbow of scented soaps.

Cassis (pronounced 'ca-see') has nothing to do with the blackcurrant liqueur (pronounced 'ca-sees') that is mixed with white wine to create the aperitif known as kir.

Orientation & Information

Cassis train station, on ave de la Gare, is just over 3km east of the centre. Buses stop at rond-point du Pressoir, five minutes' walk along ave du Professeur René Leriche and rue de l'Arène to the port. The old town surrounds the port. Its medieval chateau – privately owned and closed to visitors – peers down on the port from a rocky outcrop. Quai St-Pierre, from where boat trips depart, runs alongside the port to the beach, the sandy Plage de la Grande Mer. The pebbly Plage de Bestouan is 700m northwest of the port.

The **tourist office** *(☎ 04 42 01 71 17, fax 04 42 01 28 31; e omt-cassis@enprovence.com; quai des Moulins; open 9am-noon & 2.30pm-5.30pm Mon-Fri, 9am-noon Sat)* is in Oustaou Calendal, a reconstruction of the famous portside casino where fortunes were won and lost following its opening in 1951.

Boat Excursions

Tickets for the 15-odd daily boats that sail year-round around Les Calanques are sold at the portside **kiosk** *(information ☎ 04 42 01 90 83; square Gilbert Savon)*, opposite the boats moored alongside quai St-Pierre. A 45-minute trip to three Calanques (Port-Miou, Port-Pin and En-Vau) costs €10; a 65-minute trip covering the latter plus Oule and Devanson Calanques is €15; and a 1½-hour trip taking in seven Calanques (including

Morgiou) costs €20. Children aged two to 10 years get a small discount.

In addition to the circular boat trips, you can disembark at En-Vau (return fare €12), spend a couple of hours on the beach there, then sail back to Cassis on a later boat. Wear sturdy shoes as the climb from the boat to the beach is across rocks – a scramble not recommended for young children.

Diving

Breathtaking diving expeditions are organised by the **Centre Cassidain de Plongée** *(☎ 04 42 01 89 16, fax 04 42 01 23 76; W www.cassis-services-plongee.fr; 3 rue Michel Arnaud)*. The school is run by Henri Cosquer (see Sormiou & Morgiou earlier in this chapter for details), who leads everything from baptism dives to night dives and shipwreck expeditions.

Wine Tasting

There is no better time to taste the local *vin* than at the annual Fête des Vendanges et du Vin Cassis, celebrated to mark the grape harvest on the first Sunday in September. Failing that, you can visit one of the 13 *domaines* (wine-producing estates) that produce the Cassis appellation (AOC); the tourist office can provide you with a list. Cassis white is particularly fine drunk with *oursins*. See the Cap Couronne & Carry-le-Rouet section later in this chapter for details of this delicacy.

Places to Stay

Camping Les Cigales *(☎ 04 42 01 07 34; ave de la Marne; camping for 2 people with tent & car €14.80; open Mar–mid-Nov)*, 1km uphill from the port off route de Marseille, is the only camp site in Cassis. Buses to/from Marseilles stop outside if you ask.

Auberge de Jeunesse *(☎ 04 42 01 02 72; beds with/without HI card €8.70/11.60; reception open 7.30am-10am & 5pm-11pm daily Mar-Jan)*, 3km west of Cassis centre, is isolated in the heart of the Massif des Calanques. It has no running water (so no showers), is one hour's walk from the nearest road and you have to bring your own food. By car, follow the signs off the D559 from Marseilles, park in Port-Miou, then follow the trail from ave des Calanques.

Hôtel du Commerce *(☎ 04 42 01 09 10, fax 04 42 01 14 17; 1 rue St-Clair; doubles €47-60)* is a one-star place 20m north of the port.

Le Jardin d'Émile *(☎ 04 42 01 80 55, fax 04 42 01 80 70; W www.lejardindemile.fr; doubles with garden/sea view from €69/92)*, set beneath trees opposite Plage de Bestouan, has seven classy rooms and a highly capable chef who brews a delicious *bouillabaisse* for around €40; it must be ordered in advance.

Mahogany *(☎ 04 42 01 05 70, fax 04 42 01 34 82; e plage-bestouan@enprovence.com; doubles with sea view low/high season from €76/99)* is a white place offering a sweeping vista of sandy Plage de Bestouan from its ocean-view rooms.

Places to Eat

The quays overlooking the port are overloaded with touristy places to eat and drink. The restaurant at Le Jardin d'Émile (see Places to Stay earlier) is well worth dining at. Otherwise, there's still potential for some great gastronomic moments at the place below.

Poissonnerie Laurent *(☎ 04 42 01 71 56; 6 quai Barthélémy; plat du jour €12, menu €20)*, at Cassis port, is a pearl. Photos of the seafaring family that runs the place line the walls and the seafood platters, piled high with shellfish, are guaranteed to appease the most insatiable of seafood lovers.

Getting There & Away

Cassis is on the Bandol–Marseilles and La Ciotat–Aix-en-Provence bus routes. Buses from Marseilles/Aix arrive at rond-point du Pressoir on ave du 11 Novembre 1918; buses to Marseilles/Aix depart from the stop around the corner on ave de Provence. Cassis is served by four to six buses daily on each route.

Cassis train station is on the Marseilles–Hyères rail line and is served by regular daily trains in both directions including to/from La Ciotat (€2, six minutes), Bandol (€4, 18 minutes), Marseilles (€5.40, 22 minutes) and Toulon (€6.20, 30 minutes).

LA CIOTAT

postcode 13260 • pop 30,620

The rusty old cranes cranked up over the shipyards of La Ciotat, 16km east, lost their gleam long ago. The naval shipyards, which enjoyed their heyday in the interwar period, have since closed. Facing the shipyards is La

Ciotat's quaint Vieux Port, a favourite of Georges Braque (1892–1963), who painted it several times. Behind the yards rises the imposing 155m-high **Bec d'Aigle** (literally 'eagle's beak'), a rocky massif on Cap de l'Aigle, the peak of which resembles the head of a bird of prey – hence its name. The ensemble – protected under the Parc Marin de La Ciotat – is best viewed from **Île Verte** (Green Island), a minuscule island offshore from the cape's southeastern tip.

The world premier of the first ever movie was screened in La Ciotat in September 1895, courtesy of the pioneering Lumière brothers, who filmed the motion picture at La Ciotat train station and then showed it for the first time at their father's chateau in the town. The history of the film, entitled *L'arrivée d'un train en gare de La Ciotat* (The arrival of a train at La Ciotat station), comes to life in the **Espace Simon Lumière** (*☎ 04 42 71 61 70; rue du Maréchal Foch)*, an exhibition hall dedicated to filmography.

The **tourist office** (*☎ 04 42 08 61 32, fax 04 42 08 17 88; blvd Anatole France)*, on the headland separating the old port from the new pleasure port, distributes a free brochure that guides visitors around La Ciotat *In the Footsteps of the Lumière Brothers*.

La Ciotat hosts a morning **market** on Tuesday on place Évariste Gras, the square in front of the modern Cinéma Lumière. A well-supplied nocturnal **arts and crafts market** fills the old port quays in July and August. *Pétanque* – Provence's favourite game – was invented by *boules* player Jules Lenoir in La Ciotat in 1907 (see the boxed text 'Polish Your Boules' under Spectator Sports in the Facts for the Visitor chapter).

Getting There & Away

The train station is about a 5km trek from La Ciotat's centre. La Ciotat is served by frequent trains on the Marseilles–Hyères line (see Getting There & Away under Cassis earlier in this chapter).

Buses use the more convenient **bus station** (*☎ 04 42 08 90 90; blvd Anatole France)*, adjoining the tourist office, from where there are regular buses to/from Marseilles via Cassis and Aix-en-Provence.

La Ciotat is midway between Marseilles and Toulon; from Cassis the most direct route is the inland D559 (bypassing the route des Crêtes).

North of Marseilles

AROUND THE ÉTANG DE BERRE

Oil refineries adorn the port area around the waters of the Étang de Berre, while **Marignane** (population 34,238), on its southeastern shore, is dominated by Marseilles-Provence airport. **Istres**, on the western shore of the Étang de Berre, is best known for its military airport, which has been here since 1914.

A horrifying view of this vast industrial landscape can be scowled at from the ruins of an 11th-century Saracen tower bizarrely perched on top of a rock in **Vitrolles** (population 37,087). Across the waters, the Canal de Caronte links the reasonably attractive fishing port of **Martigues** (population 44,256), on the southwestern corner of the Étang de Berre, with Golfe de Fos in the Mediterranean. It is from Martigues that the national French flag originates. Martigues' **tourist office** (*☎ 04 42 42 31 10, fax 04 42 42 31 11; ⓔ ot.martigues@visitprovence.com; 2 quai Paul Doumer)* has more information.

Unattractive **Fos-sur-Mer** (population 14,732) is a starting point for guided forays into this industrial heartland. The **tourist office** (*☎ 04 42 47 71 96, fax 04 42 05 59 42; ⓦ www.fos-tourisme.com; place de l'Hôtel de Ville)* arranges two- to four-hour tours of the Solomat-Merex industrial waste processing plant, the Shell oil refinery, TotalfinaElf's chlorine and sodium works, and the distillation site of petroleum magnet Esso. It also takes bookings for jolly boat rides around Fos-sur-Mer's industrial port. Tours cost upwards of €5 per person.

Pockets of crystal-clear waters and blue skies still exist thanks to the **Chaîne de l'Estaque**, a harsh, uninhabitable massif that forms a natural blockade between the industrial Étang de Berre and the Mediterranean. The rocky limestone coastal stretch on the protected southern side of the massif from Cap Couronne to Marseilles is known as La Côte Bleue (the Blue Coast).

Cap Couronne & Carry-le-Rouet

From Martigues the D5 leads 10km south to Cap Couronne, a sandy cape that draws plenty of Marseillais at weekends. The waters around it are protected by the **Parc Régional Marin de la Côte Bleue**, one of the region's first marine reserves, set up in 1983 to safeguard and revive marine life. The protected zone – which does not touch the coastline – is marked with yellow buoys topped with St-Andrew's crosses.

One of the region's most unique gastronomic delights – *oursins* or sea urchins – can be sampled in Carry-le-Rouet (population 6107), a harbour town favoured by French comic actor Fernandel in the 1930s. The prickly little creatures – dubbed *châtaignes de mer* (sea chestnuts) – are only caught between September and April (fishing for them is forbidden during summertime when they reproduce).

Each year, on the first three Sundays of February, Carry-le-Rouet celebrates **L'Oursinade**, its annual sea-urchin festival, which sees a giant open-air picnic spill across the quays around the old port. Restaurants and hotels set up stalls selling urchin platters, allowing everyone – tourists and locals alike – to indulge in a *dégustation* (tasting) session around shared tables. The creatures are reportedly best served with chilled Cassis white wine.

Carry-le-Rouet's **tourist office** *(☎ 04 42 13 20 36, fax 04 42 44 52 03; W www.carry-lerouet.com – French only; ave Aristide Briand)* has accommodation details.

L'Estaque

Lying about 17km east of Carry-le-Rouet is L'Estaque, a once-untouched fishing village adjoining Marseilles' northern suburbs which, like St-Tropez, lured artists from the impressionist, Fauvist and cubist movements. Renoir, Cézanne, Dufy and Braque painted numerous canvases during their sojourns here, although the only piece that remains in the region is Dufy's *L'Usine à L'Estaque* (Factory at L'Estaque), displayed in Marseilles' Musée Cantini (see Museums in the Marseilles sections). The English-language brochure entitled *L'Estaque and the Painters*, distributed for free by Marseilles' tourist office, is handy for travellers interested in the artists' trail.

Snacks unique to L'Estaque and ideal for a munch while strolling the water's edge include *chichi frégi* (sugar-coated doughnuts) and *panisses* (chickpea-flour cakes). Both are sold at kiosks around the harbour.

Getting There & Away

Bus No 34 links Marseilles' bus station with Martigues (€6, one hour) hourly between 7.50am and 7.20pm. A couple of buses a day continue to Fos-sur-Mer.

From Marseilles more than a dozen trains daily (less in winter) trundle along La Côte Bleue as far as Port de Bouc (€6.90, 55 minutes), from where the train line heads inland to Miramas on the northern shore of the Étang de Berre. From Marseilles trains stop at L'Estaque (€2, 8 minutes), Carry-le-Rouet (€4.20, 25 minutes), La Couronne (€5.50, 35 minutes) and Miramas (€7.60, 1¼ hours).

AIX-EN-PROVENCE

postcode 13100 • pop 134,222 • elevation 206m

Aix (Ais in Provençal) was founded as a military camp under the name of Aquae Sextiae (the Waters of Sextius) in 123 BC on the site of thermal springs, which still flow. Fortunately for stuck-up Aix, the settlement consequently became known as Aix – not Sex. The city reached its zenith as a centre of art and learning under the enlightened King René (1409–80), a brilliant polyglot who brought painters to his court from all over Europe. The city remains an academic centre today thanks to the University of Aix-Marseilles, whose forerunner was established in 1409 and which attracts a student population of about 30,000.

Some 200 elegant *hôtels particuliers* (private mansions) grace Aix's squares and avenues. Many, exhibiting the unmistakable influence of the Italian Baroque and coloured a distinctive Provençal yellow, date from the 17th and 18th centuries. Tree-shaded cours Mirabeau is said by many to be Provence's most beautiful street.

Orientation

Cours Mirabeau, Aix's main boulevard, stretches from La Rotonde – a roundabout with a huge fountain on place du Général de Gaulle – east to place Forbin. Vieil Aix (Old Aix) is north of cours Mirabeau. South of cours Mirabeau is the Quartier Mazarin, whose regular street grid was laid out in the 17th century. A series of one-way boulevards rings the entire city centre.

Information

Tourist Offices The Aix-en-Provence **tourist office** *(☎ 04 42 16 11 61, fax 04 42 16 11 62; W www.aixenprovencetourism.com; 2 place du Général de Gaulle; open 8.30am-7pm*

AIX-EN-PROVENCE

PLACES TO STAY
16 Hôtel du Globe
26 Hôtel des Arts
38 Hôtel de France
42 Grand Hôtel Nègre Coste
53 Hôtel St-Christophe
57 Hôtel Cardinal
58 Hôtel Cardinal
64 Hôtel des Quatre Dauphins

PLACES TO EAT
19 Jacquou Le Croquant
22 Jacquèrres
31 Chez Maxime
33 Le Bistro Latin
35 Le Poivre d'Âne
36 Les Bacchanales
41 Monoprix Supermarket
43 Les Deux Garçons
46 Gu et Fils
54 Yôji

ENTERTAINMENT
20 The Red Clover
21 Galaxy Pub
27 Théâtre du Jeu de Paume
28 Queen's Head
45 O'Neil's
47 Cinéma Renoir
55 Le Cézanne
56 Ciné Mazarin

MUSEUMS & GALLERIES
2 Musée des Tapisseries
7 Musée du Vieil Aix; O'Neil's
30 Musée d'Histoire Naturelle
40 Galerie d'Art du Conseil Général des Bouches du Rhône
48 Musée Arbaud
62 Musée Granet

OTHER
1 Cathédrale St-Sauveur
3 Syndicat Général des Coteaux d'Aix en Provence
4 Pavillon de Vendôme
5 Thermes Sextius
6 Former University Building
8 Le Comptoir des Oliviers
9 Laundrette
10 Cycles Zammit
11 Chapelle de Ste-Catherine
12 Hublot
13 Town Hall
14 Cave du Felibrige
15 Virtu@lis
17 Laundrette
18 Savon de Marseille
23 Palais de Justice
24 Église Ste-Marie Madeleine
25 Laundrette
29 Harmonia Mundi Forum
32 La Truffe Cendrée
34 Laundrette
37 Maison de la Nature et de l'Environnement
39 L'Agence (American Express)
44 Brémond
49 Book in Bar
50 Béchaud
51 Tourist Office
52 Post Office
59 Église St-Jean de Malte
60 Place aux Huiles
61 Net Zone
63 Paradox
65 Pétanque Court
66 Bus Station

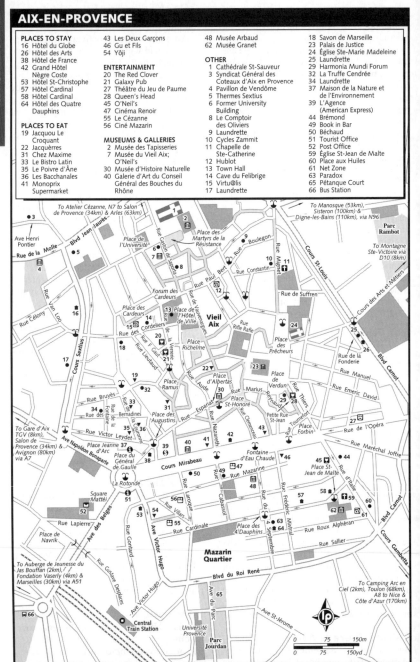

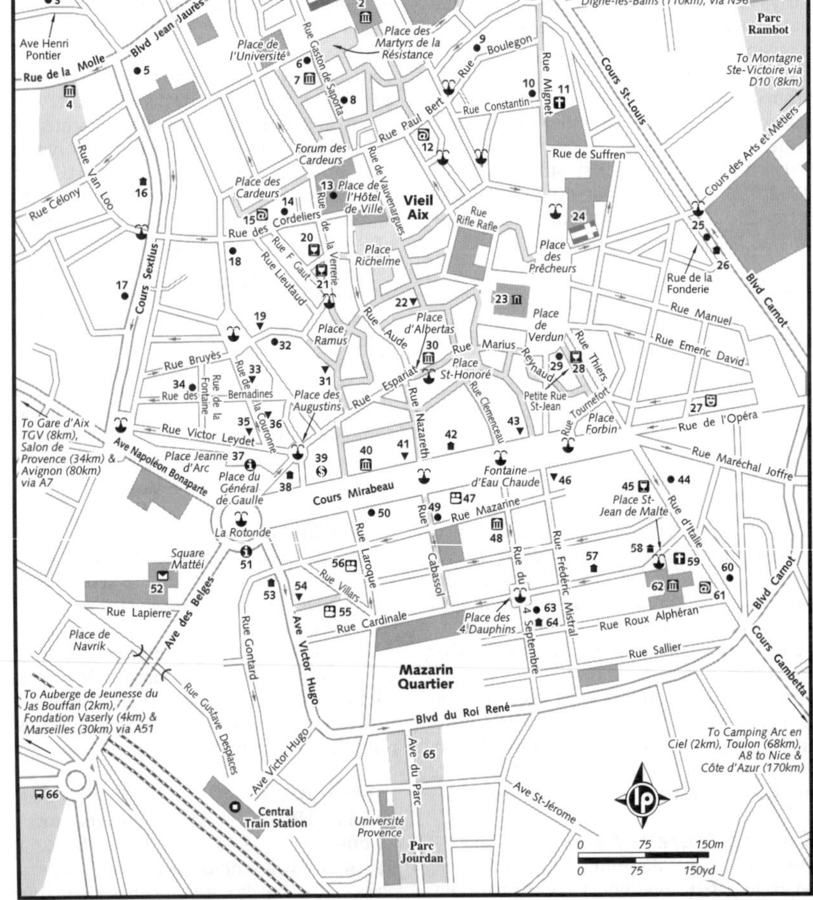

Mon-Sat, 10am-1pm & 2pm-6pm Sun Sept-June, 8.30am-10pm daily July & Aug) makes hotel reservations and runs a wealth of thematic walking tours (in English from July to November). Tours cost €8/4 per adult/under 25. Between April and mid-October it also runs bus excursions.

The **Maison de la Nature et de l'Environnement** *(☎ 04 42 93 15 80; 2 place Jeanne d'Arc; open 10am-12.30pm & 2pm-6pm Mon-Fri)* is a green source for those seeking information on the environment and ways to explore it (nature walks, discovering Mediterranean flora and so on).

Money Commercial banks amass along cours Mirabeau and cours Sextius. **L'Agence** *(☎ 04 42 26 84 77; 15 cours Mirabeau)* is an agent for American Express.

Post & Communications The city's **post office** *(square Mattéi; open 8.30am-6.45pm Mon-Fri, 8.30am-noon Sat)* overlooks ave des Belges.

Hublot *(☎ 04 42 21 37 31; ⓔ hub1@mail.vif.fr; 15-27 rue Paul Bert; open 9am-8pm Mon-Fri, 10am-8pm Sat)* charges €3.60 per hour for Internet access and throws in lots of cigarette smoke for free. The hourly rate at **Virtu@lis** *(☎ 04 42 26 02 30; ⓔ virtualis@netcourrier.com; 40 rue des Cordeliers; open 9am-1am Mon-Fri, 10am-1am Sat, 2pm-1am Sun)* is €3.80.

Net Zone *(28 rue d'Italie; open 10am-2pm & 4pm-10pm Mon-Sat, 4pm-10pm Sun)* charges €2/3/4/5 per 7/20/40/75 minutes.

Bookshops English-language novels, reference books and travel guides are stacked high at **Book in Bar** *(☎ 04 42 26 60 07; ⓦ www.bookinbar.com; 1 bis rue Cabassol; open 9am-7pm Mon-Sat Sept-June, 10am-8pm Mon-Sat July & Aug)*, an English-language bookshop and reading café.

Paradox *(☎ 04 42 26 47 99; 15 rue du 4 Septembre; open 10am-12.30pm & 2pm-6.30pm Mon-Sat)*, another English-language store in the city, also buys and sells second-hand books.

Laundry You will not have any problem finding **laundrettes** *(3 rue de la Fontaine • 34 cours Sextius • 3 rue de la Fonderie • 60 rue Boulegon; all open 7am or 8am-8pm)*. Washing a 5kg load costs around €3.

Cours Mirabeau

Aix's social scene centres on cours Mirabeau, a wide street laid out during the latter half of the 1600s and crowned by a leafy rooftop of green plane trees. A string of Renaissance *hôtels particuliers* (private mansions) lines its shady southern side, and trendy cafés adorned with young beauties basking in the shade of their sunglasses spill across pavements on the sunny northern side.

An astonishing number of people spend entire evenings strolling the length of this street. Changing art and photography exhibitions are held in the **Galerie d'Art du Conseil Général des Bouches du Rhône** *(☎ 04 42 93 03 67; 21 bis cours Mirabeau; admission free; open 10.15am-12.45pm & 13.30pm-6.30pm daily)*. The cast-iron fountain at the western end of cours Mirabeau, **Fontaine de la Rotonde** (1860) personifies justice, agriculture and fine arts. The fountain (1819) at the avenue's eastern end on place Forbin is decorated with a 19th-century statue of King René holding a bunch of Muscat grapes, a variety he is credited with introducing to the region. Moss-covered **Fontaine d'Eau Chaude** *(cnr cours Mirabeau & rue Clemenceau)* spouts 34°C water.

Quartier Mazarin & Vieil Aix

The Quartier Mazarin is also known for its aristocratic 17th- and 18th-century townhouses. Streets and squares to look out for include **rue Mazarine**, south of cours Mirabeau; **place des 4 Dauphins**, two blocks farther south; the eastern continuation of cours Mirabeau, **rue de l'Opéra**; and stunning, cobbled **place d'Albertas**, created just west of place St-Honoré for the Marquis d'Albertas in 1745. Sunday strollers should not miss a jaunt to **place de l'Hôtel de Ville**, where the city's brass band trumpets out a host of jolly tunes most Sunday mornings. From here, rue Gaston de Saporta leads to the **Cathédrale St-Sauveur**, opposite the former university building (1741).

Other Areas

South of the historic centre lies the pleasing **Parc Jourdan**, a spacious green area dominated by Aix's largest fountain and home to the town's primary *pétanque* pitch. North-westbound city walkers can take a leafy stroll to the **Pavillon de Vendôme** *(☎ 04 42 21 05 78; 32 rue Célony; open 10am-noon &*

1pm-5pm Wed-Mon Nov-Jan, 1pm-5.30pm Feb, Mar & Oct, 1pm-6pm Apr-Sept), an 18th-century house framed by a manicured French garden. Inside, contemporary art and digital exhibitions are held.

Museums

Aix's finest, the **Musée Granet** *(☎ 04 42 38 14 70; place St-Jean de Malte; open 10am-noon & 2pm-6pm Wed-Mon)* is in a 17th-century priory of the knights of Malta. Exhibits include Celtic statues from Entremont and Roman artefacts, while the museum's collection of paintings boasts 16th- to 19th-century Italian, Dutch and French works, plus some lesser-known paintings and watercolours by Aix-born Cézanne. Admission prices vary depending on what's on (free at the time of writing due to renovation works).

An unexceptional collection of artefacts pertaining to the city's history is in the **Musée du Vieil Aix** *(☎ 04 42 21 43 55; 17 rue Gaston de Saporta; adult/14-18 yrs/under 14 €4/2.50/free; open 10am-noon & 2pm-5pm Tues-Sun Nov-Mar, 2.30pm-6pm Tues-Sun Apr-Oct)*, which is housed inside Hôtel d'Estienne de St-Jean.

The **Musée des Tapisseries** *(Tapestry Museum; ☎ 04 42 23 09 91; 28 place des Martyrs de la Résistance; adult/under 25 €2/free; open 10am-11.45am & 2pm-5.45pm Wed-Mon)* is in a former archbishop's palace. Books, manuscripts and a collection of Provençal *faïence* (earthenware) fill the **Musée Arbaud** *(☎ 04 42 38 38 95; 2a rue du 4 Septembre; adult/under 10 €2.50/free; open 2pm-5pm Mon-Sat)*.

The geology of Montagne Ste-Victoire is unearthed at the **Musée d'Histoire Naturelle** *(Natural History Museum; ☎ 04 42 27 91 27; 6 rue Espariat; adult/under 25 €2/free; open 10am-noon & 1pm-5pm Mon-Sat)*, inside the 17th-century Hotel Boyer d'Eguilles.

Cathédrale St-Sauveur

Aix's cathedral incorporates architectural features representing every major period from the 5th to the 18th centuries. The main Gothic structure, built from 1285 to 1350, includes the Romanesque nave of a 12th-century church as part of its southern aisle. The chapels were added in the 14th and 15th centuries. There is a 5th-century sarcophagus in the apse. Soulful Gregorian chants and organ concerts are sometimes sung here.

The 15th-century *Triptyque du Buisson Ardent* (Triptych of the Burning Bush) in the nave is by Nicolas Froment. It is usually only opened for groups. Near it is a triptych panel illustrating Christ's passion. The tapestries encircling the choir date from the 18th century, and the fabulous gilt organ is Baroque.

Fondation Vasarely

The Vasarely Foundation *(☎ 04 42 20 01 09; W www.fondationvasarely.com; 1 ave Marcel Pagnol; adult/7-18 yrs €7/4; open 10am-1pm & 2pm-7pm Mon-Fri, 10am-7pm Sat & Sun)* is 4km west of town. It is the creation of Hungarian-born artist Victor Vasarely, the 'father of Op Art', who sought to brighten up grey urban areas with huge, colourful works that integrated art with architecture. Vasarely's works are displayed here in 14 hexagonal spaces recognisable from afar by their contrasting black-and-white, geometrical designs. Admission includes an audio-guide in English.

Take bus No 4 from La Rotonde to the Vasarely stop.

Paul Cézanne Trail

Cézanne (1839–1906), Aix's most celebrated son (at least after his death), did much of his painting in and around the city. If you're interested in the minute details of his day-to-day life follow the Circuit de Cézanne around town; ask at the tourist office for the free English-language guide *In the Footsteps of Cézanne*. Cézanne was a close friend of the French novelist Émile Zola (1840–1902), who also spent his youth in Aix.

Cézanne's last studio, set on a hill about 1.5km north of the tourist office, has been left exactly as it was when he died. Although none of his works is displayed in the **Atelier Cézanne** *(☎ 04 42 21 06 53; W www.ateliercezanne.com; 9 ave Paul Cézanne; adult/under 16 €5.50/free; open 10am-6.30pm daily mid-June–Sept, 10am-noon & 2.30pm-6pm Apr–mid-June, 10am-noon & 2pm-5pm daily Oct-Mar)*, his tools are. In the audiovisual room, films and CD-ROMs recreate the artist's life and works. Take bus No 1 to the Cézanne stop.

Thermes Sextius

Discover Aix's sexy past at Thermes Sextius *(☎ 04 42 23 81 82, fax 04 42 95 11 33; W www.thermes-sextius.com; 55 cours Sextius)*,

Calanque d'En-Vau in Les Calanques south of Marseilles

A local fisherman at Vieux Port in Marseilles

Stairs to Gare St-Charles, Marseilles' train station

ALL PHOTOGRAPHS BY JEAN-BERNARD CARILLET

DAN HERRICK

Arles' skyline from the Roman amphitheatre

MANFRED GOTTSCHALK

View from the rooftop of the 12th- to 15th-century Romanesque church, Stes-Maries de la Mer

MANFRED GOTTSCHALK

The walled city of Aigues-Mortes, the name loosely translated means 'dead waters', in Carmague

a thermal spa built on the site of the warm springs that soothed weary feet in Roman Aquae Sextiae in the 1st century BC. The excavated archaeological remains of the Roman spa are displayed beneath glass in the reception of Aix's contemporary spa, now inside an 18th-century mansion. See Activities in Facts for the Visitor for more spa details.

Special Events

Aix has a sumptuous cultural calendar. The most sought-after tickets are for June and July's **Festival d'Aix-en-Provence** *(W www.festival-aix.com)*, otherwise known as the Festival International d'Art Lyrique, which brings drama and theatre to venues across the city.

Other festivals include **Danse à Aix** in January and May; the two-day **Festival du Tambourin** (Tambourine Festival) in mid-April; the **Aix Jazz Festival and Les Festes d'Orphée** (a Baroque music festival) in July; the **Fête Mistralienne**, which marks the birthday of Provençal hero Frédéric Mistral on 13 September; and the solemn **Bénédiction des Calissons**, held the same month in Église St-Jean de Malte.

Aix's **Fête de l'Huile d'Olive Nouvelle et de la Truffe**, held on place Jeanne d'Arc in December to mark the season's new olive oil, is Aix's main gastronomic celebration.

Places to Stay

Aix might be a student town, but it is not cheap. Contact the tourist office's **reservation centre** *(☎ 04 42 16 11 84/85; e resaix@aixenprovencetourism.com)* to find out what is available in your price bracket; it has details on all types of accommodation, including university dormitories, *chambres d'hôtes* (bed and breakfast accommodation) and *gîtes ruraux* (country cottages) around Aix.

Camping Two kilometres southeast of the town, **Camping Arc en Ciel** *(☎ 04 42 26 14 28; route de Nice; camping for 2 adults with tent & car around €12; open Apr-Sept)* is at Pont des Trois Sautets. Take bus No 3 to Les Trois Sautets stop.

Hostels A hop, skip and jump from the nearby Vasarely museum (2km west of the auberge), **Auberge de Jeunesse du Jas de Bouffan** *(☎ 04 42 20 15 99, fax 04 42 59 36 12; 3 ave Marcel Pagnol; dorm bed with breakfast 1st/subsequent night €12.80/11.10; open mid-Jan–mid-Dec)* might be handy for art buffs. Rooms are locked between 10am and 5pm. Take bus No 4 from La Rotonde to the Vasarely stop.

Hotels A laid-back place (with two entrances), **Hôtel des Arts** *(☎ 04 42 38 11 77, fax 04 42 26 77 31; 69 blvd Carnot & 5 rue de la Fonderie; quiet/noisy doubles with shower & toilet €32/36)* is away from the milling crowds on the city centre's eastern fringe. It has 16 double rooms overlooking an empty backstreet while others overlook a café-filled square.

Hôtel du Globe *(☎ 04 42 26 03 58, fax 04 42 26 13 68; 74 cours Sextius; doubles €48)* is just out of the pedestrianised area.

Hôtel Cardinal *(☎ 04 42 38 32 30, fax 04 42 26 39 05; 24 rue Cardinale; doubles €50 & €60)* is a charming place, in a charming street, with 24 very charming rooms including shower, toilet and a mix of modern and period furniture. Its annexe at 12 rue Cardinale has small self-catering suites.

Hôtel de France *(☎ 04 42 27 90 15, fax 04 42 26 11 47; 63 rue Espariat; doubles with shower & toilet €44)*, in another old building bang in the heart of things, has atmospheric rooms.

Hôtel des Quatre Dauphins *(☎ 04 42 38 16 39, fax 04 42 38 60 19; 54 rue Roux Alphéran; singles/doubles from €45/61)* is a friendly, 12-room place. The two-star rooms have period furnishings.

Hôtel St-Christophe *(☎ 04 42 26 01 24, fax 04 42 38 53 17; W www.hotel-saintchristophe.com; 2 ave Victor Hugo; singles/doubles €64/70)*, with its 1930s brasserie, serves simple/full breakfasts (€4/8) on a lovely street terrace and touts comfortable rooms too.

Grand Hôtel Nègre Coste *(☎ 04 42 27 74 22, fax 04 42 26 80 93; 33 cours Mirabeau; doubles €65-90)* where, so the story goes, Louis XIV played tennis in 1660, is in a prime location with a prime view of slick cours Mirabeau. It has fanciful rooms with 18th-century furnishings.

Places to Eat

Aix's cheapest dining street is rue Van Loo which is strung with tiny restaurants offering Chinese, Thai, Italian and other Oriental cuisines. Café terraces, brasseries and bar

Calissons

These sweet almond biscuits, frosted white with icing sugar, have made mouths water since 1473, when privileged guests at the wedding banquet of King René dined on *calissons*. When the Great Plague came into town in 1630 it was calissons that supposedly staved off the terrible disease. Today, a handful of Aixois *calissonniers* (calisson makers) still bake these sweets, which must comprise 40% ground almonds and 60% melon and fruit syrup.

Traditional calisson makers include **Béchard** (*☎ 04 42 26 06 78; 12 cours Mirabeau)*; **Brémond** (*☎ 04 42 38 01 70; 16 rue d'Italie)* dating from 1830; **Roy René** (*☎ 04 42 26 67 86; 10 rue Clemenceau)*, which runs 20-minute tours of its out-of-town factory (€1; by appointment only); and **Leonard Parli** (*☎ 04 42 26 05 71; 33 ave Victor Hugo)*. The tourist office has a complete list.

Four calissons – plainly (rather than ornately) wrapped – cost €2.40.

sprawl across many of Aix's backstreet squares: place des Cardeurs, forum des Cardeurs, place de Verdun, place Richelme and place de l'Hôtel de Ville are all safe bets for a coffee or cocktail. *Calissons* (see the boxed text) are the city's sweet-as-sugar-pie speciality.

Le Poivre d'Âne (*☎ 04 42 93 45 56; 7 rue de la Couronne; 1/2/3 courses €15/20.50/26)* is quintessentially Provençal. It serves strictly local cuisine, which is mirrored in the tastebud-tickling treats – fig compote, chestnut confit, truffle oil – sold in the *épicerie* it runs across the street.

Jacquou Le Croquant (*☎ 04 42 27 37 19; 2 rue de l'Aumône Vielle; full meal around €25)*, a strictly local haunt, specialises in duck in all forms and guises at a price that will leave you coming back for more.

Le Bistro Latin (*☎ 04 42 38 22 88; 18 rue de la Couronne; menus €21 & €26)*, another hip choice, specialises in traditional French cooking.

Les Bacchanales (*☎ 04 42 27 21 06; 10 rue de la Couronne; menus €24-54)* is a classical French favourite, the priciest menu being strictly for gourmands.

Nearby rue de la Verrerie and rue Félibre Gaut flaunt various Vietnamese and Chinese options. Place Ramus, off pedestrianised rue Annonciade, is a tiny restaurant-filled square where buskers perform.

Gu et Fils (*☎ 04 42 26 75 12; 3 rue Frédéric Mistral; full meals around €25)*, a chic bistro, is laced with the scent of lavender. Gu – known as much for his handsome moustache of gigantic proportions as for his culinary skills – serves purely Provençal dishes and wonderful aperitifs *à la composition secrète*.

Yôji (*☎ 04 42 38 48 76; 7 ave Victor Hugo; lunch menus €9.50-13.79, dinner menus €20-32.50)* is a well-known Japanese and Korean sushi bar offering a succulent range of *menus*.

Chez Maxime (*☎ 04 42 26 28 51; 12 place Ramus; mains €10-20)* is an upmarket place known for the 500-odd different *crus* (wines) on its wine list. Waiter service is formal.

Les Deux Garçons (*☎ 04 42 26 00 51; 53 cours Mirabeau; lunch menu €20.10, plat du jour €11.90)* is a former intellectual hang-out with a stunning interior dating from 1792. An Aixois hot spot designed purely for the sort of people-watching and pastis-drinking that is not free of pretension, this is the place to pose and peer. Those needing an aphrodisiac can grab a six-oyster fix for €7.60.

Self-Catering Aix is among Provence's premier market towns. A mass of fruit and vegetable stands are set up every morning on place Richelme, just as they have been for centuries. Another food market fills place des Prêcheurs on Tuesday, Thursday and Saturday morning. If all else fails, try the **Monoprix** supermarket on cours Mirabeau.

Jacquèrres (*☎ 04 42 23 48 64; 9 rue Méjanes)*, a traditional *épicerie*, sells cheese, cold meats, sausages and any of the pick of 300 types of whisky.

Entertainment

Pick up a free copy of the monthly *Le Mois à Aix* at the tourist office to find out what's on when. The low-down on dance, hip hop and the clubbing scene in and around Aix is revealed in *Scapa*, a free entertainment newspaper published quarterly. Tickets for many events are sold at the tourist office. For classical concerts try **Harmonia Mundi Forum** (*☎ 04 42 38 78 30; 20 rue d'Italie)*.

The Red Clover *(30 rue de la Verrerie)* and **O'Neil's** *(15 rue d'Italia)* serve pints and host happy hours. Live bands play at **Galaxy Pub**

(38 rue de la Verrerie) several times a week. Busier still with the student set is the **Queen's Head** *(11 petite rue St-Jean)*.

Théâtre du Jeu de Paume *(☎ 04 42 99 12 00; 17-21 rue de l'Opéra)*, a stunning place, was built in 1756 on the site of a royal tennis court; the curtain rises in the ornate Italianate auditorium at 8.30pm.

Enchanting classical concerts are held in two lovely little churches, **Église Ste-Marie Madeleine** *(place des Prêcheurs)* and the 17th-century chapel **Chapelle de Ste-Catherine** *(20 rue Mignet)*; the tourist office has details.

Cinema The Aixois are fond of *le septième art* (the seventh art), and two cinemas are dedicated solely to screening nondubbed films: **Ciné Mazarin** *(6 rue Laroque)* and **Cinéma Renoir** *(24 cours Mirabeau)*; call ☎ 04 42 26 99 85 for programme details for either. Tickets cost €7.50 (under 18 €6).

The latest box office hits can often be seen in English at the 12-screen **Le Cézanne** *(☎ 08 36 68 72 70; W www.lecezanne.com – French only; 1 rue Marcel Guillaume)*.

Shopping

A flower market sets place des Prêcheurs ablaze with colour on Sunday morning. On Tuesday, Thursday and Saturday morning there's a flower market on place de Hôtel de Ville and a flea market fills place de Verdun.

Aix's chic shops (designer clothes, hats, accessories etc) cluster along pedestrianised rue Marius Reynaud, which winds its way behind (south of) the Palais de Justice on place de Verdun. Marseilles soap and a bounty of upmarket skincare products are sold at **Savon de Marseille** *(63 rue des Cordeliers)*.

Santons (see the boxed text 'Little Saints' earlier in this chapter) can be admired and bought at several workshops, including **Santons Fouque** *(☎ 04 42 26 33 38; 65 cours Gambetta)*, where the Thumbelina-sized figures have been crafted since 1934. The tourist office has a complete list.

La Truffe Cendrée *(9 rue de l'Aumône Vieille)* is the place to shop for luxury food products typical to the region, including truffles in season. Olive oil can be tasted and bought at **Le Comptoir des Oliviers** *(14 rue Gaston de Saporta)* and **Place aux Huiles** *(59 rue d'Italie)*.

For Coteaux d'Aix wine, try **Cave du Felibrige** *(8 rue des Cordeliers)* or head for the **Syndicat Général des Coteaux d'Aix-en-Provence** *(☎ 04 42 23 57 14, fax 04 42 96 98 56; 22 ave Henri Pontier)*, which has lists of wine-producing estates around Aix where you can taste and buy.

Getting There & Away

Bus From the **bus station** *(☎ 04 42 91 26 80; ave de l'Europe)* there are buses to/from Marseilles (€4.10, 35 minutes via the A51/one hour via the N8, every five to 10 minutes), Marseilles-Provence airport (€7.30, 35 minutes, two an hour between 4.45am and 10.30pm), Arles (€11.40, 1¾ hours, twice daily), Avignon (€13.50/11.70 via the A7/national road, one/1½ hours, six to 10 daily) and Toulon (€13.40, one hour, four daily).

Sumian buses serve Apt, Castellane and the Gorges du Verdon (see the Haute-Provence chapter for details).

Train Aix has two train stations: non-TGV trains chug frequently between the tiny **central station** *(ave Victor Hugo)* in town and Marseilles (€5.80, 30 minutes, 16 to 24 daily). TGV services use **Gare d'Aix TGV**, 8km west of the town centre and linked with the central bus station by bus (see the next section). The only destinations served by TGV within the region are Marseilles (€7, 15 minutes) and Avignon (€21.90, 20 minutes). There are also direct trains to/from Nice (€27.60, 3¼ hours) and coastal destinations in between.

Getting Around

Bus The city's 14 bus and three minibus lines are operated by **Aix en Bus,** which has an **information and ticketing desk** *(☎ 04 42 26 37 28; W www.aixenbus.com; open 8.30am-7pm Mon-Sat)* inside the tourist office.

La Rotonde is the main bus terminal for the city; services generally run until 8pm. A single-/10-ticket carnet costs €1.10/7.30. Minibus No 1 links the train and bus stations with La Rotonde and cours Mirabeau. Bus No 40 – also known as the Navette Aix-TGV-Aéroport – links the bus station with the TGV train station (€3.60, 20 minutes) and Marseilles-Provence airport (see Bus under Getting There & Away earlier). Shuttle buses coincide with TGV train arrivals/departures.

Camp des Milles

Les Milles' majestic red-brick tile factory, the Tuileries des Milles, manufactured 30,000 tonnes of bricks and tiles a year from 1882 until 31 August 1939 when it was turned into a WWII concentration camp. By June 1940 some 3500 artists and intellectuals – predominantly Germans living in the Marseilles region, among them Surrealist painters Max Ernst (1891–1976) and Hans Bellmer (1902–75) – had been rounded up and interned at Camp des Milles. Emotive paintings, designs and prose drawn on the walls by the prisoners in the refectory remain, as does one of the wagons used to transport prisoners by rail from Les Milles to Auschwitz via Camp Drancy in northern France.

Unnervingly, the massive red-brick complex, 6km west of Aix-en-Provence in Les Milles, remains almost wholly intact. In 1946 it briefly reopened as a factory; the refectory became a carpenter's workshop. Preserved as a moving memorial since 1993, today there's a small exhibition in the refectory. The Chemin des Déportés (Deportation Path) leads to the train wagon and a memorial to those who died during WWII, the **Mémorial des Milles** *(☎ 04 42 24 33 02; admission free; open 9am-noon & 12.45pm-5pm Mon-Thur, 6pm Fri)*. The wagon can be visited by appointment only (☎ 04 42 24 34 68).

Bicycle You can rent both road and mountain bikes at **Cycles Zammit** *(☎ 04 42 23 19 53; 27 rue Mignet; open 9am-12.30pm & 3pm-7.30pm Tues-Sat)* for €12.20/60.98 a day/week.

AROUND AIX

Mountains painted by Cézanne, a kingdom of truffles and a WWII concentration camp lie within easy reach of Aix.

Montagne Ste-Victoire

Among Cézanne's favourite haunts was Montagne Ste-Victoire, a mountain ridge immortalised on canvas numerous times by artists over the centuries. Garrigue covers its dry slopes and its foot is carpeted with 3200 hectares of vineyards, from which the local Coteaux d'Aix-en-Provence white, red and rosé wines originate.

Heading east on the D17 from Aix, you pass local artists at their easels in the roadside pine forests trying to reproduce works painted by Cézanne – including *La Montagne Ste-Victoire au Grand Pin* (1887) – along this stretch. His cubist works, *Les Baigneurs* and *Les Baigneuses* (The Bathers), were painted in the **Vallée de l'Arc** around the small mining town of **Gardanne** (population 19,679), about 10km south off the D6. Before leaving Aix-en-Provence, pick up a copy of the tourist office's *In Cezanne's Footsteps* to discover other places in the Montagne Ste-Victoire area that Cézanne painted. Between 1902 and 1906 the artist produced 11 oil and 17 watercolour paintings here.

Typical mountain flora and fauna can be found at **Écomusée de la Forêt Méditerranéenne** *(☎ 04 42 51 41 00; ⓔ institut-foret@enprovence.com; chemin de Roman; adult/under 15 €4.60/2.30; open 10am-6.45pm daily July & Aug, 9am-5.45pm daily Sept-June)* in Gardanne. The park, off the D7, is run by the people responsible for reforestation in the Provence-Alpes-Côte d'Azur region.

Montagne Ste-Victoire is prime **walking** and **mountain-biking** territory. Both Aix's tourist office and the **Maison de Ste-Victoire** *(☎ 04 42 66 84 40, fax 04 42 66 85 15; open 10am-6pm Mon & Wed-Fri, 10am-7pm Sat & Sun)* – converted stables in St-Antonin-sur-Bayon sheltering fauna and flora exhibits, a café and shop – sell the *Sainte Victoire à Pied* (€5; French only), which details walks in the area. They also stock information on the four mountain-bike trails ranging in length from 3km to 18km. The Maison de Ste-Victoire arranges guided walks. Note that the entire mountain, save the roads that cross it, is closed between 1 July and 1 September due to the threat of forest fire.

Returning to Aix via the westbound D10, you pass **Vauvenargues**, dominated by the 14th-century **Château de Vauvenargues**, in the grounds of which Pablo Picasso is buried. The red-brick castle, purchased by the artist in 1958, still belongs to the Picasso family. A sign outside bluntly states (in French): 'This castle cannot be visited. Do not insist. The museum is in Paris'

Rognes

postcode 13840 • pop 4191 • elevation 311m

Bouches-du-Rhône's truffle kingdom – alias tiny, little-known Rognes – languishes in medieval splendour 17km north of Aix-en-Provence. Originally built on the slopes of Foussa, part of the Chaîne de la Trévaresse, the village tumbled down to the bottom of the hill in 1909 after an earthquake hit.

Almost 75% of Provence's black truffles are snouted out by dogs and pigs around Rognes. The village's Grand Marché Truffes et Gastronomie (Truffle and Gastronomy Market), held each year on the Sunday before Christmas, kicks off with a solemn Bénédiction des Truffes (truffle blessing) in the village church.

The **tourist office** *(☎ 04 42 50 13 36; e office.tourisme.rogne@wanadoo.fr; 5 cours St-Étienne)* has a list of *chambre d'hôtes* in and around Rognes, including the following places.

Moulin de Rossignol *(☎ 04 42 50 16 29; chemin Font de Vabre; singles/doubles/triples €46/59/63)* has three lovely rooms in an atmospheric stone house and flowery breakfast garden. Entering Rognes from the south, turn right onto chemin de la Coulade, then left after 150m to the *moulin* (mill).

Les Olivarelles *(☎ 04 42 50 24 27; chemin Font de Vabre; menus €21-48)*, 6km northwest of Rognes along the D66, is one of several inns around Rognes to cook up the precious *Tuber melanosporum* in various guises. Truffle ice-cream, lamb roasted in truffle juice and *foie gras de canard* – another house speciality – are among the exquisite creations of highly regarded chef Pau Dietrich at his gorgeous countryside manor amid scented *garrigue*.

SALON DE PROVENCE

postcode 13300 • pop 38,137 • elevation 80m

Salon de Provence (Seloun in Provençal), 35km west of Aix and 40km east of Arles, is known for its olive-oil production and *savon de Marseille* (Marseilles soap) industry. Medieval Salon served as the residence of the Arles archbishops, and the philosopher Nostradamus (1503–66) lived and died here.

Since 1936 France's military flying school, the École de l'Air et École Militaire de l'Air, has been stationed here, bu it is very difficult to catch the Patrouille Aérienne de France – France's equivalent of the UK's Red Arrows – in flight. The school is closed to the public and France's aerial acrobatic showmasters are more often than not on tour.

The elegant roadside sculpture of a parachutist, 2km from Salon de Provence on the northbound N538 (N7), is a moving memorial to French Resistance leader Jean Moulin (1899–9143), who landed here in 1942 – a year before his arrest and death at the hands of the Gestapo – to rally together organised resistance in southern France.

Orientation & Information

Banks, the tourist office and most sights are in the Vieille Ville (old town) or on cours Gimon, cours Victor Hugo and cours Carnot, which circle it. From place Crousillat, the train station is a 1km-walk along blvd de la République.

The **tourist office** *(☎ 04 90 56 27 60, fax 04 90 56 77 09; 56 cours Gimon; open 9am-noon & 2pm-7pm or 7.30pm Mon-Sat, 10am-noon Sun)* has information on the town and its surrounds.

The **post office** *(cnr blvd Maréchal Foch & rue Massenet)* is near the bus station, and you can surf at **Plug'in** *(☎ 04 90 44 99 15; e ordikid@free.fr; 30 rue Concert; open noon-8pm Mon-Thur, noon-10pm Fri, 2pm-midnight Sat)* for €1.80/3 per 30/60 minutes.

Things to See & Do

A giant, moss-covered mushroom of a fountain, **Fontaine Moussue**, dominates place Crousillat, Salon's prettiest square tucked just outside the walled old town. To enter the old city, bear east beneath the **Tour de l'Horloge** (1626). The bells atop the clock tower have chimed every 15 minutes since 1664.

Pedestrianised rue de l'Horloge brings you to place de l'Ancienne Halle, a large square from which rue Nostradamus leads to the **Maison de Nostradamus** *(☎ 04 90 56 64 31; 11 rue Nostradamus; adult/under 7 €3.05/2.30; open 9am-noon & 2pm-6pm Mon-Fri, 2pm-6pm Sat & Sun)*, Nostradamus' former family home with 10 tableaux depicting scenes from the philosopher's life. Nostradamus lived here from 1547 until his death in 1566. His tomb rests in a side chapel dedicated to the Virgin Mary inside the imposing **Collégiale St-Laurent** *(place St-Laurent)*, a collegiate church built in 1344.

From the southern end of the place de l'Ancienne Halle, steps lead to the **Château-Musée de l'Empéri** *(☎ 04 90 56 22 36; place du Château; adult/under 7 €3.05/2.30; open 10am-noon & 2pm-6pm Wed-Mon Jan-May,*

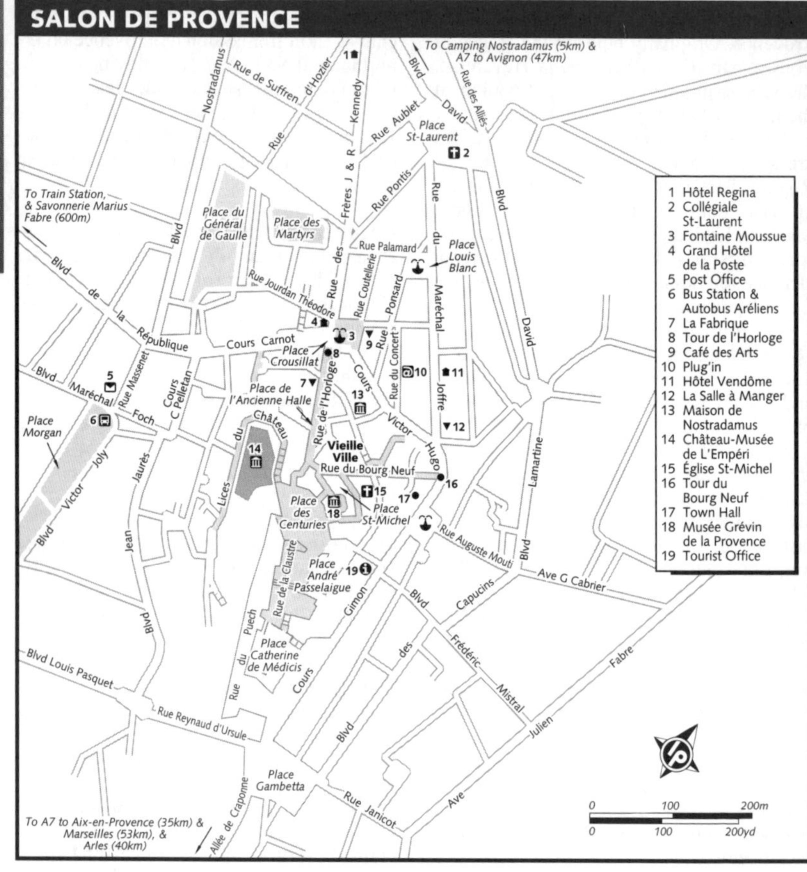

Sept, Oct & Dec, 10am-6pm Wed-Mon July & Aug). One of Provence's oldest remaining castles, it served as residence to the archbishops of Arles from the 9th to the 18th centuries. Some 30 of its spacious medieval halls are filled with over 10,000 exhibit dedicated to French military history up to WWI. Napoleon I steals the limelight. Some lovely concerts take place in the chateau courtyard in summer; the tourist office has details.

More local lore and legend is unravelled with 54 life-size waxworks at the **Musée Grévin de la Provence** *(☎ 04 90 56 36 30; place des Centuries; adult/under 7 €3.05/2.30; open 10am-noon & 2.30pm-6.30pm Wed-Mon Apr-Sept, 2pm-6pm Wed-Mon Oct-Mar)*. A combination ticket for the Musée Grévin and Maison de Nostradamus is available for €5.35/3.05 per adult/under 7.

Tour du Bourg Neuf, at the eastern end of rue du Bourg Neuf, is part of the fortified ramparts built around the city in the 12th century. In the 13th century, young women wanting to conceive venerated the statue of the Black Virgin tucked in the gate. A rare treat is the solemn Gregorian chants sung at Sunday Mass (9am) in the 13th-century **Église St-Michel** *(place St-Michel)* every first and third Sunday of the month from September to June.

One of Salon's two remaining *savonneries* (soap factories), the **Savonnerie Marius Fabre** *(☎ 04 90 53 24 77; W www.marius-fabre.fr; 148 ave Paul Borret; adult/15-18 yrs/under 15 €3.85/1.95/free)* can be visited at 10.30am on

Monday and Thursday (by appointment only). The factory produces 100 tonnes of soap a year. Exit the train station, turn right along ave Émile Zola, left along blvd Maréchal Foch, then right onto ave Paul Borret.

Places to Stay

Camping Nostradamus *(☎ 04 90 56 08 36, fax 04 90 56 65 05; route d'Eyguières; camping for 2 people with tent & car €12; open Mar-Oct)* is 5km north of Salon.

Hôtel Vendôme *(☎ 04 90 56 01 96, fax 04 90 56 48 78; 6 rue du Maréchal Joffre; doubles €40, €45 & €50, family rooms €66)*, a two-star place, markets itself as a 'garden in town'.

Grand Hôtel de la Poste *(☎ 04 90 56 01 94, fax 04 90 56 20 77; 1 rue des Frères J & R Kennedy; doubles with shower/shower & toilet €31/40)*, overlooking the Tour de l'Horloge, offers a mossy fountain view from some of its two-star rooms.

Places to Eat

La Fabrique *(☎ 04 90 56 07 39; 75 rue de l'Horloge; pasta €13.50)*, one of many terraces on pedestrianised rue de l'Horloge, stands outs. This charming Italian place has brilliantly painted walls and delicious pasta dishes. The adjoining shop, run by the same family, sells fresh pasta – including *tagliatelles au chocolat* (chocolate-flavoured pasta) – to take away.

Café des Arts *(☎ 04 90 56 00 07; place des Arts; lunch formule €13, meats €10.70-16.80)*, with its chic terrace overlooking Salon's famous mossy fountain, is an unbeatable place to lunch in summer. Meats are cooked on a wood-stoked grill and come with a choice of tasty sauces – *tapenade* (olive paste), sweet onion chutney, *pistou* (crushed basil and garlic) or *pesto* (crushed basil and pine kernels).

La Salle à Manger *(☎ 04 90 56 28 01; 6 rue du Maréchal Joffre; lunch formule €15 & €23)* is a 19th-century *hôtel particulier* wrapped around a secret garden where you can dine. A lavender dip accompanies aperitifs, and rose petals are sprinkled on the cold Indian soup. Complete your feast with one of 40 desserts – the thyme, lavender and rosemary sorbet could not be more Provençal.

An open-air food market fills place Jules Morgan on Wednesday morning.

Getting There & Away

Bus Inter-regional buses share **Autobus Aréliens' intercity bus station** *(☎ 04 90 56 50 98; cnr blvd Maréchal Foch & blvd Victor Joly)*, adjoining place Jules Morgan. From here, there are daily services to/from Aix-en-Provence, Arles (€7.30, 1¼ hours, eight daily Monday to Saturday, two a day Sunday) and Avignon.

Train From the **train station** *(ave Émile Zola)* there are some eight trains daily to Marseilles (€8.90, 1½ hours) and Avignon (€7.80, 40 minutes).

The Camargue

The sparsely populated, 780-sq-km delta of the River Rhône, known as the Camargue, is famed for its desolate beauty and the incredibly varied bird life that its wetlands support. Over 400 species of land- and water-birds inhabit the region, including storks, bee-eaters and some 160 other migratory species. Most impressive of all are the huge flocks of *flamants roses* (pink flamingos) that come here to nest during spring and summer; many set up house near the Étang de Vaccarès and Étang du Fangassier. Each year, some 30,000 flamingos winter in the Camargue and 25,000 couples hatch and raise their offspring in spring.

The Camargue has been formed by sediment deposited by the River Rhône as it flows into the Mediterranean. In the southern Camargue, the areas between the *digues à la mer* (sea-wall embankments) that line water channels are taken up by shallow salt marshes, inland lakes and lagoons whose brackish waters shimmer in the Provençal sun. The northern part of the delta is dry land, and in the years following WWII huge tracts were desalinated as part of a costly drainage and irrigation programme designed to make the area suitable for large-scale agriculture, especially the cultivation of rice. Rice production has dropped sharply since the 1960s but is still a very important part of the Camarguais economy: almost 70% of France's annual rice yield is produced here. Its other key product is salt – in times gone by a precious commodity that was transported by boat to Nice and by mule through the Vallée de Roya and beyond. This route formed one of France's many *routes du sel* (salt roads), always in remote or mountainous regions to avoid thieves and brigands.

At some places along the coast, the delta continues to grow, sweeping one-time seaside towns kilometres from the Mediterranean. Elsewhere, sea currents and storms have, in recent centuries, washed away land that had been around long enough for people to build things on it. The course of the Rhône has changed repeatedly over the millennia, but the Grand Rhône (which carries 90% of the river's flow) and the Petit Rhône have followed their present channels for about 500 years.

Highlights

- Follow Vincent van Gogh's footsteps, see Picasso sketches in the Musée Réattu and discover what the Romans called fun at the Roman amphitheatre in Arles
- Party on down at a rice or cowboy festival in Arles or at a Roma (gypsy) pilgrimage in Stes-Maries de la Mer
- View pink flamingos at close quarters in the Parc Ornithologique du Pont de Gau
- Walk atop the walled city of Aigues-Mortes
- Bird-watch and explore the wetlands on foot, by bicycle or on horseback
- Take a walk on the wild side – along the Digue à la Mer in the Camargue's untamed southern realm

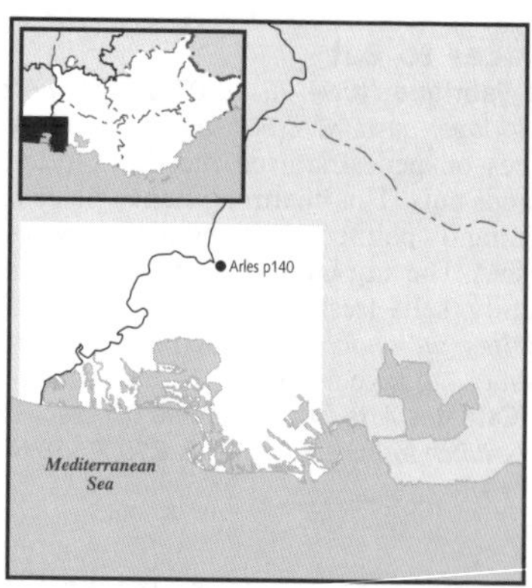

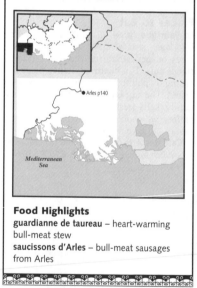

Food Highlights

guardianne de taureau – heart-warming bull-meat stew

saucissons d'Arles – bull-meat sausages from Arles

Most of the Camargue wetlands are within the Naturel Régional de Camargue (PNRC), established in 1970 to preserve the area's fragile ecosystems by maintaining an equilibrium between ecological considerations and the region's economic mainstays: agriculture, salt production, hunting, grazing and tourism. The central, 6000-hectare

Étang de Vaccarès has been protected by the Réserve Nationale de Camargue – a 135-sq-km nature reserve embracing the lagoon and its nearby peninsulas and islands – since 1927. Another 2000 hectares between Arles and Salin de Giraud in southeastern Camargue is managed by the Conservatoire de l'Espace Littoral et des Rivages Lacustres (an environmental group focusing on coastal and lakeside areas.

The Camargue's famous herds of cream-coloured horses and black bulls that roam free under the watchful eyes of the mounted *gardians* (Camarguaise cowboys) can still be seen. An equally likely sight is bulls grazing in fenced-in fields and horses saddled and tethered, waiting in rows under the blazing sun for tourists to pay for a ride. The *cheval de Camargue* (Camargue horse) – always grey-cream in colour, with a square-shaped head and about 13.1 hands in size – has been recognised as a breed in its own right since 1978. Most bulls are raised for bullfighting.

At least one traditional Camargue phenomenon is alive and well: the area's savage mosquitoes are flourishing, feeding on the blood of hapless passers-by just as they have for countless aeons. Pack *plenty* of insect repellent – then pack more.

ORIENTATION

Shaped like a giant croissant, the 850-sq-km Parc Naturel Régional de Camargue is enclosed by the Rivers Petit Rhône and Grand Rhône. The protected Étang de Vaccarès is bang in its centre.

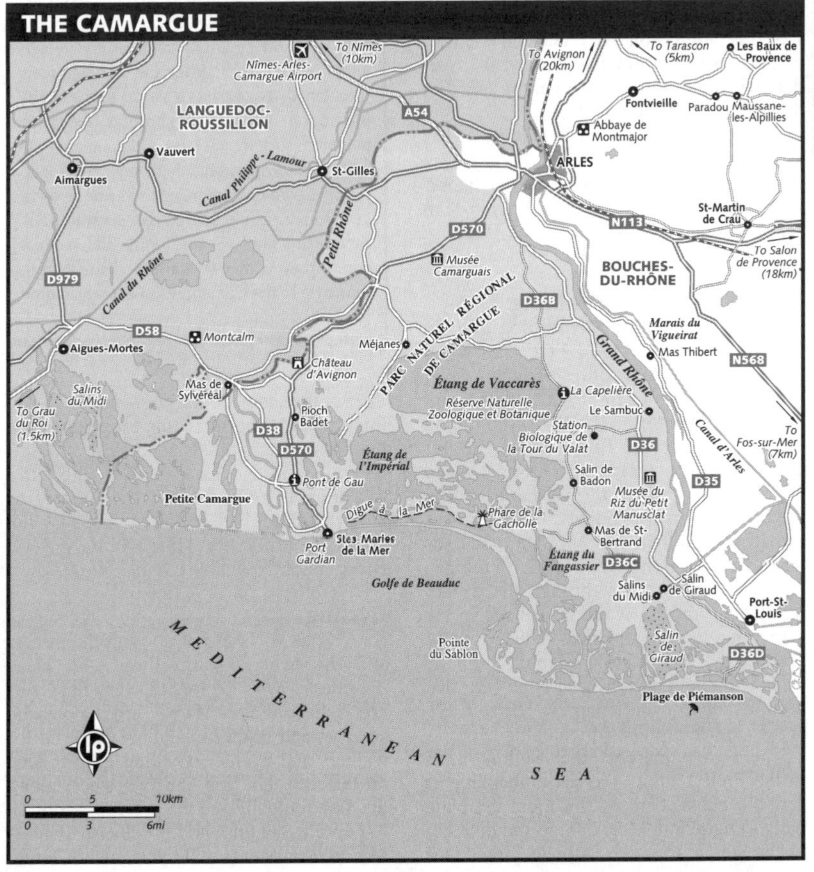

Inland, the Roman town of Arles rides on the croissant's back and is the gateway to the park. The Camargue's other two towns, both on the coast, are the resort of Stes-Maries de la Mer, 39km southwest of Arles, and the walled town of Aigues-Mortes, 45km southwest of Arles.

Rice is cultivated in the northern sections of the delta. Enormous salt evaporation pools lie around the Salin de Giraud and Aigues-Mortes.

PARK OFFICES

The Parc Naturel Régional de Camargue has an information centre, the **Centre de Ginès** *(☎ 04 90 97 86 32, fax 04 90 97 70 82; ⓔ info@parcs-naturels-regionaux.tm.fr; open 9am-6pm daily Apr-Sept, 9.30am-5pm Sat-Thur Oct-Mar)*, in Pont de Gau, 4km northwest of Stes-Maries de la Mer off the D570. Exhibits (admission free) focus on environmental issues. From the glassed-in foyer you can watch birds in the nearby marshes through powerful binoculars.

The Réserve Nationale de Camargue has an **information centre** *(☎ 04 90 97 00 97, fax 04 90 97 01 44; ⓔ snpn.reserve.de.camargue@wanadoo.fr; open 9am-1pm & 2pm-5pm Wed-Mon)* at La Capelière on the D36B.

ACTIVITIES

Bird-Watching & Walking

The 60-hectare **Parc Ornithologique du Pont de Gau** *(☎ 04 90 97 82 62; adult/under 10 €6/3; open 9am-sunset daily Apr-Sept, 10am-sunset daily Oct-Mar)*, next to the park information centre on the D570 in Pont du Gau, should be the first port of call for anyone keen to peek at the area's winged creatures or walk in the wetland. Within the ornithological park, several kilometres of paths wend their way through reed beds and marshes. Schools of pink flamingos fly overhead or wade through the watery landscape, making it the best place in the Camargue to view the birds. Guided walks around the park are available. Salin de Badon in southeastern Camargue (see that section later in this chapter) is the Camargue's other prime bird-watching spot.

There are numerous other walking trails in the PNRC, along the sea embankments and the coast. One of the most dramatic paths (Digue à la Mer) is atop the dike between Stes-Maries and Salin de Giraud (see the Southeastern Camargue section later in this chapter). Shorter nature trails start from the Musée Camarguais southwest of Arles, La Palissade and La Capelière; the latter two are both in the southeastern Camargue.

Park offices sell detailed maps of the area, including the 1:25,000 IGN Série Bleue maps, Nos 2944E and 2944O.

Pretty in Pink

The pink or greater flamingo *(Phoenicopterus ruber)* in flight is a breathtaking sight. Equally majestic is the catwalk stance – neck high, breast out – adopted by this elegant, long-legged creature when strutting through shallow waters.

Flamingo courtship starts in January, with mating taking place from March to May. The single egg laid by the female in April or May is incubated in a mud-caked nest for one month by both parents. The young chicks shakily take to the skies when they are about three months old. By the time they reach adulthood (around five years old), their soft grey down has become a fine feather coat of brilliant white or pretty rose-pink.

This well-dressed bird lives to the grand old age of 34 (longer if kept in captivity). It stands between 1.5m to 2m tall and has an average wing span of 1.9m. When the flamingo feels threatened, its loud hiss is similar to the warning sound made by a goose. It feeds on plankton, sucking in water and draining it off with its disproportionately heavy, curved bill.

Some flamingos remain in the Rhône delta year round. Come September, several thousand take flight to Spain, Tunisia and Senegal where they winter in warmer climes before returning to the Camargue in February in time for early spring.

Cycling

As long as you can put up with the insects and stiff sea breezes, travelling by bicycle is the finest way to explore the very flat Camargue. East of Stes-Maries, areas along the seafront and farther inland are reserved for walkers and cyclists. Cycling is forbidden on beaches, but you can two-wheel along the dike footpath (see the previous section).

Le Vélo Saintois and Le Vélociste in Stes-Maries de la Mer (see Bicycle under Getting

Around in that section, later in this chapter) both distribute a list of cycling itineraries – 20km to 70km in length – with route explanations in English. Both places deliver bicycles to your hotel door and open Easter to early October. Le Vélociste also organises guided bicycle rides and combined cycling and canoeing/horse riding day trips.

Rental agencies in Arles and other towns are listed in the respective Getting Around sections.

Horse Riding

Numerous farms offer *promenades à cheval* (horse riding); there are plenty along the D570 into Stes-Maries. Expect to pay €10/50 per hour/day. You can also ride at the Auberge de Jeunesse in Pioch Badet near Stes-Maries, and at the **Domaine de Méjanes** *(☎ 04 90 97 10 51, fax 04 90 77 12 42; ⓔ mejanes@archimix.com)*, a Paul Ricard leisure complex isolated on the northeastern bank of the Étang de Vaccarès in Méjanes, 20km southwest of Arles. The Domaine de la Palissade organises scenic rides in the wilder southeastern Camargue (see that section later in this chapter).

Stes-Maries' **Maison du Cheval Camargue** *(House of the Camargue Horse; ☎ 04 90 97 58 47; Mas de la Cure)*, a horse-riding and breeding centre, is the place to learn about the Camargue's grey-cream horse breed and explore the area on horseback. Guided visits (adult/child €5/3) of the horse centre depart at 10am; advance reservations are required.

For more information about equestrian activities contact the **Association Camarguaise de Tourisme Équestre** *(☎ 04 90 97 86 32)*, in the Centre de Ginès at Pont de Gau.

ORGANISED TOURS

Boat excursions can be picked up in Aigues-Mortes and Stes-Maries. **La Maison du Guide en Camargue** *(☎/fax 04 66 73 52 30, ☎ 06 12 44 73 52; ⓦ www.maisonduguide.camargue.fr)* in Montcalm, 10km northwest of Stes-Maries on the D58, organises guided tours by foot, boat and bicycle.

In Arles, **Camargue Organisation** *(☎ 04 90 96 94 44; ⓦ www.camargue-organisation.com; 14 bis rue de la Calade)* runs English-language 4WD tours around the Camargue, during March and October. Two-/three-four-hour 'safari' jeep tours cost €25/30/38. In Stes-Maries, **Camargue Safari 4x4 Gallon** *(☎ 04 90 97 86 93, 04 90 97 84 12; ⓔ camargue-safari.gallon@wanadoo.fr; 22 ave Van Gogh)* runs the equivalent into the Camargue heartland from its Stes-Maries base.

ARLES

postcode 13200 • pop 50,513 • elevation 13m

Attractive Arles, at the northern tip of the Camargue alluvial plain, sits on the River Grand Rhône just south of where the Petit Rhône splits off from it. Avignon and Nîmes are both a 30km-ride away.

Arles began its ascent to prosperity and political importance in 49 BC, when the victorious Julius Caesar – whom the city had supported – captured and plundered Marseilles, which had backed Caesar's rival, the general and statesman Pompey the Great. Arles soon replaced Marseilles as the region's major port and a Roman provincial centre that within a century and a half needed a 20,000-seat amphitheatre and a 12,000-seat theatre to entertain its citizens. Today, the two imposing structures stage cultural events and Camarguais bullfights.

The Arlésiens' most famous resident was Vincent van Gogh (1853–90), who settled in the town for a year in 1888, immortalising many of the city's most picturesque streets and surrounding rural areas on canvas. Not one of his original works remains in Arles.

Orientation

The centre of Arles is enclosed by the Grand Rhône to the northwest, blvd Émile Combes to the east and, to the south, by blvd des Lices and blvd Georges Clemenceau. It is shaped like a foot, with the train station, place de la Libération and place Lamartine (where Van Gogh once lived) at the ankle, Les Arènes at the anklebone and the tourist office squashed under the arch.

Information

Tourist Offices The **tourist office** *(☎ 04 90 18 41 20, fax 04 90 18 41 29; ⓦ www.ville-arles.fr; blvd des Lices; open 9am-6.45pm daily Apr-Sept; 9am-5.45pm Mon-Sat, 10.30am-2.30pm Sun Oct & Nov; 9am-4.45pm Mon-Sat, 10.30am-2.30pm Sun Dec & Jan-Mar)* has information on the rest of the Camargue and organises some excellent guided tours. Day trips into the Camargue and nature walks must be booked 24 hours

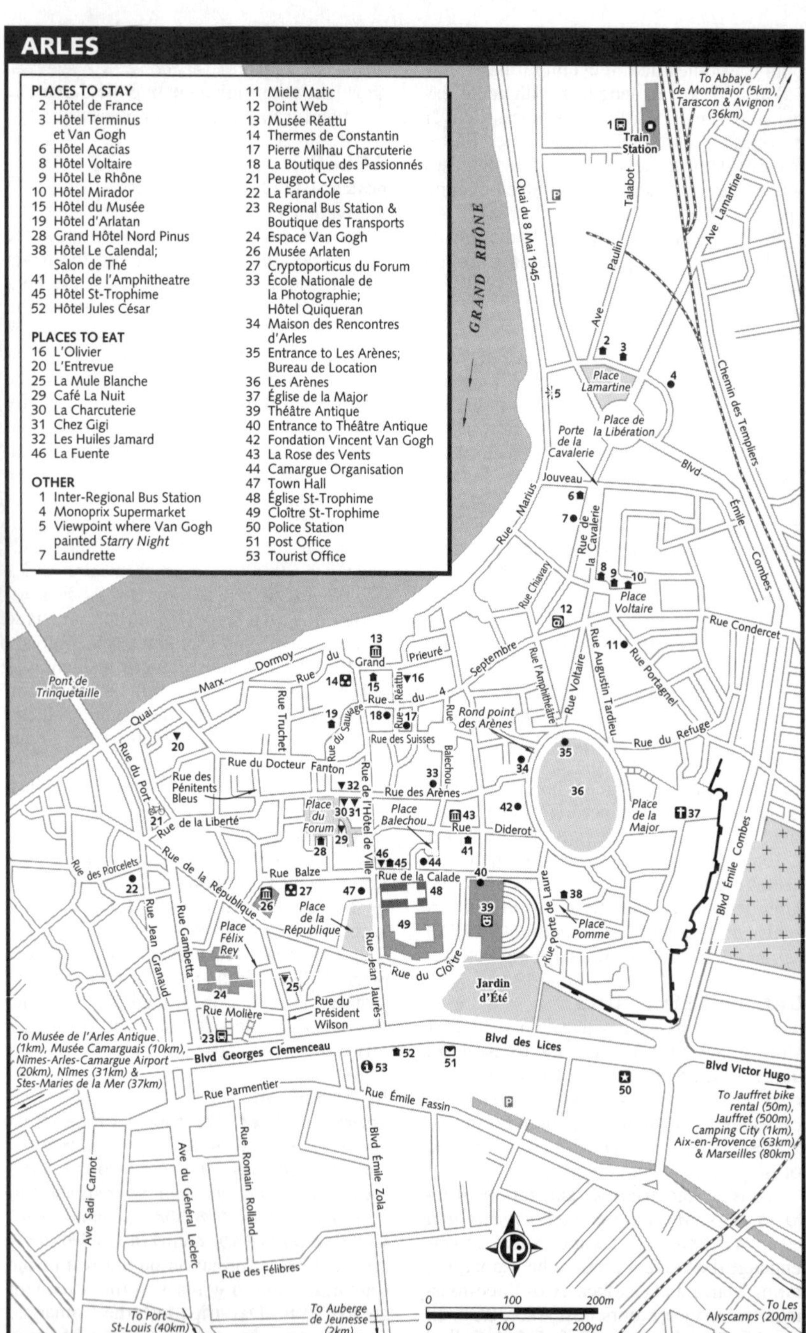
ARLES
PLACES TO STAY
2 Hôtel de France
3 Hôtel Terminus et Van Gogh
6 Hôtel Acacias
8 Hôtel Voltaire
9 Hôtel Le Rhône
10 Hôtel Mirador
15 Hôtel du Musée
19 Hôtel d'Arlatan
28 Grand Hôtel Nord Pinus
38 Hôtel Le Calendal; Salon de Thé
41 Hôtel de l'Amphitheatre
45 Hôtel St-Trophime
52 Hôtel Jules César
PLACES TO EAT
16 L'Olivier
20 L'Entrevue
25 La Mule Blanche
29 Café La Nuit
30 La Charcuterie
31 Chez Gigi
32 Les Huiles Jamard
46 La Fuente
OTHER
1 Inter-Regional Bus Station
4 Monoprix Supermarket
5 Viewpoint where Van Gogh painted Starry Night
7 Laundrette
11 Miele Matic
12 Point Web
13 Musée Réattu
14 Thermes de Constantin
17 Pierre Milhau Charcuterie
18 La Boutique des Passionnés
21 Peugeot Cycles
22 La Farandole
23 Regional Bus Station & Boutique des Transports
24 Espace Van Gogh
26 Musée Arlaten
27 Cryptoporticus du Forum
33 École Nationale de la Photographie; Hôtel Quiqueran
34 Maison des Rencontres d'Arles
35 Entrance to Les Arènes; Bureau de Location
36 Les Arènes
37 Église de la Major
39 Théâtre Antique
40 Entrance to Théâtre Antique
42 Fondation Vincent Van Gogh
43 La Rose des Vents
44 Camargue Organisation
47 Town Hall
48 Église St-Trophime
49 Cloître St-Trophime
50 Police Station
51 Post Office
53 Tourist Office
To Abbaye de Montmajor (5km), Tarascon & Avignon (36km)
Train Station
GRAND RHÔNE
Quai du 8 Mai 1945
Ave Paulin Talabot
Ave Lamartine
Chemin des Templiers
Place Lamartine
Place de la Libération
Porte de la Cavalerie
Blvd Émile Combes
Rue Marius Jouveau
Rue de la Cavalerie
Rue Chiavary
Place Voltaire
Rue Condercet
Rue Portagnel
Rue Augustin Tardieu
Rue Voltaire
Rue l'Amphithéâtre
Rue du 4 Septembre
Rue du Grand Prieuré
Rue Réattu
Quai Marx Dormoy
Pont de Trinquetaille
Rue Truchet
Rue du Sauvage
Rue des Suisses
Rond point des Arènes
Rue du Refuge
Rue Balechou
Rue du Port
Rue du Docteur Fanton
Rue des Pénitents Bleus
Rue des Arènes
Place du Forum
Place Balechou
Rue Diderot
Place de la Major
Rue de l'Hôtel de Ville
Rue de la Liberté
Rue des Porcelets
Rue de la République
Rue Balze
Rue de la Calade
Place de la République
Rue Porte de Laure
Place Pomme
Place Félix Rey
Rue Jean Granaud
Rue Gambetta
Rue Jean Jaurès
Rue du Cloître
Jardin d'Été
Rue Molière
Rue du Président Wilson
Blvd des Lices
Blvd Georges Clemenceau
Blvd Victor Hugo
To Musée de l'Arles Antique (1km), Musée Camarguais (10km), Nîmes-Arles-Camargue Airport (20km), Nîmes (31km) & Stes-Maries de la Mer (37km)
Rue Parmentier
Rue Émile Fassin
To Jauffret bike rental (50m), Jauffret (500m), Camping City (1km), Aix-en-Provence (63km) & Marseilles (80km)
Ave Sadi Carnot
Ave du Général Leclerc
Rue Romain Rolland
Blvd Émile Zola
Rue des Félibres
To Port St-Louis (40km)
To Auberge de Jeunesse (2km)
0 100 200m
0 100 200yd
To Les Alyscamps (200m)

Arles Museum Passes

The Pass Monuments (Monuments Pass) costs €12/10 per adult/12 to 18 years and is valid for three months. It covers admission to all Arles' museums and Roman relics.

Those with less time to spare can buy a cheaper Pass Antique (€9/7 per adult/12-18 years), which covers all the sights *except* the Église St-Trophime, Les Alyscamps, Musée Réattu and Musée Arlaten.

The tourist office and the museums sell both passes.

in advance. The **tourist office annexe** *(open 9am-1pm Mon-Fri)* at the train station appears to work sporadic hours, despite the times posted.

Money Commercial banks line place de la République.

Post & Communications The **post office** *(5 blvd des Lices; open 8.30am-6.30pm Mon-Sat)* has Cyberposte. Alternatively, try **Point Web** *(☎ 04 90 18 91 54; 10 rue du 4 Septembre; open 8.30am-7.30pm Mon-Sat)*.

Laundry It costs €3.50/7.40 for a 7/15kg load at the **laundrette** *(6 rue de la Cavalerie; open 7am-10pm daily)* and **Miele Matic** *(12 rue Portagnel; open 7am-9.30pm daily)*.

Les Arènes

Arles' Roman **amphitheatre** *(☎ 04 90 96 03 70; adult/12-18 yrs €4/3; open 9am-7pm daily May-Sept; 9am-6pm daily Mar, Apr & Oct; 10am-5pm daily Nov-Feb)*, built in the late 1st or early 2nd century AD to host an audience of 20,000, measures 136m by 107m, making it marginally larger than its counterpart in Nîmes. Like other such structures around the Roman empire, it was built to stage sporting contests, chariot races and the wildly popular and bloody spectacles so beloved by the Roman public. Wild animals were pitted against other animals or gladiators (usually slaves or criminals), who fought each other until one of them was either killed or surrendered (in the latter case their throat was usually then slit). Executions were carried out either by the executioner or by pushing the victim into the arena with a wild animal.

In the early medieval period, during the Arab invasions, Les Arènes was transformed into a fortress; three of the four defensive towers can still be seen around the structure. These days the amphitheatre holds over 12,000 and still draws a full house during the bullfighting season.

Opening hours at Les Arènes, which is under renovation until 2006, sometimes change during performances. The ticket office for bullfights, the Wednesday-evening *Courses Camarguaises* (see the boxed text 'Bulls & Cowboys' later in this chapter) between June and August (tickets €5) and other events are sold at the **Bureau de Location** *(☎ 04 90 96 03 70; e arenes.arles@wanadoo.fr; rond-point des Arènes; open 10am-noon & 2.30pm-6pm Mon-Fri, 10am-1pm Sat)*, next to the main entrance of the amphitheatre.

Théâtre Antique

For centuries, Arles' **Roman theatre** *(blvd des Lices; adult/12-18 yrs €3/2.20; open 9am-7pm daily May-Sept; 9am-noon & 2pm-6pm daily Mar & Apr; 9am-noon daily Oct; 10am-noon & 2pm-5pm daily Nov-Feb)*, dating from the 1st century BC, was used as a convenient source of construction materials. Nowadays little of the original structure (measuring 102m in diameter) remains, except for two imposing columns. Occasional open-air performances are hosted here; enter through the **Jardin d'Été** *(Summer Garden; blvd des Lices)*, it hosts. Ask at the tourist office for information on performances.

Église St-Trophime

This austere Romanesque church, once a cathedral (Arles was an archbishopric from the 4th century until 1790), stands on the site of several earlier churches. It was built in the late 11th and 12th centuries – perhaps using stone cut from the Théâtre Antique – and was named after St-Trophimus, a late-2nd-or early 3rd-century bishop of Arles.

Unlike the interior, almost unadorned save for a few tapestries, the western portal facing place de la République is richly decorated in 12th-century stone carvings. Two lateral chapels were added in the 14th century. The choir and the ambulatory are from the 15th century, when the structure was significantly enlarged. Across the courtyard is the serene **Cloître St-Trophime** *(rue Jean*

Bulls & Cowboys

In *mise à mort* bullfighting *(corrida)*, which is popular in Spain, Latin America and parts of southern France, a bull bred to be aggressive is killed in a bloody ceremony involving picadors, toreadors, matadors and horses. But not all bullfighting ends with a dead bull.

In a *course Camarguaise* (Camargue-style bullfight), white-clad *raseteurs* (bullfighters) try to remove ribbons or *attributs* (rosettes) tied to the bull's horns with hooks held between their fingers. It originates from the 15th century when dogs, lions and bears were let loose in a ring to chase a bull. Finally slammed as cruel in the 19th century, the other animals were then banished from the ring, leaving man alone to pit his wits against the bull *(taureau)*.

Bulls are bred, fed and tended by *gardians*, Camargue cowboys who herd the region's cattle. These mounted herdsmen are honoured by the Fête des Gardians in Arles in May, during which they parade through town on horseback – clad in leather hats, chequered shirts and dusty boots. Long ago, *gardians* lived in *cabanes de gardians*, whitewashed cottages crowned with a thatched roof and sealed with a strip of mortar.

Courses Camarguaises are common in Arles (see Les Arènes earlier in this chapter) but not so popular in Nîmes, where *férias* (bullfighting festivals) sport *corridas* and *novilladas* in which young bulls, less than four years old, are thrown in the ring to fight.

Jaurès; adult/12-18 yrs €3.50/2.60; open 9am-7pm daily May-Sept; 9am-6pm daily Mar, Apr & Oct; 10am-5pm daily Nov-Feb), a cloister surrounded by superbly sculptured columns.

Les Alyscamps

This large **necropolis** *(adult/12-18 yrs €3.50/2.60; open 9am-7pm daily May-Sept; 9am-noon & 2pm-6pm daily Mar & Apr; 9am-noon daily Oct; 10am-noon & 2pm-5pm daily Nov-Feb)*, 1km southeast of Les Arènes, was founded by the Romans and taken over by Christians in the 4th century. Les Alyscamps became a popular last resting place because of the presence of Christian martyrs among the dead, said to work miracles.

The necropolis was badly maintained during and after the Renaissance, making it a shadow of its former self. Both Van Gogh and Gauguin painted Les Alyscamps with great vividness.

Other Roman Sites

The **Thermes de Constantin** *(rue du Grand Prieuré; adult/12-18 yrs €3/2.20; open 9am-7pm daily May-Sept; 9am-noon & 2pm-6pm daily Mar & Apr; 9am-noon daily Oct; 10am-noon & 2pm-5pm daily Nov-Feb)*, Roman baths built in the 4th century, are only partly preserved. The **Cryptoporticus du Forum** *(rue Balze; adult/12-18 yrs €3.50/2.60; open 9am-7pm daily May-Sept; 9am-noon & 2pm-6pm daily Mar & Apr; 9am-noon daily Oct; 10am-noon & 2pm-5pm daily Nov-Feb)*, underground storerooms, most of which were carved out in the 1st century BC, is accessed via a 17th-century Jesuit chapel.

Museums

The **Musée de l'Arles Antique** *(☎ 04 90 18 88 88; W www.arles-antique.org; ave de la Première Division Française Libre; adult/12-18 yrs €5.35/3.80; open 9am-7pm daily Mar-Oct; 10am-5pm daily Nov-Feb)* boasts a rich collection of Pagan and Christian art, including Roman statues, artefacts, marble sarcophagi and a renowned assortment of early Christian sarcophagi from the 4th century. It is 1.5km southwest of the tourist office on the Presqu'île du Cirque Romain.

Musée Arlaten *(☎ 04 90 96 08 23; 29 rue de la République; adult/12-18 yrs €4/3; open 9.30am-1pm & 2pm-6.30pm Tues-Sun Apr & May; 9.30am-1.30pm & 2pm-7pm Tues-Sun June; 9.30am-1.30pm & 2pm-7pm daily July & Aug; 9.30am-1pm & 2pm-6.30pm daily Sept; 9.30am-12.30pm & 2pm-5.30pm Tues-Sun Oct-Mar)*, founded by Provençal poet Frédéric Mistral in 1896, is dedicated to preserving and displaying everyday objects related to traditional Provençal life: furniture, crafts, costumes, ceramics, a model of the Tarasque (a human-eating amphibious monster of Provençal legend) and so on. It's in a 16th-century townhouse built around Roman ruins.

The **Musée Réattu** *(☎ 04 90 96 37 68; 10 rue du Grand Prieuré; adult/12-18 yrs €4/3; open 10am-12.30pm & 2pm-7pm daily May-Sept; 10am-12.30pm & 2pm-5.30pm daily Mar, Apr & Oct; 1pm-5.30pm daily Nov-Feb)* is housed in a 15th-century priory. It exhibits works by some of the world's finest photographers, modern and contemporary works of art, and paintings by 18th- and 19th-century Provençal artists. It also has 57 Picasso drawings, sketched by the artist between December 1970 and November 1971. The conventional portrait of his mother, Maria, painted in Côte d'Antibes in 1923, is particularly fine.

Contemporary art exhibitions are at **Maison des Rencontres d'Arles** *(☎ 04 90 96 63 69; ⓔ r.i.p.arles@pacwan.fr; 10 rond-point des Arènes; admission €5; open 9am-noon & 2pm-6pm Mon-Fri)*, a centre that runs photography courses and also an international photography festival (see Special Events). Some shows are held at the **École Nationale de la Photographie** *(Na-tional School of Photography; 16 rue des Arènes)* in the elegant 18th-century Hôtel Quiqueran de Beaujeu.

Inside a sheep shed built in 1812, the **Camargue Museum** *(☎ 04 90 97 10 82; adult/student €4/2.30; open 9.15am-5.45pm daily Apr-Sept; 10.15am-4.45pm Wed-Mon Oct-Mar)* at Mas du Pont de Rousty (10km southwest of Arles on the D570 to Stes-Maries) is an excellent introduction to the history, ecosystems, flora and fauna of the Camargue River delta. Much attention is given to traditional life in the Camargue, such as sheep and cattle raising, salt production at Salin de Giraud and local arts. A 3.5km nature-trail leads from the museum to an observation tower.

The museum can be reached from Arles by bus (see Getting There & Away later in this section).

Van Gogh

The **Fondation Vincent Van Gogh** *(☎ 04 90 49 94 04; ⓦ www.fondationvangogh-arles.org; 24 bis rond-point des Arènes; adult/8-18 yrs €7/5; open 10am-7pm daily Apr–mid-Oct; 10am-5.40pm mid-Oct–Mar)*, inside Palais de Luppé, displays changing art exhibitions by artists inspired by Van Gogh; an updated calendar is on its website.

The gallery **La Rose des Vents** *(☎ 04 90 96 15 85; 18 rue Diderot; open 10.30am-12.30pm & 3pm-7pm Tues-Sun)* displays various Van Gogh reproductions and letters written by him. In 1888 Van Gogh wrote to his sister Willemien, 'nature in the south cannot be painted with the palette of a mauve for instance which belongs to the north…now the palette is distinctly colourful, sky blue, orange, pink, vermilion, a very bright yellow, bright green, wine red and violet'.

Various art exhibitions take place at the **Espace Van Gogh** *(☎ 04 90 49 39 39; place Félix Rey)*, a former hospital where Van Gogh spent time as a depressed patient in 1889 and painted several works, including his famous portrait of the hospital's courtyard garden, *Le Jardin de la Maison de Santé* (1989). The hospital is a cultural centre today.

Abbaye de Montmajor

Montmajor Abbey *(☎ 04 90 54 64 17; adult/under 18 €5.50/free 1st Sun of month; open 9am-7pm daily Apr-Oct; 10am-1pm & 2pm-5pm Wed-Mon Nov-Mar)*, some 5km northeast of Arles on the route de Fontvieille (the D17), is a medieval ensemble featuring an 11th-century main building and crypt, a Romanesque cloister built by Benedictine monks in the 12th century and a hermitage dedicated to St Peter. The edifice, steadily restored since 1892, hosts occasional photography exhibitions.

Special Events

Bullfights fill Les Arènes and there's bull-running in the streets during the **Féria de Pâques** at Easter.

In early July, **Les Rencontres Internationales de la Photographie** (International Photography Festival) attracts photographers and aficionados from around the world. Some screenings take place in the Théâtre Antique. The two-week **Fêtes d'Arles** at the end of June brings dance, theatre, music and poetry readings to Les Arènes.

The fascinating **Festo Vierginenco** in mid-July, celebrated since 1904, honours young girls who don the traditional Arlésienne costume (consisting of a long full skirt, lacy shawl and cap) for the first time. The week-long **Fête des Prémices du Riz** in September marks the start of the rice harvest.

Places to Stay

Camping Arle's closest camp site, **Camping City** *(☎ 04 90 93 08 86, fax 04 90 93 91 07; ⓦ www.camping-city.com; 67 route de Crau; two people with tent & car €16; open Apr-Sept)*, is 1km southeast of the centre on the Marseilles road. Take bus No 2 from blvd Georges Clemenceau to the Hermite stop.

Street Beats

Roma bands such as Los Reyes, Arles' very own Gypsy Kings (discovered while busking in St-Tropez), Chico & the Gypsies (founded by former Gypsy King, Chico Bouchikki) and Manitas de Plata have all sung on the streets of Arles and Stes-Maries de la Mer at some point in their vibrant careers. For an outstanding collection of tracks by these and other artists, shop at **La Boutique des Passionnés** *(☎ 04 90 96 59 93; W www.passionnes.com; 14 rue Réattu; open 2pm-7pm Mon, 9am-7pm Tues-Sat)*, a fabulous music shop in Arles with an online boutique.

The best time to watch Roma bands perform on the streets is during the Festival Mosaïque Gitane in Arles in mid-July and the Stes-Maries de la Mer pilgrimages in May and October. The musicians (exclusively male) are usually encircled by Roma women dancing Camargue flamenco (reminiscent of Spanish flamenco).

Hostels A 100-bed place, **Auberge de Jeunesse** *(☎ 04 90 96 18 25, fax 04 90 96 31 26; 20 ave Maréchal Foch; dorm beds with breakfast & sheets €13.50; open mid-Feb–Dec)* is 2km south of the centre. To reach the hostel, take bus No 3 from blvd Georges Clemenceau or No 8 from place Lamartine to the Fournier stop.

Hotels Above a pleasant café-bar, **Hôtel Terminus et Van Gogh** *(☎/fax 04 90 96 12 32; 5 place Lamartine; doubles with washbasin €30.50, with shower & toilet €36.50)* has 12 rooms.

Hôtel Mirador *(☎ 04 90 96 28 05, fax 04 90 96 59 89; W www.hotel-mirador.com; 3 place Voltaire; doubles with shower €30, with shower & toilet €41)* is one of a trio of two-star hotels on quaint place Voltaire.

Hôtel Le Rhône *(☎ 04 90 96 43 70, fax 04 90 93 87 03; 11 place Voltaire; doubles with washbasin €26, doubles/triples with shower €30/36, doubles/triples with shower & toilet €37.50/40.50)* is run by staff as bright and cheery as its crisp canary-yellow facade.

Hôtel Acacias *(☎ 04 90 96 37 88, fax 04 90 96 32 51; W www.hotel-acacias.com; 33 rue de la Cavalerie; doubles €46)*, painted a fresh and rosy pink, is Arles' most modern, mid-range choice. Rooms have air-con.

Hôtel du Musée *(☎ 04 90 93 88 88, fax 04 90 49 98 15; 11 rue du Grand Prieuré; singles/doubles €39/40)* is an appealing, 20-room place in a 12th- to 13th-century building. It's spacious, calm and has a terrace garden out back.

Hôtel Le Calendal *(☎ 04 90 96 11 89, fax 04 90 96 05 84; W www.lecalendal.com; 5 rue Porte de Laure; doubles from €6)* is equally well known for its tea room and restaurant, tucked beneath the shade of palm trees in a peaceful, bird-twittering walled garden. Guests can limber up with a game of giant-sized chess.

Hôtel de l'Amphithéâtre *(☎ 04 90 96 10 30, fax 04 90 93 98 69; e contact@hotelamphitheatre.fr; 5 rue Diderot; singles/doubles low season €41/45, high season €45/49, terrace suite low/high season €106/137)*, stunning inside, is decked out in a contemporary fashion to contrast with its 17th-century exterior.

Hôtel d'Arlatan *(☎ 04 90 93 56 66, fax 04 90 49 68 45; e hotel-arlatan@provnet.fr; 26 rue du Sauvage; doubles from €77)* is a historic hotel that's been operating since 1920. It has lavish rooms in the former private residence of the counts of Arlatan de Beaumont.

Hôtel Jules César *(☎ 04 90 52 52 52, fax 04 90 52 52 53; 9 blvd des Lices; doubles from €128)*, a four-star place inside a former convent with Roman-style portico, private chapel, outdoor swimming pool and sumptuous Provençal-style rooms, is worth a try for big spenders.

Places to Eat

Restaurants & Cafés Traffic-ridden blvd Georges Clemenceau and blvd des Lices are lined with plane trees and terraced brasseries. In the historic heart, place du Forum is an intimate square shaded by eight large plane trees and filled with restaurant terraces, including that of **Café La Nuit** at No 11. It's absolutely unmomentous apart from its yellow facade, which mimics the canary-yellow house (no longer standing) on place Lamartine that Van Gogh painted for his canvas *La Maison Jaune* (1888) and where he famously cut off his left ear the same year.

Les Huiles Jamard *(☎ 04 90 49 70 73; 46 rue des Arènes; sandwiches €4)* is a rustic olive-oil shop where fabulous sandwiches to take away are constructed. The mozzarella, avocado, tomato, basil and olive oil is a juicy choice.

Chez Gigi *(☎ 04 90 96 68 59; ⓔ gigietcie@wanadoo.fr; 49 rue des Arènes)*, run by French-Canadians Marcel and Gigi, is a fun 'soul food' restaurant guaranteed to please *végetariens, cannibales et amoureux de la mer* (vegetarians, cannibals and seafood lovers) alike.

La Charcuterie *(☎ 04 90 96 56 96; 51 rue des Arènes; starters/mains from €5.50/12)*, next door, is an authentic pork butcher's shop with tables to eat at. Sink your teeth into a home-made *saucisse d'Arles* (local bull-meat sausage) or a *Lyonnais andouillette* (tripe sausage typical to Lyons).

La Mule Blanche *(☎ 04 90 93 98 54; 9 rue du Président Wilson; mains from €10)* has Arles' loveliest pavement terrace – beneath a very, very, very large plane tree – and gets packed out by 12.30pm.

L'Entrevue *(☎ 04 90 93 37 28; 23 quai Max Dormoy; mains around €10)*, a stylish laid-back restaurant in an artsy cinema, bookshop and restaurant complex, serves Oriental and Caribbean cuisine. Fill up on a *tajine* or couscous, washed down with a pot of mint and pine-kernel tea.

La Fuente *(☎ 04 90 93 40 78; 20 rue de la Calade; menus €15 & €21)* cooks up king prawns (gambas) flambéed in cognac, grilled lobster tails and paella – its house specialities – in a classically square interior courtyard.

L'Olivier *(☎ 04 90 49 64 88; 1 bis rue Réattu; menus €28, €46 & €55)* is Arles' upmarket choice, known for its Provençal and Mediterranean cuisine. Period furnishings and a patio add a distinctive touch to The Olive Tree.

Self-Catering Sausage makers **La Farandole** *(11 rue des Porcelets)* and **Pierre Milhau Charcuterie** *(11 rue Réattu)* sell *saucissons d'Arles* (bull-meat sausages typical of Arles). **Les Huiles Jamard** (see Places to Eat earlier) sells olive oil by the bottle or litre.

Fruit, vegetables, olives, spices and even fish and meat are sold at the Wednesday-morning **market** *(blvd Émile Combe)* and the larger Saturday-morning **market** *(blvd des Lices & blvd Georges Clemenceau)*. **Monoprix** *(place de la Libération; open 8.30am-7.30pm Mon-Thur, 8pm Fri & Sat)* is a supermarket.

Getting There & Away

Air On the A54, the **Nîmes-Arles-Camargue airport** *(Aéroport de Nîmes-Arles-Camargue or Aéroport Nîmes-Garons; ☎ 04 66 70 49 49)* is 20km northwest of Nîmes.

Bus The Inter-Regional **bus station** *(ave Paulin Talabot)* is opposite the train station, but most buses use the bus stops on blvd George Clemenceau. The **Boutique des Transports** *(☎ 08 16 00 08 16; 34 blvd George Clemenceau)* sells tickets and has printed schedules; when the information office is closed, use the computer screen (in English) outside instead.

From Arles, there are buses to/from Stes-Maries de la Mer (€6, one hour, four to five daily), Salin de Giraud (€6.30, 40 minutes, two to four daily), Port St-Louis (€6.40, 50 minutes, two to four daily) and many places en route such as Mas du Pont de Rousty, Pioch Badet and Pont de Crau.

Outside the Camargue, you can travel by bus from Arles to/from Aix-en-Provence (€11.40, 1¾ hours, two to six daily), Marseilles (€14.60, two hours, two to six daily), Nîmes (€4.50, 50 minutes, four daily Mon-Sat), Fontvieille (€2, 20 minutes, eight daily Mon-Sat, two daily Sun), Les Baux de Provence (€4.80, 35 minutes, eight daily Mon-Sat, two daily Sun) and Salon de Provence (€7.30, 1¼ hours, eight daily Mon-Sat, two daily Sun). Eight of the 11 daily buses to/from Avignon (€8.10, 45 minutes, 11 daily) only arrive/depart from Arles bus station.

Train Arles train station, opposite the bus station, serves major rail destinations including Nîmes (€6.40, 30 minutes), Marseilles (€11.40, 50 minutes) and Avignon (€6.80, 20 to 40 minutes).

Getting Around

Bicycle Bikes can be hired from **Peugeot Cycles** *(☎ 04 90 96 03 77; 15 rue du Pont)* for upwards of €10 per day. Otherwise, try **Jauffret** *(☎ 04 90 93 50 14; 22 blvd Victor Hugo)*.

STES-MARIES DE LA MER

postcode 13460 • pop 2200

Stes-Maries de la Mer is no more than a seaside village, marooned between the Étang de l'Impérial and the sea in the Camarguaise outback. It is best known for its magnificent fortified Romanesque church, which has for centuries served as a pilgrimage site for Europe's colourful *gitan* (Roma) population. The coastline is lined with 30km of uninterrupted sandy beaches. Nudists frequent the patch near Phare de la Gacholle, a lighthouse 11km east of the village.

Orientation & Information

The amphitheatre, the tourist office and Port Gardian are lined up between ave Van Gogh and the sea. From the bus stop on ave d'Arles (the southern end of the D570), bear south along ave Frédéric Mistral then east across place des Remparts and place Portalet to get to place de l'Église.

Stes-Maries de la Mer has a **tourist office** (*☎ 04 90 97 82 55, fax 04 90 97 71 15; W www.saintesmaries.com; 5 ave Van Gogh; open 9am-8pm daily July & Aug; 9am-7pm daily Apr, May, June & Sept; 9am-5pm or 6pm daily Oct-Mar*), with an ATM outside and a **laundrette** (*24 ave d'Arles*) nearby.

Things to See & Do

Donjon-style **Église des Stes-Maries** (*place de l'Église*), built between the 12th and 15th centuries, dominates the village. Its sober, dim interior shelters a beautiful elevated choir and a crypt where the statue of St Sarah – the highly revered patron saint of the Roma – is religiously kept. Year round, a sea of smoky candles burns at the foot of the overdressed black statue, which at pilgrimage time is showered with at least 40 or 50 brightly coloured dresses (see the boxed text 'The Roma Pilgrimage' later). St Sarah's relics – discovered in the crypt by King René in 1448 – are enshrined in a gaudy wooden chest, stashed away in a hole cut in the sturdy stone wall above the choir.

A fabulous wetland panorama unfolds from the **Terrasses de l'Église** (*church terraces; adult/12-18 yrs €2/1.30; open 10am-8pm daily July & Aug; 10am-12.30pm & 2pm-6.30pm Mon-Fri, 10am-6.30pm Sat & Sun Mar-June, Sept & Oct; 10am-noon & 2pm-5pm Wed, Sat & Sun Nov-Feb*).

The **Musée de Baroncelli** (*☎ 04 90 97 87 60; rue Victor Hugo; adult/12-18 yrs €1.50/1.30; open 10am-noon & 2pm-6pm daily July & Aug, 10am-noon & 2pm-6pm Wed-Mon Apr-June & Oct*), in the 19th-century city hall, is dedicated to the Marquis of Baroncelli (1869–1943) – a *manadier* (herdsman) who devoted his life to reviving local Camarguaise culture when not herding his *manades* (herds of bulls and horses).

Les Arènes, the amphitheatre next to Port Gardian, can only be visited during bullfights; the tourist office has programme and ticket details. Bullfights are also held on Sunday, Easter to mid-July, at the **Arènes de Méjanes** (*☎ 04 90 97 10 60*), an open-air theatre at Domaine de Méjanes, the Paul Ricard complex 30km north in Méjanes.

North of Stes-Maries Roma culture is unravelled in a series of eight caravans from the 1930s to 1960s at the **Musée des Roulettes Anciennes** (*Museum of Old Caravans; ☎ 04 90 97 52 85; adult/under 14 €3.50/3; open 9am-6pm daily Sept-June; 9am-6pm daily July & Aug*), next to the hostel in Pioch Badet, 8km north of Stes-Maries.

About 2km farther north along the D570 is **Château d'Avignon** (*☎ 04 90 97 58 58; route d'Arles; adult/under 18 €3/1.50; open 10am-5pm Wed-Mon Apr-Nov*), an 18th-century chateau furnished almost exactly as it was by wealthy Marseilles merchant Louis Noilly Prat, who used the place as a hunting lodge in the 1890s. He kitted out the castle with hot and cold running water, central heating and other gadgets – all revolutionary at the time. The chateau can be visited on a guided tour (45 minutes).

Boat Trips

Several companies offer boat excursions, including **Le Camargue** (*☎ 04 90 97 84 72; 5 rue des Launes*) and **Les Quatre Maries** (*☎ 04 90 97 70 10; W www.lesquatremaries.com; 36 ave Théodore Aubanel*). Both charge around €10/5 per adult/under 18 for a 1½-hour trip. From March to November both have boats departing from Port Gardian. The **Tiki III** (*☎ 04 90 97 81 68; e tiki3@wanadoo.fr*) is docked at the mouth of the Petit Rhône 1.5km west of Stes-Maries.

Kayak Vert (*☎ 04 66 73 57 17, 06 09 56 06 47; W www.kayak.camargue.fr*) based at the Mas de Sylvéréal, 14km north of Stes-Maries, on the banks of the Petit Rhône (next to Pont du Sylvéréal) off the picturesque D38C, is a canoeing centre where you can explore Camargue's waterways by paddle power. It rents canoes for €9.50 per hour and runs half-/two-/three-/four-day guided expeditions costing €16/23/46/69. Kayak

The Roma Pilgrimage

Europe's Roma population is said to have its roots in Camargue's shifting waters, and Roma people from all over Europe flock to Stes-Maries de la Mer to honour their patron saint, Sarah, each May and October. According to Provençal legend, Sarah was the servant of Mary Jacob and Mary Salome, who (along with other New Testament figures) fled the Holy Land by boat and drifted in the open sea until landing near the River Rhône in AD 40.

Pilgrimages set the streets of Stes-Maries ablaze with song, music and dance. The May festivities last for three days, the first two of which celebrate the feast day of Mary Jacob (25 May) and see Roma party with great gusto. Many hit the road for the long journey home on the third day, which honours the Marquis de Baroncelli Jaron (1869–1943), a local herdsman who revived many Camarguaise traditions in the 19th century. Fewer travel to the autumn pilgrimage, which falls on the Sunday nearest to Mary Salome's feast day (22 October).

In anticipation of a pilgrimage, a wooden chest above the choir in Église des Stes-Maries is lowered to the altar so the pilgrims can touch it and pray by its side. The chest is believed to contain the skeletons of Sarah, Mary Jacob and Mary Salome, discovered in the church in 1448. Following a solemn mass, a black statue of Sarah is carried from the church crypt through the streets and down to the sea, to symbolise the arrival of the Roma patron saint. The procession is led by *gardians* on horseback who usher the statue to the seashore, where it is placed in a wooden fishing boat in the sea and blessed. The pilgrims pour into the sea fully clothed. The same ritual is showered upon statues of Mary Jacob and Mary Salome on 25 May when, following the benediction of the sea, the sacred relics in the church are winched back up to their safe hidey-hole.

Vert also offers a combined canoe (10km) and bicycle trip (16km), departing from Stes-Maries, for €26.

Organised Tours

For details on other tours and activities see Organised Tours at the start of the chapter.

Special Events

The village bursts with life during its annual **Roma pilgrimages** on 24–25 May and 17–18 October; see the previous boxed text for details. Bullfights animate Les Arènes during Easter, most Sundays in May and June, in mid-June for the village's five-day **Fête Votive** when it celebrates traditional Camargue traditions, and in mid-August during the **Feria du Taureau** (bull festival). The tourist office has an updated schedule.

Places to Stay

Camping With its own onsite swimming pool, **Camping La Brise** *(☎ 04 90 97 84 67, fax 04 90 97 72 01; ⓔ labrise@laposte.net; rue Marcel Carrière; camping for 2 adults with tent & car about €12)*, northeast of the centre by the seashore.

Camping Le Clos du Rhône *(☎ 04 90 97 85 99, fax 04 90 97 78 85; ⓔ leclos@laposte.net; route d'Aigues-Mortes; camping for 2 adults with tent & car about €15.50; open Mar–mid-Dec)* is likewise pool-bedecked for hot cowboys to cool down in.

Hostels In Pioch Badet, **Auberge de Jeunesse** *(☎ 04 90 97 51 72, fax 04 90 97 54 88; half-board €20.59; reception open 8.30am-11am & 5pm-10pm daily)*, is 8km north of Stes-Maries on the D570 to Arles. The hostel has bicycles to rent and organises horse riding. A hostelling card is obligatory. Les Cars de Camargue buses from Arles to Stes-Maries drop you at the door in Pioch Badet; see Getting There & Away in the Arles section earlier in this chapter.

Cabanes Aspiring cowboys can rent a *cabane de gardian* (see the boxed text 'Bulls & Cowboys' earlier in this chapter); the tourist office has details. Most cabanes sleep up to five people and can be rented on a weekly basis from April to September. There is a cluster for hire on ave Riquette Aubanel, a narrow lane (the D38) leading from Stes-Maries past the port to Aigues-Mortes.

Farmhouses Numerous *mas* (Provençal farmhouses) surround Stes-Maries.

Mas de la Grenouillère *(☎ 04 90 97 90 22, 06 80 25 68 58, fax 04 90 97 70 94; route* *d'Arles; doubles/triples/quads from €58/80/90)*, 1.5km along a dirt track signposted off the D570 1km north of Stes-Maries, has small but comfortable rooms with a terrace overlooking open fields and a choir of frogs croak guests to sleep at night. La Grenouillère (literally 'Frog Farm') has a swimming pool and organises horse riding.

L'Étrier Camarguais *(The Camargue Stirrup; ☎ 04 90 97 81 14, fax 04 90 97 88 11; W www.letrier.com; doubles low/high season €69/90; open Apr-Sept)*, a farmhouse-hotel made from 'a dream, flowers and the sun', is even more idyllic than its croaking neighbour; it's 500m before La Grenouillère along the same dirt track.

Saddled with four stars, **Mas de la Fouque** *(☎ 04 90 97 81 02, fax 04 90 97 96 84; 28 route du Petit Rhône; W www.masdelafouque.com; doubles with breakfast €275)*, falls under the umbrella of Châteaux & Hotels de Charme and is this wet region's spoil-yourself-rotten choice.

Hotels Heaps of hotels – mostly three- or four-star and costing at least €50 per night – line the D570, the main Arles–Stes-Maries road. In the village, the cheapest rooms are at one-star **Les Vagues** *(☎/fax 04 90 97 84 40; 12 ave Théodore Aubanel; doubles from €28)* on the road running along the port, west of the tourist office; and **Le Delta** *(☎ 04 90 97 81 12, fax 04 90 97 72 85; 1 place Mireille; doubles from €35)* on the right as you enter Stes-Maries from the north.

Places to Eat

The centre of Stes-Marie is loaded with unspectacular, snack-style places where you can find a cheap and speedy fill.

L'Hippocampe *(☎ 04 90 97 80 91; rue C Pelletan; menu €20.50 & €32.50)* specialises in fish fresh from the sea.

Hostellerie du Pont de Gau *(☎ 04 90 97 81 53; route d'Arles; menu €16.77; double rooms €45.74)*, a Logis de France hotel best known for its excellent restaurant, is the perfect spot for lunch after visiting the Parc Ornithologique: It is bang next door on the D570.

Getting There & Away

Stes-Maries has no bus station; buses use the shelter at the northern entrance to town on ave d'Arles (the continuation of the route d'Arles and the D570).

For bus details to/from Arles (via Pont du Gau and Mas du Pont de Rousty), see Getting There & Away in the Arles section. In summer there are two buses daily from Stes-Maries to Nîmes (1¼ hours) via Aigues-Mortes.

Getting Around

Le Vélo Saintois *(☎/fax 04 90 97 74 56; W www.levelosaintois.com; 19 rue de la République)* charges €14/34 for one/three days' bike rental. It rents children's bicycles (€12.50 per day) and tandems (€27.44 per day). Ask for a copy of its English-language tour brochure before pedalling off (free).

Le Vélociste *(☎ 04 90 97 83 26; rue de la République)* charges the same rates and likewise distributes a brochure detailing scenic rides. It also organises cycling, canoeing and horse-riding trips.

AIGUES-MORTES

postcode 30220 • pop 5000

On the Camargue's western edge, 28km northwest of Stes-Maries in the Gard *département* (department), is the curiously named walled-town of Aigues-Mortes (literally 'Dead Waters'). Sleepy Aigues-Mortes was established on marshy flat land in the mid-13th century by Louis IX so the French crown would have a Mediterranean port under its direct control. At the time, the area's other ports were governed by rival powers, including the counts of Provence. In 1248, Louis IX's ships – all 1500 of them – gathered here before setting sail to the Holy Land for the Seventh Crusade.

Aigues-Mortes' sturdy, rectangular ramparts – the tops of which afford great views over the marshlands – can be easily circumambulated from the **Tour de Constance** *(☎ 04 66 53 61 55; adult/under 18 €5.50/free; open 9.30am-8pm June-Aug; 10am-6pm Feb, Apr & Oct; 9.30am-7pm May & Sept; 10am-5pm Nov-Jan & Mar)*, named by Louis VII after his sister. Count on 30 minutes for the 1.6km wall-top walk. Inside the impregnable fortress, with its 6m-thick walls, you can visit the 32m-tall tower that served as a Huguenot women's prison after the revocation of the Edict of Nantes in 1685. The word *register* ('to resist' in old French) on the millstone in the centre of the prison was carved by heroine inmate Marie Durand, jailed here for 38 years.

The **tourist office** *(☎ 04 66 53 73 00, fax 04 66 53 65 94; W www.ot-aiguesmortes.fr; open 9am-8pm July & Aug; 9am-noon & 2pm-6pm Mon-Fri, 10am-noon & 2pm-6pm Sat & Sun Sept-June)* is inside the walled city at Porte de la Gardette.

Salins du Midi

There are magnificent views of the pink-hued saltpans that stretch south from the top of Aigues-Mortes' southern ramparts. By road, the lone D979 follows the narrow land bar that cuts across the still pools. Alternatively, hop aboard the **salt train** *(☎ 04 66 51 17 10; W www.labaleine.com)* that salt producer La Baleine operates daily between March and October. Tickets for the informative, one-hour train ride (with English commentary and a visit to La Baleine's museum and shop), cost €6.80/5 per adult/four to 15 years. Heading towards the Salins du Midi, La Baleine train stop is clearly flagged on the left just before the bridge.

Between May and August, tours of the salt works and marshes are possible. The tourist office has details.

Boat Excursions

Between March and November, boats line up at Aigues-Mortes port to take tourists on safaris around the Camargue's wild waters; the tourist office has a list of operators. Tickets cost €7/4.50 per adult/three to 12 years for a 1½-hour safari and €10/6 for a 2½-hour trip. Rîve de France (See Canal Boat under Boat in the Getting Around chapter) rents boats for two to 10 people.

Places to Stay & Eat

Chez Carrière *(☎ 04 66 53 73 07, fax 04 66 53 84 75; 18 rue Pasteur; doubles from €32)* is the cheapest for beds in Aigues-Mortes.

Hostellerie des Remparts *(☎ 04 66 53 82 77, fax 04 66 53 73 77; 6 place de France; doubles from €43)* is a three-star place overlooking Tour de Constance.

The walled city is loaded with places to eat. Pretty place St-Louis, at the southern foot of Grande Rue, has heaps of open-air cafés and terrace restaurants, most of them sporting *menus* averaging €15 and starring *guardianne de taureau* (a traditional bull-meat stew from the Camargue) for no more than €10. Bakeries and food, grocery and butcher shops bespeckle Grande Rue.

Simple but elegant, **La Salicorne** *(☎ 04 66 53 62 67; 9 rue Alsace-Lorraine; full meals around €20)* stands out. Quintessential Provençal dishes with an imaginative twist are served in an old-world yet jazzy setting.

Les Enganettes *(☎ 04 66 53 69 11; 12 rue Marceau; full meal around €20)* is known for its traditional Camargue cooking – namely, bull meat in various guises and goat's cheese from the watery region.

Getting There & Away

From Aigues-Mortes' tiny **train station** *(route de Nîmes)*, there are a handful of trains and SNCF buses to/from Nîmes (€6.10, 45 minutes).

SOUTHEASTERN CAMARGUE

The wetland is at its most savage around the eastern shores of the Étang de Vaccarès. Much of this area is protected and off limits to tourists. A memorable day trip is to head south along the D570 from Arles, turn left (southeast) onto the D36, then bear right along the narrow D36B to La Capelière, Salin de Badon and along its continuation, the D36C to Salin de Giraud. Return to Arles via the northbound D36, a larger road which shadows the Grand Rhône.

Arles to Digue à la Mer

Midway along this 48km stretch – where the D36B kisses Vaccarès' eastern shores – is **La Capelière**, a minuscule hamlet where the Réserve Nationale de Camargue runs its excellent **Centre d'Information Nature** *(Nature Information Centre; ☎ 04 90 97 00 97; adult/12-18 yrs €3/1.50; open 9am-noon & 2pm-5pm daily Apr-Sept; 9am-1pm & 2pm-5pm Wed-Mon Oct-Mar)*. As well as exhibitions, a 1.5km-long **Sentier des Rainettes** (Tree-frog Trail), studded with four wildlife observatories, enables you to discover flora and fauna native to fresh-water marshes.

The centre runs three observatories at **Salin de Badon**, former royal saltpans about 7km farther south along the D36B. Unlike at La Capelière, the bird-watching towers fall within the Réserve Nationale de Camargue. Photography is therefore forbidden and visitors need a permit (€3; issued at the Centre d'Information Nature in La Capelière) to enter. The site is accessible to permit holders Thursday to Tuesday from sunrise to 10am (11am November to 28 February) and 4pm

(3pm November to 28 February) to sunset daily.

A beautiful stroll along what seems to be the edge of the world can be enjoyed on the Digue à la Mer *(admission free; open 9am-1pm & 2pm-6pm daily Apr-Sept; 9am-1pm & 2pm-5pm daily Oct-Mar)*, a sea dike built in the 19th century to cut the delta off from the sea. An 18km-long walking and cycling track runs along the length of the dike; there's also a shorter 10km circuit and a 2.3km footpath that cuts down to a lovely sandy beach. Walking on the fragile sand dunes is forbidden. To access the dike, follow the D36B for 10km southwest to Parking de la Gacholle where motorists must park. The **Phare de la Gacholle** (lighthouse) cannot be visited.

Salin de Giraud & Beyond

The chequered evaporation saltpans *(marais salants)* of Salin de Giraud (population 2411) cover 14,000 hectares and produce about 1 million tonnes of salt per year, making them one of Europe's largest. *Sel* (salt), which takes three years to produce, is harvested in September and then stored in giant mountains. Pass the entrance to Salin de Giraud on the D36 and continue south along the D36D for a stunning panorama of the marsh village, the saltpans and the salt mountains. A couple of kilometres south of here is a **point de vue** (viewing point) where you can pull up and breathe in the salty sea air. Come here to watch the salt being harvested between August and mid-October.

The final 12km leg of this southbound journey is unforgettable. Drive slowly to enjoy the views and stop to see pink flamingos wading through the water. About 8km south of Salin de Giraud is **Domaine de la Palissade** *(☎ 04 42 86 81 28; ⓔ palissade@free.fr; route de la Mer; admission €2.30; open 9am-5pm daily Apr-Oct)*, a nature centre run by the Conservatoire de l'Espace Littoral et des Rivages Lacustres, which organises forays in the marshes on foot and horse back. There are a couple of observation towers here for nature spotting on the estate, a 1km-long **Sentier de Découverte** (discovery trail), and various audiovisual displays to help visitors learn about local flora and fauna in the main house.

The road reaches the Mediterranean about 4km farther south. Caravans and camper vans can park overnight in the camp site on the sand here, overlooking **Plage de Piémanson**. Bear east (left) from the car park and walk 1400m to get to the nudist section of the very windy beach.

Salin de Giraud is 15km east of the Digue à la Mer via the winding D36C. En route you pass the **Mas de St-Bertrand** *(☎ 04 42 48 80 69; route de Vaccarès)*, an idyllic *gîte rural* that rents rooms and bicycles from February to mid-November. The **tourist office** *(☎ 04 42 86 80 87; place des Gardians; open 9am-1pm & 2pm-6pm daily mid-June–mid-Sept)*, in a traditional cowboy's *cabane* (on the central square in Salin de Giraud), has information on the few other accommodation options in this isolated part of the world.

Back to Arles

Some 8km north of Salin de Giraud on the D36 is the **Musée du Riz du Petit Manusclat** *(☎ 04 90 97 29 44; adult/under 12 €3.10/free; open 9am-noon & 2pm-6pm Mon-Sat, Sun by appointment)* in Petit Manusclat. The history of the Camargue rice industry, which dates from the 13th century, is explained. The wetland yields 8 million *quintaux* (400,000 tonnes) of rice per year. The museum's opening hours are sporadic – call in advance to arrange a visit.

In **Le Sambuc**, 4km north along the D36, there are several places where you can horse ride.

Hôtel Longo Maï *(☎ 04 90 97 21 91, fax 04 90 97 22 92; doubles from €46)*, 1.5km south of the small hamlet, is a Logis de France hotel with pleasing rooms.

The **Station Biologique de la Tour du Valat** *(☎ 04 90 97 20 13)*, just west of here, is a biology research station. It covers an area of 2500 hectares and opens to the public one day per year (in January). In 1970 the station instigated the construction of the artificial **Étang du Fangassier**. The 4000-sq-metre island serves as a flamingo breeding colony, as a few years previously flamingos had started to breed less in the region.

On the eastern bank of the Grand Rhône is the Mas Thibert, from where the **Marais du Vigueirat** – an extensive marshland – can be explored with a local guide. Eight heron species frequent these dense swamps. Expeditions (four to six hours, April to September) have to be booked in advance through the tourist office in Arles.

Avignon Area

Avignon, the capital of the Vaucluse *département* (department), acquired its ramparts and reputation as a city of art and culture during the 14th century, when Pope Clement V and his court, fleeing political turmoil in Rome, established themselves near Avignon. From 1309 to 1377, the Holy See was based in Avignon, under seven French-born popes, and huge sums of money were invested in building and decorating the papal palace and other important church edifices.

North of Avignon, the fan-shaped Vaucluse area – with Avignon at its hinge – spreads out into a multitude of contrasting landscapes, climaxing with the stark summit of Mont Ventoux (1912m), the region's highest mountain, where the legendary mistral wind can blow at hair-raising speeds of 300km/h. Walking and cycling opportunities abound here. The sinkhole-ridden Plateau d'Albion east of here is prime spelunking territory.

South of Avignon are a cluster of towns, first settled by the Greeks and then by the Romans, who left behind a trove of archaeological treasures. The fortified village of Les Baux de Provence rakes in 2.5 million tourists a year, ranking it among France's most visited tourist attractions.

Highlights

- See how the popes lived at Avignon's Palais des Papes
- Follow in the footsteps of the Romans through Orange, Vaison-la-Romaine, Carpentras, St-Rémy de Provence and Nîmes
- Climb or cycle up Mont Ventoux or around the lacy Dentelles de Montmirail
- Sample France's most potent wine at Châteauneuf du Pape
- Think purple! Follow the lavender road

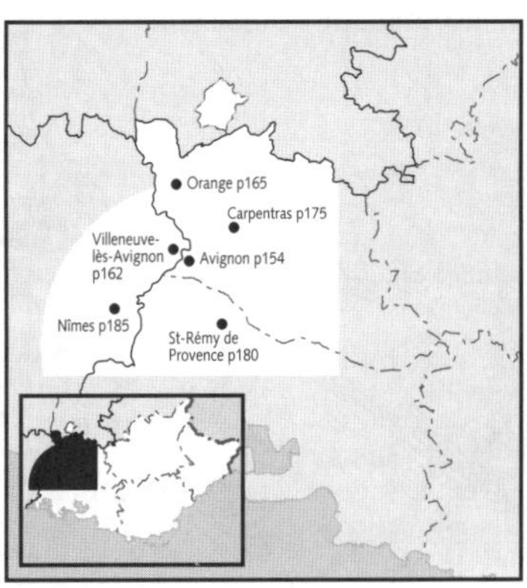

Food Highlights

papalines d'Avignon – pink chocolate balls laced with a herbal liqueur from Mont Ventoux

Châteauneuf du Pape wine, Vallée des Baux AOC olive oil and black truffles

Cantaloup melons, crystallised fruits & **berlingots** – hard caramel sweets from Carpentras

Avignon & Around

AVIGNON

postcode 84000 • pop 85,935 • elevation 21m

Avignon continues its traditional role as a patron of the arts, most notably through its annual performing arts festival. The medieval city's other attractions include a palace fit for a pope or two, fine Côtes du Rhône wines, a nursery rhyme bridge, a historic walled city – a pocket of which is under Unesco World Heritage protection – and a clutch of interesting museums, including some across the River Rhône in the town of Villeneuve-lès-Avignon.

Orientation

Avignon's main avenue – cours Jean Jaurès – runs north from the train station, outside the walled city, past the tourist office to the café-clad place de l'Horloge. Place du Palais, the square abutting the Palais des Papes, is 200m north of here.

The Quartier des Teinturiers (dyers' quarter), around rue des Teinturiers and southeast of place Pie, is Avignon's bohemian part of town.

Villeneuve-lès-Avignon and Les Angles, adjacent suburbs on the right (west) bank of the Rhône, are reached by crossing the two

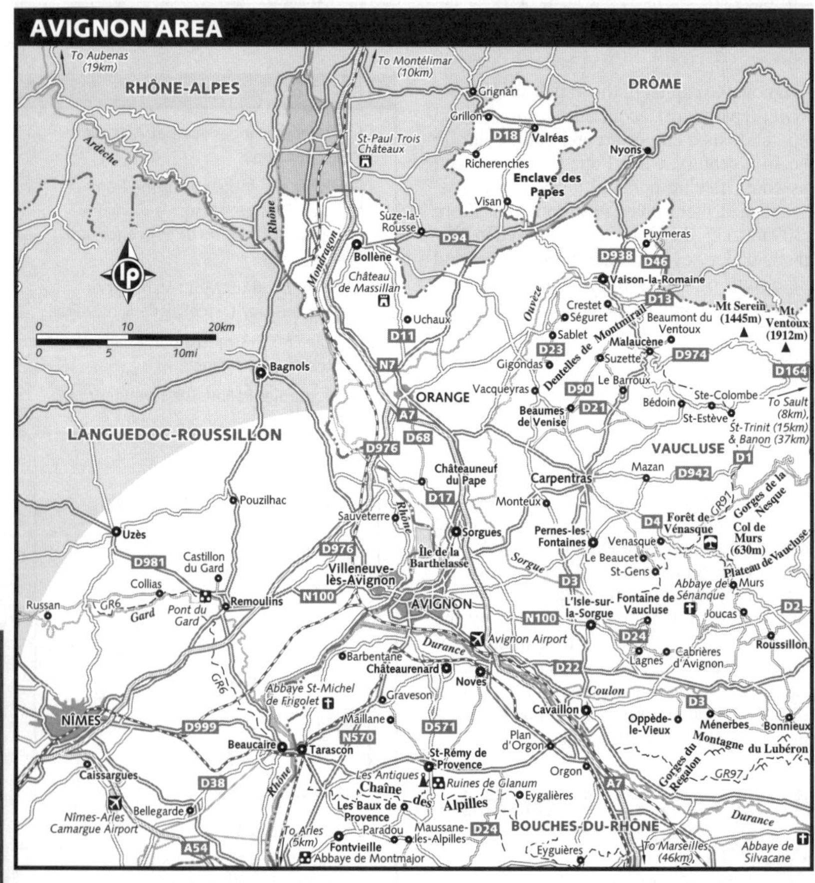

branches of the river and Île de la Barthelasse, the island that divides them.

Information

Tourist Offices The central **tourist office** *(☎ 04 32 74 32 74, fax 04 90 82 95 03;* **W** *www.avignon-tourisme.com; 41 cours Jean Jaurès; open 9am-6pm Mon-Fri, 9am-5pm Sat, 10am-noon Sun Nov-Mar; 9am-6pm Mon-Sat, 10am-5pm Sun Apr-Oct)* opens until 7pm (5pm Sun) during July's Avignon Festival. The Pont d'Avignon **tourist office** *(☎ 04 32 74 32 74; Pont St-Bénézet; open 10am-7pm Apr-Sept)* is seasonal.

Both offices take bookings for walking tours (adult/12 to 25 years €8/5) of the city (in English), which depart up to three times weekly. Both also issue the free Avignon Passion card, which, from the second sight you visit, yields a bonanza of discounts in museums and monuments.

Money There is a 24-hour banknote exchange machine outside the **Banque de Lyonnais** *(13 rue de la République)*.

Post & Communications The city's **post office** *(cours Président Kennedy; open 8am-7pm Mon-Fri, 8am-noon Sat)* is close to the central train station. For your online communication, try **G@my's** *(☎ 04 90 27 02 09; 30 rue Infirmières;* **W** *www.cyberhighway.fr.st; open 10am-9pm Mon-Sat, 2pm-9pm Sun)*, **Cyber 109** *(☎ 04 90 82 72 96; 109 rue de la Carreterie;* **W** *www.cyber109.com; open 10am-10pm Mon-Sat, 2pm-9pm Sun)*; **Cyberdrome**

(☎ *04 90 16 05 15; 68 rue Guillaume Puy; open 8am-midnight daily*); or **Arob@se** (☎ *04 90 16 02 18; 14 rue du Limas.; open 10am-10pm daily*), a trendy café and restaurant too. Expect to pay €3 to €4 per hour.

Bookshops For English-language books, try **Shakespeare** (☎ *04 90 27 38 50; 155 rue de la Carreterie; open 9.30am-12.30pm & 2pm-6.30pm Tues-Sat*).

Laundry To wash a 6kg load, most **laundrettes** (*48 rue de la Carreterie, 26 rue Lanterne & 66 place des Corps Saints; open 7am-8pm or 9pm daily*) charge around €3.

Medical Services & Emergency The **hospital** (*Hôpital Général Henri Duffaut;* ☎ *04 32 75 33 33; 305 rue Raoul Follereau*), 2.5km south of the central train station, is at the southern terminus of bus line No 1 or 3 (marked on bus maps as Hôpital Sud).

The main **police station** (☎ *04 90 16 81 00; blvd St-Roch*) is just west of the station. The **municipal police station** (☎ *08 00 00 84 00; 13 blvd quai St-Lazare*) handles lost property.

Pont St-Bénézet

Pont d'Avignon (*Avignon Bridge;* ☎ *04 90 27 51 16; rue Ferruce; adult/8-17 yrs/under 8 €3.50/3/free; open 9am-7pm Mar-July & Oct; 9am-9pm July; 9am-8pm Aug & Sept; 9am-1pm & 2pm-5pm Tues-Sun Nov-Feb*) – rarely known by its proper name, Pont St-Bénézet – was built between 1177 and 1185 to link Avignon with what later became Villeneuve-lès-Avignon. The 900m-long structure was originally made of wood and rebuilt in stone by Pope Clement VI around 1350. All but four of its 22 spans – over both channels of the River Rhône and Île de la Barthelasse in the middle – were washed away by floods in 1669.

Yes, this is the Pont d'Avignon mentioned in the French nursery rhyme, although people did not dance *sur le pont d'Avignon* (on the bridge of Avignon) but rather *sous* (under) it. Legend claims it was built by St Bénézet (St Benedict), a pious lad from Savoy, who was told in three visions to get the Rhône spanned at any cost.

Combination tickets for the bridge and the Palais des Papes are available; see that section for details.

Walled City

Avignon's most interesting bits are within the roughly oval walled city – 151 hectares of history surrounded by 4.3km of ramparts built between 1359 and 1370. The most hisoric pocket of the old city around the imposing Palais des Papes has been on Unesco's World Heritage list since 1995. To get a glimpse of Avignon's nine popes in their fashionable garbs of the day, take a gander at their trompe l'œil portrait on the side of the *conseil général* (regional council) building, off rue Viala.

The Université d'Avignon (Avignon University), founded by Pope Boniface VIII in 1303, resides in all its splendour inside Porte St-Lazare, the gate linking the eastern part of the walled city with the modern world. A short walk west from here along rue de la Carreterie and rue des Infirmières brings you to **place des Carmes**, a pretty square known for its weekend markets (see Shopping later in this section) and 14th-century **Église et Cloître des Carmes**, once part of a convent.

Palais des Papes The Papal Palace (☎ *04 90 27 50 00;* Ⓦ *www.palais-des-papes.com; place du Palais; adult/8-17 yrs/under 8 €9.50/7.50/free; open 9.30am-5.45pm daily Nov–mid-Mar, 9.30am-6.30pm daily mid-Mar–1 Apr, 9am-7pm daily Apr-June & Oct, 9am-8pm daily July-Sept*) – Europe's largest Gothic palace – was built in the 14th century as a fortified palace for the pontifical court. Papal banquets held here were of tremendous proportions. A feast to celebrate Clement VI's coronation in 1342 comprised 118 oxen, 1033 spit-roasted sheep, 1195 geese, 7428 chickens, 50,000 sweet tarts, 39,980 eggs and 95,000 loaves of bread, among numerous other things. Since 1947 the **Cours d'Honneur** (Courtyard of Honour) has hosted the Avignon theatre festival.

The basic admission fee includes an English-language audioguide to guide you around 23 of the palace's undecorated stone halls – impressive but practically empty – and the palace's **Great Chapel**, where art exhibitions are held. Self-guided tours end in **La Bouteillerie**, a wine boutique where you can pay €5.80 to taste four different wines.

Guided tours in English run once or twice every day during the summer. Alternatively, you can invest in a fascinating two-hour

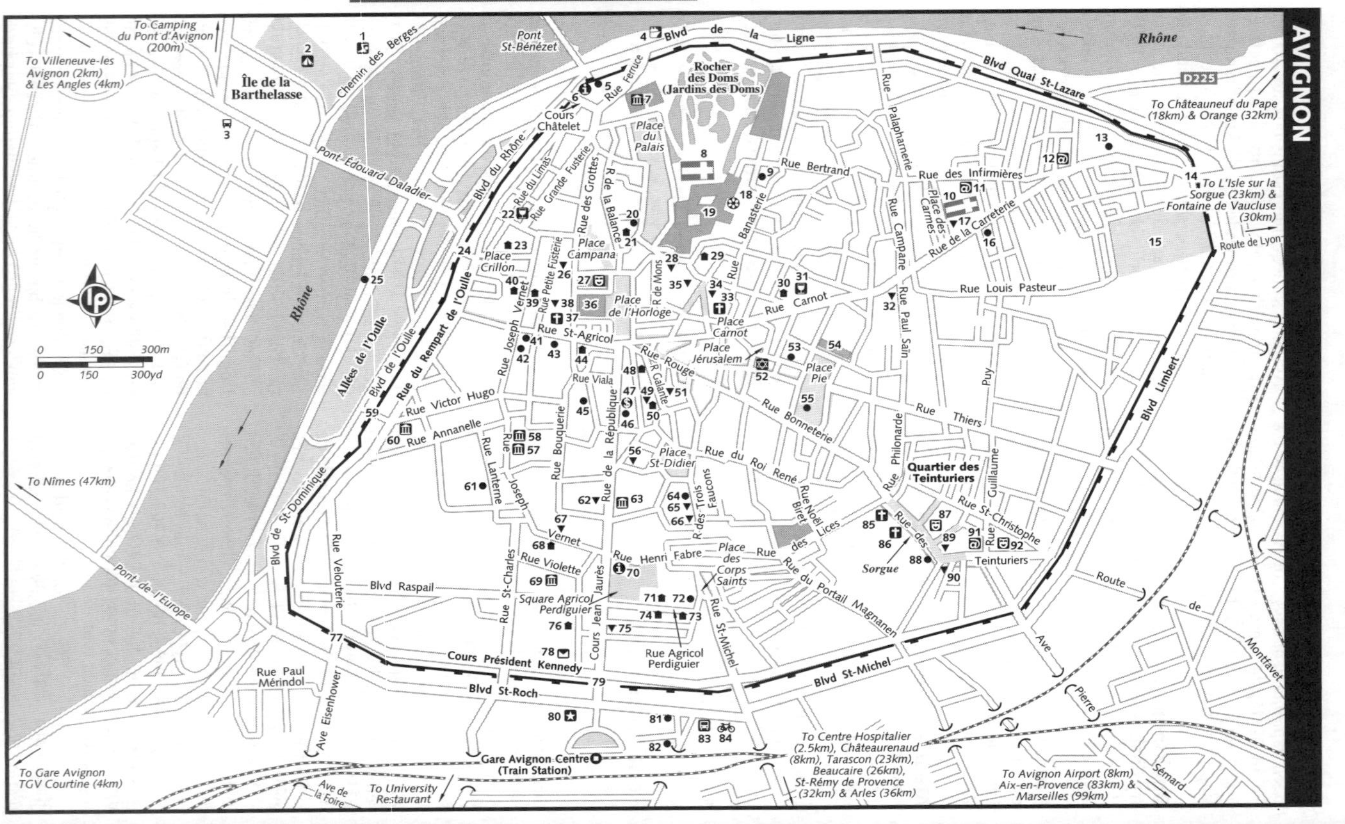
AVIGNON
To Camping du Pont d'Avignon (200m)
To Villeneuve-les Avignon (2km) & Les Angles (4km)
Île de la Barthelasse
Chemin des Berges
Pont St-Bénézet
Blvd de la Ligne
Rocher des Doms (Jardins des Doms)
Blvd Quai St-Lazare
Rhône
D225
To Châteauneuf du Pape (18km) & Orange (32km)
Rue Ferruce
Cours Châtelet
Place du Palais
Rue Bertrand
Rue Palapharnerie
Rue des Infirmières
Place des Carmes
Rue de la Carreterie
To L'Isle sur la Sorgue (23km) & Fontaine de Vaucluse (30km)
Route de Lyon
Pont Édouard Daladier
Blvd du Rhône
Rue du Limas
Rue Grande Fusterie
Rue des Grottes
R de la Balance
Banasterie
Rue Campane
Place Campana
Place Crillon
Rue Petite Fusterie
R de Mons
Rue Carnot
Rue Louis Pasteur
Place de l'Horloge
Rue Joseph Vernet
Rue St-Agricol
Place Carnot
Place Jérusalem
Rue Paul Saïn
Place Pie
Rue Rouge
R Galante
Rue Viala
Rue Victor Hugo
Rue Annanelle
Rue Bonneterie
Rue Thiers
Puy
Blvd Limbert
Allées de l'Oulle
Blvd de l'Oulle
Rue du Rempart de l'Oulle
Rue de la République
Rue Bouquerie
Rue Joseph
Rue Lanterne
Place St-Didier
Rue du Roi René
Rue Philonarde
Rue Guillaume
Quartier des Teinturiers
Rue St-Christophe
To Nîmes (47km)
Blvd de St-Dominique
Rue des Trois Faucons
Rue Noël Biret
Rue des Lices
Rue des Sorgue
Rue des Teinturiers
Rue Vernet
Rue Violette
Rue Henri Fabre
Place des Corps Saints
Rue du Portail Magnanen
Route de Montfavet
Rue Velouterie
Blvd Raspail
Rue St-Charles
Square Agricol Perdiguier
Cours Jean Jaurès
Rue St-Michel
Pont de l'Europe
Rue Agricol Perdiguier
Cours Président Kennedy
Blvd St-Michel
Ave Pierre Sémard
Rue Paul Mérindol
Blvd St-Roch
Ave Eisenhower
Gare Avignon Centre (Train Station)
To Centre Hospitalier (2.5km), Châteaurenaud (8km), Tarascon (23km), Beaucaire (26km), St-Rémy de Provence (32km) & Arles (36km)
To Avignon Airport (8km) Aix-en-Provence (83km) & Marseilles (99km)
To Gare Avignon TGV Courtine (4km)
Ave de la Foire
To University Restaurant
0 150 300m
0 150 300yd

AVIGNON AREA

PLACES TO STAY
2 Camping Bagatelle
21 Hôtel du Palais des Papes
23 Hôtel D'Europe
29 Hôtel de la Mirande
30 Hôtel Médiéval
39 Hôtel Le Provençal
40 Hôtel Mignon
44 Villa Agapé
48 Hôtel de Blauvac
50 Hôtel de Garlande
68 Hôtel Innova
76 Cloître St-Louis; Bureau du Festival

PLACES TO EAT
17 Shérazade Café; Théâtre des Carmes
26 Simple Simon
28 Restaurant Christian Étienne
32 Pick-Up Café
34 L'Epicerie
35 La Vache à Carreaux
38 Les Brantes
49 La Cave de Bancasse
51 Tapalocas
56 Maison Nani
62 Monoprix Supermarket
65 Le Caveau duThéâtre
66 Thiérry Piedoie
67 La Compagnie des Comptoirs
71 Hôtel du Parc
73 Hôtel Colbert
74 Hôtel Le Splendid
75 Erio Convert
89 L'Empreinte; Caves Breysse
90 Woolloomooloo

MUSEUMS
7 Musée du Petit Palais
57 Musée Calvet
58 Musée Requien
60 Musée Louis Vouland
63 Musée Lapidaire
69 Musée d'Art Contemporain

OTHER
1 Swimming Pool
3 La Barthelasse Bus Stop
4 Bac du Rocher des Doms
5 Tour de Châtelet; Entrance to Pont St-Bénézet
6 Tourist Office Annexe
8 Cathédrale Notre Dame des Doms
9 Ateliers de la Manutention
10 Église et Cloître des Carmes
11 G@my's
12 Cyber 109
13 Shakespeare
14 Porte St-Lazare
15 Université d'Avignon
16 Laundrette
18 Jardins des Papes
19 Palais des Papes
20 Conservatoire de Musique
22 L'Esclave; Arob@se
24 Porte de l'Oulle
25 Les Grands Bateaux de Provence
27 Opéra Théâtre d'Avignon
31 Red Zone
33 Église St-Pierre
36 Town Hall
37 Église de St-Agricol
41 La Tropézienne
42 Puyricard
43 Oliviers & Co
45 Trompe l'Œil Painting of Popes
46 FNAC
47 24-hour Banknote Exchange Machine
52 Synagogue
53 TCRA Bus Information Kiosk
54 Palais de Justice
55 Halles d'Avignon
59 Porte Ste-Dominique
61 Laundrette
64 Maison des Vins
70 Tourist Office
72 Laundrette
77 Porte St-Roch
78 Post Office
79 Porte de la République
80 Main Police Station
81 Transhumance Voyages
82 Car Rental Agencies
83 Bus Station
84 Provence Bike
85 Couvent des Cordeliers
86 Chapelle des Pénitents Gris
87 Théâtre des Roues à Aubes; L'Alibi
88 Salle Benoît
91 Cyberdrome
92 Théâtre du Chien qui Fume

Visite Palais Secrét ('secret palace' tour) – in French only – which takes visitors to some previously unexplored parts of the palace (the baths, bedrooms where the popes kept caged nightingales, secret towers, rooftop walkways etc) and ends with breakfast, lunch or an evening aperitif – plus stunning panorama – on the **Great Dignitaries' Terrace**. The tours depart up to four times daily and cost €19.50/24.50/19.50 for morning/lunchtime/early evening. Be sure to book in advance.

Combination tickets covering admission to the palace plus Pont d'Avignon (adult/seven to 18 years €11/8.50) are also available, as is a ticket covering palace, bridge and secret palace tour (€33).

Place du Palais Several 17th-century *hôtels particuliers* (private mansions) border massive place du Palais, the square of monumental proportions butting up against the Palais des Papes. The former **Hôtel des Monnaies** (mint), across the square from the palace, was built in 1619 to house a papal legation led by Cardinal Scipione Borghese. The cardinal's enormous coat of arms decorates the ornate Baroque facade of the building, today Avignon's **Conservatoire de Musique** (Conservatory of Music).

During the 14th and 15th centuries, bishops and archbishops resided in the grandiose **Petit Palace** (Little Palace) at the far northern end of place du Palais. Today, as the **Musée du Petit Palais** *(☎ 04 90 86 44 58; ⓔ musee.petitpalais@wanadoo.fr; place du Palais des Papes; adult/under 12 €6/free; open 10am-1pm & 2pm-6pm Wed-Mon June-Sept, 9.30am-1pm & 2pm-5.30pm Oct-May)*, it is home to an outstanding collection of 13th- to 16th-century Italian religious paintings.

Wedged between the two palaces is the unexciting Romanesque **Cathédrale Notre Dame des Doms**. A church stood here from the 12th century, but the current edifice dates back to 1671–72. From here, walkways lead uphill to the **Jardins des Doms**, delightful bluff-top gardens affording wonderful views of the Rhône, Pont St-Bénézet, Villeneuve-lès-Avignon and the Alpilles (see that section later in this chapter). The limestone rock top, known as **Rocher des Doms**, was inhabited by prehistoric folk. Steps link it with the riverside blvd de la Ligne.

From place du Palais, strollers can also follow the **Promenade des Papes** signposted tourist trail along the narrow rue de Mons to the **Verger d'Urbain V** – gardens since gravelled over where the popes grew sweet-smelling plants and herbs, and kept exotic caged animals such as ostriches and lions. Pope John XXII even had a camel and a bear. Cut through the park to get to the **Ateliers de la Manutention** where glass engravers, picture restorers and other artists have their workshops.

Museums Most of Avignon's museums – all but one of which focus on art – languish inside elegant *hôtels particuliers*, built for wealthy Avignonais in the 17th and 18th centuries.

Hôtel de Villeneuve-Martignan (1741–54) shelters the city's fine arts museum, the **Musée Calvet** *(☎ 04 90 86 33 84; 65 rue Joseph Vernet; adult/12-18 yrs/under 12 €6/3/free; open 10am-1pm & 2pm-6pm Wed-Mon)*, with a collection of paintings from the 16th to 20th centuries. The museum's archaeological collection of artefacts from prehistorical to Roman times slumbers in the **Musée Lapidaire** *(Statuary Museum; ☎ 04 90 86 33 84; 27 rue de la République; adult/12-18 yrs/under 12 €6/3/free; open 10am-1pm & 2pm-6pm Wed-Mon)*, in the 17th-century chapel of a former Jesuit college.

A block east, you can view artworks collected by Parisian couturier Jacques Doucet – including pieces by Van Gogh, Sisley and Cézanne – in the **Musée Angladon** *(☎ 04 90 82 29 03; W www.angladon.com; 5 rue Laboureur; adult/under 18 €5/3; open 1pm-6pm Wed-Sun Sept-June, open 1pm-6pm Wed-Sun, 3pm-6pm Tues July & Aug)*, inside yet another *hôtel particulier*.

Next door to the Musée Calvet, the **Musée Requien** *(☎ 04 90 82 43 51; 67 rue Joseph Vernet; admission free; open 9am-noon & 2pm-6pm Tues-Sun)* explores the city's natural history. The collection, founded by botanist Espirit Requien (1788–1851), has languished inside Hôtel de Raphaelis de Soissans since 1940.

Near the western city wall, the **Musée Louis Vouland** *(☎ 04 90 86 03 79; W www.vouland.com; 17 rue Victor Hugo; adult/12-18 yrs/under 12 €6/3/free; open 10am-noon & 2pm-6pm Tues-Sat May-Oct, 2pm-6pm Tues-Sat Nov-Apr)* displays a small but interesting collection of 17th- and 18th-century decorative arts.

Minimalist art, photography and video are all represented in Avignon's **Musée d'Art Contemporain** *(☎ 04 90 16 56 20; 5 rue Violette; adult/under 18 €5.50/4; open 11am-6pm or 7pm Tues-Sun)*, created by art dealer Yvon Lambert, whose passion for the avant-garde prompted him to grace Avignon with a contemporary art museum. The *hôtel particulier* in which it is housed was built for the Franque brothers, seized by the Revolution and turned into a school and then barracks.

Quartier des Teinturiers Stone-paved rue des Teinturiers follows the course of the River Sorgue through Avignon's old dyers' district which, until the 19th century, was a hive of activity. Some of the water wheels still turn. Beneath the plane trees lining the narrow street is the 16th-century **Chapelle des Pénitents Gris**. From the northern end of rue des Teinturiers, turn left along rue des Lices, right onto rue Noël Biret, then left onto rue Roi René. At No 22 on this street is **Chapelle St-Clare**, the church where the poet Petrarch first cast eyes on Laura, his muse. Laura is buried in the **Couvent des Cordeliers** *(rue des Teinturiers)*, Avignon's largest convent when it was founded in 1226. The chapel and bell tower is all that remains of it today.

Synagogue Avignon's neoclassical synagogue *(☎ 04 90 85 21 24; 2 place Jérusalem; open 10am-noon & 3pm-5pm Mon-Thur, 10am-noon Fri)* was first built in 1221. A 13th-century oven used to bake unleavened bread for Passover can still be seen, but the rest of the present round domed neoclassical structure dates from 1846; a fire destroyed the original edifice in 1845. Visitors must be modestly dressed and men have to cover their heads as is custom.

Wine Tasting

For information on where to taste Côte du Rhône wines, including the Avignon popes' favourite tipple, Châteauneuf du Pape (see that section later in this chapter), head to the **Maison des Vins** *(☎ 04 90 27 24 00; W www.rhone-wines.com; 6 rue des Trois Faucons)*. Its free 66-page booklet, *Wine Routes in Côtes du Rhône*, lists dozens of estates where you can taste and buy, and is invaluable for anyone intent on touring this wine region.

Boat Excursions

Les Grands Bateaux de Provence *(☎ 04 90 85 62 25; e bateaugbp@aol.com; allées de l'Oulle)*, based at the landing stage opposite Porte de l'Oulle, runs dinner cruises year round down the River Rhône from Avignon to Arles (four to seven hours, from €33.50). In July and August, you can simply dine in the evening aboard a boat (adult/under 12 €21.50/9.50, 1½ hours) or make a less-ambitious return trip (adult/under 12 €6/3.50, 1¼ hours, six daily) aboard its Bateau Bus between Avignon, Île de la Barthelasse and Villeneuve-lès-Avignon.

Rollerblading

Bladers can hook up with 300-odd other bladers through **Avignon en rollers** *(☎ 06 74 03 21 80; W www.avignonenrollers.asso.fr; 314 rue René Cassin)*, the local blading club that meets on Friday at 8.30pm in front of the central post office for its weekly blade.

Special Events

The world famous **Festival d'Avignon**, founded in 1947, is held each year in July. It attracts hundreds of actors, dancers, musicians and other artists who perform some 300 shows a day in every imaginable venue. Alongside this expensive, prestigious, and government-subsidised official festival runs the fringe **Festival Off** *(☎ 01 48 05 01 19; W www.avignon-off.org)*.

Tickets for official festival shows cost €12 to €33. Programme and ticket information is available online from the **Bureau du Festival** *(☎ 04 90 14 14 14; W www.festival-avignon.com; Espace St-Louis, 20 rue de laPortail Boquier; open 9am-1pm & 2pm-5pm Mon-Fri mid-June–mid-July)*, in the Cloître St-Louis hotel complex. From early June, tickets can be reserved by telephone, via the website or at branches of FNAC (€1.50 booking fee). Unsold tickets are available up to three hours before the performance starts from the Bureau du Festival, and from the actual venue 45 minutes before the performance begins.

Places to Stay

During festivals, it is impossible to find a hotel room unless you've reserved months in advance.

An excellent mid-range choice if you can't find anywhere in the city is **Le Petit Manoir** *(☎ 04 90 25 03 36, fax 04 90 25 49 13; doubles €43-57)*, across the river in Les Angles. The hotel has a shady pool, an excellent restaurant and is part of the Logis de France chain. Some rooms have their own pool-side terrace.

Places to Stay – Budget

Camping There are no fewer than five camp sites on Île de la Barthelasse, including the following two.

Camping Bagatelle *(☎ 04 90 86 30 39, fax 04 90 27 16 23; adult/tent/car low season €3.37/1.80/1, high season €3.78/2.59/1.37; reception open 8am-9pm daily)* is a shaded place north of Pont Édouard Daladier. Take bus No 10 from the main post office to La Barthelasse stop. Mobile homes cost €228 per week (€457 in high season) and there are dorm beds available in four- to eight-person rooms at the Auberge Bagatelle.

Camping du Pont d'Avignon *(☎ 04 90 82 63 50, fax 04 90 85 22 21; W www.camping-avignon.com; chemin de la Barthelasse; camping for 2 people with tent & car very low/very high season €9.50/19.65; open mid-Mar–Oct)* has five sets of prices, ranging from very low season (March) to very high season (August). Bungalows and chalets can be rented by the week *(bungalows/chalets €310/530 low season, €400/650 high season)*.

Chambres d'Hôtes The tourist office has a list of the many lovely *chambres d'hôtes* (B&Bs) around Avignon, most with pools and costing €70 to €100 per night for a double with breakfast.

Villa Agapé (*☎ 04 90 85 21 92, fax 04 32 76 34 90; e michele@villa-agape.com; 13 rue St-Agricol; doubles low/mid/high season for Caroline €90/110/140, for Olivia €80/100/120*) is a beautiful townhouse built around a pool in central Avignon. It has just two double rooms named after the host's grown-up daughters – Caroline and Olivia – whose bedrooms they once were. Its entrance is the inconspicuous wooden door next to the pharmacy on rue St-Agricol.

Hotels A trio of cheapies lies just off Avignon's main commercial shopping street.

Hôtel du Parc (*☎ 04 90 82 71 55; 18 rue Agricol Perdiguier; singles/doubles with washbasin €30/35, with shower €38/44, with shower & toilet €40/47, triples with shower & toilet €65*), the one with flowerpots for windows, has basic but acceptable rooms.

Hôtel Le Splendid (*☎ 04 90 86 14 46, fax 04 90 85 38 55; 17 rue Agricol Perdiguier; singles with washbasin/shower/shower & toilet €30/34/36, doubles/triples with shower & toilet €47*) is friendly enough for the price.

Hôtel Colbert (*☎ 04 90 86 20 20, fax 04 90 85 97 00; w www.lecolbert-hotel.com; 7 rue Agricol Perdiguier; singles/doubles/triples with shower & toilet €49/52/65*) has an interior courtyard where guests breakfast.

Hôtel Innova (*☎ 04 90 82 54 10, fax 04 90 82 52 39; 100 rue Joseph Vernet; doubles with washbasin €27.50, with shower €33, doubles/triples/quads with shower & toilet €46/50/60; reception open 7am-8pm Mon-Sat, 8am-8pm Sun*) is bright, comfortable and has soundproofed rooms. Reception is on the 1st floor.

Hôtel Mignon (*☎ 04 90 82 17 30, fax 04 90 85 78 46; w www.hotel-mignon.com; 12 rue Joseph Vernet; singles/doubles with shower & toilet €48/59*) is a one-star place tucked amid designer clothes shops; it has spotless, well-kept and soundproofed rooms. Prices include breakfast.

Places to Stay – Mid-Range

Hôtel Médiéval (*☎ 04 90 86 11 06, fax 04 90 82 08 64; 15 rue Petite Saunerie; singles/doubles/triples €35/45/63*), in a restored 17th-century mansion, has a splendid interior courtyard, and studios available on a weekly or longer-term basis.

Hôtel de Garlande (*☎ 04 90 80 08 85, fax 04 90 27 16 58; e hotel-garlande@avignon-et-provence.com; 20 rue Galante; doubles from €64*), in the same mould as Médiéval, is another lovely two-star place residing in a *hôtel particulier* in a quiet narrow street.

Hôtel de Blauvac (*☎ 04 90 86 34 11, fax 04 90 86 27 41; w www.hotel-blauvac.com; 11 rue de la Bancasse; singles/doubles/triples/quads from €52/55/75.50/86*) is the third in this trio of old and graceful twin-starred places to stay, slap-bang in the centre of things.

Hôtel du Palais des Papes (*☎ 04 90 86 04 13, fax 04 90 27 91 17; w www.hotel-avignon.com; 3 place du Palais; doubles €75-100*) is charming, old and old-worldly. The priciest rooms tout papal palace view.

Places to Stay – Top End

Hôtel d'Europe (*☎ 04 90 14 76 76, fax 04 90 14 76 71; 12 place Crillon; doubles €120-385*), with four stars, an inner courtyard to breakfast on and a fabulous €30 Sunday brunch open to all, is fit for a pope. The hotel resides inside a *hôtel particulier*, built for the Marquis de Graveson in 1580 and later host to everyone from Napoleon to Salvador Dali.

Cloître St-Louis (*☎ 04 90 27 55 55, fax 04 90 82 24 01; w www.cloitre-saint-louis.com; 20 rue du Portail Boquier; doubles low season €84-153, high season €130-214*) is a stunning four-star hotel with exquisite rooms in a Jesuit school dating from 1589. The ultra-modern wing with rooftop swimming pool was designed in 1991 by French architect Jean Nouvel.

Hôtel de la Mirande (*☎ 04 90 85 93 93, fax 04 90 86 26 85; w www.la-mirande.fr; 4 place de la Mirande; doubles low season €260-320, high season €300-430*) is Avignon's most exclusive hotel in a 14th-century cardinal's palace behind Palais des Papes. 'A place of pilgrimage for men and women of taste' was how French newspaper *Le Figaro* summed it up. Its restaurant (lunch/dinner *menus* from €28/38) is equally renowned.

Places to Eat

Restaurants Chic and hip **La Cave de Bancasse** (*☎ 04 90 86 97 02; 25 rue Bancasse; menus €11, €17, €22, €26 & €29*) bulges with antiques and art objects for diners to buy.

L'Épicerie *(☎ 04 90 82 74 22; 10 place St-Pierre; mains around €15)*, tucked in the shadow of flamboyant Église St-Pierre, dishes up bistro-style food. Beef carpaccio, pan-fried liver and a meal-sized cheese platter star here.

Tapalocas *(☎ 04 90 82 56 84; W www.tapalocas.com; 15 rue Galante; tapas €2)*, a bar-bistro hybrid, boasts a tapas menu as long as a giant's arm.

Les Brantes *(☎ 04 90 86 35 14; 2 rue Petite Fusterie; menu €12.50, lunch formule €10.50, plat du jour €7.50)* is an excellent-value pizza grill with a flower-filled courtyard out back.

La Vache à Carreaux *(☎ 04 90 80 09 05; dishes around €10)* serves cheese and wine, and wine and cheese. House wine at €2.40/7.80 a glass/bottle kicks off the wine list, which features lots of Côtes du Rhône.

Le Grand Café *(☎ 04 90 86 86 77; 4 rue des Escaliers Ste-Anne; menu €15 & €24)*, inside the La Manutention cultural centre, serves delicious cuisine in a magnificent setting. Contemporary creations hang from the red-brick, former warehouse ceiling.

Maison Nani *(☎ 04 90 82 60 90; 29 rue Théodore Aubanel; mains around €10)*, a busy place that markets itself as 'the restaurant of the Avignonnais', serves hearty salads, meat dishes and other sunny bistro-style dishes. Bold prints, paintings and murals add a flamboyant splash to its ochre interior.

Quartier des Teinturiers is the spot to let your taste buds run wild. It is also the place to drink Pernod – it was concocted in 1870 by absinthe inventor Jules Pernod in his house at 75–77 rue Guillaume Puy.

Woolloomooloo *(☎ 04 90 85 28 44; 16 bis rue des Teinturiers; lunch/dinner menus from €11/17)*, next to an old paper mill, is an Avignon institution. Its jumble of eclectic antique and contemporary furnishings is periodically rearranged to create a 'new look'. Vegetarian and Antillean dishes dominate the menu.

L'Empreinte *(☎ 04 32 76 31 84; 33 rue des Teinturiers; couscous €8.50-16)* will dazzle with its brightly coloured rugs adorning the walls, tile-topped tables and tasty Mediterranean cuisine.

Avignon's more upmarket places to dine include the following places.

La Compagnie des Comptoirs *(☎ 04 90 85 99 04; 83 rue Joseph Vernet; starters/mains from €15/20)*, in Le Cloître des Arts, is a striking minimalist place built around an 18th-century cloister. Reception flashes orange neon, the bar is a large green square and the chef cooks world cuisine.

Restaurant Christian Étienne *(☎ 04 90 86 16 50; W www.christian-etienne.fr; 10 rue de Mons; lunch/dinner menus from €28/50)* is where Avignon's best-known chef conjures up culinary creations from his eponymous rooftop restaurant overlooking Palais des Papes. The *menu homard* (€70) involves a whole lobster cooked three different ways.

Across the river in Les Angles, there is one place everyone in the know knows.

C'est La Lune *(It's the Moon; ☎ 04 90 25 40 55; montée Valadas; mains €12-15)* oozes hipness but lacks pretension of any sort. The panoramic view of Avignon and flower-bedecked swimming pool (open to lunch guests until 7pm) are as alluring as the jumbo salads and meats, laid-back beachy feel and bohemian-styled interior. Come dusk, techno beats until well into the early hours.

Cafés Most pedestrian streets and squares, including both place du Palais and place de l'Horloge, ring with the chink of coffee cups and clink of beer glasses in summer.

Simple Simon *(☎ 04 90 86 62 70; 26 rue Petite Fusterie)* is the place for an afternoon cuppa with cake, crumble or scones. A full-on English breakfast with real bacon will set you back €15 at this English tearoom.

Pick-Up Café *(☎ 04 90 85 49 77; 18 rue du Portail Matheron; dishes around €8)*, a student haunt crammed with bric-a-brac, is popular for its tummy-filling food and festival spirit year round.

Shérazade Café *(☎ 04 90 85 26 90; 2 bis place des Carmes)*, next to Théâtre des Carmes, is an atmospheric Lebanese coffee and teahouse.

Self-Catering Shop for fresh stuff at the covered market, **Les Halles** *(place Pie; open 6am-1.30pm Tues-Sun)*, and everything else at **Monoprix** *(cours Jean Jaurès)*, a supermarket opposite the Musée Lapidaire.

Erio Convert *(45 cours Jean Jaurès)* is one of Provence's top bakeries with a superb range of breads and filled baguettes to eat on the hop.

La Tropézienne *(22 rue St-Agricol)* sells *papalines d'Avignon* (pink chocolate balls laced with a liqueur concocted from 60 different Mont Ventoux plants) and other naughty-but-nice sweets and cakes.

Entertainment

Tickets for cultural events in Avignon are sold at the tourist office and at **FNAC** *(☎ 04 90 14 35 35; 19 rue de la République)*. Event listings fill the free weekly *César* magazine (W www.cesar.fr) and also the fortnightly *Rendez-vous d'Avignon*. The tourist office distributes both.

Bars & Clubs In Les Angles (see Places to Eat earlier), **C'est La Lune** throbs until the early hours and is a fabulous place to soak up the local scene.

Le Bistrot d'Utopia *(☎ 04 90 27 04 96; 4 rue des Escaliers Ste-Anne)* is a bar inside La Manutention, Avignon's most hip entertainment and cultural centre with jazz club, restaurant and cinema.

Caves Breysse *(☎ 04 32 74 25 86; 41 rue des Teinturiers)* is a trendy wine bar in the old dyers' district.

Red Zone *(☎ 04 90 27 02 44; 25 rue Carnot; W www.redzonebar.com)* is a popular music club with DJs on mix every night. Salsa, soul and dance steal the dance floor. Flyers are online.

L'Esclave *(☎ 04 90 85 14 91; 12 rue du Limas; open from 11pm daily)* is a gay hide-out, tucked inside an inconspicuous building save for the rainbow flag and a twin set of traffic lights.

AVIGNON AREA

Classical Music, Opera & Ballet The imposing **Opéra Théâtre d'Avignon** *(☎ 04 90 82 81 40; place de l'Horloge)* was built in 1847. It stages operas, plays, symphony concerts, chamber music concerts and ballet from September to June.

Theatre Avignon has dozens of theatres, including the mainstream **Théâtre du Bourg Neuf** *(☎ 04 90 85 17 90; 5 bis rue du Bourg-Neuf)* and **Théâtre des Carmes** *(☎ 04 90 82 20 47; 6 place des Carmes)*.

More alternative venues in the Quartier des Teinturiers include **Théâtre du Chien qui Fume** *(☎ 04 90 85 89 49; W www.chien-qui-fume.com; 76 rue des Teinturiers)*, literally the 'Dog that Smokes' theatre; and **Théâtre des Roues à Aubes** *(☎ 04 90 82 60 72; 29 rue des Teinturiers)*.

Jazz Inside La Manutention arts centre, **AJMI** *(☎ 04 90 86 08 61; 4 rue des Escaliers Ste-Anne)*, an abbreviation for Association pour Le Jazz & La Musique Improvisée, is a popular jazz club.

Cinema The place to go to watch new and old nondubbed films is **Cinéma Utopia** *(☎ 04 90 82 65 36; 4 rue des Escaliers Ste-Anne)* at La Manutention.

Shopping

Place des Carmes buzzes with a flower market on Saturday and a flea market on Sunday.

Avignon's classiest shopping streets, rue St-Agricol and rue Joseph Vernet, are just southwest of place de l'Horloge. The covered mall beneath the Hôtel du Petit Louvre – the private mansion at 23 rue St-Agricol where Le Félibrige (see Literature in the Facts about Provence chapter) threw extravagant banquets in the late 1880s – is laden with expensive art and antique galleries. There are many more on rue du Limas.

For luxury food stuffs, invest in designer chocolates at **Puyricard** *(33 rue Joseph Vernet)*; and olive oil from Provence and the rest of the Mediterranean at **Oliviers & Co** *(19 rue St-Agricol)*.

Getting There & Away

Air Eight kilometres southeast of Avignon, **Aéroport d'Avignon** *(Avignon airport; ☎ 04 90 81 51 51; W www.avignon.aeroport.fr)* is only served by domestic flights. See the Getting There & Away chapter for details.

Bus The **bus station** *(58 blvd St-Roch)* is in the basement of the building down the ramp to the right as you come out of the train station on blvd St-Roch. You can leave luggage at the **information desk** *(☎ 04 90 82 07 35; open 8am-6pm Mon-Fri, 8am-noon Sat)* for €2 per bag a day. Tickets are sold on board the buses.

Services include two to five daily to/from Aix-en-Provence (€11.74/13.50 via national roads/the A7 *autoroute*, one to 1½ hours), Apt (€6.70, 1¼ hours), Arles (€7.80, 1½), Cavaillon (€3.10, one hour), Vaison-la-Romaine (€6.60, 1¼ hours), Nîmes (€7.17, 1¼ hours) and Pont du Gard (€5.64, one-day return €9.70, 45 minutes). Orange (€4.70, 45 minutes) and Carpentras (€3.50, 45 minutes) are served by 20-odd buses daily.

DAN HERRICK
The 14th-century Palais des Papes, Avignon

JOHN ELK III
Roman amphitheatres, known as Les Arénes in Nîmes, were built around AD 100

NEIL IRVINE
A lone cyclist winds his way down the barren slopes of Mont Ventoux (1912m), north of Avignon

MICHAEL GEBICKI

One of the many Côtes du Lubéron vineyards around Apt, The Lubéron

JON DAVISON

Abbaye Notre-Dame de Sénanque was founded in 1148, northwest of Gordes, The Lubéron

International bus companies **Linebùs** *(☎ 04 90 85 30 48, 04 90 86 88 67)* and **Eurolines** *(☎ 04 90 85 27 60)* have offices at the far end of the bus platforms. See the Getting There & Away chapter for details.

Train Avignon has two train stations: **Gare Avignon TGV** in the southwestern suburb of Courtine, and central **Gare Avignon Centre** *(blvd St-Roch)*, a literal stone's throw from the walled city. TGV trains to/from Paris stop at both stations, but not all other TGV services do. Cities well served by TGV from Avignon include Nîmes (€12.60, 45 minutes), Marseilles (€23.90, one hour), Nice (€40.60, 2½ hours). Non-TGV services, including local trains to/from Orange (€4.70, 20 minutes) and Arles (€6.80, 20 minutes) arrive/depart from the central station.

Getting Around

Bus A one-/two-journey TCRA bus ticket costs €1/1.75 direct from the driver, and a 10-journey carnet costs €7.80 at the **TCRA office** *(☎ 04 32 74 18 32; W www.tcra.fr; ave de Lattre de Tassigny)*. Regular buses link Gare Avignon TGV with the town (€2.40, 15 minutes, two or three an hour between 6am and 11pm); in Avignon buses use the Avignon Poste stop in front of the post office on cours Président Kennedy.

Villeneuve-lès-Avignon is linked with Avignon by bus No 11, which stops in front of the post office and on the western side of the walled city near Porte de l'Oulle. Bus No 10 links Avignon Poste with Les Angles.

Bicycle In season **Provence Bike** *(☎ 04 90 27 92 61; W www.provencebike.com; 52 blvd St-Roch; open 9am-6.30pm daily Apr-Oct)*, 300m from the train station, rents town/mountain bikes for €10/17 a day and €50/95 a week. It also has 50/125cc scooters for €25/55 per day. Out of season, when the shop is shut, you can arrange wheel rental by telephone (same number).

Boat During July and August you can cross the Rhône River aboard the *Bac du Rocher des Doms*, a free shuttle boat that arrives at/departs from the jetty immediately below the Jardins des Doms on blvd de la Ligne. It runs from 11am to 9pm daily. On Île de la Barthelasse, it uses the stop in front of the restaurant Le Bercail.

VILLENEUVE-LÈS-AVIGNON

postcode 30400 • pop 12,078
• elevation 23m

Villeneuve-lès-Avignon, across the Rhône from Avignon, was founded in the late 13th century. It became known as the City of Cardinals because many primates affiliated with the papal court built large residences (known as *livrées*) in the town, despite the fact that it was in territory ruled by the French crown and not the pope.

Information

The **tourist office** *(☎ 04 90 25 61 33, fax 04 90 25 91 55; 1 place Charles David; open 9am-12.30pm & 2pm-6pm Mon-Sat Sept-June; 10am-7pm Mon-Fri, 10am-1pm & 2pm-7pm Sat & Sun July; 9am-12.30pm & 2pm-6pm daily Aug)* organises interesting two-hour guided tours (€4/3.10 for adults/12 to 18 years) of Villeneuve-lès-Avignon.

Things to See

Chartreuse du Val de Bénédiction The Val de Bénédiction Charterhouse *(☎ 04 90 15 24 24; W www.chartreuse.org; 60 rue de la République; adult/18-25 yrs/under 18 €5.50/3/free; open 9am-6.30pm daily Apr-Sept, 9.30am-5.30pm daily Oct-Mar)*, was founded in 1356 by Pope Innocent VI and, with its 40 cells and three cloisters, was once France's largest Carthusian monastery. **Cloître St-Jean** gives you an idea of the architecture and layout of the charterhouse because it was built in the same style. In the 14th-century church, the delicately carved **mausoleum** of Pope Innocent VI (died 1362) is an extraordinary example of Gothic artisanship. It was removed during the Revolution and returned in 1963.

Musée Pierre de Luxembourg This museum *(☎ 04 90 27 49 66; 3 rue de la République; adult/student/under 10 €3/1.90/free; open 10am-12.30pm & 3pm-7pm daily Apr-Sept, 10am-noon & 2pm-5.30pm Tues-Sun*

Passport for Art

A Passeport pour l'Art (Passport for Art) costs €6.86 and covers admission to each of the Villeneuve-lès-Avignon sights included in this guide. Villeneuve-lès-Avignon tourist office sells it.

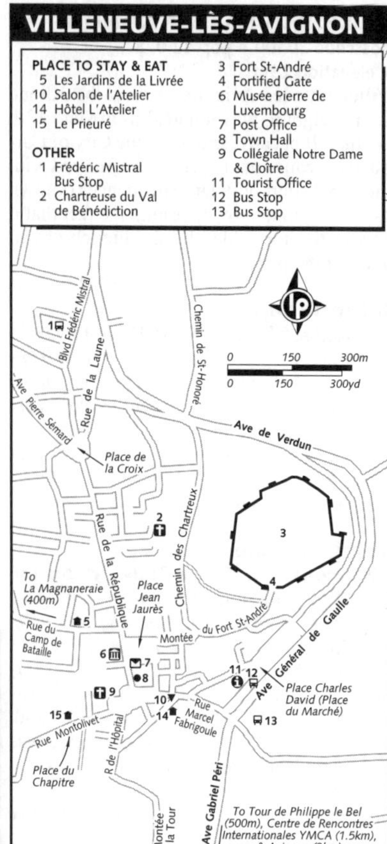

Oct-Dec, Feb & Mar) has a fine collection of religious art taken from the Chartreuse (see the previous section) during the Revolution, including 15th- to 17th-century paintings. The most exceptional works include *Vierge en Ivoire* (Ivory Virgin), a 14th-century Virgin carved from an elephant's tusk; a 15th-century *Vierge Double Face*, a marble Virgin with two faces pointing in opposite directions; and the *Couronnement de la Vierge* (Coronation of the Virgin), by Enguerrand Quarton in 1453, displayed on the 1st floor.

Tour de Philippe le Bel The defensive, 32m-tall tower *(☎ 04 32 70 08 57; adult/12-18 yrs €2/1; open 10am-12.30pm & 3pm-7pm Apr-Sept, 10am-noon & 2pm-5.30pm Tues-Sun Oct-Dec, Feb & Mar)* was built in the 14th century at what was, at the time, the western end of Pont St-Bénézet. The platform at the top of the tower – reached by a dizzying 172-step spiral staircase – affords a magnificent panorama.

Fort St-André This lumbering 14th-century fortress *(☎ 04 90 25 45 35; adult/18-25 yrs/under 18 €4/2.50/free; open 10am-noon & 2pm-6pm daily Apr-Sept, 10am-noon & 2pm-5pm daily Oct-Mar)*, built on Mont Andaon by King Philippe le Bel (1285–1314) to keep an eye on events across the river in the papal domains, has lovely views. The **fortified gate** is a fine example of medieval military architecture.

Places to Stay & Eat

The **Centre de Rencontres Internationales YMCA** *(☎ 04 90 25 46 20, fax 04 90 25 30 64; W www.ymca-avignon.com; 7 bis chemin de la Justice; singles/doubles/triples or quads low season €20/25/28, high season €30/40/52)* has a pool and organises activities, including guided tours of Avignon and its surrounds. Breakfast/dinner is €5/10. Take bus No 10 from in front of the central post office in Avignon to the Pont d'Avignon stop.

Les Jardins de la Livrée *(☎ 04 90 26 05 05; 4 bis rue du Camp de Bataille; doubles €40-76; menus €16 & €20, plat du marché €11)* is a four-room *chambre d'hôte* with stone terrace, garden, swimming pool and tasty Provençal kitchen.

Hôtel de l'Atelier *(☎ 04 90 25 01 84, fax 04 90 25 80 06; e hotel-latelier@libertysurf.fr; 5 rue de la Foire; doubles/triples low season €45/76, high season €52/84)* has charming rooms with period furnishings. Its tearoom across the street, **Salon de l'Atelier** *(☎ 04 90 15 45 37; rue de la Foire)*, serves tasty pies, tarts, salads and cakes in an equally atmospheric setting.

Le Prieuré *(☎ 04 90 15 90 15, fax 04 90 25 45 39; W www.leprieure.fr; 7 place du Chapitre; doubles €92-211, apartments €240-290; menus €34, €54 & €80)* is a bit like paradise in Provence. It was built as an archbishop's palace in 1322 and used as a priory – hence the name – from 1333.

La Magnaneraie *(☎ 04 90 25 11 11, fax 04 90 25 46 37; 37 rue du Camp de Bataille; doubles low/high season €94/106; menus €28-80)* is Villeneuve's other four-star place to sleep, eat and imagine you're in heaven.

North of Avignon

Vaucluse fans out northeast from the lucrative vineyards of Châteauneuf du Pape and the Roman treasures of Orange, through to the rocky Dentelles de Montmirail, the slopes of Mont Ventoux and the harsh and uninhabitable Plateau d'Albion (Albion plain) in the Vaucluse's easternmost corner.

If you don't have access to a car, it is possible to labour from town to town by local bus, but the frequency and pace of services are in keeping with the tempo of Provençal life – slow.

CHÂTEAUNEUF DU PAPE

postcode 84230 • pop 2098 • elevation 87m

Wealthy Châteauneuf du Pape, 18km north of Avignon, was once a humble mining hamlet called Calcernier after its limestone quarries. Then in 1317 Pope John XXII (ruled 1316–34) had a pontifical residence built in the village, around which he established a papal vineyard. Today the village is renowned worldwide for its rich, full-bodied Châteauneuf du Pape reds with a minimum alcoholic strength of 12.5% (France's highest).

The wine produced in the 18th century was called *vin d'Avignon* and then Châteauneuf du Pape-Calcernier in the 19th century. In 1923 Baron Le Roy de Boiseaumarié, who was a local *vigneron* (wine grower), wrote rules on how to produce Châteauneuf du Pape wine – prompting the establishment of an *appellation d'origine contrôlée* (AOC) in France. Châteauneuf du Pape became a certified vintage in 1929, distinguishable by its heavily embossed label bearing the pontifical coat of arms.

The Châteauneuf du Pape vineyards – usually covered with large smooth stones called *galets* – cover 3200 hectares between Avignon and Orange, on the River Rhône's left (east) bank. They are tended by some 350 *vignerons*, many of whose annual production is sold years in advance, making it impossible for tourists to taste, let alone buy, the region's top wines, which can easily command €300 or so a bottle. In the village count on paying from €11/19 for a run-of-the-mill bottle of 2001/1998 red. The year 2002 is feared to have been a catastrophic one for the appellation after flash floods in September cut off the village from the rest of the country and destroyed much of the year's crop before it was harvested.

Information

The **tourist office** *(☎ 04 90 83 71 08, fax 04 90 83 50 34; ⓔ tourisme-chato9-pape@wanadoo.fr; place du Portail; open 9.30am-1pm & 2pm-7pm Mon-Sat, 10am-1pm & 2pm-6pm Sun)* distributes a list of wine-producing estates where you can taste and buy wine.

Château des Papes

The ruins of this papal castle, built between 1317 and 1333, stand on a hillock (118m) at the northern end of the village. It was plundered and burnt during the Wars of Religion, and further destroyed by German troops on 20 August 1944.

From the foot of the castle there are sweeping views of Avignon, the Plateau de Vaucluse, the Lubéron, the River Rhône and beyond. From the car park next to the castle, steps lead to the old town.

Wine Tasting

A good place to start is the **Musée des Outils de Vignerons** *(☎ 04 90 83 70 07; ⓦ www.brotte.com; ave Louis Pasteur; open 9am or 9.30am-noon & 2pm-6pm or 7pm daily)*. The Museum of Wine Producers' Tools is essentially a ploy to sell wine from the Caves Brotte-Père Anselme. However, it's still a good opportunity to soak up the pungent smell of wine and ask 'beginner-level' questions without feeling stupid.

Most producers allow wine cellar visits and offer *dégustation gratuite* (free wine-tasting). However, some can only be visited *sur rendez-vous* (by appointment) and are closed at the weekend; others only cater to groups. Opening hours and visiting requirements are detailed in the tourist office's list of producers. In the village itself, there are a handful of *caves* (wine cellars) where you can simply stroll in, taste and buy.

Special Events

Châteauneuf du Pape celebrates a string of wine-inspired festivals; see the Wine Festivals section in the colour Food & Wine of Provence special section for details.

Places to Stay & Eat

La Mère Germaine *(☎ 04 90 83 54 37, fax 04 90 83 50 27; ⓦ www.lameregermaine.com;*

3 rue du Commandant Lemaître; doubles from €53.40; menus €31 & €39, menu pontifical without/with wine €53/79) has eight charming rooms and a splendid terrace for feasting on. The *menu pontifical* comprises seven surprise courses (trust the chef) accompanied by seven different Châteauneuf du Pape wines.

Le Verger des Papes *(☎ 04 90 83 50 40; ⓔ papeverger@aol.com; 4 montée du Château)*, an uphill climb from the village, has a shady terrace offering stunning Rhône-and-vineyard views and delicious cuisine.

La Marmite *(☎ 04 90 83 78 45; 22 rue Jospeh Ducos; plat du jour €10, menus €13.50 & €17.50)*, just off the village square, is so refreshingly simple for an upmarket place like Châteauneuf du Pape that it risks being labelled retro. It cooks up regional cuisine.

Hostellerie du Château des Fines Roches *(☎ 04 90 83 70 23, fax 04 90 83 78 42; ⓦ www.chateaufinesroches.com; standard/luxury doubles €150/192)*, 2km south of the village off the Avignon-bound D17, is a dreamlike, turreted castle set amid sprawling vineyards.

Getting There & Away

Out of Châteauneuf du Pape, **Rapides du Sud-Est** *(☎ 04 90 34 13 39)* operates buses Monday to Saturday to/from Orange €2.40, 15 minutes, one or two daily). In Châteauneuf, buses use the stop on ave du Général de Gaulle.

ORANGE

postcode 84100 • pop 28,889 • elevation 97m

Throughout a 16th-century marriage with the German House of Nassau, the House of Orange – the princely dynasty that had ruled Orange since the 12th century – became an active player in the history of the Netherlands and later, through William III (William of Orange), Britain and Ireland. Orange (Arenjo in Provençal), which had earlier been a stronghold of the Reformation, was ceded to France in 1713 by the Treaty of Utrecht, but to this day many members of the royal house of the Netherlands are known as the princes and princesses of Orange-Nassau.

Orange is best known for its magnificent Roman relics and less-than-magnificent National Front mayor. Thursday is the town's market day.

Orientation & Information

The train station is about 1km east of place de la République, the city centre, along ave Frédéric Mistral and rue de la République. The Théâtre Antique – Orange's Roman theatre – is two blocks south of place de la République.

The **tourist office** *(☎ 04 90 34 70 88, fax 04 90 34 99 62; ⓦ www.provence-orange.com; 5 cours Aristide Briand; open 9am-1pm & 2pm-7pm Mon-Sat, 10am-12.30pm & 2.30pm-6pm Sun Apr-Sept, 10am-1pm & 2pm-6pm Mon-Sat Oct-Mar)* runs a summer **annexe** *(place des Frères Mounet; open 10am-1pm & 2.15pm-7pm Mon-Sat Apr-Sept)* opposite Théâtre Antique.

There are a couple of commercial banks on place de la République and the **post office** *(blvd Édouard Daladier)* is opposite the bus station.

Théâtre Antique

Orange's Roman theatre *(☎ 04 90 51 17 60; rue Madeleine Roch; adult/7-17 yrs €7/5.50; open 9am-6pm daily Mar-Oct; 9am-7pm daily Apr, May & Sept; 9am-8pm daily June-Aug; 9am-5pm daily Nov-Feb)*, designed to seat about 10,000 spectators, was probably built during the time of Augustus Caesar (ruled 27 BC–AD 14). Its **stage wall** – the only such Roman structure still standing in its entirety (minus a few mosaics and the roof) – is 103m wide and almost 37m high. Its plain exterior can be viewed from the adjacent place des Frères Mounet to the north. Admission includes an audioguide in seven languages.

For a panoramic view of the Roman masterpiece, follow montée Philbert de Chalons or montée Lambert to the top of **Colline St-Eutrope** (97m). En route you pass the **ruins** of a **12th-century chateau**, the former residence of the princes of Orange.

Opposite the amphitheatre, in the 17th-century Hôtel Can Cuyl, is the unexciting **Musée d'Orange** *(☎ 04 90 51 18 24; rue Madeleine Roch; open 9.30am-7pm Apr-Sept, 9am-noon & 1.30pm-5.30pm Oct-Mar)*; it is known – yawn – for its Roman cadasters (land survey registers). Admission is free with a Théâtre Antique entrance ticket.

Arc de Triomphe

Orange's Roman triumphal arch is at the northern end of plane tree-lined ave de l'Arc

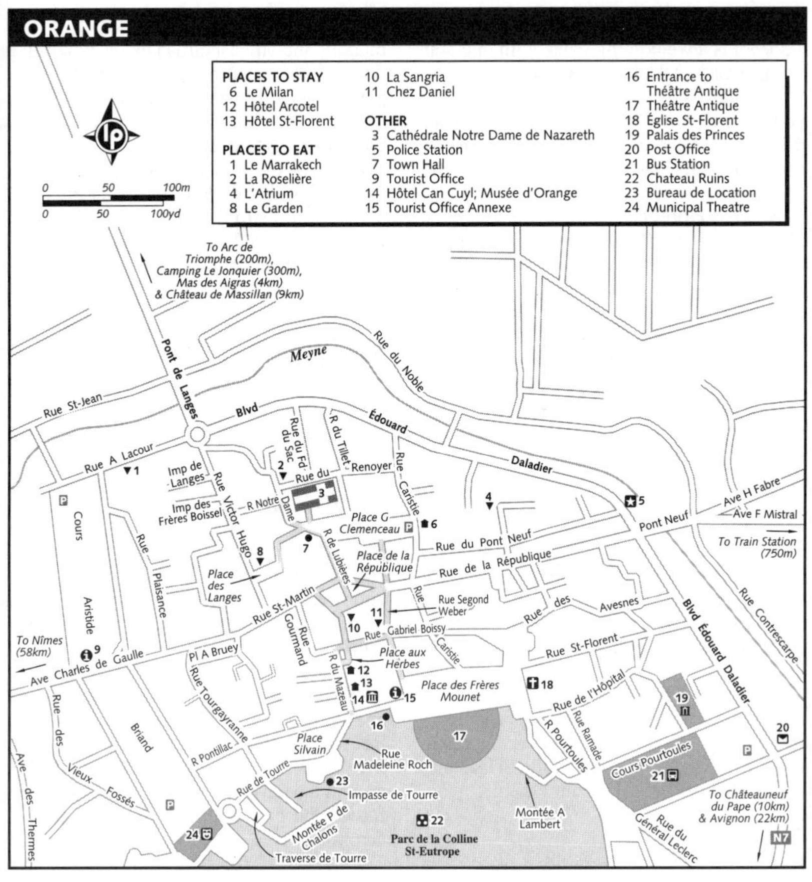

de Triomphe about 450m from the centre. Probably built around 20 BC, it is 19m in height and width and 8m thick. The exceptional friezes commemorate Julius Caesar's victories during the Gallic Wars, a series of wars fought by Caesar and his legions against various tribes in Gaul between 58 BC and 52 BC.

Special Events

In June and August, the Théâtre Antique comes alive with concerts, cinema screenings and musical events throughout Les Nuits du Théâtre Antique. During the last fortnight in July, it hosts **Les Chorégies d'Orange** (*w www.choregies.asso.fr*), a series of weekend operas, classical concerts and choral performances. Tickets are sold at the **Bureau de Location** (*☎ 04 90 34 24 24; 14 place Silvain; open 11am-1pm & 2pm-5pm Mon-Fri)*.

Places to Stay

Camping Le Jonquier (*☎ 04 90 34 49 48, fax 04 90 51 16 97; e joel.denis@waika9.com; 1321 rue Alexis Carrel; camping for 2 people with tent & car €19.50; open Apr-Sept)* is near the Arc de Triomphe. Take bus No 1 from the République stop (on ave Frédéric Mistral 600m from the train station) to the arch, then walk 100m back, turn right onto rue des Phocéens and right again onto rue des Étudiants. The site is across the football pitch.

Hôtel Arcotel (*☎ 04 90 34 09 23, fax 04 90 51 61 12; e jor8525@aol.com; 8 place aux Herbes; singles/doubles with washbasin €18/26, doubles/quads with shower & toilet from*

€35/50) is a welcoming place with one-star rooms near the Théâtre Antique.

Le Milan *(☎ 04 90 34 13 31; 22 rue Caristie; doubles with shower €26, with shower & toilet €27.50)*, above a simple bar, lacks pretension and is a what-you-see-is-what-you-get type of place.

Hôtel St-Florent *(☎ 04 90 34 18 53, fax 04 90 51 17 25; e stflorent@yahoo.fr; 4 rue du Mazeau; singles with washbasin/shower €22/27, doubles with shower/shower & toilet €34/45-53)*, with its flamboyant wall murals and fantastic *belle époque* wooden beds adorned with crushed and studded velvet, is one place you'll never forget.

Mas des Aigras *(☎ 04 90 34 81 01, fax 04 90 34 05 66; e mas-aigras@avignon-et-provence.com; chemin des Aigras, Russamp Est; doubles from €64, half-board supplement €34 per person)*, 4km north of Orange off the N7 (turn left after the Pont de l'Aygues), is a solid mid-range choice with pool, restaurant and delightful breakfast terrace.

Château de Massillan *(☎ 04 90 40 64 51, fax 04 90 40 63 85; w www.chateau-de-massillan.com; doubles from €150)*, owned by Henri II's lover Diane de Poitiers in the 16th century, is fabulous. With its glass chandeliers, turrets, bath tubs with legs and enormous park, it is everything a fairytale castle should be. The castle is 9km north in Uchaux, signposted off the D11 from Orange.

Places to Eat

La Sangria *(☎ 04 90 34 31 96; 3 place de la République; lunch formule €8.50 & €11, menus €12.50 & €19.50)* holds few gastronomic surprises but is perfectly pleasant for lunch between sights.

Le Marrakech *(rue A Lacour; couscous €10)*, with its stuff-yourself-silly offer of as much couscous as you can eat for €10, makes the mind boggle.

La Roselière *(☎ 04 90 34 50 42; 4 rue du Renoyer; mains from €10.75)*, with its bric-a-brac decor and air of rebellion blowing through the place, makes for a refreshing change from the norm. Look for the sax sign and wine bottle outside.

L'Atrium *(☎ 04 90 34 34 17; 5 impasse du Parlement; menus €14, €21, €23 & €25)*, a seafood restaurant, is Orange's choice for fish dishes – complete with garden to dine in.

Chez Daniel *(☎ 04 90 34 63 48; rue Segond Weber)* – an oyster bar – dishes up oysters, mussels and other shellfish by the bowlful or dozen. No revealing what Chez Daniel's pizzeria directly opposite serves.

Getting There & Away

Bus From the bus station on cours Pourtoules, **Rapides du Sud-Est** *(☎ 04 90 34 13 39)* runs buses to/from Avignon (€4.80, 45 minutes, about 20 daily), Châteauneuf du Pape (€2.40, 15 minutes, one or two daily), Carpentras (€3.50, 40 minutes) and Vaison-la-Romaine (€4.40, 45 minutes).

Train Trains run south from Orange's train station *(☎ 04 90 11 88 64; ave Frédéric Mistral)* to Avignon (€4.70, 20 minutes, 17 daily), Marseilles (€17.70, 1½ hours, 10 daily) and beyond.

VAISON-LA-ROMAINE

postcode 84110 • pop 5986 • elevation 193m

Vaison-la-Romaine, 23km and 50km north-east of Orange and Avignon respectively, is endowed with extensive Roman ruins, a picturesque medieval old city and too many tourists.

In the 2nd century BC, the Romans conquered an important Celtic city on this site and renamed it Vasio Vocontiorum. The Roman city flourished, in part because it was granted considerable autonomy, but around the 6th century the Great Migrations forced the population to move to the hill across the river, which was easier to defend. The counts of Toulouse built a castle atop the hill in the 12th century. The resettlement of the original site began in the 17th century. The Roman remains unearthed here include mosaic-decorated villas, colonnaded streets, public baths, a theatre and aqueduct; the latter brought water down from Mont Ventoux.

Like Malaucène and Carpentras, 10km and 27km to the south, Vaison is a good base for exploring the Dentelles de Montmirail and Mont Ventoux region. Markets fill place François Cevert on Tuesday, Thursday and Saturday morning.

Orientation & Information

Vaison is bisected by the ever-flooding River Ouvèze. The Roman city, on top of which the modern city centre has been built, is on the river's northern bank; the medieval Haute Ville (literally 'high town') is on the southern bank. In the modern city, the pedestrianised

Grande Rue heads northwest from Pont Romain (Roman Bridge), changing its name near the Roman ruins to ave du Général de Gaulle.

The **tourist office** *(☎ 04 90 36 02 11, fax 04 90 28 76 04; W www.vaison-la-romaine.com; place du Chanoine Sautel; open 9am-noon & 2pm-6.45pm Mon-Sat, 9am-noon Sun)* runs guided tours in English from April to October. It also sells the *billet tous monuments* which covers admission to all of Vaison's sights and costs €7/3.50/3 per adult/student/12 to 18 years.

Gallo-Roman Ruins

Vaison's Gallo-Roman ruins can be visited at two sites: **Fouilles de Puymin** *(adult/12-18 yrs €7/3; open 10am-noon & 2pm-4.30pm or 5.30pm Wed-Mon Oct-Feb; 10am-noon & 2pm-6pm Mar-May; 9.30am-6.15pm or 6.45pm daily June-Sept)*, the excavations on the eastern side of ave du Général de Gaulle; and **Fouilles de la Villasse** *(adult/12-18 yrs €7/3; open 10am-noon & 2pm-4.30pm or 5.30pm Wed-Mon Oct-Feb; 10am-noon & 2pm-6pm Mar-May; 9.30am-noon & 2pm-6.15pm or 6.45pm daily June-Sept)*, to the west of the same road.

Fouilles de Puymin, opposite the tourist office, is the more interesting of the pair. The site includes houses, mosaics and a theatre (designed to accommodate 6000 people) built around AD 20 during the reign of Tiberius. Among the artefacts displayed in its **Musée Archéologique** is a hefty collection of statues, including the silver bust of a 3rd-century patrician and likenesses of Hadrian and his wife Sabina.

At Fouilles de la Villasse you can visit the mosaic- and fresco-decorated house in which the bust of the patrician was discovered. Mid-June to mid-September, the tourist office runs evening tours to the site – which is particularly enchanting when illuminated. Visits depart at 10pm or 11pm and cost €6/4.50 with/without a guide.

Medieval Quarter

Across **Pont Romain**, on the south bank of the Ouvèze, lies the **Haute Ville** which dates from the 13th and 14th centuries. Narrow, cobblestone alleys lead uphill past restored houses. At the summit is the imposing 12th-century **château**, modernised in the 15th century only to be later abandoned.

Special Events

The two-week **Choralies** choral festival, held every three years in August in Vaison's Théâtre Antique (Roman theatre), is the largest of its kind in Europe. The next takes place in 2004. During the polyphonic festival some 3000 voices from across Europe sing in unison. Tickets are available from the Centre à Cœur Joie (see Places to Stay) or the **Mouvement Choral à Cœur Joie** *(☎ 04 72 19 83 40; W http://acj.musicanet.org; 24 ave Joannès Masset BP 9261, F-69264 Lyons Cedex 09)*. The latter also has details on the Festival des Chœurs Lauréats, a smaller polyphonic festival held in Cathédrale de Vaison in July.

Dance takes centre stage during the **Festival de Vaison-la-Romaine** *(W www.vaison-festival.com)*, a two-week dance festival held in the Théâtre Antique, in the northern section of the Fouilles de Puymin, in July.

Places to Stay

Camping du Théâtre Romain *(☎ 04 90 28 78 66, fax 04 90 28 78 76; chemin du Brusquet; adult/tent & car €4.30/4.20; open mid-Mar–Oct)*, opposite the Théâtre Antique in the Fouilles de Puymin, has a pool and bicycles to rent.

Centre à Cœur Joie *(☎ 04 90 36 00 78, fax 04 90 36 09 89; W http://acj.musicanet.org; ave César Geoffray; doubles/triples with half-board per person €35/32; open Apr-Nov)* is a choral centre which offers courses and accommodation. It's 500m southeast of town along the river and has great views of Mont Ventoux. Half-board is obligatory. Rates in July and August/winter are 10% more/less.

Hôtel Le Burrhus *(☎ 04 90 36 00 11, fax 04 90 36 39 05; 2 place Montfort; doubles with shower & toilet from €45)*, with a pair of stars, prides itself on its traditional Provençal feel. It has 30 rooms.

Places to Eat

The streets around the tourist office and the Gallo-Roman ruins are studded with touristy restaurants and bistros. Between June and September the Maison des Vins et des Produits du Terroir, in the basement of the tourist office, organises a Gallo-Roman dinner every Friday evening. Tickets cost €25 and include a commentary (in French) to what you are eating during dinner and a book of recipes.

Black Diamonds

Provence's cloak-and-dagger truffle trade is far from glamorous. In fact, the way these diamond dealers operate – out of a car boot (trunk), payment exclusively by cold, hard cash – is a remarkably black business.

Little known Richerenches, a deceptively wealthy village shielded within the thick walls of a 12th- to 13th-century Templar fortress, is the congruous setting for Provence's leading wholesale **truffle market**. Once a year, villagers celebrate a **truffle Mass** in the village church, during which parishioners offer truffles instead of cash. The Mass (☎ 04 90 28 02 00 at the town hall) falls on the closest Sunday to 17 January, the feast day of Antoine, the patron saint of truffles and their harvesters.

Crisp, cold Saturday mornings from November to March (10 am to noon) see ave de la Rebasse – Richerenches' main street – resound with the furtive whisperings of local *rabassaïres* (truffle hunters) gearing up to sell their weekly harvest to a big-time dealer from Paris, Germany, Italy or beyond. No more than four or five cash-laden dealers attend the weekly market. Each sets up shop – the boot (trunk) of their car – on the street, from where they carefully inspect, weigh and invariably buy kilos of the precious black fungi. Their *courtiers* (brokers) mingle with the truffle hunters to scout out the best truffles and keep tabs on deals being cut by rival dealers.

Truffle hunters, harvesters and dealers alike store the ugly, mud-caked truffles in grubby white plastic bags. Individuals seeking black diamonds generally have their own dealer whom they telephone to place an order.

At the world's largest **truffle cannery** *(☎ 04 90 46 41 44; W www.plantin.com; route de Nyons)* in Puymeras, 7km northeast of Vaison-la-Romaine, the fungus has been conserved in jars for year-round consumption since 1930. The cannery, signposted 'Plantin' just west of Puymeras village on the D46/D938 junction, opens 8 am to noon and 1.30pm to 5.30pm weekdays. The history of truffles is unearthed in the **Musée de la Truffe et du Tricastin** *(Truffle Museum; ☎ 05 75 96 61 29)*, 14km west of Richerenches in St-Paul Troix Châteaux.

JANE SMITH

Getting There & Away

From the **bus station** *(☎ 04 90 36 05 22; ave des Choralies)* there are limited services to/from Carpentras (€3.70, 45 minutes) via Crestet (€3.40, five minutes), Malaucène (€2.30, 15 minutes) and Le Barroux (€2.80, 25 minutes); Orange (€4.40, 45 minutes) and Avignon (€6.70, 1¼ hours).

ENCLAVE DES PAPES

French king Charles VII (ruled 1422–61) refused point-blank to sell any of his kingdom to the papacy, the result being the Enclave des Papes – a papal enclave in France which, from 1318 until the French Revolution in 1789, belonged to the Pope. Part of the Vaucluse since 1791, this bizarre ball of land measuring no more than 20km in diameter remains an enclave today – wholly surrounded by the Drôme department.

Medieval **Valréas** (population 9500, elevation 250m), 29km north of Vaison-la-Romaine, is the primary town in Provence's Enclave des Papes. During the 19th century, the town was known for its cardboard production, the history of which unfolds in the world's only **Musée du Cartonnage et de l'Imprimerie** *(Cardboard & Printing Museum; ☎ 04 90 35 58 75; ave Maréchal Foch; adult/12-18 yrs/under 12 €3.50/1.50/free; open 10am-noon & 3pm-6pm Tues-Sat, 3pm-6pm Sun)*. Each year, during the Nuit du Petit St-Jean on 23 June, Valréassiens in traditional dress and bearing torches parade through the old-town streets, and end with crowning a three- to five-year-old boy the new Petit St-Jean (Little St John).

Lavender fields and treasure troves of truffles buried underground (see the boxed text 'Black Diamonds') surround Valréas. Fortified **Grillon**, **Visan** and **Richerenches**, the first three to be bought by the Avignon Popes in 1318, are the only other villages in the enclave. From here, age-old olive groves stretch across the border south to Vaison-la-Romaine and east to **Nyons** (population

6948, elevation 271), 14km from Valréas, where the harvested fruits are turned into olive oil. *Saucissons aux olives de Nyons* (Nyon olive sausages) are sold at the **Boucherie Guy Dineile** *(2 rue de la Résistance, Nyons)*. Hop 3km across the enclave's western border to **Suze-la-Rousse** (population 1591, elevation 92) to learn about wine at France's **Université du Vin** *(University of Wine; ☎ 04 75 97 21 34; Ⓦ www.universite-du-vin.com)*, inside Château de la Suze, a 12th- to 14th-century feudal structure that can be visited by guided tour between 9.30am and 11.30am and 2pm to 5.30pm daily.

Valréas **tourist office** *(☎/fax 04 90 35 04 71; Ⓔ enclavedespapes@pacwan.fr; place Aristide Briand)* stocks information on accommodation in the enclave. Nyons **tourist office** *(☎ 04 75 26 10 35, fax 04 75 26 01 57; Ⓔ ot.nyons@wanadoo.fr; place de la Libération)* has a wealth of information on everything to do with olives and oils (growing, harvesting, tasting, buying and so on).

DENTELLES DE MONTMIRAIL & AROUND

Immediately south of Vaison-la-Romaine loom the pinnacles of the Dentelles de Montmirail, a series of lacy limestone rocks that thrust into the sky like needles. Vineyards cling to the lower parts of the rocky slopes, and climbers dangle perilously from the south-facing rocks around Gigondas. This area, stretching as far east as Mont Ventoux, makes great walking terrain; Régis at the Gîte d'Étape des Dentelles de Gigondas (see Places to Stay later) arranges **guided walks**, **rock climbs** and **bike rides**.

Looping the lacy outcrop of the Dentelles by car or bicycle is a good day trip: from Vaison-la-Romaine start by taking the southbound D938 to Carpentras, which snakes around the eastern side of the Dentelles to Le Barroux. Just south, follow the westbound D21 to Beaumes de Venise from where you can continue north to Gigondas, Sablet, Séguret and back to Vaison-la-Romaine. Bicycles can be hired from **Location VTT** *(☎ 04 90 46 83 25; 55 bis Grande Rue)* in Sablet. Cycling routes are mapped out on a notice board on the square in front of Sablet **tourist office** *(☎ 04 90 46 82 46; 8 place du Village)*.

Malaucène (population 2581, elevation 350m) is 10km south of Vaison-la-Romaine and the place where many people begin their forays into the Dentelles and the surrounds of Mont Ventoux, immediately east. Its **tourist office** *(☎/fax 04 90 65 22 59; Ⓔ ot-malaucene@axit.fr; place de la Mairie; open 10am-noon & 2.30pm-4.30pm Mon-Sat)* covers the entire Mont Ventoux area.

Crestet

postcode 84110 • pop 432 • elevation 310m

Art in nature and nature in art is the thematic leaning of contemporary works displayed at the **Crestet Centre d'Art** *(☎ 04 90 36 35 00; Ⓔ crestet.centre.art@wanadoo.fr; chemin de la Verrière; open 11am-7pm daily Apr-Aug, 11am-6pm daily Sept-Mar)* in the hilltop village of Crestet, 14km south of Vaison-la-Romaine. A one-hour walking trail wends its way around 12 sculptures exhibited in the woods. Works by artists in residence are displayed in the centre.

Le Barroux

postcode 84330 • pop 574 • elevation 325m

Yellow-stone Le Barroux tumbles down the hillside around the medieval **Château du Barroux** *(☎ 04 90 62 35 21; Ⓔ chateau.barroux@ifrance.com; admission €3.10; open 2pm-6pm daily Apr, May & Oct; 10am-7pm daily June-Sept)*, the hill-top village's crowning glory. The castle was built as a watchtower to protect the plain from Saracen attacks in the 12th century. Classical music concerts are held in its restored 16th-century guards' hall.

From the village's northern end, route de Suzette leads to **Abbaye Ste-Madeleine** *(☎ 04 90 62 56 31)*, a Romanesque monastery surrounded by lavender gardens. Each morning at 9.30am (10am on Sunday and holidays) the Benedictine monks – whose life revolves around hard work, poverty and prayer – sing Gregorian chants and celebrate Mass in the chapel. The shaven-headed monks get up at 3.15am and are back in bed by 8.30pm.

Beaumes de Venise & Gigondas

At the foot of the loop around the Dentelles sits Beaumes de Venise (population 2070, elevation 126m), 10km southwest of Le Barroux at the crossroads of the D21 and the D90, which leads north into the massif. The village is known for its **Or Blanc** – fruity and sweet golden Muscat wines – best drunk young, chilled to 6°C or 8°C and served as a digestif. Juicy melons from Cavaillon form the perfect partner to Beaumes de Venise's

A Village Christmas

Nowhere is a traditional Provençal Christmas celebrated more than in **Séguret** (population 892, elevation 250), a quaint yellow-tinged village that clings to a rocky outcrop 9km south of Vaison-la-Romaine.

Festivities open at dusk on Christmas Eve with *Cacho Fio*. During this Provençal ceremony, a log – usually cut from a pear, olive or cherry tree – is placed in the hearth, doused with fortified wine, blessed thrice by the youngest and oldest family members, then set alight. In keeping with tradition, the fire has to burn until the three kings arrive on 6 January.

Although many still celebrate *Cacho Fio* at home, it is only in Séguret that the village people gather to bless and burn a log together. This takes place in the Salle Delage, adjoining Chapelle Ste-Thecle on rue du Four. Later, villagers wend their way up to Église St-Denis at the top of the village where, during *Li Bergié*, the Christmas nativity scene is brought to life with real-life shepherds, lambs and a (relatively) newborn baby in a manger. This *crèche vivant* (living creche) is followed by midnight Mass, celebrated in Provençal.

After Mass, families rush home for *Caleno vo Careno*, the traditional feast of 13 desserts, which symbolises Jesus and the 12 apostles. Among the culinary delights are *pompe à huile* (leavened cake baked in olive oil and flavoured with orange blossom), sweet black-and-white nougat (home-made from honey and almonds) and an assortment of dried and fresh fruits.

wines. The **Maison des Dentelles** (☎/fax *04 90 62 94 39; place du Marché; open 9am-noon & 2pm-7pm Mon-Sat)* has a list of estates where you can taste and buy the nectar.

Beaumes' other tasty treat is olive oil. Taste it at the **Moulin à Huile de Balméenne** *(☎ 04 90 62 93 77; ave Jules Ferry)*, a mill that has been in business since 1856.

Yellow-stone Gigondas (population 648, elevation 282m), 15km northeast, offers ample wine-tasting opportunities. Wine cellars stud the central square, place du Portail, from where rue du Corps de Garde climbs to Gigondas' ruined chateau, campanile-clad church and cemetery. Contemporary sculptures en route form **Le Cheminement de Sculptures**; ask for a map of the sculpture trail at the **tourist office** *(☎ 04 90 65 85 46, fax 04 90 65 88 42; e ot-gigondas@axit.fr; place du Portail; open 10am-noon & 2pm-6pm daily Apr-June, Sept & Oct; 10am-noon & 2pm-7pm daily July & Aug)*.

Places to Stay

Camping There are several camp sites just north of Bédoin along the D974 east of Le Barroux.

Camping du Groseau *(☎ 04 90 65 10 26; route du Ventoux; adult/tent/car €2.60/2.50/2.50; open Easter-Sept)* is 1.5km east of Malaucène on the D974.

Aire Naturelle La Saousse *(☎ 04 90 65 23 52; camping for 2 adults, tent & car low/high season €8/11)*, some 4km north of Malaucène, offers lovely views in an unspoilt neck of the woods. From Malaucène, head north along the D938, turn right onto the D13, then right again at the first crossroads.

Gîte d'Étape Next to Gigondas fire station, **Gîte d'Étape des Dentelles de Gigondas** *(☎ 04 90 65 80 85, fax 04 90 65 84 63; w www.provence-trekking.com; dorm beds €11, doubles or triples with shared bathroom €13 per person)* has two 13-bed dorms and a clutch of doubles. Experienced mountain guide and rock climber Régis, who runs the place, organises hikes, mountain bike rides and climbing expeditions.

Chambres d'Hôtes Many *mas* (farmhouses) open their doors to B&B guests in summer; there are several on the northbound D23 to Séguret. Gigondas tourist office has a complete list.

Try **La Respelido** *(☎/fax 04 90 36 03 10; doubles with kitchenette/triple & Mont Ventoux view €55/60; Crestet; open Feb-Dec)*, with two guest rooms in a former oil mill. Speak sweetly to host Monsieur Veit and (in season) he might just agree to accompany you to Richerenches truffle market. Rates include breakfast.

Hotels Malaucène has a couple of unstartling but cheapish hotels. Otherwise try:

Les Géraniums *(☎ 04 90 62 41 08, fax 04 90 62 56 48; Le Barroux; doubles €42, half-board €40 per person, menus €15.25, €19 & €21; open Apr–mid-Nov)* is a charming, yellow-stone hotel with luxurious doubles furnished in traditional Provençal style. In summer half-board is obligatory. Book in advance to dine at its well-worth-a-nibble terrace restaurant.

Hôtel Montmirail *(☎ 04 90 65 84 01, fax 04 90 65 81 50; W www.hotelmontmirail.com; singles/doubles low season from €46/50, high season €63/68; open mid-Mar–Oct)* is a three-star 19th-century mansion located in a remote spot midway between Gigondas and neighbouring Vacqueyras.

Domaine de Cabasse *(☎ 04 90 46 91 12, fax 04 90 46 94 01; W www.domaine-de-cabasse.fr; route de Sablet, Séguret; singles/doubles from €82/98, half-board only July & Aug doubles from €165; open mid-Mar–Oct)* is a wine-producing estate on the plains, 800m south from Séguret village. It has 12 rooms, a pool, tennis courts and offers *dégustation* (wine-tasting).

Places to Eat

Les Géraniums, Hôtel Montmirail and Domaine de Cabasse (see the previous section) offer some delicious dining choices too. In Beaumes de Venise, **Lou Cigalou** *(☎ 04 90 62 95 95; ave Jules Ferry; lunchtime formule €12.90)* and adjoining **Lou Castelet** *(☎ 04 90 65 00 75; lunch formule €12, including 25cL of wine)*, with its outside grill and terrace, will fill you up without breaking the bank.

L'Oustalet *(☎ 04 90 65 85 30; place Gabrielle Andeol, Gigondas; 5-/6-course menu €40/50)*, the upmarket choice, has a fine wine cellar (bottles from €15.50 to €105) with plenty of Gigondas wine to accompany its stuffed pork trotters, roasted pigeon and other meaty specialities.

MONT VENTOUX

The 25km narrow ridge, dubbed the *désert de pierre* (stone desert) – a few kilometres east of the Dentelles de Montmirail – is Mont Ventoux (1912m). It is Provence's most prominent geographical feature thanks to its height and supreme isolation. The mountain's stone-capped top gives it the appearance from afar of being snow-capped, which it is anyway from December to April. The radar and antenna-studded peak, accessible by road for just a few months in summer, affords spectacular views of Provence, the southern Alps and beyond. Since 1990 the mountain and its surrounds have fallen under the protection of Unesco's Réserve de Biosphère du Mont Ventoux.

Mont Ventoux is the boundary between the fauna and flora of northern France and those of southern France. Some species, including the snake eagle, numerous spiders and a variety of butterflies, are found only here. The mountain's forests were felled 400 years ago to build ships, but since 1860 some areas have been reforested with a variety of species, including the majestic cedar of Lebanon. The mix of deciduous trees makes the mountain especially colourful in autumn. The broken white stones that cover the top are known as *lauzes*.

Since the summit is considerably cooler than the surrounding plains – there can be a difference of up to 20°C – and receives twice as much precipitation, bring warm clothes and rain gear. Areas above 1300m are generally snow-covered from December to April. With winds of up to 300km/h recorded you could say that Mont Ventoux is breezy.

Near the southwestern end of the Mont Ventoux massif is the agricultural village of **Bédoin** (population 2657, elevation 295m) and, 4km farther east along route du Mont Ventoux (D974), the neighbouring **Ste-Colombe**. Road signs here tell you if the *col* (mountain pass) over the summit is closed. At the eastern end of the Mont Ventoux massif is **Sault** (population 1190, elevation 800m), which is surrounded by a patchwork of purple lavender in July and August. In winter **Mont Serein** (1445m), 16km east of Malaucène and 5km west of Mont Ventoux's summit on the D974, is transformed into a bustling ski station.

Information

Tourist Offices Malaucène **tourist office** (see the earlier Dentelles de Montmirail section) stocks information on exploring Mont Ventoux by bicycle or on foot, including night climbs up Ventoux in July and August. Its counterparts in **Bédoin** *(☎ 04 90 65 63 95; e ot-bedoin@axit.fr; place du Marché)*, and **Sault** *(☎ 04 90 64 01 21; ave de la Promenade; open 9am-noon & 2pm-6pm Mon-Sat, 9.30am-12.30pm Sun)* organise guided mountain walks.

Walking

The GR4, running from the Ardèche River to the west, crosses the Dentelles de Montmirail before climbing up the northern face of Mont Ventoux. It then joins the GR9, and

The Perfume of Provence

If there's one aroma associated with Provence, it's *lavande* (lavender). Lavender fields – once seen, never forgotten – include those surrounding Abbaye de Sénanque near Gordes and the Musée de la Lavande in Coustellet, and those carpeting the arid Sault region, east of Mont Ventoux on the Vaucluse plateau. The vast lavender farms that sweep across the Plateau de Valensole and those at Lagarde d'Apt, are particularly memorable.

The sweet purple flower is harvested when it is in full bloom, between 15 July and 15 August. It is mechanically harvested on a hot dry day, following which the lorry-loads of cut lavender, known as *paille* (straw), are packed tight in a steam still and distilled to extract the sweet essential oils.

Authentic lavender farms, all the rage in Provence in the 1920s, are a dying breed today. Since the 1950s, lavandin – a hybrid of fine lavender and aspic, cloned at the turn of the century – has been mass produced for industrial purposes. Both blaze the same vibrant purple when in flower, but lavandin yields five times more oil than fine lavender (which produces 1kg of oil from 130kg of cut straw). Since 1997, *huile essentielle de lavande de Haute Provence* – essential lavender oil from Haute-Provence – has been protected by its own *appellation d'origine contrôlée* (AOC).

Approximately 80% of Provence's lavender farms produce lavandin today. The few remaining traditional lavender farms – such as Château du Bois, which can be visited (see the Lubéron chapter) – usually colour higher areas. Wild lavender needs an altitude of 900m to 1300m to blossom, unlike its common sister, which can grow anywhere above 800m. In 2000, the region's 400 lavender farms (covering 4500 hectares) and 150 distilleries produced 60 tonnes of essential oils, 80% of which were exported.

A complete list of lavender farms, distilleries and gardens open to visitors are listed in the English-language brochure *Les Routes de la Lavande* (The Lavender Roads), available free from tourist offices or the **Association Routes de la Lavande** *(☎ 04 75 26 65 91, fax 04 75 26 32 67; ⓔ routes.lavande@educagri.fr; 2 ave de Venterol, BP 36, F-26111 Nyons).* The latter also has information on lavender tours; some are listed in this guide under Organised Tours in the Getting Around chapter.

Several restaurants in the region – notably the Hostellerie du Val de Sault in Sault and Le Chaudron in Digne-les-Bains – dish up lavender. Lavender honey is another tasty treat. Lavender festivals *(fêtes de la lavande)* are celebrated in Valensole (3rd Sunday in July), Sault (15 August), Digne-les-Bains and Valréas (first weekend in August).

both trails follow the bare, white ridge before parting ways, with the GR4 winding east to the Gorges du Verdon. The GR9, which takes you to most of the area's ranges (including the Mont du Vaucluse and Montagne du Lubéron ranges) is arguably the most spectacular trail in Provence. The first person to climb to the top of Mont Ventoux was the Italian poet Petrarch, who scaled the mountain with a donkey in 1336, leaving everyone convinced he was mad.

At Chalet Reynard, mountain guide **Jean-Pierre Bianco** *(☎ 06 64 51 01 56; ⓔ jpbianco@club-internet.fr)* leads walks for €7.62/13.72 per half-/full day.

Before heading into the hills, find out what flora and fauna you can expect to see at the **Centre de Découverte de la Nature** *(Nature Discovery Centre; ☎ 04 90 64 13 96; ave de l'Oratoire; adult/under 8 €3/free; open 10am-noon & 2pm-7pm Tues-Sun Sept-June, 10am-noon & 3pm-7pm July & Aug)*, inside the Maison de l'Environnement et de la Chasse (Centre for the Environment & Hunting) in Sault.

Cycling

In summer cyclists labour up the sun-baked slopes of Mont Ventoux (from Chalet Reynard on the westbound D974) on the way to the summit. Many who make the journey are inspired by the British world champion cyclist Tommy Simpson (1937–67) who suffered a fatal heart attack on the mountain during the 1967 Tour de France. Most enthusiasts pedal to the top, then back-track to add their water bottle to the cycling memorabilia surrounding the roadside **memorial** to Tommy Simpson, 1km east of the summit and 1km west of Chalet Reynard. The epitaph on the stone tablet reads 'There is no mountain too high'.

In Malaucène, **AcScycles** *(☎/fax 04 90 65 15 42; ave de Verdun)* repairs and rents road/mountain bikes (from €7/8 per day). In Sault, **Albion Cycles** *(☎ 04 90 64 09 32; route de St-Trinit)* has wheels to rent (from €7 a day) and arranges bike rides. Both Malaucène and Sault tourist offices distribute *Massif du Mont Ventoux: 9 Itinéraires VTT*, a free booklet detailing nine mountain bike itineraries ranging in length from an easy 3.9km (one hour) to a gruelling 56.7km (seven to eight hours) tour of Mont Ventoux.

Skiing

Between December and March, locals flock up Ventoux to ski its slopes. **Chalet Reynard** *(☎ 04 90 61 84 55)*, at the intersection of the D974 and the eastbound D164 to Sault, is a small ski station (1440m) on the southern slopes. It has two drag lifts *(téléskis)* up to two blue runs. A half-/full day pass costs €8/13 and you can hire skis, boots and poles for €10/17 per half-/full day. Cross-country skiing is also popular. Nonskiers can test the luge (€8).

Mont Serein (1400m), 5km west of the summit on the colder northern side, is the main ski station with 12km of pistes served by eight drag lifts. Skis, ski schools, piste maps and ski passes are available from the **Chalet d'Accueil** *(☎ 04 90 63 42 02)*, in the resort centre. A half-/full-day ski pass costs €10.30/13.50 (under 6 €5) and access to the snowboard park costs €9.20 a day. Chalet Liotard (see Places to Stay & Eat following) is a mid-station, 100m farther uphill.

Places to Stay & Eat

Places listed in the Dentelles de Montmirail section also serve as a good base to explore Mont Ventoux.

Camping Municipal du Deffends *(☎ 04 90 64 07 18, fax 04 90 64 08 59; route de St-Trinit; adult/tent & car €2.90/2.40; open May-Sept)*, beneath trees in lovely Forêt du Défens, offers walking, cycling and horse-riding opportunities. In July and August you can swim in the outdoor pool (adult/three to 13 yrs €2.29/1.19). To get here, follow the D950 to St-Trinit and Banon.

Chalet Liotard *(☎ 04 90 60 68 38; doubles €50, lunch formule €10; open Dec-Sept)*, also known as Chez Coco et Mimi, is practically alpine in its cosiness with its warming cuisine *(menu €15)* and roaring winter fire. Its seven rooms sleeping two to four people get booked up quickly in winter.

Hôtel Le Louvre *(☎ 04 90 64 08 88; place du Marché, Sault; singles/doubles/triples/quads with shower & washbasin €40/45/60/70, singles/doubles/triples with bathroom €55/70/85)* is an appealing place with double rooms overlooking the village square and an excellent Provençal kitchen.

Hostellerie du Val de Sault *(☎ 04 90 64 01 41, fax 04 90 64 12 74; W www.valdesault.com; half-board per person low/mid/high season from €79.50/94/99.50; open Mar-early Nov)*, an 11-room haven of peace and tranquillity, is 2km north along the D950 towards Banon. Its restaurant, with poolside terrace, is renowned and the jacuzzi with picture-postcard view of Mont Ventoux is downright decadent – but fabulous.

Shopping

Don't leave Sault without indulging in a slab of its sweet lavender-honey and almond-flavoured nougat or bitter-sweet macaroons. Both are sold at **André Boyer** *(☎ 04 90 64 00 23; e infos@nougat-boyer.fr; place de l'Europe)*, a nougat maker featured in the *Guinness Book of Records* for cooking up the largest bar of nougat (12.45m long and 180kg in weight). Factory visits can be arranged.

For a refreshing change, taste and buy lemonade at the **Limonaderie Artisanale du Ventoux** *(☎ 04 90 64 02 28; route de St-Trinit; open 8.30am-noon & 2pm-6pm Mon-Sat)*, a traditional lemonade maker on the D950 towards St-Trinit.

Getting There & Away

If you've got a car, the summit of Mont Ventoux can be reached from Sault via the tortuous D164 or, in summer, from Malaucène or St-Estève via the switchback D974, built in the 1930s. This mountain road is often snow-blocked until as late as April. See the Carpentras section later for bus details.

CARPENTRAS

postcode 84200 • pop 27,249
• elevation 102m

Drowsy Carpentras, an important trading centre in Greek times and later a Gallo-Roman city, became the capital of the papal territory of the Comtat Venaissin in 1320. It flourished in the 14th century, when it was visited frequently by Pope Clement V. At the

Plateau d'Albion

There's more to the Plateau d'Albion than meets the eye.

France's land-based nuclear missiles were stationed on this harsh and uninhabitable moonscape from 1965 until 1996, when President Chirac ordered the missiles to be deactivated and the military site to be manned by the French Foreign Legion instead. The last nuclear missile and concrete silo was dismantled in February 1998.

What was once France's biggest secret is riddled with natural pot-holes and caverns. The plain can be uncovered – above or below ground – with the **Association Spéléologique du Plateau d'Albion** *(☎ 04 90 76 08 33, fax 04 90 75 09 86; W www.aspanet.net; 2 rue de l'Église)*, a spelunking club in the plain's only real village, **St-Christol d'Albion** (population 555, elevation 850m), 11km south of Sault. Spelunking costs from €50 per day; the association also arranges mountain-biking expeditions. Basic accommodation (€10/5/25 for bed/breakfast/half-board) is available in the club's *refuge* (hut).

same time, Jews expelled from territory controlled by the French crown (especially in Provence and Languedoc) sought refuge in the Comtat Venaissin, where they could live under papal protection – subject to certain restrictions. The Comtat Venaissin became part of France in 1791 after the French Revolution. Today, Carpentras' 14th-century synagogue is France's oldest such structure still in use.

Carpentras is 25km from both Avignon and Orange. Easy to navigate on foot, the agricultural town is known for its bustling Friday morning market on place Aristide Briand, where you can buy everything from truffles (November to March) to locally made *berlingots* (hard-boiled sweets).

Orientation

In the 19th century, the city's 16th-century fortifications and walls were replaced by a ring of boulevards: ave Jean Jaurès, blvd Alfred Rogier, blvd du Nord, blvd Maréchal Leclerc, blvd Gambetta and blvd Albin Durand. Inside, is the partly pedestrian old city. The northern Porte d'Orange (1560) still stands.

If you arrive by bus, walk northeast to place Aristide Briand, a major traffic intersection at the southernmost point on the heart-shaped ring of boulevards. Pedestrian-only rue de la République heads north to the cathedral and the Palais de Justice.

Information

The **tourist office** *(☎ 04 90 63 00 78, fax 04 90 60 41 02; e tourist.carpentras@axit.fr; place Aristide Briand; open 9.30am-12.30pm & 2pm-6pm Mon-Sat Oct-May, 9am-7pm daily June-Sept)* runs themed city tours on foot (adult/10 to 18 years €4/2.50), as well as *berlingot* factory tours (admission free), three-hour guided bike rides along the Canal de Carpentras (adult/10 to 18 years €9/6, plus bike hire €8), 1½-hour wine-tasting workshops (€4 per person), 2½-hour truffle hunts in the Massif du Ventoux (adult/10 to 18 years €9/6, 2½ hours) and September grape-harvest trips (€5 per person). Trips must be booked in advanced.

Commercial banks line place Aristide Briand and blvd Albin Durand. Surf at the **post office** *(65 rue d'Inguimbert; open 8.30am-7pm Mon-Fri, 8.30am-noon Sat)* or the **Web Center** *(☎ 04 90 67 32 64; 290 blvd Albin Durand; open 10.30am-7.30pm Mon-Sat)*, which charges €5.30 an hour.

Synagogue

Carpentras synagogue *(☎ 04 90 63 39 97; place Juiverie; admission free; open 10am-noon & 3pm-5pm Mon-Fri)*, inconspicuous as it is (look for the stone plaque inscribed with Hebrew letters), was founded in 1367, rebuilt between 1741 and 1743, and restored in 1929 and again in 1954. The 1st-floor sanctuary in France's oldest remaining synagogue is decorated with wood panelling and liturgical objects from the 18th century. Down below, there's an oven that was used until 1904 to bake matzo *(pain azyme* in French), the unleavened bread eaten at Passover.

Cathédrale St-Siffrein

Carpentras' one-time cathedral *(open 10am-noon & 2pm-6pm Tues-Sat)*, which dominates place Charles de Gaulle, was built in the Méridional (southern French) Gothic style between 1405 and 1519. The classical doorway was added in the 17th century. Inside, the **Trésor d'Art Sacré** (Treasury of Religious Art) displays liturgical objects

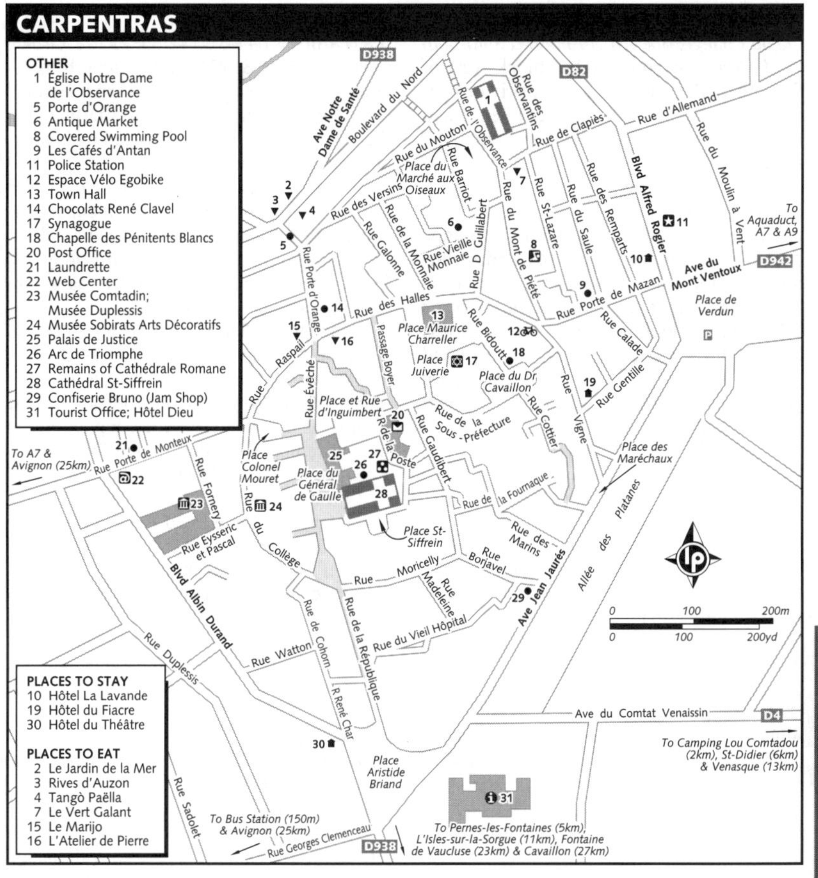

and reliquaries from the 14th to 19th century, including St-Mors, the Holy Bridle-bit supposedly made by St-Helen for her son Constantine from a nail taken from the True Cross.

Arc de Triomphe

Hidden in a corner off rue d'Inguimbert – next to the cathedral and behind the **Palais de Justice** in an episcopal palace built in 1801 – what's left of this triumphal arch is the town's only Roman relic. Built under Augustus in the 1st century AD, it is little more than a convenient public urinal today. Facing the arch on the opposite side of the square are the paltry remains of a 7th-century **Cathédrale Romane**, most of which was destroyed in 1399.

The northern outskirts of Carpentras are crossed by its most impressive stone relic, the remains of a 10km-long **aqueduct** that supplied water to the city between 1745 and 1893. For a heady glimpse of all 48 of the structure's arches, follow the Orange road signs from the centre.

Museums

The **Musée Comtadin** *(234 blvd Albin Durand; open 10am-noon & 2pm-6pm Wed-Mon, 4pm in winter),* which displays artefacts related to local history and folklore, and the **Musée Duplessis** *(☎ 04 90 63 04 92; 234 blvd Albin Durand; open 10am-noon & 2pm-6pm Wed-Mon, 10am-noon & 2pm-4pm in winter),* which houses a bunch of paintings, share the same building.

The **Musée Sobirats Arts Décoratifs** *(112 rue du Collège; open 10am-noon & 2pm-6pm Wed-Mon, 4pm in winter)*, a block west of the cathedral, is an 18th-century private residence crammed with furniture, faïence and *objets d'art* in the Louis XV and Louis XVI styles.

Swimming

Art Deco fans who enjoy taking a plunge should head for the lovely **covered swimming pool** *(piscine couverte; ☎ 04 90 60 92 03; rue du Mont de Piété; adult/3-15 yrs €2/1.50)*, overlooking place Capponi. It was built by the Caisse d'Épargne in 1930 and has since been restored to its geometric glory. The water temperature is 20°C. Opening hours vary.

Places to Stay

The tourist office has a long list of *chambres d'hôtes* in and around town.

Camping Lou Comtadou *(☎ 04 90 67 03 16, fax 04 90 86 62 95; 881 ave Pierre de Coubertin; camping for 2 people with tent & car €8, four-person mobile homes from €350 per week; open Easter-Oct)*, 2km east of town, has a *pétanque* court where campers can take a spin.

Hôtel du Théâtre *(☎ 04 90 63 02 90; 7 blvd Albin Durand; doubles with washbasin €30, with shower & toilet €43)*, a friendly, one-star place overlooking place Aristide Briand, is arguably the best place in town to stay for travellers watching their wallets. Rooms are large.

Hôtel La Lavande *(☎ 04 90 63 13 49, fax 04 90 63 55 12; 282 blvd Alfred Rogier; singles/doubles/triples €26/31.25/30.50)* is an eight-room place straddling a busy road. Rooms have bathrooms.

Hôtel du Fiacre *(☎ 04 90 63 03 15, fax 04 90 60 49 73; 153 rue Vigne; singles/doubles/triples low season €46/50/85, high season €49/55/95)* offers a bunch of bathroom-clad rooms above a restaurant and piano bar.

Château de Mazan *(☎ 04 90 69 62 61, fax 04 90 69 76 62; W www.chateaudemazan.fr; place Napoléon; doubles from €110, with private garden €185)*, in Mazan village, 7km east of Carpentras along the D942, is a regal and historic choice. In the 18th century this charming *demeure* (residence) belonged to the notorious Marquis de Sade (see the boxed text 'Sadism' in the Lubéron chapter).

Places to Eat

Le Marijo *(☎ 04 90 60 42 65; 73 rue Raspail; menus €17.50 & €27)* serves superb three- and four-course *menus* laden with regional fare. Finish with goat's cheese marinated in herbs and olive oil and sprinkled with *marc*, a local eau de vie.

Rives d'Auzon *(☎ 04 90 60 62 62; 47 blvd du Nord; lunch formule €17, menus €22, €26.50 & €29)*, a colourful place next door, is another prized restaurant. On Friday and Saturday evening it serves an 'eat-as-much-as-you-can' shellfish buffet.

L'Atelier de Pierre *(☎ 04 90 60 75 00; 30 place de l'Horloge; menus €26, €34 & €54)*, cooks up imaginative and mouth-watering creations on Carpentras' finest terrace – at the foot of a 16th-century belfry, topped by an ornate campanile dating from 1572. Its seasonal truffle *menu* (€58) is worth every cent.

Le Vert Galant *(☎ 04 90 67 15 50; 12 rue de Clapiès; menus €25.30 & €43)* serves up very palatable truffles – prepared and dressed by chef Michel Castelain.

Tangò Paëlla *(☎ 04 90 67 05 93; 48 blvd du Nord; paella €4.50)* looks uncannily like a laundrette but is, in fact, a fast-food paella place that also doles out *tajines* and couscous by the dishful.

Shopping

The **antique market** *(place du Marché aux Oiseaux)*, Friday morning from April to October, is worth a browse.

Chocolats René Clavel *(☎ 04 90 63 07 59; 30 rue Porte d'Orange)* is packed with fantastical sculptures carved from *berlingot*, a hard caramel candy created in Carpentras in 1844. The largest weighs 56kg and was a *Guinness Book of Records* record-breaker in 1992.

Confiserie Bruno *(☎ 04 90 63 04 99; 280 ave Jean Jaurès)* has cooked up *berlingots* since 1925.

Getting There & Away

From the **bus station** *(place Terradou)*, **Trans Vaucluse** *(☎ 04 90 63 01 82)* runs hourly services to/from Avignon (€3.50, 45 minutes) and less frequent buses to/from Orange (€3.90, 40 minutes), Cavaillon (€ 4.30, 45 minutes), L'Isle-sur-la-Sorgue (€1.80, 20 minutes), Sault (€4.80, 1¼ hours), Venasque (€2.50, 30 minutes) and Sablet (€1.80, 40 minutes) via Beaumes de Venise (€1.50, 20 minutes), and Gigondas (€1.30, 30 minutes).

Getting Around

Mountain-bike specialist **Espace Vélo Egobike** *(☎ 04 90 67 05 58; e felbaum@caramail.com; 64 rue Vigne; open 10am-noon & 2.30pm-7pm Tues-Fri, 2.30pm-7pm Sat)* rents bikes, arranges guides and can transport you and your bike to the top of Mont Ventoux, allowing you to whiz downhill in unexhausted splendour.

AROUND CARPENTRAS

From Carpentras, a circular day trip takes travellers through a water world of fountains and water wheels, gushing springs and breathtaking gorges.

Pernes-les-Fontaines

postcode 84210 • pop 10,309 • elevation 75m

A former capital of the Comtat Venaissin, Pernes-les-Fontaines (Perno la Font in Provençal), 5km south of Carpentras, is named after the 40 fountains that spring from its stone walls and decorate its squares. Upon discovering the Font de Bouvery source in the 18th century, the town mayor graced the town with monumental mushrooms of fountains, extravagantly decorated and sprouting from 3m-wide bases: the grandiose, moss-covered **Fontaine du Cormoran, Fontaine Reboul** and **Fontaine du Gigot** are the result – ask at the **tourist office** *(☎ 04 90 61 31 04, fax 04 90 61 33 23; w www.ville-pernes-les-fontaines.fr; place Gabriel Moutte; open 9am-12.30pm & 2.30pm-7pm Mon-Fri, 9am-12.30pm & 2.30pm-6pm Sat)* for a map marked with all 40 fountains.

L'Isle-sur-la-Sorgue

postcode 84800 • pop 17,443

A farther 11km south sits L'Isle-sur-la-Sorgue, a chic spot known for its antique shops and graceful waterways. L'Isle dates from the 12th century when villagers built huts on stilts above what was then a swampy marshland. By the 18th century it was a thriving silk-weaving centre surrounded by canals ploughed by water wheels powering its paper mills and silk factories.

On Sunday morning the quays are swamped with book and antique sellers, and a host of market stalls selling other wares. A food market fills the streets on Thursday morning. **Le Quai de la Gare** *(☎ 04 90 20 73 42; 4 ave Julien Guigue)*, opposite the train station, is an old warehouse housing 35 antique dealers. Another 100 or so can be found in **Le Village des Antiquaires** *(☎ 04 90 38 04 57; w www.villagegare.com; 2 bis ave de l'Égalité)*, an antique shopping mall fronted by an 18th-century mill. Don't expect any bargains.

The **tourist office** *(☎ 04 90 38 04 78, fax 04 90 38 35 43; w www.ot-islesurlasorgue.fr; place de la Liberté; open 9am-12.30pm or 1pm & 2pm or 2.30pm-6pm or 6.30pm Mon-Sat, 9.30am-12.30pm or 1pm Sun)* has plenty of information on L'Isle-sur-la-Sorgue hotels, upmarket *chambres d'hôtes* and restaurants around town.

Fontaine de Vaucluse

postcode 84800 • pop 61 • elevation 75m

The mighty spring that gives Fontaine de Vaucluse (Vau-Cluso La Font in Provençal) its name is the spot where the River Sorgue ends its subterranean course and gushes to the surface. At the end of winter and in early spring, up to 200 cubic metres of water per second spill forth from the base of the cliff, forming one of the world's most powerful springs. During drier periods, the reduced flow seeps through the rocks at various points downstream from the cliff and the spring becomes little more than a still, very deep pond. Following numerous unsuccessful human and robotic attempts to reach the bottom, a remote-controlled submarine touched the 315m-deep base in 1985.

Some 1.5 million visitors descend upon Fontaine de Vaucluse each year to stroll its streets and throw pebbles in its pond. The **tourist office** *(☎ 04 90 20 32 22, fax 04 90 20 21 37; e officetourisme.vaucluse@wanadoo.fr; chemin de la Fontaine; open 9am-1pm &*

Canoeing

Ploughing the 8km of water between Fontaine de Vaucluse and L'Isle-sur-la-Sorgue is an ideal way of discovering this busy part of Provence in peace. Late April to early November, **Canoë Évasion** *(☎ 04 90 38 26 22, fax 04 90 38 51 79; route de Fontaine de Vaucluse)*, next to Camping de la Coutelière on the D24 from Fontaine de Vaucluse towards Lagnes; and **Kayak Vert** *(☎ 04 90 20 35 44, fax 04 90 20 20 28; w www.canoefrance.com)* in Fontaine de Vaucluse, both rent canoes and organise river expeditions. A canoe or kayak with guide costs €18 per person.

2pm-8pm Mon-Sat) is southeast of central place de la Colonne.

Museums Fontaine's two museums deal with the Resistance movement at the **Musée de la Résistance 1939–45** *(☎ 04 90 20 24 00; chemin de la Fontaine; adult/12-16 yrs/under 12 €3.50/1.50/free; open 10am-noon & 2pm-5pm or 6pm Wed-Mon Oct-May, 10am-6pm Wed-Mon June-Sept)*, next door to the tourist office; and with earthly stalactites and speleology at the **Écomusée du Gouffre** *(☎ 04 90 20 34 13; chemin de la Fontaine; adult/7-18 yrs €5/3.25; open 9.30am-noon & 2pm-6pm daily Feb-May, Oct & Nov; 9.30am-7pm daily June-Sept)*.

The **Moulin à Papier Vallis Clausa** *(☎ 04 90 20 34 14; chemin de la Fontaine; open 9am or 10am-12.20pm & 2pm-6.50pm daily)*, opposite the tourist office, is a reconstruction of a paper mill, built where Fontaine de Vaucluse's old mill was located from 1522 to 1968. Flower-encrusted paper, made by hand as it was in the 16th century, is sold in its boutique.

The Italian Renaissance poet Petrarch (Pétrarque in French) lived in Fontaine de Vaucluse from 1337 to 1353 where he immortalised his true love, Laura, wife of Hugues de Sade, in verse. The **Musée Pétrarque** *(☎ 04 90 20 37 20; adult/12-16 yrs/under 12 €3.50/1.50/free; open 10am-noon & 2pm-6pm Wed-Mon)*, on the left bank of the Sorgue, is devoted to his work, sojourn and broken heart. A combined ticket covering admission to the Musée Pétrarque and the Musée d'Histoire costs €4.20/2.50 per adult/12 to 16 years.

Pays de Venasque

The hill-top villages sprinkled around **Venasque** (population 980, elevation 320m), 13km southeast of Carpentras, form what is known as the Pays de Venasque, literally 'Venasque Country'. Seldom explored yet beautiful, they are well worth the drive. Venasque's village **baptistry** *(adult/under 12 €3/free; open 9.15am-noon & 1pm-5pm daily Jan-Apr; 9am-noon & 1pm-6.30pm daily Apr-Oct; 9.15am-noon & 1pm-5pm daily Oct-Dec)*, was built in the 5th century on the site of a Roman temple and is one of France's oldest structures.

The fortress village of **Le Beaucet** (population 354, elevation 300m), tumbles down the hillside 6km south via the winding D314. Two kilometres south along chemin des Oratoires (the D39A) in the hamlet of **St-Gens** is a small Romanesque basilica, rebuilt in 1884. The hermit Gens, who lived with wolves and performed rain-making miracles, died here in 1127.

The **Forêt de Vénasque**, crossed by the GR91 walking trail, lies to the east of Venasque. Heading across the Col de Murs (627m) mountain pass to the pretty village of **Murs** (population 420), 5km east, you can see remains of the **Le Mur de la Peste** (literally 'Wall of Plague'; see the boxed text 'What a Pest' in the Lubéron chapter). Continuing north, the GR91 makes a beeline for the magnificent **Gorges de la Nesque**, from where Sault and the eastern realms of the Ventoux can be accessed. On the scenic **Col des Abeilles**, immediately north of the gorges on the D1, you can hire a donkey to accompany you along the gorges or up Mont Ventoux at **Les Ânes des Abeilles** *(☎ 04 90 64 01 52)*. Donkeys can carry up to 30kg and walk between 3km and 4km per hour; a day/weekend costs around €40/60.

Venasque **tourist office** *(☎ 04 90 66 11 66; Grande Rue; open 10am-noon & 2pm-6pm Mon-Sat Apr, May, Sept & Oct; 10am-noon & 2.30pm-6.30pm Mon-Sat June; 10am-12.30pm & 2.30pm-6pm Mon-Sat July & Aug)* has information on the Pays de Venasque. There is a *gîte d'étape* (hiker's accommodation), **Les Hauts de Rémourase** *(☎/fax 04 90 72 64 05; Quartier Les Beylons; bed in 4- to 8-bed dorm €11, sheets/breakfast €3/5)* in Murs.

Places to Stay

Camping Municipal Les Coucourelles *(☎ 04 90 66 45 55; ave René Char, Pernes-les-Fontaines; adult/tent & car €3.10/3.10; open Apr-Sept)*, probably the area's best-value site, offers the sixth night for free. It has space for three and is just opposite the municipal open-air swimming pool.

Auberge de Jeunesse *(☎ 04 90 20 31 65, fax 04 90 20 26 20; chemin de la Vignasse; dorm bed €8, breakfast/sheets €3.05/2.90; open Feb–mid-Nov, reception open 8am-10am & 5pm-10pm daily)* is 800m south of Fontaine de Vaucluse towards Lagnes (walk uphill from the bus stop). Pitch your tent for €4.80 per person.

The tourist offices have details on the dozens of *chambres d'hôtes* around Carpentras.

Hotel-wise, avoid L'Isle-sur-la-Sorgue: it's stupidly expensive. The cheapest of Fontaine de Vaucluse's three overpriced hotels is **Hôtel Les Sources** (*☎ 04 90 20 31 84, fax 04 90 20 39 09; route de Cavaillon; doubles €47.50*), with 12 rooms.

Mas La Bonoty (*☎ 04 90 61 61 09, fax 04 90 61 35 14; W www.bonoty.com; chemin de la Bonoty, Pernes-les-Fontaines; doubles/triples with breakfast from €69/115*), a farmhouse hotel with apricot groves, lavender fields, pool and elegant rooms is worth the splurge.

Places to Eat

In Venasque, there are a couple of places well worth the drive.

Auberge La Fontaine (*☎ 04 90 66 02 96, fax 04 90 66 13 14; place de la Fontaine; doubles €125, bistro/restaurant menu €18/38*), in the heart of this charming village, runs cookery courses and hosts a rash of elegant and atmospheric dinner-concerts (€43 without wine).

Cybercafé de l'Olivianne (*☎ 04 90 66 64 85; place de la Fontaine; brunch €10, savoury tart & salad €9*) is a sweet spot for a light lunch, cooling *citron pressé* (freshly squeezed lemon juice) or an aperitif and dinner come dusk. It has one computer to access the Internet (€6.10/hour) and hosts jazz concerts.

Getting There & Away

Fontaine de Vaucluse is 21km southeast of Carpentras and about 7km east of L'Isle-sur-la-Sorgue. From Avignon, **Voyages Arnaud** (*☎ 04 90 38 15 58*) runs three to four buses daily to L'Isle-sur-la-Sorgue (€3.20, 40 minutes) and Fontaine de Vaucluse (€4, one hour). The bus then continues to Lagnes (€4.40, 1¼ hours) in the Lubéron. There are also Voyages Arnaud buses between Carpentras and L'Isle-sur-la-Sorgue (20 minutes). A one-way L'Isle-sur-la-Sorgue–Fontaine de Vaucluse fare is €3.20.

L'Isle-sur-la-Sorgue train station is not served by passenger trains.

Getting Around

Easy riders can hire wheels to scoot around Pernes-les-Fontaines from **Vélo & Oxygène** (*☎ 04 90 61 37 37; 284 rue Émile Zola*) for €10/8 for one/subsequent days. In L'Isle-sur-la-Sorgue, try **Christophe Tendil** (*☎ 04 90 38 19 12; 10 ave Julien Guigue*).

Les Alpilles

South of Avignon is the Chaîne des Alpilles, a barren chain of wild limestone rocks, carpeted in parts with herbal *garrigue* (scrubland) and studded with oil mills. To the north and south sits St-Rémy de Provence and Maussane-les-Alpilles respectively, a town and a village linked by the Vallée des Baux, which safeguards its own culinary secret. Les Alpilles stretch east to the River Durance and west to the River Rhône.

ST-RÉMY DE PROVENCE

postcode 13210 • pop 10,007 • elevation 60m

St-Rémy de Provence – the main starting point for forays into the Chaîne des Alpilles – is a colourful place with a colourful past. The Greeks and then the Romans settled Glanum on the city's southern fringe. The philosopher Nostradamus (1503–66) was born in a house on rue Hoche in St-Rémy, only later moving to Salon de Provence to compile his influential prophecies. Three centuries on, a tormented Vincent van Gogh (1853–90) sought refuge in St-Rémy, painting some of his best-known works here in 1889–90.

Moutons (sheep), *moutons* and more *moutons* fill the streets each year on Pentecost Monday during the Fête de la Transhumance, which marks the movement of the flocks to pastures new. On 15 August St-Rémy celebrates its Carreto Ramado, which sees 50 horses lug a cart laden with local produce through town. September closes with a 10-day festival in honour of St-Rémy's patron saint.

More recently, St-Rémy has become something of a gastronomic mecca, luring notable chefs and one of France's best chocolate-makers into its fold. The famed, smooth, rich oils from the Vallée des Baux – credited with their own *appellation d'origine contrôllée* (AOC) since 1997 – can also be tried and tasted here. Wednesday is market day.

Orientation & Information

Glanum is 2km south of the centre. From the ruins, ave Vincent van Gogh (D5) and its continuation, ave Pasteur, leads north to place Jean Jaurès and farther to blvd Victor Hugo, the street encircling the old town.

You can buy maps at the St-Rémy **tourist office** (*☎ 04 90 92 05 22, fax 04 90 92 38 52;*

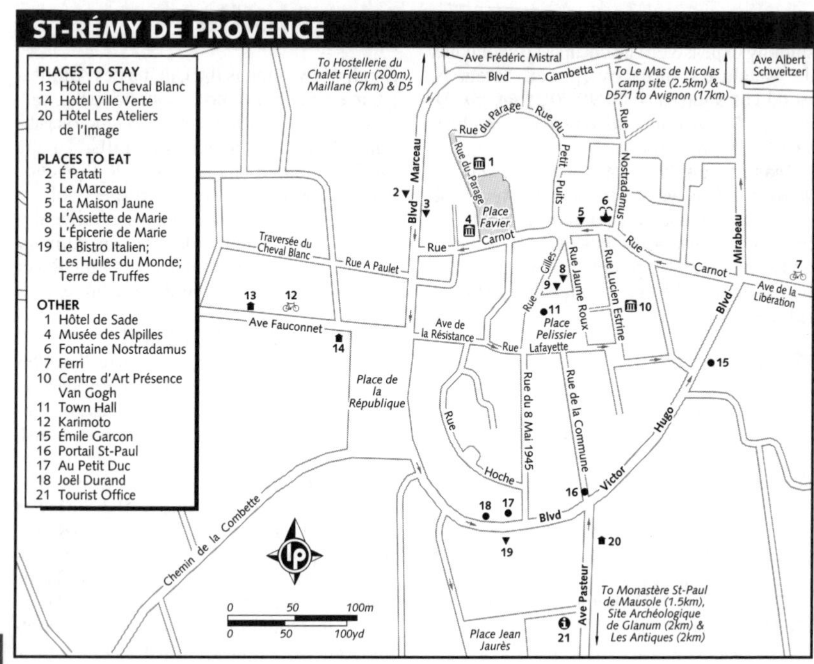

www.saintremy-de-provence.com; place Jean Jaurès; open 9am-noon & 2pm-7pm Mon-Sat, Sun 9am-noon mid-June–mid-Sept; 9am-noon & 2pm-6pm Mon-Sat mid-Sept–mid-June)*. It also runs one-hour guided tours, including one in the footsteps of Van Gogh (adult/12-18 yrs €6.40/3.65), and organises nature walks in the surrounding Alpilles (adult/student/under 12 €6.10/3.10/free).

Site Archéologique de Glanum

The Glanum archaeological site *(☎ 04 90 92 23 79; adult/18-25 yrs/under 18 €5.49/3.51/free; open 9am-7pm daily Apr-Sept, 9am-noon & 2pm-5pm Oct-Mar)* sits at the foot of Mont Gaussier. The excavated remains date from the Gallo-Greek era (3rd to 1st centuries BC) to the Gallo-Roman era (1st century BC to 3rd century AD). The Celto-Ligurians first inhabited the site, which they called Glaniques, around the 1st century BC. Among the archaeological finds uncovered are parts of Glanum's temple, public baths dating from 50 BC and the forum. Smaller fragments of treasure dug up are displayed in the Renaissance **Hôtel de Sade** *(☎ 04 90 92 64 04; 1 rue du Parage; adult/under 18 €2.50/free; open 10am-noon & 2pm-5pm or 6pm daily)*, in the centre of St-Rémy.

The roadside opposite the entrance to the archaeological site on ave Van Gogh (the southbound D5) is dominated by Provence's two most spectacular Roman monuments: the **triumphal arch** and **mausoleum**. **Les Antiques**, as the majestic pair is known, date from AD 20 and 30–20 BC respectively.

Van Gogh

The Dutch-born artist retreated to **Monastère St-Paul de Mausole** *(☎ 04 90 92 77 00; e maison.sante.st.paul@wanadoo.fr; adult/12-16 yrs €3/2.20; open 9.30am-7pm daily Apr-Oct, 10.30am-1pm & 1.30pm-5pm daily Nov-Mar)*, a monastery that served as an asylum from the 18th century. Van Gogh voluntarily admitted himself on 3 May 1889 and stayed here until 16 May 1890. During this time, he accomplished 100 drawings and about 150 paintings, including the well-known *Les Iris* (Still Life with Iris, 1890) and *Le Champ de Blé au Cyprès* (Yellow Cornfield, 1889). During WWI, the building was a prison camp. Today it is a clinic, but the **Romanesque cloister** and **Centre**

Valetudo, where patients' artwork is exhibited, can be visited. There is also a **reconstruction of Van Gogh's room** to see.

From the monastery entrance, information boards mark the **Promenade sur les lieux peints par Van Gogh**, a trail that leads you to the places where Van Gogh painted some of his most famous works. In town, the life and works of van Gogh are unravelled at the **Centre d'Art Présence Van Gogh** *(☎ 04 90 92 34 72; 8 rue Lucien Estrine; adults €3.20; open 10.30am-12.30pm & 2.30pm-6.30pm Tues-Sun late Mar-Dec)*.

Places to Stay

Le Mas de Nicolas *(☎ 04 90 92 27 05, fax 04 90 92 36 83; ⓔ camping-mas-de-nicolas@wanadoo.fr; ave Plaisance du Touch; two adults, tent & car €13; open mid-Mar–mid-Oct)*, St-Rémy's municipal camp site, is just north of the centre.

Hôtel Ville Verte *(☎ 04 90 92 06 14, fax 04 90 92 56 54; ⓦ www.hotel-villeverte.com; 18 place de la République; doubles with shower €36m, with shower & toilet €41, studios for 2/3/4 people €300/360/390)* is a charming place with a pool, 37 double rooms and 17 self-catering studios that can only be rented by the week.

Hôtel du Cheval Blanc *(☎ 04 90 92 09 28, fax 04 90 92 69 05; 6 ave Fauconnet; singles/doubles €45/50)* is a large, green-shuttered place with 22 rooms for rent. Dogs and parking are free.

Hostellerie du Chalet Fleuri *(☎ 04 90 92 03 62, fax 04 90 92 60 28; 15 ave Frédéric Mistral; doubles with shower €34, with shower & toilet €46; menu €19)*, part of the Logis de France chain, is a cosy place with prettily furnished rooms. Provençal cuisine is served in the flowery garden restaurant.

Hôtel Les Ateliers de l'Image *(☎ 04 90 92 51 50, fax 04 90 92 43 5; ⓔ ateliers-images@pacwan.fr; 5 ave Pasteur; doubles €150-280)* is a photography hotel that runs photography workshops (see Courses in the Facts for the Visitor chapter) – and a contemporary architectural gem.

Places to Eat

É Patati *(blvd Marceau; plat du jour €13, pasta €13)*, easily spotted by its pea-green wooden shutters and the old Simla Cinq car parked out front, oozes charm. Come here for pasta and potato dishes.

A Tasty Shopping Spree

Shop for...

...**chocolates to die for at Joël Durand's boutique** *(☎ 04 90 92 38 25; 3 blvd Victor Hugo)*. His astonishing use of Provençal herbs and plants – lavender, rose petals, violet, thyme etc – ranks him among France's top 10 chocolate-makers.

...**historical biscuits** baked by food historian Anne Daguin using old Roman, Renaissance, Alpine and Arlésien recipes. Her shop is **Au Petit Duc** *(☎ 04 90 92 08 31; 7 blvd Victor Hugo)*.

...**olive oil** from Provence and the Mediterranean at **Olive: Huiles du Monde** *(☎ 04 90 92 53 93; 16 blvd Victor Hugo)*. Taste 30 different oils at its *bar à huiles* (oil bar). Enter via the courtyard.

...**truffles** at **Terre de Truffes** *(16 blvd Victor Hugo)* is a classy boutique inspired by chef Bruno that sells conserved truffles year round, fresh ones in season and truffle oil.

L'Assiette de Marie *(☎ 04 90 92 32 14; 1 rue Jaume Roux; menu €29)*, a bistro cluttered with knick-knacks from another era, serves local cuisine in an old-world setting.

Le Bistro Italien *(☎ 04 90 92 05 95; 16 blvd Victor Hugo; pasta/pizza €10/9-12)* has a flower-filled terrace and a menu crammed with typical Italian temptations.

Le Marceau *(☎ 04 90 92 37 11; 13 blvd Marceau; menu €23 & €36)* is a simple yet refined place where you can dine beneath age-old beams. *Anchoïade* (anchovy paste) and *aïoli* (garlic mayonnaise) star on chef Alain Assaud's menu.

La Maison Jaune *(☎ 04 90 92 56 14; ⓔ lamaisonjaune@wanadoo.fr; 15 rue Carnot; menus €29, €44 & €52)*, named after Van Gogh's well-known *Yellow House* painting, is another tasty stop. François Perraud cooks up traditional cuisine with a twist in an interior decked out in a stark, contemporary style.

Getting There & Away

Buses to Tarascon and Nîmes operated by **Cévennes Cars** *(☎ 04 66 29 27 29)* depart from the bus stop outside the Bar du Marché on place de la République. Avignon-bound buses run by **Sociétés Rapides du Sud-Est** *(☎ 04 90 14 59 00)* leave from in front of the École de la République on blvd Victor Hugo.

Getting Around

Karimoto *(☎ 04 90 92 54 00; 29 ave Fauconnet)* rents bicycles for €15/70 a day/week, as does **Ferri** *(☎ 04 90 92 10 88; 35 ave de la Libération)*.

AROUND ST-RÉMY DE PROVENCE

Several tip-top tourist sights lie within easy reach of St-Rémy. The surrounding countryside is composed of vineyards and garrigue – whose herbal vegetation gives off a powerful fragrance in spring and early summer.

Les Baux de Provence

postcode 13520 • pop 443 • elevation 185m

Some 10km southwest of St-Rémy de Provence is Les Baux de Provence – a hilltop village that gave its name to bauxite, the chief ore of aluminium first mined in the village in 1822. In Provençal, *baou* means 'rocky spur'.

Its chief attraction is **Château des Baux** *(☎ 04 90 54 55 56; adult/student/7-17 yrs €6.50/5/3.50, family ticket €17; open 9am-6.30pm daily Mar-Nov; 9am-8.30pm daily July & Aug; 9am-5pm daily Dec-Feb)*, the former feudal home of Monaco's Grimaldi royal family, whose ruins sprawl across some seven rocky hectares and afford an unbeatable view of the surrounding Chaîne des Alpilles. A clutch of medieval war machines, a small history museum and a slide show of Provence through painters' eyes are other on-site attractions.

A dramatic portrait of Provence is projected across 4000 sq metres of rock at **Cathédrale d'Images** *(☎ 04 90 54 38 65; ⓦ www.cathedrale-images.com; route de Maillane; adult/8-16 yrs €7/4.10; open 10am-7pm daily Mar-Sept, 10am-6pm daily Oct-Feb)*, at La Baux's northern foot. The Image Cathedral, in a redundant quarry (bring a sweater), screens 3000 different images during its 30-minute sound-and-light show.

The **tourist office** *(☎ 04 90 54 34 39, fax 04 90 54 51 51; ⓦ www.lesbauxdeprovence.com; Maison du Roy, rue Porte Mage)* has information on Les Baux's limited (and expensive) accommodation. Taste olive oil from the valley at **Olive: Huiles du Monde**, midway along Grande Rue.

Les Variétés *(☎ 04 90 54 55 88; 29 rue du Trencat; menu €14.50;)* stands out from all the terribly ticky-tacky tourist restaurants. Simple but hearty cuisine is cooked up without pretence at this down-to-earth eatery with hidden terrace.

Maussane-les-Alpilles

postcode 13520 • pop 2003 • elevation 35m

Maussane-les-Alpilles, 3km south of Les Baux on the Alpilles' southern fringe, shelters some of Provence's best-known *moulins d'huile* (oil mills), where five different types of freshly harvested olives are pummelled and pressed into smooth, golden olive oil. You cannot tour the mills here, but you can buy olive oil.

The **Moulin Coopérative Jean-Marie Cornille** *(☎ 04 90 54 32 37; ⓦ www.moulin-cornille.com; rue Charloun Rieu; open 8am-noon & 2pm-6pm Mon-Sat, 11am-8pm Sun)*, in a 17th-century mill named after the original owner, was founded in 1924. Its olive oil – just 120,000L of which are produced each year – costs €17.50 per litre. Depending on the harvest, it can sell out by mid-August. New stock goes on sale from 15 December.

Lunch afterwards at **Le Bistrot du Paradou** *(☎ 04 90 54 32 70; lunch/dinner menu €32/36)*, an authentic Provençal bistro 3km west along the D78 in Paradou. Every table is snapped up by 12.30pm by courageous diners, determined to savour every last *morceau* (bite) of the fixed *menu*, which includes wine, a choice of starters and home-made desserts, a no-choice main course and a fantastic array of ponging cheeses.

From Maussane, stunning views of the fierce, silver-ridged Alpilles can be enjoyed along the eastbound D78. The village of **Eyguières** (population 5392, elevation 75) is dominated by the Alpilles' highest point (493m). Nearby **Eygalières** (population 1851, elevation 134) is home to a **Jardin de l'Alchimiste** *(☎ 04 90 90 67 77; ⓔ contact@jardin-alchimiste.com; Mas de la Brune; adult/student €5/4, guided visit €8 open 10am-7pm Tues-Sat May–mid-Sept, 10am-5pm Tues-Sat mid-Sept–mid-Oct)*, where alchemist herbs and plants blossom. **Orgon** (population 2268), 9km farther north, is guarded by **Notre Dame de Beauregard** (1878), a church perched up high on a needle of rock and proffering a stunning panorama of the Alpilles, TGV railway line and highway. By foot, the GR6 traverses the Alpilles' entire length.

The villages of **Maussane** *(☎ 04 90 54 52 04; e contact@maussane.com; place Laugier de Monblan)* and **Orgon** *(☎ 04 90 73 09 54; ave Georges Coste)* have small tourist offices.

Fontvieille

postcode 13990 • pop 3566 • elevation 20m

Sleepy Fontvieille, 10km west of Maussane-les-Alpilles along the D17, is famed for its windmill immortalised by Alphonse Daudet in his collection of short stories *Lettres de mon Moulin* (Letters from my Windmill), published in 1869. Despite the French author being born in Nîmes and spending most of his life in Paris, he shared a strong spiritual affinity with Provence and is regarded as a Provençal writer.

Contrary to popular belief, **Le Moulin de Daudet** (Daudet's windmill), which dates back to 1814 and houses the **Musée de Daudet** *(adult/under 12 €2/1; open 9am-7pm daily June-Sept, 10am-noon & 2pm-5pm daily Nov, Dec & Feb-May)*, is not the windmill where the writer spent hours sunk in literary thought. From the windmill-museum, a 1½-hour circular trail leads past the ruined **Moulin Ramet** to **Moulin Tissot-Avon** – Daudet's true haunt, defunct since 1905. The trail continues to **Château de Montauban**, home to Daudet's cousins with whom he stayed when in town. It is currently closed for renovation. The **tourist office** *(☎ 04 90 54 67 49, fax 04 90 54 69 82; e ot.fontvieille@visitprovence.com; 5 rue Marcel Honorat; open 9am-noon & 2pm-6pm Mon-Sat)* has details.

Places to Stay & Eat **Camping Municipal Les Pins** *(☎ 04 90 54 78 69, fax 04 90 54 81 25; rue Michelet; adult, tent & car €7; open Easter–mid-Oct)*, tucked amid trees behind the chateau de Montauban, has a pool.

Le Ripaille *(☎ 04 90 54 73 15, fax 04 90 54 60 69; route des Baux; doubles €41; open mid-Mar–Nov)* is a two-star hotel with heated pool, horses, ping pong and a *pétanque* court.

Le Homard *(The Lobster; ☎ 04 90 54 75 34; route du Nord; menus €22 & €30)* specialises in Provençal cuisine *à l'huile d'olive* (cuisine that uses only olive oil).

Maillane to the Rhône

Provençal poet and 1904 winner of the Nobel Prize for Literature, Frédéric Mistral (1830–1914), was a native of **Maillane** (population 1880, elevation 14m), 7km northwest of St-Rémy de Provence. He was born in the Mas du Juge, a farmhouse on its outskirts. After his father's death, he and his mother moved into the centre of the village. Upon marrying, 46-year-old Mistral left home – moving with his newly wed Marie Rivière (aged 19) into a house opposite his mother's. Today it is a **house museum** *(11 rue Lamartine; open 9.30am-11.30am & 2.30pm-6.30pm Tues-Sun Apr-Sept, 10am-11.30am & 2pm-4.30pm Tues-Sun rest of year)*. Look out for the lizard and short verse written in Provençal that he engraved on his mother's house. Mistral is buried in the village cemetery.

Continuing 3km north towards the River Rhône, you hit **Graveson** (population 3188, elevation 14m), worth sniffing out for its **Musée des Arômes et du Parfum** *(Museum of Aromas & Perfumes; ☎ 04 90 95 81 55; W www.viearome.com; petite route du Grès; adult/under 12 €3.05/free; open 10am-noon & 2pm-6pm daily)*. Herbs and plants traditionally used to create perfumes grow in the medieval garden; distillation is demonstrated on Monday. In July, during the colourful Fête de St-Éloi, a flower-decorated cart is pulled through the village by 20 galloping horses.

From Graveson, the scenic D81 meanders through the **Massif de la Montagnette**, gently rolling hills that proved inspirational to both Mistral and Daudet. Hidden in the south of the massif is the **Abbaye St-Michel de Frigolet** *(☎ 04 90 95 70 07; W www.frigolet.com)* a neo-Gothic abbey built between 1863 and 1866. You can stroll in the grounds, but the church and cloisters can only be visited on Sunday at 4pm, September to Easter. You can dine in the abbey restaurant, **Le Relais de la Treille** *(☎ 04 90 90 52 70; menus €12.50 & €16.50)* and sleep at the **Hostellerie St-Michel** *(☎ 04 90 90 52 70, fax 04 90 95 75 22; doubles from €41.50)*, the abbey hotel with comfortable rooms overlooking the gardens, or in one of the towers, year round.

Barbentane (population 3780, elevation 40m), a medieval village dominated by the 28m Tour Anglica (Anglica Tower), sits near the river in the north of the massif. The tower – also mused upon by Mistral – was built in 1385 as the donjon of Barbentane's original chateau, since destroyed save for two gates. The classical 17th-century **Château de Barbentane** *(☎ 04 90 95 51 07; adult/6-15 yrs €6/4.50; open 10am-noon & 2pm-6pm daily July-Sept, 10am-noon & 2pm-6pm*

Thur-Tues Apr, June & Oct) remains home to the Marquis de Barbentane.

TARASCON & BEAUCAIRE

The mighty chateaux of Tarascon (population 12,991) and Beaucaire (population 13,940) peer at each other across the Rhône. Each year during June's Fête de la Tarasque, a Chinese-style dragon parades through Tarascon to celebrate St-Martha's slaying of Tarasque, a dragon that lurked in the Rhône according to Provençal legend.

Louis II had **Château de Tarascon** *(☎ 04 90 91 01 93; adult/18-25 yrs/under 18 €5.50/3/free; open 9am-noon & 2pm-5pm daily Oct-Mar, 9am-7pm daily Apr-Sept)* built in the 15th century to defend Provence's political frontier, which was marked by the Rhône. The interior was richly decorated under King René (1434–80), but later stripped and used as a mint, then, from the 18th century until 1926, as a prison.

Shabby and dusty Beaucaire was plagued by a dragon, Drac de Beaucaire, who slept in the Rhône but prowled the streets of Beaucaire by day disguised as a man. Or so legend says. One day Drac snatched a washerwoman and took her back to his filthy hovel where she tended his baby son, Le Draconnet, for seven years. Years after her release, she spotted Drac in Beaucaire. Upon greeting him, Drac was so horrified to have his disguise blown that he poked out the woman's eyes. A sculpture of him can be seen on place de la République.

Beaucaire's ruined 11th-century castle, **Château de Beaucaire** *(☎ 04 66 59 26 72; Ⓦ www.aigles-de-beaucaire.com; place du Château; adult/5-11 yrs €7.50/5)* can only be entered during falconry displays, mid-March to November. The town's other animal spectacle is its running through the streets of 100 bulls, accompanied by Camargue cowboys on horseback, which opens the week-long Foire de Beaucaire in mid-July.

Southwest of Beaucaire on the D38 towards Bellegarde is the **Mas des Tourelles** *(☎ 04 66 59 19 72; Ⓦ www.tourelles.com; adult/5-16 yrs €4.60/1.60; open 2pm-6pm daily Apr-June, Sept & Oct; 10am-noon & 2pm-6pm daily July & Aug)*, a farm where you can learn how the Romans made wine in the 1st and 2nd centuries. In the cellar, taste farm-made Roman *mucsum* (honeyed wine) and *defrutum* (grape juice).

Accommodation in the twin towns is limited, but Tarascon does have an **Auberge de Jeunesse** *(☎ 04 90 91 04 08, fax 04 90 91 54 17; Ⓔ tarascon@fuaj.org; 31 blvd Gambetta; dorm bed in 8–12-bed room €8, breakfast/sheets €3.20/2.70; reception open 7.30am-10am & 5.30pm-11pm daily)*. The hostel is a 15-minute walk from Tarascon train station.

The tourist offices in Beaucaire *(☎ 04 66 59 71 34, fax 04 66 59 68 51; Ⓦ www.ot-beaucaire.fr; 24 cours Gambetta)* and Tarascon *(☎ 04 90 91 03 52, fax 04 90 91 22 96; Ⓦ www.tarascon.org; 59 rue des Halles)* have more accommodation details.

Across the River Rhône

On the western bank of the River Rhône sits the Roman town of Nîmes and the Roman aqueduct known as the Pont du Gard – two fabulous sights which, though not part of Provence-Alpes-Côte d'Azur *région* (both are in Languedoc-Roussillon), make an easy day trip from Avignon.

NÎMES

postcode 30000 • pop 137,740 • elevation 40m

Lazy, laid-back Nîmes, a little bit Provençal but with a soul as Languedocien as *cassoulet*, is graced by some of Europe's best-preserved Roman public buildings. Founded by Augustus, the Roman Colonia Nemausensis reached its zenith in the 2nd century, receiving its water supply from a Roman aqueduct system that included the Pont du Gard, an awesome bridge 23km to the northeast. The sacking of the city by the Vandals in the early 5th century began a downwards spiral in fortunes, from which Nîmes never recovered.

The city is also known for its contemporary architectural creations, most notably the Carrée d'Art. Nîmes' coat of arms, featuring a palm tree and a crocodile, was redesigned by Philippe Starck in 1987. The French designer, who is best known for his furniture creations, also was resonsible for *Abribus* – the region's most attractive bus stop, on ave Carnot. The fountain-decorated **place d'Assas** (1989) is the creation of new realist painter Martial Raysse.

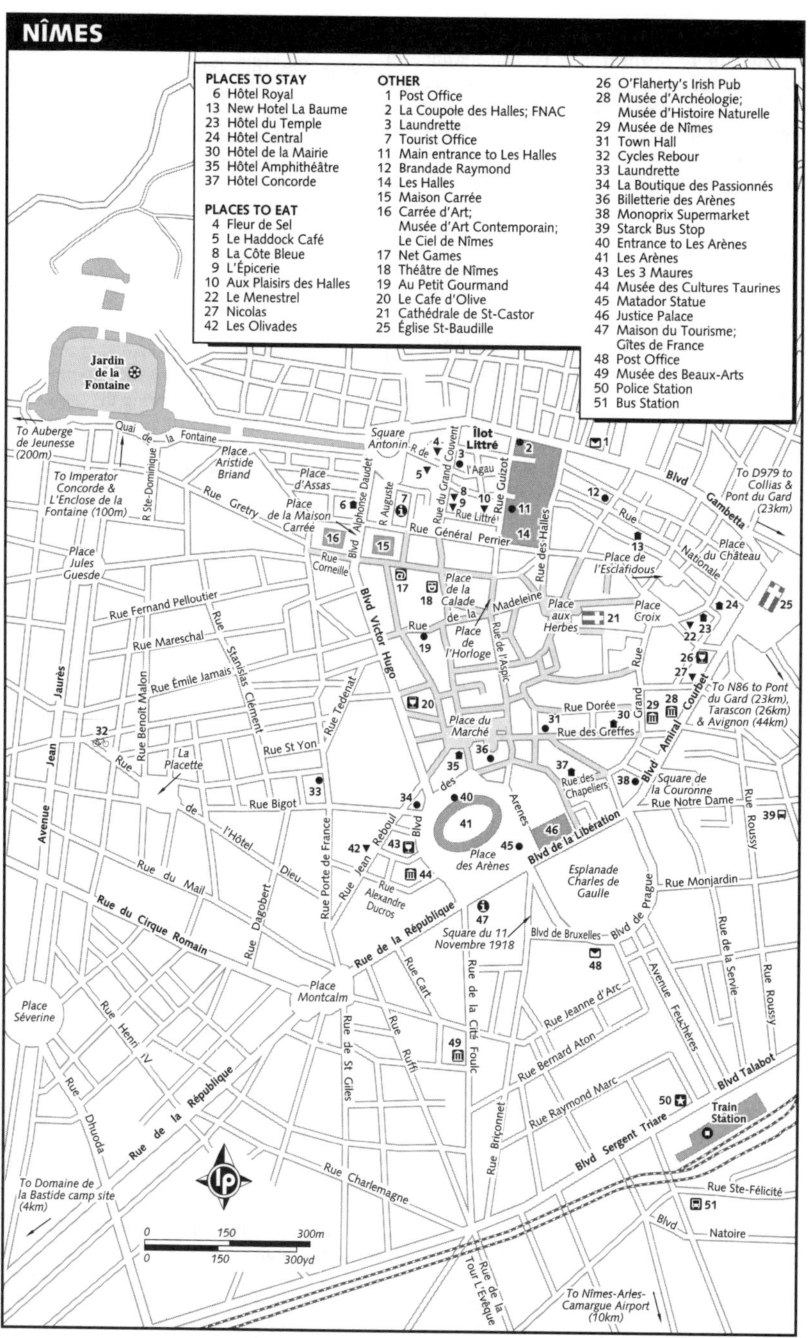
NÎMES
PLACES TO STAY
6 Hôtel Royal
13 New Hotel La Baume
23 Hôtel du Temple
24 Hôtel Central
30 Hôtel de la Mairie
35 Hôtel Amphithéâtre
37 Hôtel Concorde
PLACES TO EAT
4 Fleur de Sel
5 Le Haddock Café
8 La Côte Bleue
9 L'Épicerie
10 Aux Plaisirs des Halles
22 Le Menestrel
27 Nicolas
42 Les Olivades
OTHER
1 Post Office
2 La Coupole des Halles; FNAC
3 Laundrette
7 Tourist Office
11 Main entrance to Les Halles
12 Brandade Raymond
14 Les Halles
15 Maison Carrée
16 Carrée d'Art; Musée d'Art Contemporain; Le Ciel de Nîmes
17 Net Games
18 Théâtre de Nîmes
19 Au Petit Gourmand
20 Le Cafe d'Olive
21 Cathédrale de St-Castor
25 Église St-Baudille
26 O'Flaherty's Irish Pub
28 Musée d'Archéologie; Musée d'Histoire Naturelle
29 Musée de Nîmes
31 Town Hall
32 Cycles Rebour
33 Laundrette
34 La Boutique des Passionnés
36 Billetterie des Arènes
38 Monoprix Supermarket
39 Starck Bus Stop
40 Entrance to Les Arènes
41 Les Arènes
43 Les 3 Maures
44 Musée des Cultures Taurines
45 Matador Statue
46 Justice Palace
47 Maison du Tourisme; Gîtes de France
48 Post Office
49 Musée des Beaux-Arts
50 Police Station
51 Bus Station
Jardin de la Fontaine
To Auberge de Jeunesse (200m)
To Imperator Concorde & L'Enclose de la Fontaine (100m)
Quai de la Fontaine
Place Aristide Briand
Place d'Assas
Place de la Maison Carrée
Square Antonin
Îlot Littré
To D979 to Collias & Pont du Gard (23km)
Blvd Gambetta
Rue Nationale
Place du Château
Place de l'Esclafidous
Place aux Herbes
Place Croix
Place de la Calade
Place de l'Horloge
Place du Marché
Place Jules Guesde
Rue Fernand Pelloutier
Rue Mareschal
Rue Émile Jamais
Rue Stanislas Clément
Rue Tedenat
Blvd Victor Hugo
Rue St Yon
La Placette
Rue Bigot
Rue de l'Hôtel Dieu
Rue du Mail
Rue du Cirque Romain
Rue Dagobert
Rue Porte de France
Rue Jean Reboul
Rue Alexandre Ducros
Place des Arènes
Blvd de la Libération
Esplanade Charles de Gaulle
Square de la Couronne
Rue Notre Dame
Rue Monjardin
Blvd de Prague
Blvd de Bruxelles
Square du 11 Novembre 1918
Rue de la République
Place Montcalm
Place Séverine
Rue Henri IV
Rue Dhuoda
Rue Jeanne d'Arc
Rue Bernard Aton
Rue Raymond Marc
Avenue Feuchères
Blvd Talabot
Train Station
Blvd Sergent Triare
Rue Charlemagne
Rue Briçonnet
Rue de la Cité Foulc
Rue Tour L'Évêque
Rue Ste-Félicité
Blvd Natoire
Avenue Jean Jaurès
To N86 to Pont du Gard (23km), Tarascon (26km) & Avignon (44km)
Blvd Amiral Courbet
Rue Dorée
Rue des Greffes
Rue des Chapeliers
Rue des Arènes
Rue de la Servie
Rue Roussy
To Domaine de la Bastide camp site (4km)
To Nîmes-Arles-Camargue Airport (10km)
0 150 300m
0 150 300yd

Nîmes, just 44km southwest of Avignon, becomes more Spanish than French during its *férias*, the city's bullfighting festivals (see Special Events later in this chapter). During the flash floods that struck the Gard department in September 2002, Nîmes' monumental central square – place de la Maison Carrée – was one big swimming pool.

Orientation

Everything, including traffic, revolves around Les Arènes. Just north of the amphitheatre, the fan-shaped, largely pedestrianised old city is bounded by blvd Victor Hugo, blvd Amiral Courbet and blvd Gambetta. North of place aux Herbes, one of the main squares, lies the carefully preserved Îlot Littré – the old dyers' quarter.

Southeast of Les Arènes is esplanade Charles de Gaulle, a large open square, from where ave Feuchères leads southeast to the train and bus stations.

Information

Tourist Offices The Nîmes **tourist office** *(☎ 04 66 58 38 00, fax 04 66 58 38 01; W www.ot-nimes.fr; 6 rue Auguste; open 8.30am-7pm Mon-Fri, 9am-7pm Sat, 9am-5pm Sun Sept-June; 8am-8pm Mon-Wed & Fri, 8am-9pm Thur, 9am-7pm Sat, 10am-5pm Sun July & Aug)* takes bookings for various guided tours, including thematic literary strolls in the city (€5.50) and day trips to the Camargue (€13).

Information on the Gard department is available at the **Maison du Tourisme** *(☎ 04 66 36 96 30, fax 04 66 36 13 14; W www.cdt-gard.fr; 3 place des Arènes; open 8.45am-6pm Mon-Fri, 9.30am-noon Sat)*.

Money Commercial banks line blvd Amiral Courbet and the western side of Blvd Victor Hugo.

Post & Communications The city's **post office** *(1 blvd de Bruxelles; open 8am-6.30pm Mon-Fri, 8am-noon Sat)* has Cyberposte. Alternatively, try **Net Game** *(25 rue de l'Horloge; open 10am-1am May–mid-Sept, 10am-9.30pm Mon-Sat, 2pm-9.30pm Sun mid-Sept–Apr)* which charges €2/3 per 30/60 minutes.

Laundry There are several **laundrettes** *(30 rue du Grand Couvent • 26 rue Porte de France; open 7am or 8am-8.30pm or 9pm)* around the city.

Denim

During the 18th century, Nîmes' sizeable Protestant middle class, barred from government posts and various forms of employment, turned its energies to trade and manufacturing. Among the products made in the Protestant-owned factories was a twilled fabric known as *serge*. The soft but durable material became very popular among workers and, stained blue, was the 'uniform' of the fishermen of Genoa.

When Levi Strauss (1829–1902), a Bavarian-Jewish immigrant to the USA, began producing trousers in California during and after the gold rush of 1849, he soon realised that miners needed garments that would last. After trying tent canvas, he began importing the *serge de Nîmes*, now better known as denim (a short form of *de Nîmes* meaning 'from Nîmes').

Les Arènes

This superb Roman amphitheatre *(places des Arènes; adult/10-16 yrs €4.45/3.20; open 9am-6pm daily mid-Sept–Mar, 9am-7pm daily Apr–mid-Sept)*, reminiscent of the Colosseum in Rome, was built around AD 100 on place des Arènes to seat 24,000 spectators. It isbetter preserved than any other such structure in France, even retaining its upper storey – unlike its Arles counterpart. The interior has four tiers of seats and a system of exits and passages designed so that patricians attending the animal and gladiator combats never had to rub shoulders with the plebeians. In July and August free guided tours in English depart four times daily. A ticket covering admission to Les Arènes and the Tour Magne is also available – see the Jardin de la Fontaine section.

Throughout the year Les Arènes, which is covered by a high-tech removable roof from October to April, is used for theatre performances, music concerts and bullfights. Tickets, available until 30 minutes before closing time, are sold at the **ticket office** *(☎ 04 66 21 80 52)*, tucked in the amphitheatre's northern walls.

Maison Carrée & Carré d'Art

The rectangular, Greek-style temple known as the Maison Carrée *(Square House; place de la Maison Carrée; open 9.30am-6.30pm daily Apr–mid-Sept, 9am-5pm daily mid-Sept–Mar)*

AVIGNON AREA

is one of the world's most remarkably preserved Roman temples. Built around AD 5 to honour Augustus' two nephews, Gaius and Lucius, it survived the centuries as a meeting hall (during the Middle Ages), a private residence, a stable (in the 17th century), a church and, after the Revolution, an archive. The Maison Carrée, host to occasional free exhibitions of a historical nature, is entered through six symmetrical Corinthian columns.

The striking glass-and-steel building directly opposite is the modern Carrée d'Art *(Square of Art; ☎ 04 66 76 35 77; 15 place de la Maison Carreé)*, home to the municipal library, mediatheque, and Musée d'Art Contemporain (see Museums later in this section). The creation of British architect Sir Norman Foster (1935–1993), it perfectly reflects the Maison Carrée and is everything modern architecture should be: innovative, complementary and beautiful.

Jardin de la Fontaine

The Fountain Garden, home to Nîmes' other important Roman monuments, was laid out around the Source de la Fontaine (the site of a spring, temple and baths in Roman times). It retains an elegant air, with statue-adorned paths running around deep, slimy-green waterways. Don't miss the **Temple de Diane** to the left of the main entrance.

A 10-minute walk uphill through the terraced garden takes you to the crumbly white shell of **Tour Magne** *(adult/10-16 yrs €2.40/1.90; open 9am-6pm daily mid-Sept–June, 9am-7pm daily July–mid-Sept)*, the largest of the many towers that once ran along the city's 7km-long Roman ramparts. A spiral staircase of 140 exhausting steps leads to the top of the tower. A combination ticket that also covers Les Arènes costs €5.40/4.45.

Museums

Museum buffs can buy a three-day pass (adult/10 to 16 years €9.55/4.80), covering admission to all museums, from the tourist office or any museum.

A wonderful Roman mosaic uncovered here in 1883 and an unsurprising collection of Flemish, Italian and French works are in the **Musée des Beaux-Arts** *(Fine Arts Museum; ☎ 04 66 67 38 21; ⓔ musee.beauxarts@ville-nimes.fr; 20-22 rue de la Cité Foulc; adult/10-16 yrs €4.45/3.20, admission free 1st Sun of month; open 11am-6pm Tues-Sun)*.

The modern face of art can be enjoyed at the **Musée d'Art Contemporain** *(Contemporary Art Museum; ☎ 04 66 76 35 80; ⓔ carreart@mnet.fr: place de la Maison Carrée; adult/10-16 yrs €4.45/3.20, admission free 1st Sun of month; open 11am-6pm Tues-Sun)*, which is on the 2nd floor of the Carrée d'Art. The permanent collection features works from the 1960s to 1990s.

The city's former 17th-century Jesuit college shelters three sights: the **Musée d'Archéologie** *(Archaeological Museum; ☎ 04 66 76 74 80; 18 bis blvd Amiral Courbet; adult/10-16 yrs €4.45/3.20; open 11am-6pm Tues-Sun)*, which brings together columns, mosaics and sculptures from the Roman and pre-Roman periods; a **Musée d'Histoire Naturelle** *(Natural History Museum; ☎ 04 66 76 73 45; 13 bis blvd Amiral Courbet; adult/10-16 yrs €4.45/3.20; open 11am-6pm Tues-Sun)*; and the impressive **Chapelle des Jésuits**, host to art exhibitions and cultural happenings.

Special Events

The three *férias* – the three-day Féria Primavera (Spring Festival) on the last weekend in February, the five-day Féria de Pentecôte (Pentecost Festival) in June, and the three-day Féria des Vendanges to mark the start of the grape harvest on the third weekend in September – revolve around a series of *corridas* (bullfights), one or two of which are held on each of the days. Tickets to a *corrida* cost €15 to €85; reservations must be made months ahead via the **Billetterie des Arènes** *(☎ 04 66 02 80 80; ⓦ www.arenesdenimes.com; 4 rue de la Violette; open 10am-6pm Mon-Fri, 10am-noon Sat, from 9am during férias)* or from branches of FNAC (see Entertainment later in this section).

Courses Camarguaises (see the boxed text 'Bulls & Cowboys' in the Camargue chapter) are held on the weekend before a *féria* and at other times during the bullfighting season. Tickets cost €10. The best bulls are rewarded with a couple of bars from Bizet's opera *Carmen* as they leave the arena.

In July and August during Les Jeudis de Nîmes festival, concerts set the streets rocking on Thursday evening.

Places to Stay

For *chambres d'hôtes* and self-catering accommodation, contact **Gîtes de France**

(☎ *04 66 27 94 94, fax 04 66 27 94 95;* ⓦ *www.gites-de-france-gard.asso.fr; 3 place des Arènes)*, on the 1st floor of the Maison du Tourisme.

Camping From the train station, take bus No 1 in the Caremeau direction to get to **Domaine de la Bastide** (☎ *04 66 38 09 21; route de Générac; camping for 2 adults with tent & car €11.58)*. At the Jean Jaurès stop, change to bus D and get off at La Bastide.

Hostels About 2.5km northwest of the train station, **Auberge de Jeunesse** (☎ *04 66 68 03 20, fax 04 66 68 03 21;* ⓔ *nimes@fuaj.org; 257 chemin de la Cigale; beds in 2- to 6-bed room €8.65)* has 80 beds. Sheets/breakfast cost €2.70/3.20. Internet access, laundry and bicycle rental (€8 per day) likewise cost extra. Bikes can only be rented between 9am and 10am, so get up early. From the train station, take bus No 2 (Alès or Villeverte direction) to the Stade stop, from where it is a 500m walk uphill; follow the hostel signs.

Hotels At the less-than-inspiring **Hôtel de la Mairie** (☎ *04 66 67 65 91; 11 rue des Greffes; singles with washbasin/shower €21/28, doubles/quads with shower & toilet €37/40)* there is an assortment of dreary rooms to assure an unexciting stay.

Hôtel Amphithéâtre (☎ *04 66 67 28 51, fax 04 66 67 07 79;* ⓔ *hotel-amphitheatre@wanadoo.fr; 4 rue des Arènes; singles/doubles/triples €33.55/42.70/56.40)*, just up the road from its namesake, touts 17 rooms with eclectic furnishings. Internet access is available to guests.

Hôtel du Temple (☎ *04 66 67 54 61, fax 04 66 36 04 36;* ⓦ *www.hotel-du-temple.com; 1 rue Charles Babut; doubles with washbasin/shower €30/32, with shower & toilet €34, quad with shower & toilet €65)*, a nice cheery establishment, has been run by the same family since 1960.

Hôtel Royal (☎ *04 66 58 28 27, fax 04 66 58 28 28; 3 blvd Alphonse Daudet; singles/doubles €42/58)* is a fine three-star place with good-value rooms and terrace-restaurant overlooking place d'Assas. The latter hosts flamenco, jazz and salsa evenings.

New Hotel La Baume (☎ *04 66 76 28 42, fax 04 66 76 28 45;* ⓔ *nimeslabaume@new-hotel.com; 21 rue Nationale; singles/doubles €85/95, during férias €120/150)*, where the period-furnished rooms (some with frescoed ceilings) encircle a 17th-century courtyard, is a stylish and sumptuous choice.

Imperator Concorde (☎ *04 66 21 90 30, fax 04 66 67 70 25;* ⓔ *hotel.imperator@wanadoo.fr; quai de la Fontaine; doubles €90-160)* is a dreamy four-star, honeymooners' type of pad, with Nîmes' most exquisite garden-restaurant.

Places to Eat

Place aux Herbes, place du Marché with its crocodile and very large palm tree, and the western side of place de la Maison Carrée buzz with café life. Several cosy dining spots are hidden on place de l'Esclafidous, a real gem once found.

Le Ciel de Nîmes (☎ *04 66 36 71 70; place de la Maison Carrée; mains €10)*, a chic 3rd-floor hang-out in the Carré d'Art, offers a stunning view of the Roman temple. Anglophones call it 'The Sky of Nîmes'.

Le Haddock Cafe (☎ *04 66 67 86 57; 13 rue de l'Agau; lunch/dinner menus €9/11.40, €14.50 & €18.30)* hosts theme nights and chalks up excellent-value lunchtime deals on a board outside. The place is trendy among students.

Fleur de Sel (☎ *04 66 76 04 19; 29 rue du Grand Convent; lunch/dinner menus €9/15.50 & €20)*, run by Bruno and his Russian wife Svetlana, cook up traditional fish and meat dishes – washed down with a dozen or so different vodkas!

Le Menestrel (☎ *04 66 67 54 45; 6 rue École Vieille; menus €13, €19 & €26.50)* serves the meatiest of meat dishes – piggies' trotters and pan-fried bull chops.

L'Épicerie (☎ *04 66 67 22 50; 10 rue Littré; menu €11-16)*, also called Del Sud, serves Mediterranean cuisine in a flowery 15th- to 18th-century courtyard. It's particularly known for its lunchtime deals.

Les Olivades (☎ *04 66 21 71 78; 18 rue Jean Reboul; lunch formule €11, menu €16.50)*, a specialist in local wine, is a packed spot just west of place des Arènes.

Aux Plaisirs des Halles (☎ *04 66 36 01 02; 4 rue Littré; menus €16, €22, €31, €36 & €45)* lives up to its name (literally 'Pleasures of the Market Hall'), with its *menu de la ballade des halles* – a gastronomic stroll through the market hall, served on a quiet terrace save for a tinkling fountain and clinking wine glasses.

Nicolas *(☎ 04 66 67 50 47; 1 rue Poise; menus €11.45, €16 & €22.90)* is known among Nîmois foodies for its homemade *clafoutis* (fruit-and-custardy batter dessert) and *bourride de lotte* (monkfish soup). Fancy sinking your teeth into a grilled bull chop? Go for the most expensive *menu*.

Entertainment

What's-on listings fill *Nîmescope*, a fortnightly entertainment magazine that is freely distributed at the tourist office. FNAC's **Billetterie de Spectacles** *(☎ 04 66 36 33 33; 22 blvd Gambetta)*, in La Coupole des Halles indoor shopping centre, sells tickets for most other cultural events.

Plays, ballets, modern dance and music recitals are held at the **Théâtre de Nîmes** *(☎ 04 66 36 65 00; 1 place de la Calade)*. Interesting documentaries and films (French only) are screened in the **auditorium** *(☎ 04 66 76 35 36)* inside the Carré d'Art.

O'Flaherty's Irish Pub *(☎ 04 66 67 22 63; 21 blvd Amiral Courbet)* is the place to meet Anglophone travellers and foreign students; local bands play here.

During *férias*, it is the brash, brasserie-style **Les 3 Maures** *(☎ 04 66 36 23 23; 10 blvd des Arènes)* – easily distinguished by the stuffed bull outside – that fills up.

Shopping

During *férias* Arles-based music boutique **La Boutique des Passionnés** *(5 rue Jean Reboul; open 10am-10pm)* sets up shop in Nîmes (see the boxed text 'Street Beats' in the Camargue chapter).

Caladons – hard, honey-and-almond biscuits, typical to Nîmes – are sold at **Au Petit Gourmand** *(27 rue de la Madeleine)*. Rival *croquants Villaret* – drier finger-shaped almond biscuits – have been baked by the Villaret family at **La Maison Villaret** *(cnr rue de la Madeleine & place de l'Horloge)* since 1775.

Brandade de Nîmes is the trademark of **Brandade Raymond** *(☎ 04 66 67 20 47; 34 rue Nationale)*, a veteran *traiteur* (delicatessen and caterer) who has made the traditional salted cod paste since 1879. A 125g tin costs around €1.90.

Costières de Nîmes wine sold by knowledgeable staff can be found at the Vinothèque adjoining Les Olivades (see Places to Eat earlier in this section).

Getting There & Away

Air Also called Aéroport Nîmes-Garons, **Aéroport de Nîmes-Arles-Camargue** *(Nîmes-Arles-Camargue Airport; ☎ 04 66 70 49 49)* is 10km southeast of the city on the A54 towards Arles.

Bus From the **bus station** *(☎ 04 66 29 52 00; rue Ste-Félicité)* there are five buses daily to/from Pont du Gard (€5.50, 45 minutes, five to six daily), Avignon (€7.10, 30 minutes, 10 or more daily) and Arles (€5.40, 30 to 45 minutes, four to eight daily).

International bus operators **Eurolines** *(☎ 04 66 29 49 02)* and **Linebùs** *(☎ 04 66 29 50 62)* have neighbouring offices at the far end of the terminal.

Train The city's **train station** *(blvd Talabot)* is at the southeastern end of ave Feuchères. Destinations include Avignon (€12.60, 45 minutes, 10 or more daily), Arles (€6.40, 30 minutes, nine daily) and Marseilles (€15.70, 1¼ hours, 12 daily). A number of SNCF buses and trains head to Aigues-Mortes (€6.10, 40 minutes/one hour by train/bus) in the Camargue.

Getting Around

To/From the Airport From the bus station, **STD Gard** *(☎ 04 66 29 27 29; www.stdgard.com)* runs shuttle buses to/from the airport (€4.30, 30 minutes) to coincide with flight times. Bus drivers sell tickets.

Bicycle You can rent bikes at **Cycles Rebour** *(☎ 04 66 76 24 92; 38 rue de l'Hôtel Dieu)* for around €15 per day.

PONT DU GARD

The well-preserved, three-tiered Roman aqueduct known as the Pont du Gard – photographs of which consistently appear in texts on Western European history – was once part of a 50km-long system of canals built around 19 BC by Agrippa, Augustus' powerful deputy and son-in-law, to bring water from the Eure Springs in Uzès, 25km northwest, to Nîmes. The 35 small arches of the 275m upper tier of the *pont*, 49m above the River Gard, contain a 1.2m by 1.75m watercourse that, for a century and a half, carried 35,000 cubic metres of water a day. The Romans took 15 years to build the aqueduct which remained in use until the 3rd century.

From a large car park on the northern (*rive gauche*; left bank) side of the river, paths lead through scented garrigue to the shores of the River Gard, from where you can view both the aqueduct and the road bridge, built in 1743 alongside the top of the aqueduct's lower tier on the Gard's upstream side. The best view of the Pont du Gard is from the hill on the left bank. The Pont du Gard is only illuminated from 40 minutes after dusk until midnight on Friday and Saturday, June to September.

On hot days you can swim in the river. The Pont du Gard – the fifth most-visited site in France – is frequented by two million people a year (averaging 5000-plus visitors a day). Admission to the site is free, but you have to pay €5 to park (irrespective of whether you stay one hour or five), plus €5 if you want to join a guided tour (in English). Tours depart from Le Portal, designed by French architect Jean-Paul Viguier on the left bank. Inside is **La Grande Expo du Pont du Gard** *(☎ 08 20 90 33 30; adult/6-21 yrs €7/4)*, a museum that explores the history of the Pont du Gard and Nîmes' Roman aqueduct. The admission fee includes a 30-minute film shown on a 45-sq-metre screen and admission to Ludo – a museum-cum-play centre designed especially for children where they can learn about the Romans' watery way of life.

Between July and September, visitors can try their hand at laying a Roman mosaic, making Roman jewellery or fighting the Roman way. Workshops cost €1 to €3 and bookings can be made at the Accueil du Pont du Gard in Le Portal (see Information). In summer, gladiator combats (€2, 30-45 minutes) take place several times daily near the Pont du Gard on the left bank. While the Romans' mammoth aqueduct managed to weather the ferocious flash floods that swept across the region in September 2002, their modern-day predecessor's somewhat flimsier construction efforts on the southern (*rive droite*; right bank) riverbank were smashed to smithereens. In early 2003 the Pont du Gard site could still not be accessed from the flood-damaged right bank; check with the Accueil du Pont du Gard (see next section) for the latest update.

Information

The **Accueil du Pont du Gard** *(Pont du Gard Welcome Centre; ☎ 08 20 90 33 30)*, inside Le Portal on the left bank, sells tickets for the museum, workshops and guided tours. Directly opposite, **Richesses du Pont du Gard** *(☎ 04 66 37 03 77; open 10am-6pm daily)* doles out tourist information on the entire Gard department.

Remoulins **tourist office** *(☎ 04 66 37 22 34, fax 04 66 37 22 01; place des Grands Jours)* is another information source.

Canoeing & Cycling

The beautiful, wild River Gard, which descends from the Cévennes mountains, flows through the hills in a long gorge, passing under the Pont du Gard. Hire canoes to paddle around beneath the aqueduct from **Kayak Vert** *(☎ 04 66 22 80 76; ⓔ kayak.vert@wanadoo.dr)* or **Canoë Le Tourbillon** *(☎ 04 66 22 85 54; ⓔ location@canoe-le-tourbillon.com)*, both based in neighbouring Collias, 4km upstream, under the village's single bridge. Both places are open between March and October only.

Between March and October, you can paddle the 6km from Collias to the Pont du Gard with a group in half a day (€16 per person). March to May and September and October you can be dropped off 22km upstream in **Russan**, from where there's a great descent back to Collias (€23) – a full-day trip.

The region is known for its unpredictable weather. Torrential rains or floods in the case of 2002 rapidly raise water levels by 2m to 5m, while during long, dry spells, the Gard can almost disappear.

Kayak Vert and Canoë Le Tourbillon also rent mountain bikes. From the Pont du Gard, a 30km signposted circuit heads northwest towards Uzès in Languedoc; ask at Richesses du Pont du Gard for a brochure outlining the route.

Places to Stay & Eat

Camping La Sousta *(☎ 04 66 37 12 80, fax 04 66 37 23 69; ⓦ www.lasousta.fr; ave du Pont du Gard; camping for 2 people with tent & car low/high season €10.50/15; open Mar-Oct)* is a three-star site, five minutes' walk from the aqueduct on the south side (follow the D981).

Le Mas de Castille *(☎ 04 66 22 97 72; ⓔ mas-castille@avignon-et-provence.com; Quartier du Château, Argilliers; doubles with breakfast €65, four-course evening meal with aperitif €22)*, 4km west of the Pont du Gard in the tiny hamlet of Argilliers (signposted off the D981 along the D3 bis), is a charming *chambre d'hôte* where tasty evening meals are cooked up and guests have run of the garden and pool, alongside Ernest, the ball-catching black lab.

Hôtel Restaurant Le Colombier *(☎ 04 66 37 05 28, fax 04 66 37 35 75; route du Pont du Gard; doubles/triples €45/58)*, a rambling building with terracotta-tiled roof and sunny terrace, is walking distance of the aqueduct, on the D981 on Remoulins' western fringe. It is part of the Logis de France chain.

Getting There & Away

The Pont du Gard is 23km northeast of Nîmes and 26km west of Avignon. Buses from Avignon and Nîmes stop 1km north of the bridge. To get to Collias (€5, one hour) take bus No 168 (two daily) from Nîmes' bus station – or hitch.

Parking in the car park on the left riverbank costs €5 a day. The right-bank car park and pedestrian access to the Pont du Gard were closed following the flash floods that swept through in September 2002.

The Lubéron

The Lubéron hills (Montagne du Lubéron) stretch from Cavaillon in the west to Manosque in the east, and from Apt south to the River Durance and the Romanesque Abbaye de Silvacane. The area is named after the main range, a compact massif with the gentle summit of Mourre Nègre (1125m). Its oak-covered northern face is steep and uneven, while its southern face is drier and more Mediterranean in both climate and flora. Fruit orchards and vineyards carpet the lower slopes. The Combe de Lourmarin (Loumarin Coomb) divides the Petit Lubéron in the west from the Grand Lubéron in the east. The entire region is crisscrossed with walking trails and a circular 230km-long cycling route.

The Lubéron – much of which is protected by the Parc Naturel Régional du Lubéron – is greener, less densely populated and extremely affluent compared to the rest of the Vaucluse *département* (department), of which it is a part. Most of its lower lying land is farmed, forming a rich, manicured patchwork of vineyards, olive groves and fruit farms as toy-like as the perfectly restored, golden-stone *mas* (farmhouses). *Bories* dot the northern part of the region, while ochre sands – sculpted by the wind and rain over the centuries into fantastic formations – colour it a fantastic fire-red.

Highlights

- Take a walk on the colourful side: through red Rustrel, purple lavender fields in Lagarde d'Apt, and around silver-stone *bories* (old shepherds' huts) in Viens
- Tour the dramatic gorges and grand fortresses of the Grand Lubéron
- Reel in the sacred splendour of the Romanesque Abbaye Notre-Dame de Sénanque
- Explore the Petit Lubéron by bicycle

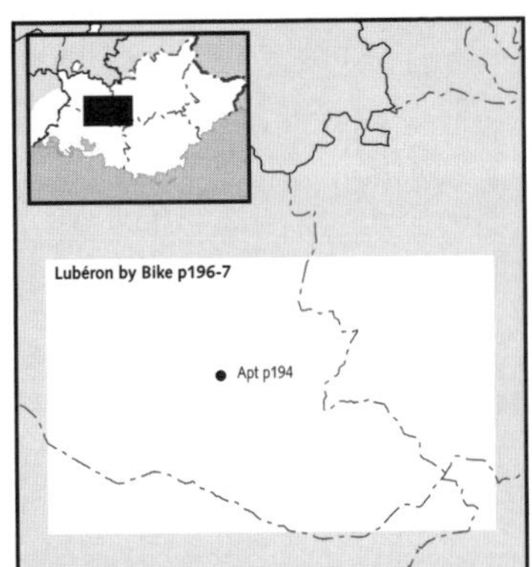

Food Highlights

Cherries and **fruits confits** (crystallised fruits) from Apt

APT

postcode 84400 • pop 11,500 • elevation 250m

Apt, a small town founded by the Romans in 45–30 BC, is considered Lubéron's capital and a solid base for exploring. The town itself is largely unexceptional beyond its grapes, cherries and *fruits confits* (crystallised fruits), all of which are still candied by a bunch of veteran sweet-makers. The popular 'Lubéron by Bike' cycling itinerary passes through Apt (see the boxed text later in this chapter), as does the GR9, which links Apt with hill-top Buoux, 8km south, and Villars, 7km north.

Information

The **tourist office** *(☎ 04 90 74 03 18, fax 04 90 04 64 30; ⓔ tourisme.apt@pacwan.fr; 20 ave Philippe de Girard; open 9am-noon & 2pm-6pm Mon-Sat Sept-June; 9am-7pm Mon-Sat, 9am-noon Sun July & Aug)* has lots of information on walking and cycling in the area.

Commercial banks frame the western side of place de la Bouquerie. The **post office** *(105 ave Victor Hugo; open 9am-noon & 2pm-7.30pm Mon-Fri, 8.30am-noon Sat)* is nearby. Internet access at **Infotelec** *(☎ 04 90 04 46 40; 88 rue de la Sous-Préfecture; open 9am-noon & 2pm-5pm or 6pm Mon-Fri, 9.30am-1pm Sat)* costs €5 per hour.

Things to See & Do

The tourist office distributes a free map marked with three one- to 1½-hour walking itineraries signposted around Apt. The **Ancienne Cathédrale Ste-Anne** *(cnr rue Ste-Anne & rue St-Pierre)* is a highlight. Dating back to

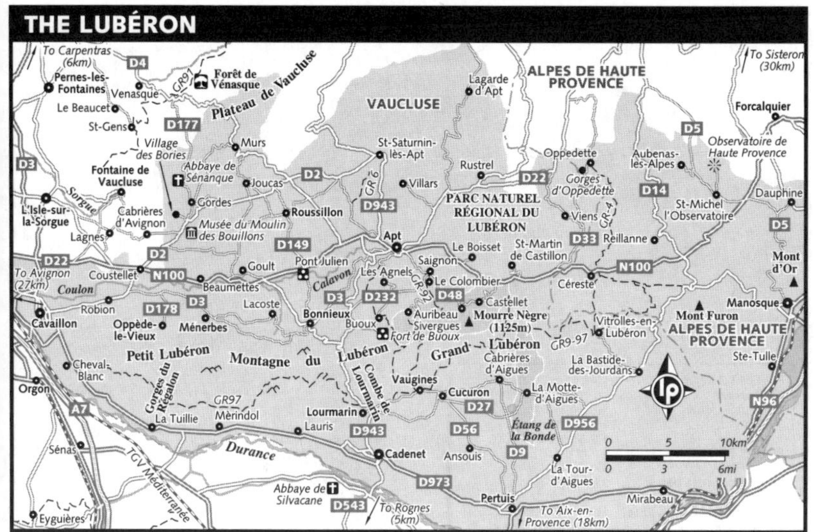

the 11th century, the old cathedral shelters Saint Anne's relics and several illuminated 11th- and 12th-century manuscripts.

Remnants from the Roman Apta Julia are exhibited in the **Musée d'Histoire et d'Archéologie d'Apt** *(History & Archaeology Museum; ☎ 04 90 04 76 65; 27 rue de l'Amphithéâtre; adult/12-18 yrs/under 12 €2/1/free; open 10am-noon & 2pm-5.30pm Wed-Sat & Mon, 2pm-6pm Sun)*. The museum stands on the site where gladiators were once pitted against beasts in the Roman amphitheatre.

Prehistoric beasts (fauna) and beauties (flora) can be seen at Apt's **Musée de Paléontologie** *(Palaeontology Museum; ☎ 04 90 04 42 00; 60 place Jean Jaurès; adult/under 18 €1.50/free; open 8.30am-noon & 1.30pm-7pm Mon-Sat Apr-Sept; 8.30am-noon & 1.30pm-6pm Mon-Fri Oct-Mar)*, inside the Maison du Parc (see the boxed text 'Parc Naturel Régional du Lubéron' later in this chapter).

Tasting and buying traditional *fruits confits* is Apt's sweetest past-time. **Confiserie Kerry Aptunion** *(☎ 04 90 76 31 43; e shop@kerryaptunion.com; quartier Salignan)*, west of town, is the largest crystallised fruits factory in the world and can be visited by guided tour (advance reservations only). In town, taste figs, cherries and other fruits at **Marcel Richaud** *(☎ 04 90 74 43 50; 112 quai de la Liberté)* or **La Bonbonnière** *(☎ 04 90 74 12 92; 57 rue de la Sous-Préfecture)*.

Special Events

Apt marks Ascension in May with a jazz festival and enjoys a **Fête de la Cerise** (Cherry Festival) in June. Its fabulous Cavalcade d'Apt in June has celebrated Pentecost since 1883 and climaxes with a grand evening ball.

Market Days

Fruit and vegetables fresh from the farm are sold at a *marché paysan* (farmers' market), held in the morning from May/June to October/November (relevant town names are in italics in the list below). Regular morning markets (town names that are not italicised) feature plenty of fresh produce too.

Monday – Cadenet, Cavaillon and Lauris
Tuesday – Apt, Cucuron, Gordes, Lacoste, St-Saturnin-lès-Apt and La Tour d'Aigues
Wednesday – Mérindol and Pertuis
Thursday – Ansouis, La Motte d'Aigues and La Tour d'Aigues
Friday – Bonnieux, Lourmarin, Pertuis and Roussillon
Saturday – Apt, Cadenet, Lauris, Manosque, Pertuis and Vaugines
Sunday – Coustellet, Vaugines and Villars

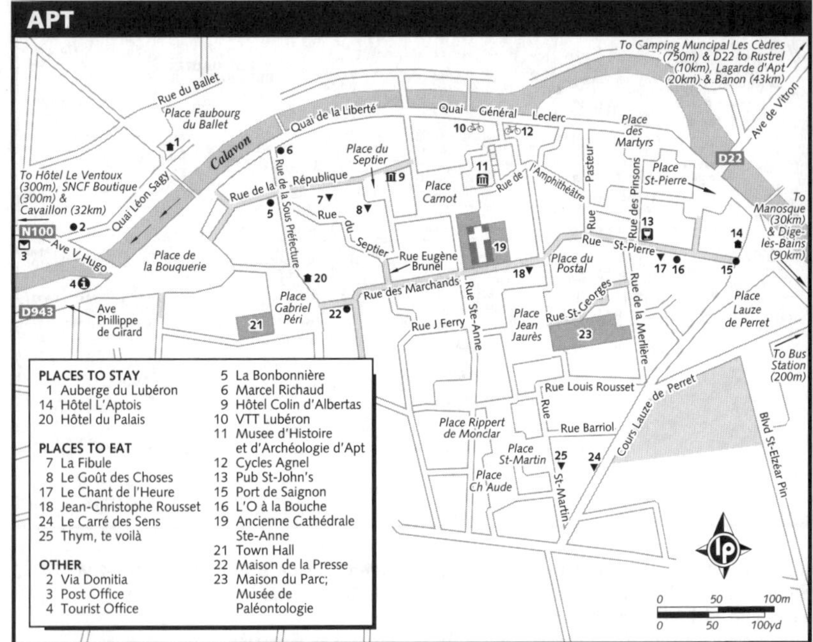

Places to Stay

Apt has no hostel but there are dorm beds in Buoux, Sivergues, Le Colombier (near Saignon) and Auribeau (see Le Grand Lubéron later in this chapter), all 6km to 8km south of Apt.

Camping Municipal Les Cèdres *(☎ 04 90 74 14 61; route de Rustrel; camping for 2 adults, tent & car €7.30; open mid-Feb–mid-Nov)* is by the river out of town on the D22.

Hôtel du Palais *(☎ 04 90 04 89 32, fax 04 90 04 71 81; place Gabriel Péri; doubles with washbasin €32, with shower €35, singles/doubles/triples/quads with shower & toilet €30/45/52/80)* is a welcoming pet-friendly place in the heart of old Apt.

Hôtel L'Aptois *(☎ 04 90 74 02 02, fax 04 90 74 64 79; W www.aptois.fr.st; doubles with washbasin €29, with shower & toilet €42.60)* is cyclist-friendly hotel belonging to the Vélo Loisir en Lubéron scheme. It rents bikes (but only to hotel guests) and tandems, prepares picnic hampers for cycling guests and provides a breakdown service.

Auberge du Lubéron *(☎ 04 90 74 12 50, fax 04 90 04 79 49; W www.auberge-luberon-peuzin.com; 8 place Faubourg du Ballet; doubles/triples €45/99; menus €26, €42 & €54)*, a cosy place on the opposite side of the river, is part of the Logis de France chain. Its restaurant is expensive but renowned.

Places to Eat

Place de la Bouquerie abounds with café and restaurant terraces in summer. Rue St-Pierre is another hot spot. The pavement terrace at **Pub St-John's** *(☎ 04 90 74 58 59; place St-Pierre)* is busy day and night.

Le Carré des Sens *(☎ 04 90 74 74 00; cours Lauze du Perret; menu €28, plat du jour €11, gourmet platters €8)* is unique. In a series of neoclassical buildings encircling a beautiful interior courtyard, the 'Square of Senses' comprises the Carré Gourmand restaurant; the less formal L'Orangeraie where you can have a light lunch, coffee or aperitif; and the elegant Bistro à Vins wine bar where you can taste regional wines and enjoy *assiettes gourmands* (gourmet platters).

Thym, te voilà *(☎ 04 90 74 28 25; 59 rue St-Martin)*, a lovely little tea room, with an inviting open kitchen, rustic-inspired decor and oodles of charm. Refreshing cold soups, ice cream and milkshakes are on its menu.

Parc Naturel Régional du Lubéron

The 1200-sq-km Lubéron Regional Park, created in 1977 and recognised as a Biosphere Reserve by Unesco in 1997, encompasses 67 villages (population 155,000), desolate forests and unexpected gorges. The GR6, GR9, GR92 and GR97 walking trails all cross it, as does a 230km-long cycling route (see the boxed text 'Lubéron by Bike'). For amblers, there are short thematic paths with information panels – a botanical trail through the park's oldest cedar forest (Bonnieux); a trail around ochre cliffs (Roussillon); and a *bories* discovery path (Viens). See the relevant sections in this chapter for details.

Information and maps can be picked up at the **Maison du Parc** *(☎ 04 90 04 42 00, fax 04 90 04 81 15; W www.parcduluberon.org; 60 place Jean Jaurès; open 8.30am-noon & 1.30pm-6pm Mon-Fri)*. From March to June, those not keen to go it alone can join a free organised nature workshop conducted in French (advance reservations only). The eagle owl, wild boar, bonelli eagle and etruscan honeysuckle are some of species you will learn about – and maybe see.

Guides sold at the Maison du Parc and the **Maison de la Presse** *(☎ 04 90 74 23 52; 28 rue des Marchands)* include topoguide *Le Parc du Lubéron à pied* (PN07), detailing 24 walks including the GR trails (available in English); and the topoguide *Walks in Provence* (PN04), which outlines 24 shorter walks (3km to 20km) and includes panels on the park's flora, fauna, ochre production and so on.

Le Goût des Choses *(☎ 04 90 74 27 97; 3 place du Septier)*, a rustic, unpretentious tea-room and *saladerie* (salad house) in a court-yard wrapped around a small fountain, is a fine place for lunch in the shade.

La Fibule *(☎ 04 90 74 05 29; 28 rue de la République)* is a Moroccan place serving spicy *tajines* and couscous in a warm, ochre-painted interior. Evening reservations are essential.

Jean-Christophe Rousset *(196 rue des Marchands)* is a cake shop and tea room where you can sample Apt treats such as crystallised figs and cherry or lavender ice cream.

The Saturday morning market on rue St-Pierre and the Tuesday farmers' market (see the boxed text 'Market Days' earlier in this chapter) are perfect for shopping for goat cheese, truffles (seasonal), marinated olives, fruit and vegetables. Otherwise, try **L'O à la Bouche** *(☎ 04 90 74 19 45; 98 rue St-Pierre)*; **Via Domitia** *(☎ 04 90 74 40 69; 19 quai Léon Sagy)* or **La Galerie du Carré** inside Le Carré des Sens – a trio of *épiceries fines* (upmarket grocery shops).

Getting There & Away

Apt's train station is no longer in use but tickets can be bought at the **SNCF boutique** *(☎ 04 90 74 00 85; 26 blvd Victor Hugo; open 8.30am-5.50pm Mon-Fri, 8.30am-4.50pm Sat)*, in the old station building.

Buses leave from the **bus station** *(☎ 04 90 74 20 21; 250 ave de la Libération)*, east of the centre. Daily bus services include buses to/from Avignon (€6.70, 1¼ hours, five daily) via Coustellet (€3.10, 40 minutes) and Cavaillon (€4.40, 50 minutes); Digne-les-Bains (€9.45, two hours); and Manosque (€6.40, one hour, twice daily). Twice-daily buses between Apt and Marseilles (€8.45, 2½ hours) stop in Bonnieux, Lourmarin, Cadenet, Pertuis and Aix-en-Provence.

Getting Around

Cycles Agnel *(☎ 04 90 74 17 16; 86 quai Général Leclerc; open 8.30am-noon & 2.15pm-7pm Tues-Fri, 8.30am-12.15pm & 2.15pm-5.30pm Sat)* hires mountain or road bikes per half-day/day/week for €8/13.50/76.50. Posters advertising group rides organised by local cycling club **VTT Lubéron** *(☎/fax 04 90 74 62 02; 62 quai Général Leclerc; open 8am-noon Tues & Thur-Sat)* plaster its windows.

AROUND APT

From Apt a good day trip is to head northwest to Roussillon, Gordes and the Abbaye de Sénanque – three of Provence's hottest tourist spots – and return via the pretty villages of **Joucas** (population 321), **St-Saturnin-lès-Apt** (population 2393) and hill-top **Villars** (population 700).

Heading in the opposite direction, Provence's very own Colorado makes for a colourful day trip. Alternatively, go walking with a donkey with **Association Vivre** *(☎/fax 04 90 75 12 49; Hameau Le Jas)*, a farm where you can hire donkeys to ride or bear the load for €5/8/20/35 per 30 minutes/hour/half-day/day. Bear 10km east along the N100 and after the first left-hand turning for St-Martin de Castillon, turn left towards Le Jas.

Roussillon

postcode 84220 • pop 1190 • elevation 360m

Some two millennia ago, the Romans used the distinctive ochre earth around Roussillon, set in the valley between the Plateau de Vaucluse and the Lubéron range, for producing pottery glazes. These days the whole village – even gravestones in the cemetery – is built of the reddish local stone. The red and orange hues are especially striking given the yellow-white bareness of the surrounding area and the green conifers sprinkled around town.

From the village, a 1km-long **Sentier des Ocres** *(Ochre Trail; adult/under 10 €2/free;*

Lubéron by Bike

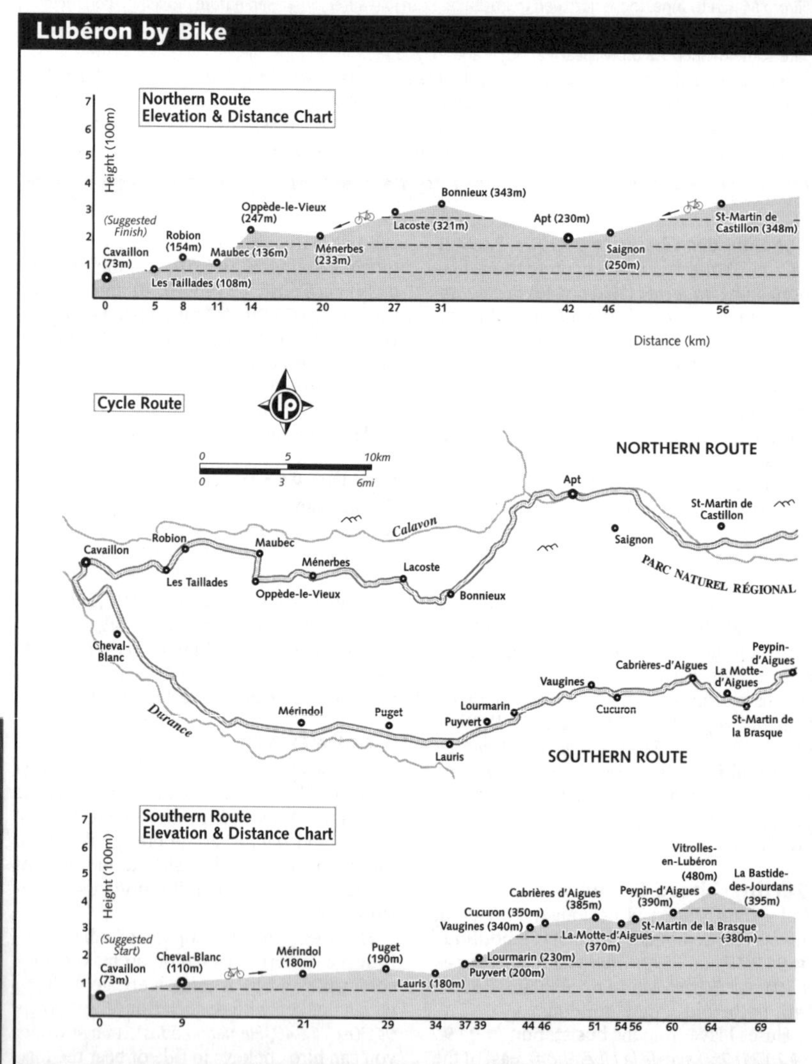

THE LUBÉRON

open 9am-7.30pm daily July & Aug; 10am-5.30pm daily Sept-mid–Nov & Mar-June; 9am-noon & 1pm-5pm Tues-Sun mid-Nov–Feb) leads you through fairytale groves of chestnuts, maritime pines and scrub to the bizarre and beautiful ochre formations created by erosion and winds over the centuries. Avoid wearing white: you'll return rust-coloured.

Workshops (some in English) exploring the colouring properties of ochre, first realised in the 18th century, are held at the **Conservatoire des Ocres et Pigments Appliqués** *(Applied Pigment & Ochre Conservatory; ☎/fax 04 90 05 66 69; ⓔ info@okhra.com; route d'Apt)*, on the D104 east towards Apt. Guided tours of the ochre conservatory depart four or five times daily, July to October, and once or twice monthly, the rest of the year.

The **tourist office** *(☎ 04 90 05 60 25, fax 04 90 05 63 31; ⓔ ot-roussillon@axit.fr; place de la*

Lubéron by Bike

Cyclists can cross the Parc Naturel Régional du Lubéron by following a circular 230km-long itinerary. Roads – steep in places – have little traffic and pass through many beautiful villages, vineyards and olive groves, lavender fields and fruit farms.

The northern route pedals cyclists 111km from Forcalqieur to Cavaillon via Apt, Bonnieux, Lacoste and Ménerbes; and the southern route links the two towns by way of Lourmarin, Vaugines, Cucuron and Manosque.

Hardened cyclists who enjoy a stiff climb should tackle the northern route east to west (signposted with white markers). Freewheelers should opt for the easier westbound route, which is marked by orange signs. For day-trippers already in Cavaillon, the 40km round-trip to Ménerbes and back again makes for an exhilarating bike ride.

Information boards posted along both routes provide details on accommodation, places to eat, and sights to see; as does **Vélo Loisir en Lubéron** *(☎ 04 92 79 05 82; Ⓦ www.veloloisirluberon.com; BP 14, F-04280 Céreste)*, which also has information on bicycle rental and technical support to saddle-sore cyclists.

Another cycling itinerary, Ocres en Lubéron, forms a 50km circle around the region's ochre fields: rocky-red Roussillon, Rustrel, Gargas, Apt and Villars. The Maison du Parc (see the boxed text 'Parc Naturel Régional du Lubéron' earlier in this chapter) has details.

Poste; open 9am-noon & 1.30pm-6.30pm Tues-Fri, 10am-noon & 2pm-5.30pm Mon & Sat) has accommodation details.

Roussillon, 9km east of Gordes, is inaccessible by public transport bar one bus to/from Apt (information ☎ 04 90 74 20 21) on Saturday morning. The GR6 footpath passes through Roussillon and you can rent bicycles from Camping Arc en Ciel (see Places to Stay later).

Gordes

postcode 84220 • pop 2127 • elevation 372m

On the white, rocky southern face of the Vaucluse plateau, the tiered village of Gordes, 20km west of Apt on the Lubéron slopes, forms an amphitheatre over the Rivers Sorgue and Calavon. The village is crowned by a sturdy 11th-century chateau, rebuilt in 1525. It houses art exhibitions and the **Musée Pol Mara** *(☎ 04 90 72 02 75; place du Château; adult/10-17 yrs €4.50/3; open 10am-noon & 2pm-6pm daily)*, with 200-odd paintings. The bright-blue piece of monumental art at the foot of the village is the creation of Hungarian sculptor Victor de Vasarely, an honorary citizen of Gordes since 1983.

This once typical Provençal village is overrun with tourists in summer but is still worth a wander. The **tourist office** *(☎ 04 90 72 02 75, fax 04 90 72 02 26; W www.gordes-village.com; place du Château; open 9am-noon & 2pm-6pm Mon-Sat, 10am-noon & 2pm-6pm Sun)*, inside the chateau, has plenty of information on places around Gordes.

South of Gordes, 3.5km along route de St-Pantaléon (D148) and just west of St-Pantaléon, is the **Moulin des Bouillons** *(☎ 04 90 72 22 11; adult/10-17 yrs €4.50/3, guided tour €3; open 10am-noon & 2pm-6pm Wed-Mon Apr-Oct)*, a preserved oil mill that can be visited. The 10m-long press weighs seven tonnes. The gastronomic thrill of locally milled olive oil (and some 200 wines) can be sampled at the Mas de Tourteron – see Places to Eat later in this section.

Buses, operated by Cavaillon-based **Les Express de la Durance** *(☎ 04 90 71 03 00)*, link Gordes with Cavaillon two to four times daily.

Village des Bories

The walled Village des Bories *(☎ 04 90 72 03 48; adult/10-17 yrs €5.50/3; open 9am-sunset daily)* is 4km southwest of Gordes off the D2 towards Cavaillon. *Bories* are one- or two-storey beehive-shaped huts constructed without mortar using thin wedges of limestone. They were first built in the area in the Bronze Age and were continuously lived in, renovated and even built anew until as late as the 18th century. It is not known what purpose they first served but over the centuries they were used as shelters, workshops, wine cellars and storage sheds. The 'village' contains about 20 such structures, restored to the way they were about 150 years ago.

Abbaye Notre-Dame de Sénanque

Some 4km northwest of Gordes off the D177 is the Cistercian Abbaye Notre-Dame de Sénanque *(☎ 04 90 72 05 72; W www.senanque.fr; adult/6-18 yrs €5/2; open 10am-noon & 2pm-6pm Mon-Sat, 2pm-6pm Sun Feb–mid-Nov; 2pm-5pm or 6pm daily mid-Nov–Jan)* which, in July, is framed by fields of lilac lavender. The abbey was founded in 1148 and today is inhabited by six young monks. Mass is celebrated at noon on weekdays and 9am Sunday.

St-Saturnin-lès-Apt

Rooftop views of St-Saturnin-lès-Apt, 9km north of Apt, and the surrounding Vaucluse hilltops can be enjoyed from the **17th-century windmill**, 1km north of the village off the D943 to Sault. Follow signs for Le Château Les Moulins.

Down in the village, you can shop for honey, lavender and truffles (when in season), taste wine round stone tables at the **Caveau des Aiguiers** *(37 ave Jean Geoffroy)*; and learn how olives are turned into oil (which costs about €15 per litre) at the **Moulin à Huile Jullien** *(☎ 04 90 75 45 80; 1 rue Albert Trouchet)*. The shop opens year round but the mill can only be visited during the olive harvest in November.

Rustrel & Around

The main reason for visiting Rustrel (population 621), 10km northeast of Apt, is to gaze in awe at the breathtaking rock formations of the **Colorado Provençal** (see the boxed text 'Provence's Colorado' later in this section). For aerial views, head for the paragliding school **Rustr'aile Colorado** *(☎ 04 40 04 96 53; W www.sud-parapente.com; Le Stade, 84400 Rustrel)*.

Provence's Colorado

Appearing unexpectedly in the Lubéron's neat patchwork of vineyards and fruit orchards is an extraordinary collection of rock formations known as the Colorado Provençal *(☎ 04 90 04 96 07; open 9am-dusk daily)*. The site is an old quarry in Rustrel, where ochre was mined from the 1880s until 1956, but what visitors see now is more like part of the Grand Canyon than a relic of an industrial past.

Although ochre has been used in the Lubéron since Roman times, it was not until 1785 that large deposits of the hydrated oxidised iron-and-clay sands were mined industrially. Traditionally used as a pigment to colour pots and buildings, ochre comes in some 25 shades, ranging from delicate yellow to vivid orange and fire red, colours that stain the interesting (and occasionally suggestive) rock formations. Men are known to stare wistfully at the **Cheminée de Fées** (literally 'Chimney of Fairies'), a fiery pillar that protrudes in all its erect magnificence from a savage landscape of red-ochre sand.

Many of these hues can be discovered first-hand along seven **short walking trails** that wind through the Colorado. The trails for two of the most dramatic – the **Sentier des Cheminées de Fées** (1km, 30 minutes) and the **Sentier du Sahara** (1.5km, 45 minutes) – start from the municipal car park in Bouvène, immediately south of Rustrel village along a narrow road signposted off the D22. Parking costs €2.50 and includes a free map detailing all seven walks.

The eastbound D22 and winding D33 links Rustrel with **Viens** (population 500), a good starting point for forays into the **Gorges d'Oppedettes**, a limestone canyon. From the northern end of the village, a circular footpath (4km, 1½ hours) marked with yellow blazes takes strollers past several *bories*. The GR4 passes through **Céreste** (population 1045, elevation 370m), 8km south. In Roman times the Via Domitia passed through the village of Céreste. Its **tourist office** *(☎ 04 92 79 09 84; place de la République; open 10am-6pm Mon-Fri, 10am-noon & 2pm-6pm Sat, 10am-noon Sun)* rents mountain bikes for €15/80 per day/week.

From Céreste the N100 pushes on east to Haute-Provence (see that chapter). Lavender fiends might want to access this neighbouring region via the northbound D14, a scenic road strung with purple in season (see the boxed text 'The Perfume of Provence' in the Avignon Area chapter for details). **Reillanne** village, 8km east of Céreste off the D14, has a couple of gorgeous places to stay and eat (see those sections later).

These villages are inaccessible by public transport – walking and cycling are invigorating alternatives.

Places to Stay

Camping Arc en Ciel *(☎ 04 90 05 73 96; route de Goult; adult/tent/car around €12.90/1.55/1.55; open mid-March–Oct)*, 5km south of Roussillon towards Goult, is a pretty site with plenty of green, natural charm and mountain bikes to rent.

Camping des Sources *(☎ 04 90 72 12 48, fax 04 90 72 09 43; route des Murs, Gordes; adult/tent/car low season €3.30/4/free, high season €4.30/5/free; open Mar-Oct)* is a large pool-clad site with four- to six-person mobile homes and chalets too.

Hôtel Aiguebelle *(☎ 04 92 79 00 09; place de la République, Céreste; singles/doubles with shower €31/34, with shower & toilet €46/48; menus €15, €23 & €30)* is a true village inn with a lovely restaurant. The grilled duck with lavender honey is worth the trip.

Le St-Hubert *(☎ 04 90 75 42 02; place de la Fraternité, St-Saturnin-lès-Apt; doubles/triples with shower & toilet €46/60)*, above a busy bar-cum-café, touts eight good-value rooms. Don't check in on Monday without a reservation – the bar is closed.

La Bastide de Gordes *(☎ 04 90 72 12 12, fax 04 90 72 05 20; W www.bastide-de-gordes.com; Gordes; doubles with village/valley view low season from €140/191, high season €155/209)* ranks among the region's most heavenly four-star pads.

Auberge de Reillanne *(☎/fax 04 92 76 45 95; Reillanne; singles/doubles €45/63-68; breakfast €7.50)*, down a gravel track off the D14 south of Reillanne, will charm the socks off the fussiest of guests. The stone manor has a rustic but luxurious interior, and is surrounded by green fields.

Places to Eat

In Roussillon, lunch on one of the many pavement terraces in the village or try the following places.

Micka's *(place de la Mairie)*, one of a clutch of cheapish places to eat on the town hall square, will teach you a thing or two about herbs – which grow around you on the terrace as you dine.

David *(☎ 04 90 05 60 13; place de la Poste; menus €21.40, €28 & €30.70)*, perched on an ochre cliff, dishes up sophisticated cuisine and a magnificent vineyard panorama.

Gordes' tastiest restaurants are in stone farmhouses a short drive from the village.

L'Estellan *(☎ 04 90 72 04 90; chemin des Escortiels; lunch/dinner menu €23/33)*, signposted off the D2 towards Cavaillon, is quiet, peaceful and full of natural charm.

Mas de Tourteron *(☎ 04 90 72 00 16; chemin de St-Blaise; menus €28 & €42)*, an upmarket choice, serves typical Provençal cuisine against a backdrop of opulent, flower-laden gardens.

Auberge Perry *(☎ 04 92 76 51 95; cnr N100 & D214 to Reillanne; lunch menu Mon-Thur €13, menus €16, €26, €23 & €35)* is beautifully placed in the countryside, east of Céreste. It's an atmospheric farmhouse with a rustic-inspired menu to match. Its *terrine de lapin aux pignons de pin* (rabbit terrine with pine kernels) will appease the most sophisticated of palates.

LE PETIT LUBÉRON

The rocky landscape of the 'little Lubéron' embraces the western part of the massif and is studded with *villages perchés*. These hilltop villages are perched aloft stony spurs and offer good views of the region's lower-lying treasures, including its thick cedar forests.

Côtes du Lubéron vineyards – covering 3500 hectares – line the southbound route de Bonnieux (D3) from Apt to Bonnieux; Bonnieux tourist office has a list of estates where you can taste and buy. The Lubéron's other nectar is honey. Try it and buy it at **Le Mas des Abeilles** *(☎ 04 90 74 29 55; ⓔ info@mas-des-abeilles.com)*, a farmhouse on the Col du Pointu (accessed via the D943, which runs parallel to the D3), on Bonnieux's northern fringe.

Bonnieux

postcode 84220 • pop 1436 • elevation 425m

Bonnieux, 11km southwest of Apt and 26km east of Cavaillon, is Le Petit Lubéron's best-known village. Eighty-six steps lead from place de la Liberté and rue de la Mairie to its 12th-century **Église Vieille du Haut**, host to some lovely classical music concerts in July. The history of bread-making is unravelled in the **Musée de la Boulangerie** *(☎ 04 90 75 88 34; 12 rue de la République)*, a former bakery.

From Bonnieux, the D36 to Buoux leads southwest to the **Forêt des Cèdres**, a protected cedar forest dating back to 1861. Part of its 250 hectares is crossed by a two-hour **Sentier Botanique** (botanical trail).

Pont Julien, 6km north of Bonnieux on the D149, is a three-arched Roman bridge built between 27 BC and AD 14. Five kilometres north of Bonnieux towards Goult on the D36 is **La Gare de Bonnieux**, home to the old village train station, an art gallery and the local wine cooperative **Caves des Vignerons de Bonnieux** *(☎ 04 90 75 80 03; ⓦ www.cave-bonnieux.com; open 9am-noon & 2.30pm-6pm Mon-Sat)* where you can fill up your plastic container with wine for €1/1.13 for a litre of red/rosé table wine. AOC wine costs upwards of €2.90 a bottle.

Bonnieux **tourist office** *(☎ 04 90 75 91 90, fax 04 90 75 92 94; ⓦ www.provenceguide.com; place Carnot; open 9.30am-12.30pm & 2pm-6.30pm Mon-Sat)* has information on the entire area. Nearby, **Mountain Bike Lubéron** *(☎ 04 90 75 89 96, 06 83 25 48 07; ⓦ www.mountainbikeluberon.com; rue Marceau)* rents road and mountain bikes for €14/23/74 per day/weekend/week, and delivers bikes within a 15km radius for free.

Buses to/from Apt and Marseilles stop in Bonnieux (see Getting There & Away in Apt earlier in this chapter).

Places to Stay There are dozens of luxurious *chambres d'hôtes* (bed and breakfast accommodation) around the village; the tourist office has a list.

Camping Municipal du Vallon *(☎/fax 04 90 75 86 14; route de Ménerbes; adult/tent/car €2.20/1.70/1.40; open 15 Mar-15 Nov)* is at the foot of the village, along the D3 to Lacoste.

Les Termes Blanches *(☎/fax 04 90 75 88 42; route de Ménerbes; dorm beds €17, half-board €30)* is a *gîte d'étape* (hiker's accommodation), 2km from Bonnieux along the westbound D3. Sleep in a bunk-bed dorm or – if you're lucky – in a two- to three-bed room. Breakfast is included.

Hôtel Le César *(☎ 04 90 75 96 35, fax 04 90 75 86 38; ⓦ www.hotel-cesar.com; place* *de la Liberté; singles/doubles with shower €31/38, with shower & balcony €46, with shower, toilet & terrace €70 or €92)* is Bonnieux's cheapest hotel.

Hostellerie du Prieuré *(☎ 04 90 75 80 78, fax 04 90 75 96 00; rue Jean Baptiste Aurard; doubles €65, €92 & €129; menu €30)* is in a beautiful 18th-century priory with a peaceful walled garden and a talented chef heading its treat-worthy restaurant.

Places to Eat A simple restaurant, **La Flambée** *(☎ 04 90 75 82 20; 2 place du 4 Septembre; menus €14.50 & €21)* is well worth frequenting for the stunning panorama that can be enjoyed from its 1st-floor terrace. Pizza (€7 to €11), truffles, game and goat-cheese bread get cooked up here.

Le Fournil *(The Bakehouse; ☎ 04 90 75 83 62; 5 place Carnot; lunch/dinner menu €24/34; open Tues evening-Sun)*, next to the tourist office, is a cut above the average village restaurant. Its interior is cut into a rock face with a trickling fountain in front. Provençal highlights served with a flourish include a tasty courgette *gâteau* (cake) garnished with tiny prawns, thyme-dressed shoulder of lamb, and *soupe de cerise au vin rouge* (cherry- and red-wine soup). Advance reservations are essential.

Restaurant de la Gare *(☎ 04 90 75 82 00; lunch/dinner menus from €11/20 & €23)* in La Gare de Bonnieux, 5km north along the D36 to Goult, serves delicious food and rents bicycles for guests to wobble around on in the countryside afterwards. Advance reservations are essential.

Auberge de l'Aiguebrun *(☎ 04 90 04 47 00, fax 04 90 04 47 01; doubles low season €120-180, high season €130-200; menu €45)* is a truly delightful *bastide* (country house) set in the remote and dramatic heart of the Combe de Lourmarin, 6km southeast of Bonnicux off the D943 towards Apt. Its restaurant is nothing short of exquisite.

Lacoste

postcode 84220 • pop 417 • elevation 320m

It was to 9th-century Château de Lacoste, 6.5km west of Bonnieux, that the notorious Marquis de Sade retreated in 1771 when his writings became too scandalous for Paris. His 45-room palace, once maintained by 20 servants, remained nothing more than an eerie ruin until 2002 when French designer Pierre Cardin stepped in. So captivated was the couturier with the stone pile that he bought it immediately – and transformed it into a theatre and opera stage. The month-long Festival de Lacoste, held each year around the still partially ruined chateau in July, is magnificent and rewards audiences – after a steep climb up – with unbeatable valley views.

Places to Stay & Eat At the foot of the village, **Café de Sade** *(☎ 04 90 75 82 29, fax 04 90 75 95 68; rue Basse; dorm beds €12.50, doubles with/without shower & toilet €46/42; menu du jour €12; open mid-Feb–Dec)* runs a *gîte d'étape* with 32 dorm beds. It also has basic doubles and a cheap restaurant set beneath a leafy trellis.

Hôtel de France *(☎ 04 90 75 82 25; doubles €30, with shower €37, with shower & toilet €45)*, in the village centre, is excellent value and has six simple but charming double rooms. The village visible from the terrace is Bonnieux.

Relais du Procureur *(☎ 04 90 75 82 28; rue Basse; doubles €80-137)* is an 11th-century manor with terrace and pool. Its restaurant, **Table du Procureur** *(☎ 04 90 75 84 78; mains around □15)* is Lacoste's upmarket dining choice.

Ménerbes

postcode 84560 • pop 1007 • elevation 230m

Continue 6km west of Lacoste on the D109 to Ménerbes, a pretty hill-top village marked firmly on the tourist trail by British novelist Peter Mayle, who lived here between 1986 and 1993. (His former *mas*, 2km southeast of the village on the D3 to Bonnieux, is the second house on the right after the football pitch.)

Sample local Côtes du Lubéron wine and stare agog at over 1000 different corkscrews at the **Musée du Tire-Bouchon** *(Corkscrew Museum; ☎ 04 90 72 41 58)*, in the chateau of Domaine de la Citadelle, at the village's western foot on the D3 to Cavaillon. The museum is the brainchild of Yves Rousset-Rouard, village mayor and former French MP who resides in the restored chateau at the top of Ménerbes. In the 1970s he produced films, notably the soft porn film *Emmanuelle* (1974).

Wholesome lunches and snacks are dished up on the flowery terrace of **Café du Progrès**

Sadism

The Marquis de Sade (1740–1814) was a complex character whose research into pleasure led to an eroticisation of pain. He was considered a sadist, hence the word. His sexually explicit novels – *120 Journées de Sodome* (120 Days of Sodom; 1785), *Justine* (1791) and *Juliette* (1798) – caused an outrage and were banned when published in the late 18th century. Equally shocking were the sex scandals surrounding de Sade's own life, 27 years of which were spent in prison.

De Sade spent parts of his childhood in Provence where his family had owned Château de Lacoste since 1627. Family members included the ancestors Hugues de Sade and his wife Laura, a lifelong muse for Italian poet Petrarch. At the age of 22, de Sade wed Parisian bourgeoisie Renée Pélagie de Montreuil, although marriage never tampered with his love for orgies. In 1771, following his ostracism by Parisian society for accosting and flagellating a woman who took him to court for rape, de Sade moved to Château de Lacoste with his wife and three children. He was later tried on charges of sodomy and attempted poisoning after indulging in a whipping session with four prostitutes and his manservant in Marseilles.

Château de Lacoste was looted by revolutionaries in 1789, and subsequently sold by de Sade who spent the last 11 years of his life in a mental asylum where he died, far from mad, aged 74. His works weren't freely published until after WWII.

(☎ *04 90 72 22 09; place Albert Roure)*, the tobacconist in the village centre.

Oppède-le-Vieux

postcode 84580 • pop 1246 • elevation 300m

Large car parks that are designated for the use of tourist traffic sit at the foot of Oppède-le-Vieux, 6km southwest of Ménerbes. This medieval village (located on a rocky outcrop) was abandoned around 1910 by the villagers who moved down the valley to the cultivated plains to earn their livings. A steep rocky path leads to the hillside **ruins**. The 16th- to 18th-century **church**, which is under constant restoration, hosts concerts during August and celebrates mass in honour of Oppède's patron saint (Saint Laurent) on 10 August.

From the car parks, signs lead you to the starting point for the **Sentier Vigneron d'Oppède**, a delightful 1½ hour winegrowers' trail through olive groves, cherry orchards and vineyards. Panels along the way tell you what grape varieties you are looking at, how to train a vine 'lyre' style etc. An explanatory brochure (in English) is doled out to motorists when they park (€2).

Oppède-les-Poulivets, the new village, is 1km north of Oppède-le-Vieux.

Coustellet

Coustellet, on noisy route de Gordes (N100) about 6km north of Oppède-les-Poulivets, is uninspiring beyond its **Musée de la Lavande** *(☎ 04 90 76 91 23; W www.museedelalavande.com; adult/under 15 €4/free; open 10am-noon & 2pm-6pm or 7pm Feb-Dec)*. The museum has stills used to extract the sweet-smelling scent, and a boutique selling lavender-scented products. Most informative is the short video (in English), which explains how the purple flower is harvested and distilled (see the boxed text 'The Perfume of Provence' in the Avignon Area chapter).

Thirsty travellers can fill up their water bottles with Côtes du Lubéron wine for around €1.50 per litre or table wine for no more than €1 per litre at the **Cave du Lubéron** *(☎ 04 90 76 90 01)*, at the southern end of Coustellet on the D2. The Sunday-morning **farmers' market** (see the boxed text 'Market Days' earlier in this chapter) takes place in the village centre, at the intersection of the N100 and the D2.

Cabrières d'Avignon & Lagnes

Cabrières d'Avignon (population 1431, elevation 167m), 5km north of Coustellet, was one of the Waldensian villages in the Lubéron to be destroyed in 1545 under the terms of the *Arrêt de Mérindol* (see Cavaillon to Cadenet later in this chapter). Troops stormed its 12th-century chateau (1182), which has since been restored and is privately owned.

The northern part of the village is shrouded in beautiful pine and cedar forests, crisscrossed with walking paths, and has picnic tables and a small amphitheatre made from the same dry stone as the region's *bories*. Herbs and flowers typical to this pocket of Provence are used to flavour delicious honey, made and sold at **Miel de Cabrières** *(☎ 04 90 76 83 52; chemin de la*

Pourtalette) in the village. Pass by here early in the morning in late June and you might just get to see what exactly is done with the nectar once it's been harvested.

Le Bistrot à Michel *(☎/fax 04 90 76 82 08; Cabrières d'Avignon; meals about €20; open Wed-Sun Oct-Dec & Feb-May; Wed-Mon June-Sept)* is a delightful restaurant, renowned for its excellent Provençal cuisine served in summer on a flower-filled terrace. Aperitifs come with a *confiture d'oignons* (sweet onion chutney) to die for. You should book tables days in advance.

Yellow-brick Lagnes (population 1509, elevation 110m), 5km west, offers little to do beyond strolling its cobbled streets and visiting occasional art exhibitions hosted in its *vieux lavoir* (old wash house) off place du Fontaine.

From Lagnes, **Voyages Arnaud** *(☎ 04 90 38 15 58)* operates three to four buses daily to/from L'Isle-sur-la-Sorgue (€3.20, 25 minutes) and Avignon (€4.40, 1¼ hours).

CAVAILLON

postcode 84300 • pop 25,058 • elevation 75m

Acting as the Lubéron's western gateway, Cavaillon is 28km southeast of Avignon. The market town is best known for its sweet melons, mountains of which are sold at the early morning Monday market in season, May to September. Melons abound during mid-July's Fête du Melon and the **tourist office** *(☎ 04 90 71 32 01, fax 04 90 71 42 99; e o.t.cavaillon@wanadoo.fr; place François Tourel; 3hr tour adult/under 12 €6/free; open 9am-12.30pm & 2pm-6.30pm Mon-Sat)* arranges melon-tasting tours.

Things to See & Do

An **arch** built by the Romans in the 1st century BC adorns place François Tourel, the square in front of the tourist office, at the western end of cours Bournissac, Cavaillon's main shopping street. Three blocks north is the 12th-century **Cathédrale St-Véran** with its fine Roman cloister. Cavaillon's beautiful **synagogue** (1772–74) and adjoining **Musée Juif Comtadin** *(Jewish Museum; ☎ 04 90 76 00 34; rue Hébraïque; adult/under 12 €3/free; open 9am-noon & 2pm-5pm Tues-Fri)*, inside the former bakery of the Jewish community, are also worth visiting.

What a Pest

The plague, brought to the region in 1720 aboard a ship from Asia, was such a terrible scourge that the king of France ordered a 1.5m-high dry stone wall to be built in 1721 to prevent the killer disease spreading further into Papal-controlled Comtat Venaissin.

About 6km of the **Mur de la Peste** (literally 'Wall of the Plague') remains standing today – in Cabrières d'Avignon, around Lagnes and in the Pays de Venasque (see that section in the Avignon Area chapter earlier).

Cheval-Blanc, 3km southeast of Cavaillon, is the starting point for walks into the majestic **Gorges du Régalon**. The gorges, up to 30m high and as narrow as 50cm in places, are protected by a geological nature reserve. A footpath leads from the car park in La Tuillie, 9km east of Cheval-Blanc off the D973.

The tourist office takes bookings for half-day guided walks in the Petit Lubéron with a guide from the Office National des Forêts de Cavaillon (National Forestry Office), departing on Tuesday, Wednesday and Thursday morning at 9.30am. Walks cost €5.50/free per adult/under 12.

Places to Stay & Eat

There are **camp sites** in Robion, 6km east of Cavaillon, and Maubec, 9km east.

Central hotels in Cavaillon include **Hôtel Le Provence** *(☎ 04 90 78 03 38; 9 cours Bournissac; doubles from €25)*, with nine doubles above a snack bar; and **Hôtel Le Forum** *(☎ 04 90 78 37 55; 68 place du Clos; singles/doubles €28/39)*, with 18 rooms.

Auzet Cavaillon *(☎ 04 90 78 06 54; 61 cours Bournissac)* bakes 15 types of bread (garlic, walnut, wholemeal, bran, rye and so on) plus exotic loaves like Roquefort, thyme and onion, which must be ordered in advance. The bakery has a sit-down café.

La Fin de Siècle *(☎ 04 90 71 12 27; 42-46 place du Clos; menus €14.50, €21.35 & €46)* is a popular brasserie dating from 1900. It has a lovely people-watching pavement terrace and a few hotel rooms.

Jean-Jacques Prévôt *(☎ 04 90 71 32 43; 353 ave de Verdun; lunch/dinner menus from €25/40)*, who is Cavaillon's best-known chef, adores melons. Throughout the melon season (mid-May–mid-Oct) he conjures up a fabulous melon-inspired *menu* (€70). Truffles (January and February), game (November and December) and asparagus (March and April) are other local products he honours with their own *menus*. Prévôt's €85 *menu carte blanche* is a series of really fabulous surprises.

Getting There & Away

From the bus stop beside the train station, there are daily bus services *(☎ 04 90 63 01 82)* to/from L'Isle-sur-la-Sorgue (€1.90, 15 minutes, three or four daily), Aix-en-Provence (€9.90, 1½ hours, three daily), Marseilles (€11.70, one hour, three daily) and Avignon (€3.10, one hour, five to 20 daily).

From the **train station** *(place de la Gare)*, at the eastern end of ave Maréchal Joffre, there are trains to/from Marseilles via Miramas (€11.20, 1½ hours, eight or so daily) and Avignon (€5.30, 30 minutes, seven daily).

Getting Around

The friendly and efficient **Cyclix Cavaillon** *(☎ 04 90 78 07 06; Ⓦ www.cyclix.fr.st; 166 cours Gambetta)* rents tandems for €28/50/140 per day/weekend/week and road bikes for €19/31/92.

CAVAILLON TO CADENET

Southeast of Cavaillon, the busy D973 skims the Lubéron's southern boundary, delineated by the River Durance and the valley it carves. Some 243 species of birds typical of the river-banks can be seen from the **Observatoire Ornithologique**, an ornithological centre run by the Parc Naturel Régional du Lubéron near the Mérindol-Mallemort dam. Spot herons and great cormorants in abundance along the 3km-long **bird sanctuary trail** (1½ hours) marked with yellow blazes.

Mérindol (population 1800, elevation 200m) itself, about 15km east of Cavaillon, was one of 11 Lubéron villages destroyed by troops under the terms of the Aix parliament's *Arrêt de Mérindol* bill in 1545 that condemned Vaudois heretics to death. The Vaudois (Waldenses) were a minority group who sought refuge in the Lubéron hills following the excommunication of their leader, Pierre Valdès, from the Church by Pope Lucius III in 1184. The Vaudois joined the Reformation in 1532, leading to their eventual massacre on the 19 and 20 April 1545. In Mérindol, surviving villagers later rebuilt their village lower down the hillside. All that remains of the original *castrum* (fort) – a couple of ruined walls at the top of the new village – guards a memorial to the 3000 Lubéron people murdered and a further 600 sent to the galleys. Their unfortunate history is unravelled in **La Muse** *(☎ 04 90 72 91 64; Ⓔ contact@routevaudoisluberon.com; 3 rue du Four)*, a Waldensian library and research centre.

The GR6 runs through Mérindol. Ask at the **tourist office** *(☎ 04 90 72 88 50, fax 04 90 72 90 06; Ⓔ ot-merindol@axit.fr; route du Four)* for information on walking and mountain-biking in the area.

Lauris (population 1800, elevation 200m), 10km farther east, has an 18th-century **chateau** surrounded by fine gardens and a church topped by a typical wrought-iron campanile. The **tourist office** *(☎ 04 90 08 39 30, fax 04 90 08 28 36; Ⓔ ot-lauris@axit.fr; Cour Nord du Château)* has details on open-air concerts, theatrical performances and the Hot Jazz Festival held around the chateau.

Wickerwork has been the mainstay industry of **Cadenet** (population 3937), 7km upstream (east), for centuries. The cultivation of osier (wicker) on the river banks and its exploitation is explored in the **Musée de la Vannerie** *(☎ 04 90 68 24 44; ave Philippe de Giraud; adult/12-18 yrs/under 12 €3/1.50/free)*. The little drummer boy, alias André Estienne (1777–1837), is Cadenet's other known product. A drummer in the Lubéron regiment from the age of 14, Estienne's ferocious drumbeat, assured victory for Napoleon I over the Austrians at Arcole (Italy) who thought it was gunfire, in 1796. A statue of **Le Tambour d'Arcole** (the drummer of Arcole) stands on place du Tambour and there are others in Paris. In 1804 Estienne was decorated with the Légion d'Honneur.

Six cycling itineraries from Cadenet can be picked up at the **tourist office** *(☎ 04 90 68 38 21, fax 04 90 68 24 49; Ⓔ ot-cadenet@axit.fr; 11 place du Tambour)*. The latter also rents wheels for €9.15/13.72/22.87 per half-day/day/weekend from its rental outlet at 3 rue Hoche.

Abbaye de Silvacane

Lovely Silvacane Abbey *(☎ 04 42 50 41 69; adults/students & under 26/under 17 €5.50/*

3.50/free; open 9am-6pm daily Apr-Sept; 10am-1pm & 2pm-5pm Wed-Mon Oct-Mar) is the third in the trio of the medieval Provençal abbeys built in an austere Romanesque style in the 12th century. It sits south of the Durance, 7km southeast of Cadenet. The Cistercian monks, responsible for the magnificent architectural creations, built Abbaye de Silvacane between 1175 and 1230. Work on the large refectory that joins the cloister's northern side did not begin until 1420. The abbey hosts various classical music concerts in summer – and year round three colonies of bats (several hundred in total) in its cloister!

Just 10km or so southeast of Silvacane is **Rognes**, renowned for its truffle market (see the Marseilles Area chapter).

LE GRAND LUBÉRON

The deep **Combe de Lourmarin**, which cuts through the massif in an almost perfect perpendicular from Bonnieux to Lourmarin, marks the great divide between Le Petit and Le Grand Lubéron. Dramatic gorges and grand fortresses are the trademarks of the 'Big' Lubéron.

Buoux

postcode 84480 • pop 117

Several kilometres northeast of Bonnieux and 8km south of Apt is Buoux, dominated by the splendid hill-top **ruins of Fort de Buoux** (550m). As a traditional Protestant stronghold, Buoux was destroyed in the 1545 Waldensian massacres and again in 1660. The fort and old village ruins, perilous in places due to loose rocks and so on, can be explored on foot. Painted white arrows mark an optional return route via a magnificent 'hidden' spiralling staircase cut in the rock.

Améthyste *(☎/fax 04 90 74 05 92; ⓔ amethyste1901@hotmail.fr; La Baume)* is a local climbing club that organises rock climbing, walks and nature activities.

Places to Stay & Eat An upmarket *gîte d'étape* in a stone building, **La Sparagoule** *(☎/fax 04 90 74 47 82; dorm bed €11.50, singles/doubles/triples/quads €26/35/46/57)* is just up the hill from Auberge de la Loube (see later) in the village. Breakfast costs an extra €4.50 and you can get a picnic/evening meal for €6/12.

Auberge des Seguins *(☎ 04 90 74 16 37, fax 04 90 74 03 26; dorm bed with half-board €30, doubles with shower/shower & toilet with half-board €38/43 per person; menus €20, €25.50 & €29; open Mar–mid-Nov)*, 2.5km from Buoux village, is a rambling *gîte d'étape* in the middle of nowhere (beneath cliffs in the Vallée de l'Aiguebrun to be precise) with an outdoor pool.

Auberge de la Loube *(☎/fax 04 90 74 19 58; lunch/dinner menu €21/27.50, with cheese €29.50; no credit cards)* is an atmospheric inn surrounded by flowers and a couple of horse-drawn carriages collected by Maurice, the chef and owner. The house speciality in season is *hors d'œuvres Provençaux de la Loube* – a wicker tray of Provençal treats such as tapenade, *anchoïade* (anchovy sauce), quail eggs, melon slices, cherry tomatoes and fresh figs.

Plateau de Claparèdes

Lavender fields carpet this plateau to form a purple oval between Buoux (west), Sivergues (south), Saignon (north) and Auribeau (east). Beyond cycling (see the boxed text

Lavender Trail

From **Buoux**, an invigorating cycling or driving route takes you north on the D113 to a set of crossroads straddled by lavender fields – blazing blue in July. From here, you can bear west along the D232 to Bonnieux; northeast to the hill-top village of **Saignon** and **Le Boisset** (from where you can link up with the N100); or east along the D48 to **Auribeau** (4.3km) and **Castellet** (7km). Otherwise you can continue on a northbound lavender trail to Apt.

After passing more lavender fields, the D113 climbs to **Les Agnels**, where lavender, cypress leaves and rosemary are distilled at the **Distillerie Agnel** *(☎ 04 90 74 22 72, route de Buoux)*. It dates from 1895 and can be visited by guided tour (three times daily July & Aug, three times daily Tues-Sun May, June & Sept).

Lavender lovers should not miss the **Musée de la Lavande**, 22km west of Apt, and its 80-hectare lavender farm, **Château du Bois** *(☎ 04 90 76 91 23)*, 25km north of Apt in Lagarde d'Apt. On the farm a 2km-long trail (signposted 'Parcours Lavande'), passes field upon field of purple lavender, abuzz with bees and aflutter with butterflies from late June until mid-July when the sweet-smelling flower is harvested.

'Lavender Trail' earlier) or walking, the star attraction of this flat pocket and its tiny hamlets is the incredible hostel-style accommodation it offers.

Auberge de Jeunesse Regain *(☎ 04 90 74 39 34, fax 04 90 74 50 94; Le Colombier; B&B in 3- to 9-bed dorm €14; open mid-Feb–mid-Jan)* is 6km southeast of Apt on a farm in Le Colombier. From Apt, follow the southbound D48 through Saignon, then turn right (west) onto the westbound D232 to Bonnieux. Dinner/sheets cost €9.20/3 and you can camp here for €4 a night.

Les Castelas *(☎/fax 04 90 74 60 89; Sivergues; dorm bed €15.50, doubles with shower & toilet €46; lunch/dinner menu €13/23.50; open Mar-Dec)* is a goat farm. Feast on fresh farm produce (the cheese is superb) but be prepared to taste all – there's one fixed *menu*.

Les Grottes *(☎ 04 90 74 09 59; Sivergues; dorm bed €18, including breakfast, doubles/quads with shower & toilet €48/83; open Easter-Nov)*, a *gîte d'étape*, commands great views of Mourre Nègre from its 17th-century farmhouse windows.

Auberge de Presbytère *(☎ 04 90 74 11 50, fax 04 90 04 68 51; ⓔ auberge.presbytere@provence-luberon.com; place de la Fontaine, Saignon; doubles €52-110)* is an inn with rooms and a terrace restaurant overlooking the village wash house.

Le Moulin des Fondons *(☎/fax 04 90 75 10 63; Auribeau; bed in 2- to 6-bed room €15.50, B&B €21, half-board €36)* is a three-room *gîte d'étape* in a former mill. It arranges horse riding, and walking opportunities are plentiful as it borders the GR92.

To get to all these places without a car or bicycle, use your feet or thumb.

Lourmarin

postcode 84160 • pop 1127 • elevation 230m

The main draw of Lourmarin, 6.5km south of Bonnieux and another massacre victim of 1545, is its Renaissance **chateau** *(☎ 04 90 68 15 23; adult/student/10-18 yrs €5/3/2.50; guided visits every 30 min 10am-11.30am & 3pm-6pm July & Aug; 4 to 6 times daily Oct-Dec, Feb-June & Sept)*. The **tourist office** *(☎/fax 04 90 68 10 77; 9 ave Philippe de Giraud; open 9.30am-1pm & 3pm-7pm Mon-Sat, 9.30am-noon Sun)* has information on castle classical music concerts.

Nobel Prize winning writer Albert Camus (1913–60) and his wife are buried in the village cemetery; his tombstone is planted with rosemary, hers with lavender. In recent years, Lourmarin gained fame as the setting for French car manufacturer Renault's 'Papa! Nicole!' Clio TV commercials and as the adopted home of British novelist Peter Mayle.

Moulin de Lourmarin *(☎ 04 90 68 06 69, fax 04 90 68 31 76; ⓦ www.moulindelourmarin.com; doubles €190-655)*, back in Lourmarin, is a grandiose place with rooms in a restored 18th-century oil mill.

Vaugines & Cucuron

From Lourmarin the D56 follows the GR97 footpath 5km east to Vaugines (population 469), the village where parts of Claude Berri's Pagnol films *Manon des Sources* and *Jean de Florette* (1986) were shot. Take one look at the giant horse-chestnut tree and fabulous moss-covered fountain that fills central place de la Fontaine and you'll understand why.

Cucuron (population 1792, elevation 350m), 2km farther east, is the starting point for walks up **Mourre Nègre** (1125m). The **tourist office** *(☎ 04 90 77 28 37, fax 04 90 77 17 00; ⓔ ot.cucuron@axit.fr; rue Léonce Brieugne; open 9am-12.15pm & 2pm-6.30pm Mon-Sat)* sells maps and walking and cycling guides.

Pays d'Aigues

Many consider rugged Pays d'Aigues the last remaining stronghold in Lubéron yet to be colonised by *résidence secondaire* (second-home) owners. The **Étang de la Bonde**, a lake with a beach 3km south of Cabrières d'Aigues on the D9, is one of the few spots to swim and sunbathe.

In **Ansouis** (population 1057), **Château d'Ansouis** *(☎ 04 90 09 82 70; adult/student/child €6/4.50/3; open 2.30pm-6pm Sun Nov-Easter; 2.30p-6pm Wed-Mon Easter-June & Oct; 2.30pm-6pm daily July-Sept)* remains inhabited by the original de Sabran family but can be visited by guided tour. Classical music concerts are held in its manicured gardens in August.

Eccentrics will adore Ansouis' **Musée Extraordinaire** *(☎ 04 90 09 82 64; open 2pm-6pm or 7pm daily)*, set up by Marseilles-born painter and diver Georges Mazoyer, whose passion for the sea is reflected in the museum's fossilised exhibits.

La Tour d'Aigues (population 4010, 270m), 10km farther east, is dominated by the Renaissance **Château de Tour d'Aigues** *(☎ 04 90 07 50 33; W www.chateau-latourdaigues.com; adult/student €4.50/2; open 9.30am-noon & 2pm-6pm Wed-Fri, 2pm-6pm Sat & Sun, 9.30am-noon Tues)*. Visits of the 12th- to 15th-century castle take in temporary exhibitions and a **Musée des Faïences**, full of 18th-century earthenware. Concerts are held in its court of honour. **Sud Lubéron Tourisme** *(☎ 04 90 07 30 00, fax 04 90 07 59 72; W www.provence-luberon.net)*, in the chateau, provides tourist information and organises gastronomic, walking and cycling trips.

MANOSQUE

postcode 04100 • pop 20,309
• elevation 387m

Manosque is a perfect stepping stone between toy-town Lubéron and its wilder eastern neighbour (Haute Provence). Provençal writer Jean Giono (1895–1970) was born and bred here, and has an arts centre dedicated to him. **Mont d'Or**, meaning 'mount of gold', immediately north, offers good views of the town's red rooftops and Lubéron hills beyond, and there are unparalleled panoramic views from **Mont Foron** (600m), 10km west.

Cycling routes are mapped on a board in front of the **tourist office** *(☎ 04 92 72 16 00, fax 04 92 72 58 98; W www.ville-manosque.fr; place du Docteur Joubert; open 9am-12.15pm & 1.30pm-6.30pm Mon-Sat, 10am-noon Sun)*.

Manosque has an **Auberge de Jeunesse** *(☎ 04 92 87 57 44, fax 04 92 72 43 91; ave de l'Argile, Parc de la Rochette; dorm beds adult/child €8/4; open Feb-Nov)*, 1km west from the centre; and a couple of cheap hotels.

Hostellerie de la Fuste *(☎ 04 92 72 05 95, fax 04 92 72 92 93; e lafuste@aol.com; route d'Oraison; doubles €115-150)*, inside a 17th-century manor, 6km east on the D4, is the most prestigious place to eat and sleep.

Getting There & Away

The **bus station** *(☎ 04 92 87 55 99; blvd Charles de Gaulle)* is 500m from the centre. Exit the station, turn left on blvd Charles de Gaulle, then right to ave Jean Giono. Buses are run by the **Société des Cars Alpes Littoral** *(☎ 04 92 51 06 05)* and **Digne-based Société des Autocars Dignois** *(☎ 04 92 31 50 00)*. About 10 daily buses go to/from Marseilles (€8.30, 1½ hours) via Aix-en-Provence.

From the **train station** *(place Frédéric Mistral)*, 2km south of the centre, there are six daily trains to/from Marseilles (€13.50, 1¼ hours) and Sisteron (€7.40, one hour).

Haute-Provence

Haute-Provence is Provence at its rawest. Mass tourism has yet to touch these mountainous 'Alpes d'Azur', and peace, tranquillity and isolation are not hard to find. The splendid snowcapped peaks of the southern Alps dominate the north, while its southeastern valleys are sprinkled with hill-top villages, where the tempo of life has barely shifted gear since medieval times. Southwest lies the land of lakes, gorges and Europe's grandest canyon. Lavender is a purple trait of the lower-lying Plateau de Valensole, on the left bank of the River Durance, which skirts the region's western side.

A large part of Alpes-de-Haute-Provence *département* (department) is protected by the Parc National du Mercantour. Spread-eagled in an arc along the French-Italian border, it is Provence's largest national park and offers a rich variety of outdoor activities – walking, cycling, climbing and white-water rafting in summer, snow-trekking and skiing in winter.

The Monte Carlo Rally tears round Haute-Provence's overdose of hairpin bends in January. Part of the region is also crossed by an enchanting narrow-gauge railway, and a steam train huffs and puffs along a small section of it. Exploring is tough without your own wheels and a sturdy set of walking boots.

Highlights

- Discover Europe's grandest gorges – on foot, by canoe or by bicycle; watch vultures in Rougon or go wolf-watching in the Vallée de la Tinée
- Take a ride into the wild side of Provence with Digne-les-Bains' mountain railway – stunning views guaranteed!
- Track down prehistoric rock drawings in the Réserve Géologique de Haute-Provence
- Sniff Provence's perfumes at Salagon priory or sniff out the region's tasty goat cheese in Banon
- Scale new heights – cross Europe's highest bridge, Pont de l'Artuby (182m) and highest mountain pass, the Col de Restefond la Bonette (2802m)

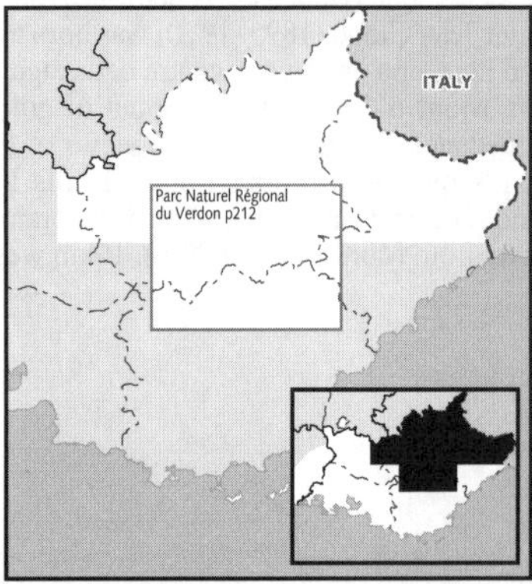

Food Highlights

banon – goat cheese wrapped in a chestnut leaf

olive oil – AOC Haute-Provence

secca de bœuf – mountain-dried beef

GORGES DU VERDON

The georgeous 25km of the Gorges du Verdon – Europe's largest canyon – slice through the limestone plateau midway between Avignon and Nice on Haute-Provence's southernmost fringe. The gorges actually begin at Rougon – near the confluence of the Rivers Verdon and Jabron – and continue until the Verdon River flows into Lac de Ste-Croix. Castellane (northeast) and Moustiers Ste-Marie (west) are the main gateways into the region's most fabulous sight.

Since 1997 the Parc Naturel Régional du Verdon has protected the 250m- to 700m-deep gorges, carved by the green waters of the River Verdon. The gorges are 8m to 90m wide at the bottom and the rims are 200m to 1500m apart. It is the water's unusually high fluorine content that gives the river its magnificent green colour.

Information

Tourist Offices The tourist offices in **Castellane** (*☎ 04 92 83 61 14, fax 04 92 83 76 89; W www.castellane.org; rue Nationale; open 9am-12.30pm & 2pm-7pm Mon-Sat, 10am-12.30pm Sun*) and **Moustiers Ste-Marie** (*☎ 04 92 74 67 84, fax 04 92 74 60 65; e moustiers@wanadoo.fr; rue de la Bourgade;*

open 10am-12.30pm & 2pm-7.30pm daily) organise excursions into the gorges and stock information on outdoor activities.

The Canyon

The bottom of the gorges can be visited on foot or by raft. Motorists and cyclists can enjoy spectacular views from two cliff-side roads that link Moustiers Ste-Marie and Castellane.

The **route des Crêtes** (the D952 and D23) follows the northern rim and passes the **Point Sublime** viewing point at the canyon's entrance, from where the GR4 walking trail leads to the bottom of the canyon. At its eastern end, the steep and narrow D317 climbs 3km to the quaint village of **Rougon** (population 85, elevation 963m).

The **Corniche Sublime** (the D19 to the D71) skims the southern rim and takes you to such landmarks as **Balcons de la Mescla** (Mescla Terraces) and **Pont de l'Artuby**, Europe's highest bridge (182m).

A complete circuit of the Gorges du Verdon involves about 140km of relentless driving along winding roads. The only real village en route is **La Palud-sur-Verdon** (population 300, elevation 930m), 2km northeast of the northern bank of the gorges. The **Maison des Gorges du Verdon** *(☎/fax 04 92 77 32 02)*, inside a 17th-century chateau, hosts exhibitions on gorge flora, fauna and geology, and organises guided walks in the gorges, among other things.

The bottom of the canyon, which was first explored in its entirety in 1905, presents walkers and white-water rafters with an overwhelming series of cliffs and narrows to negotiate. You can walk most of it along the often-difficult GR4, a route covered by Didier-Richard's 1:50,000-scale map No 19, *Haute-Provence-Verdon*. The full GR4 takes two days to complete, though short descents into the canyon are possible from a number of points. Bring a torch (flashlight) and drinking water. Camping on gravel beaches along the way is illegal.

The water level of the river in the upper part of the canyon can rise suddenly if France's electricity company, Électricité de France (EDF), opens the hydroelectric dams upstream, making it difficult, if not impossible, to cross the river. Check water levels and weather forecasts with the tourist office before you set out.

Starry Starry Night

In July and August during the Nuits du Cinéma en Plein Air, films are shown at least once a week on giant screens beneath the stars in a clutch of villages across the region, including Annot, Allemagne-en-Provence, Banon, Castellane, Forcalquier and Moustiers Ste-Marie. A particularly breathtaking venue is the Centre d'Astronomie, up high near St-Michel l'Observatoire. Films start at 9.30pm and admission costs €4. Programme details are available online at W www.cinepays.fr.st. Alternatively, call festival organiser **Le Cinéma de Pays** *(☎ 08 92 61 05 79, 04 92 72 97 81; e cinepays@wanadoo.fr)*.

Castellane

postcode 04120 • pop 1539 • elevation 730m

Small-town Castellane is unmomentous beyond its favoured status as the starting point for expeditions into the gorges. The central place Marcel Sauvaire and adjoining place de l'Église shelter several hotels and white-water sports shops.

The **Musée Sirènes et Fossiles** *(☎ 04 92 83 19 23; e sirenes@club-internet.fr; place Marcel Sauvaire; adult/7-15 yrs €3.85/2.75; open 10am-1pm & 2pm-6pm daily May-Sept, open 9am-noon & 2pm-6pm Mon-Fri Apr & Oct)* combines mermaid mythology with fossils. The **Musée de la Résistance** *(☎ 04 92 83 78 25; route de Digne; adult/12-18 yrs/under 12 €3/1.50/free; open 9am-7.30pm daily Apr-Sept, by appointment only rest of year)* is dedicated to the Resistance's war-time heroics.

Peering down on Castellane from its 180m-high perch is the **Chapelle Notre Dame du Roc**, dating from 1703 and precariously built on a needle-shaped rock. A 45-minute walking trail leads from place de l'Église to the chapel. Each year on 15 August (Assumption Day), pilgrims process by torch-light up to the rock to celebrate Mass.

Moustiers Ste-Marie

postcode 04360 • pop 635 • elevation 634m

Pretty Moustiers Ste-Marie is a quaint crop of houses nestled on a rocky shelf beneath a backdrop of two towering cliffs. A 227m-long gold chain bearing a star hangs between the rocks – suspended, so legend claims, by a brave knight who, after being imprisoned by Saracens during a crusade, vowed to hang

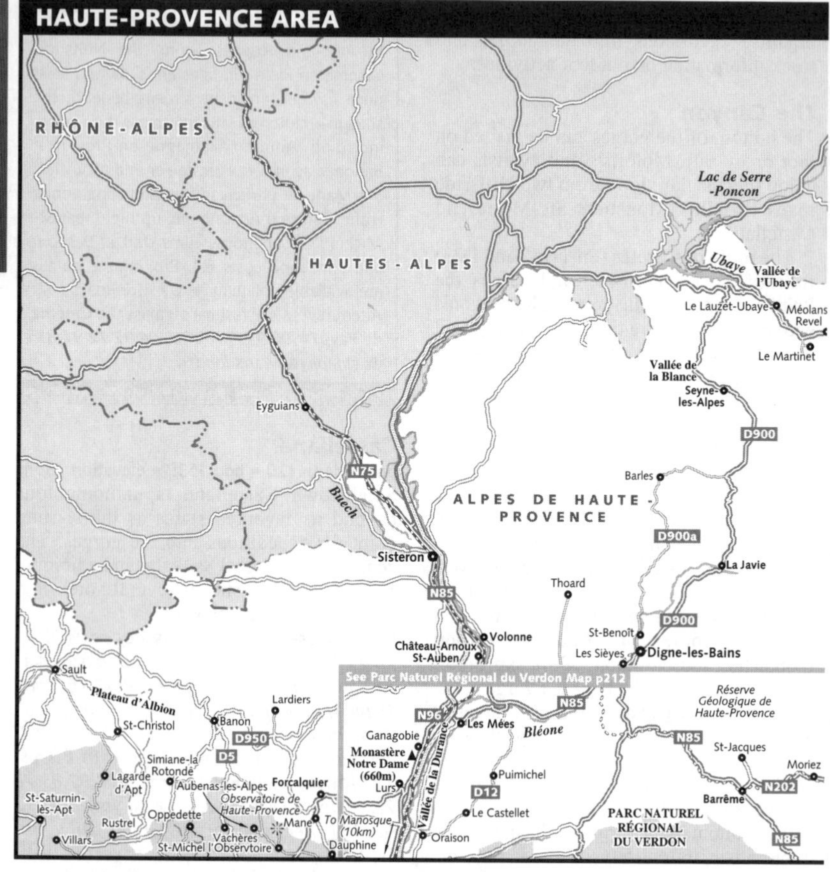

up a star should he return home. The 12th-century **Chapelle Notre Dame de Beauvoir**, with its waterfall, is perched on a ledge on one of the limestone cliffs. A steep trail leads up from rue Bourgade, passing 14 stations of the cross en route; count on at least about 30 minutes' climbing.

In the 17th century, Moustiers earned itself European recognition for its decorative Provençal *faïence* (earthenware), a tradition that is kept alive today by potters who turn out tourist souvenirs rather than more artistic masterpieces. The latter can be admired in the **Musée de la Faïence** (*☎ 04 92 74 61 64; rue Bourgade; adult/16-18 yrs/under 16 €2/1/free; open 9am-noon & 2pm-6pm Wed-Mon Apr-June, Sept & Oct; 9am-noon & 2pm-7pm Wed-Mon July & Aug*).

Activities

Most water-sport centres have a base in Castellane and a website outlining their deals, all of which are pretty similar and include a guide: half-/full-day **rafting** (€30/70) and **canyoning** (€45/65) expeditions, **hot-dogging** – bombing down the river in an inflatable canoe (€30) – and **hydrospeed** trips – with a bodyboard – (€45). Adventurous cyclists can try **water-rambling** with mountain bikes (€10/20 per half-/full day). Trips run from April to September and must be booked in advance.

Outlets providing water-sports actvities are plentiful and include **Aboard Rafting** (*☎/fax 04 92 83 76 11; W www.aboard-rafting.com; 8 place Marcel Sauvaire*), which also has mountain bikes to rent; **Aqua Viva Est**

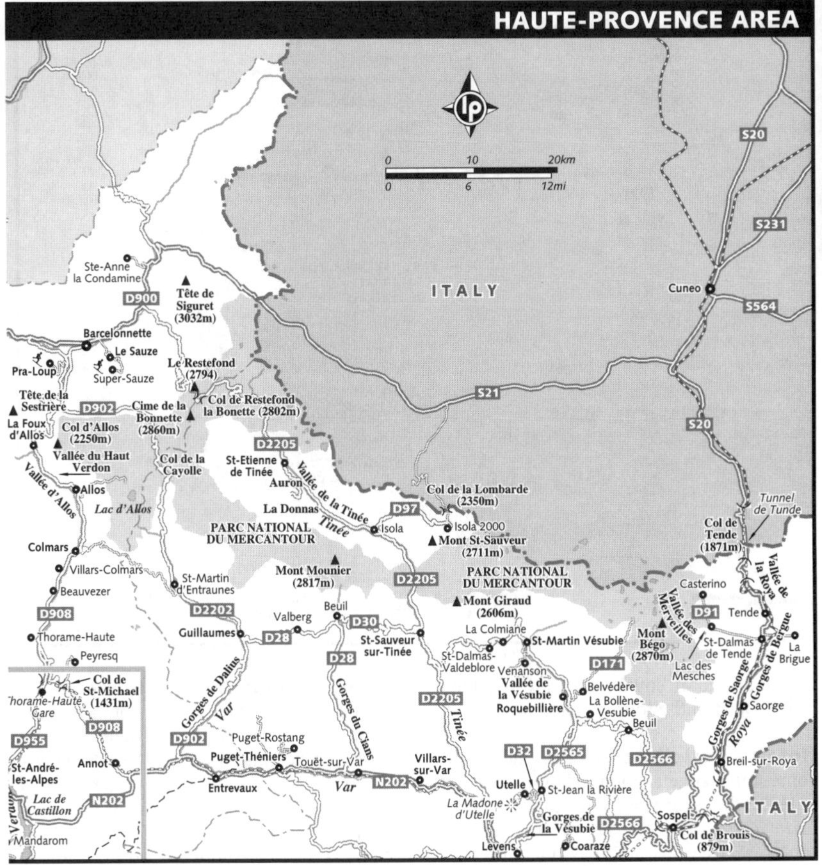

(☎/fax 04 92 83 75 74; W *www.aquavivaest.com; 12 blvd de la République*); **Montagne & Rivière** (☎/fax 04 92 83 67 24; W *www.rafting-castellane.com; 20 rue Nationale*); **Action Adventure** (☎ *04 92 83 79 39;* W *www.action-adventure.com; 12 rue Nationale*); **Aqua Verdon** (☎ *04 92 83 72 75;* W *www.aquaverdon.com; 9 rue Nationale*); and **Acti-Raft** (☎ *04 92 83 76 64;* W *http://actiraft.com; route des Gorges du Verdon*).

Discovering the gorges on horseback is another option. Contact **La Ferme Équestre du Pesquier** (☎ *04 92 83 63 94;* W *www.cheval-verdon.com; route de Digne*) in Castellane.

Places to Stay

Camping Along the approach to Castellane, the river is lined with some 15 crowded and pricey seasonal camp sites. Count on paying at least €12 for two adults with a tent and car.

Gîte d'Étape Nine kilometres from Castellane, in La Baume, is **Gîte de la Baume** (☎/fax *04 92 83 70 82;* W *www.gite-de-la-baume.com; dorm bed & breakfast €15, picnic/dinner €7/14, double room with breakfast €48, half-board in double room €74 per person*). Dorm beds are in two- or four-bed rooms and B&B is in a separate house.

Chambres d'Hôtes Pays du Verdon offers ample B&B options – ask at the tourist office.

Gîte de Chasteuil (☎/fax *04 92 83 72 45; www.gitedechasteuil.com; Hameau de Chasteuil; singles/doubles/triples with breakfast €39/48/62.50*), in the 16th-century village of

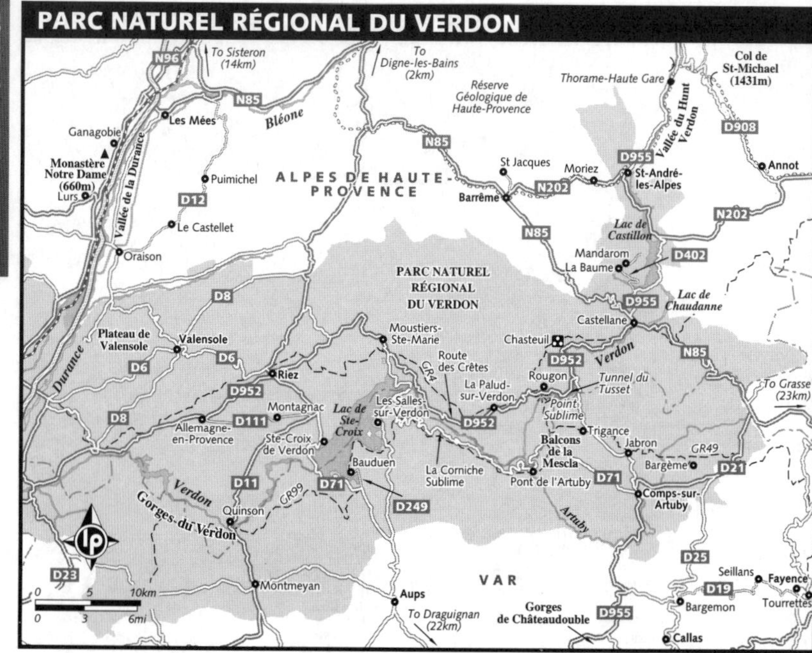

Chasteuil, 8km southwest of Castellane, offers B&B in the former schoolhouse.

Hotels – Castellane You can find wholesome, mid-range accommodation here.

Hôtel du Levant *(☎ 04 92 83 60 05, fax 04 92 83 72 14; place Marcel Sauvaire; doubles/triples/quads €40/71/75)* is an impressive pile with particularly good-value doubles.

Auberge du Bon Accueil *(☎/fax 04 92 83 62 01; place Marcel Sauvaire; doubles/triples/quads €45/56/65, 2-/4-person studios from €31/65, menus €14 & €22)* is another solid choice with a cheap(ish) restaurant.

Ma Petite Auberge *(☎ 04 92 83 62 06, fax 04 92 83 68 49; e mapetite.auberge@libertysurf.fr; rue de la République; singles/doubles/triples/quads €49/49/56/64)* teeters on the edge of being upmarket and is Castellane's most stylish joint.

Auberge au Point Sublime *(☎ 04 92 83 60 35, fax 04 92 83 74 31; e point-sublime@wanadoo.fr; La Palud-sur-Verdon; doubles from €45; open Mar-Oct)*, a roadside inn with 14 rooms at the foot of the D317 route to Rougon, is a delightful place to sleep and eat.

Hotels – Moustiers Ste-Marie In the village there are three pricey hotels that fill up fast; the tourist office has details.

La Clos des Iris *(☎ 04 92 74 63 46, fax 04 92 74 63 59; e closdesiris@wanadoo.fr; chemin de Quinson; doubles €60)*, down the same country lane as La Bastide (see the next entry), is a blue-shuttered house with an untamed flowery garden dotted with blue-tiled tables.

La Bastide de Moustiers *(☎ 04 92 70 47 47, fax 04 92 70 47 48; w www.bastide-moustiers.com; chemin de Quinson; doubles €145-250)* is run by French chef Alain Ducasse, off the northbound route de Riez (the D952). The Red Poppy Room in the 17th-century country house has a Starck-designed bathtub.

Places to Eat

For a cuisine so Provençal that even Frédéric Mistral would be truly proud, head for the **Restaurant du Commerce** *(☎ 04 92 83 61 00; place de l'Église, Castellane; menus €20 & €27)*.

Le Mur d'Abeilles *(☎ 04 92 83 76 33; e murabeille@wanadoo.fr; Rougon; pancakes €4-7.50)*, close to the Point Sublime at the gorge's eastern end, is worth the steep climb. The *crêperie* serves sweet and savoury pancakes on a terrace boasting views to kill. Taste and buy honey here – fresh from the hives embedded in the wall.

Les Santons de Moustiers *(☎ 04 92 74 66 48; place de l'Église, Moustiers Ste-Marie; menus €26, €39 & €53)*, firmly planted on the tourist trail, is tasty nonetheless. Try for a table above the moss-covered waterfall.

La Ferme Ste-Cécile *(☎ 04 92 74 64 18; quartier St-Michel, Moustiers Ste-Marie; lunch menu €20)* oozes charm. Fresh fish with garlic ice-cream is among the unexpected, delicious culinary surprises to be enjoyed at this authentic *ferme auberge* (farmhouse restaurant).

Getting There & Away

Bus Public transport is limited. **Autocars Sumian** *(☎ 04 42 67 60 34)* runs weekly buses from Marseilles to Castellane via Aix-en-Provence, La Palud-sur-Verdon and Moustiers. **VFD** *(☎ 04 93 85 24 56)* operates a daily bus from Grenoble to Nice via Digne-les-Bains and Grasse, stopping in Castellane en route. Tourist offices in Castellane and Moustiers have schedules.

LACS DU VERDON

The Verdon lakes – dams created by the national electricity company – are a spectacular, sparkling green.

Lac de Ste-Croix

Pretty **Bauduen** (population 276) sits on the southeastern banks of the largest lake, Lac de Ste-Croix, which stretches 10km southwest of Moustiers Ste-Marie. Covering 2200 hectares, the lake was created in 1974. Camp sites dot the lakeside D71 and D249, leading to the village. There's a small tourist office in Bauduen *(☎/fax 04 94 84 39 02; rue de Juterie)* and **Les Salles-sur-Verdon** *(☎ 04 94 70 21 84, fax 04 94 84 22 57; ⓔ verdon83@clubinternet.fr; place Fontfreye)*.

On the western banks, **Ste-Croix de Verdon** (population 103, elevation 525m) is the only village. At the lake shore you can hire electric boats, sailboards and catamarans, and bounce on floating trampolines.

Lac de Quinson

Lac de Quinson sits at the southernmost foot of the lower Gorges du Verdon. The lake is crossed by the D11, the main road that cuts through **Quinson** (population 354). Here, the **Musée de la Préhistoire des Gorges du Verdon** *(☎ 04 92 74 09 59; ⓦ www.museeprehistoire.com; route de Montmeyan; adult/6-18 yrs/under 6 €7/5/free, family ticket €19; open 10am-6pm Wed-Mon Feb, Mar & Oct–mid-Dec, 10am-7pm Wed-Mon Apr-June & Sept, 10am-8pm daily July & Aug, closed mid-Dec–end Jan)* – designed by British architect Norman Foster – explores the gorges' prehistoric past and archaeological treasures. In July and August, it runs expeditions to the **Grotte de la Baume Bonne**, a prehistoric cave discovered by archaeologists in the 1960s. Twice-weekly guided tours (adult/six to 18 years €3.80/3.10, three hours) entail a two-hour walk through rocky terrain (difficult in places) and up metal staircases. Walking shoes, a hat and water are essential. Reserve in advance at the museum. Quinson **tourist office** *(☎ 04 92 74 01 12, fax 04 92 74 00 03; place de la Mairie)* also has details.

Endearing **Montagnac** (population 326), 11km north off the D11, is known for its fresh truffles, available November to March. Eight kilometres west is **Allemagne-en-Provence** (population 384). The village adopted its German-influenced name during the Wars of

Vulture Culture

Not seen in Haute-Provence for more than a century, the griffon vulture was reintroduced into the region in 1999: By 2002 the 12 vultures put into the wild in Rougon, in the Gorges du Verdon, had multiplied into a colony of 50-odd.

The griffon vulture weighs up to 10kg, has a wing span of almost 3m, feeds on mammal carcasses and lives up to 40 years.

Between June and September, the Association Vautours en Haute-Provence, together with regional branches of the Office National des Forêts and the **Ligue pour la Protection des Oiseaux** *(☎ 04 92 83 69 55)*, organises guided vulture-watching around Rougon. Half-day walks depart on Wednesday (and Tuesday and Thursday in July and August) at 9am from Castellane's tourist office (9.30am from Rougon Village). It costs €6/3 for adults/students (under-10s free), and walkers need a sturdy pair of walking boots.

Religion (1562–98), when the Baron of Germany besieged the place. Its centrepiece is the privately owned 12th- to 16th-century **Château d'Allemagne** *(☎ 04 92 77 46 78; guided tours 4pm & 5pm Wed-Sun July–mid-Sept, 4pm & 5pm Sat & Sun Apr-June & mid-Sept–Oct)*, a donjon-style building that is still inhabited.

Lacs de Chaudanne & Castillon

The eastern end of the Gorges du Verdon is adorned with Lac de Chaudanne. Four kilometres north is Lac de Castillon, a steep-banked lake. You can swim and hire paddle boats (€12 per hour) from the beach just south of St-André-les-Alpes on its north-western shore; from St-Julien de Verdon's Plage du Touron; and from the beach on Castillon lake's southwestern tip.

From the latter, the single-track D402 cuts into the mountains to the walled **Cité Ste-de Mandarom Shambhasalem** *(Holy City of Mandarom Shambhasalem; ☎ 04 92 83 63 83; W www.aumisme.org; open 10am-11.15am & 3pm-4.15pm Sat & Sun, 10am-11.15am & 3pm-4.15pm daily during Easter and summer school holidays)*. The oversized Buddha and temple relics that glitter and sparkle from Castillon's western shores are worshipped by the Aumist cult (founded in 1969). Its garishly dressed members adhere to a cocktail of world religions. Visits are by guided tour (in English).

St-André-les-Alpes (population 832, elevation 914m) is at the northern tip of Lac de Castillon and is France's leading paragliding centre. Spread your wings at **Aérogliss** *(☎ 04 92 89 11 30, fax 04 92 89 02 36; W www.aerogliss.com; chemin des Iscles)*. In the village heart, the **tourist office** *(☎ 04 92 89 02 39, fax 04 92 89 19 23; W www.ot-st-andre-les-alpes.fr; place Marcel Pastorelli; open 9am-noon & 2pm-5pm Mon-Fri year-round; 10am-12.30pm & 4pm-6pm Sat mid-Apr–mid-June; 10am-1pm Sun mid-June–mid Sept)* has more information on activities.

Local culinary specialities sold at the **Maison du Saucisson** *(House of Sausages; ☎ 04 92 89 03 16; place de Verdun)* include donkey and wild-boar sausages (from €22 per kg).

St-André is linked with eastern Provence and the coastal resort of Nice by a narrow-gauge railway (see the boxed text 'Along the Mountain Railway' later in this chapter).

Places to Stay

There are numerous camp sites in and around Ste-Croix de Verdon; ask at the Castellane tourist office.

Camping Les Iscles *(☎ 04 92 89 02 29, fax 04 92 89 02 56; route de Nice, St-André-les-Alpes; car & tent/adult €1.75/3.65; open May-Sept)* is in a well-kept site next to St-Andre's paragliding school.

Les Cougnas *(☎/fax 04 92 89 18 78; e lescougnas@club-internet.fr; route de Nice, St-André-les-Alpes; bed in 4- to 6-bed room €11.50, bed in double room €16.50, breakfast/dinner €4/12.50)* is a *gîte d'étape* (hiker's accommodation) overlooking Lac de Castillon. Watch paragliders drop from the sky while you breakfast.

Hôtel Lac et Forêt *(☎ 04 92 89 07 38, fax 04 92 89 13 88; e lacforet@club-internet.fr; route de Nice; doubles with toilet & washbasin €26, doubles/triples with bathroom from €39/43)*, next door to Les Cougnas, is a family-run hotel with a tasty restaurant, TV room and plenty of pensioners taking full board in July and August.

Places to Eat

The places to stay already listed are solid eating options too. For something out of the ordinary try the following place.

Domaine d'Aiguines *(☎ 04 92 34 25 72; St-Jacques; menus €15, €20 & €23)* is for duck lovers – on a plate. Home to 400 to 650 ducks, this duck farm cooks up splendid feasts of farm-made *foie gras*, pan-fried duck salad, oven-baked duck and other ducky dishes. A peacock, chickens and dogs amuse guests in the yard out front. To get here, follow the N202 for 13km west from St André-les-Alpes and just before Barrême, turn left (north) along the narrow D118 to the hamlet of St-Jacques.

DIGNE-LES-BAINS

postcode 04000 • pop 17,680
• elevation 608m

The land of snow and melted cheese meets the land of sun and olives around Digne-les-Bains. The town is named after its thermal springs, which are visited annually by 11,000 people seeking a water cure for rheumatism, respiratory ailments and other medical conditions.

Digne itself is unremarkable. But it was home to a remarkable woman, Alexandra

Along the Mountain Railway

The Digne–Nice railway operated by Chemins de Fer de Provence chugs from the mountains to the sea, crossing five valleys en route and affording breathtaking views of dramatic landscapes scarcely navigable by road. The 150km narrow-gauge track was built between 1890 and 1911, and passes 25 tunnels, 16 viaducts and 15 metal bridges on its mountain journey. From May to October passengers can travel along part of the route with a 1909 steam locomotive.

Eastbound, the journey takes you from **Digne-les-Bains** to **St-André-les-Alpes** (50 minutes; see the Lacs du Verdon section earlier in this chapter). The next stop is **Thorame-Haute** (population 174, elevation 1012m), a village at the foot of the Vallée du Haut Verdon, which despite its pinprick size serves as a vital link on bus routes between southern Provence and the Allos ski resorts. After Thorame-Haute, the Col de St-Michel (1431m) and the ancient shepherds' village of **Peyresq** flash past. The 3.5km-long tunnel here took 400 workers some two years to construct.

Annot (population 1020, elevation 700m), the next halt, has a sweet old town and a couple of interesting 17th-century chapels, both a short walk from the village. The **tourist office** *(☎ 04 92 83 23 03, fax 04 92 83 30 63; W www.annot.fr; blvd St-Pierre)* has details.

Entrevaux (population 752), 7km east, tumbles dramatically down the hillside from a Vauban-built citadel. Across the drawbridge, outside the 17th-century fortifications surrounding the village, is an oil and flour mill that can be visited. The **tourist office** *(☎ 04 93 05 46 73, fax 04 93 05 40 71; W www.entrevaux.info)* is inside the old city gate.

The steam train *Train des Pignes* is stationed at **Puget-Théniers** (population 1624, elevation 405). From May to October it shunts between Puget and Annot (€16.80 return, 50 minutes). Passengers seeking hearty Haute-Provence fodder in Puget – including *secca de bœuf* (mountain-dried beef) from the region – should head for the charming **Auberge des Acacias** *(☎ 04 93 05 05 25; lunch/dinner menu €12.20/17.55)*, 1km east of Puget on the N202 (get off at 'Le Planet' train stop). In Puget itself, **Edelweiss** *(☎ 04 90 05 01 00; 1 place Adolphe Cornil; lunch/dinner menus €11.50/16 & €24)* cooks up lamb kidneys in nut-flavoured wine and tasty lamb in lavender pastry.

Picking up the eastward trail again, you reach the mountain villages of **Touët-sur-Var** (population 445) and **Villars-sur-Var** (population 584) before plunging south along the Var River through **St-Martin du Var** and **Colomars** (population 385) to Nice. The **Auberge des Chasseurs** *(☎ 04 93 05 71 11; menus €15 & €30)*, in Touët-sur-Var, is known for its game dishes in season – don't miss the wild boar.

The entire trip from Digne-les-Bains to Nice takes 3¼ hours. There are four or five trains daily and a single fare is €17.65. A single Annot-Nice fare is €10.10 (€24.40 with the steam train between Puget and Annot). Updated fares and schedules are on Chemins de Fer de Provence's website at W www.trainprovence.com.

David-Neel, whose travels to Tibet brought her wide acclaim. The shale around Digne is rich in fossils and is protected by the Réserve Géologique de Haute-Provence (150,000 hectares). The area is also known for its production of lavender, which is harvested in July or August and honoured in town with the five-day Corso de la Lavande, the town's lavender festival on the first weekend of August.

Route Napoléon (the N85), which Bonaparte followed in 1815 on his way to Paris after his escape from Elba, passes though Digne-les-Bains. The D900 heading north takes you past the mountain village of **La Javie** to **Seyne-les-Alpes** (population 1230, elevation 1200m), 42km north in the Vallée de la Blanche, where you can ski in winter.

Orientation & Information

Digne-les-Bains is on the eastern bank of the Bléone. The major roads into town converge at rond-point du 11 Novembre 1918, 400m northeast of the train station. Blvd Gassendi heads northeast from the roundabout to place du Général de Gaulle, the main square.

The **tourist office** *(☎ 04 92 36 62 62, fax 04 92 32 27 24; W www.ot-dignelesbains.fr; place du Tampinet; open 8.45am-noon & 2pm-6.30pm Mon-Sat, 10.30am-noon Sun May-Oct, 8.45am-noon & 2pm-6pm Mon-Sat Nov-Apr)* overlooks the rond-point du 11 Novembre 1918.

Musée Alexandra David-Néel

Paris-born writer and philosopher Alexandra David-Néel (1868–1969), who spent her last years in Digne (reaching the age of 101), is known for her early-20th-century incognito voyage to Tibet. Her memory and all-consuming passion for Tibet are kept alive by the Musée Alexandra David-Néel *(☎ 04 92 31 32 38; W www.alexandra-david-neel.org; 27 ave Maréchal Juin; admission free; guided tours 10.30am, 2pm & 4pm daily Oct-June, 10.30am, 2pm, 3.30pm & 5pm daily July-Sept)*, in her erstwhile residence. Tours last 1¼ hours – some are in English. The museum is just over 1km from town on the Nice-bound N85. By bus, take TUD bus No 3 to the Stade Rolland stop.

The Journées Tibetaines (Tibetan Days), an annual celebration of Tibetan culture, is held over three days in August.

Réserve Géologique de Haute-Provence

Digne-les-Bains is in the middle of the 190,000 hectare-large Réserve Géologique de Haute-Provence, whose spectacular fossil deposits include the footprints of prehistoric birds as well as ammonites (spiral shells that look something like a ram's horn). You'll need a detailed regional map or topoguide (sold at the tourist office) to the Digne and Sisteron areas and your own transport to get to the 18 sites. Most of the sites are around **Barles** (population 114), 24km north of Digne, and **Barrême** (population 442), 28km southeast. There's an impressive limestone slab with some 500 ammonites 3km north of Digne on the road to Barles. The reserve runs museums in Sisteron and Castellane (see those sections).

The reserve has its headquarters in the **Centre de Géologie** *(☎ 04 92 36 70 70; W www.resgeol04.org; Parc St-Bénoît; museum open 9am-noon & 2pm-5.30pm daily Apr-Oct; 9am-noon & 2pm-5.30pm Mon-Thur, 9am-noon & 2pm-4.30pm Fri Nov-Mar; park open 8am-7pm daily Apr-Oct, 8am-7pm Mon-Fri Nov-Mar)*, 2km north of town off the road to Barles in St-Bénoît. Take TUD bus No 2 to the Champourcin stop (across the bridge), then follow the road to the left that's signposted 'Musée-Promenade' – a dramatic 15-minute walk along a rocky overhang above the river (cars aren't allowed up).

Activities

Between mid-February and early December, you can enjoy a **thermal bath** (29° to 49°C) at **Les Thermes de Digne-les-Bains**; see Spas in the Facts for the Visitor for details. Visitors (rather than those seeking cures) can visit at 2pm Thursday, March to August and November.

The more active can soar with **Dinovol** *(☎/fax 04 92 32 42 06; e parapente.dinovol@wanadoo.fr; 9 rue de Provence)*, a paragliding school based at 10 ave du Maréchal Juin (route de Nice). Next door, **Rando Lavande** *(☎ 04 92 32 27 44, 06 12 73 43 70; e bietrix@free.fr; 7 rue de Provence)* organises tailor-made mountain walks and snow-shoeing expeditions (from €16 per person a day).

Half-day rambles with a donkey are run by **Lambert Âne** *(☎ 04 92 31 60 37; W www.lambertane.com; Le Château-Lambert)* and **Poivre d'Âne** *(☎ 04 92 34 87 12; Les Férauds)*, northwest of Digne in Thouard. Donkey hire costs €30/45 per half-/full day.

In winter, you can **ski** at the mountain resort of Seyne-les-Alpes, 42km north of Digne.

Places to Stay & Eat

Camping du Bourg *(☎ 04 92 31 04 87; route de Barcelonnette; camping for 2 people with car & tent or caravan €10.50; open Apr-Oct)*, 2km northeast of Digne, charges €0.50 less if you're taking a cure at Les Thermes de Digne-les-Bains. Take bus No 2 to the Notre Dame du Bourg stop, from where it is a 600m walk.

Hôtel Central *(☎ 04 92 31 31 91, fax 04 92 31 49 78; W www.hotel-central.fr.st; 26 blvd Gassendi; doubles with washbasin €27, with shower €31, with shower & toilet €40)* is a two-star place. Reception is on the 1st floor; guests need a code to enter after dark.

Hôtel du Petit St-Jean *(☎ 04 92 31 30 04, fax 04 92 36 05 80; 14 cours des Arès; singles/doubles/triples/quads with washbasin & bidet €20/23/29/37, with shower €25/29/37/40; lunch/dinner menus from €9/14)* is a budget inn where at €4.60, even breakfast is cheap. It overlooks the central place du Général de Gaulle and serves *aïoli Provençale* once a week.

Le Chaudron *(☎ 04 92 31 24 87, 40 rue de l'Hubac; menus €14 & €22, plat du jour €10)* serves traditional Provençal cuisine featuring lots of Dignois lavender. Its interior is rustic and beamed.

Ma Petite Auberge *(☎ 04 92 35 56 52; Chabrières; mains around €10)*, about 15km southeast on the N85, appears to be little more than a ramshackle roadside hut. Step inside and allow yourself to be wooed by excellent cuisine served in a refined and easy-going setting.

A **food market** fills place du Général de Gaulle on Wednesday and Saturday morning.

Getting There & Away

Bus From the **bus station** *(☎ 04 92 31 50 00; place du Tampinet)*, there are buses to/from Nice (€14.30, 2¼ hours, one or two daily), Marseilles (€13.50, 2¼ hours, two to four daily), Castellane (€10.90, one hour, twice daily), La Foux d'Allos (☎ 04 92 83 95 81; €9.60, two hours, two or three weekly during the ski season, plus July & August) via Colmars and Allos, Barcelonnette (€8.10, 1½ hours, one bus daily), Manosque (€5.30, 1¼ hours, two to four daily) and Apt (€9.45, two hours, twice daily).

During the ski season, **Société des Cars Alpes Littoral** *(SCAL; ☎ 04 92 51 06 05)* runs a daily bus in either direction between Marseilles and Pra-Loup (€24.10, 4½ hours) via Digne-les-Bains (€13.50, 2¼ hours) and Barcelonnette (€21.60, four hours). Transporting a pair of skis costs €2.50.

Train From the train station, a 10-minute walk west of the tourist office on ave Pierre Sémard, there are four daily trains to/from Marseilles (€18.60, 2¼ hours); some require a change in Château-Arnoux St-Auban.

Digne-les-Bains is also served by two-car diesel trains, operated by **Chemins de Fer de la Provence** *(☎ 04 92 31 01 58)*, which chug along a scenic narrow-gauge line from Digne to Nice (see the boxed text 'Along the Mountain Railway' following).

VALLÉE DE LA DURANCE

The Durance Valley ploughs along Haute-Provence's western fringes. The River Durance, an affluent of the Rhône, follows a 324km course from its source in the southern Alps to the Camargue. Its impetuous waters, slammed by Frédéric Mistral in the 19th century as one of Provence's great three curses (along with the Aix Parliament and the mistral wind), were partly tamed by Électricité de France in the 1960s.

Manosque, on the eastern edge of the Lubéron (see that chapter); industrial **Château-Arnoux** (population 5000) with its modern Elf-Atochem complex and 16th-century castle on the confluence of the Rivers Durance and Bléone; and Sisteron are the three main towns along this 100km stretch. East of Manosque, the D6 cuts across the **Plateau de Valensole**, famed for its fields of lavender, to **Valensole** (population 2358). The village celebrates a Fête de la Lavande on the 3rd Sunday in July; its annual Fête du Goût (Festival of Tastes) in October or November is a good chance to taste lavender honey.

Sisteron (population 7232, elevation 485m) is unstartling beyond its 13th- to 16th-century **Château de Sisteron**, perched on a rock above the *cluse* (transverse valley) in which sunken Sisteron sits. The open-air classical music concerts hosted here during the Nuits de la Citadelle (Citadel Nights), a festival held each year from mid-July to mid-August since 1928, are worth the ticket price (€25 to €50); the **tourist office** *(☎ 04 92 61 12 03, fax 04 92 61 19 57; ⓔ office-de-tourisme-sisteron@wanadoo.fr; Hôtel de Ville)* has details.

Sisteron's other lure is its **Musée Terre et Temps** *(Museum of Earth & Time; ☎ 04 92 61 61 30; ⓔ musee_terre_et_temps@libertysurf.fr; 6 place du Général de Gaulle; open 10am-1pm & 3pm-7pm daily July & Aug; 9.30am-12.30pm & 2pm-6pm Wed-Sun Apr & Oct; 9.30am-12.30pm & 2pm-6pm daily May, June & Sept)*, inside a former chapel dating from 1631. From here, motorists can follow the **Route du Temps** (Time Road) – a marked itinerary that follows the eastbound D3 to remote **St-Geniez**, from where it climbs over the Col de Font-Belle (1708m) before plummeting south to the medieval fortified village of **Thoard** and Digne-les-Bains. Information panels en route highlight geological sights.

In **Les Mées** (population 2973), 20km south of Sisteron, is the **Rocher des Mées**, a row of rocky pinnacles that stand 100m tall. The rock formations, also called Les Pénitents des Mées, were created from a gaggle of monks who were turned to stone for lusting after Saracen women, so legend claims.

Ten kilometres south in Ganagobie, on the Durance's western bank, the 10th-century, Benedictine **Monastère Notre Dame** *(☎ 04 92 68 00 04; ⓔ ste.madeleine@ndganagobie.com; open 3pm-5.30pm Tues-Sun in summer, 3pm-5pm Tues-Sun in winter)*, showcases an exquisite 12th-century floor mosaic – the largest of its kind in France – in its chapel.

Forcalquier

postcode 04300 • pop 4375 • elevation 550m

Forcalquier sits atop a rocky perch 19km southwest of Ganagobie. Steep steps lead to the citadel and octagonal-shaped chapel at the top of the village, where carillon concerts are held. The **tourist office** *(☎ 04 92 75 10 02, fax 04 92 75 26 76; W www.forcalquier.com; 13 place du Bourguet; open 9am-noon & 2pm-6pm Mon-Sat mid-Sept–mid-June; 9am-12.30pm & 2pm-7pm Mon-Sat, 10am-1pm Sun mid-June–mid-Sept)*, overlooking the Gothic **Église Notre Dame**, has details. The village **cemetery** *(place du Souvenir Français; open 9am-5pm daily)*, 1km north of the centre, is France's only listed cemetery – distinguished by its age-old yew trees that are cut to form high, decorative alleys.

Fiery liqueurs like La Farigoule (thyme liqueur), *amandine* (almond liqueur) and *eau de vie de poires* (pear brandy) have been distilled at the **Distilleries et Domaines des Provences** since 1898. Taste and buy a bottle at its **Espace Dégustation** *(☎ 04 92 75 15 41; 9 ave St-Promasse; open 9am-noon & 2pm-6pm Mon & Wed-Sat)*, or sample one as an aperitif at **Le Lapin Tant Pis** *(☎ 04 92 75 38 88; 10 ave St-Promasse; menu €35, with cheese €42.50; open Thur, Fri & Sat eve)*, a boldly unconventional village restaurant run by quirky French chef Gérard Vives. The AOC Haute-Provence olive-oil harvest can be tested at **Oliviers & Co** *(☎ 04 92 75 00 75; 5 rue des Cordeliers; menus around €17)*, an oil shop that dishes up light Mediterranean cuisine in its adjoining bistro.

Around Forcalquier

The **Prieuré de Salagon** *(☎ 04 92 75 70 50; e musee.salagon@wanadoo.fr; adult/12-18 yrs/under 12 €4.60/2.40/free; open 10am-noon & 2pm-7pm daily May-Sept, 2pm-6pm daily Oct, 2pm-6pm Sat & Sun Nov-Apr)*, 4km south in Mane, is a 13th-century priory on a farm estate. Aromatic herbs for traditional remedies grow in a medieval garden and perfumes typical of Provence – lavender, mint, mugwort, sage – fill its Jardin de Senteurs.

A bunch of villages peek at Forcalquier from their hill-top perches west of the town: **Vachères** (population 260, elevation 830m), 30km west; **Oppedette** (population 40, elevation 525m) with its lovely gorges crossed by the GR4; **Lurs** (population 347, elevation 600m); and **Simiane-la-Rotonde** (population 532), host to the international music festival Les Riches Heures Musicales in August. Tickets costing €26 are sold at Forcalquier tourist office.

Observatories

The **Observatoire de Haute-Provence** *(☎ 04 92 70 64 00; W www.obs-hp.fr)*, 10km southwest of Forcalquier at the end of the D305 from St-Michel l'Observatoire, is a national research centre that can be visited by a 30-minute guided tour between 1.30pm and 4.30pm on Wednesday in July and August. Wednesday morning visits can also be reserved in advance (☎ 04 92 76 69 09). Tours for adults/six to 12 years cost €2.30/1.50 and shuttle buses run every 30 minutes between St-Michel l'Observatoire village and the observatory.

From St-Michel l'Observatoire, the eastbound D5 flashes past **Centre d'Astronomie** *(☎ 04 92 76 69 69; W www.astrosurf.com/centre.astro; Plateau du Moulin à Vent)*, an astronomy centre that organises star-filled, multimedia events and educational workshops. Learn how to watch stars with the naked eye and telescopes at 9pm or 9.30pm on Friday and Saturday (adult/six to 12 years €8/6.50).

Accommodation and food are available in St-Michel l'Observatoire at the friendly **Hôtel-Restaurant l'Observatoire** *(☎/fax 04 92 76 63 62; place de la Fontaine; singles/doubles €27/32, lunch/dinner menu €12/21)*. Gilles the chef has been cooking up simple yet satisfying dishes for 25 years.

Getting There & Away

There are buses that leave from the **Sisteron bus station** *(☎ 04 92 61 22 18)* to and from Aix-en-Provence (€10.40, 2½ hours, four daily), Marseilles (€13.30, two hours, four daily) and Nice (€17.90, 3¾ hours, one daily) via Digne-les-Bains (€3.60, 45 minutes).

From the stop on place Martial Sicard in Forcalquier, **Voyages Brémond** *(☎ 04 92 75 16 32)* runs buses to/from Marseilles (€10.30, two hours, up to five daily) and Manosque (€3.20, 35 minutes, three daily). Daily services to/from Avignon (€11, two hours) and Digne-les-Bains (€7, one hour) are by **Rapides du Sud-Est** *(☎ 04 32 76 00 40)*.

St-Michel l'Observatoire is accessible by one daily bus from Manosque (30 minutes) and Forcalquier (15 minutes).

A Delicious Detour

From Forcalquier, a delicious detour can be made to **Banon** (population 940, elevation 760m), unremarkable save for its cheesy pleasures and blazing lavender fields that carpet its southern foot.

Banon is a type of cheese that comes wrapped in a chestnut leaf. Traditionally made from *chèvre* (goats' milk) in summer and *brebis* (sheep's milk) in winter, the 6cm- to 8cm-diameter and 3cm-thick cheese patties can taste *doux* (mild) or *fort* (strong), depending on the ripening process. A *Banon à la feuille* is dipped in eau de vie before being packaged in its leaf. In May, Banon celebrates its annual Fête du Fromage (Cheese Fair).

The **Fromagerie de Banon** *(☎ 04 92 73 25 03; route de Carniol)* makes the best *Banon*. Its cheeses are sold at the Tuesday morning market on place de la République, Banon's central square; and at **Chez Melchio** *(☎ 04 92 73 23 05; place de la République; open 7.30am-12.30pm & 2.30pm-7pm Mon & Wed-Sat)*, a fabulous meat shop and grocery. Cheese aside, Maurice Melchio is known for his *brandilles* – extraordinary long (about 60cm) and skinny goat or donkey sausages, flavoured with pine kernels, walnuts or herbs.

The **tourist office** *(☎ 04 92 73 36 37; place de la République; open 10am-noon & 2pm-4.20pm Mon & Wed-Fri, 9am-noon & 2pm-4.20pm Thur)* has a list of farms in the surrounding countryside where you can taste and buy fresh cheese.

Banon is 25km northwest of Forcalquier along the winding D950; the two towns are not linked by public transport.

PARC NATIONAL DU MERCANTOUR

The Mercantour National Park is Provence at its most majestic. Its uninhabited heart covers 68,500 hectares in the northeast of the region and embraces six valleys. The park abuts Italy's Parco Naturale delle Alpi Marittime to the east and is surrounded by a 146,500-hectare partially protected and inhabited peripheral zone.

Europe's highest mountain pass, Col de Restefond la Bonette (2802m), strides through the Vallée de l'Ubaye, the park's most northern and wildest valley. Come winter, the Ubaye and its southern sisters, the Vallées du Haut Verdon and de la Tinée, offer fine skiing. Farther south sit the Vallées de la Vésubie, des Merveilles and de la Roya – a heady mix of gorges, ageless rocks and white waters, all within easy reach of the Côte d'Azur.

The national park has information offices in St-Martin-Vésubie, Tende and Valberg; summer bureaux in St-Étienne de Tinée, St-Sauveur-sur-Tinée, Isola 2000 and at Lac d'Allos; its headquarters in Nice (see the Nice to Menton chapter); and a website at **W** www.parc-mercantour.fr.

Vallée de L'Ubaye

The River Ubaye, a tributary of the Durance, skirts Provence's northern tip between Lac de Serre-Poncon and Barcelonnette and offers top white-water rafting. The Ubaye Valley, shielded by the southern Alps, is sandwiched between the Parc Régional du Queyras (north) and the Parc National du Mercantour (south). It is crossed by the D900, which closely shadows the riverbanks.

Barcelonnette (population 3316, elevation 1135m), founded by the count of Barcelona in 1231, is the only town in this desolate valley. From the 18th century until WWII, some 5000 Barcelonnettais followed in the footsteps of the enterprising Arnaud brothers who emigrated to Mexico in 1805 to seek their fortunes in the silk and wool-weaving industry. Their colourful history unfolds in the **Musée de la Vallée** *(☎ 04 92 81 27 15; **e** musee.vallee@wanadoo.fr; 10 ave de la Libération; adult/child €3.10/1.60; open 9.30am-noon & 2.30pm-7pm daily July & Aug; 3pm-7pm Tues-Sat June & Sept; 2.30pm-6pm daily during school holidays & 3pm-6pm Wed, Sat, Thur & Sat during non-school holidays Oct-May)*.

Information Barcelonnette **tourist office** *(☎ 04 92 81 04 71, fax 04 92 81 22 67; **W** www.barcelonnette.net; place Frédéric Mistral; open 9am-noon & 2pm-6.30pm Mon-Sat)* has a list of guides who organise walks, mountain bikes and canoeing trips.

Alternatively, contact the **Maison de la Vallée de l'Ubaye** *(☎ 04 92 81 03 68, fax 04 92 81 51 67; 4 ave des Trois Frères Arnaud)*. The walking and climbing club **Club Alpin**

Wildlife & Where to See It

The Parc National du Mercantour is home to a dazzling array of birds, including the golden and short-toed eagle, the buzzard, black grouse and the nutcracker. Its higher-altitude plains in the southern Alps shelter marmot, mouflon and chamois (a mountain antelope), as well as the *bouquetin* (Alpine ibex), reintroduced into the region in the early 1990s. In the lower-altitude wooded areas, the red and roe deer are common. Wild boar roam throughout.

The bearded vulture, extinct in the Alps in the 19th century, was reintroduced into the Mercantour in 1993. Since then at least seven vultures have been born in the wild. In 2001, the park released two more vultures that were bred in Vienna, Austria.

The wolf, which disappeared from France in 1930, has been spotted in the Parc National du Mercantour near Utelle. Wolf-watching expeditions are among the many guided nature walks organised by the park. Full-day wolf walks (€20 per person) depart once weekly from St-Étienne de Tinée's **Maison du Parc** *(☎ 04 93 02 42 27, fax 04 93 02 41 33; open 9.30am-12.30pm & 2.30pm-6.30pm daily July & Aug)*.

From the **Maison du Parc** *(☎ 04 93 03 23 15; e mercantour.vesubie@wanadoo.fr; 8 rue Kellermann Sérurier; open 9am-noon & 2pm-6.30pm Mon-Sat)* in St-Martin-Vésubie, park wardens lead weekly walks into the Vallée des Merveilles (€24.50), including flower-, insect- and bird-discovery walks (adult/under 18s €19/15); walks to learn about mammals and birds of prey (€19/15); and four-day donkey-accompanied treks (€140/90).

Français *(☎ 04 92 81 28 18; w www.cafubaye.com)* is in the same building.

White-Water Sports Canoe-rental places line the D900 between Le Lauzet-Ubaye and Barcelonnette. In **Le Martinet**, just south off the D900, 6km east of Le Lauzet-Ubaye, is **AN Rafting** *(☎ 04 92 85 54 90; w www.an-rafting.com; Pont du Martinet)* and **River** *(☎ 04 92 85 53 99; w www.river.fr)*. Both arrange two- to three-hour rafting (€35), hot-dogging (€35 to €40) and canyoning (€35) expeditions, and a multitude of other white-water activities. **Adventure Rio Raft** *(☎ 04 92 81 91 15)*, the adjoining Camping du Rioclar in Méolans-Revel, 12km west of Barcelonnette, sports similar rates.

Cycling The Vallée de l'Ubaye is linked to the outside world by seven mountain passes. Cyclists tough enough to conquer them all, including Col de Restefond la Bonette – Europe's highest pass at 2808m – are given a medal; the Maison de la Vallée de l'Ubaye in Barcelonnette (see Vallée de l'Ubaye earlier in this chapter) has details.

In Le Martinet, both white-water sports bases (see the previous section) rent mountain bikes (€8/26 per hour/day) and arrange guided rides; River has a mini-VTT course for kids, 20km of forest trails, 1.7km of downhill tracks and a 500m bi-cross (scramble) circuit for adult riders.

Skiing Pra-Loup is the main resort in the Vallée de l'Ubaye, 8.5km from Barcelonnette, connected by a lift system across the Vallon des Agneliers with La Foux d'Allos resort in the Vallée du Haut-Verdon (see that section later). Pra-Loup has 170km of runs – 73 pistes (35 of which are red or black) – and is suited for both intermediate and advanced skiers. Boarders can surf in the snow park. Nearby Super-Sauze (1400m) is smaller.

A six-day Ski Pass Vallée covering the above resorts plus Ste-Anne La Condamine (1800m) costs €111/135 in low/high season. Pra-Loup's **École du Ski Français** *(ESF; ☎ 04 92 84 11 05; w www.esf-praloup.com; Les Mélèzes bldg)* charges around €82/99 in low/high season for six group-skiing lessons and €91/122 for the equivalent on a snowboard. Skis, boots and poles can be hired for around €20 per day.

Pra-Loup's **tourist office** *(☎ 04 92 84 10 04, fax 04 92 84 02 93; w www.praloup.com; Maison de Pra-Loup; open 9am-7pm daily)* has information on the entire valley.

Places to Stay & Eat In Méolans-Revel, **Camping du Rioclar** *(☎ 04 92 31 20 30; ave Georges Pompidou; camping for 2 adults, tent & car from €12)* is a large site ideally set next to the hamlet's water-sports centre. It only opens in summer.

The tourist offices have accommodation lists for the ski resorts already mentioned.

Pyjama *(☎ 04 92 81 12 00, fax 04 92 81 03 16; Super-Sauze; doubles from €47)* is a delightful place to stay in Super-Sauze. Furnishings are old style and family rooms have mezzanines.

Tisane *(☎ 04 92 84 10 55; Pra-Loup; menus from €15)*, in the heart of Pra-Loup, is an atmospheric choice for traditional mountain cooking.

Getting There & Away The nearest train station is Gap, 60km north.

From Barcelonnette, **Autocars SCAL** (*☎ 04 92 81 00 20)* runs buses to/from Marseilles and Digne-les-Bains. During the ski season, there are direct buses between Pra-Loup and Marseilles (€21.60, four hours), departing daily from Marseilles at 7am and from Pra-Loup at 3.50pm.

Buses in the Vallée de l'Ubaye are run by **Autocars Maurel** *(☎ 04 92 81 20 09)*. There are three Barcelonnette–La Martinet buses a day, and four daily shuttle buses between Barcelonnette and Sauze. Shuttles between Sauze (3.5km south of Barcelonnette) and Super-Sauze (5km farther south) are free.

Vallée du Haut Verdon

The breathtaking **Col d'Allos** (2250m) links Vallée de l'Ubaye with its southern neighbour, the Vallée du Haut Verdon, which penetrates the Parc National du Mercantour. The mighty River Verdon has its source here at La Tête de la Sestrière (2572m).

Immediately after crossing the mountain pass (snow-blocked in winter), is **La Foux d'Allos** (elevation 1800m), an unattractive ski resort 23.5km south of Pra-Loup and connected to it by cable car. Its **tourist office** *(☎ 04 92 83 02 81, fax 04 92 83 06 66; W www.valdallos.com)* is in the Maison de la Foux on the main square. In the upper village close to the lift stations, there's an **Auberge de Jeunesse** *(☎ 04 92 83 81 08, fax 04 92 83 83 70; e la-foux-allos@fuag.org; Sat €48, 3 nights full board €106-116, 6 nights full board €240-262 Dec-Apr, dorm bed/breakfast/sheet hire €8.40/3.25/2.75 mid-June–mid-Sept; reception open 10am-noon & 4pm-10pm daily mid-Dec–late-Apr & mid-June–mid-Sept)*. HI cards are obligatory but non-HI members can stay for an extra €2.90 per night in summer. The hostel overlooks Les Chauvets ski slope.

Allos (population 650, elevation 1400m), 8km farther south on the D908, bears the same concrete-block architectural stamp as its ugly sister and is just as deserted outside of the ski season, except in July and August when hotels reopen their doors to walkers.

Lac d'Allos – Europe's largest Alpine lake at 62 hectares – is the valley's main draw. The lake is 12km east of Allos along the D226. From Parking du Laus (the car park at the end of the road on Plateau du Laus), a trail leads to Lac d'Allos (2226m) – an approximate 40-minute walk. Route maps and walking information are available from the **Parc National du Mercantour office** *(☎ 04 92 83 06 34)* that operates from the car park in July and August.

Lower in the valley, Colmars-les-Alpes and **Beauvezer** (population 287) are ideal retreats. **Colmars-les-Alpes** (population 385), 24km south of Allos, is a fortified village surrounded by high thick walls built by Vauban. The Savoy fort at the top can be visited by guided tour (adult/under 16 €4/1.50) in July and August; the **tourist office** *(☎ 04 92 83 41 92, fax 04 92 83 52 31; open 9am-12.15pm & 2pm-5.45pm Mon-Sat Sept-June, 8am-12.30pm & 2pm-7pm daily July & Aug)* has details. In July and August it takes bookings for the shuttle bus (adult/five to 18 years €6/3, three times weekly) linking Colmars with Lac d'Allos (Parking du Laus).

Getting There & Away In Colmars-les-Alpes, **Haut Verdon Voyages** *(☎ 04 92 83 95 81)* runs buses between Digne-les-Bains and La Foux d'Allos (€9.60, two hours, one daily), stopping at St-André-les-Alpes, Thorame-Haute Gare, Colmars and Allos.

On Saturday during the ski season (usually mid-December to early April), direct shuttle buses link La Foux d'Allos with Nice and Marseilles airports. Fares and schedules change every year – check with Haut Verdon Voyages or the tourist office in La Foux.

By train, you can take the mountain railway (see the boxed text 'Along the Mountain Railway' earlier in this chapter) from Nice to Thorame-Haute.

Vallée de la Tinée

Europe's highest mountain pass, the **Col de Restefond la Bonette** (2802m) links Barcelonnette and the Vallée de l'Ubaye with the tamer, more southern Vallée de la Tinée. In winter, when the snowy pass is closed, the 149km-long Tinée Valley can

Via Ferrata

During WWI, Italian troops moved swiftly and safely through the Dolomites – the natural frontier between Italy and Austria – using iron-rung ladders and steel cables bolted into the rocky mountainside. Today, similar routes known as *via ferrata* (meaning 'iron way' in Italian) allow adventurous tourists to scale rock faces in the Alps without knowing the first thing about rock-climbing.

Haute-Provence sports a clutch of *via ferrata* courses, rigged at dizzying heights and guaranteed to get the blood pumping. Anyone (with guts) can do it: Harnessed climbers are attached to the rock by two lines. To move along the rock face safely, climbers unclip the karabiner of one line then attach it further along the steel cable, before unclipping and then clipping the second.

Courses range in length from 3½ hours to 5½ hours; first-timers can tackle short sections. Giddying elevations of up to 2274m are reached and *ponts Himalayen* (rope bridges with steel cables at waist height), *ponts de singe* (monkey bridges with steel cables above your head) and *tyroliennes* (zip lines, requiring climbers to pull themselves along, legs dangling) are hair-raising features of most.

Climbers need a *casque* (helmet), *mousquetons* (a harness attached to two cables with shock-absorbers and karabiners), and a sturdy pair of walking shoes. Gloves also come in handy. Everything but boots and gloves can be hired on-site for around €9. Course admission costs an additional €3. Tickets and equipment hire are generally handled by the local tourist office.

There are *via ferrata* in the **Vallée de la Vésubie** *(Via Ferrata du Baus de la Frema near La Colmiane; ☎ 04 93 02 89 54)*; in **Puget-Théniers** *(Les Demoiselles du Castagnet; ☎ 04 93 05 05 05)*; and in the Vallée de la Tinée *(in Auron; ☎ 04 93 23 02 66)*. The Circuit des Comtes Lascaris is split across three sites – in La Brigue and Tende in the Vallée de la Roya, and in Peille (see the Arrière-Pays Niçois section in the Nice to Menton chapter). The Peille section is not recommended for beginners.

Those who'd rather not scale new heights alone can hook up with a local mountain guide; see the Vallée de la Tinée and Vallée de la Roya sections in this chapter for details. Online, see W www.viaferrata.org.

only be accessed up its southern leg from Nice. The narrow road (D2205) is laced with hairpins and wiggles along the French-Italian border for the duration of its journey from the mountain pass to **Isola** (875m), where it plummets sharply south towards the coast.

The steep D97 makes an eastbound climb to **Isola 2000** (population 536, elevation 2000m), a purpose-built ski resort from where the **Col de la Lombarde** (2350m) crosses into Italy.

St-Étienne de Tinée (population 1684), 15km northwest of Isola village on the D2205, is a lovely Alpine village offering endless walking opportunities in summer around the Cime de la Bonette (2860m). Thrill-seekers can scale new heights here at the **Via Ferrata d'Auron**; see the boxed text 'Via Ferrata' earlier in this chapter.

Southbound, the road twists through beautiful gorges to **St-Sauveur-sur-Tinée** (population 459, elevation 490m), gateway to the Parc National du Mercantour.

St-Sauveur to Guillaumes From St-Sauveur-sur-Tinée, the spectacular D30 takes you 24km west to **Beuil** (population 334, elevation 1450m), from where you can access the dazzling **Gorges du Cians**, carved from burgundy-coloured rock.

Flora typical to this neck of the woods can be viewed in the **Arboretum Marcel Kroenlein** *(☎ 04 93 35 00 50)* in Roure, a few kilometres west of St-Sauveur off the D30. From the 1920s until 1961 villagers here used a 1850m-long cable to transport their milk and cheese down the mountain and food provisions up – you can still see the cable.

Dozens of twists farther west is **Valberg** (elevation 1700m), a ski resort that lures walkers and mountain bikers in summer. At the **Espace Valberg Aventure** *(☎ 04 93 02 60 07; open July & Aug)* you can scale trees, cross rope bridges and monkey around dozens more Tarzan-inspired obstacles. The forested site can be accessed via the Croix du Sapet chairlift at the resort's southern end off ave de Valberg; a single ride with/without a mountain bike costs €4/3.50. Valberg also has a summer luge (€2.80/7.50 for one/three rides).

Guillaumes (elevation 800m), 20km west again, is the starting point for forays into the

Gorges de Dalius, also chiselled from the burgundy-coloured rock. Thrill-seekers can **bungee jump** *(☎ 04 93 73 50 29)* from Pont de la Mariée, an 80m-high stone footbridge across the gorges.

Pont de Berthéou, another bridge 8km south of Guillaumes on the D2202, is the starting point for the scenic **Sentier du Point Sublime** (4km, 1½ hours), a beautiful walk that takes you through oak and pine forest and past red rock formations to the 'sublime point', from where there is a stunning clifftop view. Panels on the way highlight flora and fauna species you might see. Guillaumes' **tourist office** *(☎ 04 93 05 57 76, fax 04 93 05 54 75; W www.pays-de-guillaumes.com; place Napoléon III)* has more information.

Information Parc National du Mercantour has several information centres in the valley; see the boxed text 'Wildlife & Where to See It' earlier in this chapter for details. In July and August, it runs small offices in Isola 2000; **Valberg** *(☎ 04 93 02 58 23; rue Jean Mineur)*; and **St-Sauveur-sur-Tinée** *(☎ 04 93 02 10 33; 11 ave des Blavets)*.

Tourist offices in **Isola 2000** *(☎ 04 93 23 15 15, fax 04 93 23 14 25; W www.isola2000.com; Galerie Marchande)* and **Valberg** *(☎ 04 93 23 24 25, fax 04 93 02 52 27; W www.valberg.com; place du Quartier)* also stock information on outdoor activities.

Places to Stay & Eat Isola 2000 has a host of unappealing concrete blocks.

Hôtel La Renaissance *(☎ 04 93 05 59 89; doubles from €30)* is in Guillaumes, 44km west at the northern mouth of the Gorges de Dalius, opposite the sheep folds where the weekly village sheep fair takes place.

Auberge de la Gare *(☎ 04 93 02 00 67; ave des Blavets (the D2205), St-Sauveur-sur-Tinée; plat du jour €8.50, menu €12)* in the village of St-Sauveur-sur-Tinée, is a cheap and simple place to enjoy filling food like your mum would make – almost.

Le Valbergan *(☎ 04 93 02 50 28; 2 ave Valberg, Valberg)* cooks up mountain cuisine guaranteed to warm the cockles – cheesy *raclettes* and fondues, meaty *fondues bourguignonnes* and *pierrades* (meat grilled on a stone slab).

Getting There & Away Three daily buses run between Nice and Isola 2000 (€27.10, 2½ hours) from December to April, and one or two daily the rest of the year. Call ☎ 04 93 85 92 60 for information. During the ski season, buses serve Nice-Côte d'Azur airport (€27.10, two hours).

Société Broch *(☎ 04 93 31 10 52)* operates one daily bus year-round between Nice's bus station, Nice-Côte d'Azur airport and Valberg (€10, two hours).

Vallée de la Vésubie

The Vésubie, a dead-end valley that has to be accessed from the south, is less wild than its northwestern neighbours, Vallées de la Tinée and du Haut Verdon, primarily due to its proximity to Nice and the Côte d'Azur.

The hairpin-laced **Gorges de la Vésubie** weaves its way from the Vésubie Valley's southern foot, which kicks off at Plan du Var, 20km north of Nice on the busy N202. For a stunning aerial view of the gorge and surrounding valley, head for **La Madone d'Utelle** (1181m), a pilgrimage site settled by Spanish sailors in the 9th century, which since 1806 has been crowned with a chapel. Sung masses attended by hundreds of pilgrims mark 15 August (Assumption Day) and 8 September (Nativité de la Vierge; Nativity of the Virgin). From the mountain village of **St-Jean la Rivière** (D2565), a stone bridge crosses the River Var, from where a steep, winding mountain pass (D32) leads west to **Utelle** (population 489), 6km northeast of La Madone.

About 18km north of the St-Jean along the D2565, just past the turning for **La Bollène-Vésubie** (elevation 964m), you arrive at a cross-roads. Bear east along the snakelike D171 to get to **Belvédère** (population 495, elevation 820m), a hill-top village where you can learn how milk is made in the **Musée du Lait** (Milk Museum); visits are arranged by the **tourist office** *(☎ 04 93 03 51 66; 1 place du Colonel Baldoni)*.

Small old **St-Martin-Vésubie** (population 1089, elevation 1000m), 13km north of Belvédère, is the valley's primary outdoor activity base. The **tourist office** *(☎/fax 04 93 03 21 28; place Félix Faure)* has a list of mountain guides who lead walks and ski tours. Otherwise, try the **Maison du Parc** (see the boxed text 'Wildlife & Where to See It' earlier in this chapter) which recommends guides and organises some excellent guided hikes. For a panorama of the village, follow

Shut Up!

Green 'bods' in St-Martin-Vésubie have come up with a cunning idea to shut up noisy motorists and stop their green and peaceful valley from being polluted – the electric car.

Between June and September, visitors can hire an electric car from the tourist office in St-Martin-Vésubie (see Vallée de la Vésubie earlier in this chapter). Four different full-day itineraries are available, each including an optional lunch in a traditional inn, bistro or mountain hut. Car rental costs €23/31/38/46 per person (€41/67/92/118 with lunch). Reserve wheels at least 48 hours in advance.

the steep D31 up to **Venanson** (elevation 1164m), a hamlet perched on a rock above St-Martin.

A good map for walks in the area is Didier-Richard's No 9 or IGN's Série Bleue map No 3741OT *Vallée de la Vésubie, Parc National du Mercantour*.

Activities The small **ski** station of La Colmiane, 7km west of St-Martin-Vésubie across Col de St-Martin, has one chair lift that whisks skiers and walkers up to Pic de la Colmiane (1795m). From here, 30km of ski slopes and several **walking and mountain-bike trails** can be accessed. A single/eight-ride card costs €3.50 and a one-day pass is available for €9.50. The chair lift runs from 10am to 6pm daily.

The **Via Ferrata du Baus de la Frema** *(☎ 04 93 02 89 54)* is 3km from La Colmiane ski station along an unpaved track (see the boxed text 'Via Ferrata' earlier in this chapter). **Igloo Sports** *(☎ 04 93 02 83 43)* and **Ferrata Sport** *(☎ 04 93 02 80 56)* both rent Via Ferrata and ski gear as well as mountain bikes (€22 per day).

The **Bureau des Guides** *(☎ 04 93 02 88 30, fax 04 93 02 84 16)* in La Colmiane can guide you around the Via Ferrata for €39, and organises guided climbs for €30 per half-day. It also arranges canyoning and white-water rafting (from €35).

High-flyers can paraglide in St-Dalmas-Valdeblore (elevation 1350m), 5km farther west. The **tourist office** *(☎ 04 93 23 25 90, fax 04 93 23 25 91; W www.colmiane.com)* in La Roche, a hamlet 4km west of St-Dalmas-Valdeblore, has a list of paragliding schools.

Places to Stay Beneath trees next to a river, **Camping La Merio** *(☎ 04 93 03 30 38; 133 route de la Colmiane, St-Martin-Vésubie; tent & two adults/car €9.50/4.50; open June-early Sept)* is just 1km southwest of the village on the road to Colmiane.

Gîte d'Étape RandoSportNature *(☎ 04 93 02 82 86; e lorenzo.garofalo@libertsurf.fr; St-Dalmas-Valdeblore; dorm bed €15, breakfast €4, meal €14, half-board €28)* sports five shared rooms in a little stone house. The place is run by an experienced mountain guide who organises mountain walks, fishing, mushrooming and mountain-bike expeditions (from €15.50 per person) for anyone interested.

La Rouguière *(☎ 04 93 03 29 19, 06 07 41 92 08; e rougiere@aol.com; 6 rue Kellermann Sérurier, St-Martin-Vésubie; bed in 3-, 4- or 5-bed room €11)* is next to the Maison du Parc. In winter there's an additional charge of €0.85 per night to cover wood and electric heating.

Gîte du Boréon *(☎ 04 93 03 27 27; e gite duboreon@free.fr; 248 route de Salèse, Le Boréon; dorm bed €12.50, half-board €30)*, 5km northwest of St-Martin on the D89, is a *gîte d'étape* with lake view. Picnics/breakfast cost an extra €6/4.50. The place opens in winter, too, providing you reserve in advance.

Places to Eat In the family-run village restaurant **La Trappa** *(☎ 04 93 03 21 50; place du Marché, St-Martin-Vésubie; menus €13 & €19)* you can eat snails in garlic butter, game terrine, mountain ham and other 'mountain' food.

Auberge del Campo *(☎ 04 93 03 13 12; menus from €20)*, a charming farmhouse inn run by a very humorous patron, is 2km west of St-Jean la Rivière on the D32. The stone farmhouse dates from 1785 and offers sweeping views of the gorges and village from its hillside terrace. A roaring fire warms the place in winter and the menu oozes fresh local produce.

Getting There & Away Two to three weekly buses are run by **Transport Régional des Alpes-Maritimes** *(☎ 04 93 89 41 45)* between Nice and La Colmiane (€13.20, two hours), plus one a day on weekends only to/from La Colmiane via St-Martin-Vésubie (€9.80, 1¾ hours).

Vallée des Merveilles

Sandwiched between the Vésubie Valley and the Roya Valley is the 'Valley of Wonders'. It lies at the heart of the Parc National du Mercantour and protects one of the world's most precious collections of Bronze Age petroglyphs. The rock engravings of human figures, bulls and other animals, spread over 30 sq km around Mont Bégo (2872m), date from between 1800 and 1500 BC and are thought to have been made by a Ligurian cult. The area is sprinkled with lakes.

The main access routes into the valley are the eastbound D91 from St-Dalmas de Tende in the Vallée de la Roya, or the dead-end D171, which leads north to the valley from **Roquebillière** (population 1513) in the Vallée de la Vésubie. The moonscape valley is snow-covered much of the year and the best time to visit is July to September. Access is restricted: Walkers can only use authorised footpaths and are encouraged by park authorities to only visit the valley with a guide. See Activities under Vallée de la Roya following for information on guided walks.

IGN's Série Bleue map No 3841OT *Vallée de la Roya, Vallée des Merveilles* covers the area in a scale of 1:25,000.

Vallée de la Roya

The Roya Valley once served as a hunting ground for King Victor Emmanuel II of Italy and only became part of France in 1947. In this valley is the pretty **Breil-sur-Roya** (population 2023, elevation 280m), 62km northeast of Nice. There are good views from the Col de Brouis (879m), which links **Sospel** (population 2937), 21km south, with the Roya Valley.

The dramatic **Gorges de Saorge**, 9km north of Breil-sur-Roya, lead to fortified **Saorge** (population 398, elevation 520m), which overlooks the valley and is set in a natural amphitheatre. The village is a maze of narrow, stepped streets and 15th- to 17th-century houses. A Baroque church and cloister decorated with 17th-century frescoes form part of the **Monastère de Saorge** *(☎ 04 93 04 55 55; adult/18-25 yrs/under 18 €4/2.50/free; open 10am-noon & 2pm-6pm Wed-Mon Apr-Oct, 2pm-6pm Wed-Mon Nov-Mar)*. The monastery was founded by the reformed Friars Minor of the Observance in 1633.

Immediately north, the **Gorges de Bergue** lead to **St-Dalmas de Tende**, which is the main gateway into the Vallée des Merveilles. From St-Dalmas de Tende, the D91 winds 10km west along the Vallon de la Minière to **Lac des Mesches** (1390m), from where trails lead into the valley past the Refuge des Merveilles (2111m). Alternatively, continue 5km to the mountain resort of **Casterino** to pick up more northern trails.

Equally scenic is the eastbound D143 from St-Dalmas de Tende to **La Brigue** (elevation 770m) and 4km farther on to **Notre Dame des Fontaines**, a fabulous church hidden at the foot of the mountain. Dubbed the Sistine Chapel of the southern Alps, it shelters beautifully preserved frescoes by 15th-century Piedmontese painters Jean Canavesio and Jean Baleison. Contact the tourist office in La Brigue (see Information later in this section) for a guided visit (four daily, €3.20/1.50 with/without commentary).

In **Tende** (population 1890, elevation 830m), 4km north of St-Dalmas de Tende, the **Musée des Merveilles** *(☎ 04 93 04 32 50; W www.museedesmerveilles.com; ave du 16 Septembre 1947; adult/7-16 yrs €4.55/2.30, admission free 1st Sun of the month; open 10am-6.30pm Wed-Mon May–mid-Oct, 10am-5pm Wed-Mon mid-Oct–Feb & Apr)*, gives the natural history of the valley and exhibits numerous archaeological finds.

Foodies can learn about how the region's tastebud-tickling honey is made at the small but sweet **Maison du Miel et de l'Abeille** *(House of Honey & Bees; ☎ 04 93 04 76 22; descente aux Moulins; adult/child €1.50/0.75; open 10am-5pm Thur, 10am-6pm Wed & Fri-Sun in winter, 10am-6pm daily in summer)* in Tende; and shop for cheese and smoked ham at **La Maison du Fromage** *(☎ 04 93 04 64 82; 13 ave du 16 Septembre 1947)*, a fabulous cheese shop.

The valley celebrates Les Baroquiales, a Baroque art and music festival, in July. Concerts *(☎ 04 93 04 24 41; W www.lesbaroquiales.org; tickets €10-20)* are held in churches, and on squares such as Sospel's place St-Michel there are art exhibitions and costumed street parades.

Just 5km north of Tende, the **Tunnel de Tende** – engineered in 1882 – provides a vital link into Italy.

Information There are small but efficient tourist offices in **Breil-sur-Roya** *(☎/fax 04 93 04 99 76; W www.breil-sur-roya.fr; place*

Biancheri); **Sospel** *(☎ 04 93 04 15 80, fax 04 93 04 19 96; Le Pont-Vieux)*, inside the city gate on the old bridge; **La Brigue** *(☎ 04 93 04 36 07, fax 04 93 04 36 09; place St-Martin)*; and **Tende** *(☎ 04 93 04 73 71, fax 04 93 04 35 09; W www.tendemerveilles.com; ave du 16 Septembre 1947)*.

Activities Breil-sur-Roya is a water-sports base. **Roya Évasion** *(☎ 04 93 04 91 46; W www.royaevasion.com; 1 rue Pasteur)* organises kayaking, canyoning and rafting trips on the River Roya, as well as walks and mountain-bike expeditions. **AET Nature** *(☎/fax 04 93 04 47 64; W http://aetcanyoning.com; 392 chemin du Foussa)*, with a bureau on central place Biancheri, likewise organises white-water and walking trips. A day's canyoning typically costs €40.

Guides for walks and 4WD jeep expeditions in the Vallée des Merveilles can be hired in St-Dalmas de Tende and Tende. **Merveilles, Gravures & Découvertes** *(☎ 06 83 03 90 13, fax 04 93 04 20 75; e gravureinfo@yahoo.fr; 18 rue Antoine Operti, Tende)* runs daily guided archaeological walks to Mont Bégo (adult/12 to 18 years €8/4) and weekly night visits (€4 per person) in July and August. **Luc Fioretti** *(☎ 06 82 19 61 55, fax 04 93 04 69 11; e lucfioretti@9online.fr; 56 rue Béatrice Lascaris, Tende)* runs one-day 4WD jeep tours (€61 per person).

In July and August, the **Parc National du Mercantour office** *(open 10am-1pm & 3pm-7pm daily mid-June–mid-Sept)*, inside Sospel's old city gate, organises guided walks and distributes a map detailing 19 mountain-biking itineraries. Cycling club **Sospel VTT** *(☎ 06 70 76 57 05)* rents wheels. In Tende, the **Maison de la Montagne et des Sports** *(☎/fax 04 93 04 77 73; e mmstende@aol.com; 11 ave du 16 Septembre 1947)* rents bikes and can tell you about 23 bike trails departing from Tende, Col de Tende, La Brigue and Casterino.

The Maison de la Montagne et des Sports also rents equipment for Tende's dizzying **Via Ferrata des Comtes Lascaris** (see the boxed text 'Via Ferrata' earlier in this chapter) and can provide you with a guide.

Places to Stay & Eat Signposted from Breil-sur-Roya train station, **USBTP** *(☎ 04 93 04 46 66, fax 04 93 04 92 22; 55 route des Vacances; camping per adult/car/tent from €2.80/1.85/2.45)* is a camp site with a pool.

Neige et Merveilles *(☎ 04 93 04 62 40, fax 04 93 04 88 58; W www.neige-merveilles.com; La Minière de Vallauria; dorm bed or doubles per person with half-board €32.50; open Apr-late Oct)* is a mountain activity centre in St-Dalmas de Tende.

Hôtel Le Roya *(☎ 04 93 04 48 10, fax 04 93 04 92 70; place Bianchéri; doubles €41.16, formule gîte €15.25 per person)* is a simple inn in Breil-sur-Roya that also offers a nifty *formule gîte* for breakfast-keen walkers happy to share a room with a stranger.

Castel du Roy *(☎ 04 93 04 43 66, fax 04 93 04 91 83; route de Tende; doubles/triples low season €65/71, high season €81/82, half-board per person low/high season €70/98)*, signposted off the Tende-bound N204 from Breil-sur-Roya centre, is known as much for its delicious restaurant as for its charming hotel rooms and five acres of green and flowery grounds.

Restaurant Le Roya *(☎ 04 93 04 47 38; place de Brancion; menu €20, trout €11.50, plat du jour €7, lunchtime formule €11)* and the hotel of the same name sit either side of the church in Breil-sur-Roya. The restaurant serves food in a 16th-century mill where you can pick your own trout – then pick one of eight toppings.

Getting There & Away There is an SNCF train station in Sospel, Breil-sur-Roya, St-Dalmas de Tende and Tende – all served by the Nice-Turin line that runs several times per day from the coast, along the Roya Valley and into Italy.

Buses *(☎ 04 93 04 01 24)* link Sospel with Menton on the coast (€4.50; 40 minutes, four to five daily).

Nice to Menton

Nice and Menton (and the 30km of towns in between) are linked by three *corniches* (coastal roads), each higher and more hazardous than the last. They are particularly celebrated for their breathtaking sea views, luxurious seaside villas and – in July and August – hellish traffic, which moves at a snail's pace in the searing heat. In the 1920s motorists raced the coastal *Train Bleu* (Blue Train) from Paris along these roads. Speed fiends today should opt for the inland A8, which continues east to Ventimiglia (Vintimille in French) in Italy.

Nice makes an ideal base for exploring the rest of the Côte d'Azur. The city has plenty of relatively cheap places to stay and is only a short train or bus ride from Monaco (see the Monaco chapter), Cannes and other Riviera hot spots. Away from the coast's body-packed beaches is the Niçois hinterland, an inland maze of remote *villages perchés* (hill-top villages) and hairpin mountain passes, guaranteed to send a chill through the raciest of drivers.

Highlights

- Gape at Nice's wedding-cake mansions and *belle époque* follies
- Find out what made Matisse tick in Cimiez; visit his modern friends at the Musée d'Art Moderne et d'Art Contemporain in Nice
- See how the rich lived: visit the lush interiors and gardens of Cap Ferrat's Villa Rothschild, the Villa Grecque Kérylos in Beaulieu-sur-Mer and Menton's bushel of gardens
- Walk around a cape and discover Mediterranean flora – take your pick from Cap Martin, Cap d'Ail and Cap Ferrat
- Tour a hill-top village then lunch at the Beau Séjour in Gorbio

Food Highlights

pissaladière – Niçois onion, anchovy and black olive tart

salade niçoise – green salad with tuna, egg and anchovies

socca – griddled chickpea flour and olive oil pancake from Nice

Nice

postcodes 06000 & 06300 • pop 342,738

Nice is nice (Nissa in Niçois, Nizza in Italian) – the fifth-largest town in France – and is considered the capital of the Côte d'Azur. Fashionable but relaxed, it is fun fun fun, and especially in the height of summer when backpackers flock here in droves to dip their toes in its sparkling waters and sample the best of southern France's sky-blue coast.

The city's pebble beach may not be worth a postcard home, but the city's fantastical architecture from the early 20th-century *belle époque*, art museums and buzzing cultural scene most certainly are. The famous Nice Carnival sets the streets ablaze each year at Mardi Gras with a merry-go-round of masked parades and colourful floats.

Nice was founded by seafaring Greeks, who named it Nikaia to commemorate a victory (*nike* in Greek) over a nearby town. The Romans followed in 154 BC, settling Cemenelum (now Cimiez). The city become part of France in 1860. See the Facts about Provence chapter for more about the city's history.

ORIENTATION

Ave Jean Médecin runs south from near the train station to place Masséna. The modern city centre, the area north and west of place Masséna, includes the pedestrian streets of rue de France and rue Masséna. The bus

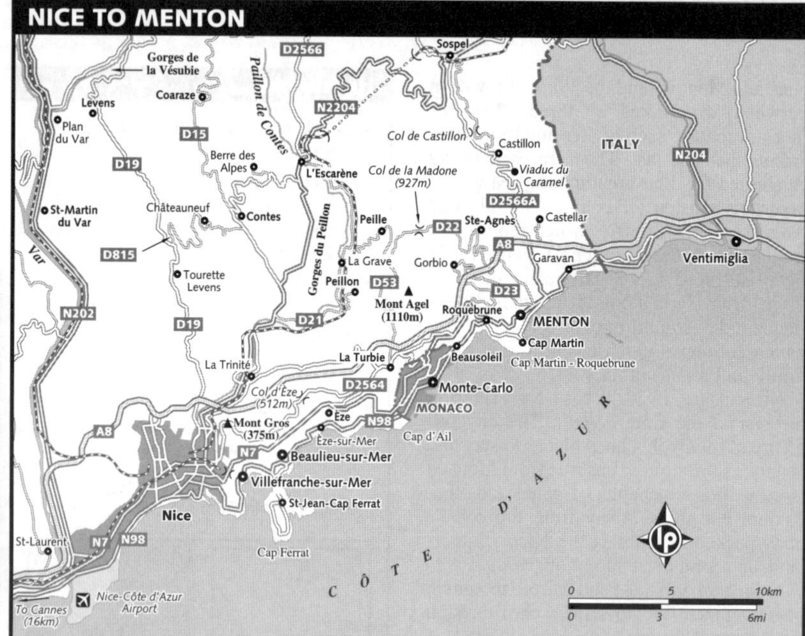

terminal on square Général Leclerc and the local bus station are east of place Masséna.

Famous promenade des Anglais follows the beachfront west from the port, past the city centre to the airport, 6km west. Vieux Nice (Old Nice) is delineated by blvd Jean Jaurès, quai des États-Unis and the hill known as Colline du Château.

The wealthy neighbourhood of Cimiez, home to several outstanding museums, is north of the centre.

INFORMATION

Tourist Offices

There's always a queue for information at the **tourist office** *(☎ 04 93 87 07 07; W www.nicetourisme.com; ave Thiers; open 8am-8pm Mon-Sat, 9am-7pm Sun)*, which is to the left as you exit from the train station. Its beachfront **annexe** *(☎ 04 92 14 48 00; 5 promenade des Anglais; open 8am-8pm Mon-Sat, 9am-7pm Sun)* is less frantic. At the airport, there is a **tourist office** *(☎ 04 93 21 44 11; open 8am-10pm daily)* in the arrivals hall of terminal 1. All three offices dole out free city maps and will also make hotel reservations for free.

The **Comité Régional du Tourisme Riviera-Côte d'Azur** *(☎ 04 93 37 78 78, fax 04 93 86 01 06; W www.guideriviera.com; 55 promenade des Anglais)* runs an **information desk** *(☎ 04 93 21 80 95; open 8am-10pm daily)* next to the tourist office at the airport.

The **Parc National du Mercantour** *(☎ 04 93 16 78 88, fax 04 93 88 79 05; W www.parcmercantour.fr; 23 rue d'Italie; open 9am-6pm Mon-Fri)* has its headquarters here.

Money

American Express *(☎ 04 93 16 53 53; 11 promenade des Anglais; 9am-9pm daily May-Sept, open 9am-8pm daily Oct-Apr)* overlooks the sea.

At the train station, there is a convenient **Thomas Cook** *(☎ 04 93 82 13 00; 12 ave Thiers; open 7.30am-9.30pm daily May-Sept, 8am-8pm daily Oct-Apr)* exchange bureau in the car-rental building (to the right as you are leaving the station) and another at the top of the stairs leading from 13 ave Thiers *(open 8am-10pm daily May-Sept, 9am-5.30pm daily Oct-Apr)* to rue de Belgique and ave Durante.

There's a 24-hour currency exchange machine outside the **Banque Populaire de la Côte d'Azur** *(17 ave Jean Médecin)*.

Post & Communications

The postcode for central Nice north and west of blvd Jean Jaurès and ave Galliéni is 06000. The postcode for Vieux Nice and the ferry port is 06300.

The **post office** *(23 ave Thiers; open 8am-7pm Mon-Fri, 8am-noon Sat)* has a **branch office** *(2 rue Louis Gassin; open 8.30am-6pm Mon-Fri, 8.30am or 9am-noon Sat)* in Vieux Nice.

Near the train station, **Web Store** *(☎ 04 93 87 87 99; e info@webstore.fr; 12 rue de Russie; open 10am-noon & 2pm-7pm Mon-Sat)* charges €4.50/7.50 per 30/60 minutes. **3.W.O** *(☎ 04 93 80 51 12; 32 rue Assalit; open 10am-8pm daily)* and bamboo-decked **Planète Nature** *(☎ 04 93 16 89 81; 16 rue Paganini; open 9am-9.30pm daily)*, which also serves organic food and drink, both charge €5 per hour.

Opposite the bus station, **@ Cyber Point** *(☎ 04 93 92 70 63; 10 ave Félix Faure; open 9.30am-7.30pm Mon-Sat)* has the choice of French or American keyboards and touts a €6 hourly rate.

By the sea, **Panini & Web** *(☎ 04 93 88 72 75; 25 promenade des Anglais; open 10am-9pm daily)* charges €4 per 30 minutes, or €6 for one hour and a free drink. Alternatively, invest €3.80 in a *panino* (Italian-style sandwich).

Travel Agencies

Reliable travel agencies include **USIT Connections** *(☎ 08 25 08 25 25; 15 rue de France)*; **OTU Voyages** *(☎ 08 25 00 25 88; 48 rue de France)*; and **Wasteels** *(☎ 08 03 88 70 54; 32 rue Hôtel des Postes)*.

Bookshops

New and second-hand English-language novels and guides are sold at **The Cat's Whiskers** *(☎ 04 93 80 02 66; 30 rue Lamartine; open 2pm-6.45pm Mon, 9.30am-noon & 2pm-6.45pm Tues-Fri, 9.30am-noon & 3pm-6.30pm Sat)*. For second-hand reference books in English try **Brouillon de Culture** *(☎ 04 93 62 28 32; 23 rue de l'Hôtel des Postes; open 9am-noon & 2.30pm-7pm Mon-Sat)*.

Travel bookshop **Magellan** *(☎ 04 93 82 31 81; 3 rue d'Italie; open 9.30am-1pm & 2pm-7pm Tues-Sat)* sells IGN maps, Didier-Richard walking maps, topoguides and travel guides (including Lonely Planet) in English.

Cultural Centres & Libraries

The ornate **Holy Trinity Anglican Church** *(☎ 04 93 87 19 83; 11 rue de la Buffa)* functions as an Anglophone cultural centre. Sunday Mass is celebrated at 11am. Among the 'pioneer' expatriate graves from the 19th and 20th centuries in the adjoining cemetery is that of Henri Francis Lyte (1793–1847), a British vicar from Devonshire who wrote the hymn *Abide with Me* only three weeks before dying from tuberculosis in Nice.

To get to the adjoining **Anglo-American library** *(12 rue de France; open 10am-11am & 3pm-5pm Tues-Thur & Sat, 3pm-5pm Fri)* cut through the passageway opposite 17 rue de France.

Nice's hi-tech **Bibliothèque Louis Nucéra** *(☎ 04 97 13 48 00; 2 place Yves Klein; open 1pm-6pm Tues-Sat July & Aug, 10am-7pm Tues & Wed, 2pm-7pm Thur & Fri, 10am-6pm Sat Sept-June)*, next to the Musée d'Art Moderne et d'Art Contemporain, is shaped like a big square head atop a neck (the neck being underground).

Laundry

Self-service laundrettes include **Taxi Lav'** *(22 rue Pertinax)* and another at 13 rue du Pont Vieux in Vieux Nice, both open 7am to 9pm or 10pm daily. Count on paying €3 for a 5kg wash.

Medical Services

Pharmacie Riviera *(☎ 04 93 62 54 44; 66 ave Jean Médecin)* and **Pharmacie Masséna** *(☎ 04 93 87 78 94; 7 rue Masséna)* are 24-hour pharmacies. **Hôpital St-Roch** *(☎ 04 92 03 33 75; 5 rue Pierre Dévoluy)* has a 24-hour emergency service. For an emergency home visit, call **SOS Médecins** *(☎ 08 01 85 01 07)*.

Emergency

The **police headquarters** *(☎ 04 92 17 22 22; 1 ave Maréchal Foch)* has a special **foreign tourist department** *(☎ 04 92 17 20 63; open 8am-noon & 2pm-6pm daily)*; report lost or stolen passports here. Other lost property is handled by the **police station** *(☎ 04 93 80 65 50; 10 cours Saleya)* in Vieux Nice.

NICE

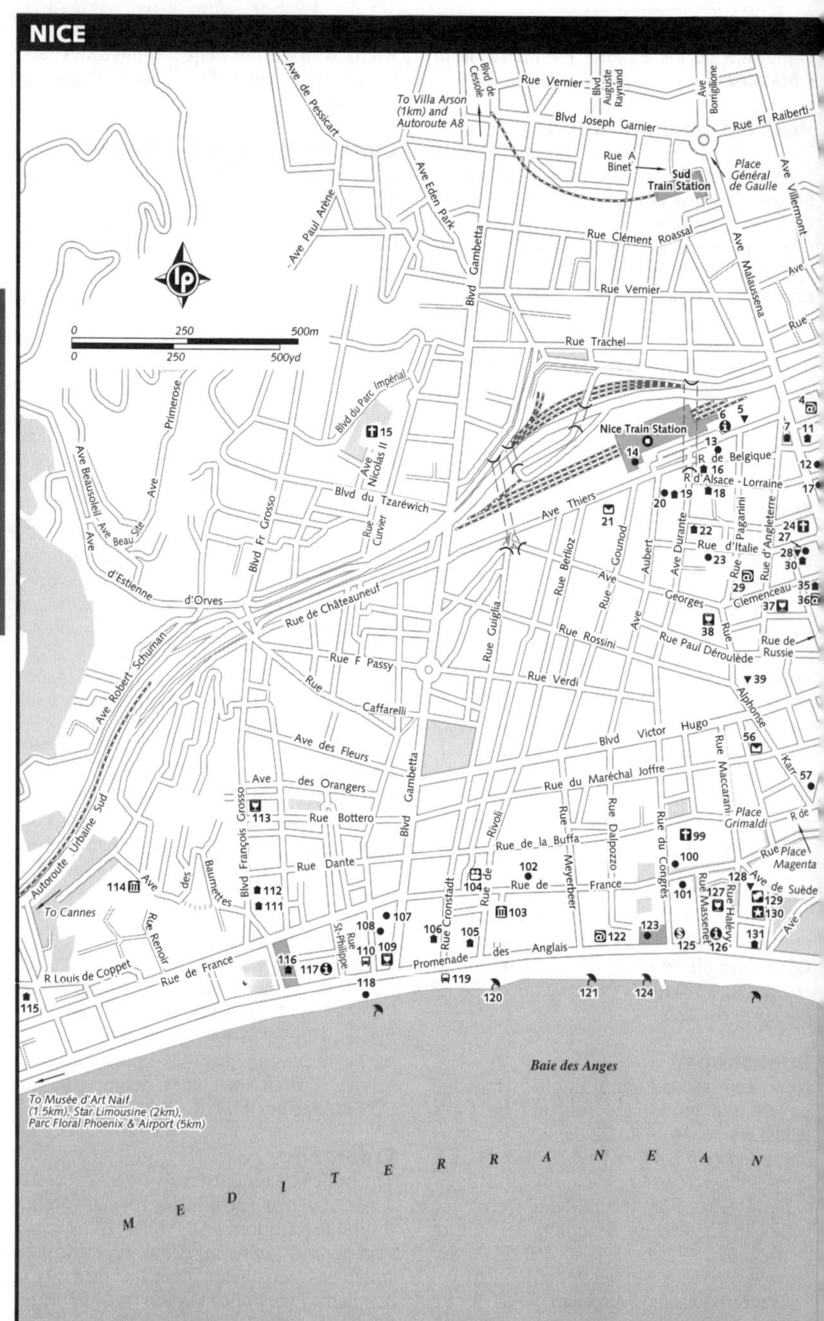

Rue Vernier
Blvd de Cessole
Blvd Auguste Raynaud
Ave Borriglione
To Villa Arson (1km) and Autoroute A8
Blvd Joseph Garnier
Rue Fl Raiberti
Ave de Pessicart
Rue A Binet
Sud Train Station
Place Général de Gaulle
Ave Villermont
Ave Eden Park
Ave Paul Arène
Rue Clément Roassal
Blvd Gambetta
Ave Malausséna
Rue Vernier
Rue Trachel
0 250 500m
0 250 500yd
Blvd du Parc Impérial
Ave Primerose
Nice Train Station
R de Belgique
R d'Alsace - Lorraine
Ave Nicolas II
Blvd du Tzaréwich
Ave Beausoleil
Ave Beau Site
Blvd Fr Grosso
Rue Curvier
Ave Thiers
Rue Paganini
Rue d'Angleterre
Rue d'Italie
Ave Durante
Rue Aubert
Rue Gounod
Rue Berlioz
Ave d'Estienne d'Orves
Rue de Châteauneuf
Ave Georges Clemenceau
Rue Rossini
Rue Paul Déroulède
Rue de Russie
Rue F Passy
Rue Guiglia
Rue Verdi
Ave Robert Schuman
Rue Caffarelli
Rue Alphonse Karr
Ave des Fleurs
Blvd Victor Hugo
Rue Maccarani
Ave des Orangers
Rue du Maréchal Joffre
Rue Bottero
Place Grimaldi
R de
Rue Dalpozzo
Rue du Congrès
Rue Meyerbeer
Rue de Rivoli
Rue de la Buffa
Autoroute Urbaine Sud
Blvd François Grosso
Rue Dante
Place Magenta
Ave de Suède
Ave des Baumettes
Rue Cronstadt
Rue de France
Rue Massenet
Rue Halévy
To Cannes
Rue Renoir
Rue St-Philippe
R Louis de Coppet
Rue de France
Promenade des Anglais
Baie des Anges
To Musée d'Art Naïf (1.5km), Star Limousine (2km), Parc Floral Phoenix & Airport (5km)
MEDITERRANEAN

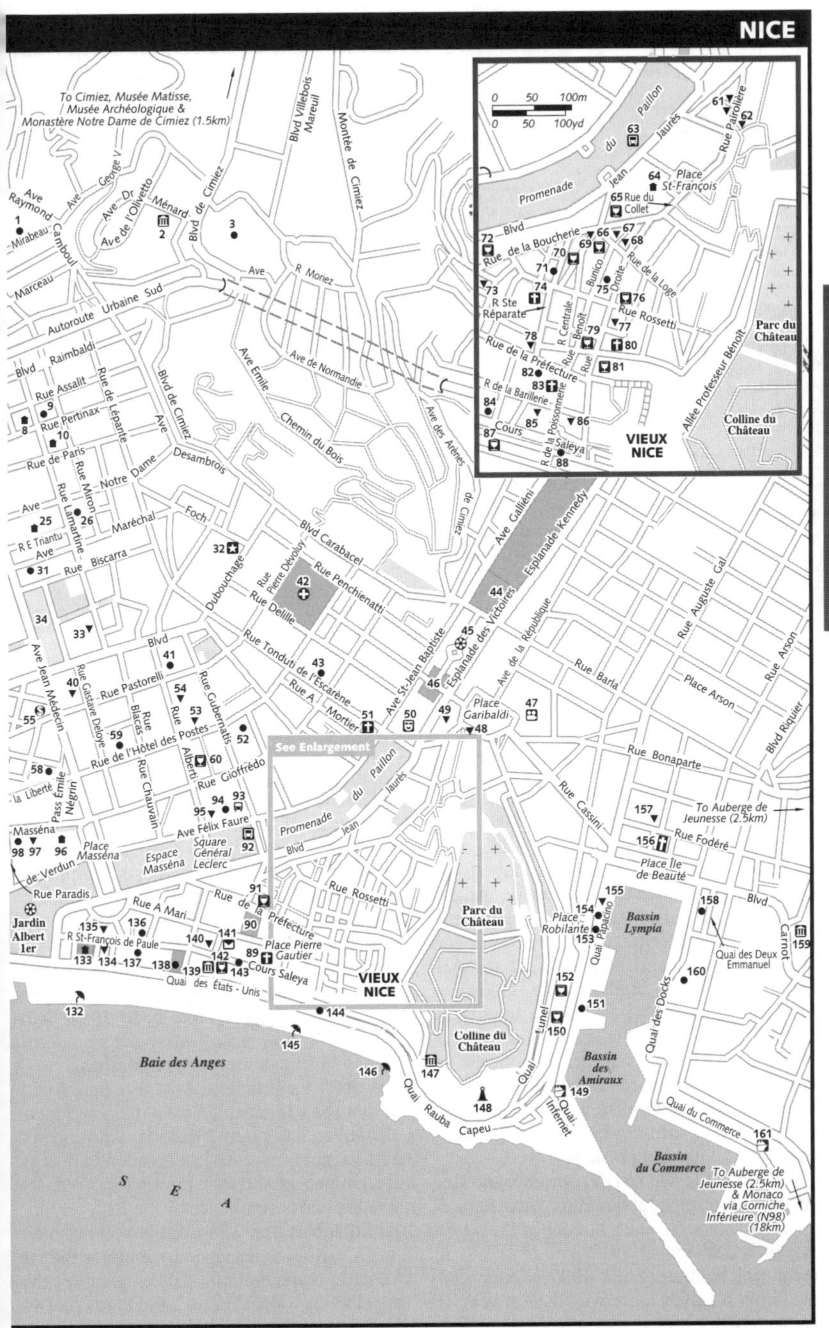
NICE
To Cimiez, Musée Matisse, Musée Archéologique & Monastère Notre Dame de Cimiez (1.5km)
Ave Raymond Comboul
Mirabeau
Ave George V
Ave Dr Ménard
Ave de l'Olivetto
Blvd de Cimiez
Blvd Villebois Mareuil
Montée de Cimiez
Marceau
Autoroute Urbaine Sud
Ave R Moriez
Blvd Raimbaldi
Rue Assalit
Rue Pertinax
Rue de Paris
Rue de Lépante
Rue Miron
Rue Lamartine
Ave Notre Dame
Ave Maréchal Foch
Desambrois
Ave Emile
Ave de Normandie
Chemin du Bois
Ave des Arènes de Cimiez
R E Triantu
Ave
Rue Biscarra
Dubouchage
Rue Pierre Dévoluy
Rue Delille
Blvd Carabacel
Rue Penchienatti
Rue Tonduti de l'Escarène
Rue A Mortier
Ave Jean Médecin
Rue Gustave Deloye
Rue Pastorelli
Rue Blacas
Rue Alberti
Rue Gubernatis
Rue de l'Hôtel des Postes
Rue Chauvain
Rue Gioffredo
Ave Félix Faure
la Liberté
Pass Émile Négrin
Masséna
Place Masséna
Espace Masséna
Square Général Leclerc
de Verdun
Rue Paradis
Jardin Albert 1er
Rue A Mari
Rue de la Préfecture
R St-François de Paule
Place Pierre Gautier
Cours Saleya
Quai des États - Unis
Ave St-Jean Baptiste
Esplanade des Victoires
Ave Galliéni
Esplanade Kennedy
Ave de la République
Place Garibaldi
Rue Barla
Place Arson
Rue Arson
Rue Auguste Gal
Blvd Riquier
Rue Bonaparte
Rue Cassini
To Auberge de Jeunesse (2.5km)
Rue Fodéré
Place Île de Beauté
Place Robilante
Quai Papacino
Bassin Lympia
Blvd Carnot
Quai des Deux Emmanuel
Quai des Docks
Bassin des Amiraux
Quai Lunel
Quai Infernet
Quai du Commerce
Bassin du Commerce
To Auberge de Jeunesse (2.5km) & Monaco via Corniche Inférieure (N98) (18km)
See Enlargement
Promenade du Paillon
Blvd Jean Jaurès
Rue Rossetti
Parc du Château
Colline du Château
VIEUX NICE
Quai Rauba Capeu
Baie des Anges
S E A
0 50 100m
0 50 100yd
Place St-François
Rue du Collet
Rue Pairolière
Rue de la Boucherie
Rue Bunico
Rue Droite
Rue de la Loge
R Ste Réparate
R Centrale
Rue Benoît
Rue de la Préfecture
R de la Barillerie
R de la Poissonnerie
Cours Saleya
Allée Professeur Bénoît
1 2 3 8 9 10 25 26 31 32 33 34 40 41 42 43 44 45 46 47 48 49 50 51 52 53 54 55 58 59 60
61 62 63 64 65 66 67 68 69 70 71 72 73 74 75 76 77 78 79 80 81 82 83 84 85 86 87 88
89 90 91 92 93 94 95 96 97 98 132 133 134 135 136 137 138 139 140 141 142 143 144 145 146 147 148 149 150 151 152 153 154 155 156 157 158 159 160 161

NICE

7 Hôtel Darcy; Restaurant de Paris
8 Hôtel Astrid
10 Hôtel Plaisance
11 Backpackers' Hotel – Chez Patrick; Le Faubourg Montmartre
16 Hôtel d'Orsay
18 Hôtel du Piémont
19 Hôtel Belle Meunière
22 Hôtel Les Orangers
25 Le Petit Louvre
30 Hôtel Lyonnais; Hôtel Notre Dame
35 Hôtel Clemenceau
64 Hôtel St-François
96 Hôtel Rex
105 Hôtel Négresco; Chantecler
106 Hôtel Cronstadt
111 Hôtel Carlone
112 Résidence Hôtelière Astoria
115 Centre Hébergement Jeunes
116 Four Points Elysée Palace
131 Hôtel Le Méridien
133 Hôtel Beau Rivage

PLACES TO EAT
5 Flunch
28 Auberge au Soleil
33 Le Speakeasy
39 Les Viviers
40 Indyana
48 Grand Café de Turin
49 Prisunic
53 Maí"l's
54 Le Cantine de Lulu
61 Chez René
62 L'Escalinada
66 Lou Philha Leva
67 Oliviera
68 Chez Palmyre
73 Casalinga
77 Chez Thérésa
78 Nissa Socca
85 Le Living Room
86 La Mezzanine; Ghost House
95 Sud
97 Boccaccio
128 La Cigale Orientale
134 Le Comptoir
135 Terre de Truffes
140 Le Pain Quotidien
155 Zucca Magica
157 Café Borghese

MUSEUMS
2 Musée National Message Biblique Marc Chagall
46 Musée d'Art Moderne et d'Art Contemporain; Bibliothèque Louis Nocera
103 Musée d'Art et d'Histoire; Palais Masséna
114 Musée des Beaux-Arts
147 Musée de la Marine; Lift; Tour Bellanda
159 Musée de Paléonthologie Humaine de Terra Amata

BARS & CLUBS
37 Plasma Café
38 Le Grand Escurial
60 Entre Mets & Vins
65 William's Pub
69 Jonathan's Live Music Pub
70 Pub Oxford; De Klomp
72 McMahons Pub
76 O'Hara's
79 Karma
81 O'Neill's
87 La Casa del Sol
91 Wayne's; Master Home
109 Forum
113 Blue Boy
127 Le Klub
142 Thor Pub
150 Dizzy Club
152 The Seventies

OTHER
1 Club Alpin Français des Alpes-Maritimes
3 Conservatoire de Musique
4 3.W.O
6 Tourist Office
9 Taxi Lav'
12 Pharmacie Riviera
13 Nicea Location Rent
14 ADA, Avis, Budget & Europcar; Thomas Cook

PROMENADE DES ANGLAIS

Palm-lined Promenade of the English, paid for by Nice's English colony in 1822 as a shoreside strolling path, is a fine stage for a stroll along the beach and the Baie des Anges (Bay of Angels). Don't miss the magnificent facade of **Hôtel Negresco**, built in 1912 for the Romanian Henri Negresco, or the Art Deco **Palais de la Méditerranée**, gradually becoming prime real-estate apartments at nos 13–17. The Mediterranean Palace – a 1930s casino – was the prize property of American millionaire Frank Jay Gould, whose seafront enterprise was France's top-earning casino until the 1970s when his luck changed and he shut up shop.

East towards Vieux Nice, promenade des Anglais becomes **quai des États-Unis**, named after the United States in honour of President Wilson's decision in 1917 to join WWI. A memorial honouring the 4000 Niçois who died in WWI (plus those who died in WWII) is carved in the rock at the quay's eastern end.

Galerie des Ponchettes *(☎ 04 93 62 31 24; 77 quai des États-Unis; admission free; open 10am-6pm Tues-Sat, 2pm-6pm Sun)* is a 19th-century vaulted hall that hosts temporary contemporary art exhibitions. The building was used as an arsenal for the Sardinian navy, then as a fish market until 1950 when Matisse persuaded the council to revamp it. **Galerie de la Marine** *(☎ 04 93 62 37 11; 59 quai des États-Unis; admission free; open 10am-6pm Tues-Sat, 2pm-6pm Sun)* is another seaside art gallery hosting temporary exhibitions.

Just off the Promenade at the southern end of **ave Jean Médecin**, Nice's main commercial street, sits **place Masséna**, whose early 19th-century, neoclassical arcaded buildings are painted in shades of ochre and red. Its western end is dominated by the 19th-century **Jardin Albert 1er**. The giant arc languishing on the lawn was designed by sculptor Bernar Venet to commemorate the centenary of the appellation 'Côte d'Azur', the brainchild of French poet Stéphane Liégeard (1830–1925).

NICE

15 Cathédrale Orthodoxe Russe St-Nicolas
17 J Multari (Bakery)
20 Holiday Bikes; JML
21 Post Office
23 Parc National du Mercantour Headquarters
24 Église Notre Dame
26 The Cat's Whiskers
27 Magellan
29 Planète Nature
31 Monoprix Supermarket
32 Police Headquarters
34 Centre Commercial Nice Étoile; FNAC
36 Web Store
41 Laundrette
42 Hôpital St-Roch
43 J Multari (Bakery)
44 Acropolis
45 Jardin Maréchal Juin
47 Cinéma Nouveau Mercury
50 Théâtre de Nice
51 Église du Voeu
52 Brouillon de Culture
55 Banque Populaire de la Côte d'Azur (24-Hour Currency Exchange Machine)
56 Branch Post Office
57 J Multari (Bakery)
58 SNCF Boutique
59 Wasteels
63 Intercity Bus Station
71 Laundrette
74 Cathédrale Ste-Réparate
75 Palais Lascaris
80 Église St-Jacques Le Majeur
82 Caves Caprioglio
83 Église St-Giaume
84 Fruit & Vegetable Market
88 Roller Station
89 Chapelle de la Misericode
90 Palais de Justice; Palais de Lap Préfecture
92 City Bus Station (Station Centrale)
93 @ Cyber Point; Sunboutique
94 Airlib Express
98 Pharmacie Masséna
99 Holy Trinity Anglican Church
100 USIT Connections
101 Anglo-American Library
102 OTU Voyages
104 Cinéma Rialto
107 Intermarché Supermarket
108 Cycles Mach 2
110 Airport Buses
117 Comité Régional du Tourisme Riviera-Côte d'Azur
118 Public Showers & Toilets
119 Airport Buses
120 Plage du Neptune
121 Plage du Sporting
122 Panini & Web; Always
123 Palais de la Méditerranée
124 Lido Plage
125 American Express
126 Tourist Office Annexe
129 US Consulate
130 Police Station
132 Plage Publique de Beaurivage
136 Town Hall
137 Moulin à Huile d'Olive Alziari
138 Opéra de Nice
139 Galerie des Ponchettes
141 Branch Post Office
143 Flower Market
144 Galerie de la Marine
145 Plage Publique de l'Opéra
146 Plage Publique des Ponchettes
148 WWI Memorial
149 Ferry Terminal (Terminal 2)
151 Trans Côte d'Azur; Corsica Ferries Ticket Office; Le Poseidon
153 Les Puces des Nice (Antique Shops)
154 Confiserie Florian
156 Eglise Notre Dame de l'Immaculée Conception
158 François Lejeune Centre de Plongee
160 Nice Diving
161 Ferry Terminal (Terminal 1)

Espace Masséna, a public square enlivened by fountains, a rollerblading dome and ornamental gardens, straddles the eastern side of place Masséna.

VIEUX NICE

This area of narrow, winding streets between quai des États-Unis and the Musée d'Art Moderne et d'Art Contemporain has looked pretty much the same since the 1700s. The arcade-lined **place Garibaldi**, built during the late 18th century, is named after one of the great heroes of Italian unification, Giuseppe Garibaldi (1807–82), born in Nice and buried in the cemetery in the Parc du Château.

Cours Saleya and rue de la Préfecture, the old city's main artery, are dominated by the imposing **Palais de la Préfecture**, built at the beginning of the 17th century for the princes of Savoy.

Interesting churches in Vieux Nice include the Baroque **Cathédrale Ste-Réparate** *(place Rossetti)*, which was built between 1650 and 1680 in honour of the city's patron saint; blue-grey and yellow **Église St-Jacques Le Majeur** *(place du Gésu)*, (1650) with Baroque ornamentation dating from the mid-17th century; **Église St-Giaume** *(1 rue de la Poissonnerie)*; and **Chapelle de la Miséricorde** *(cours Saleya)* built between 1740 and 1780.

Rue Bénoît Bunico, perpendicular to rue Rossetti, served as Nice's Jewish ghetto after a 1430 law restricted where Jews could live. South along the parallel rue Droite, you reach the Baroque **Palais Lascaris** *(☎ 04 93 62 05 54; 15 rue Droite; admission free; open 10am-6pm Wed-Mon)*, named after the Lascaris-Ventimiglia family who owned the house in the 17th century. A monumental staircase leads up to state apartments, the ceilings of which are richly decorated with elaborate frescoes depicting ancient mythology. Fine Flemish tapestries line the walls and an 18th-century pharmacy is on the ground floor.

Vieux Nice's eastern extremity, at the end of quai des États-Unis, is flagged by the **Parc**

du Château, a public park atop a 92m-high hill that offers panoramic views of Nice and the sparkling Baie des Anges. You can also visit the **Cascade Donjon**, an artificial waterfall crowned with a viewing platform. Open-air concerts are held here in summer.

The 12th-century castle, after which the hill and park are named, was razed by Louis XIV in 1706. In the one remaining tower, 16th-century Tour Bellanda, is the **Musée de la Marine** *(Naval Museum; ☎ 04 93 80 47 61; adult/student/under 18 €2.28/1.37/free; open 10am-noon & 2pm-7pm Wed-Sun June-Sept, 10am-noon & 2pm-5pm Wed-Sun Oct-May)*, with naval exhibits for dyed-in-the-wool Sinbads. The cemetery where Garibaldi is buried covers the northwestern section of the park. To get here, ride the **lift** *(ascenseur du château; rue des Ponchettes; single/return €0.60/0.90, children 4-10 years €0.30/0.45; open 10am-6pm daily Oct-Mar; 9am-7pm daily Apr, May & Sept; 9am-8pm June-Aug)* from beneath Tour Bellanda. Alternatively, plod up the staircase on montée Lesage or at the eastern end of rue Rossetti.

MUSEUMS

Musée d'Art Moderne et d'Art Contemporain

The Museum of Modern and Contemporary Art *(Mamac; ☎ 04 93 62 61 62; W www.mamac-nice.org; promenade des Arts; adult/student/under 18 €3.80/2.30/free; open 10am-6pm Tues-Sun)* specialises in European and American avant-garde works from the 1960s to the present. Glass walkways connect the four marble towers, which are topped with a rooftop garden and gallery featuring works by Nice-born Yves Klein (1928–62).

Temporary exhibitions fill the ground and 1st floors. Highlights in the permanent 2nd- and 3rd-floor exhibits include Andy Warhol's *Campbell's Soup Can* (1965), a shopping trolley wrapped by Christo, *Entablature* (1971) by pop artist Roy Lichtenstein, and a pea-green model-T Ford pressed to a 1.60m-tall block by Marseillais sculptor César.

The hall, dedicated to the 1960s New Realism movement, features works by Nice-born Arman, known for encasing mountains of mundane objects such as kitchen trash, letters or children's toys in monumental perspex containers. Born as Armand Fernandez, a printer's mistake in 1958 inspired Arman to drop the 'd' from his name.

Art films and cult movies are screened twice a month in the auditorium. The **Jardin Maréchal Juin**, a modernist red concrete garden, hugs Mamac's eastern side.

Museums in Nice

Municipal museums in Nice are free on the first and third Sunday of the month (or daily for those aged under 18). Beyond that, you have to pay to view Matisse's *Blue Nude*, Warhol's *Dollar Sign* or Christo's wrapped shopping trolley.

Tourist offices sell the **Carte Passe Musées** costing €6 (no concession) and allowing its holder one visit to each of Nice's museums (excluding the Chagall and Asian Arts museums, which aren't run by the municipality) during seven consecutive days. Museum aficionados can invest in the €18.30 version (students €9.15), valid for a year and allowing card-holders 15 museum visits.

If you intend straying farther afield, invest in **La Carte Musées Côte d'Azur** (see the Facts for the Visitor chapter for details).

Musée National Message Biblique Marc Chagall

The Marc Chagall Biblical Message Museum *(☎ 04 93 53 87 20; 4 ave Docteur Ménard; adult/18-25 yrs & Sun/under 18 permanent collection €5.02/4/free, temporary exhibitions €6.70/5.20/free; open 10am-7pm Wed-Mon July-Sept)* is on the corner of blvd de Cimiez. It houses the largest public collection of works by Russian painter Marc Chagall (1887–1985), who lived in St-Paul de Vence from 1950 until his death.

Floating humans, goats and green-headed violins characterise Chagall's work. His *Biblical Message Cycle*, displayed in the severe, purpose-built museum, includes 12 canvases illustrating scenes from the Old Testament. Don't miss the second version of the *Blue Rose* mosaic (1958) of the rose window at Metz Cathedral, viewed through a plate-glass window and reflected in a small pond.

Take bus No 15 from place Masséna to the stop in front of the museum; or walk (signposted from ave de l'Olivetto).

Musée d'Art et d'Histoire

Nice's Art & History Museum, also called Musée Masséna *(☎ 04 93 88 11 34; 65 rue de*

Absolutely Fabulous

Belle époque Nice was ab fab. The wedding-cake mansions, palaces and pastel-painted concrete gateaux that sprang up in abundance were not just fabulous: they were fantastical.

The Cimiez quarter remains the pearl of this lavish, pre-WWI legacy. The **Haussmann-style Conservatoire de Musique** *(8 blvd de Cimiez)* dates from 1902. At No 46 is **L'Alhambra** (1901), an opulent private mansion set on a small, palm tree-studded mound and surrounded by a high wall, though not high enough to hide the Moorish minarets that rise from the sparkling white building. **Villa Raphaeli-Surany** (1900), opposite at No 35, is adorned with intricate mosaic reliefs. The boulevard's crowning jewel is **Hôtel Excelsior Régina** *(71 ave Régina)*, built in 1896 to welcome Queen Victoria to Nice (a statue of the queen stands in front). Henri Matisse later lived here. This titanic of a building houses private apartments and a handful of medical practices today.

The pink confection you see from Nice ferry port, atop star-studded Mont Boron, where celebrities such as Elton John reside, is **Château de l'Anglais**, built in 1859 for an English engineer called Robert Smith, renowned at the time as being the only foreigner to live in Nice year round. Locals quickly dubbed his castle – now protected as a historical monument – Smith's folly. It has since been split into private apartments.

France), inside the Palais Masséna, is closed for renovation. When it reopens, expect an eclectic collection of paintings, furniture, icons, ceramics and religious art – all in a marvellous Italian-style villa from 1898.

Musée des Beaux-Arts

This Fine Arts Museum *(☎ 04 92 15 28 28; 33 ave des Baumettes; adult/student/under 18 €3.80/2.30/free; open 10am-6pm Tues-Sun)* lives in a fantastic cream-and-apricot 19th-century villa built for the Ukrainian princess Elisabeth Vassilievna Kotschoubey in 1878. Its decorative stucco friezes and six-column rear terrace overlooking luxuriant gardens are typical of houses dating from Nice's *belle époque*.

The collection includes works by Dutch artist Kees van Dongen (1877–1968) and Fauvist Raoul Dufy; several Flemish tapestries; Pierre Bonnard's 20th-century *Window Opening onto the Seine at Vernonnet*; some late impressionist pieces by Monet and Sisley; numerous works by Jules Chéret (1836–1932), the creator of modern poster art; and local works of art by Alexis Mossa (1844–1926) – a Niçois artist better known for introducing wildly decorated floats to the Nice Carnival than for his watercolours.

Bus No 38 from the local bus station stops outside.

Musée International d'Art Naïf Anatole Jakovsky

A collection of naive art from all over the world can be seen at the Anatole Jakovsky International Naive Art Museum *(☎ 04 93 71 78 33; ave de Fabron; adult/under 18 €3.80/free; open 10am-6pm Wed-Mon)*, less than 2km west of the city centre. The very pink Château Ste-Hélène, in which the museum is housed, was built in the 19th century atop Mont Fabron by François Blanc, who founded the casino in Monte Carlo; it later served as the country home of a perfume manufacturer. The collection was donated to the museum by Romanian art critic Anatole Jakovsky (1909–83), who lived in southern France with his wife, Renée, from 1932 onwards.

To get to the museum, take bus No 10 or 12 from the local bus station to the Fabron stop, then walk or take bus No 34 to the Musée Art Naïf stop.

Villa Arson

Sensational temporary photographic and contemporary art exhibitions can be seen at the **Centre National d'Art Contemporain** *(☎ 04 92 07 73 73; 20 ave Stéphane Liégeard; W www.cnap-villa-arson.fr; admission free; open 2pm-7pm Wed-Mon July-Sept & 2pm-6pm Wed-Mon Oct-June)*, inside the 18th-century Villa Arson, about 1km north of the town centre.

Take bus No 36 to the Villa Arson stop, or bus No 4, 7 or 26 to the Fanny stop on blvd de Cessole.

Musée des Arts Asiatiques

A striking white-marble building designed by Japanese architect Kenzo Tange houses

Nice's Museum of Asian Arts *(☎ 04 92 29 37 00; W www.arts-asiatiques.com; 405 promenade des Anglais; adult/students & 6-18 yrs €5.35/3.80; open 10am-6pm Wed-Mon May-Sept, 10am-5pm Wed-Mon Oct-Apr)*. It showcases Oriental art. The museum is in Nice's spacious **Parc Floral Phoenix**, near the airport.

Musée de Paléonthologie Humaine de Terra Amata

Just east of the port, this museum *(☎ 04 93 55 59 93; 25 blvd Carnot; adult/student/under 18 €3.80/2.30/free; open 10am-6pm Tues-Sun)*, displays objects from a site inhabited some 400,000 years ago by the predecessors of *Homo sapiens*. Bus No 32 links the local bus station and the museum; alight at the Carnot stop.

Cathédrale Orthodoxe Russe St-Nicolas

The multicoloured Russian Orthodox Cathedral of St-Nicolas *(☎ 04 93 96 88 02; ave Nicolas II)*, opposite 17 blvd du Tzaréwich, is crowned by six onion domes and was built between 1903 and 1912 in early 17th-century style. Step inside and you are transported to Imperial Russia. Shorts, miniskirts and sleeveless shirts are forbidden.

CIMIEZ

Nice's wealthiest residential district, 2.5km from the train station, is known for its mesmerising chocolate-box creations surrounded by vast grounds and high walls.

Musée Matisse

The Matisse Museum *(☎ 04 93 81 08 08; W www.musee-matisse-nice.org; 164 ave des Arènes de Cimiez; adult/student/under 18 €3.80/2.30/free; open 10am-6pm Wed-Mon Apr-Sept, 10am-5pm Wed-Mon Oct-Mar)*, houses a fine collection of works by Henri Matisse. Its permanent collection is displayed in an ochre 17th-century Genoese villa overlooking the olive tree-studded **Parc des Arènes**. Temporary exhibitions are hosted in the futuristic basement building. The reception hall of the museum is dominated by a colourful, 4.1m by 8.7m, paper cut-out frieze entitled *Flowers and Fruits* and designed by Matisse for the inner courtyard of a Californian villa in 1953.

Well-known pieces in the permanent collection include Matisse's blue paper cut-outs of *Blue Nude IV* (1952) and *Woman with Amphora* (1953). To get here, take bus No 15, 17 or 20 from the local bus station to the Arènes Musée Matisse stop.

Monastère Notre Dame de Cimiez

Stairs lead from the eastern end of Parc des Arènes (end of allée Miles Davis) to the 16th-century Monastère Notre Dame de Cimiez *(☎ 04 93 81 00 04; e franciscaincimiez@libertysurf.fr; ave Bellanda)*. Matisse is buried

Matisse – the Essential Elements

Henri Matisse (1869–1954) was passionate about pure colour. His paintings epitomised the radical use of violent colour, heavy outlines and simplified forms characteristic of Fauvism.

Matisse was a latecomer compared to contemporaries such as Picasso, not becoming interested in painting until he was 20. He studied art for many years under the symbolist painter Gustave Moreau. While visiting Brittany, he met Australian artist John Russell, who introduced him to the works of Van Gogh, Monet and other impressionists, prompting Matisse's change from a sombre palette to brighter colours.

By the early 1900s Matisse was well known in Paris but was still struggling financially. It wasn't until the first Fauvist exhibition in 1905, which followed a summer of innovative painting in the fishing village of Collioure in Roussillon, that his financial situation improved. By 1913 he had paintings on display in London and New York.

In the 1920s Matisse moved to the Côte d'Azur but still travelled widely. During these years he painted prolifically but was less radical; his work's characteristic sensuality and optimism, however, were always present. The 1930s saw him return to more experimental techniques and a renewed search for simplicity, in which the subject matter was reduced to essential elements. In 1948 he began working on a set of stained-glass windows for the Chapelle du Rosaire in Vence (see the Cannes Area chapter). He died and was buried in Nice (see the Monastère Notre Dame de Cimiez section in this chapter) in 1954.

in the cemetery here; his grave is signposted '*sépulture Henri Matisse*' from the graveyard's main entrance. Raoul Dufy (1877–1953), who spent many years in Nice, is also buried here.

Inside the monastery, the **Musée Franciscain** *(☎ 04 93 81 00 04; ave Bellanda; open 10am-noon & 3pm-6pm Mon-Sat)* recounts the history of the monastery's Franciscan monks. Three pieces of precious medieval art by Nice artist Louis Bréa hang in the adjoining **Église Notre Dame** *(admission free; open 9am-6pm daily)*. The monumental Baroque altar, carved in wood and decorated with gold leaf, dates from the 17th century. Surrounding the monastery, the beautiful **Jardin du Monastère** – studded with cypress trees and an abundance of sweet-smelling roses – offers a sweeping panorama of the Baie des Anges.

Take bus No 32 from the train station to the Monastère stop.

Musée d'Archéologie

The ruins of the ancient Roman city of Cemenelum lie on the eastern side of the Parc des Arènes. Discover its rocky history in the Archaeology Museum *(☎ 04 93 81 59 57; 160 ave des Arènes de Cimiez; adult/student/under 18 €3.80/2.30/free, guided tours €3; open 10am-6pm Wed-Mon)*. Both the public baths and the amphitheatre – the venue for outdoor concerts during the Nice Jazz festival (see Special Events later) – can be visited.

ACTIVITIES

For information on mountain-biking and walking, try the headquarters of the Parc National du Mercantour (see Information earlier) or the **Club Alpin Français des Alpes-Maritimes** *(☎ 04 93 62 59 99; Ⓦ http://cafnice.free.fr; 14 ave Mirabeau; open 4pm-8pm Mon-Fri)*.

Beaches & Boats

If you don't like the feel of sand between your toes, Nice's **beaches** – covered with smooth, round pebbles – are for you. Free public sections of beach alternate with 15 private beaches that cost upwards of €10 per day to use (around €15 with sun-lounger and parasol). **Lido Plage** *(☎ 04 93 87 18 25; ⓔ lidoplage@wanadoo.fr)*, opposite the Palais de la Méditerranée, hosts romantic candle-lit dinners, discos and salsa evenings on the beach. **Plage Publique des Ponchettes**, opposite Vieux Nice, gets the most packed with oiled bodies laid out to bake.

From June to mid-September you can take to the air in a parachute strung to the back of a motorboat from the public sections of Lido Plage, Plage du Neptune (opposite Hôtel Negresco) and Plage du Sporting (opposite 25 promenade des Anglais). All three charge €40/55 for a parachute ride for one/two people, €20 for a hair-raising ride in rubber ring *(bouée)* and €22 to water-ski.

Trans Côte d'Azur *(☎ 04 92 00 42 30; Ⓦ www.trans-cote-azur.com; quai Lunel)* runs one-hour **boat trips** along the coast, departing from the port at 3pm Tuesday to Sunday, mid-June to September. Tickets cost €10/5 for adults/four to 10 years. It also runs weekly excursions to Île Ste-Marguerite (€23/16), St-Tropez (€38/23), Monaco (€20/15) and San Remo (€32/20) in Italy.

Diving & Snorkelling

Day- and night-time dives are organised by the **François Lejeune Centre de Plongée** *(☎ 06 03 54 42 21; ⓔ francois.b.lejeune@wanadoo.fr; 3 quai des Deux Emmanuel)*, based at the 3B Plongée diving shop. Count on paying €40/35 for a baptism/night dive and €264 for a six-dive course. **Le Poseidon** *(☎ 06 11 80 81 81, 04 92 00 43 86; Ⓦ www.poseidon-nice.com; quai Lunel)* and **Nice Diving** *(☎ 04 93 89 42 44; Ⓦ www.nicediving.com; 14 quai des Docks)* are other port-side diving schools.

Rollerblading

Promenade des Anglais is the place to blade. Hire blades from **Roller Station** *(☎ 04 93 62 99 05; 49 quai des États Unis)* for €5 a day, or a skateboard or micro-scooter *(trottinette)* for €5/10/15 an hour/four hours/day. Nicea Location Rent (see Car & Motorcycle later in this section) also rents rollers and micro-scooters.

Between June and September, local blading association **Nice Roller Attitude** *(☎ 06 09 07 57 19; Ⓦ www.nice-roller-attitude.com; 48 rue Gioffrédo)* runs weekly blades around town, departing from quai des États Unis at 9.30pm on Friday. From October to May, bladers meet every first and third Friday of the month.

SPECIAL EVENTS

The celebrated two-week **Carnaval de Nice** (Nice Carnival) has been held each year around Mardi Gras (Shrove Tuesday) since 1294. The highlight is its *bataille de fleurs* (battle of flowers), when hundreds upon thousands of fresh flowers are tossed into the crowds from passing floats. A mock carnival king is burned and fireworks are lit on promenade des Anglais.

The week-long **Nice Jazz Festival** jives in July, its main venue being the olive grove behind the Musée Matisse in Cimiez. Equally atmospheric is the two-day **Fête au Château**, an outdoor music festival held in Parc du Château in mid-June. During the **Festival de Musique Sacrée** (Festival of Sacred Music), Russian sacred chants meet with Mozart's *Requiem* for two weeks in late June. During the three-week **Les Nuits Musicales de Nice** in mid-July/early August, classical musical concerts are held in the cloisters of Monastère Notre Dame de Cimiez, the olive grove in Cimiez and in the gardens around the Musée d'Art Moderne et d'Art Contemporain .

PLACES TO STAY

Nice has a surfeit of reasonably priced places to stay, although cheap accommodation can be hard to find in July and August when most hostels brandish *complet* (full) signs by 10am. Sleeping on the beach is illegal.

Places to Stay – Budget

Hostels A couple of budget hotels near the train station have dorm beds; see the following section.

Auberge de Jeunesse *(☎ 04 93 89 23 64, fax 04 92 04 03 10; route Forestière du Mont Alban; dorm bed with breakfast €13.50; reception open 7am-noon & 5pm-midnight daily Jan-Oct)*, 5km east of the train station, offers stunning views of downtown Nice. Curfew is at midnight and rooms are locked from 10am to 5pm. Take bus No 14 from the local bus station (linked to the train station by bus Nos 15 and 17) and get off at L'Auberge stop.

Backpackers' Hotel *(☎ 04 93 80 30 72, 06 13 25 29 31; ⓔ chezpatrick@voila.fr; 32 rue Pertinax; dorm bed €18)*, just off ave Jean Médecin, is run by cheery Patrick, whom guests say is a real darling. Internet and laundry facilities are available.

Hotels – Train Station Area The quickest way to get to these hotels is to cut down the steps opposite the train station onto ave Durante.

Hôtel Belle Meunière *(☎ 04 93 88 66 15, fax 04 93 82 51 76; 21 ave Durante; bed in three-, four- or five-bed dorm with/without shower €18/13, including breakfast, doubles/triples with shower & toilet from €47/72 including breakfast; reception open 7.30am-midnight daily Feb–mid-Nov)* is a busy place with a tree-studded garden with tables and chairs for guests to lounge on. Safety deposit boxes (€2 per day) are available.

Hôtel Les Orangers *(☎ 04 93 87 51 41, fax 04 93 87 57 82; 10 bis ave Durante; dorm beds €14, singles/doubles/triples/quads with shower €16/34/44/55; open Dec-Oct)* in a late-19th-century townhouse almost opposite, is equally popular. Snug four- to six-bed dorms have a shower and big windows. Some rooms have a balcony overlooking a palm-tree garden. A fridge and hotplate are available upon request.

Rue d'Alsace-Lorraine is dotted with several two-star hotels, including:

Hôtel du Piémont *(☎ 04 93 88 25 15; 19 rue d'Alsace-Lorraine; singles/doubles with washbasin €19/24, with shower €22/26, with shower & toilet €35/38.50)*, down an alley, is among the cheapest. It rents rooms on a longer-term basis too.

Hôtel d'Orsay *(☎ 04 93 88 45 02, fax 04 93 82 30 28; 20 rue d'Alsace-Lorraine; singles/doubles/triples/quads with washbasin low season €21/27/37/43, high season €21/31/39/49, singles/doubles/triples/quads with shower & toilet low season €26/34/44/52, high season €29/39/46/55)* has 32 rooms and is on the same street as the Hôtel du Piémont.

Hotels – City Centre Midway between the sea and the train station is **Le Petit Louvre** *(☎ 04 93 80 15 54, fax 04 93 62 45 08; 10 rue Emma Tiranty; singles/doubles with shower €31/37, with shower & toilet €34/42, triples with shower €46; open Feb-Oct)*, a colourful backpacker-favourite run by a humorous musician (Monsieur Vila played sax and clarinet). A faceless Mona Lisa greets guests as they enter and corridors are adorned with an eclectic mix of paintings. Breakfast comprises cereal and fruit as well as the usual *baguette*, croissant and coffee.

Hôtel Lyonnais (☎ *04 93 88 70 74, fax 04 93 16 25 56; 20 rue de Russie; singles/doubles/triples/quads with washbasin low season €24/25/38/49, high season €31/36/49/61, singles/doubles/triples/quads with shower & toilet low season €34/39/47/61, high season €43/49/56/75)*, amid its mind-boggling set of rates, has a list of cheaper prices for long-term stays. Use of the corridor shower costs a cheeky €2.

Places to Stay – Mid-Range

Near the train station, there are plenty of two-star hotels on rue d'Angleterre, rue d'Alsace-Lorraine, rue de Suisse, rue de Russie and ave Durante.

Hôtel Plaisance (☎ *04 93 85 11 90, fax 04 93 80 88 92; 20 rue de Paris; singles from €53.36/70.89)*, in the centre, is a pleasing two-star pile with 34 air-conditioned rooms.

Hôtel Notre Dame (☎ *04 93 88 70 44, fax 04 93 82 20 38; 22 rue de Russie; singles/doubles/triples/quads with shower & toilet €39/42/54/67)* is a clean and modern place named after its location near Église Notre Dame. Rooms are spacious.

Hôtel Carlone (☎*/fax 04 93 44 71 61; 2 blvd François Grosso; singles/doubles/triples/quads €40/50/60/70)*, a stone's throw from the sea and the Musée des Beaux-Arts, has light and airy rooms, and private parking for an extra €7 per night.

Résidence Hôtelière Astoria (☎ *04 95 15 25 45; mini-studio per night/week low season €26/170, high season €34/250; studios per night/week low season €35/210, high season €48/298; reception open 8.30am-7.30pm daily)*, almost next door to the Carlone, has studios with bathroom, fridge and hotplate to let on a short- and long-term basis. There are no monthly rentals in August. The Astoria also has a pretty garden where guests can breakfast.

Hôtel Cronstadt (☎ *04 93 82 00 30, fax 04 93 16 87 40;* ⓔ *reservation@hotelcronstadt.com; 3 rue Cronstadt; doubles/triples from €56/73, including breakfast)*, hidden in a mansion with a marble-decorated garden, is just like home. Rooms are quiet and graceful. Press the buzzer to enter via the porch.

Places to Stay – Top End

The **Hôtel Negresco** (☎ *04 93 16 64 00, fax 04 93 88 35 68;* ⓦ *www.hotel-negresco-nice.com; 37 promenade des Anglais; doubles with courtyard/garden & sea view from €213/297)* is Nice's fanciest – and privately owned at that. Van Loo paintings, Aubusson carpets and crystal chandeliers furnish its lavish *belle époque* interior, and doormen wear knickerbockers and feathered caps.

Hôtel Le Méridien (☎ *04 97 03 44 44, fax 04 97 03 44 45;* ⓦ *www.lemeridien-nice.com; 1 promenade des Anglais; doubles from €175)* is a stylish four-star hotel with a rooftop pool.

Hôtel Beau Rivage (☎ *04 92 47 82 82, fax 04 92 47 82 83;* ⓦ *www.nicebeaurivage.com; 24 rue St-François de Paule; doubles low/high season €122/160)* was used by Matisse in 1916. Russian playwright Anton Chekhov (1860–1904) graced the place with his presence in 1891.

Four Points Elysée Palace (☎ *04 93 97 90 90, fax 04 93 44 50 40;* ⓦ *www.elysee-palace.com; 59 promenade des Anglais; doubles low/high season from €175/220)* reflects the modern face of Nice in its Art Deco-style glass walls. The building's concrete rear is adorned with a giant statue of Venus baring a breast to passers-by on rue de France.

PLACES TO EAT

Restaurants

Train Station Area All the places to eat listed here offer a cheap fill within five minutes' walk of the train station. Vietnamese and Chinese restaurants are clustered on rue Paganini, rue d'Italie and rue d'Alsace-Lorraine.

Auberge du Soleil (☎ *04 93 88 77 74; 7 bis rue d'Italie; menu €11, plat du jour €7)* has been run by the same husband-and-wife team since 1960. The smiling pair serve local cuisine, including an all-day omelette breakfast for €5.50 and a hearty *menu* that includes a 25cL *pichet* (jug) of wine.

Le Faubourg Montmartre (☎ *04 93 62 55 03; 32 rue Pertinax; menu €11)* essentially caters to backpackers staying in the hostel above. You can leave your bags here for €1.50 a day and taste a cheap version of traditional bouillabaisse for around €15 for two.

City Centre Pedestrianised rue Masséna and its nearby streets and squares, including rue de France and place Magenta, are crammed with cafés and restaurants. Most don't offer particularly good value, but there are exceptions.

Cantine de Lulu *(☎ 04 93 62 15 33; 26 rue Alberti; starters/mains around €7/12)* dishes up all the great classics such as *escalope de veau à la crème* (veal escalop in a cream sauce) and local specialities like stuffed courgette flowers and octopus *à la niçoise*. Lulu's is commended for upholding the great old tradition of the *cuisine nissarde* (Nice cuisine).

Grand Café de Turin *(☎ 04 93 62 66 52; ⓔ bdudoignon@aol.com; 5 place Garibaldi; full meal around €25)* sports an authentic 1900 interior and is one of Nice's most traditional seafood spots. Shellfish, including sea urchins when in season, are prepared beneath the arches on the pavement terrace.

Boccaccio *(☎ 04 93 87 71 76; ⓔ bocaccio@club-internet.fr; 7 rue Masséna; seafood platters €31-92)* serves *plateaux de fruits de mer* (seafood platters) and fish dishes. The polka-dotted fish swimming in a tank inside are purely decorative. Seafood paella/*bouillabaisse* swim in at €25/€50, and six oysters will set you back €11.

Les Viviers *(☎ 04 93 16 00 48; 22 rue Alphonse Karr; lunch/dinner menu from €16/25)* is a temple to seafood with its magnificent choice of oysters, urchins and other shellfish. Its good old-fashioned *bourride* (fish soup) and bouillabaisse are notable – consume to the sweet tinkle of a pianist. Diners seeking a less full-on affair can try its Viviers' bistro next door.

Le Comptoir *(☎ 04 93 92 08 80; 20 rue St-François de Paule; lunch/dinner menu €15/30)* is a graceful place with adjoining nightclub and terrace decked out in Art Deco style. The cuisine is classical.

La Cigale Orientale *(☎ 04 93 88 60 20; ⓦ www.la-cigale-orientale.com; 7 ave de Suède; full meal around €20)* cooks up Lebanese cuisine in a hip and modern interior. Dine in or stock up on stuffed vine leaves, falafel et al to eat from the front-of-house shop or to munch on the move. Dining reservations are essential, particularly on Friday and Saturday evenings when belly dancers dance.

Indyana *(☎ 04 93 80 67 69; 11 rue Gustave Deloye)* cleverly mixes the oriental with the minimalist to create one of Nice's most chic spots. Sushi (€24/26 for 14/17 pieces) is among the world cuisines the chef cooks up. Forget about coming here without a reservation.

Terre de Truffes *(☎ 04 93 80 28 69; 20 rue de la Barillerie)*, a classy boutique-restaurant by acclaimed chef Bruno, serves the region's most expensive fungi in all forms and guises – in tiramisu, with eggs or, for the ultimate in decadence, encased whole inside puff pastry (€18.50/35 for a *Tuber aestiuum/melamosporum*).

Chantecler *(☎ 04 93 16 64 00; 37 promenade des Anglais; lunch/dinner menus €40/75 & €90)*, inside Hôtel Negresco, is a mind-blowing extravaganza. Impeccable service and tantalising cuisine equal two Michelin stars. Lunch in the nearby La Rotonde – which is decorated like an old-fashioned carousel – is cheaper (*plat du jour* €19).

Vieux Nice Vieux Nice's narrow streets are crammed with restaurants, cafés, pizzerias and so on that draw locals and visitors alike. In summer, the dozens of outdoor places to eat and drink on cours Saleya, place Pierre Gautier and place Rossetti buzz with activity until well past midnight.

Chez René *(1 rue Pairolière)*, a perennial favourite with bench seating on both sides of rue Miralhet, is the spot to sample *socca*, a giant-sized chickpea flour and olive oil pancake fried on a griddle above a wood-stoked fire. Select a plateful of *socca* (€2) to eat with other typical Niçois treats such as *beignets de courgettes* (slices of zucchini fried in batter), *beignets d'aubergines* (battered eggplant slices) or *pissaladière* (onion, anchovy and black olive tart). Wash the whole lot down with a €2.15 glass of Côtes de Provence wine.

Lou Pilha Leva *(place Centrale)* is a similar spot, which is always busy. Buy your food at the bar before sitting down; waiters only serve drinks. A plate of battered and deep-fried sardines, squid or eggplant etc costs €4.

Nissa Socca *(☎ 04 93 80 18 35; 5 rue Ste-Réparate; meat/pasta dishes €12/8.50)* is where *salade niçoise* (green salad with tuna, egg and anchovies), ratatouille and other traditional dishes draw crowds.

L'Escalinada *(☎ 04 93 62 11 71; 22 rue Pairolière; full meal around €30)* is an enchanting place, with smiling staff and a candlelit terrace. It serves all of the usual Niçois delicacies plus its house speciality, *testicules de mouton panés* (sheep testicles in batter).

Chez Palmyre *(3 rue Droite; four-course menu €11.50)*, with its unpretentious slipper-shuffling clientele, makes a refreshing change from old Nice's dozens of tourist-targeted establishments. The fare is *cuisine familiale* – think grandmother-style.

Casalinga *(☎ 04 93 80 12 40; 4 rue de l'Abbaye; menu €19)* is a pocket-sized place praised for its homemade pasta dishes.

La Mezzanine *(☎ 04 93 80 10 68; ⓔ mezzanine2@wanadoo.fr; 5 rue de la Barillerie; open 7pm-11.30pm Tues-Sun)* takes it name from the mezzanine floor perched above the bar. Food is traditional and the crowd, hip, at this ambient joint.

Le Living Room *(☎ 04 93 80 28 69; 20 rue de la Barillerie; open 8pm-11.30pm Tues-Sun)*, another slightly alternative evening-only venue, touts an imaginative chef who can conjure up impressive creations from around the globe.

Port Area Bursting with vegetarian surprises and guaranteed to thrill, **Zucca Magica** *(Magic Pumpkin; ☎ 04 93 56 25 27; 4 bis quai Papacino; three-/four-course menu with dessert €15/22)* offers just one fixed *menu confiance*. Italian chef Marco Folicardi moved from Rome to Nice to open this highly praised egg, cheese and vegetable restaurant.

Cafés & Fast Food

There are numerous sandwich stalls and snack bars around the train station.

J Multari *(58 bis ave Jean Médecin)*, a top-notch bakery with in-house café, is always packed to the rafters. Sample traditional *michettes* (savoury bread stuffed with cheese, olives, anchovies and onions) and other local breads. It offers tasty breakfasts too (€2.15, €2.75 and €4).

Chez Thérésa *(☎ 04 93 85 00 04; 28 rue Droite)* doles out socca through a hole in the wall. The socca maker, whose family business dates back to 1925, has a stall at the cours Saleya food market.

Terrace cafés and bars just made for beer quaffing and cocktail sipping abound on Cour Saleya.

Le Speakeasy *(☎ 04 93 85 59 50; 7 rue Lamartine; starters/mains €3/6.50 & €7.50; open Mon-Sat)* is a highly vocal vegetarian place, run by an American who cooks up dishes for organic vegetarians.

Nice Markets

There's always a market on Vieux Nice's cours Saleya, be it the chaotic **fruit and vegetable market** on Tuesday to Sunday mornings, or the colourful **daily flower market**. Some stalls at the latter sell *fruits glacés* (glazed or candied fruits), a speciality of the region.

For the catch of the day, delve further into the old town to the **fresh fish market**, Tuesday to Sunday morning, on fountain-clad place St-François.

Café Borghese *(☎ 04 92 04 83 83; 9 rue Fodéré)*, behind Église Notre Dame de l'Immaculée Conception at the port, is a trendy bohemian café-cum-bar that serves food until 11pm and caters to a stylish in-the-know set.

Maïl's *(☎ 04 93 85 28 17; 26 rue de l'Hôtel des Postes; plat du jour €9)* entices a hip bunch with its swings at the bar and funky interior furnishings. Come here for coffee, tea, cocktails or a light lunch.

Oliviera *(☎ 04 93 13 06 45; ⓦ www.oliviera.com; 8 bis rue du Collet; platters €8-18)* is a modern olive-oil parlour where you can sample five different French AOC oils in a series of light lunchtime platters. Its oil-doused fig and parmesan cheese plate is particularly memorable.

Le Pain Quotidien *(☎ 04 93 62 94 32; 1 rue St-François de Paule; salads/sandwiches from €15.50/4; open 7am-9pm daily)*, in a similar vein, serves healthy salads, open sandwiches *(tartines)* mixing beef tartar with capers and the like, and one of the city's best organic breakfasts (€7.50) and brunches (€18).

Self-Catering

Rue du Collet and its continuation, rue Pairolière, is lined with cheese shops, bakeries and fruit shops. There is an **Intermarché** supermarket at the southern end of blvd Gambetta and a **Monoprix** supermarket opposite 33 ave Jean Médecin. Both open 8am or 8.30am to 8pm Monday to Saturday.

ENTERTAINMENT

Cinema and theatre schedules are online at ⓦ www.nice.webcity.fr (French only). Drinking and clubbing venues are listed in *Excés*

(☎ www.exces.com), a free entertainment mag published monthly.

Tickets for most events are sold at **FNAC** (*☎ 04 92 17 77 74*), inside the Centre Commercial Nice Étoile (see Shopping later in this section).

Pubs & Bars

The Seventies (*☎ 04 93 55 14 42; 24 quai Lunel; starters €9.50-17, mains €14-25*), at the port, is as much a bar as restaurant with its kiss-me-quick red-lip sofa and other 1970s pop design furnishings. Tasty morsels include stuffed artichoke hearts and *foie gras*-filled ravioli.

Plasma Café (*☎ 04 93 16 17 32; www.plasmacafe.com; 11 rue Offenbach*) has super powerful air-conditioning and lures a laid-back crowd with its lounge music, sushi station, art exhibitions and minimalist decor. Pick up club flyers here. See its website for what's on.

La Casa del Sol (*☎ 04 93 62 87 28; 69 quai des États Unis*), a Moroccan-inspired tapas bar, is a mellow, early-evening port of call with trendy locals. The house DJ lets rip from midnight on.

Karma (*☎ 04 93 62 52 70; 24 rue Benoît Bunico*) entices an equally chic crowd with its sushi fare.

Entre Mets & Vins (*☎ 04 93 13 96 78; 12 rue Alberti*) makes a refreshing break from the norm with wine tasting in a refined setting.

Vieux Nice boasts a bounty of pubs that sport happy hours, host live bands and are crammed with Anglophones; most open 11am to 2am daily.

Wayne's (*☎ 04 93 13 46 99; www.waynes.fr; 15 rue de la Préfecture*) has live music from 9.30pm, throws happy hours with pints of cocktails at drink-silly prices, and hosts DJ-driven beach parties (€10 including one free drink).

Master Home (*☎ 04 93 80 33 82; www.master-home.com; 11 rue de la Préfecture*), next door, is a good spot to relax over a pint between pubs, and watch the crowds pile into Wayne's. It has a couple of computers to access the Net (€5.50 per hour), 30 types of beers and more than 20 different whiskies.

Oxford Pub (*☎ 04 93 92 24 54; 4 rue Mascoïnat*) sells itself as a traditional English pub.

De Klomp (*☎ 04 93 92 42 85; 6 rue Mascoïnat*), next door, is a Dutch place that lures punters with 18 beers on tap, 100 types of bottled beers, 60 whiskies and a 'little café of Amsterdam' slogan.

Jonathan's Live Music Pub (*☎ 04 93 62 57 62; 1 rue de la Loge*), **William's Pub** (*☎ 04 93 85 84 66; 4 rue Centrale*) and **Thor Pub** (*☎ 04 93 62 49 90; www.thor-pub.com; 34 cours Saleya*) are other popular places on the backpacker circuit.

Guinness-serving Irish pubs include **McMahons Pub** (*☎ 04 93 13 84 00; 50 blvd Jean Jaurès*), which dishes up fish 'n' chips in newspaper; fireplace-ornamented **O'Neill's** (*☎ 04 93 80 06 75; 40 rue Droite*), which runs the occasional pub quiz and charges €6.20 a pint; and **O'Hara's** (*☎ 04 93 80 43 22; 22 rue Droite*), which serves pub grub until 1.30am and shows the BBC on the box.

Discos & Clubs

Dizzy Club (*☎ 04 93 26 54 29; 26 quai Lunel; open 11.30pm-early morning Wed-Sun*), at the port, features a stunning 1930s decor and DJs that spin everything from jazz and house to techno. A drink is included in the entrance fee; otherwise count on paying €12 an orgasm.

Ghost (*☎ 04 93 92 93 37; 3 rue de la Barillerie*) in Vieux Nice is an essential stop on the local clubber's weekend circuit.

La Suite (*☎ 04 93 92 92 91; 2 rue Bréa*), an early closer for night owls, draws a buoyant crowd nonetheless.

Le Grand Escurial (*☎ 04 93 82 37 66; 29 rue Alphonse Karr*) is a huge industrial-style complex with nightclub, restaurant, bar, live bands and so on.

Le Saramanga (*☎ 04 93 96 68 00; 45-47 promenade des Anglais*), opposite the beach, plays mainly house behind its steely grey doors. Admission (€15) includes a free drink.

Gay & Lesbian Venues

Le Klub (*☎ 06 60 55 26 61; www.leklub.net; 6 rue Halévy; open 11pm-5am Wed-Sun*) is Nice's hippest gay clubbing venue where house and techno rules. Admission costs anything from nothing to €15 depending on what's on – an updated programme is on its website.

Blue Boy (*☎ 04 93 44 68 24; 9 rue Jean-Baptiste Spinetta; open from 9.30pm daily*) is another gay club.

Cherry's Café (*☎ 04 93 13 85 45; 35 quai des États Unis; open from noon daily*) is an essential dining-and-dancing stop on the city's gay circuit.

Opera, Ballet & Classical Music

Operas and orchestral concerts are held at the Garnier-designed **Opéra de Nice** *(Opera House; ☎ 04 92 17 40 00; 4-6 rue St-François de Paule)*, dating from 1885. Opera tickets, available at the **box office** *(☎ 04 92 17 40 40; ⓔ opera-billetterie@ville-nice.fr; open 10-5.30pm Mon, 10am-6pm Tues-Thur & Sat, 10am-8pm Fri, and 1 hour before performances begin)* inside the opera house, cost €7 to €72.

Theatre

The modern **Théâtre de Nice** *(☎ 04 93 80 52 60; esplanade des Victoires)*, a block west of place Garibaldi, hosts first-rate plays and concerts.

Cinema

Nice has two cinemas screening original-language films, often in English: **Cinéma Nouveau Mercury** *(☎ 08 36 68 81 06; 16 place Garibaldi)*, and **Cinéma Rialto** *(☎ 04 93 88 08 41; 4 rue de Rivoli)*. Tickets cost around €7.

Art films (in French or with French subtitles) are shown at the Musée d'Art Moderne et d'Art Contemporain (see that section earlier).

SHOPPING

To tour, taste and buy chocolate-coated orange slices, cocoa-covered almonds, figs and tangerine slices, visit **Confiserie Florian** *(☎ 04 93 55 43 50; ⓦ www.confiserieflorian.com; 14 quai Papacino)*; free kitchen tours are run 9am to noon and 2pm to 6.30pm daily.

Fill your water bottle with wine (from €1.20 per litre) at **Caves Caprioglio** *(16 rue de la Préfecture)*, an excellent wine shop lined with a dozen or so enormous vats of wine. It also sells olive oil (€4.25 per litre), as does **Moulin à Huile d'Olive Alziari** *(☎ 04 93 85 76 92; 14 rue St-François de Paule)*.

Quality antique shops cram the streets immediately west of the port, around rue Emmanuel Philibert. Shop for antiques under one roof at portside **Les Puces de Nice** *(place Robilante; open 10am-6pm Tues-Sat Oct-May, 10am-7pm daily June-Sept)*.

Designer names abound above the beautiful fashion boutiques that line rue Paradis, ave de Suède, rue Alphonse Karr, and rue du Maréchal Joffre. **Centre Commercial Nice Étoile** *(☎ 04 92 17 38 17; 30 ave Jean Médecin; open 10am-7.30pm Mon-Sat)*, an indoor shopping centre, has mainstream fashion shops, FNAC and so on.

GETTING THERE & AWAY

Air

You can Kiss & Fly (as the drop-off point outside Terminal 1 departure hall is called) from **Aéroport International Nice-Côte d'Azur** *(Nice-Côte d'Azur International Airport; information ☎ 08 20 42 33 33, recorded flight information ☎ 08 36 69 55 55; ⓦ www.nice.aeroport.fr)*, 7km west of Nice city centre.

Domestic carrier **Airlib Express** *(☎ 08 25 09 090 09; ⓦ www.airlibexpress.com; ave Félix Faure; open 9am-5.30pm Mon-Fri)* has a ticketing office in town and at the airport *(☎ 08 25 09 09 09; open 5am-9pm daily)*.

For details on helicopter flights to/from Nice, see the Getting Around chapter.

Bus

Lines operated by some two dozen bus companies use the **intercity bus station** *(5 blvd Jean Jaurès)*. Check with the **information counter** *(☎ 04 93 85 61 81; open 8.30am-5.30pm Mon-Fri, 9am-noon & 1pm-4pm Sat)*.

Slow but frequent coastal services are operated by **Rapides Côte d'Azur** *(☎ 04 93 85 64 44, 04 97 00 97 00; ⓦ www.rca.tm.fr)*. It runs at least 15 buses daily to/from Cannes (€5.80, 1¼ hours) via Marineland in Biot (€3.70, 40 minutes), Antibes (€4.10, 50 minutes) and Golfe-Juan (€5, one hour); to/from Menton (€4.90 return, 1¼ hours, every 20 minutes between 6am and 8pm) via the Corniche Inférieure villages (see that section later in this chapter); nine daily to/from Beaulieu-sur-Mer via Villefranche-sur-Mer and St Jean-Cap Ferrat (45 minutes). Less frequent buses serve the Moyenne and Grande Corniche (see those sections later in this chapter).

There are daily buses to Vence (€4.50, one hour), Cagnes-sur-Mer (€2.90, 25 minutes) and St-Paul de Vence (€4.10, 45 minutes) every half-hour between 6.55am and 8.15pm. Buses to/from Grasse (€6.20, 1¼ hours, eight to 10 buses daily) run by Soma CFTI (☎ 04 92 96 88 88) stop in Cagnes-sur-Mer too.

Phocéens Cars *(☎ 04 93 85 66 61)* handles services between Nice and Hyères (€22, two hours, six daily Monday to Saturday), Toulon (€22, 2½ hours, six daily Monday to Saturday), Aix-en-Provence (€22.50, 2¼ hours, up to three daily), Marseilles (€22.50, 2½ hours, up to three daily) and Avignon (€27, 5½ hours, one daily).

Heading north into Haute-Provence, **Transport Régional des Alpes-Maritimes** *(☎ 04 93 89 41 45)* runs two to three weekly buses to La Colmiane (€13.20, two hours), plus one a day on weekends to/from La Colmiane via St-Martin-Vésubie (€9.80, 1¾ hours). Buses depart up to three times daily to/from Isola 2000 (€27.10, 2½ hours), and once or twice daily to/from Valberg (€10, two hours). For sporadic buses to the mountain villages north of Nice, see the Arrière-Pays Niçois section later in this chapter.

Société des Cars Alpes-Littoral *(☎ 04 92 51 06 05)* operates one bus a day Monday to Saturday to/from Sisteron (€17.90, 3¾ hours) and one or two daily to/from Digne-les-Bains (€14.30, 2¼ hours).

For long-haul travel, **Intercars** *(☎ 04 93 80 08 70)* at the bus station, takes you to various European destinations (see the Getting There & Away chapter).

Train

Nice's main train station, **Gare de Nice** *(Gare Thiers; ☎ 08 36 35 35 35; ave Thiers)* is 1200m north of the beach. Left luggage lockers in the ticket hall can be accessed 7am to 10.30pm (€3/4.50/6.10 for a small/medium/large locker per 72 hours. In town, tickets are sold at the **SNCF Boutique** *(cnr rue de la Liberté & passage E Negrin; open 9.30am-6.30pm Mon-Sat)*.

There is a fast, frequent service – up to 40 trains daily in each direction – to towns along the coast between St-Raphaël and Ventimiglia (across the Italian border), including Antibes (€3.40, 30 minutes), Cannes (€5.10, 40 minutes), Menton (€3.90, 35 minutes), Monaco (€3, 20 minutes) and St-Raphaël (€9, 45 minutes).

The mountain railway operated by **Chemins de Fer de la Provence** *(☎ 04 97 03 80 80)* offers a scenic trip four or five times daily from Nice's **Gare du Sud** *(☎ 04 93 82 10 17; 4 bis rue Alfred Binet)*. See the boxed text 'Along the Mountain Railway' in the Haute-Provence chapter for details.

Boat

At Nice's **ferry terminal** *(Gare Maritime; ☎ 04 93 13 78 78)*, SNCM ferries to/from Corsica (see the Getting There & Away chapter) sail in and out of **terminal 1** *(quai du Commerce)*. Corsica Ferries uses **terminal 2** *(quai Infernet)*. Both ferry companies have ticketing offices at the port.

GETTING AROUND

To/From the Airport

Sunbus No 99 provides a speedy link between Nice's train station and the airport (15 minutes), departing every 30 minutes between 8am and 9pm. Bus No 98 runs between the airport and the Intercity bus station (15 minutes) every 20 minutes between 6am and 9pm. Bus drivers on both routes sell tickets (€3.50). Otherwise, there's the cheaper – and substantially slower – bus No 23, which runs every 10 minutes between 6am and 9pm between the airport and train station; a single fare is only €1.30.

Buses operated by **Auto Nice Direct** (ANT; 04 92 29 88 88) also link the airport with town, stopping at the train and bus stations and various other strategic points in the centre. Journey time is about 30 minutes and buses depart about every 20 minutes between 6am and 11.45pm. A single/return fare is €3.50/6.40.

From the **airport bus station**, next to Terminal 1 at Nice airport, there are daily buses to countless other destinations, including Cannes via the coastal N7 (€3.20, one hour, every 30 minutes between 8am and 7pm) or via the A8 (€9.50, 50 minutes); Grasse (€3.20, one hour, 18 daily); Isola 2000 (€27.10, two hours, twice daily); Menton (€15.70/25.90 single/return, 1¼ hours, departures to coincide with flight times); Vence (€5.20, 45 minutes, eight daily); and Valberg (€10.20, one daily).

A taxi from the airport to Nice centre costs between €20 and €30, depending on the time of day, which terminal you're at and whether you're being ripped off or not.

To/From the Port

Free shuttle buses operated by the Chamber of Commerce & Industry shunt ferry passengers between the port, train station and a handful of upmarket hotels. Alternatively, bus Nos 1 and 2 run between the Port stop and ave Jean Médecin.

Bus

City buses are run by Sunbus, which has its main hub (the Station Centrale) on square Général Leclerc, sandwiched between ave Félix Faure and blvd Jean Jaurès. Tickets (€6.22/8.29 for a six-/eight-ticket carnet) are sold at the **Sunboutique** *(☎ 04 93 13 53 13; W www.sunbus.com; 10 ave Félix Faure; open 7.15am-7pm Mon-Fri, 7.15am-6pm Sat)*. Bus drivers sell single tickets for €1.30 and a one-day travel pass for €4. After you time-stamp your single ticket, it's valid for one hour and can be used for one transfer.

Bus No 12 links the train station with promenade des Anglais. To get from the train station to Vieux Nice and the local bus station, take bus No 2, 5 or 17. At night, Noctambus buses run north, east and west from place Masséna.

Plans are afoot for a tramway in Nice.

Car & Motorcycle

Most car rental agencies – including **ADA** *(☎ 04 93 82 27 00)*, **Avis** *(☎ 04 93 87 90 11)*, **Budget** *(☎ 04 93 16 24 16)* and **Europcar** *(☎ 04 93 82 17 34)* – have an office in the annexe adjoining the train station at 12 ave Thiers, as well as in town and at the airport.

Opposite the station, **Holiday Bikes** *(☎ 04 93 16 01 62; W www.holiday-bikes.com; 34 ave Aubert)* and neighbouring **JML** *(☎ 04 93 16 07 00; 34 ave Aubert)* rent scooters/125cc motorcycles for around €29/55 a day. **Nicea Location Rent** *(☎ 04 93 82 42 71; W www.nicealocationrent.com; 12 rue de Belgique)* is also competitive.

Always *(☎ 04 93 16 10 32; e always@wgn.net; 25 promenade des Anglais)* rents 50/100/125cc scooters for €38/53/60 a day and also has hip buggy-style scoot cars for €60/80 per half-/full day. For limousine hire, contact **Star Limousine** *(☎ 04 92 29 44 44; e info@starlimousine.fr; 455 promenade des Anglais)*.

Taxi

Nice has numerous **taxi ranks** *(☎ 04 93 13 78 78)*, including outside the train station, near place Masséna on ave Félix Faure and on promenade des Anglais.

Bicycle

Always, JML and Nicea Location Rent (see Car & Motorcycle earlier in this section) rent road and mountain bikes too. Always charges €5/8/15/70 per hour/half-day/day/week for their bikes.

Mountain bikes at **Cycles Mach 2** *(☎ 04 97 07 03 43; W www.mach2-nice.com; 2 rue St-Philippe)* cost €5/10/15 per hour/half-day/day. The bike specialist repairs bikes too.

The Three Corniches

The Corniche Inférieure, also called the Basse Corniche (Lower Corniche; the N98) sticks closely to the nearby train line and villa-lined waterfront. The Moyenne Corniche, the middle and least exciting coastal road (the N7), clings to the hillside, affording great views if you can find somewhere to pull over. The Grande Corniche, whose panoramas are by far the most spectacular, leaves Nice as the D2564 and passes the Col d'Èze (512m), La Turbie and Le Vistaëro, all of which offer breathtaking coastline views.

Accommodation here is pricey and limited. The cheapest option is to stay in Nice from where easy day or half-day trips can be made. The Corniche Inférieure, the lowest of the trio, is well served by train from Nice; the higher two roads, and the entire Niçois hinterland, are practically inaccessible by public transport.

CORNICHE INFÉRIEURE

Heading east from Nice to Menton, the Corniche Inférieure – built in the 1860s – passes through Villefranche-sur-Mer, St-Jean-Cap Ferrat, Beaulieu-sur-Mer, Èze-sur-Mer, Cap d'Ail and Monaco. Look for pretty-pink Château de l'Anglais (see the boxed text 'Absolutely Fabulous' earlier in this chapter) flash past atop Mont Boron as you are leaving Nice.

Getting There & Away

The lower coastal road is well served by bus and train. Bus No 100 operated by Rapides Côte d'Azur (see the Nice Getting There & Away section earlier in this chapter) runs the length of the Corniche Inférieure between Nice and Menton, stopping at all the villages along the way (every 15 or 20 minutes between 6am and 8pm). To/from Nice, bus No 111 serves Villefranche-sur-Mer (€1.70, 10 minutes), Beaulieu-sur-Mer (€2.10, 45 minutes) and St Jean-Cap Ferrat (€2.10, 25 minutes) six to nine times daily.

Trains run from Nice along the coast to Ventimiglia, Italy, every 10 to 20 minutes between 6am and 6pm (every 30 to 50 minutes from 6pm to 1am). Most stop at:

destination	Cost (€)	time (min)
Villefranche-sur-Mer	1.30	8
Beaulieu-sur-Mer	1.70	14
Cap d'Ail	2.50	21
Monaco	3.00	25
Cap Martin-Roquebrune	3.60	32
Carnolès	3.90	36
Menton	3.90	38

Between July and September, buy a Carte Isabelle (see Train Passes in the Getting Around chapter) if you intend making several train trips along the coast in one day. If you're merely making a return daytrip to Menton however, stopping en route in Villefranche-sur-Mer and Beaulieu-sur-Mer, it's cheaper to buy a straightforward Nice-Menton return ticket.

Villefranche-sur-Mer

postcode 06230 • pop 6877

Set in one of the Côte d'Azur's most charming – and unspoilt – harbours, this port village overlooks the Cap Ferrat peninsula and is a popular port of call for passing cruise ships. It has a well-preserved, 14th-century old town with a rash of evocatively named tiny streets, broken up with steps. Arcaded **rue Obscure**, the street a block in from the water, is a classified historical monument.

Keep a look out for occasional glimpses of the sea as you wander through the streets that lead to quai Amiral Courbet and the old fishing harbour, **Port de la Santé**. The houses that peep through wooden shutters at the water here are painted in a rainbow of muted colours, ranging from bedtime-pink to peppermint green. On Sunday morning, an art and antique **market** fills place Amélie Pollonnais, the old-town square above the water.

From here, a **coastal path** runs around the citadel to Port Royal de la Darse, fortified between 1725 and 1737 and sheltering pleasure boats today. En route there are picture-taking opportunities and good views of Cap Ferrat and the wooded slopes of the Gulf of Villefranche (Golfe de Villefranche), which served as a naval base for the Russians during their conflicts with the Turks in the 19th century.

Orientation & Information From Villefranche-sur-Mer train station, steps lead to quai Amiral Courbet and Plage des Marinières, a shallow shingle beach with no shade. To get to rue Obscure, walk up the staircase at 7–9 quai Amiral Courbert (between La Mère Germaine and L'Oursin Bleu restaurants), then turn immediately right onto rue Obscure. Follow it to its dark and eerie end and you come out onto rue du Poilu, the main street in the old town.

The **tourist office** *(☎ 04 93 76 33 33, fax 04 93 76 33 28; W www.villefranche-sur-mer.com; Jardin François Bacon; open 9am-9pm daily)* runs guided tours of the citadel and old town.

Citadel The imposing **Fort St-Elme** *(place Emmanuel Philibert)* was built by the duke of Savoy between 1554 and 1559 to defend the gulf. In true Monégasque style, you can watch the **changing of the guard** – a 15-minute spectacle – at 7pm in July and August.

Inside the fortress is Villefranche's town hall; the open-air **Théâtre de la Citadelle,** where films are screened daily at 9.30pm in July and August (tickets €6); public gardens; and the **Musée Volti** *(☎ 04 93 76 33 27; admission free; open 9am-noon & 2pm-5.30pm Tues-Sat, 1.30pm-6pm Sun Oct-May; 9am-noon & 2.30pm-6pm Tues-Sat, 2.30pm-7pm Sun June & Sept; 10am-noon & 2.30pm-7pm Tues-Sat, 2.30pm-7pm Sun July & Aug)*, an art museum displaying bronze sculptures of voluptuous female forms in all shapes, sizes and postures. Most are the work of sculptor Antoniucci Volti (1915–89), who was born in Villefranche-sur-Mer.

During Les Petits Matins de la Citadelle (Citadel Early Mornings), on Friday from April to September, you can breakfast in the museum garden at 9am, then have a tour of the fortress and old town from 9.30am. Tickets (☎ 04 93 01 73 68) cost €8.

Chapelle de St-Pierre Villefranche was a favourite of Jean Cocteau (1889–1963), who sought solace here in 1924 following the death of his companion Raymond Radiguet. In 1957 Cocteau decorated the inside of Chapelle de St-Pierre *(☎ 04 93 76 90 70;*

admission €2; open 9.30am-noon & 3pm-9pm Tues-Sun Apr-June, 10am-noon & 4pm-8.30pm Tues-Sun July-Sept, 9.30am-noon & 2pm-6pm Tues-Sun Oct, 9.30am-noon & 2pm-5pm Tues-Sun Dec-Mar, closed Nov), a derelict 14th-century Romanesque chapel used by local fishermen to store their nets until the 68-year-old artist got his hands on it. The engraving above the entrance to the waterfront chapel reads 'Enter this building as if it were made of living stone'. The interior, the pastel-coloured frescoes, the altar – carved out of a rock from La Turbie – and its cloths, crucifix and candelabra were all designed by Cocteau. Mass is celebrated here once a year – on 29 June, the feast day of St Peter, the patron saint of fishermen.

When in town, Cocteau stayed at Hôtel Welcome (see Places to Stay later in this section), a restored 17th-century convent opposite the chapel. Here he wrote the play *Orphée* (Orpheus), and the libretto for Stravinsky's *Oedipus Rex*.

Activities From the Gare Maritime at Port de la Santé, at the western end of quai Amiral Courbet, **Affrètement Maritime Villlefranchois** *(☎ 04 93 76 65 65; e amv.sirenes@wanadoo.fr; open 9am-noon & 2pm-6pm Tues-Sun June-Sept)* runs weekly boat trips to Cap Ferrat (€8/5, one hour) and Monaco (€14/10, two hours), June to September. It also sells tickets for dolphin- and whale-watching expeditions; see the boxed text 'Whale-Watching' later.

Dark Pelican *(☎/fax 04 93 01 76 54; W www.darkpelican.com; Port de la Santé)* rents boats of all shapes and sizes, starting at €60/110 per morning/day for a five-person, no-licence-required Fun Yak 450.

Underwater photography is one of the many activities offered by the diving centre **Aqua Pro Dive International** *(☎ 04 93 01 71 04; e apdi-pantxoa@wanadoo.fr; 16 rue du Poilu)*. It rents all the gear.

Places to Stay With its warm mustard-coloured facade and family-run atmosphere, **Hôtel Provençal** *(☎ 04 93 76 53 53, fax 04 93 76 96 00; W www.hotelprovencal.com; ave Maréchal Joffre; doubles with sea/village view from €61/49)* oozes charm. **Hôtel Welcome** *(☎ 04 93 76 27 62, fax 04 93 76 27 66; W www.hotelwelcome.com; 1 quai Amiral Courbet; doubles weekday/weekend low season from €99/110, with balcony €117/130, doubles with/without balcony high season €150/125)*, a former Cocteau haunt, has rooms with balconies over the old port.

Whale-Watching

There's no guarantee that you'll see one (binoculars are a smart idea), but the whale- and dolphin-spotting expeditions organised by **Acti'Loisirs** *(☎ 04 92 47 75 00, 06 03 78 30 85; W www.actiloisirs.com)* from Villefranche-sur-Mer are exciting nonetheless.

Boats depart daily June to September (twice daily in July and August) from Port de la Santé. An English-speaking marine biologist is planted on board to tell you what's what. Cetacean species typical to the Mediterranean include the long-finned pilot whale, sperm whale and several types of dolphin. Expeditions last four hours and tickets cost €40/29 for adults/children.

Places to Eat English-inspired **Chez Net** *(☎ 04 93 01 83 06; 5 place du Marché)* is a café-cum-bar frequented by a backpacking crowd for its Internet access, big-screen TV and traditional English breakfast.

Quai Amiral Courbet is lined with terraces where you can eat the catch of the day or crack open a crustacean.

La Mère Germaine *(☎ 04 93 01 71 39; 9 quai Amiral Courbet; menu €34)* is the great-grandmother of Villefranchois cuisine. She has cooked up her prized *bouillabaisse* and other fishy delights since 1938.

Carpaccio *(☎ 04 93 01 72 97; W www.restaurant-carpaccio.com; 17 quai Amiral Courbet; menus €16 & €28)*, named after Italian painter Vittore Carpaccio (who lent his name to the meaty dish), is the spot to dine for those who like raw sliced fish. The tuna carpaccio (€19) melts in your mouth.

St-Jean-Cap Ferrat

postcode 06230 • pop 2555

Once a fishing village, St-Jean-Cap Ferrat lies on the spectacular wooded peninsula of Cap Ferrat, which conceals a bounty of millionaires' villas and a star-studded past. Charlie Chaplin, Churchill and Cocteau all holidayed here. King Leopold II of Belgium and *Pink Panther* actor David Niven (1910–83) retired here. Writer Somerset

Maugham (1874–1965) lived and died at the luxurious Villa Mauresque; Noël Coward, Ian Fleming, TS Eliot and Evelyn Waugh were among his regular house guests. British film director Michael Powell ran a hotel at the port. In 1938 Murray Burnett wrote the play *Everybody Comes to Rick's* (the basis for the classic film *Casablanca*) here.

Some 14km of marked walking paths cross the cape. A coastal path links **Plage de Passable** – a fine shingle beach (part public, part paying – €5.20 a day) – on the cape's western shore with the café-lined port on its eastern side. From the latter it is an easy 2.5km (30 minutes) stroll to Beaulieu-sur-Mer. An 8km-walk (two to three hours) takes you right around the cape. Other trails take you inland – routes are clearly marked on a map distributed at the **tourist office** *(☎ 04 93 76 08 90, fax 04 93 76 16 67; 59 ave Denis Séméria; open 8.30am-noon & 1pm-5pm Mon-Sat)*. On a clear day scale the 164 steps of the *phare* (lighthouse) on the cape's most southern tip for a stunning panorama of the coast from Italy to the Ésterel.

Villa Ephrussi de Rothschild On the narrow isthmus of Cap Ferrat is the **Musée de Béatrice Ephrussi de Rothschild** *(☎ 04 93 01 33 09; admission to gardens & ground floor adult/7-17 yrs €8/6, 1st-floor collections €2; open 10am-7pm daily July & Aug, 10am-6pm daily Feb-June & Sept-Oct, 10am-6pm Sat & Sun Nov-Feb, gardens only 2pm-6pm Mon-Fri Nov-Feb)*, in a *belle époque* villa built for the Baroness de Rothschild in 1912. Her house was designed in the style of the great Renaissance houses of Tuscany and took 40 architects seven years to build. It abounds with paintings, tapestries, porcelain and antique furniture and is surrounded by seven beautiful gardens. The central garden was landscaped like a ship's deck so that the baroness could imagine herself aboard a ship. On her ship's prow stands an enchanting temple of love, behind which sprawl Spanish, Japanese, Florentine, cactus and oriental gardens. Different herbs, oleanders and an olive grove adorn the Provençal garden.

Bus No 111 linking Nice and St-Jean-Cap Ferrat stops at the foot of the driveway leading to the villa, at the northern end of ave Denis Séméria (the D25). By train, get off at Beaulieu-sur-Mer from where it is a 20-minute walk: from the seafront follow promenade Maurice Rouvier south and turn right along the second alley way (just before the melon pink villa built on the rocks). Con-tinue uphill along ave Honoré Sauvan (note the round-shaped villa on the left through the trees) to the D25.

Places to Stay & Eat On the western side of the port, **La Frégate** *(☎ 04 93 76 04 51, fax 04 93 76 14 93; 11 ave Denis Séméria; rooms with shower/shower & toilet €42/57)* is a one-star place with 10 shower-equipped rooms.

L'Oursin *(☎ 04 93 76 04 65, fax 04 93 76 12 55; ⓔ oursin@wanadoo.fr; 1 ave Denis Séméria)* is another good 'cheapie' by local standards.

La Voile d'Or *(☎ 04 93 01 13 13, fax 04 93 76 11 17; ⓦ www.lavoiledor.fr; ave Mermoz; doubles from with/without balcony low season €368/202, mid-season €489/291, high season €645/365)*, Michael Powell's former haunt, overlooking the port from its eastern quay, boasts four stars, a private beach and sky-high prices to match.

Grand Hôtel du Cap Ferrat *(☎ 04 93 76 50 50, fax 04 93 76 04 52; 71 blvd Général de Gaulle)*, an equally dreamy paradise, charges similar rates to La Voile d'Or.

La Civette *(☎ 04 93 76 04 14; 1 place Clemenceau)*, occupying a prime spot just back from the water since 1946, dishes up delicious salads, sandwiches, devilish ice cream and other lunchtime fillers.

Beaulieu-sur-Mer

postcode 06310 • pop 3701

Upmarket Beaulieu-sur-Mer never witnessed such a grand time as during the pre-WWI flamboyant *belle époque*, when Europe's wealthy and aristocratic flocked to the resort.

French architect Gustave Eiffel lived at the waterfront Villa Durandy from 1896 until his death in 1923; the Florentine-style villa was consequently converted into luxury holiday apartments (see Places to Stay & Eat following). Next door is the Villa Grecque Kérylos, Beaulieu's main draw.

Tamer remnants of the resort's golden age include the **Grand Casino** *(☎ 04 93 76 48 00; ⓦ www.casinobeaulieu.com; 4 ave Fernand Dunan)*, built in 1928 and still drawing wildcards until 4am or 5am daily; and neighbouring La Rotonde (1899), a domed structure built as a hotel, used as a hospital during WWII and housing a small local history museum today. Across from the harbour are the **Jardins de L'Olivaie**, the venue for a two-week Jazz Parade in August.

Beaulieu's shingle **beach** overlooks the Baie des Fourmis (Bay of Ants). From here, **promenade Maurice Rouvier** leads southwest beneath a hedgerow of *lauriers-roses* (oleanders) to the port of St-Jean-Cap Ferrat, making for a pleasant 30-minute stroll (2.5km). Several more scenic seaside walks, 4km to 8km long, are detailed (in English) on the reverse side of the free map distributed by the **tourist office** (*☎ 04 93 01 02 21, fax 04 93 01 44 04; W www.ot-beaulieu-sur-mer.fr; place Georges Clemenceau; open 9am-12.30pm & 2pm or 3pm-7pm Mon-Sat, 9am-12.30pm Sun)*, next to the train station.

Villa Grecque Kérylos This luxurious villa, perched on the rocky Baie des Fourmis peninsula, is a reconstruction of an ancient Greek dwelling, built in 1902 for scholar and archaeologist Théodore Reinach (1860–1928). The villa took seven years to complete building and is a near-perfect reproduction of an Athenian villa from the 1st and 2nd centuries BC.

The rooms retain their original Hellenic name and purpose. From the marble bath tub decorated with mosaics of splashing dolphins in the *balanéion* (bathroom), Reinach's male guests retired to the *triklinos* (dining room) and afterwards to the *andron*, a large parlour clad in yellow marble from Siena. It appears Reinach saw no need to invite women to the villa where he lived, given it has no *gynaeceum*, the parlour to which women retired after dinner in ancient Greece. In the gardens, a botanical trail highlights the ancient uses of plants typical to Greece and the French coast.

Villa Grecque Kérylos (*☎ 04 93 76 44 09; W www.villa-kerylos.com; ave Gustave Eiffel; adult/child €7/5.50; open 10am-7pm daily July & Aug; 10am-6pm daily Feb-June, Sept & Oct; 2pm-6pm Mon-Fri & 10am-6pm Sat & Sun Nov-Jan)* hosts concerts year round; details are on its website.

Places to Stay & Eat North off blvd du Maréchal Leclerc, the one-star **Hôtel Riviera** (*☎ 04 93 01 04 92, fax 04 93 01 19 31; 6 rue Paul Dommer; doubles with washbasin & bidet €33, doubles/triples with shower & toilet €55/58)* is Beaulieu's bargain-basement hotel. Some rooms have been renovated with sparkling modern fittings and those that haven't will be completed by the end of 2003.

Hôtel Résidence Eiffel (*☎ 04 93 76 46 46, fax 04 93 76 46 00; W www.residence-eiffel.com; rue Gustave Eiffel; studios per week low/high season from €651/924)*, at the former family home of Gustave Eiffel, has weekly rates for four-person self-catering studios. Anyone can feast on the magnificent sea views in its terrace restaurant and tea salon.

La Réserve (*☎ 04 93 01 00 01, fax 04 93 01 28 99; W www.reservebeaulieu.com; 5 blvd du Maréchal Leclerc; doubles with port/sea view from €270/380, suite from €1080)* has been Beaulieu's decadent hang-out since its grand opening in the late 1870s. It's famed, four-star and very pink.

Cap d'Ail

postcode 06320 • pop 4565

There is little to do on the unpoetically named Cape of Garlic (a name actually derived from the Provençal 'Cap d'Abaglio' meaning Cape of Bees) except stroll or swim.

Greta Garbo and Valentina Schlee (the well-known fashion designer) both hung out on this lush, heavily vegetated headland of palm trees and pines, bespeckled with villas, in the 1960s. The house built in 1902 for Auguste Lumière still stands in all its grandeur at 8 ave Charles Blanc, while the spectacular **amphitheatre** that Cocteau designed is used as a youth theatre by the **Centre Méditerranéen d'Études Françaises** (*☎ 04 93 78 21 59, fax 04 93 41 83 96; e centremed@monte-carlo.mc; chemin des Oliviers)*.

Smoking and dogs are banned on **Plage Mala**, Cap d'Ail's shingle beach tucked in a cove. From Cap d'Ail train station, walk down the steps to ave Raymond Gramaglia, a promenade from where Cap d'Ail's splendid **Sentier du Littoral** (coastal path) can be accessed. Information panels along the way explain the lush flora and plush villas you pass; during rough seas, the seaside path is closed. Bear west (right) for a 20-minute amble around rocks to the beach, or east for a more strenuous stroll to Monaco. The **tourist office** (*☎ 04 93 78 02 33, fax 04 92 10 74 36; W www.cap-dail.com; 87 bis ave du*

3 Septembre), in the village centre on the N98, has plenty more information on walks in the area.

July kicks off with a three-day Fête de l'Abeille (Bee Festival). Throughout the month, Tuesday-evening jazz concerts fill the seaside **Amphithéâtre de la Mer** *(☎ 04 93 78 02 33, fax 04 92 10 74 36; place Marquet)*, overlooking Cap d'Ail's small port. Concerts generally start at 9.30pm and tickets cost €8.

Places to Stay & Eat On the coast in a villa overlooking the sea, **Relais International de la Jeunesse** *(☎ 04 93 78 18 58, fax 04 93 53 35 88; ave Raymond Gramaglia; bed in 6- to 12-bed dorm with breakfast €13)* is Cap d'Ail's stunning seaside hostel. Prices include breakfast and sheets. Travellers have to vacate their rooms between 9.30am and 5pm, and a curfew is enforced from 11pm.

Restaurant La Pinède *(☎ 04 93 78 37 10; 10 blvd de la Mer; menus €36 & €46, lobster €75)*, a former fisherman's hut in rocks overlooking the sea on Cap d'Ail coastal path, is a great spot to splash out on a refined and delicious fish lunch and while away the afternoon on a cool sea-facing terrace. From the train station, walk down the steps and head straight for the sea.

Cap Martin

Cap Martin is the coastal quarter of Cap Martin-Roquebrune (see the Grande Corniche later). The green headland is best known for its sumptuous villas, presumptuous collection of royal honorary citizens and famous past residents – among them Winston Churchill, Coco Chanel, Marlène Dietrich, the architect Le Corbusier, designer Eileen Gray and the Irish poet WB Yeats.

Exploring on foot is a pleasurable pastime. Ave Le Corbusier follows the coast east, around Baie de Roquebrune to the northern end of the cape where it turns into promenade Le Corbusier. The beach, **Plage du Buse**, is a two-minute stroll from the train station on ave de la Gare. The hill-top village of Roquebrune is an hour's walk (2km) – up numerous staircases – from the station, while Monte Carlo is three hours (7km) away by foot.

The **tourist office** *(☎ 04 93 35 62 87, fax 04 93 28 57 00; 218 ave Aristide Briand)*, at the northern end of the cape, midway between Carnolès and Cap Martin-Roquebrune train stations, distributes a free map of walking trails to/from and around Cap Martin. It also arranges guided tours (adult/six to 18 years €5/2) of medieval Roquebrune (see the Grande Corniche later) and Corbusier's seashore studio (see the boxed text 'Trailing Le Corbusier' under Architecture in the Facts about Provence chapter).

Cap Martin's medieval counterpart (see Cap Martin-Roquebrune in the Grande Corniche section later) has a couple of delightful eating options.

MOYENNE CORNICHE

Cut through rock in the 1920s, the Moyenne Corniche takes you from Nice past the Col de Villefranche (149m), Èze and Beausoleil, the French town up the hill from Monaco's Monte Carlo.

Getting There & Away

To/from Nice, bus No 112 operated by Rapides Côte d'Azur (see the Nice Getting There & Away section earlier in this chapter) serves the Moyenne Corniche, stopping at Èze village (€1.70, 20 minutes) and Beausoleil (€2.10, 40 minutes). Buses run seven times a day Monday to Saturday, and three times daily on Sunday and holidays.

By train from Nice, get off at Èze-sur-Mer train station on the Corniche Inférieure, from where shuttle buses transport tourists up and down the hill between May and October (eight buses in either direction daily, coinciding with train arrivals/departures). Failing that, it's a 3km uphill trudge on foot to Èze village.

Èze

postcode 06360 • pop 2604 • elevation 429m

Perched on a rocky peak is picturesque Èze, a village once occupied by Ligurians and Phoenicians and grossly overrun with tourists today. Below is its modern coastal counterpart, Èze-sur-Mer, accessible by road or train from the Corniche Inférieure.

When German philosopher Friedrich Nietzsche (1844–1900) stayed here, he started writing *Thus Spoke Zarathustra*; the path that links Èze-sur-Mer and Èze is named after him. Walt Disney holidayed in Èze, and in 2002, U2 guitarist (The Edge) got married on a luxury yacht moored off the coast here.

Ask at the **tourist office** *(☎ 04 93 41 26 00, fax 04 93 41 04 80; Ⓦ www.eze-riviera.com; place du Général de Gaulle)* for details of thematic nature walks (flora, fauna, geology etc).

Things to See & Do Steep narrow streets lead to the medieval hill-top village, which is crammed with art galleries, souvenir shops and pricey cafés. Its crowning glory are chateau ruins, brightened up with a cactus-laden **Jardin Exotique** *(☎ 04 93 41 10 30; adult/11-16 yrs (€2.50/1.50; open 9am-dusk daily)*. Those keen to savour the marvellous panorama of Cap Ferrat to the Massif de l'Ésterel have no choice but pay the cheeky admission fee.

Perfumery Fragonard (see Grasse in the Cannes Area chapter) has an outlet in Èze where the subtleties of its sweet-smelling products can be discovered. The **Fragonard factory** *(☎ 04 93 36 44 65; admission free; open 8.30am-noon & 2pm-6.30pm daily Nov-Jan, 8.30am-6.30pm daily Feb-Oct)*, on the eastern edge of Èze on the Moyenne Corniche, can be visited by guided tour. Rival perfumery **Galimard** *(☎ 04 93 41 10 70; admission free; place Général de Gaulle)* also has an outlet that can be visited.

Places to Stay & Eat At the western end of the Col d'Èze, **Camping Les Romarins** *(☎/fax 04 93 01 81 64; Col d'Èze; camping for 2 adults, tent & car low/high season €16.50/19.50; open Apr-Oct)* is above the village.

Hôtel du Golf *(☎ 04 93 41 18 50, fax 04 93 41 29 93; place de la Colette; doubles €53)* is Èze village's cheapest option. It has 11 rooms and is always booked months in advance.

Hermitage du Col d'Èze *(☎ 04 93 41 00 68, fax 04 93 41 24 05; Col d'Èze; doubles €30-45)*, 2.5km from the village centre, is an old-style 10-room inn spectacularly set at the top of the mountain pass and featuring unbeatable views from its terrace. Food is strictly local fare and delicious to boot – a guaranteed taste of the region.

Château de la Chèvre d'Or *(☎ 04 92 10 66 66, fax 04 93 41 06 72; Ⓦ www.chevredor.com; rue du Barri; doubles low/high season from €260/350, menus from €54)*, first and foremost a gastronomic restaurant of the highest calibre, is strictly for those with a bottomless wallet – but guaranteed to thrill.

GRANDE CORNICHE

The Grande Corniche, built by Napoléon along part of the Roman via Julia Augusta, is shot with spectacular (and dangerous) tunnels and blinding hairpin bends – all of which proved sufficiently cliff-hanging in the 1950s to act as a backdrop to Hitchcock's film *To Catch a Thief* (1956), starring Cary Grant and Grace Kelly. Ironically, the Hollywood actress, who met her Monégasque Prince Charming while shooting the film, died in 1982 after crashing her car on this very same road.

Getting There & Away

To/from Nice, Rapides Côte d'Azur's bus No 116 stops at La Turbie (35 minutes, four buses per day) Monday to Saturday en route to Peille (one hour). Other than that, you need your own wheels.

Observatoire de Nice & Astrorama

The Observatoire de Nice *(☎ 04 92 00 30 11; Ⓦ www.obs-nice.fr)*, a 19th-century, classical domed observatory 5km northeast of Nice centre at the top of Mont Gros (375m), was designed by French architects Gustave Eiffel and Charles Garnier. It sits amid 35 hectares of landscaped parkland. When the observatory opened in 1887, its telescope – 76cm in diameter – was among the largest in Europe. Guided tours (adult/child €4.50/2.50, 1½-hours) of the observatory depart at 3pm on Saturday.

Stargazers can also observe the skies at Astrorama *(☎ 04 93 41 23 04; Ⓦ www.astrorama.net; adult/student & child 7-10 yrs €6/4.50, 'spectacles aux étoiles' €9/6; open 6pm-10pm Fri & Sat Sept-June, 6pm-10pm Mon-Sat July & Aug)*, a planetarium and astronomy centre 8km farther northeast along the Grande Corniche in La Trinité.

A combined ticket allowing guided visits to both of the observatories costs €9 (there are no concessions).

La Turbie

postcode 06320 • pop 3043 • elevation 480m

La Turbie teeters on a promontory above Monaco and offers a stunning night-time vista of the principality. By day, an unparalleled aerial view can be had from the gardens of the **Trophée d'Auguste** *(Augustus' Trophy; ☎ 04 93 41 20 84; 18 ave Albert I; adult/under*

18 €4/free; open 9.30am-6pm daily Apr–mid-June; 9.30am-7pm daily mid-June–mid-Sept; 10am-5pm Tues-Sun mid-Sept–Mar), a trophy monument on the highest point of the old Roman road. It was built by Roman Emperor Augustus in 6 BC to celebrate his victory over the Alps. The 45 Alpine tribes he conquered are listed on the 9m-wide inscription carved on the western side of the monument. Restoration work started on the trophy in the 1920s. Steps lead to the top of the shoddily reconstructed monument and there is a history museum at its base. The site's entrance is on place Théodore de Banville.

La Turbie village is unexciting bar its small but intact old town, neatly packed around the Baroque-style **Église St-Michel** (1777). From the village, a mountain road leads to the top of **Mont Agel** (1110m), the slopes of which are graced with the greens of **Monte Carlo Golf Club** *(04 93 41 09 11; route du Mont Agel)*, an elite 11-hole golf club dating to 1911.

Roquebrune

postcode 06190 • pop 11,966

Cap Martin-Roquebrune, sandwiched between Monaco and Menton, became part of France in 1861; prior to that it was a free town following its revolt against Grimaldi rule in 1848. The town stretches north from the exclusive suburb of Cap Martin on the coast (see the Corniche Inférieure section earlier in this chapter) to the hill-top village perched at 300m.

A donjon complete with a re-created feudal castle dating from the 10th century crowns medieval Roquebrune. The mock-medieval **Tour Anglaise** (English Tower) near the entrance was built by wealthy British lord William Ingram, who bought the chateau in 1911. His fairytale tower caused such an outrage in the village that the state almost immediately classified **Château de Roquebrune** *(☎ 04 93 35 07 22; place Ingram; adult/7-18 yrs €3.50/1.50; open 10am-12.30pm & 2pm-5pm or 6pm Sept-Mar, 10am-12.30pm & 3pm-6pm or 7.30pm Apr-Aug)* as a historical monument to protect it from further fantastical modifications. Its four floors can be visited.

Of all Roquebrune's steep and tortuous streets, rue Moncollet – with its arcaded passages and stairways carved out of the rock – is the most impressive. The architect Le Corbusier is buried in the cemetery at the top of the village – see the boxed text 'Trailing Le Corbusier' under Architecture in the Facts about Provence chapter.

Places to Stay & Eat Boasting 10 lovely seaview rooms, **Hôtel-Restaurant Les Deux Frères** *(☎ 04 93 28 99 00, fax 04 93 28 99 10; W www.lesdeuxfreres.com; place des Deux Frères; singles/doubles high season €65/83; lunch/dinner menu €20/45)* also has a stylish restaurant terrace perched above the water and an excellent-value lunchtime menu that includes half a bottle of wine; don't miss the grapefruit sorbet.

Au Grand Inquisiteur *(☎ 04 93 35 05 37; 18 rue du Château; menus €24 & €35)* could be a film set. Dine in a rock cave and watch your food be carried from the kitchen across the street. Menus include cheese or dessert – add another €4 if you want both.

ARRIÈRE-PAYS NIÇOIS

The Niçois hinterland stretches inland from Nice to Menton. It is studded with medieval hill-top villages, which were perched aloft rocky crags as a safeguard and lookout point.

Getting There & Away

To/from Nice, Transport Régional des Alpes-Maritimes operates hourly buses Monday to Saturday (five on Sunday) to Contes (€3.30, 45 minutes), two or three of which continue Monday to Saturday to Coaraze (€4.50). For bus information of daily services between Nice and Tourrette Levens (€2.50, 45 minutes), call ☎ 04 93 85 61 81.

From Menton, there are buses to/from Ste-Agnès (€7 return, 45 minutes, two or three daily), Gorbio (€6.20 return, 30 minutes) and Castellar (€5.80 return, 25 minutes). A pass covering return transport from Menton all three villages costs €13.50.

Contes to Coaraze

Roman Contes (population 7000), 16km north of Nice, sits on a ship-shaped rock above the River Paillon de Contes. Before plodding up, nip into the **tourist office** *(☎ 04 93 79 13 99; place A Olivier; open 2pm-7pm Mon-Fri)*, level with the D15 below the village. Olives have been crushed at the still-functioning **Moulin à Huile de la Laouza** *(☎ 04 93 79 19 17; ave Raiberti; admission €1; open 9.30am-12.30pm & 2pm-5pm Sat)*, at the northern end of Contes on the D15, since the 13th century. Discover the ins and outs of olive-oil making here and buy locally made olive oil in its shop. Neighbouring **Forge de Bracco** *(ave Raiberti; admission €1; open 9.30am-12.30pm & 2pm-5pm Sat)*, a 13th- to 14th-century smithy where agricultural tools were made, shelters a recreation of a 19th-century Contoise kitchen.

Châteauneuf de Contes, 6km west, is a hamlet at the foot of the overgrown ruins of an older village, abandoned prior to WWI. A path, occasionally barred by a territorial pack of goats, leads from the road to the crumbling ruins, which – territorial goats allowing – can be freely explored on foot. To get to the ruins, follow route de Châteauneuf (the D815) through Châteauneuf de Contes, and bear left at the wrought-iron roadside cross along route des Chevaliers de Malte. The ruins are signposted and located 2km from here.

Continuing west along the D815, then south along the D19, you come to **Tourrette Levens** (population 4000, elevation 390m), a particularly dramatic hill-top village crowned with a **Château Musée** *(Castle Museum; ☎ 04 93 91 03 20; place du Château; admission free; open 2pm-5pm or 7pm daily)*, which houses an exotic butterfly collection and natural history museum. Enchanting concerts are held in its grounds during Les Nuits Musicales (Musical Nights) in July and August. The **Maison des Cantons des Alpes d'Azur** *(☎ 04 93 08 76 31, fax 04 93 29 23 10)*, 10km west on the N202 in **Colomars** (population 2885, elevation 334m), has information on all these villages.

In Coaraze (population 659, elevation 640m), 9km north of Contes on the Col St-Roch (D15), a Provençal poem engraved in stone next to a green lizard mosaic on place Félix-Giordan, tells the tale of how villagers trapped the devil and demanded he sacrifice his lizard-like tail to be set free. Coaraze is derived from the Provençal words '*coa raza*' meaning 'cut tail'. The village celebrates an olive festival on 15 August. Its small **tourist office** *(☎/fax 04 93 79 37 47; 7 place Ste-Catherine)* has details.

Truly fantastic works fill the **Musée Figas** *(☎ 04 93 79 31 87; Engarvin; adult/7-18 yrs €4/2; open 2pm-5pm or 6pm Sat & Sun*, home to oils by fantastic painter Marcel Figas, born in Nice in 1935. From Coaraze, continue north along the D15 towards Col St-Roch and after 6km turn left to Engarvin.

Places to Stay & Eat Tucked at the top of Coaraze, the **Auberge du Soleil** *(☎ 04 93 79 08 11, fax 04 93 79 37 79; half-board €60 per person; open mid-Mar–mid-Nov)* has 10 lovely double rooms, a garden and pool. Its terrace overlooking mountains makes for a very tasty lunch.

Lou Madonics *(☎ 04 93 79 03 52; place des Barbets, Châteauneuf de Contes; full meal around €15)*, with its pea-green shutters, candy-striped covered terrace, *pétanque* (boules) pitch and simple *cuisine familiale* (family kitchen), has all the ingredients for a long and lazy informal lunch.

Peille & Peillon

Quaintly restored Peille (population 2055, elevation 630m) is quite untouched by tourism tack despite the raving reports it gets as being among the hinterland's most intact hill-top villages. Its eastern entrance is guarded by the 12th-century **Chapelle St-Roch** *(place Jean Mioul)*.

In the teeny **Musée du Terroir** *(open 2pm-6pm in summer)*, captions are written in Pelhasc. This is a dialect specific to Peille and distinguishable from the Niçois dialect by its absent 'r's and silent 'l's. For instance, the Peillasques say *carriea* instead of *carriera* (Niçois for *rue*, meaning street). Peille celebrates a Fête du Blé et de la Lavande (Wheat & Lavender Festival) in early August.

Not for the faint-hearted is the **Via Ferrata de Peille**, cut into rock above Peille. The course is a 10-minute walk from the village and scales the Baous de Caster and Barma de la Sié rock formations. The full monty takes 3½ hours to conquer, but it's possible to tackle just one or two of the four sections (each 45 minutes to an hour long). Admission and equipment hire costs €17/25 for a half-/full day. Advance reservations (recommended), tickets and equipment hire are handled by **Havana K'Fe** *(☎ 04 93 91 91 39; 42 rue Centrale)*, a café and ice-cream parlour in the village.

Six kilometres of hairpins southwest of Peille on the D53 towards Peillon, is **La Grave** (population 500), a blot-on-the-landscape cement works where the hinterland's limestone is turned into cement. The best aerial view of Peille and La Grave is from the

Col de la Madone (927m), a beautiful – and hair-raising to drive – stone-tunnelled mountain pass (the D22) that runs east from Peille to Ste-Agnès.

Peillon (population 1229, elevation 456m), 14km northeast of Nice, is known for its precarious *nid d'aigle* (eagle's nest) location. From the village car park, a footpath leads to the **Chapelle des Pénitents Blancs**, noteworthy for its set of macabre 15th-century frescoes. Longer trails lead to Peille, La Turbie and Chapelle St-Martin. North of Peillon, the **Gorges du Peillon** (D21) cuts through the Peillon Valley to **L'Escarène** (population 2138), an important mule stop in the 17th and 18th centuries for traders working the Route du Sel (salt road) from Nice to Turin in Italy.

Places to Stay & Eat At the foot of the village of Peillon, **Auberge de la Madone** *(☎ 04 93 79 91 17, fax 04 93 79 99 36; ⓔ info@ch-demeure.com; Peillon; doubles from around €60; menu €29)* is an upmarket hotel and restaurant with three-star doubles and delicious local Peillonnais cuisine that draws diners from far and wide. Both rooms and tables need booking well in advance.

Gorbio & Ste-Agnès

The flowery hill-top village of Gorbio (population 1162, elevation 360m), 10km northwest of Menton and 2km west of Ste-Agnès as the crow flies, is best known for its annual Fête Dieu in June. On this feast day, during a traditional Procession aux Limaces, villagers light up Gorbio's medieval cobble streets with snail shells set in pots of sand and filled with burning olive oil. Other than that, exploring its maze of cobbled streets and lunching away several lazy hours at Beau Séjour (see the following Places to Stay & Eat section) are its chief attractions.

A trail leads from Gorbio to Ste-Agnès (population 1200, elevation 780m), supposedly Europe's highest 'seaside village'. From montée du Souvenir, 187 perilously rocky steps lead to the scanty 12th-century **chateau ruins** *(open 2pm-5pm Tues-Sun; admission by donation)*. Stones from here were used to build the present-day village in the 15th century. Goats and a donkey graze between the rocks, there's a well-manicured medieval garden to visit and views of the coastline are breathtaking.

Beneath the village, **Fort Ste-Agnès** *(adult/7-14 yrs €3.05/1.52; open 3pm-6pm daily July-Sept, 2.30pm-5.30pm Sat & Sun Oct-June)*, a 2500-sq-metre underground fort, was built between 1932 and 1938 as part of a series of fortifications intended to defend Nice and its coastline from the Italians (who nonetheless overcame Nice immediately following Nazi Germany's invasion of Vichy France in 1942). Close to the drawbridge, the reinforced concrete bunkers of one of four artillery blocks are clearly visible.

For information on both villages, go to Ste-Agnès **tourist office** *(☎ 04 93 35 87 35; ⓔ association.les.peintres.du.soleil@wanadoo.fr; rue du Seigneur Baroum; open 9.30am-5pm Tues-Sat, 2pm-5pm or 6pm Sun)*, inside the Espace Culture et Tradition along with a small art gallery, archaeology museum and exhibition of traditional tools (admission free).

Places to Stay & Eat Probably the busiest camp site along this stretch of coast, **Camping Fleur de Mai** *(☎ 04 93 57 22 36, fax 04 93 57 22 36; route du Val de Gorbio; adult/tent/car low season €10/3.50/12, high season €11/3.50/13; open mid-Sept–mid-Apr)* is midway between Menton and Gorbio. Another site is signposted off the central village square in Gorbio village.

Hôtel St-Yves *(☎ 04 93 35 91 45; rue des Sarassins, Ste-Agnès; menu €12, doubles €29, half-/fullboard €39/43 per person)*, halfway up steep Ste-Agnès, is definitely not for the unenergetic.

Beau Séjour *(☎ 04 93 41 46 15; menus €21, €24 & €30)*, meaning 'Beautiful Stay', is the stuff of Provençal dreams. The Gorbio auberge, run by the same family for four generations, is a village inn dating back to 1880 and has a beautiful jasmine-covered terrace overlooking the quiet village square. Inside, a pianist plays while diners enjoy regional fare cooked with a twist.

Menton & Around

MENTON

postcode 06500 • pop 29,266

Menton is reputed to be the warmest spot on the Côte d'Azur (particularly in winter). Only a few kilometres from the Italian border, it is popular with older holiday-makers,

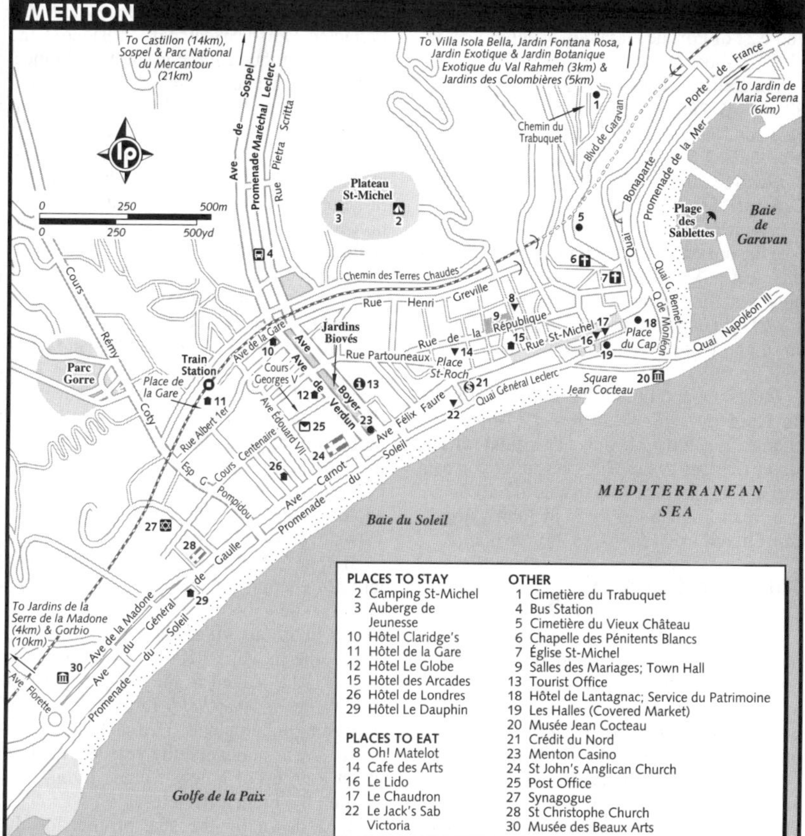

whose way of life has made the town's after-dark life tranquil compared with other coastal hot spots.

Gustave Flaubert, Guy de Maupassant, Katherine Mansfield, and Robert Louis Stevenson all found solace in Menton in the past. Today, the town mainly draws Italians from across the border and retains a magnetic charm free of the airs, graces and pretensions so prevalent elsewhere on the coast.

Historically, Menton, along with neighbouring Cap Martin-Roquebrune, found itself under Grimaldi rule until 1848, when its people rebelled and declared a new independent republic under the protection of Sardinia. In 1861, the two towns voted to become part of France, forcing Charles III of Monaco to sell Menton to Napoleon III for four million FF; he also sold Cap Martin-Roquebrune at the same time.

Above all, Menton is famed for its cultivation of lemons. Giant, larger-than-life sculptures made from lemons, lemons and more lemons (about 130 tonnes) take over the town for two weeks during Menton's fabulous Fête des Citrons (Lemon Festival) in February.

Orientation & Information

The old town and port are wedged between Baie de Garavan, to the east, and Baie du Soleil, which stretches 3km west to Cap Martin-Roquebrune. Promenade du Soleil and its continuations quai Général Leclerc and quai de Monléon skirt the length of Menton's shingle beach. There are more beaches directly northeast of the old port and east of Port de Garavan, Menton's main pleasure-boat harbour.

The **tourist office** *(☎ 04 92 41 76 76, fax 04 92 41 76 78; W www.villedementon.com; Palais de l'Europe, 8 ave Boyer; open 9am-7pm Mon-Sat, 9.30am-12.30pm Sun May-Sept; 8.30am-12.30pm & 1.30pm-6pm Mon-Sat Oct-Apr)* arranges guided tours of *belle époque* Menton and visits to its many gardens (see the boxed text 'Menton Gardens' later in this section). It has information and takes bookings for one-day canyoning, rafting and *via ferrata* expeditions (€34 to €46 per person), and half-day guided walks in the area (€17 to €19).

Banks abound on rue Partouneaux. **Crédit du Nord** *(place St-Roch)* has a 24-hour exchange machine outside. The **post office** *(cours Georges V)* has Cyberposte, or you can surf at Café des Arts (see Places to Eat) There is a small English library in **St John's Anglican Church** *(☎ 04 93 57 20 25; ave Carnot).*

Things to See & Do

Down by the port, a small 17th-century fort crowns the tip of land wedged between Menton's two bays, behind which the old town sprawls. It was built in 1636 to defend Menton and was later used as a salt cellar, prison and lighthouse. Today, the seafront bastion houses the **Musée Jean Cocteau** *(☎ 04 93 57 72 30; square Jean Cocteau; adult/under 25 €3/2.25, admission free 1st Sun of month; open 10am-noon & 2pm-6pm Wed-Mon)*, in which drawings, tapestries and ceramics by the French artist are displayed. Cocteau restored and refurbished the building himself, decorating the outer walls and reception hall with pebble mosaics. His gravestone, tucked in the shade of the bastion walls and looking out to sea, reads *Je reste avec vous* (I stay with you). In 1957 Cocteau decorated Menton's **Salles des Mariages** *(Marriage Hall; place Ardoïno; admission €2; open 8am-noon & 2pm-5.30pm Mon-Fri)* inside the town hall.

From the bastion, walk south along quai de Monléon then cut across place du Marché, an outdoor marketplace adjoining **Les Halles**, Menton's bustling indoor market. Walk under the arches at the eastern end of the square and cross café-filled **place aux Herbes** to get to rue St-Michel, the main pedestrianised street in the **old town**.

From place du Cap a ramp leads up to the Italianate **Église St-Michel**, considered the grandest Baroque church in southern France. Its creamy facade is flanked by a 35m-tall clock tower and a 53m-high steeple, constructed between 1701 and 1703. The square in front of the church hosts a music festival in August; see Special Events later. Above St-Michael's Church on place de la Conception is apricot-coloured **Chapelle des Pénitents Blancs** (1689).

Farther uphill via montée du Souvenir is the cypress-shaded **Cimetière du Vieux Château**, home to the graves of English, Irish, Americans, New Zealanders and other foreigners who died in Menton in the 19th century. The inventor of rugby, the Reverend William Webb Ellis (1805–72), is buried in the cemetery's southwestern corner. Continue north along the steep chemin du Trabuquet to the **Cimetière du Trabuquet**, another cemetery with stunning panoramic views over Menton, the sea and into Italy.

Blvd de Garavan, which runs north parallel with chemin du Trabuquet, leads to the upmarket neighbourhood of **Garavan**, known for its luxurious villas. Between 1920 and 1921, the novelist Katherine Mansfield (1888–1923) stayed in the **Villa Isola Bella** *(ave Katherine Mansfield)* to try to ease her worsening tuberculosis. Her short story *The Doves' Nest*, published the year she died, is about a group of lonely women living in a villa on the French Riviera.

Back down by the sea, promenade du Soleil leads southwest to the early 18th-century Palais Carnolès, a former summer residence of Monaco's royal family, which nowadays houses Menton's **Musée des Beaux-Arts** *(☎ 04 93 35 49 71; 3 ave de la Madone; admission free; open 10am-noon & 2pm-6pm Wed-Mon)*. Its surrounding **Jardin de Sculptures** features sculptures set amid a lemon and orange grove.

Special Events in Menton

Menton's **Fête des Citrons** (Lemon Festival) in February kicks off around the ornamental Jardins Biovès on Mardi Gras. Mid-July brings contemporary dance and jazz to the Jardin Fontana Rosa during the **Rencontres de Danse Contemporaine**. Tickets costing €14 (students €7) are available at the **Service du Patrimoine** *(☎ 04 92 10 97 10; Hôtel de Lantagnac, 24 rue St-Michel)*. The

Menton Gardens

The green-thumbed can lose themselves in a maze of beautiful gardens in Menton, each oozing a different horticultural appeal and historical charm. Many are in the wealthy northern quarter of Garavan.

The **Jardin Botanique Exotique du Val Rahmeh** *(☎ 04 93 35 86 72; ave St-Jacques)* was laid out in 1905 for Lord Radcliffe, the governor of Malta. In 1967, financial debts forced its botany-mad English owner, Maybud Campbell, to sell her prized garden to the state. Since then, the beautiful one-hectare garden, known for its exotic fruit tree collection and sub-tropical plants, has formed the Mediterranean branch of Paris' National Natural History Museum. The tourist office runs guided visits (€7) here at 3pm on Monday.

The neighbouring **Jardin Fontana Rosa** *(ave Blasco Ibañez)*, created by Spanish novelist Vicente Blasco Ibañez in the 1920s, features fanciful benches, pergolas, pools and columns made from ceramic. Watching a contemporary dance or jazz performance (see Special Events later in this section) here is particularly memorable. On the same street, **Parc du Pian** *(ave Blasco Ibañez)* comprises a 1000-year-old grove of 530 olive trees spread across three hectares; the park can be freely visited.

In France's most temperate garden, the **Jardin de Maria Serena** *(21 promenade Reine-Astrid)* the temperature never falls below 5°C. The garden, known for its palm trees, frames the white Villa Maria Serena, designed in a grandiose Second Empire style by Charles Garnier in 1866. French engineer Ferdinand de Lesseps stayed here after overseeing the building of the Suez Canal. Musical recitals are likewise hosted here in summer. Guided visits (€5) depart at 10am on Tuesday; the tourist office has details.

Olive trees, cypresses, lavender and other non-exotic plants feature in the **Jardins des Colombières** *(route des Colombières Garavan)*, a series of lovely little gardens 5km north of town, each inspired by a different personality in Greek mythology. They were designed by Ferdinand Bac (1859–1952), comic writer and the illegitimate son of Napoleon III, between 1918 and 1927. In July and August the tourist office runs a daily visit at 4pm (€5).

It was an American gardener, Lawrence Johnston, who made **Jardin de la Serre de la Madone** *(☎ 04 93 57 73 90; route de Gorbio; admission €8; guided visits 2.30pm Tues-Sun Feb & Mar; 2.30pm & 4.30pm Apr & May; 10am & 4pm June & Sep, 10am & 5pm July & Aug)* the historic garden it is today. After laying out the gardens at Hidcote Manor in Gloucestershire, UK, the botanical buff moved to the coast where he planted dozens of rare plants, picked up from his travels around the world. The seven-hectare garden, abandoned for decades, was bought by the Conservatoire du Littoral in 1999 and is now slowly being restored by a small but enthusiastic army of gardeners. The villa on the estate will eventually house a tea room and international centre for rare-plant enthusiasts.

Festival de Musique, held in front of Église St-Michel throughout August, is an even more stunning affair.

Places to Stay

Camping The two-star **Camping St-Michel** *(☎ 04 93 35 81 23; route des Ciappes de Castellar; camping for 2 adults, tent & car from €12; open Apr–mid-Oct)* is 1km northeast of the train station up plateau St-Michel.

Hostels A sweaty walk uphill from the train station is the **Auberge de Jeunesse** *(☎ 04 93 35 93 14, fax 04 93 35 93 07; plateau St-Michel; dorm bed with breakfast €11.35; reception open 7am-noon & 5pm-11pm or midnight)* with 80 beds and lots of steps to carry your pack up. You have to be in by the midnight curfew.

Hotels Located at the train station, **Hôtel de la Gare** *(☎/fax 04 93 57 69 87; place de la Gare; singles/doubles €28/40)*, has nine rooms above Le Chouchou sandwich bar. Advance payment is a must and rooms are strictly nonsmoking.

Hôtel Claridge's *(☎ 04 93 35 72 53, fax 04 93 35 42 90; W www.claridges-menton.com; 39 ave de Verdun; singles/doubles from €39.54/49.58)* is a two-star place near the sea. Air-conditioning costs an extra couple of euros, and it touts a tasty in-house restaurant (*menus* €13.50 & €18).

Hôtel Le Globe *(☎ 04 92 10 59 70, fax 04 92 10 59 71; 21 ave de Verdun; singles/doubles low season €45.73/48.73, high season €48.78/53.36)*, is a member of the reliable Logis de France chain and has one of the most complicated price lists ever, has quite comfortable rooms that would warrant no complaints.

Hôtel de Londres (☎ *04 93 35 74 62, fax 04 93 41 77 78;* Ⓦ *www.hotel-de-londres.com; 15 ave Carnot; doubles low/high season from €44/55)*, another Logis de France safe bet, is a pretty hotel with flower boxes and a small garden set off the road.

Hôtel Le Dauphin (☎ *04 93 35 76 37, fax 04 93 35 31 74; 408 promenade du Soleil; singles/doubles low season €49/51, mid-season €53/55, high season €58/60)* overlooks the sea and has three giant palm trees out front. A seaview costs €6 to €10 more than inland-facing rooms.

Hôtel des Arcades (☎ *04 93 35 70 62, fax 04 93 35 35 97; 41 ave Félix Faure; doubles with washbasin/shower & toilet €56/59, including breakfast; lunchtime plat du jour €9.50, menus €14 & €21.50)*, under the arches in town, is one of Menton's most picturesque options. Its restaurant is equally popular.

Places to Eat

There are places to eat galore – at any time of day – along ave Félix Faure and its pedestrianised continuation, rue St-Michel. Place Clemenceau and place aux Herbes in the Vieille Ville are equally table-packed. Several spots on place du Cap dish up Italian-inspired *bruschetta* (toasted bread piled with a savoury topping) for €5 per meal-sized slice. Pricier places to eat with terraces that are fanned by cool sea breezes line promenade du Soleil.

Valle Boulangerie-Pâtisserie *(ave Felix Faure)*, a traditional Italian-run bakery, cooks up crunchy €2 *sacristains* (sticks of twisted pastry entwined with chocolate, almonds or cheese), olive-oil bread, and juicy €2 to €3.50 slices of aubergine and parmesan *fougasse* (a Niçois interpretation of pizza).

Oh! Matelot (☎ *04 93 28 45 40; place Loredan Larchey; menu €12.50)* serves salads, open (and closed) sandwiches and *bruschetta* all day long. Inside, this cheap and cheerful bistro is decorated like a boat.

Café des Arts (☎ *04 93 35 78 67; 16 rue de République; pasta/salads/meats €8/8/12)* lures a young and trendy crowd with its stylish traditional-with-a-twist interior, laidback attitude and computers to access the Net.

Le Jack's Sab Victoria (☎ *04 93 57 91 22; promenade du Soleil; menu €12.50)* is an upbeat spot with beachfront terrace and plenty of light snacks to appease the trendy crowd who lunch here.

Le Chaudron (☎ *04 93 35 90 25; 28 rue St-Michel; menu €19.95)* serves traditional fare, including well-stuffed courgette flowers (€10.35).

Le Lido (☎ *04 93 28 48 71; 24 rue St-Michel; menus €15 & €30)*, a bustling seafood bar, is the spot to savour oysters, lobsters and other crustacean friends, piled high on seafood platters (€16 per person).

Menton has a covered food market, **Les Halles** *(quai de Monléon; open 5am-1pm Tues-Sun)*, and an open-air equivalent that sets up shop beneath the bridge on ave de Verdun on Saturday morning.

Getting There & Away

Bus From the **bus station** (☎ *04 93 28 43 27; 12 promenade Maréchal Leclerc)* there are buses to/from Monaco (€2.10, 30 minutes), Nice (€5, 1¼ hours), Nice-Côte d'Azur airport (€15.70/25.90 single/return, 1¼ hours, departures to coincide with flight times), Ste-Agnès (€7 return, 45 minutes) and Sospel (€4.50 one-way, 45 minutes).

Train Trains to Ventimiglia across the border cost €2 and take 10 minutes. For information on Côte d'Azur train services see earlier Getting There & Away sections earlier in this chapter.

AROUND MENTON

A string of mountain villages peer down on Menton from the **Col de Castillon** (707m), a hair-raising pass (the D2566) that wends its way up the Vallée du Carei from the coast to Sospel, 21km north of Menton and gateway to the Parc National du Mercantour (see the Haute-Provence chapter). The road cuts through **Forêt de Menton**, a thick forest traversed with walking trails, following which you pass the **Viaduc du Caramel**. In former times, the viaduct was used by the old Menton–Sospel tramway, which used to trundle along the valley.

Castillon (population 280), just south of the top of the pass, is considered a model of modern rural planning. The village was destroyed by an earthquake in 1887, then bombed in 1944. It was built anew in 1951, perched on the mountain slopes in true Provençal fashion. It has a small **tourist**

office *(☎ 04 93 04 32 03, fax 04 93 04 32 09; W www.castillon06.com; rue de la République)*. The Sospel-Menton bus stops in Castillon.

About 5km northeast of Menton along the skinny route de Castellar (the D24) is **Castellar**. En route you pass by the former home of designer Eileen Gray (see the boxed text 'Trailing Le Corbuiser' under Architecture in the Facts about Provence chapter). Climb the steep and narrow streets, scale stairs and cut through tiny covered passages to reach place Clemenceau, the square at the top of the hill-top village from where there is a magnificent panorama across the valley. Both the GR51 and GR52 walking paths pass through Castellar.

Cannes Area

Cannes is famous for its cultural activities, the most renowned being the 10-day International Film Festival in mid-May, which sees the city's population quadruple overnight. One spin-off of all this party madness, which lasts year round, is an ultra-hip and chic night life centred around a clutch of lounge bars in Cannes' so-called 'Magic Square'.

Art-wise, Cannes has just one museum and, since its speciality is ethnography, the only art you'll encounter is in the many rather chichi galleries scattered around town or on the promenade where henna tattooists draw elaborate patterns on suntanned skins. The town's adopted slogan may well be 'life is a festival', but the main tourist season only runs from May to October.

Offshore from Cannes lie the two Lérins islands. Continuing northeast along the coast, you arrive at Antibes and its singing cape, Vallauris and Golfe-Juan (which is Picasso territory). Then there's a cluster of arty, inland villages crowned with Matisse's Vence, Chagall's St-Paul de Vence and Renoir's Cagnes-sur-Mer. Inland is smelly Grasse.

The most stunning natural feature of the entire Côte d'Azur – apart from the sky-blue sea, of course – is the lump of red porphyritic rock known as the Massif de l'Estérel. At its foot is St-Raphaël, a beachside resort town a couple of kilometres southeast of Roman Fréjus.

Highlights

- Stroll the length of La Croisette, the Riviera's classiest promenade, then head up to le Suquet, Cannes' old quarter
- Sail to the Lérins islands to see where the man in the iron mask rotted in hell
- View Picassos in Antibes and Vallauris, Renoirs in Cagnes, and works by Matisse in Vence
- Gawk at palatial seaside villas, mansions and fabulous gardens on Cap d'Antibes
- Take a walk on the wild side in red-rocked Massif de l'Estérel
- Create a perfume you can call your own in smelly Grasse

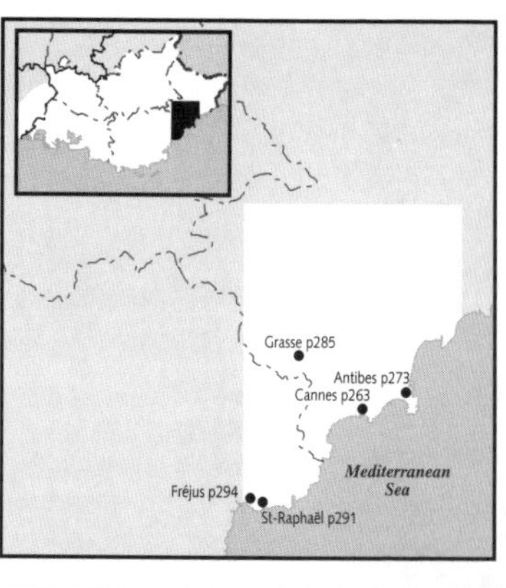

Cannes to Nice

The 32km-stretch of coast that lies between Cannes and Nice is heavily developed – unlike in the late 1940s, when Picasso had a studio in Antibes (an upmarket port midway between the two), lived in the neighbouring potters village of Vallauris, and quite often lunched (in exchange for a painting) with other then-impoverished artists such as Matisse, Marc Chagall and Fredinand Leger in the hill-top village of St-Paul de Vence.

CANNES

postcode 06400 • pop 67,304

It's the money of the affluent, readily spent with fashionable nonchalance, that keeps Cannes' expensive hotels, restaurants and exorbitant boutiques in business and ocean-liner-sized yachts afloat. But the harbour, the bay, the old quarter of Le Suquet, the beachside promenade, the beaches and the sunworshippers laid out on them, provide more than enough natural beauty to make at least a day trip here well worth the effort.

Orientation

Don't expect to be struck down by glitz 'n' glamour the minute you step foot in Cannes. Seedy sex shops and peep shows abound around the train station and bus stop on rue Jean Jaurès. Things glam up along

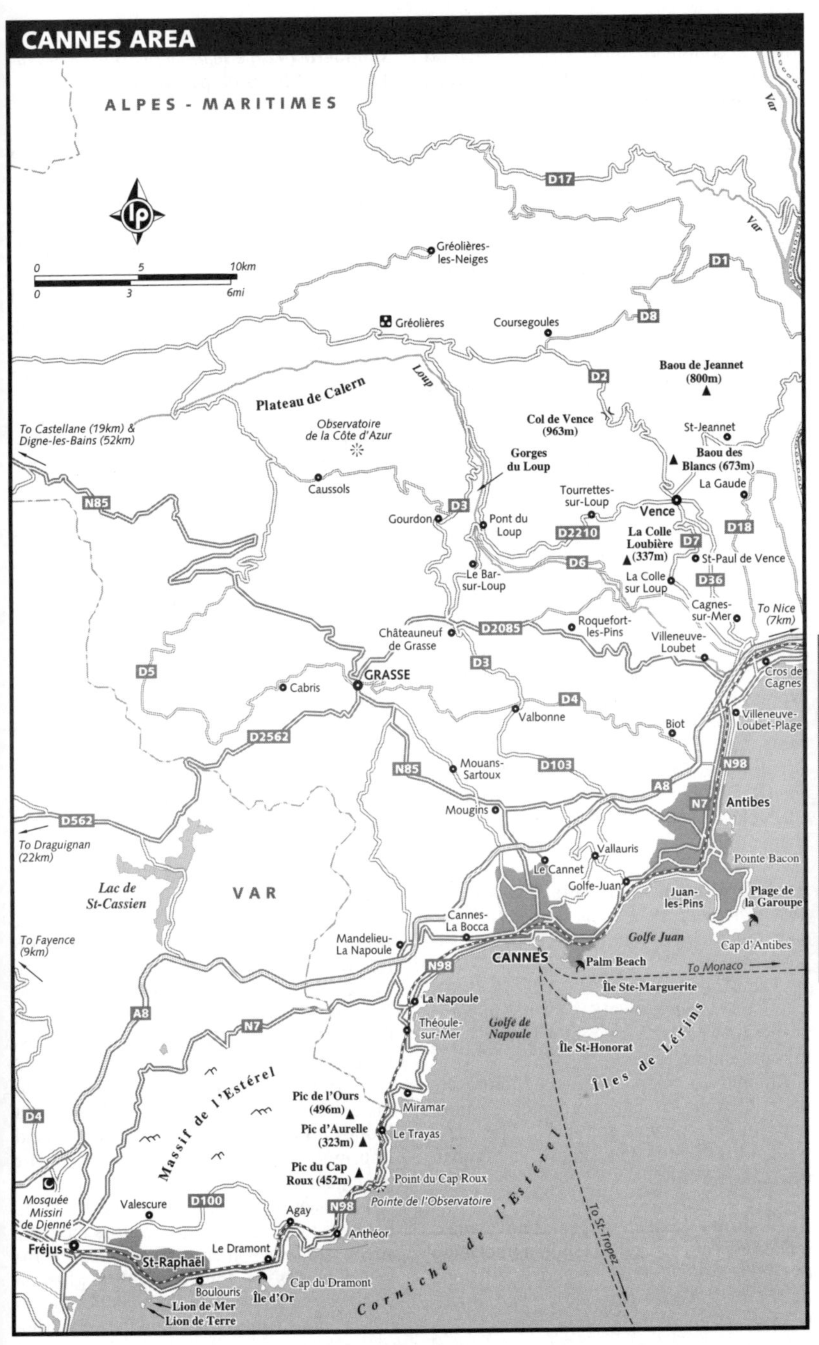
CANNES AREA
ALPES - MARITIMES
VAR
Var
D17
D1
D8
D2
Gréolières-les-Neiges
Gréolières
Coursegoules
Baou de Jeannet (800m)
Loup
Plateau de Calern
Observatoire de la Côte d'Azur
Col de Vence (963m)
St-Jeannet
Baou des Blancs (673m)
Gorges du Loup
To Castellane (19km) & Digne-les-Bains (52km)
Caussols
La Gaude
Tourrettes-sur-Loup
Vence
N85
D3
Gourdon
Pont du Loup
D2210
La Colle Loubière (337m)
D7
D18
St-Paul de Vence
D6
Le Bar-sur-Loup
La Colle sur Loup
D36
Cagnes-sur-Mer
To Nice (7km)
Châteauneuf de Grasse
D2085
Roquefort-les-Pins
Villeneuve-Loubet
D5
GRASSE
Cros de Cagnes
Cabris
D4
Valbonne
Villeneuve-Loubet-Plage
Biot
D2562
N85
Mouans-Sartoux
D103
N98
A8
N7
Antibes
D562
Mougins
To Draguignan (22km)
Vallauris
Le Cannet
Pointe Bacon
Lac de St-Cassien
Golfe-Juan
Juan-les-Pins
Plage de la Garoupe
To Fayence (9km)
Cannes-La Bocca
Mandelieu-La Napoule
Golfe Juan
Cap d'Antibes
CANNES
Palm Beach
To Monaco
N98
Île Ste-Marguerite
La Napoule
A8
Théoule-sur-Mer
Golfe de Napoule
N7
Île St-Honorat
Îles de Lérins
Massif de l'Estérel
Pic de l'Ours (496m)
Miramar
D4
Pic d'Aurelle (323m)
Le Trayas
Pic du Cap Roux (452m)
Point du Cap Roux
Mosquée Missiri de Djenné
Valescure
D100
Agay
N98
Pointe de l'Observatoire
Corniche de l'Estérel
To St-Tropez
Anthéor
Fréjus
Le Dramont
St-Raphaël
Boulouris
Île d'Or
Cap du Dramont
Lion de Mer
Lion de Terre
0 5 10km
0 3 6mi

rue d'Antibes, the main shop-till-you-drop street a couple of blocks south. Several blocks south again is Palais des Festivals, east of the Vieux Port (old port).

Cannes' famous promenade, the magnificent blvd de la Croisette, begins at Palais des Festivals and continues east along Baie de Cannes to Pointe de la Croisette. Place Bernard Cornut Gentille, home to the main bus station, fills the northwestern corner of the Vieux Port. Perched on a hill west of the Vieux Port is the less crowded, pedestrianised quarter of Le Suquet.

Information

Tourist Offices The Cannes **tourist office** *(☎ 04 93 39 24 53, fax 04 92 99 84 23; W www.cannes.fr; open 9am-7pm daily)*, on the ground floor of Palais des Festivals, runs weekly organised tours of the bunker (see the boxed text 'Starring at Cannes' later), June to August. Tours costs €2 and last 45 minutes. It runs an **annexe** *(☎ 04 93 99 19 77; rue Jean Jaurès; open 9am-7pm Mon-Sat)* next to the train station.

Money Commercial banks are dotted along rue d'Antibes and rue Félix Faure. **American Express** *(Amex; ☎ 04 93 38 15 87; 8 rue des Belges; open 9am-5.45pm Mon-Fri, 9am-11.45 Sat May-Sept, 9am-5.45pm Mon-Fri Oct-Apr)* and **Thomas Cook** *(8 rue d'Antibes; open 9am-10pm daily)* cash all types of travellers cheques; the latter levies a commision charge of 6%.

CANNES AREA

Post & Communications The Cannes **post office** *(22 rue Bivouac Napoléon; open 8am-7pm Mon-Fri, 8am-noon Sat)* has Cyberposte facilities.

The **Mondega Café** *(☎ 04 93 68 19 21; e yallah@wanadoo.fr; 15 place Mérimée)*, a proper Internet café, charges €4/8 for 30/60 minutes online.

Alliance Location (see Car & Motorcycle under Getting Around later in this section) rents mobile phones for €11/63 per day/week, plus €0.80/1.85 a minute for national/international calls.

Bookshops English-language novels and guides are sold at **Cannes English Bookshop** *(☎ 04 93 99 40 08; e cannesbooks@wanadoo.fr; 11 rue Bivouac Napoléon; open 10am-6.30pm or 7pm Mon-Sat)*.

Laundry Wash your glad rags at **Laverie Gambetta** *(42 rue Jean Jaurès; open 8.30am-8pm daily)* for €5/8 per 6/12kg.

Walking Tour

The obvious place to take a people-watching stroll is **blvd de la Croisette** – the Riviera's classiest promenade, known locally as La Croisette. Start at the pine- and palm-shaded promenade's westernmost end, **La Malmaison** *(☎ 04 93 99 04 04; 47 blvd de la Croisette; adult/18-25 yrs/under 18 €3/2/free; open 10am-1pm & 3pm-7pm Tues-Sun June-Aug; 10am-1pm & 2.30pm-6.30pm Tues-Sun Apr, May & Sept, to 5.30pm Oct-Mar)*, a tiny (relatively-speaking, that is) seaside house built in 1863 between the Grand Hôtel and flashy Noga Hilton. Temporary art exhibitions are held here. Continuing east, you pass the sparkling windows of real-estate agent **John Taylor & Son** *(☎ 04 93 38 00 66; e jgil@john-taylor.fr; 55 blvd de la Croisette)*, founded in 1864 and an agent for Christie's auction house. The photographs of the absolutely fabulous properties displayed are likely to be the closest glimpse you'll get of the domiciles of the rich and famous.

When it all gets too much, backtrack east a tad for tea on the terrace of Cannes' most famous hotel, the **Carlton Inter-Continental** *(58 blvd de la Croisette)*. Its twin cupolas, erected in 1912, were modelled on the breasts of La Belle Otéro, infamous for the string of lovers – including Spain's Alphonso XIII, Tsar Nicholas II and Leopold II of Belgium – she picked up at the legendary gambling tables of Monte Carlo.

Once refreshed (and still reeling in shock from the price of that cuppa), stride with renewed vigour west along La Croisette to the legendary **Palais des Festivals** (Festival Palace), plonked on the headland between the Vieux Port and Baie de Cannes. Most pose for a photograph on the familiar 22 steps (minus the red carpet) leading up to the entrance, then totter along the **allée des Étoiles du Cinèma**, a path of celebrity hand imprints, embedded in concrete on the pavement.

From here, you can gawk at the big boats bobbing in the **Vieux Port** or cross the busy street and watch men play *pétanque* (Provençal boules) on **square Lord Brougham**, a large gravel area where the kids ride on an old-fashioned merry-go-round, teens drink

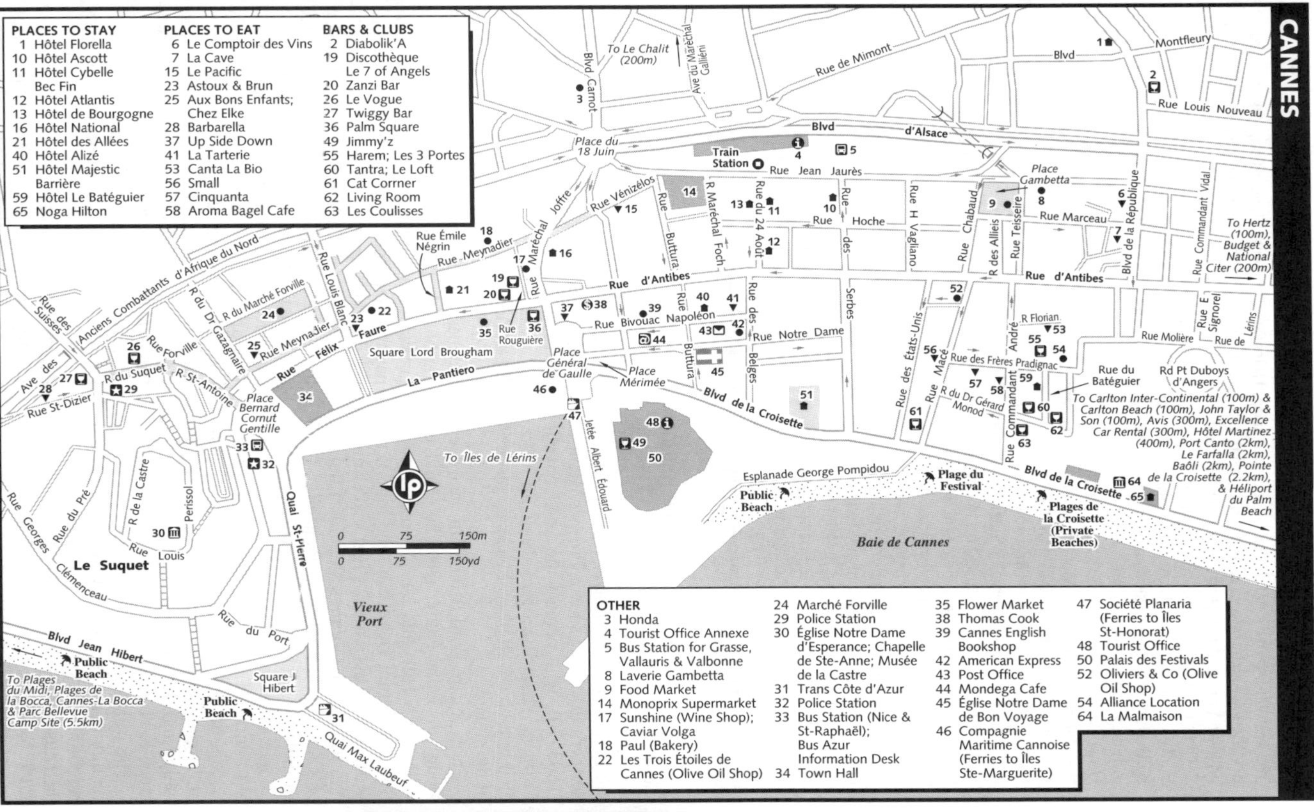
CANNES
PLACES TO STAY
1 Hôtel Florella
10 Hôtel Ascott
11 Hôtel Cybelle Bec Fin
12 Hôtel Atlantis
13 Hôtel de Bourgogne
16 Hôtel National
21 Hôtel des Allées
40 Hôtel Alizé
51 Hôtel Majestic Barrière
59 Hôtel Le Batéguier
65 Noga Hilton
PLACES TO EAT
6 Le Comptoir des Vins
7 La Cave
15 Le Pacific
23 Astoux & Brun
25 Aux Bons Enfants; Chez Elke
28 Barbarella
37 Up Side Down
41 La Tarterie
53 Canta La Bio
56 Small
57 Cinquanta
58 Aroma Bagel Cafe
BARS & CLUBS
2 Diabolik'A
19 Discothèque Le 7 of Angels
20 Zanzi Bar
26 Le Vogue
27 Twiggy Bar
36 Palm Square
49 Jimmy'z
55 Harem; Les 3 Portes
60 Tantra; Le Loft
61 Cat Corrner
62 Living Room
63 Les Coulisses
OTHER
3 Honda
4 Tourist Office Annexe
5 Bus Station for Grasse, Vallauris & Valbonne
8 Laverie Gambetta
9 Food Market
14 Monoprix Supermarket
17 Sunshine (Wine Shop); Caviar Volga
18 Paul (Bakery)
22 Les Trois Étoiles de Cannes (Olive Oil Shop)
24 Marché Forville
29 Police Station
30 Église Notre Dame d'Esperance; Chapelle de Ste-Anne; Musée de la Castre
31 Trans Côte d'Azur
32 Police Station
33 Bus Station (Nice & St-Raphaël); Bus Azur Information Desk
34 Town Hall
35 Flower Market
38 Thomas Cook
39 Cannes English Bookshop
42 American Express
43 Post Office
44 Mondega Cafe
45 Église Notre Dame de Bon Voyage
46 Compagnie Maritime Cannoise (Ferries to Îles Ste-Marguerite)
47 Société Planaria (Ferries to Îles St-Honorat)
48 Tourist Office
50 Palais des Festivals
52 Oliviers & Co (Olive Oil Shop)
54 Alliance Location
64 La Malmaison

Starring at Cannes

The Festival International du Film is a closed shop. Unless you're Gérard Depardieu, Brigitte Bardot or otherwise rich, beautiful and worth a tabloid splash, you have absolutely no chance of scoring an invitation to the legendary Cannes film festival.

The 10-day festival revolves around the ugly, 60,000-sq-metre Palais des Festivals, called 'the bunker' by local Cannois. At the centre of the competition is the prestigious Palme d'Or, awarded by the jury and its president to the winning film – generally not a box office hit. Notable exceptions include Coppola's *Apocalypse Now* (1979), *Sex, Lies & Video Tape* (1989), David Lynch's *Wild at Heart* (1990) and Tarentino's *Pulp Fiction* (1994). An equally integral part of the annual festival is the Marché du Film (Film Market) where an estimated US$200 million worth of business takes place.

Around 7000 'names', trailed by 3000 journalists, attend the star-studded spectacle. Most stay at the Carlton, Majestic or Noga Hilton hotels. They eat at Eden Roc on the Cap, Alain Ducasse's Le Louis XV in Monaco and Roger Vergé's Moulin de Mougins, 8km north of Cannes.

Starlets have always stripped off at Cannes. In the early days dropping your top shocked. The 1954 festival, for example, saw the unknown Simone Sylva drop her top in front of actor Robert Mitchum who, being a gentleman and all that, had his hands covering her boobs within seconds to hide them from the public eye. The cameras clicked, it hit the headlines, Mitchum's wife was mortified – and Simone Sylva committed suicide six months later. The line of glamour girls who pose topless on the beach today (snapped mainly by tourists) is passé.

The Festival International du Film was created in 1939 to counter Mussolini's fascist propaganda film festival in Venice. It was not until after WWII, however, that the first festival starred at Cannes. Tickets (to be pitched for no later than 31 March) are issued by the **Association France du Festival International du Film** (*☎ 01 53 59 61 00; W www.festival-cannes.fr; 3 rue Amélie, F-75007 Paris*).

shakes outside McDonald's, and aspiring models wait to be spotted on the terrace of Palm Square (see Entertainment later in this section). A morning **flower market** fills the northern side of the square. Prosper Mérimée (1803–70), who penned the 1845 novella *Carmen*, which Bizet turned into an opera, died in a house on place Mérimée, just east of the square.

From square Lord Brougham, bear west along rue Felix Faure, past the **Hôtel de Ville** (town hall) and bus station on place Bernard Cornut Gentille, to the foot of rue St-Antoine. This narrow street snakes north into the hilly **Le Suquet**, the oldest quarter of Cannes where British chancellor Lord Brougham – the first foreigner to live in Cannes (after whom the square is named) – built himself the **Villa Eleanore** (1862). Locals thought the former lord chancellor of England totally nutty (and quintessentially English) when he insisted on laying a green lawn around his abode.

The hill is topped by the majestic, 12th-century **Église Notre Dame d'Esperance** and adjoining **Chapelle de Ste-Anne**, home to the **Musée de la Castre** (*☎ 04 93 38 55 26; adult/18-25 yrs/under 18 €3/2/free, free 1st Sun of month; open 10am-noon & 3pm-7pm Tues-Sun June-Sept, 10am-noon & 2pm-6pm Tues-Sun Apr & May, to 5pm Oct-Mar*). Inside is a diverse collection of Mediterranean and Middle Eastern antiquities, and objects of ethnographic interest from all over the world.

Beaches

Unlike Nice, Cannes is endowed with sandy beaches. Unfortunately most of the sand lining blvd de la Croisette is sectioned off for guests of fancy hotels. Here, sunworshippers pay for a cushioned sun-lounger – from €10 per day on **Plage du Festival** to an astonishing €35-odd on **Carlton Beach** – and lap up the beachside equivalent of room service (lunch delivered to your deck chair, strips of carpet leading to the water's edge and so on). This arrangement leaves only a relatively small strip of sand near the Palais des Festivals for the bathing pleasure of the picnicking hoi polloi. However, free public beaches, **Plage du Midi** and **Plage de la Bocca**, stretch for several kilometres west from the Vieux Port along blvd Jean Hibert and blvd du Midi.

Boat Excursions

The regular boats to/from the Îles de Lérins (see that section later) make great boat trips.

Between June and September, **Compagnie Maritime Cannoise** (CMC; see Getting There & Away in the Îles de Lérins section later) also runs day trips by boat from Cannes to Monaco (once weekly) and St-Tropez (twice weekly). A return fare to either costs €27/13.50 per adult/five to 10 years.

Trans Côte d'Azur (see Getting There & Away in the Îles de Lérins section later) runs once-weekly boat excursions to Île de Porquerolles (adult/four to 10 years €45/21), Monaco (€29/14) and San Remo in neighbouring Italy (€40/19) in July and August; twice-weekly along the Corniche de l'Estérel (€14/8). mid-June to September; and three-times weekly to St-Tropez (€30/15), June to September.

There are also seasonal boats from Juan-les-Pins (see Beaches & Boats in the Antibes section, later in this chapter), Golfe-Juan (see Boat Excursions under Vallauris, later) and the seaside resorts of Mandelieu-La Napoule and Théoule-sur-mer (see those sections under the Massif de l'Estérel, later).

Places to Stay – Budget

Camping In Cannes-La Bocca, **Parc Bellevue** *(☎ 04 93 47 28 97, fax 04 93 48 66 25; 67 ave Maurice Chevalier; camping for 2 adults, tent & car around €15; open Apr-Oct)* lies about 5.5km west of Cannes centre. Bus No 9 from the port-side bus station stops 400m from the site.

Hotels Several budget hotels are clustered around the train station, including:

Hôtel Cybelle Bec Fin *(☎ 04 93 38 31 33, fax 04 93 38 43 47; 14 rue du 24 Août; doubles with washbasin €23.50, with shower €28, with shower & toilet €37.50)* is a simple but atmospheric choice with a lively adjoining restaurant (*menus* €18 & €22.50) strung with celluloid.

Hôtel de Bourgogne *(☎ 04 93 38 36 73, fax 04 92 99 28 41; 11 rue du 24 Août; singles/doubles with washbasin from €30/35, doubles with shower €37, doubles/triples with shower & toilet €45/50)* is another good-value spot to rest party-tired bones.

Hôtel National *(☎ 04 93 39 91 92, fax 04 92 98 44 06; ⓔ hotelnationalcannes@wanadoo.fr; 8 rue Maréchal Joffre; doubles with washbasin €45, doubles/triples with shower & toilet €55/78)* is a spic-and-span, one-star place. Reception is on the 1st floor – ring the bell.

Hôtel Le Batéguier *(☎ 04 93 68 90 00, fax 04 93 38 83 33; ⓔ 10 rue du Batéguier; singles/doubles €35/45)* might be run by a cranky guy, but its location – a mere stumble away from Cannes' most hip bars – makes it well worth a mention.

Places to Stay – Mid-Range

Don't even consider staying in Cannes during the May festival unless you have booked months in advance. Prices listed in this section do not cover the film festival or congress periods when rates shoot out of the roof and many places only accept 12-day bookings.

Hôtel Atlantis *(☎ 04 93 39 18 72, fax 04 93 68 37 65; 4 rue du 24 Août; doubles with shower/shower & toilet €31/38)*, as with many hotels along the coastal area, has rooms not nearly as modern as its renovated reception suggests. They are quite adequate nonetheless.

Hôtel Alizé *(☎ 04 93 39 62 17, fax 04 93 39 64 32; ⓦ www.alizecannes.com; 29 rue Bivouac Napoléon; singles/doubles €44-80)*, opposite the central post office, touts air-conditioned rooms with all mod cons.

Hôtel Ascott *(☎ 04 93 38 48 79, fax 04 93 99 12 26; 27 rue des Serbes; singles with shower €43, doubles/triples with shower & toilet €47/76)* is a bright and airy option across from the train station. Internet access is available in the lobby.

Hôtel des Allées *(☎ 04 93 39 53 90, fax 04 93 99 43 25; ⓦ www.hotel-des-allees.com; 6 rue Émile Négrin; singles/doubles €56.40/71.80)*, a Swiss-run place, offers clean and comfortable mid-range accommodation on a pedestrian street in the heart of central Cannes.

Hôtel Florella *(☎ 04 93 38 48 11, fax 04 93 99 22 15; ⓦ www.hotelflorella.com; 55 blvd de la République; singles/doubles €55/61)*, rated highly by many readers, is a family-run place. Friendly Irish owners Brian and Mairead have 12 double rooms available with shower, TV and toilet in their excellent-value hotel-like-home.

Places to Stay – Top End

During the film festival, Cannes' horribly expensive hotels buzz with the frantic comings and goings of journalists, paparazzi and stars. Fortunately for their fans – who can only dream of staying in such places during Cannes' precious days of May – all of the top-end hotels are historic buildings in prime positions on blvd de la Croisette.

Noga Hilton *(☎ 04 92 99 70 00, fax 04 92 99 70 11; W www.hiltoncannes.com; 50 blvd de la Croisette; doubles from €150)*, with its blue glass facade, is bold, modern and big. It touts four restaurants up top and the modern building stands on top of a theatre and car park.

Carlton Inter-Continental *(☎ 04 93 06 40 06, fax 04 93 06 40 25; W www.cannes.interconti.com; 58 blvd de la Croisette; doubles from €240)* stands pert and tall among the world's most photographed hotels – see the Walking Tour, earlier in this section, for one reason why.

Hôtel Martinez *(☎ 04 92 98 73 00, fax 04 93 39 67 82; W www.hotel-martinez.com; 73 blvd de la Croisette; doubles from €310)* is crowned with two presidential suites, each with a 500-sq-metre terrace. The hotel dates to 1929 and its restaurant bears the most stars in Cannes.

Hôtel Majestic Barrière *(☎ 04 92 98 77 00, fax 04 93 38 97 90; e majestic@lucienbarriere.com; 10 blvd de la Croisette; doubles from €220)* was built in 1863 but received a massive facelift in 1912 to transform it into the Art Deco palace it is today.

Places to Eat

Restaurants Not far from the train station, **Le Pacific** *(☎ 04 93 39 46 71; 14 rue Vénizélos; menu €10)* is a favourite with locals for its eat-on-the-cheap, three-course *menu*. A 10-*menu* carnet costs €90.

There are a few inexpensive restaurants around rue du Marché Forville and lots of little (but not necessarily cheap) restaurants along pedestrian rue St-Antoine, rue du Suquet and rue Meynadier.

Aux Bons Enfants *(80 rue Meynadier; menu €15.50)* serves regional dishes such as *aïoli garni* and *mesclun* (a salad of dandelion greens and other roughage) in a convivial atmosphere.

Chez Elke *(☎ 04 93 68 35 39; 76 rue Meynadier; starters/mains/desserts€7/15/7)*, next door, is another pocket-sized place where you can feast on quintessential French dishes – onion soup, grilled sardines etc.

Barbarella *(☎ 04 92 99 17 33; 16 rue St-Dizier; menu €24.50)*, decked out 1970s style – complete with a monumental plastic ceiling lamp – is a trendy music restaurant with innovative cuisine and wines from around the world.

Astoux & Brun *(☎ 04 93 39 21 87; 27 rue Félix Faure; full meal around €30)* is the place for fish lovers. Every type and size of oyster is available, as well as elaborate fish platters. In summer, chefs draw a crowd by preparing shellfish on the pavement outside.

Among the rash of tasty places to eat and be seen around Cannes' *carré magique* (see the Entertainment section later) is loungy bar-cum-restaurant **Harem** *(☎ 04 93 39 62 70; 15 rue des Frères Pradignac)*, with its white minimalist decor; neighbouring **Les 3 Portes** *(☎ 04 93 38 91 70; 16 rue des Frères Pradignac)*; equally trendy **Tantra** (listed under Entertainment later).

Small *(☎ 04 93 39 58 36; 14 rue Macé; menus from €15)* cooks up 'fine food' in a rich and lavish interior, studded with beautiful diners.

Canta La Bio *(☎ 04 93 39 49 40; W www.restaurantbio.com; 6 rue Florian; vegetarian/meat plat du jour €11.30/13.50, menu €21.40)*, headed by chef Marc André Vial, is the French Riviera's most prized organic restaurant.

La Cave *(☎ 04 93 99 79 87; 9 blvd de la République; lunch menu €23)* is a tasty little number for hearty Provençal dishes in a rustic beamed-ceiling setting.

Le Comptoir des Vins *(☎ 04 93 68 13 26; 13 blvd de la République; lunch menu €23)*, not to be confused with La Cave nearby, is a well-stocked wine cellar run by knowledgeable staff. Better still, it hides a delicious little bistro out the back where you can eat and drink wine.

Cafés There is no shortage of cafés.

Up Side Down *(☎ 04 93 99 27 70; 5 place du Général de Gaulle)*, with another entrance at 45 rue d'Antibes (look for the Häagen Dazs shop front), lures a buoyant crowd – day and night – with its contemporary furnishings and young 'n' swish waiters in black.

Cinquanta *(☎ 04 93 39 00 01; 10 rue des Frères Pradignac)*, high-heeled strolling distance from the hip crowd's magic square, is a bold and striking Italian-inspired café-stroke-bar, otherwise called '50'.

Aroma Bagel Café *(22 rue Commandant André)* serves giant-sized bagels crammed with delectable goodies (such as cheese, cream and basil) to eat in or take away (€7 to €9).

La Tarterie *(☎ 04 93 39 67 43; 33 rue Bivouac Napoléon; eat in/take away menu €6.90/8.40)* cooks up delicious sweet and savoury tarts. Don't miss its pear, cinnamon and chocolate creation.

Self-Catering Cannes' main markets are the morning **food market** *(daily summer, Tues-Sun winter)* on place Gambetta and the **Marché Forville** *(rue du Marché Forville; open Tues-Sun)*, a covered fruit and vegetable market.

Specialist food shops include the **Sunshine** wine cellar and neighbouring **Caviar Volga** *(5 rue Maréchal Joffre)*, a caviar emporium; **Paul** *(10 rue Meynadier)* where honey, olive oil and various other types of bread are baked and delicious sandwiches to take away are filled; **Les Trois Étoiles de Cannes** *(43 rue Meynadier)*, an oil and liqueur shop where you can fill your bottle with lavender vinegar, truffle oil or a fruity liqueur; and **Oliviers & Co** *(☎ 04 93 39 00 38; 4 rue Macé)*, an olive oil shop that offers *dégustation* (tasting) for customers.

The supermarket **Monoprix** has entrances on rue Jean Jaurès, rue Maréchal Foch and rue Buttura.

Special Events

The Cannes **Festival International du Film** (International Film Festival) is held over 10 days in May; see the boxed text 'Starring at Cannes' earlier in this chapter. In mid-July, concerts and plays are held in the square in front of Église Notre Dame d'Ésperance during the 10-day **Nuits Musicales du Suquet**.

Entertainment

The tourist office knows what's on where. Tickets for many events are at the **box office** *(☎ 04 92 98 62 77; open 10am-7pm Mon-Sat)*, inside the Palais des Festivals tourist office.

Bars & Clubs Rue Commandant André, rue des Frères Pradignac, rue du Batéguier and rue du Dr Gérard Monod form the so-called *carré magique* (magic square) – jam-packed with Cannes' hippest haunts.

Le Loft *(☎ 04 93 39 40 39; 13 rue du Dr Gérard Monod)* above the equally popular **Tantra** *(☎ 04 93 39 40 39)* restaurant, is a lounge bar where celebrities playing truant from official functions often congregate.

Living Room *(☎ 04 93 68 22 24; 17 rue du Dr Gérard Monod)* is another star-studded bet where a nonchalant atmosphere shields an ultra-posey crowd.

Les Coulisses *(☎ 04 92 99 17 17; 29 rue Commandant André)*, a hot spot on Cannes' clubbing circuit, is clad with zebra-skin seating and crowds of beautiful Cannois.

In-vogue bars elsewhere in and around Le Suquet include:

Twiggy Bar *(☎ 04 93 99 13 32; 3 rue des Suisses; open 3pm-12.30am daily)*, a temple to 1970s pop, is a hip record shop and bar up the hill from the water.

Le Vogue *(☎ 04 93 39 99 18; 20 rue du Suquet)*, another ambient bar, lures a young and trendy, but down-to-earth, crowd.

Palm Square *(☎ 04 93 06 78 27; W www.palm-square.com; 1 allées de la Liberté; menu €20)* is a lavish bar-cum-restaurant-cum-club where the trendy gather for lunch and stars sip cocktails on fake leopard-skin seating.

Clubs and discos guaranteed to draw a crowd (and stars when they roll into town) include **Cat Corrner** *(☎ 04 93 39 31 31; 22 rue Macé)*; and **Baôli** *(☎ 04 93 43 03 43)* and **Le Farfalla** *(☎ 04 93 68 93 81)*, both at 1 blvd la Croisette near Port Canto. **Jimmy'z** *(☎ 04 92 98 78 00; La Croisette)*, inside the Palais des Festivals, is the Cannes version of Monaco's legendary Jimmy'z nightclub, both run by the same team.

Gay & Lesbian Venues Said to be France's oldest gay bar, (**Zanzi Bar** *☎ 04 93 39 30 75; 85 rue Félix Faure; open 6pm-6am daily)* dates from 1885 and has been gay since the end of WWII.

Around the corner is Cannes' premier gay club, **Discothèque Le 7 of Angels** *(☎ 04 93 39 10 36; 7 rue Rouguière)*, known simply as '7' and attracting an increasingly mixed crowd. Otherwise try **Diabolik'A** *(☎ 04 93 68 23 23; 48 blvd de la République)*, inside the Espace Eiffel.

Getting There & Away

Air Nice Hélicoptères (see Air in the introductory Getting Around chapter) flies in and out of **Héliport du Palm Beach** *(☎ 04 93 43 42 42; blvd de la Croisette)*.

Bus Buses leave from the bus station (marked 'Hôtel de Ville' on bus timetables) on place Bernard Cornut Gentille to Nice (€5.80, 1¼ hours, every 20 minutes 6.10am to 9.45pm Mon to Saturday, every 30 minutes 8.30am to 9.40pm Sunday), Nice-Côte d'Azur airport (€3.20/9.50 via N7/A8, one hour/50 minutes, every 30/50 minutes 8am to 7pm), Cagnes-sur-Mer, Antibes and Golfe-Juan. For westbound buses along the coast to St-Raphaël, see Getting There & Away in that section later in this chapter.

Buses to Grasse (€3.70, 45 minutes) via Mougins (€1.70, 20 minutes) and Mouans-Sartoux (€2.10, 25 minutes) and Vallauris (€2.40, 30 minutes) depart from Cannes' second bus station, next to the train station on rue Jean Jaurès. It also has an **information desk** *(☎ 04 93 39 11 39; open 8.30am-11.10am & 2.30pm-6.45pm Mon, Tues, Thur & Fri)*.

Train Destinations within easy reach of Cannes **train station** *(rue Jean Jaurès)* include St-Raphaël (€5.40, 30 minutes, two per hour) from where you can get buses to St-Tropez and Toulon; and Marseilles (€23.30, two hours). Most trains to and from Nice (€5.10, 40 minutes) stop in Antibes (€3.90, 15 minutes).

CANNES AREA

Getting Around

Bus Cannes and destinations up to 7km from town are served by **Bus Azur** *(☎ 04 93 45 20 08; place Bernard Cornut Gentille; open 7am-7pm Mon-Fri, 8.30am-6.30pm Sat)*, with an information desk at the bus station. A ticket/10-ticket carnet costs €1.25/8.30. A weekly Carte Palm'Hebdo/monthly Carte Croisette costs €9.20/31.30.

Bus No 8 runs along the coast from place Bernard Cornut Gentille to the port and Palm Beach Casino on Pointe de la Croisette; bus Nos 2 and 9 run from the train station, via the bus station, to/from the beaches in Cannes La Bocca; line 620 follows the same route but continues farther southwest along the coast to Théoule-sur-Mer.

Car & Motorcycle All the major car-rental companies have offices in Cannes, including **Avis** *(☎ 04 93 94 15 86; 69 blvd de la Croisette)*, next to Hôtel Martinez **Budget** *(☎ 04 93 99 44 04; 160 rue d'Antibes)*; **National Citer** *(☎ 04 93 94 64 41; 160 rue d'Antibes)*; and also **Hertz** *(☎ 04 93 99 04 20; 145 rue d'Antibes)*. **Excellence** *(☎ 04 93 94 67 67; 66 blvd de la Croisette)* rents Ferraris, Bentleys and other dream machines.

Alliance Location *(☎ 04 93 38 62 62; w www.alliance-location.com; 19 rue des Frères Pradignac)* rents 50cc scooters/125cc motorcycles starting at €26/46 per day. North of the train station, **Honda** *(☎ 04 97 06 61 00; e teamfb@wanadoo.fr; 9 blvd Carnot)* charges €58 a day for a 125cc scooter.

Bicycle & Rollerblades Alliance Location also rents mountain bikes for €15 per day. Rollerblades and micro-scooters both costs €8 a day.

ÎLES DE LÉRINS

The two islands making up Lérins – Île Ste-Marguerite and Île St-Honorat – lie within a 20-minute boat ride of Cannes. Known as Lero and Lerina in ancient times, these tiny, traffic-free oases of peace and tranquillity remain a world away from the glitz, glamour and hanky-panky of cocky Cannes.

Wild camping, cycling and smoking are forbidden on both islands (well, theoretically, anyway – visitors still light up). There are no hotels or camp sites on either island and St-Honorat, the smaller of the two, has nowhere to eat either. Take a picnic and good supply of drinking water with you.

Neither island has a wildly fantastic beach. Pretty coves can be found on the southern side of Ste-Marguerite (a 45-minute walk from the harbour). On the northern side, sunworshippers lie on rocks and mounds of dried seaweed.

Île Ste-Marguerite

The Eucalyptus- and pine-covered Île Ste-Marguerite is 1km from the mainland. The island is famed as the place where the enigmatic Man in the Iron Mask – immortalised by Alexandre Dumas (1802–70) in his novel *Le Viscomte de Bragelonne* (1847) – was held in the late 17th century (see boxed text later).

The island, home to 20 families, is crossed by walking trails and paths. Its centrepiece is 17th-century **Fort Royal**, built by Richelieu to defend the islands from the Spanish (who still managed to occupy the fort from 1635 to 1637), with later additions by Vauban. Today it houses the **Musée dela Mer** *(☎ 04 93*

The Man in the Iron Mask

More than 68 names have been suggested for this prisoner whose name no one knows, whose face no one has seen: a living mystery, shadow, enigma, problem.

Victor Hugo

The Man in the Iron Mask was imprisoned by Louis XIV (1661–1715) in the fortress on Île Ste-Marguerite from around 1660 until 1690, when he was transferred to the Bastille in Paris. Only the king knew the identity of the man behind the mask, prompting a rich pageant of myth and legend to be woven around the mysterious, ill-fated inmate.

Political and social satirist Voltaire (1694–1778) claimed the prisoner was the king's brother – a twin or an illegitimate older brother. In 1751 he published *Le Siècle de Louis XIV* which attested that Louis XIV's usurped brother, face shrouded in iron, arrived on the island in 1661, was personally escorted to the Bastille by its new governor in 1690, and died in 1703 aged around 60. His featureless mask was lined with silk and fitted with a spring mechanism at the chin to allow him to eat. Prison guards had orders to kill anyone who dared remove his iron face.

JANE SMITH

Countless other identities were showered on the masked prisoner, among them the Duke of Monmouth (actually beheaded under James II), the Comte de Vermandois (son of Louis XIV, said to have died from smallpox in 1683), the Duc de Beaufort (killed by the Turks in 1669) and Molière. Some theorists claimed the man in the iron mask was actually a woman.

The storming of the Bastille in 1789 fuelled yet more stories. Revolutionaries claimed to have discovered a skeleton, the skull of which was locked in an iron mask, when plundering the prison, while others focused on a supposed entry found in the prison register which read *détenu 64389000: l'homme au masque de fer* (prisoner 64389000: the man in the iron mask). To the contrary, others provoked a storm with their allegations that there was *no* iron mask entry in the prison register – just a missing page. In 1855, an iron mask was found in a scrap heap in Langres, north of Dijon, and displayed in the town museum as the ill-fated mask.

Voltaire's tragic tale of a usurped heir sentenced to a life behind iron inspired a flurry of theatrical tragedies. With the 1850 publication of Alexandre Dumas' novel *Le Vicomte de Bragelonne*, the last of his musketeers trilogy, the royal crime became written in stone: in 1638 Anne of Austria, wife of Louis XIII (1617–43) and mother of Louis XIV, gives birth to twins; one is taken away from her, leaving her to bear the secret alone until an old friend uncovers the terrible truth. The rest is history.

Dozens of iron mask films have been made this century, starring Richard Chamberlain as the masked prince/evil king in 1976 and Leonardo DiCaprio in 1998.

43 18 17; adult/18-25s yrs/under 18 €3/2/ free, admission free 1st Sun of month; open 10.30am-1.15pm & 2.15pm-5.45pm Tues-Sun Apr-Sept, to 4.45pm Oct-Mar), a museum with exhibits on the fort's history and shipwrecks. A door to the left in the museum's reception hall leads to the **state prisons**, built below by Louis XIV. Infamous inmates include steamboat inventor, Claude François Dorothée, who allegedly came up with his idea while watching slaves row to the island during his imprisonment here between 1773 and 1774; and the Man in the Iron Mask.

Île St-Honorat

Forested St-Honorat, 1.5km by 400m, is the smallest and most southern of the two Lérins islands. It was the site of a powerful monastery in the 5th century. Today it is home to 30-odd Cistercian monks who own the island but welcome people to visit their monastery and the seven small chapels dotted around, which have drawn pilgrims since the Middle Ages.

The **donjon** *(fortified tower; admission €2; open 10.30am-4pm daily Oct-June)* guarding the island's southern shores is all that remains of the original monastery. Visits from July to September are by guided tour only between 10.30am and 12.30pm, and 2.30pm and 4.45pm, from Monday to Saturday, and from 2.30pm to 4.45pm Sunday. Built in 1073 to protect the monks from pirate attacks, its entrance stood 4m above ground level and was accessible only by ladder (later replaced by the stone staircase evident today). The elegant arches of the vaulted **cloître de la prière** (cloister of prayer) on the 1st floor date from the 15th century. A magnificent panorama of the Côte d'Azur from the Estérel to Cap d'Antibes can be enjoyed from the donjon terrace.

In front of the donjon is the walled, 19th-century **Abbaye Notre Dame de Lérins** *(☎ 04 92 99 54 21; ⓦ www.abbayedelerins.com)*. Monks celebrated mass in their 19th-century church here at 11.25am weekdays and 9.50am Sunday. In the souvenir shop you can buy the 50% alcohol *Lérina*, a pea-green liqueur concocted by the monks from 44 different herbs.

The Byzantine-inspired **Chapelle de la Trinité** *(visits by guided tour only 10.30am-12.30pm & 2.30pm-4.45pm Mon-Sat, 2.30pm-4.45pm Sun, July-Sept)* was built between the 5th and 11th centuries on the island's eastern tip.

Getting There & Away

From Cannes, **Compagnie Maritime Cannoise** *(CMC; ☎ 04 93 38 66 33; ⓔ cmcrgm@aol.com)* runs daily ferries from jetée Albert Édouart to Île Ste-Marguerite year round (adult/five to 10 years €8/4 return; 15 minutes). Tickets are sold at the kiosk overlooking place du Général de Gaulle on jetée Albert Édouart.

Based at the other end of the port, **Trans Côte d'Azur** *(☎ 04 92 98 71 30; quai St-Pierre)*, opposite Hôtel Sofitel, charges €9/6 per adult/four to 10 years for the return voyage to Ste-Marguerite. Its boats sail from quai Max Laubeuf.

Hourly boats between 8am to 5.30pm (4.30pm in winter) to Île St-Honorat (20 minutes) are run by **Société Planaria** *(☎ 04 92 98 71 38; ⓔ info@abbayedelerins.com)*, the abbey boat service. A return fare costs €8/5 per adult/five to 10 years. Boats sail/dock next to its kiosk on jetée Albert Édouard.

VALLAURIS & GOLFE-JUAN

postcode 06220 • pop 25,931

The traditional potters town of Vallauris is as closely associated with Picasso as Antibes, 7km east. The town itself has little charm beyond three memorable museums, one of which is dedicated to the eccentric artist who lived in Vallauris with Françoise Gilot from 1948 until 1955.

Clay pots have been churned out in Vallauris since Roman times. A declining trade in the 16th century was boosted by a group of Genoese potters who moved their studios to Vallauris in order to exploit its clay-rich soil. An artistic revival in the 1940s, spearheaded by Picasso, ensured the trade's survival. Today, it is tourism that potters rely on, as visitors flock to Vallauris to visit the museums and buy a signature *marmite* (giant pot, only glazed on the inside and used for cooking Provençal stew).

Vallauris' satellite resort of Golfe-Juan, 2km south on the coast, is unmonumental beyond its historic claim to fame as the spot where Napoleon landed following his return from exile in 1815. Boats sail from here to the Îles de Lérins in summer.

Orientation & Information

Vallauris bus station adjoins place de la Libération, the central square in the northern part of town. From here, ave George Clémenceau, the main street, leads south to the **tourist office** *(☎ 04 93 63 82 58, fax 04 93 63 95 01; ⓔ tourisme.vgj@wanadoo.fr; square du 8 Mai)*, in the car park off the D135.

The closest train station is in Golfe-Juan. From Vallauris tourist office continue south along the D135 to Golfe-Juan's central square Nabonnand, then continue south along ave de la Gare (past Golfe-Juan train station) to the seafront; Golfe-Juan **tourist office** *(☎ 04 93 63 73 12; ave des Frères Roustan)* is here.

Château Musée de Vallauris

The Vallauris Castle Museum *(☎ 04 93 64 16 05; place de la Libération; adult/under 17 €3/free; open 10am-12.15pm & 2pm-5pm or 6pm Wed-Mon)* hosts three museums: the **Musée National Picasso** (National Picasso

Museum), which is based around Picasso-decorated Chapelle La Guerre et La Paix (War and Peace Chapel); the **Musée Magnelli**, devoted to the works of Italian artist Albert Magnelli (1899–1971); and a **Musée de la Céramique** (Ceramic Museum), in which the history of Vallauris' age-old craft is unravelled.

Picasso (1881–1973) was 71 years old when he started work on what he dubbed his *temple de la paix* (temple of peace), a 12th-century chapel built on the site of an abbey dating from the Middle Ages. He painted his dramatic murals on plywood panels secured to the church's stone walls.

The museum is next to Vallauris bus station; steps lead from the station to place de la Libération.

Galerie Madoura

A handful of licensed copies of ceramics cast by Picasso while in Vallauris are on sale at Galerie Madoura *(☎ 04 93 64 66 39; W www.madoura.com; ave Suzanne Ramié; admission free; open 10am-12.30pm & 2.30pm-6pm or 7pm Mon-Fri)*, the pottery where, in 1946, Picasso first dabbled in the clay medium under the guidance of local potters Georges and Suzanne Ramié. He consequently granted the Ramiés the exclusive right to reproduce his work, resulting in a limited edition – between 25 and 500 in number – of 633 different Picasso pieces being cast between 1947 and 1971.

The gallery is off ave des Anciens Combattants d'Afrique du Nord. From the bus station, walk south along ave George Clémenceau, then west (right) along ave des Anciens Combattants d'Afrique du Nord.

The ungainly statue of *L'Homme au Mouton* – a bronze stick figure clutching a sheep by its hind legs – on place Paul Isnard (the tree-filled square adjoining place de la Libération) was a gift from Picasso to Vallauris.

Maison de la Pétanque

Everything from its invention to its contemporary champions can be discovered in the quaint House of Provençal Boules *(☎ 04 93 64 11 36; e contact@masiondelapetanque.com; 1193 chemin de St-Bernard; admission €3; open 9am-noon & 2pm-6.30pm Mon-Sat Apr-Sept, Mon-Fri only Oct & Dec-Mar)*, a museum dedicated to the region's most popular sport. Amateurs can have a spin on the *pétanque* pitch here, and enthusiasts can get their own set of boules made to measure. See Spectator Sports in the Facts for the Visitor chapter.

The museum is 2km north of Vallauris bus station. From the station, head north along ave de Grasse and at the roundabout bear east (right) along chemin St-Bernard.

Boat Excursions

In summer, **Maritime Cap d'Antibes** *(☎ 04 93 63 45 94; e cmcrgm@aol.com)* sails daily from quai St-Pierre at the Vieux Port in Golfe-Juan to Îles Ste-Marguerite. May to October, there are four crossings daily (50 minutes). A return ticket to Ste-Marguerite costs €10/5 per adult/five to 10 years. In July and August, there are a couple of weekly boat trips to St-Tropez (€28) and also to Monaco (€42).

To get to the port from the Golfe-Juan train station, turn right (east) along ave de Belgique, then turn right again (south) onto ave de la Gare, which cuts underneath the train track towards the sea. At the end of the street, bear south again onto blvd des Frères Roustan, the promenade fronting the Vieux Port.

Places to Stay & Eat

Bar Hôtel du Stade *(☎ 04 93 64 91 27; 48 ave Georges Clémenceau; doubles with washbasin €25-35)* is a cheap nine-room place above a local bar in Vallauris centre. Shared showers and toilets are in the corridor.

Hôtel Le Provence *(☎ 04 97 21 85 30, fax 04 97 21 85 43; e leprovence@wailka9.com; 17 ave de la Gare; doubles €49-75)*, near Golfe-Juan train station, is another cheapie with no-frills rooms.

Maison Lascasse *(☎ 04 93 63 14 14; 62 ave Georges Clémenceau)*, a master bakery, is where a staggering choice of bread is baked before your eyes. It usually stocks 35 of its 55 bread types.

Getting There & Away

Golfe-Juan train station, from where trains go in both directions along the coast, is 3km south of Vallauris town, making bus the most convenient way of getting to/from Vallauris.

From Vallauris **bus station** *(☎ 04 93 64 18 37; cnr ave de la Grasse & ave Aimé Berger)*, bus No 6V goes to Cannes train station (about every 30 minutes 7.15am to 7pm). Bus No 5V serves Antibes bus station (€2.65, hourly 7am to 6pm). Buses are less frequent on Sunday.

Getting Around

There is a regular Sillages/STGA bus between Vallauris bus station and Golfe-Juan train station (every 15 minutes 6am to 7.40pm). Journey time is 15 minutes.

ANTIBES

postcodes 06600 (Greater Antibes) & 06160 (Cap d'Antibes) • pop 72,412

Antibes, the next coastal hot spot northeast of Cannes and across the Baie des Anges from Nice, has as many attractions as its larger neighbours but is not as crowded. It has sandy beaches, 16th-century ramparts along the shore, an attractive pleasure-boat harbour (Port Vauban) and an old city with narrow streets and flower-bedecked houses. Picasso, Max Ernst and Nicolas de Staël all found an appealing charm in Antibes. Between 1966 and 1990, globetrotter and writer Graham Greene chose Antibes as his base.

Greater Antibes embraces the modern beach resort of Juan-les-Pins as well as Cap d'Antibes, the exclusive green cape on which Antibes and Juan-les-Pins sit.

Juan-les-Pins sprang up west of Antibes in the 1880s. It is known for its beautiful 2km-long sandy beach backed by pine trees, and outrageous night life – a legacy of the 1920s when Americans swung into town with their jazz music and oh-so-brief swimsuits. Party madness peaks in late July when the resort hosts Jazz à Juan, a week-long jazz festival attracting musicians and music lovers worldwide.

Cheap accommodation here is particularly scarce; try the hostel on Cap d'Antibes or a camp site in Biot (see that section following).

Orientation

Antibes is made up of three parts: the commercial centre around place du Général de Gaulle; Vieil Antibes (old Antibes) south of Port Vauban and the Vieux Port; and, to the southwest, Cap d'Antibes and the contiguous community of Juan-les-Pins.

Ave Robert Soleau links the Antibes train station with place du Général de Gaulle, where the tourist office is located. From here, Juan-les-Pins is a straight 1.5km walk along blvd du Président Wilson, which runs southwest off Antibes' central square.

Information

Tourist Offices Antibes **tourist office** *(☎ 04 92 90 53 00, fax 04 92 90 53 01; W www.antibesjuanlespins.com; 11 place du Général de Gaulle; open 9am-7pm daily July & Aug, 8am-12.30pm & 2pm-6.30pm Mon-Fri, 9am-noon & 2pm-6pm Sat Jan-June & Sept-Dec)* sells tickets for cultural events and has information on some interesting three-hour guided tours (reservations ☎ 04 93 34 56 82; €7.50). Its **train station annexe** *(☎ 04 92 90 53 00; open 9am-12.30pm & 1.30pm-5pm Mon-Fri)* doubles as a bus-information desk.

In Vieil Antibes, the **tourist office** *(☎ 04 93 34 65 65; W www.vieil-antibes.org; 32 blvd d'Aguillon; open 9.30am-noon & 2pm-5.30pm Mon-Fri)* is inside Porte Marine.

Juan-les-Pins **tourist office** *(☎ 04 92 90 53 05, fax 04 93 61 55 13; 51 blvd Charles Guillaumont; open 9am-7pm daily July & Aug, 9am-noon & 2pm-6pm Mon-Fri, 9am-noon Sat Jan-June & Sept-Dec)* is on the seafront.

Money In Antibes centre, commercial banks are on ave Robert Soleau. Exchange bureau **Eurochange** *(4 rue Georges Clémenceau; open 9am-7pm Mon-Sat)* charges €2 commission to change amounts under €100.

Post & Communications The **post office** *(place des Martyrs de la Résistance; open 8am-7pm Mon-Fri, 8am-noon Sat)* is in Antibes centre. Juan-les-Pins' **post office** *(square Pablo Picasso; open 8am-noon & 2pm or 2.30pm-6pm Mon-Fri, 8am-noon Sat)* has Cyberposte.

In Vieil Antibes, the **ASA Cyber Café** *(☎ 04 93 34 55 84; 6 rue du Marc; open 9am-1pm & 3pm-8pm Tues-Sat, 10am-1pm & 4pm-7pm Sun)* charges €6.90 per hour for online access.

Bookshops For an excellent selection of English-language books, try **Antibes Books** *(☎ 04 93 34 74 11; 24 rue Aubernon; open 10am-7pm daily)*, otherwise known as Heidi's English Bookshop.

Laundry Wash your socks and smocks at **Laverie du Port** *(14 rue Thuret; open 8am-8pm Mon-Fri, 9am-8pm Sat)*.

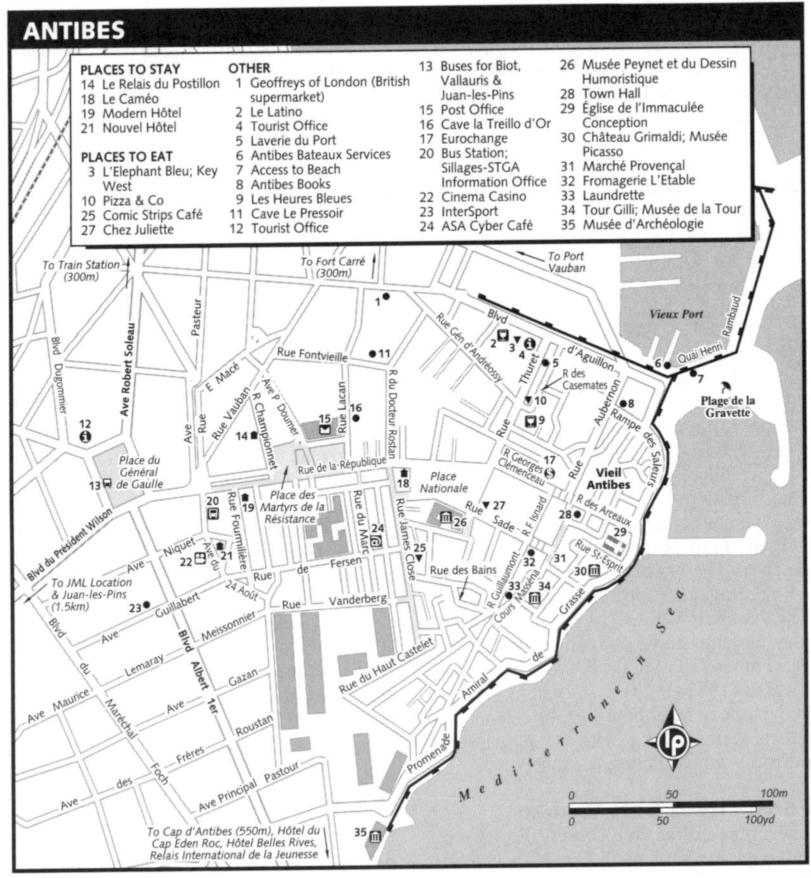

Vieil Antibes

Because of Antibes' position on the border of France and Savoy, it was fortified in the 17th and 18th centuries, but these fortifications were ripped down in 1896 to give the city room to expand. From the tourist office on place du Général de Gaulle, bear east along rue de la République to **Porte de France**, one of the few remaining parts of the original city walls.

The **Musée Peynet et du Dessin Humoristique** *(☎ 04 92 90 54 30; place Nationale, adult/student €3/1.50; open 10am-noon & 2pm-6pm Tues-Sun)* should make you smile. It displays over 300 pictures, cartoons, sculptures and theatrical costumes by Antibes-born cartoonist Peynet, best known for his *Lovers* series.

A hectic morning **Marché Provençal** (Provençal market) sprawls the length of cours Masséna, Tuesday to Sunday, September to May. At the southern end of cours Masséna, 19th-century Tour Gilli houses a small arts and traditions museum called **Musée de la Tour** *(☎ 04 93 34 50 91; 2 rue de l'Orme; open 4pm-7pm Wed, Thur & Sat June-Sept, 3pm-5pm Wed, Thur & Sat Oct-May)*.

East of cours Masséna (entrance on montée de la Souchère), is Antibes' **Église de L'Immaculée Conception** *(rue St-Esprit)*, built on the site of an ancient Greek temple with an ochre neoclassical facade. Its tall, square Romanesque bell tower dates from the 12th century.

Southwest is the **Musée d'Archéologie** *(☎ 04 92 90 54 35; promenade Amiral de*

Grasse; adult/under 18 €3/free; open 10am-6pm Tues-Thur, Sat & Sun, 10am-10pm Fri June-Sept, 10am-noon & 2pm-6pm Tues-Sun Oct-May), inside the Vauban-built Bastion St-André. Its displays are devoted to Antibes' Greek history.

Musée Picasso

From the cathedral, steps lead to **Château Grimaldi**, set on a spectacular site overlooking the sea. This 12th-century castle served as Picasso's studio from July to December 1946. Today it houses the Picasso Museum *(☎ 04 92 90 54 20; adult/under 7 €4.60/2.30; open 10am-6pm Tues-Sun June-Sept, 10am-noon & 2pm-6pm Tues-Sun Oct-May)*, boasting an excellent collection of Picasso's paintings, lithographs, drawings and ceramics as well as interesting displays about his life. A collection of contemporary art by other artists graces the sculpture-lined terrace facing the Mediterranean.

Particularly poignant is Picasso's *La Joie de Vivre* (The Joy of Life), one in a series of 25 paintings that form *The Antipolis Suite*. The young flower girl, surrounded by flute-playing fauns and mountain goats, symbolises Françoise Gilot, the 23-year-old love of Picasso (1881–1973), with whom he lived at the time in neighbouring Golfe-Juan. The entire series, along with its preparatory drawings and sketches, are displayed.

Fort Carré & Port Vauban

The impregnable 16th-century Fort Carré, enlarged by Vauban in the 17th century, dominates the approach to Antibes from Nice. Port Vauban, one of the first pleasure ports to be established on the Mediterranean, is between the fort and Antibes old town.

Inside the fortress, which can be visited by guided tour, a pedestrian walkway takes visitors around the stadium hidden within the star-shaped walls. The guided tours depart every 30 minutes between 10am and 4.30pm Tuesday to Sunday, September to April; and between 10am and 6pm Tuesday to Sunday, from May to August. The tourist office has details.

Cap d'Antibes

You feel like a shrunken Alice in Wonderland on this select peninsula where larger-than-life villas and pine trees loom above you at every turn. The sense of wonder at the sheer luxury is further exacerbated by the constant buzz of cicadas (see the boxed text 'Love Song' later) whose frenzied chants reach a shrilling crescendo around the time of the midday sun.

The southwestern tip of the cape is crowned by the legendary **Hôtel du Cap Eden Roc**, Côte d'Azur's most exclusive hotel, dating from 1870 (see Places to Stay later in this section). It made a name for itself in 1923 when its Italian owner, Antoine Sella, kept his doors open in July and August, heralding the start of a summer season on the coast. Hôtel du Cap Eden Roc was consequently immortalised in F Scott Fitzgerald's novel *Tender is the Night* (1934) under the guise of the fictional Hôtel des Étrangers. By 1925 the luxury complex, sporting the first open-air swimming pool on the Riviera (built in 1914 for WWI servicemen), was known as Eden Roc. Other notable names on Cap d'Antibes' guestbook include Cole Porter who rented **Château de la Garoupe** in 1922; and novelist Jules Verne (1828–1905) who lived at **Les Chênes Verts** *(152 blvd John F Kennedy)*.

Immediately northwest of the hotel is the **Musée Napoléonien** *(☎ 04 93 61 45 32; adult/student €3/1.50; open 9.15am-11.45am & 2pm-5.45pm Mon-Fri, 9.15am-11.45 Sat Nov-Sept)*, a naval museum inside Tour Sella, and off blvd John F Kennedy. The museum documents Napoleon's return from exile in 1815.

The centre of the cape is dominated by beautiful **Jardin Botanique de la Villa Thuret** *(☎ 04 93 67 88 66; ⓔ thuret@antibes.inra.fr; 41 blvd du Cap; admission free; open 8am-5pm or 6pm Mon-Fri)*, 3.5 hectares of botanical garden embracing 2500 species and dating from 1857. Another lovely garden to visit is the 11-hectare landscaped park around **Villa Eilenroc** *(☎ 04 93 67 74 33; ave de Beaumont; park open 9am-5pm Tues & Wed Sept-June, guided tours of villa 9.30am-noon & 1.30pm-5pm Wed Sept-June)*, on the tip of Cap d'Antibes. Eilenroc was designed by Garnier for a Dutchman who scrambled the name of his wife Cornélie to come up with the villa's name.

Sweeping views of the coastline, from St-Tropez to Italy, can be enjoyed from **Chapelle de la Garoupe**, a chapel atop a hillock off route du Phare. The neighbouring lighthouse can't be visited. From here, steps lead downhill to ave Aimé Bourreau; bear right, then turn left along ave Guide to get to sandy **Plage de la Garoupe**, first raked clear of seaweed in 1922 by Cole Porter and American artist Gerald Murphy. A coastal path snakes from here to **Cap Gros**, the cape's southeasternmost tip.

Beaches & Boats

Antibes has a small beach, sandy **Plage de la Gravette**, accessible from quai Henri Rambaud at the Vieux Port. You can rent a 6cv boat (without licence) to go to sea at **Antibes Bateaux Services** *(☎ 06 15 75 44 36; W www.antibes-bateaux.com; quai Henri Rambaud)* for €70/125 per half-/full day.

In Antibes, rollerblades can be hired for about €10 per day at **InterSport** *(☎ 04 93 34 20 14; e antibes@atsat.com; 10 & 12 ave Guillabert; open 9am-12.15pm & 2.30pm-7.15pm Mon-Sat)*.

Juan-les-Pins' long sandy beaches buzz with business from sunrise to sunset. From the Ponton Courbet, opposite the tourist office on blvd Charles Guillaumont, glass-bottomed boats (adult/two to 12 years €11/5, 1¼ hours) sail around Cap d'Antibes, May to September. From May to October, ferries also sail to the Îles de Lérins (see that section earlier).

Special Events

Antibes' premier occasion is **Jazz à Juan**, also known as the Festival de Jazz d'Antibes Juan-les-Pins, which kicks off the third week in July. Juan-les-Pins' **Eden Casino** *(☎ 04 92 93 71 71; blvd Édouard Baudoin)* and the gardens fronting the beach on square Gould are leading venues. Festival programmes and tickets are available from FNAC in Nice or Antibes and Juan-les-Pins tourist offices.

Places to Stay

Hostel The cheapest option is **Relais International de la Jeunesse** *(☎ 04 93 61 34 40, fax 04 90 83 65 33; 60 blvd de la Garoupe; camping per person €6, B&B €14; open Mar-Oct, reception open 8am-11am & 5.30pm-11pm)*, in Cap d'Antibes south of the centre. Sheets cost €2. Campers can pitch their tent here, and breakfast is included. Guests have to evacuate their rooms from 10am to 5.30pm. From Antibes' bus station, take bus No 2A (direction Eden Roc) to L'Antiquité stop.

Love Song

The frenzied buzz that serenades sunny days in Provence's hot south is, in fact, *cigales* (cicadas) on the pull.

Cicadas (Family Cicadidae) are transparent-winged insects, most common in tropical or temperate climes. The male cicada courts when the temperatures is above 25°C in the shade. Its shrill love song is produced with tymbals, vibrating music-making plates attached to the abdomen. Female cicadas do not sing.

The life span of a cicada is three to 17 years, all but four to six weeks of which is spent underground. Upon emerging from the soil to embark on its adult life, the cicada attaches itself to a tree where it immediately begins its mating rituals. It dies just weeks later.

Hotels Notable choices in central Antibes include:

Nouvel Hôtel *(☎ 04 93 34 44 07; 1 ave du 24 Août; singles/doubles with washbasin €30.49/42.68, doubles with shower/shower & toilet €50.38/53.38)* is a quintessential French bar with rooms up top. Late arrivals can collect a key from the Casino cinema across the street.

Le Caméo *(☎ 04 93 34 24 17, fax 04 93 34 35 80; 62 rue de la République; doubles/triples with shower €46/54, with shower & toilet €54/64)* is a large place overlooking Vieil Antibes' central square.

Modern Hôtel *(☎ 04 92 90 59 05, fax 04 92 90 59 06; 1 rue Fourmilière; singles/doubles low season €53/68, high season €61/80)* is a small and sweet choice, hidden down a narrow pedestrian street in the old town. Rooms have TV and air-con.

Le Relais du Postillon *(☎ 04 93 34 20 77, fax 04 93 34 61 24; W www.relais-postillon.com; 8 rue Championnet; double rooms with courtyard/parkside view from €43/59)* is well priced for the comforts offered. Its 15 cosy rooms are named after beautiful cities, islands or villages (Florence, Malta, Vallauris and so on) to reflect their significance.

Two of the Riviera's most notable hotels are in Juan-les-Pins and Cap d'Antibes.

Hôtel Belles Rives *(☎ 04 93 61 02 79, fax 04 93 67 43 51; W www.bellesrives.com; 33 blvd Édouard Baudoin; singles/doubles* *from €125/200)* is a four-star oasis of luxury with its own private jetty, beach and pool. F Scott and Zelda Fitzgerald stayed at Villa St-Louis – then an untouched spot of paradise – in 1926. Three years later, their humble abode reopened as a hotel.

Hôtel du Cap Eden Roc *(☎ 04 93 61 39 01, fax 04 93 67 76 04; W www.edenroc-hotel.fr; blvd Kennedy; singles/doubles from €280/420)* is expensive, exquisite and on a par with paradise. Ride the teak-seated cable car down from the hotel to the private beach below and pretend you're in a James Bond movie.

Places to Eat

Terrace restaurants and cafés lace Antibes' old-town streets. Plenty of places on blvd d'Aguillon serve brunch and/or late breakfasts, including **Key West** *(☎ 04 93 34 58 20; blvd d'Aguillon)*, which fries up a jumbo English breakfast for €9.50.

Chez Juliette *(☎ 04 93 34 67 37; e chezjuliette@wanadoo.fr; 18 rue Sade; menus €12.96, €19.06 & €25.16)* is popular for its wide choice of guaranteed-to-fill Provençal dishes, including tripe, rabbit stew with polenta or stuffed sardine fillets in tomato sauce. Juliette opens evenings only.

L'Elephant Bleu *(The Blue Elephant, ☎ 04 93 34 28 80; 28 blvd d'Aguillon; lunch menu €13, dinner meat/vegetarian menu €18/16)* cooks up tasty Chinese, Vietnamese and Thai cuisine on one of Antibes' trendiest streets.

Comic Strips Cafe *(☎ 04 93 34 91 40; 4 rue James Close)*, a playful and fun place, sees smiling punters lick through their childhood greats, albeit Tintin, Astérix or the more sophisticated Sempé.

For self-caterers, **Cave le Pressoir** *(rue Fontvieille)* and **Cave la Treillo d'Or** *(12 rue Lacan)* both sell wine; **Fromagerie L'Etable** *(cnr rue Sade & rue Guillaumont)* sells cheese; and **Geoffreys of London** *(Galerie du Port)* is the place for British foodstuffs (baked beans, marmite etc).

CANNES AREA

Entertainment

Pedestrian blvd d'Aguillon, immediately south of the old city wall by the port, is lined with busy bars.

Le Latino *(☎ 04 93 34 44 22; W www.lelatino.com; 24 blvd d'Aguillon; tapas €7)*, a busy tapas bar, is popular for that ever-essential, early-evening aperitif.

KE-OPS *(☎ 04 93 67 24 12; 21 blvd Guy Maupassant)* in Juan-les-Pins, is a gay and gay-friendly nightclub.

Les Heures Bleues *(☎ 04 93 34 50 61; 2 rue des Casemates)* is a lively café-theatre. Stroll home afterwards munching a €2 slice of fire-baked pizza from **Pizza & Co** opposite the nightclub.

Cinéma Casino *(☎ 04 93 34 04 37; 6 ave du 24 Août)* screens films in their original language (usually English) with French subtitles on Tuesday at 8.30pm.

Getting There & Away

Bus Antibes **bus station** *(☎ 04 93 34 37 60)*, just off rue de la République, has buses leaving/arriving every 20 minutes or so between 6am and 8pm to/from Nice (€4.10, 50 minutes), Cagnes-sur-Mer (€2.10, 20 minutes), Golfe-Juan (€1.70, 15 minutes) and Cannes (€2.10, 30 minutes).

Buses to/from Biot (line 10A, €1.10, 20 minutes, seven to 11 buses daily) and Vallauris (line No 5V, €2.20, 30 minutes, hourly 7am to 6pm) use the bus stops on place du Général de Gaulle.

Train From Antibes **train station** *(place Pierre Semard)*, at the end of ave Robert Soleau, there are frequent trains to/from Nice (€3.40, 30 minutes) and Cannes (€2.20, 15 minutes).

Unlike Antibes where many TGVs stop, the smaller **train station** *(ave de l'Estérel)* in Juan-les-Pins is only served by local trains.

Getting Around

Bus In summer a minibus shuttles travellers between Antibes centre and Vieil Antibes. The Centre Ville line (shaded blue on the route maps displayed at bus stops) links the train station with place du Général de Gaulle and the bus station. The Vieil Antibes line (shaded red) links the train station with Fort Carré. The bus stop is immediately on the right as you exit the train station on ave Robert Soleau. Free minibuses run every 10 minutes between 7.30am and 7.30pm Monday to Saturday.

A ticket/10-ticket carnet for other city buses run by **Sillages-STGA** *(☎ 04 93 64 88 84; W www.sillages-stga.tm.fr)* costs €1.10/10. One-/three-/eight-day passes are available for €4.20/10/20. Bus Nos 1A, 3A and 8A link Antibes bus station and place du

Général de Gaulle with square du Lys in Juan-les-Pins. Buses run every 10 to 20 minutes.

Bus No 2A to Eden Roc on Cap d'Antibes departs every 30 minutes from Antibes bus station. Between 15 June and 15 September, bus No 2A bis circles the Cap, continuing along the coast from Eden Roc to Juan-les-Pins before returning to Antibes.

Bicycle You can rent bikes/scooters/125cc motorcycles at **JML Location** *(☎ 04 92 93 05 06; 93 blvd du Président Wilson)*. The tourist office has a list of other rental outlets.

BIOT

postcode 06410 • pop 7849 • elevation 80m

This charming hill-top village was once an important pottery-manufacturing centre specialising in large earthenware oil and wine containers. Metal containers brought an end to this industry, but Biot is still active in handicraft production. Its streets are pleasant to stroll around; get there early to beat the hordes. **Place des Arcades** dates from the 13th century.

The history of the old Templar village comes to life in the **Musée d'Histoire et de Céramique Biotoise** *(☎ 04 93 65 54 54; 9 rue St-Sébastien)*. At the foot of the village, the **Verrerie de Biot** *(☎ 04 93 65 03 00; e verrie@verreriebiot.com; chemin des Combes)* runs glass-blowing workshops and has a small glass ecomuseum and modern glass-art galleries on site. A complete list of glass-blowing workshops *(verreries)* is available at the **tourist office** *(☎ 04 93 65 78 00, fax 04 93 65 78 04; w www.biot-coteazur.com; 46 rue St-Sébastien; open 10am-7pm Mon-Fri, 2.30pm-7pm Sat & Sun July & Aug, 9am-noon & 2pm-6pm Mon-Fri, 2pm-6pm Sat & Sun Sept-June)*.

Musée National Fernand Léger

The National Fernand Léger Museum *(☎ 04 92 91 50 30; chemin du Val de Pôme; adult/under 18 €4/free; open 11am-6pm Wed-Mon July-Sept, 10am-12.30pm & 2pm-5.30pm Wed-Mon Oct-June)*, 2km from Biot centre, contains some 350 works by Fernand Léger (1881–1955), including paintings, mosaics, ceramics and stained-glass windows. The museum was built by Léger's wife following his death. Léger had bought the land one month earlier to build himself a studio. The foundation stone was laid by Braques, Chagall and Picasso in 1957.

Colourful Léger mosaics decorate the museum facade. The predominant mosaic above the entrance was intended for a sports stadium. Several Léger sculptures bespeckle the surrounding park.

Bonsaï Arboretum

This Japanese garden *(☎ 04 93 65 63 99; 209 chemin du Val de Pôme; adult/student €4/2; open 10am-noon & 2pm or 3pm-5.30pm or 6.30pm Wed-Mon)*, created from the private collection of the Okonek family, displays a wealthy array of Bonsaï trees. Its centrepiece is Europe's largest Bonsaï forest – 6m long. In addition to strolling the sculpted gardens, green-fingered visitors can buy their own Bonsaï tree.

Marineland

Well distanced from the hill-top village is the Disneyland-style **Parc de la Mer** *(Sea Park; ☎ 04 93 33 49 49)*, a giant amusement complex offering a mind-boggling spectacle of games, shows and activities to amuse. Waterworld Marineland *(adult/3-12 yrs low season €22/15, high season €28/21; open 10am-midnight July & Aug, 10am-8pm Sept-June)* is the park's main drawcard. Acrobatic killer-whale/dolphin shows are held several times daily in summer. Sharks can be viewed through a transparent, underwater tunnel.

To get to Marineland take bus No 10A from Antibes bus station to the Marineland stop. By train, turn right out of Biot train station, walk 50m along route de Nice (N7), then turn right along the D4 signposted 'Marineland & Biot'.

Getting There & Away

Biot village is a good 4km from Biot train station. From Antibes, take bus No 10A from the bus station or place du Général de Gaulle to Biot village (€1.10, 20 minutes, 11 buses daily).

CAGNES-SUR-MER

postcode 06800 • pop 44,207

Cagnes-sur-Mer comprises **Haut de Cagnes**, the old hill-top town; **Le Cros de Cagnes**, the former fishing village by the beach; and **Cagnes Ville**, a fast-growing modern quarter. The old city, with its ramparts, is dominated by the 14th-century Château Grimaldi.

Near Cagnes Ville, the Renoir Museum is dedicated to the artist who spent his last 12 years in Cagnes-sur-Mer. The magnificent olive and orange groves around the Provençal *mas* (farmhouse; today the boutique) and bourgeois house are as much an attraction as the museum itself.

The **tourist office** *(☎ 04 93 20 61 64, fax 04 93 20 52 63; ⓔ info@cagnes-tourisme.com; 6 blvd Maréchal Juin; open 9am-7pm Mon-Sat, 9am-noon Sun July & Aug, 9am-noon & 2pm-6pm or 7pm Mon-Sat Sept-June)*, just off the A8 in Cagnes Ville, runs annexes in both **Haut de Cagnes** *(☎ 04 92 02 85 05; place du Château)* and **Le Cros de Cagnes** *(☎ 04 93 07 67 08; 20 ave des Oliviers)*.

Château Musée

Home to the Grimaldi family until the French Revolution, the Castle Museum *(☎ 04 92 02 47 30; place du Château; one/two museums €3/4.50; open 10am-noon & 2pm-5pm or 6pm Wed-Mon)*, at the top of the village, houses a **Musée de l'Olivier** (Olive Tree Museum) featuring paintings of olive groves as well as the predictable ethnographic collection; and a **Musée d'Art Méditerranéen Moderne** (Museum of Modern Mediterranean Art) dedicated to the host of 20th-century artists inspired by the Côte d'Azur. Between July and September, the permanent art collection is replaced by exhibits of the Festival International de la Peinture (International Painting Festival).

The castle was restored in the early 1900s. Its grandiose banquet hall is dominated by a 17th-century ceiling fresco depicting the Greek mythological fall of Phaeton. The marquise of Grimaldi's old boudoir is filled with a bizarre collection of portraits featuring **Suzy Solidor** (1900–85), a cabaret singer who spent the last 25 years of her life living in Cagnes-sur-Mer. When not starring in Parisian cabarets, sexy Suzy starred on the canvases of Europe's leading artists. Among the 40 portraits she donated to the museum before her death (out of the 224 she possessed) are pieces by Brayer, Cocteau, Dufy, Kisling and Van Dongen.

Musée Renoir

La Domaine des Collettes, today the Renoir Museum *(☎ 04 93 20 61 07; chemin des Collettes; adult/under 12 €3/1.50; open 10am-noon & 2pm-6pm Wed-Mon May-Sept, to 5pm Oct-Apr)*, served as home and studio to an arthritis-crippled Renoir (1841–1919), who lived here with his wife and three sons from 1907 until his death.

It has retained its original decor. The wheelchair-bound artist painted, with a brush bandaged to his fingers, in the north-facing, 2nd-floor studios. The chicken wire covering the window protected Renoir from his children's mis-hit tennis balls.

Several of the artist's works are on display, including *Les Grandes Baigneuses* (The Women Bathers; 1892), a reworking of the 1887 original. Photographs documenting his life are dotted around the house, as well as some of Renoir's sculptures, notably *Vénus Victorieuse* (Venus Victorious), a Renoir statue of a fashionably rounded, nude Venus cast in bronze.

To get to the museum from Cagnes bus station on place du Général de Gaulle, walk east along ave Renoir and its continuation, ave des Tuilières, then turn left (north) onto chemin des Collettes. From here, the museum is 500m uphill.

Places to Eat

Cagnes Ville centre has plenty of typically unstartling, seaside resort-style restaurants and cafés. Those seeking food to remember can scale new gastronomic heights in Haut de Cagnes.

Le Cagnard *(☎ 04 93 20 73 21; ⓦ www.le-cagnard.com; 1 rue du Ponti Long, Haut de Cagnes; menus from around €55)* resides inside a stylish 14th-century nobleman's residence (today a Relais & Châteaux hotel) in castle walls. Black-truffle lasagne is among its house specialities and the fabulous Renaissance-styled ceiling of the restaurant is drawn back in summer.

Josy-Jo *(☎ 04 93 20 68 76; place Notre Dame de la Protection, Haut de Cagnes; full meal around €45)* lacks pretension, oozes charm and is the hill-top town's simple-yet-stately place to dine.

Getting There & Away

Cagnes-sur-Mer is served by two train stations, Gare Cagnes-sur-Mer, and Gare Le Cros de Cagnes. Most Cannes–Ventimiglia trains stop at both (they're two to three minutes apart).

Buses from Cannes to Nice (every 20 minutes) stop outside Cagnes-sur-Mer (52 minutes) and Le Cros de Cagnes train stations (one hour), and at Cagnes' central bus station on place du Général de Gaulle. The Grasse–Nice bus (No 500) only stops outside Cagnes-sur-Mer train station (35 minutes, about 10 daily).

From Vence, bus No 400 departs every 30 minutes to Cagnes-sur-Mer (20 minutes) via St-Paul de Vence. Cheap day passes are available on this route (see the St-Paul de Vence section).

ST-PAUL DE VENCE

postcode 06570 • pop 2900 • elevation 125m

This picturesque and touristy medieval hilltop village, 10km north of Cagnes-sur-Mer, has been a haven to a great many artists and writers over the centuries and is a must for any art lover following in the footsteps of the 20th-century's great masters. Some of their works are exhibited at the extraordinary Fondation Maeght and, for those into fine dining, at La Colombe d'Or.

St-Paul de Vence was home to Russian artist Marc Chagall (1887–1985) who is buried in the village cemetery. The African-American novelist James Baldwin (1924–85) also spent the last years of his life in St-Paul. Yves Montand (1921–91) was a frequent visitor here for many years. The French singer/actor was best known for his roles in the 1986 film adaptations of Pagnol's novels *Jean de Florette* and *Manon des Sources* (and in the late 1990s for the controversial exhumation of his corpse for DNA testing as part of a 10-year paternity suit filed against him). He met his wife, the actress Simone Signoret, for the first time in St-Paul in 1949. They threw their wedding reception at La Colombe d'Or.

The **tourist office** *(☎ 04 93 32 86 95, fax 04 93 32 60 27; ⓔ artdevivre@wanadoo.fr; 2 rue Grande; open 10am-7pm daily June-Sept, to 6pm Oct-May)*, on your right as you enter the old village through its northern gate, organises guided tours of the old village and a local artist's studio (€8, one hour).

The Village

Strolling the narrow streets packaged within 15th-century ramparts is how most visitors pass the time in St-Paul. No less than 36 of its 64 **art galleries** are on rue Grande; the tourist office has a list. Steps from rue Grande lead east to St-Paul's crowning glory, the **Église Collégiale** and adjoining **Chapelle des Pénitents**, place de l'Église. Free organ recitals are held here in July and August.

Marc Chagall and his wife, Vava, are buried in the **cemetery** at the village's southern end. Beach pebbles are scattered on top of their plain tombs. From the main cemetery entrance, turn right, then left; the Chagall graves are the third on the left.

The mosaic mural by Fernand Léger, *Les Femmes au Perroquet* (Women with a Parrot), is among a handful of pieces of modern art that can be viewed at **La Colombe d'Or** (see Places to Stay & Eat later in this section) on place des Ormeaux. This upmarket restaurant is where Braque, Chagall, Dufy, Picasso and other then-impoverished artists dined in the post-WWI years in exchange for one of their humble creations – which today form one of France's largest private art collections. Viewing is strictly for diners.

Yves Montand was among the handful of celebrities captured on black-and-white film while playing **pétanque** on the gravel square in front of La Colombe d'Or. The tourist office hires balls (€3 a set) and arranges games with local *pétanque* champs (€61 per hour).

Fondation Maeght

One of the foremost centres in France for contemporary art, the Maeght Foundation *(☎ 04 93 32 81 63; ⓔ contact@fondation-maeght.com; adult/under 10 €10/free; open 10am-7pm daily July-Sept, 10am-12.30pm & 2.30pm-6pm daily Oct-June)*, is in a futuristic building on a hill in beautiful countryside amid gardens embellished with sculptures and fountains. It hosts an exceptional permanent collection of 20th-century works featuring Braque, Bonnard, Chagall, Matisse, Miró and Léger. Its temporary exhibitions are equally extraordinary.

In the gardens behind the museum, visitors can stroll through the **Miró Labyrinth**, a terraced area laid out by Catalan architect José Luis Sert, a pupil of Le Corbusier. The route is studded with gigantic sculptures and mosaics – some spouting water – by Spanish surrealist Joan Miró (1893–1983), who frequently visited the Côte d'Azur to see Picasso and other artists living on the coast.

The centre, signposted from rond point St-Claire, is 800m from the bus stop. A steep driveway leads up to the Foundation. Approaching St-Paul by car, turn left off the D7 from La-Colle-sur-Loup.

Galerie Guy Pieters

This modern art gallery *(☎ 04 93 32 06 46; w www.modern-art-foundation.com; chemin des Trious; open 10am-7pm daily June-Oct, 10am-12.30pm & 2pm-6pm daily Nov-May)*, at the foot of the driveway leading to Fondation Maeght, is a must for big spenders. Stunning (and often monumental) pieces of contemporary work are displayed here; many are for sale. Some of the star pieces exhibited in the gallery (not for sale) include Andy Warhol's *La Grande Passion* (1984), Tom Wesselmann's *Smoker* (1998) and Arman's 2.8m-tall *Music Power*, which the Nice-born artist created from a dozen violins in 1985.

Places to Stay & Eat

St-Paul de Vence is strictly for the rich and well-to-do. The tourist office stocks a list of hotels.

Hostellerie Les Remparts *(☎ 04 93 32 09 88, fax 04 93 32 06 91; e h.remparts@wanadoo.fr; 72 rue Grande; doubles from €30)* is among the cheapest places, and is cosy to boot.

Le St-Paul *(☎ 04 93 32 65 25, fax 04 93 32 52 94; e stpaul@relaischateaux.fr; 86 rue Grande; doubles from €220)*, the only four-star hotel within the village walls, is one of the Riviera's most exclusive.

Café de la Place *(☎ 04 93 32 80 03; place de Gaulle; lunch special €8.50)*, overlooking the boules pitch, is St-Paul's humblest – in inverted commas – joint. Daily specials make for a satisfying lunch.

La Colombe d'Or *(The Golden Dove; ☎ 04 93 32 80 02, fax 04 93 32 77 78; w www.la-colombe-dor.com; place de Gaulle; doubles €214)* is best known for its legendary restaurant. Tables must be booked at least eight days (months for July and August) in advance. To wine and dine your sweetheart will set you back at least €100 per head (excluding wine).

Getting There & Away

St-Paul de Vence (St-Paul on bus timetables and road signs) is served by bus No 400 from Nice (€4.10, 45 minutes, every half-hour from 6.55am to 8.15pm).

VENCE

postcode 06140 • pop 17,184 • elevation 325m

Vence is a pleasant inland town, 4km north of St-Paul de Vence. The area is typically built up with holiday homes and villas, but the medieval centre is perfect for strolling past art galleries and through street markets.

The exceptional Chapelle du Rosaire, designed and decorated by Matisse, is tended today by the community of Dominican nuns for whom the 77-year-old Matisse created the chapel between 1947 and 1951. Matisse lived in Vence for six years, accomplishing works such as *Lemons and Mimosas Against a Black Background* (1943), *Yellow and Blue Interior* (1946) and *Still Life with Pomegranates* (1947) while he was here. His home and studio, called Le Rêve (The Dream) was a villa 200m from the Chapelle du Rosaire, opposite 320 ave Henri Matisse.

Music fills the streets of Vence during its music festival, **Nuits du Sud**, which occupies place du Grand Jardin during the last two weeks of July and the first week of August. At other times, a morning fruit and vegetable market fills the central square on Tuesday and Sunday.

Orientation & Information

Large place du Grand Jardin is Vence's central square, overlooked by the **tourist office** *(☎ 04 93 58 06 38, fax 04 93 58 91 81; w www.ville-vence.fr; place du Grand Jardin; open 9am-1pm & 2pm-7pm Mon-Sat July & Aug, 9am-12.30am & 2pm-6pm Mon-Sat Sept-June)*.

To get to the old city, turn left onto ave Marcellin Maurel, which skirts the medieval city's southern wall. Port du Peyra, the main city entrance, is at the western end of ave Marcellin Maurel. Place Clémenceau lies at the heart of the medieval city.

Medieval Vence

Porte du Peyra, the main gate of the 13th-century wall that encircles the old city, leads to place du Peyra and its **fountain** (1578). Gate and square are named after the execution block that once adorned place du Peyra. The western edge of the square is dominated by imposing **Château de Villeneuve** and adjoining 12th-century **watchtower**. The castle houses the **Fondation Émile Hughes** *(☎ 04 93 24 24 23; 2 place du Frêne; adult/student*

€5/2.50; open 10am-6pm Tues-Sun July & Aug, 10am-12.30pm & 2pm-6pm Tues-Sun Sept-June), a cultural centre with 20th-century art exhibitions. In front stands a 400-year-old ash tree.

From place du Peyra, narrow **rue du Marché** – dotted with delectable food shops selling fresh pasta, fish, fruit and so on – leads east. Cut along rue Alsace-Lorraine to reach **place Clémenceau**, the central square and market place. The **Romanesque cathedral** on the eastern side of the square was built in the 11th century on the site of an old Roman temple.

The best panorama of medieval Vence can be had from Matisse's Chapelle du Rosaire. The watchtower provides a ready landmark.

Matisse's Chapelle du Rosaire

Matisse moved from war-torn Nice to Vence in June 1943. Upon his arrival he was reunited with Monique Bourgeois, his former nurse and model who had since become a Dominican nun under the name Sœur Jacques-Marie. She persuaded the artist to design a chapel for her community, the result being the striking Chapelle du Rosaire *(Chapel of the Rosary; ☎ 04 93 58 03 26; 468 ave Henri Matisse; adult/6-16 yrs €2.50/1; open 10am-11.30am & 2pm-5.30pm Tues & Thur, 2pm-5.30pm Mon, Wed & Sat Dec-Oct)*. Matisse was 81 when he completed the project in 1951.

The chapel is still used by the Dominican nuns of the Rosary today. Blue-and-white ceramic tiles coat the low roof, which is topped by a 13m-tall wrought-iron cross and bell tower. Inside, stark white walls provide a dramatic contrast to the stained-glass windows, through which the sun's rays glow. A line image of the Virgin Mary and child is painted on white ceramic tiles on the northern interior wall. The western wall is dominated by the bolder *Chemin de Croix* (Stations of the Cross), numbered in Matisse's frenzied handwriting. St-Dominic overlooks the altar.

Matisse also designed the chapel's stone altar, candlesticks, cross, and the colourful priests' vestments displayed in an adjoining hall. Many of his preparatory sketches and models for the four-year project are here too, as is a photograph of the artist with Sister Jacques-Marie, arms linked in friendly companionship.

The chapel is about 800m north of Vence on route de St-Jeannet (the D2210). From place du Grand Jardin, head east along ave de la Résistance then turn right (north) along ave Tuby. At the next junction, bear right (northeast) along ave de Provence then left (north) onto ave Henri Matisse. During French school holidays, it also opens 2pm to 5.30pm Friday. Sunday Mass (open to everyone) is celebrated at 10am, followed by a guided tour at 10.45am.

Places to Stay & Eat

Maison Lacordaire *(☎ 04 93 58 03 26, fax 04 93 58 21 10; 466 ave Henri Matisse; half-/full board per person €27/36)*, adjoining the Chapelle du Rosaire, belongs to the Dominican nuns where they offer beds for the night. Rooms *must* be reserved three to eight days in advance.

Hôtel La Victoire *(☎ 04 93 58 61 30, fax 04 93 58 74 68; place du Grand Jardin; singles/doubles from €27/32)* is above a busy bar.

Le P'tit Provençal *(☎ 04 93 58 50 64; 4 place Clémenceau; menus €19 & €26)*, tucked beside the town hall, serves local cuisine on a pavement terrace. Notable highlights include quail salad with grated turnips, and roasted rabbit pie with onions and basil.

Le Pêcheur du Soleil *(☎ 04 93 58 32 56; place Godeau; pizzas €7.10-12.80)* is a pizzeria with tasty fare.

Nicole & Christian Marchisio *(☎ 04 93 58 08 25; 2 place Surian)* should be the first port of call (along with the morning markets) for picnic goodies. The delicatessen sells an excellent choice of savoury tart slices to take away.

Getting There & Away

Bus No 400 to/from Nice (€4.50, one hour) uses the stop on place du Grand Jardin, in front of No 14 (a few doors down from the tourist office).

AROUND VENCE

Varied walking, cycling and soft-top motoring surrounds Vence. The northbound D2 from Vence leads to the **Col de Vence** (963m), a mountain pass 10km north offering good views of the *baous* (rocky promontories), typical of this region. At the foot of the pass is the **Baou des Blancs** (673m), crowned by the stony remains of the **Bastide St-Laurent**, inhabited by the Templars in the

13th century. Marked walking trails around the pass follow part of the GR51.

Coursegoules (pop 323, elevation 1020m), 6km farther north along the D2, is a typical Provençal hill-top village with 11th-century castle ruins and fortifications. From here, head west along the D2 to **Gréolieres** (pop 455), yet another fabulous hill-top village. Walkers can then follow the GR4 north to **Gréolieres-les-Neiges** (elevation 1450m), a small ski station equipped with 14 lifts (and eight snow canons!), on the northern face of Montagne Cheiron; the GR4 scales Cheiron's 1778m-high peak.

Several hairpin bends and 7km south of Gréolieres along the D603, you hook up with the dramatic **Gorges du Loup**. The road along the western side of the gorges (the D3) crescendos with the village of **Gourdon** (pop 384, elevation 758m). Art deco works, including pieces from designer Eileen Gray's Paris apartment and seaside villa on Cap Martin (see the boxed text 'Trailing Le Corbusier' under Architecture in the Facts about Provence chapter), can be viewed in the **Musée des Arts Décoratifs et de la Modernité** *(☎ 04 93 09 68 02; ⓔ chatewaudegourdon@hotmail.com; place du Château; open 10am-1pm & 2pm-7pm daily July & August)* inside Château de Gourdon. Aspiring 'noses' can see what happens to freshly picked lavender, genista, thyme and orange-tree leaves at **La Source Parfumée** *(☎ 04 93 09 68 23; ⓔ lasourceparfumee@wanadoo.fr; rue Principale; admission free; open 10am-6pm daily)*, a distillery run by the Galimard perfumery (see the boxed text 'Follow Your Nose' in the Grasse section later in this chapter).

From Gourdon, stargazers can detour 15km west to the **Observatoire de la Côte d'Azur** *(1270m; ☎ 04 93 40 54 54)*, which is the region's highest observatory atop the Plateau de Calern near Caussols. Alternatively, the D6 leads to **Pont du Loup**, mostly visited for its factory of **Confiserie Florian** *(☎ 04 93 59 32 91; admission free; open 9am-noon & 2pm-6.30pm daily)*, in a lovely old flour mill built in 1868. A 10-minute tour gives you an idea of how the traditional sweet house makes its crystallised fruits, jams, jellied flowers and other sweet treats. Lemon trees and other citrus-fruit plants are grown in the pleasant Jardin d'Agrumes and there is – of course – a shop where you can buy Florian products.

From Pont du Loup, the eastbound D2210 snakes to Tourrettes-sur-Loup. Some 5km before the village is **Ferme des Courmettes** *(☎ 04 93 59 31 93)*, a 600-hectare **goat farm** where cheese is made. Guided tours and *dégustation* sessions are available; Vence tourist office has details. **Tourrettes-sur-Loup** (pop 3921, elevation 400m), dubbed the 'city of violets' after its production of the purple flower, is a picturesque, 15th-century hill-top village crammed with art galleries and craft shops. Violet flowers are crystallised and its leaves, harvested in May and August, are sold to perfumeries in Grasse for the extraction of essential oils. Tourrettes' annual **Fête des Violettes** (violet festival) on the first or second Sunday in March closes with a flower battle. The **tourist office** *(☎ 04 93 24 18 93, fax 04 93 59 24 40; ⓦ www.tourrettessurloup.com; 2 place Libération)* has more information.

Six kilometres northeast of Vence, at the foot of **Baou de Jeannet** (800m), is the village of **St-Jeannet** (pop 3647, elevation 400m), the setting for Peter Mayle's fictional *Chasing Cézanne*. A 45-minute marked trail leads from central place Ste-Barbe to the summit of the promontory. Top off the trip with a visit to **La Gaude** (pop 6217), a less-touristy hill-top village 1.5km south of St-Jeannet.

Inland to Grasse

From Cannes, an inland journey takes you along the same road Napoleon Bonaparte trod on his return from exile in 1814. From the island of Elba, he landed at Golfe-Juan (see that section earlier in this chapter), from where he and a clutch of faithful followers marched for six days north to Lyons. They took what is called **La Route Napoléon** or the N85 today – at that time a remote route passing through a couple of medieval villages, Grasse with its skilled perfumers and then beyond into the mountains of Haute-Provence.

MOUGINS

postcode 06250 • pop 16,287 • elevation 260m

Elite and elegant Mougins, 7km north of Cannes, prides itself on two things: art and gastronomy. Picasso, who discovered the spot in 1935 with lover Dora Marr and surrealist photographer Man Ray (1890–1976), lived in Mougins with his final love, Jacqueline Roque, from 1961 until his death.

Today the village is known for the culinary wonders cooked up by French chef Roger Vergé and for its innovative photography museum. Bugatti, Rolls-Royce and Ferrari race into gear 5km south in the **Musée de l'Automobiliste** *(☎ 04 93 69 27 80; W www.museauto.fr.st; 772 chemin de Font de Currault; adult/12-18 yrs €7/4; open 10am-6pm or 7pm daily)*, an automobile museum just off the A8.

May to October, art exhibitions (free) are held in the 19th-century **lavoir** *(public wash-house: ☎ 04 92 92 50 42; 15 ave Jean-Charles Mallet)*. The **tourist office** *(☎ 04 93 75 87 67, fax 04 92 92 04 03; W www.mougins-coteazur.org; parking du Moulin de la Croix; open 10am-5.30pm daily)*, in the car park at the foot of the village, has a list of no less than 30 art galleries in the village that can be visited.

Musée de la Photographie

Celebrated Riviera photographer Jacques Henri Lartigue (1894–1986) is among the wealth of known photographers represented in this fabulous museum *(☎ 04 93 75 85 67; admission €2; open 10am-8pm daily July-Sept, 10am-noon & 2pm-6pm Wed-Sat, 2pm-6pm Sun Oct & mid-Dec–May)*, inside Mougin's medieval Porte Sarrazine, behind the church bell tower. The museum was set up in 1989 by André Villers, best known for photographing Picasso, to whom the 2nd floor is dedicated. A collection of antique cameras and a series of aerial photographs of Mougins in the early 1900s are displayed on the 1st floor, and temporary photographic exhibitions fill the ground floor.

Places to Stay

L'Eau Vive *(☎ 04 93 75 36 35; 713 chemin des Cabrières; camping for 2 people, tent & car €14)*, is the nearest camp site, 1.5km south of Mougins off ave Maréchal Foch (N85).

Beyond that one low-cost option, four-star hotels rule in Mougins.

Moulin de Mougins *(☎ 04 93 75 78 24, fax 04 93 90 18 55; W www.moulin-mougins.com; ave Notre Dame de Vie; doubles from €137, lunch/dinner menus from €44/90)*, Roger Vergé's illustrious place, is in a 16th-century oil mill, crammed with original works by César, Picasso and so on. Menus feature Provençal delights like courgette flowers with black truffles. The mill is 2.5km southeast off the D3.

Places to Eat

Gourmet Collection *(☎ 04 93 75 30 14; 11 rue Honoré Henry)* is a small boutique where you can shop for kitchen utensils and taste different types of beans in its coffee shop out the back.

L'Amandier *(The Almond Tree; ☎ 04 93 90 00 91; place du Commandant Lamy; menus from €25)*, in the village centre, is Vergé's affordable option. Here you can dine on light but traditional Provençal creations, followed by a shopping spree for wine in Vergé's wine cellar and for stylish tablecloths and other household nonessentials in Madame Vergé's upmarket boutique.

La Ferme de Mougins *(☎ 04 93 09 03 74; W www.lafermedemougins.fr; 10 ave St-Basile; menus from €30)*, out of the village on a farm, is an upmarket haven of peace, tranquillity and unforgettable cuisine.

Getting There & Away

Mougins is on the Cannes–Grasse bus route. From the bus station next to Cannes train station, buses depart every half-hour (hourly on Sunday) between 6.30am and 7.30pm to Mougins (€1.70, 20 minutes). Grasse is a 20-minute bus ride from Mougins (€2).

MOUANS-SARTOUX

postcode 06370 • pop 9031 • elevation 120m

The main draw of Mouans-Sartoux, 4km north, is its **Espace de l'Art Concret** *(Centre of Concrete Art; ☎ 04 93 75 71 50; e espace.art.concret@wanadoo.fr; place Suzanne de Villeneuve; adult/12-18 yrs €2.30/ 1.15; open 11am-7pm Wed-Sun June-Sept, to 6pm Oct-May)*. Bold, gigantic, geometric shapes, use of industrial materials, and mischievous tampering with natural light and space create a grandiose juxtaposition with the its unfabricated setting – 16th-century Château de Mouans (1504–10). Concrete art, which focuses on the intellectual aspect of art (as opposed to emotional or aesthetic), was coined by Theo van Doesburg in the 1930s.

Places to Stay & Eat

The **tourist office** *(☎ 04 93 75 75 16, fax 04 92 92 09 16; W www.mouans-sartoux.com;*

258 ave de Cannes), on the main road through town, has information on accommodation in the region.

Hôtel de la Paix *(☎ 04 92 92 42 80, fax 04 92 92 42 99; 45 rue de Cannes; doubles with toilet €28, with shower & toilet €43)*, likewise on the busy central street, is a cheap choice.

Restaurant du Château *(☎ 04 93 75 54 50; 1 place Suzanne de Villeneuve; plat/menu du jour €8.50/12)* serves an excellent *plat du jour* (dish of the day) and *menu du jour*; both include a 25cL jug of house wine. Its shaded terrace overlooks Château de Mouans.

Getting There & Away

Mouans-Sartoux is on the same Cannes–Grasse bus route as Mougins (see that section earlier). A single Mouans-Sartoux–Grasse fare costs €1.10.

GRASSE

postcode 06130 • pop 44,790 • elevation 250m

If it weren't for the scents around Grasse, 17km north of the Mediterranean, you could probably detect a sea breeze. For centuries Grasse, with its distinct red- and orange-tiled roofs rising up pre-Alpine slopes, has been one of France's leading centres of perfume production.

Founded by the Romans, Grasse had become a small republic by the early Middle Ages, exporting tanned hides and oil (from which it may have earned its name since *gras* or *matière grasse* means 'fat' in French). With the advent of perfumed gloves in the 1500s (the doing of France's queen at the time, Catherine de Medicis, who detested the smell of raw leather on her hands), Grasse discovered a new wealth. Glove-makers quickly split from the tanners and set up a separate industry, leading to the eventual creation of perfumeries. In the 18th century, with perfume suddenly becoming all the rage, these blossomed.

Grasse and its surrounds produce some of France's most highly prized flowers, including lavender, jasmine, centifolia roses, mimosa, orange blossom and violets. Cut flowers are sold at the *marché Provençal* (Provençal market) that brings a splash of colour to cours Honoré Cresp on the first and third Saturday of the month. In springtime, the green-fingered should take a stroll around **Jardin de la Villa Noailles** *(☎ 04 93 36 07 77; 59 ave Guy de Maupassant; admission €10; open 2pm-4pm Fri Apr-June)*, English- and Italian-inspired gardens created in 1947 by Charles de Noailles, since restored and protected as a historic monument.

Orientation & Information

The N85 (the route Napoléon), which leads north to Castellane and Digne-les-Bains and south to Cannes, runs into Grasse, where it becomes the town's main (and often congested) thoroughfare, blvd du Jeu de Ballon. The steep stairways and roads of old Grasse, densely packed into the hillside, are best explored on foot.

The **tourist office** *(☎ 04 93 36 66 66, fax 04 93 36 86 36; ⓔ tourisme.grasse@wanadoo.fr; 22 cours Honoré Cresp; open 9am-7pm Mon-Sat, 9am-1pm & 2pm-6pm Sun July–mid-Sept, 9am-12.30pm & 1.30pm-6pm Mon-Sat rest of year)* has information on factory visits. Near the bus station, try **Grasse Espace Accueil***(☎ 04 93 36 21 68, fax 04 93 36 21 07; 3 place de la Foux; open 9am-7pm Mon-Sat, 9am-12.30pm & 1.30-6pm Sun July–mid-Sept, 9am-12.30pm & 1.30pm-6pm Mon-Sat rest of year)*.

Commercial banks are dotted along blvd du Jeu de Ballon and there's a **post office** *(blvd Fragonard)*.

Museums

Those who are intending to visit more than one museum can buy an €8 ticket (10 to 16 years/under 10 €4/free) covering admission to all three museums; it is available at any museum.

Musée Jean-Honoré Fragonard Named after the artist Jean-Honoré Fragonard, who was born in Grasse in 1732, the villa where the artist lived for a year in 1790 has been turned into a house-museum *(☎ 04 93 36 01 81; 23 blvd Fragonard; adult/10-16 yrs/under 10 €4/2/free; open 10am-7pm daily June-Sept, 10am-12.30pm & 2pm-5.30pm Wed-Sun Oct-May)*. His paintings, famous for their licentious scenes, are on display inside the museum.

Musée Provençal du Costume et du Bijou Visiting Grasse's colourful costume and jewellery museum comes as a breath of fresh air after touring the town's perfumeries. The museum *(☎ 04 93 36 44 65;*

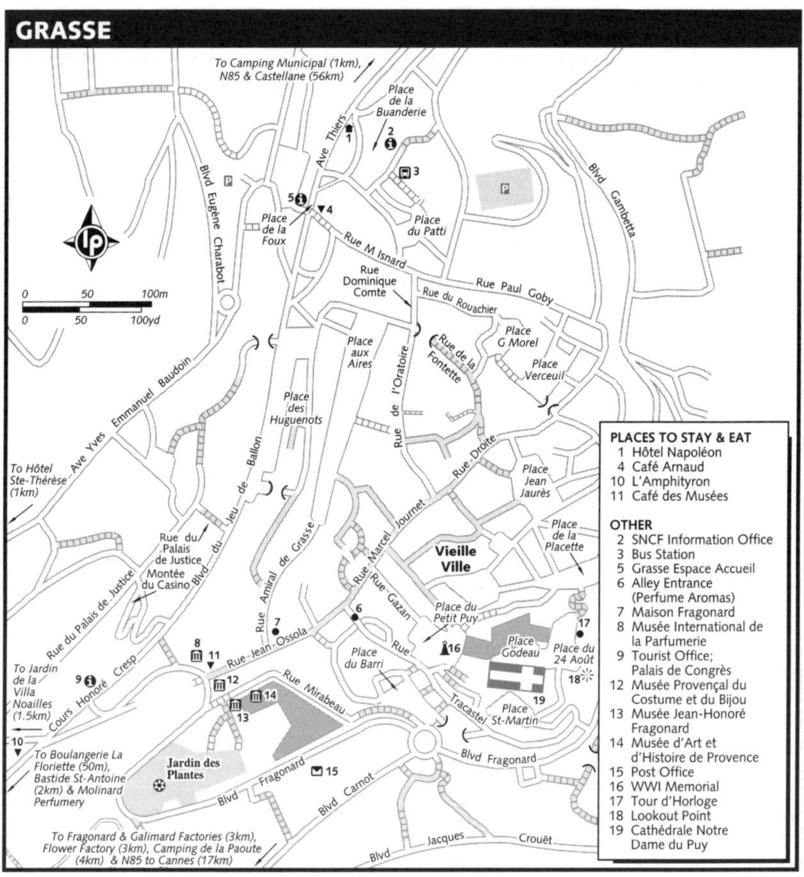

2 rue Jean Ossola; admission free; open 10am-6pm daily Feb-Oct, 10am-noon & 2pm-6pm Nov-Jan), run by Fragonard, is inside stately Hôtel de Clapiers Cabris, the private mansion of the sister of revolutionary Mirabeau, the marquise de Cabris, who lived in Grasse from 1769.

Musée d'Art et d'Histoire de Provence Just around the corner, regional art and history is the mammoth topic touched upon by this small museum *(☎ 04 93 36 01 61; 2 rue Mirabeau; adult/10-16 yrs/under 10 €4/2/free; open 10am-7pm daily June-Sept, 10am-12.30pm & 2pm-5.30pm Wed-Sun Oct-May)*. Furniture, paintings, costumes and ornamental figures form a large part of the collection.

Musée International de la Parfumerie
This museum *(☎ 04 93 36 80 20; 8 place du Cours Honoré Cresp; adult/10-16 yrs/under 10 €4/2/free; open 10am-7pm daily June-Sept, 10am-12.30pm & 2pm-5.30pm Wed-Sun Oct-May)* examines every detail of perfume production – from extraction techniques right through to sales and publicity – and traces its 400 years of history in Grasse. One of the most appealing parts of the museum is the rooftop conservatory, where lavender, mint, thyme and jasmine are grown in a heady mix of aromatic scents.

Cathédrale Notre Dame du Puy

Although rather uninteresting in itself, the cathedral, built in Provençal Romanesque style in the 12th and 13th centuries and

Follow Your Nose

Don't expect to sniff out Chanel, Giorgio Beverley Hills or Guerlain here: Grasse's 40 or so *parfumeries* (perfumeries) sell their essence to factories or by mail order and are practically unknown.

Sales-driven guided tours of three of the biggest names – tourist showcases rather than working factories – take you through every stage of perfume production, from extraction and distillation to the work of the perfumer or *nez* (nose). At the end you'll be squirted with several house scents, invited to purchase as many as you'd like, and leave reeking. With many 'big name' perfumes today, 60% of what you pay is for the fancy bottle.

Galimard *(☎ 04 93 09 20 00; W www.galimard.com; 73 route de Cannes; open 9am-6pm daily)*, with a *savonnerie* (soap factory) in Èze (see the Nice to Menton chapter) and its flower distillery in Gourdon, is 3km from Grasse centre on the southbound N85. At its nearby **Studio des Fragrances** *(☎ 04 93 09 20 00; 5 route de Pégomas; sessions 2pm & 4pm Mon-Sat)*, you can create your own fragrance under the guidance of a professional *nez* (nose), as perfumers are called. There are 250 noses (of which 30 are women) and five famous master noses in the world. Noses combine a natural gift with 10 years of study (five years of which are spent at a special nose school in Chicago, Zürich or Versailles near Paris) and a meagre lifestyle (no smoking, alcohol, coffee, garlic, spicy food) to identify – from no more than a whiff – 6000 or so scents. Somewhere between 200 and 500 of these fragrances are used to make just one perfume; 'create-your-own' sessions give you the choice of 127 different scents to use. Workshops last two hours and cost €34, including a 30ml bottle of your scent; you must reserve in advance.

Fragonard *(☎ 04 93 36 44 65; 20 blvd Fragonard; W www.fragonard.com; admission free; open 9am-6.30pm daily Feb-Oct, 9am-12.30pm & 2pm-6.30pm Nov-Jan)*, a perfume house dating back to 1926, is named after one of the town's original perfume-making families. These perfumers left fresh

reworked in the 18th century, contains a painting by Fragonard entitled *Washing of the Feet*, and several early paintings by Rubens, including *The Crown of Thorns* and *Christ Crucified*. Summer concerts are occasionally held here.

Special Events

Grasse's two main events – related to flowers and scents *naturellement* – are **Exporose** in May and **La Jasminade**, a jasmine festival, the first weekend in August.

Places to Stay

Camping Municipal *(☎ 04 93 36 28 69, fax 04 93 36 90 54; 27 blvd Alice de Rothschild; camping for 2 adults, tent & car €12)*, 1km northeast of the bus station, is a two-star place. Bus No 8 marked 'Piscine' leaves from the bus station and stops in front of the site.

Hôtel Napoléon *(☎ 04 93 36 05 87, fax 04 93 36 41 09; 6 ave Thiers; singles/doubles €21.35/29)*, a one-star place, is the cheapest option in town. It has a handful of triples and quads.

Just over a kilometre up the hill from the Grasse tourist information office, the **Hôtel Ste-Thérèse** *(☎ 04 93 36 10 29, fax 04 93 36 11 73; e hotelstetherese@wanadoo.fr; 39 ave Yves Emmanuel Baudoin; singles/doubles from €26/35)* has a panoramic view of the valley and dusty, orange-roofed town.

Bastide St-Antoine *(☎ 04 93 70 94 94, fax 04 93 70 94 95; W www.jacques-chibois.com; 48 ave Henri Dunant; doubles low/high season from €150/201, menus €45, €107 & €135)*, a four-star Relais & Chateaux pad, is Grasse's most upmarket dining and sleeping choice. To say that the rooms in this 18th-century country house, overlooking a vast olive grove, are lavish would be something of an understatement. Gastronomic temptations are created by well-known French chef Jacques Chibois.

Places to Eat

Café des Musées *(☎ 04 92 60 99 00; 1 rue Jean Ossola; mains €11)* is the best bet for a quick and tasty lunch. Sit on a yellow Jacobsen chair in its modern interior and pick a Mediterranean-inspired *assiettes* (platters).

Café Arnaud *(☎ 04 93 36 44 88; 10 place de la Foux; menu €27.50)*, a traditional bistro, cooks homemade gnocchi and ravioli and serves it beneath a vaulted ceiling.

L'Amphityron *(☎ 04 93 36 58 73; 16 blvd Victor Hugo; lunch/dinner menus €25/29)*, in

Follow Your Nose

flower petals to rest in animal fat for three months, then mixed the fatty substance with alcohol to extract the essences. Unlike today (synthetic products are used in the main), they created perfumes exclusively from flowers; 600kg of fresh flower petals yields just 1L of essence. Perfume contains up to 24% pure essence (and lasts up to 10 hours on the skin), compared to eau de parfum, which contains 12% (and lasts six hours), and eau de toilette or eau de Cologne with 2% to 6% concentrate and a skin life of two or three hours. Fragonard 'factory' tours at 20 blvd Fragonard take visitors through a former 16th-century tannery; production takes place at the modern **Fabrique des Fleurs** *(Flower Factory; route de Cannes; admission free; open same hours)*, out of town on the southbound N85; and at its plant in Èze (see the Nice to Menton chapter).

Molinard *(☎ 04 93 36 01 62; W www.molinard.com; 60 blvd Victor Hugo; open 9am-6.30pm daily Apr-Sept, 9am-6pm Mon-Sat Oct-Mar)*, a ritzier affair, is in a turreted, Provençal-style villa surrounded by immaculate lawns and a blaze of flowers. In its factory-museum, you can learn what flowers from Provence – jasmin, lavender, orange-tree leaves, mimosa and so on – are traditionally used, and how the region's olive oil is turned into soap. The perfume house was founded in 1849 and the copper stills used prior to industrialisation in the 1970s are displayed in its former distillery, designed by architect Gustave Eiffel in 1890. Molinard offers numerous packages, including 1½-hour 'create your own perfume' sessions (€32, including 50ml bottle of eau de parfum); combined with a visit to a rose or jasmine field (€40, May to September); and 40-minute aerial visits in a six-seater, twin-engine plane of Grasse's flower fields (€216/108/86 per person for two/four/five passengers).

Grasse's perfume industry employs 3000 and averages an annual gross revenue of €5.2 million; 60% of its products (perfumes and alimentary aromas) are exported, mainly to Germany, the USA, the UK and Switzerland.

the centre of town, is the spot if you're seeking a tasty lunch at a price that won't leave you choking.

Shopping

Perfume shopping aside (see the boxed text 'Follow Your Nose'), shop for stylish tablecloths, Provençal recipe books, reproductions of 18th-century jewellery, embroidered laundry sacks and other household items at **Maison Fragonard** *(☎ 04 93 40 12 04; 2 rue Amiral de Grasse)*.

Getting There & Away

Bus From the **bus station** *(☎ 04 93 36 08 43; place de la Buanderie)*, there are eight to 10 buses daily to/from Nice (€10.20, 1¼ hours) and Cannes (€3.70, 45 minutes) via Mouans-Sartoux and Mougins (see those sections earlier for details).

Train The train line no longer continues to Grasse, but there are plans are afoot to re-open the section of track between Grasse and Cannes by 2004; hourly trains will run between the two towns. The **SNCF information office** *(☎ 04 93 36 06 13; open 8.30am-5.30pm Mon-Sat)*, near the bus station, has details.

Massif de l'Estérel

Covered by pine, oak and eucalyptus trees until the devastating fires of 1985 and 1986 and now beginning to return to life, this spectacular range sprawls immediately southwest of Cannes. It is roughly marked by Mandelieu-La Napoule to the north and St-Raphaël to the south. The latter, together with its Roman neighbour, Fréjus, serves as the main gateway to the Massif de l'Estérel and St-Tropez. Its inland boundary is hugged by noisy La Provençale (the A8 motorway), immediately north of which spills Lac de St-Cassien, where you can swim, sail and windsurf.

There are all sorts of walks to enjoy in the Massif de l'Estérel, but for the more difficult trails you will need to come equipped with a good map, such as IGN's *Série Bleue* (1:25,000) No 3544ET, which costs 45FF. Those not keen to go alone can link up with an organised walk; tourist offices in Mandelieu-La Napoule, Agay, St-Raphaël and Fréjus have details (see later).

CORNICHE DE L'ESTÉREL

The coastal road that runs along the base of the massif is called the Corniche de l'Estérel (also known as the Corniche d'Or and the N98). A drive or walk along this winding road is not to be missed as the views are spectacular. Small summer resorts and inlets (good for swimming) are dotted the length of the 40km-odd coastal stretch, all of which is easily accessible by bus or train (see Getting There & Away later in this section).

If the snail-paced traffic amid the searing heat gets too much in summer, opt for the inland N7. This quieter road runs through the hills and transports you into an entirely different world.

Mandelieu-La Napoule

'Once upon a time' is an apt label for the turreted, 14th-century **Château de la Napoule** *(☎ 04 93 49 95 05; ave Henry Clews; adult/under 10 €4.60/3, gardens only €3; open 2pm-6.30pm daily July & Aug, 2pm-5.30pm Wed-Mon Sept-June)* that dominates this small seaside village. The fanciful castle was the creation of Henry and Marie Clews, an American couple who arrived on the coast in 1918 and spent 17 years rebuilding the sea-facing Saracen tower. Above the main entrance to the chateau, considered a folly by many, are carved the words 'once upon a time'.

The interior and the gardens are adorned with fantastical sculptures created by Henry Clews (1876–1937). The monumental statue, *The God of Humormystics*, which stands in the courtyard, was the sculptor's wedding present to his wife. Château de la Napoule was occupied during WWII (forcing the widowed Marie to move into the gatehouse). In 1951, Marie Clews established the **Fondation d'Art de la Napoule** in commemoration of her husband's eccentric art. His gravestone in the castle grounds reads 'Poet, Sculptor, Actor, Grand Knight of La Mancha, Supreme Master Humormystic, Castelan of Once upon a time, Chevalier de Marie'.

The chateau, which remains privately owned, can be visited with or without a guided tour; tours depart at 3pm and 4pm (5pm in July and August), March to October. Its sturdy garden wall is laced by **Plage du Château**, a sandy beach where coastal paths to the neighbouring beaches of **Plage de la Raguette** (10 minutes) and **Plage de la Rague** (30 minutes) start. Pick up more information on coastal walks in the area – including guided nature walks by the Office National des Forêts – at the **tourist office** *(☎ 04 93 49 95 31; 272 ave Henry Clews; open 10am-12.30pm & 2pm-6pm Mon-Fri)* on the other side of the street to the castle.

From adjacent Port de la Napoule, **Compagnie Maritime Napouloise** *(☎ 04 93 49 15 88)* runs seasonal boats to/from Île Ste-Marguerite. Boats sail one to three times daily, April to September (adult/four to eight years €10/5 return).

Théoule-sur-Mer

Neighbouring Théoule-sur-Mer, 2.5km south along the coast, is dominated by **Château de la Théoule**, another privately owned folly built in the same architectural style as its better-known sister. In the 18th century it was a soap factory. An even bigger folly, the very round **Palais Bulles**, lies well-hidden amid trees 5km west of the small seaside-resort. The fantastical bubble palace was designed in the 1960s by architect Antti Lovag (born in Hungary in 1925 to a Russian father and Finnish mother) and bought by Pierre Cardin in 1989. Lovag lives in Tourettes-sur-Loup where he also designed a couple of habitats. Unfortunately, the only chance to get a glimpse of his fanciful palace (other than online at Ⓦ www.palaisbulles.com) is during the handful of cultural events it hosts in June andJuly; the **tourist office** *(☎ 04 93 49 28 28, fax 04 93 49 00 04; Ⓦ www.theoule-sur-mer.org; 1 corniche d'Or; open 9am-7pm Mon-Sat, 9am-2pm Sun)* has details.

Seasonal boats likewise sail from the small port here to Île Ste-Marguerite. There are three or four departures Monday and Wednesday to Sunday, April to May, and five or six daily in July and August (adult/five to eight years €10/5 return). Between April and September, shorter boat excursions with guided commentary also sail along the Corniche d'Or (adult/five to eight years €10/5; 1¾ hours).

Théoule tourist office rents bicycles for €9/14 per half-day/24 hours.

Le Trayas

Seven kilometres south of Théoule-sur-Mer is Le Trayas, the highest point of the corniche, from where the road gets more dramatic as it twists and turns its way past the **Forêt Domaine de l'Estérel** along the jagged coastline. Needles of red rock strike out amid the splashing sea, hugging small sheltered

Aerial view of Gorges du Verdon, Haute-Provence

DAVID TOMLINSON

Villa Ephrussi de Rothschild, St Jean-Cap Ferrat

DAN HERRICK

Musée d'Art Moderne et d'Art Contemporain, Nice

NICOLA WILLIAMS

Lamps line the winding streets of Old Nice

DAN HERRICK

VERONICA GARBUTT

The public beach along blvd de la Croisette, Cannes

DAN HERRICK

Umbrellas adorn the beach at Cannes

DAN HERRICK

Musicians along the beach in Cannes

DAN HERRICK

The flashy Cannes Carlton Inter-Continental

anses (coves). There is a largish beach at **Anse de la Figueirette**, at the northern end of Le Trayas.

There are several parking areas along this stretch of the corniche where you can stop to picnic and take snaps of the red rocks. There are good views of the spectacular **Rocher de St-Barthélemy** (St-Bartholomew's Rock) and Cap Roux from the **Pointe de l'Observatoire**, 2km south of Le Trayas.

Agay

The village resort of Agay, 10km or so south of Le Trayas, is celebrated for its fine views of the **Rade d'Agay**, a perfect horseshoe-shaped bay embraced by sandy beaches and abundant pine trees. Numerous water sports and boat excursions are on offer at busy central Plage d'Agay. The **tourist office** *(☎ 04 94 82 01 85; 577 blvd de la Plage)*, opposite the beach, has details.

From Agay, route de Valescure leads inland into the massif, from where various walking trails are signposted, including to **Pic de l'Ours** (496m), **Pic du Cap Roux** (452m) and **Pic d'Aurelle** (323m). All three *pics* (peaks) offer stunning panoramas of the Massif de l'Estérel. Guided nature walks (€8, 2½ hours), led by forest rangers, depart from the tourist office.

Le Dramont

Cap du Dramont, also called Cap Estérel, is crowned by a military semaphore and sits at the southern end of the Rade d'Agay. From the semaphore there are unbeatable views of the Golfe de Fréjus flanked by the **Lion de Terre** and the **Lion de Mer** – two red porphyry rocks jutting out of the sea – to the west. Trails lead to the semaphore from **Plage du Débarquement** in Le Dramont on the western side of the cape. In Agay, a path starts from the car park near **Plage du Camp Long**, at the eastern foot of the cape. Both beaches are accessible from the N98.

From Plage du Débarquement you can sail (15 minutes) to **Île d'Or** (Golden Island), a pinprick island, uninhabited bar a small stone fort that is someone's summer house. You can hire catamarans (about €30/110 for one/five hours) and sailboards (from €10 per hour) from the **Accueil Base Nautique**, a wooden hut on the beach.

Overlooking Plage du Débarquement, 1km west of Boulouris on the Corniche de l'Estérel (N98), is a large **memorial park** *(blvd de la 36ème DI du Texas)*, which commemorates the landing of the 36th US Infantry Division on the beach here on 15 August 1944. A monumental landing craft faces out to sea. Steps lead from here down to the beach.

Places to Stay

Camping The bounty of coastal camp sites in and around Agay (all clearly signposted along the N98) include:

Campéole Le Draumont *(☎ 04 94 82 07 68, fax 04 94 82 75 30; ⓔ contact@campeoples.fr; camping for 2 people with tent & car low/mid/high season €15.50/24.20/28.50, mobile home for 3-5 people low/mid/high season €51/60/80; open mid-Mar–mid-Oct)*, a pretty site next to Plage du Débarquement on the western side of Cap du Dramont, has numerous facilities, including tennis courts and an onsite diving school. Mobile homes are only let for two nights or more in high season.

Royal Camping *(☎ 04 94 82 00 20, fax 04 94 82 00 20; camping for 2 people with tent & car €16; open Feb-Oct)*, prettily set beneath trees off the N98 road, is a stone's throw – quite literally – from the sandy Plage du Camp Long; a snack kiosk is all that stands between the two.

Camping Agay Soleil *(☎ 04 94 82 00 79; 1152 blvd de la Plage; camping for 2 people with tent & car €20.20; reception open 9am-noon & 3pm-7.30pm daily Mar–mid-Nov)*, also signposted off the N98, is a small place with sandy tent sites by the water's edge.

Hostels A coastal youth hostel in Le Trayas, **Villa Solange** *(☎ 04 93 75 40 23, fax 04 93 75 43 45; 9 ave de la Véronèse; camping/dorm bed with breakfast €8.30/11.50; open mid-Feb–end Dec, closed 10am-5pm)* is on an idyllic site overlooking Ansc de la Figueirette. The hostel is 1.5km up the hill from the Auberge Blanche bus stop. Non-HI card-holders pay €2.90 more a night. Sheets cost €3.70. Telephone reservations are not accepted.

Hotels Opposite Château de la Napoule in La Napoule, **Hôtel La Calanque** *(☎ 04 93 49 95 11, fax 04 93 49 67 44; ave Henry Clews; doubles with/without sea view low season €50/39, high season €58/47)* is a two-star place.

Le Relais des Calanques *(☎ 04 94 44 14 06, fax 04 94 44 10 93; route des Escalles; doubles low/high season from €50/70)*, at the southern end of Le Trayas on the N98, offers striking views of the red-rocked sea. The hotel has a pool and private beach.

Getting There & Away

Bus Frequent daily buses run by **Société Varoise d'Autocars BELTRAME** *(☎ 04 94 83 87 63)* travel along the Corniche d'Estérel to/from Cannes to St-Raphaël (eight between 8am and 7pm Monday to Saturday, five on Sunday; plus seven additional buses daily from Le Trayas and/or Agay to St-Raphaël).

From Cannes, buses on this route (labelled 'Ligne de la Corniche d'Or' on timetables) stop at La Napoule, Théole-sur-Mer, Le Trayas, Agay, Cap du Dramont, Le Dramont and Boulouris.

Train There is a train station at Mandelieu-la-Napoule, 4km north of La Napoule, and at Théoule-sur-Mer, Le Trayas, Agay, Le Dramont and Boulouris. These stations are served by the Nice–St-Raphaël–Fréjus-Les Arcs–Draguignan coastal train route (nine to 11 trains between 8.15am and 8.45pm Monday to Saturday; less frequently on Sunday and in winter). There are many more trains from Cannes to St-Raphaël (see Getting There & Away under Cannes earlier in this chapter), from where there are regular buses.

ST-RAPHAËL

postcode 83700 • pop 31,196

The old port here was where Napoleon landed in 1799 upon his return from Egypt, and from where he set sail for exile in Elba in 1814. During WWII, it was one of the main landing bases of US and French troops in August 1944.

Created by Félix Martin (1842–99), mayor of the then-small fishing commune, St-Raphaël resort is 2km southeast of Fréjus. A fabulous place to be seen in the 1920s, the suburbs of contemporary St-Raphaël are so intertwined with those of its Roman neighbour Fréjus that the two places almost form a single town.

From St-Raphaël, it is a pleasant 10-minute walk west along blvd de la Libération to Fréjus Plage (beach). By bicycle, you can cycle westbound along the coast to Toulon on a silky-smooth, two-lane cycling track.

Orientation

The new centre of St-Raphaël is neatly packed between rue Waldeck Rousseau and promenade de Lattre de Tassigny, which leads west to the Vieux Port (old port); the old town is immediately north of rue Waldeck Rousseau off rue de la Liberté. St-Raphaël's beach activities sprawl as far east as Port Santa Lucia, a modern pleasure port 2km southeast along the coast from the centre.

Information

The **tourist office** *(☎ 04 94 19 52 52, fax 04 94 83 85 40; W www.saint-raphael.com; rue Waldeck Rousseau; open 9am-7pm daily July & Aug, 9am-12.30pm & 2pm-6.30pm Mon-Sat Sept-June)*, opposite the train station, organises two-hour guided tours (€2.29) of St-Raphaël on Wednesday, departing at 10am. Hotel rooms can be booked across the street through the accommodation service, **Centrale de Reservation: Terre et Mer** *(☎ 04 94 19 10 60, fax 04 94 19 10 67; e reservation@saint-raphael.com; rue Waldeck Rousseau; open 9am-12.30pm & 2pm-6.30pm Mon-Sat)*.

The **post office** *(ave Victor Hugo)* is east of the tourist office. Log in at **Cyber Bureau** *(☎ 04 94 95 29 36; e info@bureauworks.com; 123 rue Waldeck Rousseau; open 8.30am-noon & 2pm-7pm Mon-Fri, 8.30am-noon Sat)*, inside the train-station shopping mall.

Beaches & Boat Excursions

St-Raphaël has excellent sandy beaches including **Plage du Veillat**, the main beach. To the east, **Plage Beaurivage** is covered in small pebbles. You can parachute behind a speedboat and ride the waves in a rubber tyre from most beaches along this stretch of coastline.

Port Santa Lucia, farther east, is a water-sports hub. **Club Nautique St-Raphaël** *(☎ 04 94 95 11 66; blvd Général de Gaulle)* offers sailing, surfing and kayaking lessons. In July and August, it rents surfboards/catamarans for around €50/100 per five hours.

St-Raphaël is a leading **dive** centre, thanks in part to the **WWII shipwrecks** off the coast. Most diving clubs in town organise dives to the wrecks, ranging from a 42m-long US minesweeper to a landing craft destroyed by a rocket in 1944 during the Allied landings. **Plongée 83** *(☎ 04 94 95 27 18; 29 rue Waldeck Rousseau)*, the diving shop, runs night/all-day dives (€34/42) as well as baptism dives (€26). Equipment hire is an extra €12.

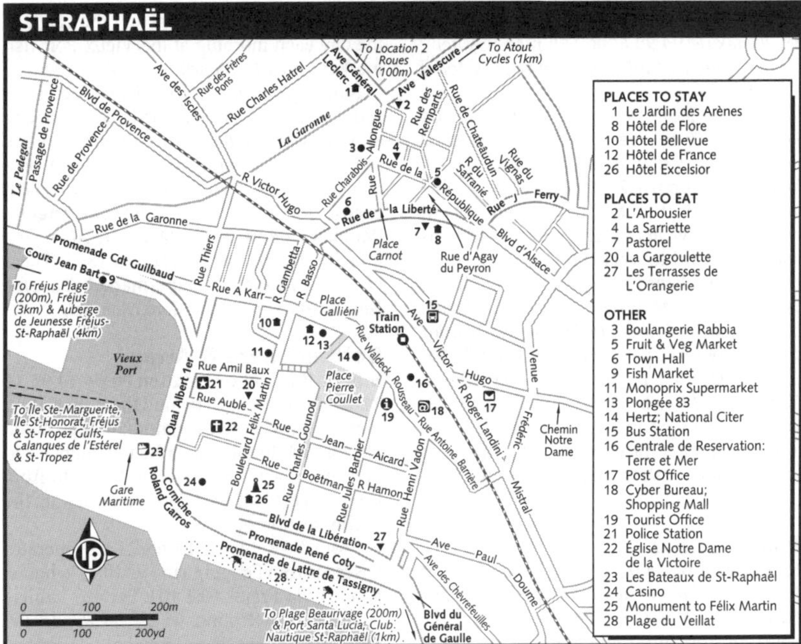

Les Bateaux de St-Raphaël (☎ *04 94 95 17 46*), based at the Gare Maritime at the Vieux Port, has daily boat excursions in summer to Île Ste-Marguerite (adult/two to nine years €22/11 return), the Fréjus and St-Tropez gulfs (€12/6), the Calanques de l'Estérel (€10/6) and Corniche de l'Estérel (€13/7). It also runs daily boats to/from St-Tropez (see the St-Tropez to Toulon chapter).

Special Events

St-Raphaël's strong fishing community honours its patron saint, St-Peter, every August with a two-day **Fête de la St-Pierre des Pêcheurs**. Local fishermen, dressed in traditional costume, joust Provençal-style from flat-bottomed boats moored in the harbour.

Every year, St-Raphaël hosts a number of Provençal **jousting competitions**; during the summer watch out for members of the Société des Joutes Raphaëloises (Raphaëloises Jousting Society) practising in boats around the Vieux Port.

Places to Stay

The Fréjus section later in this chapter lists camp sites.

Hostels Near Fréjus Ville, **Auberge de Jeunesse Fréjus-St-Raphaël** (☎ *04 94 53 18 75, fax 04 94 53 25 86; chemin du Counillier; dorm beds with breakfast €12*) is set in a seven-hectare park. HI cards are obligatory. Guests are evacuated and the hostel closed from 10am to 6pm; check in between 7.30am and 10am or 6pm and 9pm. From St-Raphaël bus station, bus No 7 departs at 8.30am and 6pm (6pm only Sunday) to Les Chênes stop, from where it is a 1km walk uphill along chemin du Counillier. From Fréjus' train or bus station, bus No 3 is the best option.

Hotels The cheapest joint in town must be **Le Jardin des Arènes** (☎ *04 94 95 06 34, fax 04 94 83 18 97; 31 ave du Général Leclerc; doubles with washbasin €21.24, with shower €30.34, with shower & toilet €39.48; reception open 7.30am-12.30pm & 1.30pm-11pm daily*).

Hôtel Bellevue (☎ *04 94 19 90 10, fax 04 94 19 90 11; 24 blvd Félix Martin; singles/doubles/triples from €34.30/40.40/45.77*) is a two-star place with good-value rooms; it also has rooms for four and five people.

Nearby is **Hôtel de France** *(☎ 04 94 95 19 20, fax 04 94 95 61 84; 25 place Galliéni; singles/doubles/triples with shower & toilet €40/50/63)*.

Hôtel de Flore *(☎ 04 94 95 90 00, fax 04 94 83 75 57; 56 rue de la Liberté; singles/doubles/triples low season from €52/62/72, high season from €75/89/98)* is very blue and mirrored. It touts four different sets of rates plus low and high season, and runs some good-value weekend deals.

Hôtel Excelsior *(☎ 04 94 95 02 42, fax 04 94 95 33 82; W www.excelsior-hotel.com; promenade René Coty; singles with washbasin/shower low season €40/50, high season €50/65, doubles with bathroom low/high season from €105/120)*, by the seashore, is an elegant old pile next to the casino, graced with a beautiful tea terrace overlooking the azure sea. Its bathroomless single rooms are extraordinarily good value.

Places to Eat

La Sarriette *(☎ 04 94 19 28 13; 45 rue de la République; menu €15)* is a pretty place tucked in the shade of a plane tree in the heart of the old town. Dishes are well doused with Provençal herbs and spices.

Pastorel *(☎ 04 94 95 02 36; 54 rue de la Liberté; lunch/dinner menu €16/28)*, a traditional place dating from 1922, is an institution. Its *menu du marché* (market menu) is well worth every cent, as is the jumbo *aïoli* it makes every Friday. Tempting cooking smells waft from here.

La Gargoulette *(☎ 04 94 95 48 18; 29 rue Pierre Aublé; menus €30.50 & €39.63)*, known for its truffle *menu* in season, also cooks imaginative fish dishes such as monkfish braised in *jus de coquillages* (shellfish juice) and sea bream carpaccio.

L'Arbousier *(☎ 04 94 95 25 00; 4 ave Valescure; lunch menu €26, evening menus €34, €42 & €55)* has a melon-pink and baby-blue facade, a fabulous flowery garden to dine in, and is this seaside town's gastronomic choice.

Les Terrasses de l'Orangerie *(☎ 04 94 83 10 50; promenade René Coty; full meal from €20)*, a lovely brasserie that has looked out to sea since the *belle époque* days of F Scott Fitzgerald et al, is a fine seaside dining spot.

Self-Catering A good **fruit and vegetable market** fills place de la République and place Victor Hugo. Fishmongers sell the catch of the day each morning at the Vieux Port **fish market** *(cours Jean Bart)*.

Stock up on a *tarte Tropézienne* (a creamy, sponge cake sandwich topped with sugar and almonds), *farinette Niçois* (Niçois bread), *pain blanc bio* (organic white bread) or a choice of olive, bacon bits, anchovy or goat cheese *fougasse* at splendid **Boulangerie Rabbia** *(☎ 04 94 95 07 82; 29 rue Allongue)*, a family bakery dating back to 1885. There is also a **Monoprix supermarket** *(58 blvd Félix Martin; open 9am-8pm Mon-Sat)*.

Getting There & Away

Bus St-Raphaël **bus station** *(☎ 04 94 95 16 71; ave Victor Hugo)*, behind the train station (accessible via the escalators on the station platforms), doubles as Fréjus' main bus station too. For information on buses to/from Fréjus see Getting There & Away in the Frèjus section next.

From St-Raphaël, **Estérel Cars** operates buses to/from Draguignan (€5.40, 1¼ hours, hourly) via Fréjus (€1.10). **Société Varoise d'Autocars Beltrame** *(☎ 04 94 83 87 63)* runs buses along the Corniche de l'Estérel (see that section earlier in the chapter) to Cannes. **Sodetrav** *(☎ 04 94 97 88 51)* runs buses to St-Tropez (€8.40, 1¼ hours, eight to 10 daily) via Port Grimaud or Grimaud (€7.50, 55 minutes) and Ste-Maxime (€4.20, 35 minutes). Services are less frequent in winter.

Train There is a frequent service to/from Nice (every 30 minutes) from the **Gare de St-Raphaël-Valescure** *(rue Waldeck Rousseau)*. Some of the trains stop at the village train stations along the Corniche d'Estérel (see that section).

Getting Around

Major car rental agencies are clustered around the train station: Budget, ADA and Avis have an office in the station; Hertz and National Citer are opposite. **Location 2 Roues** *(☎ 04 94 53 65 99; 199 ave Général Leclerc)* rents 50/100cc scooters for €30/40 a day.

Location 2 Roues also has mountain bikes to rent for €12/13 per half-/full day. Alternatively, go to **Atout Cycles** *(☎ 04 94 95 56 91; 330 blvd Jean Moulin)* where you can pick up a pair of wheels for €10/15/23 per half-day/day/weekend.

FRÉJUS

postcode 83600 • pop 47,897 • elevation 250m

Fréjus, first settled by Massiliots (the Greek colonists from Marseilles) and then colonised by Julius Caesar around 49 BC as Forum Julii, is known for its Roman ruins. Once an important port, the town was sacked by various invaders from the 10th century onwards. Much of the town's commercial activity ceased after its harbour silted up in the 16th century.

Fréjus' golden-sand beach Fréjus Plage is lined with buildings from the 1950s. Its chic port – full of expensive places to eat offering every shellfish imaginable at unimaginable prices – was built in the 1980s.

Place Paul Albert Février, in the old heart of Fréjus Ville, hosts various markets: flowers on Wednesday, Saturday and Sunday morning; fruit and veg every morning, Tuesday to Sunday, June to September; and a Provençal market with a bit of everything on Wednesday and Saturday morning, year round. You'll find a *marché nocturnal* (night market) spilling across the sand at Fréjus Plage most evenings, June to September.

Orientation

Fréjus comprises hillside Fréjus Ville, 3km from the seafront, and Fréjus Plage, on the Gulf of Fréjus. Fréjus' modern port is at the western end of blvd de la Libération and its continuation, blvd d'Alger. The Roman remains are almost all in Fréjus Ville.

Information

Fréjus tourist office *(☎ 04 94 51 83 83, fax 04 91 51 00 26; 🅦 www.ville-frejus.fr; 325 rue Jean Jaurès; open 9am-noon & 2pm-7pm Mon-Sat, 10am-noon & 3pm-6pm Sun June–mid-Sept, 9am-noon & 2pm-6pm Mon-Sat mid-Sept–Apr)* runs a summertime **kiosk** *(☎ 04 94 51 48 42; open 10am-12.30pm & 3pm-6.30pm daily June–mid-Sept)* on the beach, opposite 11 blvd de la Libération. Its **annexe** *(☎ 04 94 17 27 93; Fréjus Port; open 8.30am-12.30pm & 1.30pm-5.30pm Mon & Wed, 8.30am-12.30pm & 1.30pm-4.30pm Fri, year round)*, distributes maps and takes bookings for guided tours of Fréjus' archaeological treasures (adult/12 to 18 years €5/3) and thematic nature walks in the Massif de l'Estérel (adult/under 12 €8/5). Seasonal themes include the mimosa (March), the Estérel at sunset (July), the war cry of the mating stag (October) and mushrooms (November).

For changing money **Banque National de Paris** *(BNP; 232 rue Jean Jaurès)* is convenient. Check email at the **post office** *(ave Aristide Briand; open 8.30am-6.30pm Mon-Fri, 8.30am- noon Sat)* or **Esp@ce Cyber** *(☎ 04 94 52 17 16; 🅔 info@okdak.com; 220 ave de Port-Fréjus; open 9am-1pm & 2pm-9pm Mon-Sat)* at the port.

Roman Ruins

West of Fréjus' old city, past the ancient **Porte des Gaules**, is the mostly rebuilt 1st- and 2nd-century **Les Arènes** *(amphitheatre; ☎ 04 94 51 34 31; rue Henri Vadon; admission free; open 9am-noon & 2pm-6pm Wed-Mon Apr-Nov, to 4.30pm Dec-Mar)*. It once sat an audience of 10,000 and is used for rock concerts and bullfights today.

At the southeastern edge of the old city is the 3rd-century **Porte d'Orée** *(rue des Moulins)*, the only arcade of the monumental Roman thermal baths still standing. North of the old town are the remains of a **Roman theatre** *(☎ 04 94 53 58 75; rue du Théâtre Romain; admission free; open 10am-1pm & 2.30pm-6.30pm Wed-Mon Apr-Nov, 10am-noon or 12.30pm & 1.30pm-5.30pm Wed-Mon Dec-Mar)*. Part of the stage and the outer walls are all that can be seen today.

Northeast, towards La Tour de Mare, you pass a remaining section of a 40km **aqueduc** *(aqueduct; ave du 15 Corps d'Armée)*, which once carried water to Roman Fréjus. Continuing 500m farther north along ave du 15 Corps d'Armée, across the roundabout, onto ave du General Calliès, you reach **Villa Aurèlienne**, built in 1880, that today hosts temporary photography exhibitions. In its 22-hectare park there's another section of the aqueduct, complete with five arches.

Le Groupe Épiscopal

In the centre of town, occupying the site of a Roman temple, is an Episcopal ensemble *(☎ 04 94 51 26 30; 58 rue de Fleury; adult/12-18 yrs €4/2.50; open 9am-7pm daily Apr-Sept, 9am-noon & 2pm-5pm Tues-Sun Oct-Mar)* comprising an 11th- and 12th-century **cathedral** *(58 rue de Fleury)* that was one of the first Gothic buildings in the region (though it retains certain Roman features). The carved wooden doors at the main

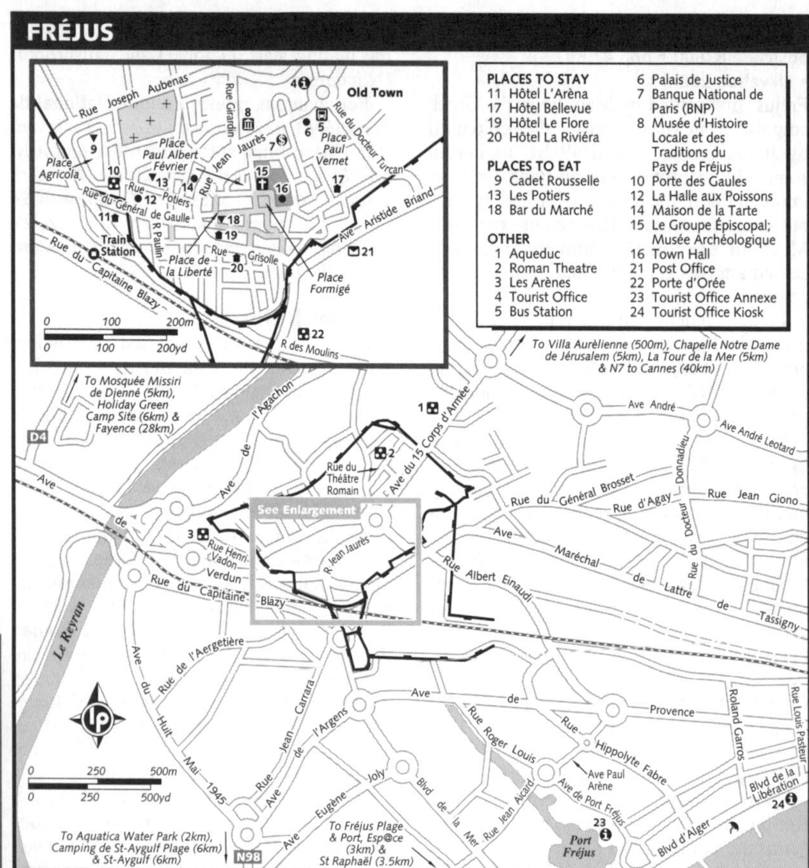

entrance were added during the Renaissance. Concerts are occasionally held here.

Left of the cathedral is the octagonal 5th-century **baptistry**, with a Roman column at each of its eight corners. Stairs from the narthex lead up to the stunning 11th- and 13th-century **cloister**, whose features include some of the columns of the Roman temple and painted wooden ceilings from the 14th and 15th centuries. It looks onto a fine courtyard with a well-tended garden and well.

Museums

Adjoining Fréjus' episcopal treasures is the **Musée Archéologique** (*☎ 04 94 52 15 78; place Calvini; admission free; open 10am-1pm & 2.30pm-6.30pm Mon & Wed-Sat Apr-Oct, 10am-noon & 1.30pm-5.30pm Nov-Mar*). A marble statue of Hermes, a head of Jupiter and a magnificent 3rd-century mosaic depicting a leopard are displayed here.

The town's history is illustrated in the **Musée d'Histoire Locale et des Traditions du Pays de Fréjus** (*Local History & Fréjus Traditions Museum; ☎ 04 94 51 64 01; 153 rue Jean Jaurès; admission free; open 10am-1pm & 2.30pm-6.30pm Mon & Wed-Sat July & Aug, 10am-1pm Mon & Wed-Fri, 10am-1pm & 2.30pm-6.30pm Sat Apr, June, Sept & Oct, 1.30pm-5.30pm Mon-Fri, 9.30am-12.30pm & 1.30pm-5.30pm Sat Nov-Mar*).

Chapelle Notre Dame de Jérusalem

This small chapel (*☎ 04 94 53 27 06; ave François Nicolaï; open 1.30pm-5.30pm Mon &*

Wed-Fri, 9.30am-12.30pm & 1.30pm-5.30pm Sat Nov-Apr, 2.30pm-6.30pm Mon & Wed-Fri, 10am-1pm & 2.30pm-8.30pm Sat May-Oct) was one of the last pieces of work embarked upon by Jean Cocteau (1889–1963). Cocteau, best known for the fishermen's chapel he decorated farther up the coast in Villefranche-sur-Mer (see the Nice to Menton chapter), began work on Chapelle Notre Dame in Fréjus in 1961. It was not completed until 1988 however when Cocteau's legal heir, Édouard Dermit, completed his former companion's work. The altar is made from a millstone.

The chapel is about 5km northeast of the old city in the quarter of La Tour de Mare (served by bus No 13 – see Getting Around), on the N7 towards Cannes.

Mosquée Missiri de Djenné

Along route de Bagnols-en-Forêt (the D4 towards Fayence), 5km north of Fréjus, is this mosque *(rue des Combattants d'Afrique du Nord)*, built in 1930 for Sudanese troops stationed at a marine base in Fréjus. It is a replica of a mosque in Djenné, Mali.

Aquatica

You can bomb down giant water slides, ride rubber rings and go wave-crazy on dozens of different wet and slippery rides and attractions at this large water park *(☎ 04 94 51 82 51; W www.parc-aquatica.com; adult/under 12 €22/18; open 10am-7pm daily July & Aug, to 6pm June & Sept)*, out of town on the southbound N98.

Places to Stay

Hostellers note: it is equally feasible to stay in the hostel in St-Raphaël (see Hostels under St-Raphaël earlier).

Camping Fréjus has a dozen or so camping grounds:

Holiday Green *(☎ 04 94 19 88 30, fax 04 94 19 88 31; rue des Combattants d'Afrique du Nord; camping for 2 adults, tent & car low/high season €19.60/28; open Apr-Sept)*, on the D4 towards Fayence, is a four-star place, 7km from the beach but with its own large pool.

Camping de St-Aygulf Plage *(☎ 04 94 17 62 49, fax 04 94 81 03 16; 270 ave Salvarelli; camping for 2 adults, tent & car low/high season €11.80/23; open Apr-Oct)* in St-Aygulf, south of Fréjus, is a huge place with 1100 tent sites practically on the beach.

Hotels In Fréjus Ville, **Hôtel La Riviéra** *(☎ 04 94 51 31 46, fax 04 94 17 18 34; 90 rue Grisolle; doubles with washbasin €26.85, with shower €31.40, with shower & toilet €36, 3- or 4-person rooms with bathroom €39.50, menu €11)* is a popular backpacker's choice. Its ground-floor restaurant serves a hearty, guaranteed-to-fill *plat du jour* (€8.40) which includes 25cL of wine.

Hôtel Bellevue *(☎ 04 94 17 16 10; place Paul Vernet; singles/doubles/triples with washbasin €32/35/40, with shower & toilet €38/40/45)* is a zero-star, 11-room place overlooking men playing *pétanque* and a large car park. Reception is in the adjoining bar.

Hôtel Le Flore *(☎ 04 94 51 38 35, fax 04 94 52 28 20; 35 rue Grisolle; doubles from €50)* is an unmomentous two-star choice, again in the centre of town.

Hôtel L'Arèna *(☎ 04 94 17 09 40, fax 04 94 52 01 52; W www.arena-hotel.com; 145 rue du Général de Gaulle; singles/doubles/triples/quads low season from €61/80/100/105, mid-season from €61/86/115/120, high season from €77/95/135/150)*, a three-star Logis de France inn with charming rooms, is where Napoleon stayed on his way through town in October 1799. The hotel is known for its excellent **restaurant** *(starters/mains €20/25)*.

Places to Eat

For a handful of cafés and restaurants, with a view of bobbing boats, try Port Fréjus. In Fréjus Ville, **Bar du Marché** *(place de la Liberté)* serves giant pizzas and bowlfuls of *moules frites* (mussels and fries) on its busy terrace. The restaurant inside Hôtel L'Arèna is a delicious upmarket choice.

Cadet Rousselle *(☎ 04 94 53 36 92; place Agricola; menu €10.50)*, with dozens of different sweet/savoury crepes (from €3.10/3.25), makes for a cheap lunch.

Les Potiers *(☎ 04 94 51 33 74; 135 rue Potiers; menu €21.50)*, tucked down a quiet narrow backstreet, is a quaint spot with desserts such as a spiced wine and strawberry soup with old-fashioned rice pudding, or *crème brulée* flavoured with lavender, orange, rosemary or chocolate.

Maison de la Tarte *(☎ 04 94 51 17 34; 33 rue Jean Jaurès)*, a top-quality boulangerie-cum-tarterie, sells well-filled baguettes and a peachy array of sweet tarts (peach, strawberry, pear and chocolate, pine kernel, fig and almond, and so on), sold by the slice (€1.90 to €2.20) to take away. Be prepared to queue.

Buy fresh fish at **La Halle aux Poissons** *(☎ 04 94 51 36 44; 122 rue du Général de Gaulle)*.

Getting There & Away

Bus Fréjus **bus station** *(☎ 04 94 53 78 46; place Paul Vernet)* – a humble series of bus stops around a roundabout – is served by buses to/from Draguignan (€5.40, one hour, hourly) and buses to/from St-Raphaël (€1.10, 20 or 27 minutes). Estérel Bus No 5 links the bus station with St-Raphaël's bus station and Fréjus' train station. Buses Nos 6 and 7 link place Paul Vernet and St-Raphaël – No 6 via the coastal road and No 7 via ave de Provence.

Train The town's **train station** *(rue du Capitaine Blazy)* is on the Nice–Marseilles train route, although few trains stop here beyond services to/from St-Raphaël (€1.20, two minutes, hourly).

Getting Around

Bus No 6 links the beaches of Fréjus-Plage with place Paul Vernet in Fréjus-Ville. Bus No 13 runs between the Fréjus train station, the bus station and Cocteau's Chapelle Notre Dame de Jérusalem. Tickets can be purchased from bus drivers (€1.10/8.40 for one/carnet of 10).

Close to the beach, **Holiday Bikes** *(☎ 04 94 52 30 65; ⓔ hb-frejus@wanadoo.fr; 41 blvd Severin Decuers)*, overlooking rond point des Moulins, rents cars from around 200FF per day and 50/100cc scooters for €35/45 per day.

Holiday Bikes also rents road/mountain bikes for €8/10 per half-day or €14/20 per 24 hours.

CANNES AREA

St-Tropez to Toulon

In 1956 St-Tropez was the setting for the film *Et Dieu Créa la Femme* (And God Created Woman), starring Brigitte Bardot. Its stunning success brought about St-Tropez's rise to stardom – or destruction – depending on your viewpoint. But one thing is clear: the peaceful little fishing village of St-Tropez, somewhat isolated from the rest of the Côte d'Azur at the end of its own peninsula, suddenly became the favourite of the jet set. The Tropeziens have thrived on their sexy image ever since.

Inland from St-Tropez, medieval Les Arcs-sur-Argens is equidistant (31km) from the coastal towns of St-Raphaël and Ste-Maxime. Ten kilometres north is Pays Dracénois (literally 'country of Draguignan people'), with Draguignan at its heart, which embraces some of the region's least-spoilt villages.

West from St-Tropez sprawls a wild, remote and heavily forested massif, smothered with fine pine, chestnut and cork oak trees. Its vegetation makes it appear almost black and gives rise to the name Massif des Maures, which is derived from the Provençal word *mauro* (dark pine wood). The arc-shaped massif stretches from Fréjus in the northeast to pretty palm-tree lined Hyères – a launch pad for day trips to the golden Île d'Hyères – in the southwest.

Toulon, 20km farther west along the coast, is a base for the French navy's Mediterranean fleet and as such is France's most important naval port. The city's run-down centre is grim compared to Nice, Cannes or even Marseilles. Continuing west, the islands off Toulon's shores, dubbed the Îles du Fun (Islands of Fun), have been transformed into concrete playgrounds by 1950s French industrialist Paul Ricard.

Highlights

- View works by the world's great pointillists, the Nabis, Fauvists and cubists at St-Tropez's Musée de l'Annonciade
- Go island-hopping around the golden Îles d'Hyères
- Walk around the Chartreuse de la Verne monastery in the Massif des Maures
- Window-shop in St-Tropez and sip *pastis* at its Vieux Port
- Explore the drowsy hill-top villages and abbeys of the northern Var; shop for black truffles in Aups, wine in La Celle and terracotta tiles in Salernes
- Sample a dozen different Côtes de Provence wines in Les Arcs-sur-Argens, then lunch at the Domaine de la Maurette

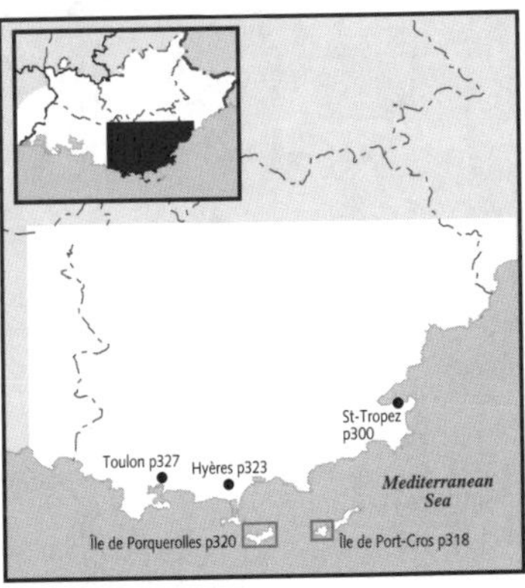

Food Highlights

Tarte Tropézienne – sponge-cake sandwich filled with custard-cream and topped with sugar and almonds

Marrons glacés, glace aux marrons glacés, crème de marrons and **liqueur de châtaignes** – candied chestnuts, chestnut ice cream, chestnut cream & chestnut liqueur

Bouillabaisse from Toulon – Provençal fish stew with potatoes at L'Oursinade on Cap de Carqueiranne

St-Tropez & Around

ST-TROPEZ

postcode 83990 • pop 5542

Attempts to keep St-Tropez small and exclusive have created at least one tangible result: huge traffic queues into town. Yachts, way out of proportion to the size of the old harbour, chased away the simple fishing boats a long time ago. Artists jostle each other for

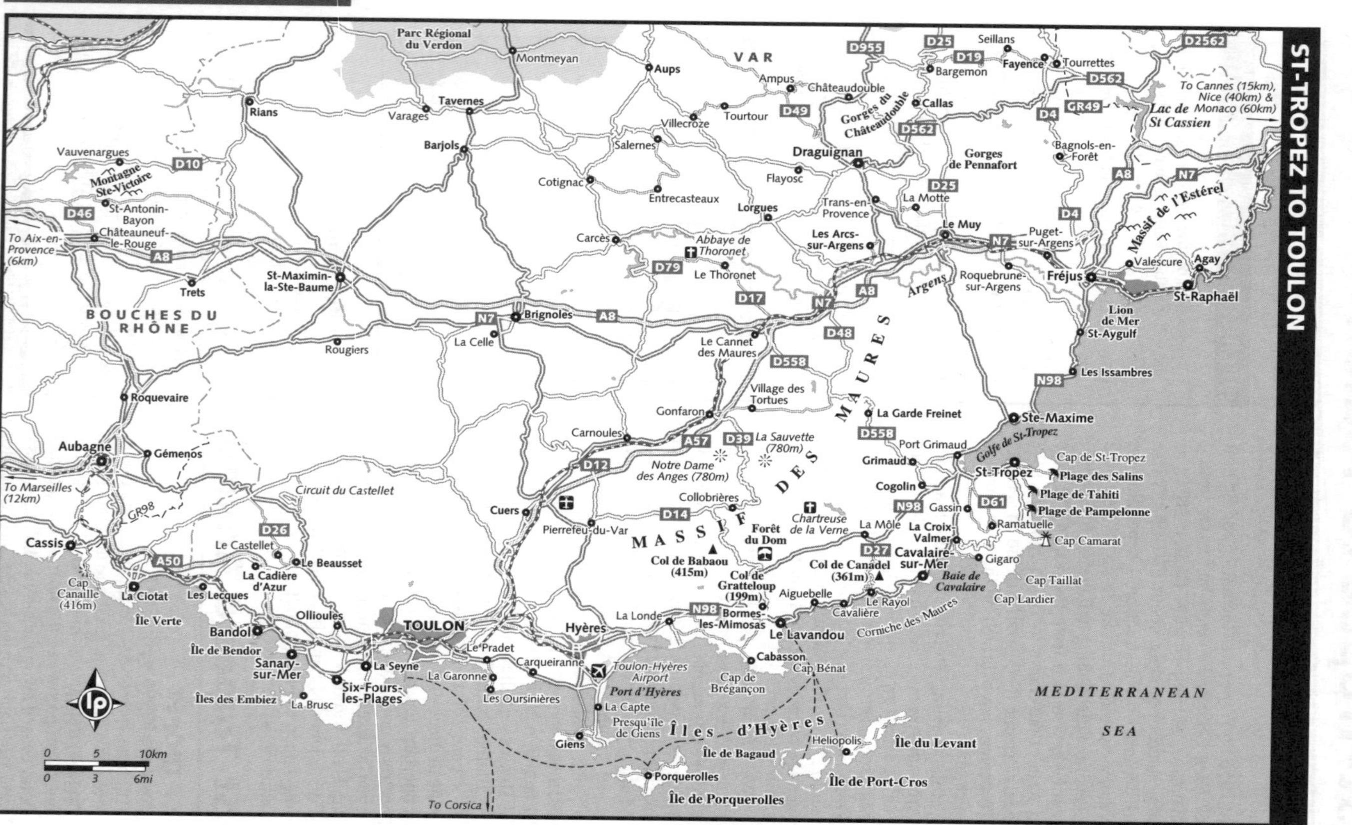
ST-TROPEZ TO TOULON
Parc Régional du Verdon
Montmeyan
Aups
VAR
Ampus
Châteaudouble
Gorges du Châteaudouble
Seillans
Fayence
Tourrettes
Bargemon
Callas
To Cannes (15km), Nice (40km) & Monaco (60km)
Lac de St Cassien
Bagnols-en-Forêt
Gorges de Pennafort
Massif de l'Estérel
Rians
Varages
Tavernes
Villecroze
Tourtour
Barjols
Salernes
Draguignan
Vauvenargues
Montagne Ste-Victoire
Cotignac
Flayosc
La Motte
Entrecasteaux
Lorgues
Trans-en-Provence
St-Antonin-Bayon
Châteauneuf-le-Rouge
To Aix-en-Provence (6km)
Carcès
Abbaye de Thoronet
Les Arcs-sur-Argens
Le Muy
Puget-sur-Argens
Valescure
Agay
Trets
St-Maximin-la-Ste-Baume
Le Thoronet
Argens
Roquebrune-sur-Argens
Fréjus
St-Raphaël
BOUCHES DU RHÔNE
Brignoles
La Celle
Rougiers
Le Cannet des Maures
Lion de Mer
St-Aygulf
Les Issambres
Village des Tortues
Roquevaire
Gonfaron
La Garde Freinet
Ste-Maxime
Carnoules
La Sauvette (780m)
MASSIF DES MAURES
Aubagne
Gémenos
Port Grimaud
Golfe de St-Tropez
Notre Dame des Anges (780m)
Grimaud
Cap de St-Tropez
St-Tropez
Plage des Salins
To Marseilles (12km)
Circuit du Castellet
Collobrières
Cogolin
Plage de Tahiti
GR98
Cuers
Chartreuse de la Verne
Gassin
Plage de Pampelonne
Forêt du Dom
La Môle
La Croix-Valmer
Ramatuelle
Cassis
Le Castellet
Pierrefeu-du-Var
Cap Camarat
Le Beausset
Col de Babaou (415m)
Col de Canadel (361m)
Cavalaire-sur-Mer
Gigaro
Cap Canaille (416m)
La Ciotat
Les Lecques
La Cadière d'Azur
Col de Gratteloup (199m)
Baie de Cavalaire
Cap Taillat
Aiguebelle
Le Rayol
Cap Lardier
Île Verte
Ollioules
La Londe
Bormes-les-Mimosas
Cavalière
Bandol
TOULON
Hyères
Le Lavandou
Corniche des Maures
Île de Bendor
Le Pradet
Sanary-sur-Mer
La Seyne
Carqueiranne
Cabasson
Cap Bénat
La Garonne
Toulon-Hyères Airport
Cap de Brégançon
Six-Fours-les-Plages
Îles des Embiez
La Brusc
Les Oursinières
Port d'Hyères
MEDITERRANEAN SEA
La Capte
Presqu'île de Giens
Îles d'Hyères
Giens
Heliopolis
Île du Levant
Île de Bagaud
Porquerolles
Île de Port-Cros
Île de Porquerolles
To Corsica
0 5 10km
0 3 6mi
D955
D25
D19
D2562
D562
D49
D4
GR49
D562
D10
D25
A8
N7
D46
D4
A8
N7
D79
D17
A8
N7
D48
D558
N98
D558
D39
A57
D12
D26
D14
N98
D61
D27
A50
N98

easel space along the quay, and in summer there's little of the intimate village air that artists such as the pointillist Paul Signac found so alluring.

Still, sitting in a café on place des Lices in late May, watching people playing *pétanque* in the shade of the age-old plane trees, is pleasant enough – as is that seductive image of St-Tropez from out at sea. Arriving by boat, you see the yellow-and-orange church tower crowned with a Provençal campanile standing majestically over the sloping roofs and sprawling citadel.

The food, flower, clothing and antique market extravaganza that fills place des Lices on Tuesday and Saturday morning is unforgettable. Equally memorable is the spectacle of rich people dining aboard their floating palaces, within spitting distance of the crowds gathered on the portside to gawk at them twirling their silver knives and forks.

Tropeziens call St-Tropez 'St-Trop' (literally 'St-Too Much'). Beautifully apt.

History

The Greeks founded Athenopolis here and were followed by the Romans in 31 BC who called it Heraclea. St-Tropez gained its contemporary name in AD 68 when a boat landed on its shores bearing the decapitated body of the Roman officer Torpes, whom Nero had beheaded in Pisa for his conversion to Christianity. The village adopted the headless Torpes as its saint.

A syphilis-ridden Maupassant (1850–93) arrived in St-Tropez in 1887. Signac (1863–1935) followed in his boat *L'Olympia* five years later, exclaiming upon arrival, *'Je ne fais pas escale. Je me fixe'* ('I'm not just stopping here. I'm staying'). Sexy St-Tropez has not looked back since, with visitors such as Colette, Pagnol, Matisse, Marlène Dietrich, Bardot, Johnny Hallyday, Pink Floyd ('As I reach for a peach/Slide a line down behind a sofa in San Tropez'), George Michael, Joan Collins, Mohammad Al-Fayed...

And it's not only glitzy, but explosive too: Torpedoes have been manufactured at the Usine de Gassin in St-Tropez since 1912.

Orientation

St-Tropez lies at the southern end of the narrow Golfe de St-Tropez, within easy reach of the Massif des Maures. The old city is packed between quai Jean Jaurès, the main quay of the Vieux Port (old port); place des Lices, a vast shady rectangular square a few blocks inland; and what remains of the 16th-century citadel overlooking the town from the northeast. Visiting floating palaces moor in the old port alongside quai Suffren.

Information

Tourist Offices City tours on foot (adult/under 12 €5/free; 10.30am Thursday April to September) depart from in front of the **tourist office** *(☎ 04 94 97 45 21, fax 04 94 97 82 66; W www.ot-saint-tropez.com; quai Jean Jaurès; open 9.30am-8.30pm daily July & Aug, 9.30am-12.30pm & 2pm-7pm daily Sept, 9am-noon & 2pm-6pm daily Oct-June)*.

Tours of Gassin and Ramatuelle are by prior arrangement only.

Money Portside **Change Cambio** *(18 rue Allard; open 9.15am-7pm daily)* exchanges currency and cashes travellers cheque with no commission.

Post & Communications The St-Tropez **post office** *(place Celli; open 8.30am-noon & 2pm-5pm Mon-Fri, 8.30am-noon Sat)* is not far from the bus station and port. Internet cafés include **Le Girafe** *(☎ 04 94 97 13 09; 36 rue du Portail Neuf)*, which charges €2.50 for 15 minutes, then €0.12 per minute; and **FCDCI** *(☎ 04 94 54 84 81; e infos@fcdci.com; 2 ave Paul Roussel; open 9.30am-12.30pm & 2.30pm-7.30pm daily)* where one hour online costs €9.

Laundry Wash your glad rags for €8 a 7kg wash at **La Bugade** *(5 rue Quaranta; open 7am-9pm daily)*. At the port, **Laverie du Port** *(13 quai de l'Épi; open 7am-9pm daily)* charges €5/12.50 per 5/16.5kg wash.

Medical Services For medical emergencies **Hôpital de St-Tropez** *(☎ 04 94 79 47 00; ave Foch)* runs a 24-hour emergency service *(☎ 04 94 79 47 30)*.

Walking Tour

Vieux Port – the heart of Tropezien life – is as good a place as any to kick off a stroll. On quai Suffren, a **statue of the Bailli de Suffren** cast from a 19th-century cannon peers out to sea. The bailiff of Suffren (1729–88) was a sailor who fought with a

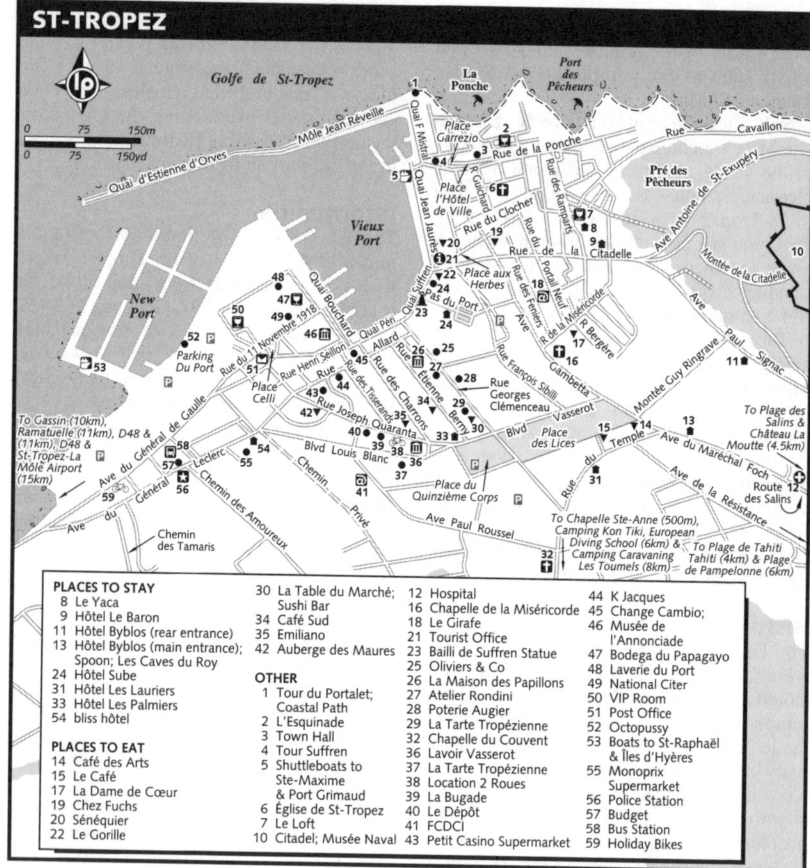

Tropezien crew against Britain and Prussia during the Seven Years' War.

In a backstreet, a block southwest, is **La Maison des Papillons** *(House of Butterflies; ☎ 04 94 97 63 45; 9 rue Étienne Berny; adult/under 10 €3.05/free; open 10am-noon & 2pm-7pm Wed-Mon June-Aug, 10am-noon & 2pm-6pm Wed-Mon Sept-May)*. Some 4500 of the creatures are pinned to the wall. The collection of European species is that of Dany Lartigue, son of Riviera photographer Jacques Henri Lartigue (1894-1986). Dany – by appointment – runs guided tours of the cottage-museum. It was the former Lartigue home and family photos line the staircase.

The old fishing quarter of **La Ponche** is northeast of the Vieux Port. To get to the harbour (where Signac and company docked) from quai Suffren, walk to the northern end of its continuations – quai Jean Jaurès and quai Frédéric Mistral. At the 15th-century **Tour du Portalet**, turn right (east) to the sandy fishing cove. From here, a coastal path snakes its way around the St-Tropez peninsula (see Coastal Walks later).

From the southern end of quai Frédéric Mistral, place Garrezio sprawls east from the 10th-century **Tour Suffren** to place de l'Hôtel de Ville. From here, rue Guichard leads southeast to the 18th-century **Église de St-Tropez**, built in 1785 in an Italian Baroque style on place de l'Ormeau. Inside is the bust of St-Tropez, honoured during Les Bravades (see Special Events later).

A 16th-century **citadel** dominates the hillside overlooking St-Tropez to the east.

Steps lead from the eastern end of rue de la Citadelle, up montée de la Citadelle, to the citadel. Its former dungeons house a **Musée Naval** *(☎ 04 94 97 59 43; adult/8-18 yrs €3/2; open 10am-12.30pm & 1.30pm-5.30pm or 6.30pm daily)*, dedicated to the town's maritime history and the Allied landings in August 1944.

Back on rue de la Citadelle, and a few blocks south, is **Chapelle de la Miséricorde** *(rue Miséricorde)*, built in 1645, with its pretty bell tower and dome, decorated with coloured ceramic tiles. One block farther south is **place des Lices**, whose 200m length is lined with plane trees and *pétanque* players. The 1757 **Chapelle du Couvent** *(ave Augustin Grangeon)* and **Chapelle Ste-Anne** *(ave Augustin Grangeon)*, built in 1618, lie south of here. Inside Chapelle Ste-Anne, there is an impressive collection of ex-votive paintings and centuries-old miniature boats given by Tropezien fishermen. They can be viewed once a year – 26 July, the feast day of St Anne.

Musée de l'Annonciade

The graceful Musée de l'Annonciade *(☎ 04 94 97 04 01; place Georges Grammont; adult/under 10 €4.60/free; open 10am-noon & 3pm-7pm Wed-Mon June-Sept, 10am-noon & 2pm-6pm Wed-Mon Oct & Dec)*, in an early-16th-century chapel at the Vieux Port, contains an impressive collection of modern art, with works by Matisse, Bonnard, Dufy, Derain, Rouault and Signac.

The pointillist collection on the 2nd floor includes Signac's *St-Tropez, L'Orage* (1895), *St-Tropez, Le Quai* (1899) and *St-Tropez, Le Sentier Côtier* (1901). Another room is dedicated to the self-named Nabis group and displays works by painters such as Vuillard, Bonnard, Maurice Denis and Valloton. A third room features the Fauvists: Matisse spent the summer of 1904 in St-Tropez, starting preliminary studies for *Luxe, Calme et Volupté*. Cubists George Braque and Picasso are also represented.

In summer, art exhibitions are also held in the 19th-century **Lavoir Vasserot** *(rue Quaranta; admission free)*, the former communal washhouse. Genre of the exhibitions and opening hours vary.

Beaches

About 4km southeast of the town is the start of the magnificent sandy **Plage de Tahiti**, and its continuation, **Plage de Pampelonne**, overlooking Baie de Pampelonne (Pampelonne Bay). The beach runs for about 9km between Cap du Pinet and Cap Camarat, a rocky cape dominated by France's second-tallest **lighthouse** *(☎ 04 94 79 80 65; admission free; open 2pm-5pm or 6pm daily)*. Fabulous views can be enjoyed from the platform at the top of 84 steps. To get to the beach on foot, head out of town along ave de la Résistance (south of place des Lices) to route de la Belle Isnarde and then route de Tahiti. Otherwise, the bus to Ramatuelle stops at points along a road that runs about 1km inland from the beach.

Closer to St-Tropez, **Plage des Salins** is a long, wide sandy beach 4.5km east of town at the southern foot of Cap des Salins. To get here, follow route des Salins to its end. En route you pass **La Treille Muscate** (The Wine Trellis), a rambling villa framed with red-ochre columns wrapped in honeysuckle. Here in 1927 Colette wrote *La Naissance du Jour*, which evokes a 1920s unspoilt St-Tropez. She left town in 1938.

At the northern end of Plage des Salins, on a rock jutting out to sea, is the **tomb of Émile Olivier** (1825–1913), who served as first minister to Napoleon III until his exile in 1870. Olivier's 17-volume *L'Empire Libéral* is preserved in the library of **Château La Moutte**, his former home on Cap des Salins. Musical concerts are also held here in summer. Its unmarked entrance is on chemin de la Moutte. A sandy track leads from the car park at the end of chemin de la Moutte to the beach.

Olivier's sea-facing tomb looks out towards **La Tête de Chien** (The Dog's Head), named after the legendary dog who, along with a cock, was flung into the boat carrying St-Torpes' remains, to eat the body Nero had decapitated. Thankfully for the Tropeziens, neither did, and Torpes became their saint. Farther south, **Pointe du Capon** is a beautiful cape crisscrossed with walking trails. BB – Brigitte Bardot – lives here.

Catch 22

Tuesday is a tricky day for St-Tropez–bound tourists – its museums are shut but the place des Lices market is on.

Museums are closed every day in November.

Beach Legends

If you really want to spot a star, hang out at **La Voile Rouge** *(The Red Sail; ☎ 04 94 79 84 34; route des Tamaris; open Apr-Sept)* or **Le Club 55** *(☎ 04 94 55 55 55; 43 blvd Patch; open lunch only Mar–mid-Nov; advance reservations essential)*, St-Tropez's two most legendary bars on Plage de Pampelonne, southeast of town. Both jet-set joints, bang-slap on the sand, have played decadent host to celebrities since the 1950s.

Vadim shot parts of Bardot in *And God Created Woman* at La Voile Rouge (little more than a beach hut at the time) in 1955, while his film crew haggled for drinks at Le Club 55 (hence its name, so the story goes). Boobs and bums were flashed here first, with the advent of topless bathers at La Voile Rouge in 1970 (prompting founder and current owner Paul Tomaselli to be taken to court for allowing such indecent exposure) and, a decade or so on, the g-string bikini.

The antics of the filthy rich and famous remain as hedonistic as ever. Attempts by Ramatuelle's socialist mayor to shut down La Voile Rouge in summer 2000 backfired after Tomaselli appealed against the court decision to close his famous bar – and won.

Bathers can swim in the buff on aptly named **Plage de la Liberté**, a nudist beach on Pampelonne's northern end, **Plage de la Moutte** on Cap des Salins, or the more secluded **Plage de l'Escalet**, on the southern side of Cap Camarat.

Coastal Walks

A picturesque coastal path leads 35km south from St-Tropez to the beach at Cavalaire-sur-Mer, and around the St-Tropez peninsula as far west as Le Lavandou (60km), passing rocky outcrops and hidden bays en route.

In St-Tropez the path, flagged with a yellow marker, starts at **La Ponche**, immediately east of Tour du Portalet at the northern end of quai Frédéric Mistral. From here, trails lead to Baie des Cannebiers (2.7km, 50 minutes), La Moutte (7.4km, two hours), Plage des Salins (8.5km, 2½ hours) and Plage de Tahiti (12km, 3½ hours). Alternatively, drive to the end of route des Salins, from where it is a shorter walk along the coastal path to Plage de Tahiti (2.7km, 45 minutes) and nudist Plage de la Moutte (1.7km, 30 minutes) on Cap des Salins.

Cap Lardier, the peninsula's southernmost cape, is protected by the Parc National de Port-Cros (see Île de Port-Cros later in this chapter).

Diving & Snorkelling

Discover St-Tropez's underworld with **Octopussy** *(Ramatuelle ☎ 04 94 79 92 58, St-Tropez ☎ 04 94 56 68 71, 06 10 25 61 26; W www.octopussy.fr)*, a Ramatuelle-based diving school with a kiosk in the portside car park, Parking du Port, from May to October. Dives cost from €30. The **European Diving School** *(☎ 04 94 79 90 37; W www.EuropeanDiving.com)*, based at Camping Kon Tiki, also organises dives; Kon Tiki campers get cheaper rates.

Boat Excursions

Boat trips around the glamorous Baie des Cannebiers – otherwise dubbed the 'Bay of Stars' after the many celebrity villas that peep out along the coast here – are advertised on boards along quai Suffren. Trips typically last one hour (adult/five to 10 years €8/4; four to five departures daily April to September). **MMG** (see Boat under Getting There & Away later in this section) runs daily boat trips around Baie des Cannebiers (adult/four to 12 years €8/4 March to October).

Les Bateaux Verts (see Boat Excursions under Ste-Maxime later in this chapter) runs 1¼-hour boat trips (€9/4.50 for adult/four to 10 years) in a glass-bottomed boat around the Bay of St-Tropez. June to September, it operates four weekly boat trips to Port-Cros (€26/16.50) and Porquerolles (€30/19). The boats depart from St-Tropez at 8.30am Monday, Thursday, Friday and Sunday morning. Other day trips from St-Tropez include Cannes (€26/16.50, twice weekly) and Ste-Marguerite (€26/16.50, twice weekly). Both latter as well as island boats depart from the new harbour (opposite Parking du Port).

Vedettes Îles d'Or et Le Corsaire (see Boat Excursions in Le Lavandou section later in this chapter) runs seasonal boat trips from St-Tropez to Cavalaire-sur-Mer (adult/four to 12 years €30/21.50; 1¼ hours, once weekly April to September) and Le Lavandou.

Otherwise, shuttleboats between St-Tropez, St-Raphaël, Ste-Maxime and Port Grimaud make for a jolly day out. See Getting There & Away later.

Special Events

Guns blaze and flags flutter in St-Tropez on 15 June during **Les Bravades des Espagnols**, a festival held to mark St-Tropez's victory over 21 Spanish galleons that attacked the port on 15 June 1637. The militaristic street processions are led by a nominated *capitaine de ville* (town captain) who, between 1481 and 1672, when St-Tropez enjoyed a special autonomy, served as captain of the town.

The most important *bravades* (Provençal for 'bravery'), however, fall on 16, 17 (St Torpes' day) and 18 May. These have been celebrated since 1558 and see Tropeziens process through the streets wearing traditional costume. During this festival the town captain, followed by an army of 140 musket-firing *bravadeurs*, moves through the street bearing a bust of the town's saint.

Places to Stay – Budget & Mid-Range

St-Tropez touts no cheap hotels or hostels, and camping on the beach is illegal. Contact the tourist office for information on self-catering accommodation.

Camping The closest camp sites are on the road to Plage de Pampelonne; both rent chalets and mobile homes too.

Camping Kon Tiki (*☎ 04 94 55 96 96. fax 04 94 55 96 95; ⓔ kontiki@wanadoo.fr; route des Tamaris; camping for 2 people with tent & car low/mid/high season €15/20/35; reception open 8am-8pm daily mid-Mar–Oct*), overlooking the sand at the northern end of Plage de Pampelonne, sports a diving school, supermarket, beach huts, Internet station and plenty of other fun 'n' games to keep campers happy.

Camping Caravaning Les Tournels (*☎ 04 94 55 90 90, fax 04 94 55 90 99; ⓦ www.tournels.com; route de Camarat; adult/tent/car low season €5/5.90/2.60, high season €6.80/8.40/3.20, reception open 9am-8pm daily mid-Feb–Dec*), near the lighthouse on Cap Camarat, is very much in the middle of nowhere. It has a pool, shopping centre, disco, four- to six-person chalets and mountain bikes (€10/35 per day/week) for exploring the cape's green surrounds.

Hotels At the foot of the citadel, **Hôtel Le Baron** (*☎ 04 94 97 06 57, fax 04 94 97 58 72; ⓦ www.hotel-le-baron.com; 23 rue de l'Aïoli; doubles low/mid/high season from €46/53/69*) is an unpretentious place with 10 comfortable double rooms.

Hôtel Les Lauriers (*☎ 04 94 97 04 88, fax 04 94 97 21 87; rue du Temple; doubles €55-70*) is an equally comfy, two-star place.

Hôtel Les Palmiers (*☎ 04 94 97 01 61, fax 04 94 97 10 02; ⓦ www.hotel-les-palmiers.com; 24-26 blvd Vasserot; doubles €70, suite €172*) offers a prime view of place des Lices' *pétanque* players from its rooms overlooking the square.

Places to Stay – Top End

bliss hôtel (*☎ 04 98 12 91 12, fax 04 98 12 91 13; ⓔ contact@blisshotel.fr; 1 ave du Général Leclerc; doubles low/mid/high season from €150/240/330*), in a beautifully restored mansion built in 1850, prides itself on being a 'boutique hotel' – whatever that means.

Hôtel Sube (*☎ 04 94 97 30 04, fax 04 94 54 89 08; ⓔ sube@nova.fr; quai Suffren; rooms with garden view low/high season €65/90, with sea view €150/250*) is behind the Bailli de Suffren statue at the Vieux Port. Pricier rooms are plusher and have boat-harbour views.

Le Yaca (*☎ 04 94 55 81 00, fax 04 94 97 58 50; ⓦ www.hotel-le-yaca.fr; 1 blvd d'Aumale; singles/doubles/apartments low season €250/300/550, high season €300/380/750; open Mar-early Jan*) has a decor that combines old world with new, and a clientele that 'famous or not, is chic and beautiful' (according to the hotel brochure).

Hôtel Byblos (*☎ 04 94 56 68 00, fax 04 94 56 68 01; ⓦ www.byblos.com; ave Paul Signac; doubles €435; open mid-Apr–mid-Oct*) is one of the Riviera's choicest spots. Its facade – a rainbow of pastels from terracotta to lavender-blue – shields luxurious rooms warranting no complaints.

Places to Eat

Don't leave St-Tropez without sampling a sweet and creamy *tarte Tropézienne*, a sponge-cake sandwich filled with custard cream and topped with sugar and almonds.

Restaurants Quai Jean Jaurès is lined with restaurants; most have €20 *menus* and a strategic view of the silverware and crystal of those dining on the decks of their yachts. At the northern end of rue des Remparts in the old town, there is a lesser-known cluster

BB

Brigitte Bardot epitomised sex appeal in the 1950s and 1960s. An icon of sexual liberation, the Paris-born model-turned-actress sprang to stardom in 1956 as a young woman, baring more than most, in Vadim's *Et Dieu Créa la Femme* (And God Created Woman). She moved to St-Tropez in 1958.

A year later she met French singer Serge Gainsbourg with whom she went on to record several tracks, including in 1967 the breathlessly erotic *Je t'aime...moi non plus,* which she refused to release (the BBC and Vatican promptly banned the re-recorded version with Jane Birkin), and the raunchy *Harley Davidson,* which saw the starlet clad in leather coquetting a motorbike. Serge Gainsbourg's subsequent hit called *Initials BB* (1968) – a melodious tribute to the Bardot myth – became a legend in its own time.

Animals became Bardot's passion after she retired from the screen. She founded the **Fondation Brigitte Bardot** *(☎ 01 45 05 14 60, fax 01 45 05 14 80; 45 rue Vineuse, F-75116 Paris)* in 1986, subsequently donating her celebrated 1960s St-Tropez home – Villa La Madrague overlooking Baie des Cannebiers – to the animal-activist campaign group. From her Pointe du Capon seaside villa, where she lives with a menagerie of furry friends, Bardot continues to campaign tirelessly for the foundation.

The 1990s saw the actress – now in her sixties – in court. In 1998 she was found guilty of inciting racial hatred during a public criticism of the Muslim ritual involving slaughter of sheep and was fined €3000. The previous year, her ex-husband (one of three) and son successfully sued her for libellous comments made in the first of her two-volume autobiography. The media pounced on Bardot's fourth marriage to National Front politician Bernard d'Ormale in 1992 as ultimate proof that the 1960s icon leans very heavily (politically speaking) towards the extreme right.

JANE SMITH

of places overlooking Port des Pêcheurs at La Ponche.

La Dame de Cœur *(☎ 04 94 97 23 16; 2 rue de la Miséricorde; mains €10)* caters to a budget-oriented crowd. No name is signposted outside; look for the Queen of Hearts playing card.

Chez Fuchs *(☎ 04 94 97 01 25; 7 rue des Commerçants; menu €30)*, a truly authentic affair where Tropeziens hang out, ranks among St-Tropez's least pretentious places.

La Table du Marché *(☎ 04 94 97 85 20; 38 rue Georges Clémenceau; menus €18 & €25)* is an informal bistro where traditional Provençal dishes are concocted from market produce. The same team also runs the neighbouring **Sushi Bar** *(☎ 04 94 97 85 20; 6-piece/8-piece sushi €19/22)*, a temple to clam-stuffed dim sum.

Auberge des Maures *(☎ 04 94 97 01 50; rue du Docteur Bourtin; menu €39)* is an old favourite. The decor is quaintly Provençal and the food is delicious. Opt for a traditional *menu* or go for the *carte barbecue* – a choice of grilled meats, lobster (€46 per 600g), monkfish (€29) etc.

Café Sud *(☎ 04 94 97 42 52; 12 rue Étienne Berny; menu €35)* is a tasteful restaurant set in a star-topped courtyard. Specialities include clam carpaccio with a citrus-fruit dressing, *petits farcis Provençaux* (Provençal filled vegetables) and grilled seafood. Café Sud's other outlet, **La Plage des Jumeaux** *(☎ 04 94 79 84 21; route de l'Épi)* is on Plage Pampelonne.

Emiliano *(☎ 04 94 97 09 99; 26 rue des Charrons; starters/mains €15/25)*, in an intimate walled garden, is an oasis of calm where you can tuck into world cuisine. Locally inspired tasty choices include *supions* (pan-fried squid with garlic and parsley) with aubergine charlotte, or king prawns skewered on vanilla sticks and served with a gingered pear.

Spoon *(☎ 04 94 56 68 20; ⓔ spoonbyblos@byblos.com; ave du Maréchal Foch; starters/mains/desserts €20/35/15, menu €59)*, inside the Hôtel Byblos, is this minimalist Ducasse creation where you can feast on world food at low tables. Follow the numbered columns horizontally for the chef's choice or zigzag to create the culinary unthinkable.

Cafés Count on as much as €5 for a five-sip *café* (small black coffee) at some of the trendy sipping spots. St-Tropez's most famous café is Café des Arts, next to the cinema on place des Lices, where artists and intellectuals have been meeting for years. Today the historic café is called **Le Café** *(☎ 04 94 97 44 69; W www.lecafe.fr)*; aspiring *pétanque* players can ask at the bar to borrow a set of boules to have a spin alongside the square's legendary *pétanque* players. Don't confuse this legendary place with the newer, red-canopied **Café des Arts** *(☎ 04 94 97 02 25; cnr place des Lices & ave du Maréchal Foch)*, which (despite its copycat name) has no connection with the former haunt of BB and her glam friends and foes.

Sénéquier *(☎ 04 94 97 00 90; quai Jean Jaurès)* is where Sartre wrote parts of *Les Chemins de la Liberté*. It's another buzzing, people-watching spot, boasting a large terrace filled with red tables and chairs. It serves breakfast from 7.30am or 8am.

Le Gorille *(☎ 04 94 97 03 93; 1 quai Suffren; open 24 hrs)* is a hot spot for a pastis at dusk, sunrise or any other time of day.

Self-Catering A morning **fresh fish market** fills place aux Herbes daily (Tuesday to Sunday in winter); walk under the archway directly behind the tourist office on rue de la Citadelle. Place aux Herbes is also home to an excellent **fromagerie**. On Tuesday and Saturday morning, a massive **market** selling everything from fruit, veg and olives to clothes, antique mirrors and slippers fills place des Lices.

La Tarte Tropézienne *(36 rue Georges Clémenceau)* sells the traditional cream-filled sandwich cake, originally cooked by *boulanger* Micka in Cogolin in 1955. Its **larger outlet** *(9 blvd Louis Blanc)* sells freshly baked breads of all shapes and sizes; arrive early for a loaf straight from the oven.

In-town supermarkets include **Monoprix** *(9 ave du Général Leclerc)* and **Petit Casino** *(39 rue Allard)*.

Entertainment

For years the 'in' spots to dance and rub shoulders with stars have been **Les Caves du Roy** *(☎ 04 94 97 16 02; ave Foch)*, inside the Hôtel Byblos (see Places to Stay) and **VIP Room** *(☎ 04 94 97 14 70; blvd 11 Novembre 1918)*, at the old port, is St-Tropez's other star-studded nightclub. It is only at open weekends outside the high season.

Bodega du Papagayo *(☎ 04 94 97 76 70; Résidence du Port, quai Bouchard; starters/mains €15/20)*, overlooking the old port, is a trendy restaurant, nightclub and terrace rolled into one. The leopard-skin toilet seats in the ladies' (which cost an outrageous €1 to use) add a sweet touch. You can dine here until 1am.

L'Esquinade *(2 rue du Four)*, tucked near the water in the old fishing quarter of La Ponche, was hot stuff when this book was researched; as was **Le Loft** *(☎ 04 94 97 60 50; 9 rue des Ramparts)*, another La Ponche nightclub.

Shopping

St-Tropez is loaded with expensive boutiques, gourmet food shops and galleries overflowing with bad art. The covered Grand passage, linking rue Allard with rue Georges Clémenceau, is crammed with designer fashion shops. Second-hand designer labels can be picked up at **Le Dépôt** *(☎ 04 94 97 80 70; rue Quaranta)*, next to La Bugade laundrette.

Traditional sandals, said to have been inspired by a simple leather pair brought by Colette from Greece to show her local cobbler, are all part of the St-Tropez myth. Buy a pair costing from €80 at **Atelier Rondini** *(16 rue Georges Clémenceau)*, where the strappy footwear has been crafted since 1927; or **K Jacques** *(25 rue Allard)* whose family has cobbled since 1933.

Poterie Augier *(19 rue Georges Clémenceau)* is a pottery with plenty of giant-sized urns to lug home. **Oliviers & Co** *(11 rue Georges Clémenceau)* sells olive oil and offers *dégustation* (tasting).

Getting There & Away

Air The closest airport is **St-Tropez–La Môle Airport** *(Aéroport International St-Tropez–La Môle; ☎ 04 94 54 76 40; W www.st-tropez-airport.com)*, 15km west of St-Tropez on the westbound N98. See the Getting There & Away chapter for details.

Bus From St-Tropez **bus station** *(☎ 04 94 97 88 51; ave du Général de Gaulle)*, buses to/from Ramatuelle (€2.80, 40 minutes, five daily) and Gassin (€2.80, 50 minutes, twice weekly September to June, four daily July and August) run parallel to the coast about 1km inland.

There are also buses to/from St-Raphaël (€8.30, 1¼ hours, six to eight daily) via Grimaud and Port Grimaud (€3.20, 20 minutes), Ste-Maxime (€4.10, 40 minutes) and Fréjus (€4.10, one hour). Buses to/from Toulon (€15.90, 2¼ hours, seven daily) go inland before joining the coast at Cavalaire-sur-Mer (€4.30, 1½ hours); they also stop at Le Lavandou (€9, one hour) and Hyères (€13, 1¼ hours). Services are less frequent in winter.

Car & Motorcycle They're all here: **National Citer** *(☎ 04 94 54 85 19; rue du 11 Novembre 1918)*, **Budget** *(☎ 04 94 54 86 54; 2 ave du Général Leclerc)*, **Hertz** *(☎ 04 94 55 83 00; rue de la Poste)* and **Avis** *(☎ 04 94 97 03 10; ave du 8 Mai 1945)*.

Boat **Les Bateaux de St-Raphaël** *(☎ 04 94 95 17 46)* runs two boats daily from St-Tropez to St-Raphaël (adult/two to nine years €15/10 same-day return, 50 minutes), April to August, and boats twice a week in September and October. Boats depart from the new port, from the jetty off ave du 8 Mai 1945, opposite the bus station.

Between March and October, **MMG** *(☎ 04 94 96 51 00; ⓔ mmgtrans@aol.com)* runs *navettes* (shuttleboats) to/from Ste-Maxime (adult/four to 12 years €5.10/2.60 one way, 30 minutes, at least hourly) and Port Grimaud (€4.20/2.30, 20 minutes, nine to 11 daily); shuttles to/from Les Issambres (€5.50/2.80, 20 minutes, eight or nine daily) only sail mid-June to mid-September. Boats depart from the pier off quai Jean Jaurès at *the* Vieux Port. Tickets are sold five minutes before departure from the portside kiosk.

Shuttleboats between St-Tropez and Ste-Maxime operated by Les Bateaux Verts (see Boat Excursions under Ste-Maxime later in this chapter) sail year round; the fare is the same as MMG's.

See Boat Excursions, earlier in this section, for boats to/from the Îles d'Hyères (Porquerolles and Port-Cros).

Getting Around

To/From the Airport Shuttle buses between Aéroport-International St-Tropez–La Môle and St-Tropez bus station (€16, one hour) coincide with flight arrivals/departures.

Bus Mid-March to October, shuttle buses run from the car park (Parking du Port) opposite the bus station to/from ave du Général Leclerc, ave Gambetta (place des Lices) and quai Suffren (Vieux Port). A single ticket/carnet of 10 costs €1/8 and there are buses every 20 minutes between 10am and 1pm and 3pm and 6.30pm daily mid-March to June, September and October, and every 20 minutes from 10am to 11pm daily in July and August (from 9am on Tuesday and Saturday).

The Ramatuelle bus (see Getting There & Away earlier) stops at Plage de Pampelonne (€1.40) – there are bus stops on route des Plages (the D93) and blvd Patch.

Taxi There is a **taxi rank** *(☎ 04 94 97 05 27)* in front of the Musée de l'Annonciade at the Vieux Port.

Car & Motorcycle Cool dudes can hire a roofless, four-wheel buggy from **Too's Car** *(☎ 04 94 97 61 24; route de Tahiti)* to cruise between beaches; it costs €45 for two hours and €70/100/600 for a half-day/24 hours/week.

Holiday Bikes *(☎ 04 94 97 09 39; ⓔ hbtropez@wanadoo.fr; 14 ave du Général Leclerc)*, with a **beachside outlet** *(☎ 04 94 79 87 75; route des Tamaris)* by Plage de Pampelonne, rents 50cc scooters/600cc motorcycles.

Bicycle In town, **Location 2 Roues** *(☎ 04 94 97 00 60; 3-5 rue Joseph Quaranta; open 9am-7pm Mon-Sat, 9am-3pm Sun)* rents road/mountain bikes/80cc scooters for €8/12/35 per day and €38/69/215 per week. Otherwise, both outlets of Holiday Bikes (see Car & Motorcycle above) rent bicycles.

GASSIN & RAMATUELLE

The sparsely populated interior of the **Presqu'île de St-Tropez** (St-Tropez peninsula) is crossed by sprawling vineyards and a handful of roads that link the villages of Gassin and Ramatuelle to the coast.

In medieval Gassin (pop 2752, elevation 200m), 11km southwest of St-Tropez, narrow streets wend up to the village **church** (1558), atop the rocky promontory on which the village is built. From Gassin, route des Moulins de Paillas snakes 3km southeast, past the remains of ancient **windmills** (some are being rebuilt), to Ramatuelle (pop 2174, elevation 136m), 10km from St-Tropez via the D61. Each year in early August, jazz and theatre liven up the tourist-packed streets during the two-week Festival de Ramatuelle.

The fruits of the peninsula's lush vineyards – Côtes de Provence wines – can be tested at various chateaux along the D61; **Ramatuelle tourist office** *(☎ 04 94 79 26 04, fax 04 94 79 12 66; ⓔ ot.ramatuelle@worldonline.fr; place de l'Ormeau; open 9am-1pm & 3pm-7.30pm daily July & Aug, 9am-1pm & 3pm-7pm Mon-Sat Apr, June & Sept, 8.30am-12.30pm & 2pm-6pm Mon-Fri Oct-Mar)* has a list of estates and cellars where you can taste and buy.

Places to Stay & Eat

The camp sites listed under Places to Stay in the St-Tropez section serve the peninsula villages too.

Le Giulià *(☎ 04 94 79 20 46; 31 ave Georges Clémenceau; doubles €50, menus €15.50 & €23)* is Ramatuelle's cheapest hotel – and a friendly place at that. Its six rooms are above a simple bar-cum-restaurant.

Le Vesuvio *(☎ 04 94 79 21 60; ave Georges Clémenceau; plat du jour €11, menus €15.50, €18.50 & €21)* has been around for 25 years and is guaranteed to please. It dishes up Italianate pizzas and pasta dishes as well as seafood treats such as king prawn and clam skewered kebabs.

GOLFE DE ST-TROPEZ

The Gulf of St-Tropez, northwest of St-Tropez, is dominated by the brash resort of Ste-Maxime at the northern end of the bay, and the more pleasing, architectural wonder of Port Grimaud, 8km southwest. In summer, boats plough their way back and forth across the gulf between St-Tropez and the two resorts.

Accommodation can be booked through the **Golfe de St-Tropez tourist office** *(☎ 04 94 55 22 02, fax 04 94 55 22 03; ⓦ www.golfeinfos.com; open 9am-8pm Mon-Fri, 10am-7pm Sat & Sun July & Aug, 9am-7pm Mon-Fri, 10am-6pm Sat Sept-June)*, overlooking the busy roundabout in Carrefour de la Foux, 2km south of Port Grimaud, on the N98.

Ste-Maxime

postcode 83120 • pop 11,978

Sandy-beached Ste-Maxime, 24km south of St-Raphaël and 14km northwest of St-Tropez, is a crowded, modern, ugly resort with few thrills greater than those offered at the countless water-sports clubs that line the beachfront.

Ste-Maxime's old town, centred around rue Gambetta, is crammed with touristy cafés, craft stalls and souvenir shops. Giant pans of paella, fruit stalls and pastry shops line rue Courbet, a cobbled street that leads to the town's main market square, place du Marché. Flowers, fish, olives, oil, wine, *tartes Tropéziennes* and other culinary delights are sold in the **covered market** *(4 rue Fernard Bessy)*.

The **tourist office** *(☎ 04 94 96 19 24, fax 04 94 49 17 97; promenade Simon Lorière)* has information on water sports and other seafaring activities.

Boat Excursions April to September, **Les Bateaux Verts** *(☎ 04 94 49 29 39; ⓔ bateaux.verts@wanadoo.fr; 14 quai Léon Condroyer)* runs boat excursions from its portside base to the Baie des Cannebiers (adult/four to 12 years €11.80/5.50); the Gulf of St-Tropez (€13/7.80 with or without a stop in St-Tropez); the Calanques de l'Estérel (€15.30/9.15); and around the capes of Camarat, Taillat and Lardier (€15.30/9.15). There are also return sailings four times per week to Port-Cros (€28/16.50) and Porquerolles (€30/19), and two times per week to Cannes (€26/16.50) and the Îles de Lérins (€26/16.50).

Getting There & Away There are regular buses and shuttleboats between St-Tropez and Ste-Maxime (see Getting There & Away under St-Tropez earlier in this chapter). In Ste-Maxime boats depart from 14 quai Léon Condroyer at the port.

Port Grimaud

Pretty little Port Grimaud was built in the 1960s on top of a 100-hectare swamp. Within the high wall that barricades the floating village, Provençal cottages – painted all colours – stand gracefully alongside yacht-laden waterways. On Thursday and Sunday morning a market fills place du Marché, from where a wooden bridge leads to Port Grimaud's modernist **church**. Inside, sunbeams shine through a stained-glass window designed by Vasarely. A panorama of red rooftops fans out from the **bell tower** (€1).

Alsatian architect Francis Spoerry (1912–99), who conceived the entire project, fought for four years (1962–96) to get the authorities to agree to his water-world proposal. Pictures of prehistoric lagoon towns displayed in Zürich's Landesmuseum were apparently Spoerry's inspiration. Spoerry, who went on to design Port Liberty in New York, is buried in Port Grimuad's church.

Cars are forbidden to enter this Venice of Provence. Bronzed residents generally cruise around in speedboats. Port Grimaud is endowed with 12km of quays, 7km of 4m-deep canals and mooring space for 3000 luxury yachts – gaped at by 400,000 visitors a year. *Tenue correcte* (correct dress) is insisted upon, except on the wide sandy beach which can be accessed on foot from Grand rue.

In summer, a small **tourist office** *(☎ 04 94 56 02 01; chemin Communal; open 9am-12.30pm & 2.30pm-6.15pm Mon-Sat June-Sept)* operates on the roadside (N98) in St-Pons Les Mûres, opposite the Porte de Poterne, the main pedestrian entrance into Port Grimaud.

Places to Stay & Eat There are a couple of camp sites immediately north of Port Grimaud on the N98; buses to/from St-Raphaël and Ste-Maxime stop in front of both.

Camping des Mûres *(☎ 04 94 56 16 97, fax 04 94 56 37 91; W www.camping-des-mures.com; camping for 2 people with tent & car low/high season €19/23; open Apr-Sept)* sports three stars and plenty of facilities to ensure a happy holiday.

Hôtel Giraglia *(☎ 04 94 56 31 33, fax 04 94 56 33 77; W www.hotelgiraglia.com; place du 14 Juin; doubles low/high season from €200/250)*, Port Grimaud's only hotel, is a four-star place with rooms oozing romance. Delicious culinary creations are served with a flourish by waiters in dinner jackets at its poolside restaurant.

Getting There & Away There are buses between Port Grimaud and Grimaud (€1.10, 10 minutes, five daily) and St-Tropez (€3.20, 20 minutes, eight to 10 daily).

April to mid-October, an **electric tourist train** *(☎ 04 94 54 09 09)* shunts visitors between Port Grimaud and Grimaud (50 minutes). From Port Grimaud, there are five daily trains between 10.15am and 6.25pm, with extra evening trains until sometime around 10pm mid-June to August. A one-way/return ticket costs €3/5.30 (four to 12 years €2/2.80). In Port Grimaud, the stop is opposite Porte de Poterne, the pedestrian entrance to the marine village; in Grimaud it's on central place Neuve.

March to October, there are shuttleboats to/from St-Tropez (see Getting There & Away in that section earlier). A combined ticket covering a return ride on the Port-Grimaud–Grimaud train and St-Tropez shuttleboat costs €12.60/6.75 for adults/four to 12 years.

Getting Around From mid-June to mid-September, **Les Coches d'Eau** *(☎ 04 94 56 21 13; 12 place du Marché)* runs 20-minute boat tours of Port Grimaud, departing from place du Marché every 10 minutes between 9am and 10pm daily; they are at 10am to noon and 2pm to 6pm, the rest of the year. The tickets are €3.50/2 for adults/three to 12 years.

Across the bridge on place de l'Église you can hire an electric boat *(barque électrique)*, costing €18 per 30 minutes for up to four people, between Easter and mid-November.

Inside Porte de Poterne, **Nautic Location** *(☎ 04 94 43 47 27; W www.nauticlocation.com; 22 place du Sud)* rents speedboats (for licence-holders) and less powerful six-person Zodiacs (without licence); the latter costs €40/50 per half-day in low/high season, plus €750 deposit.

L'Amiral *(☎ 04 94 43 47 32; 47 Grand Rue)* rents bikes for €6/18 per hour/day.

Grimaud

postcode 83310 • pop 3847 • elevation 105m

Port Grimaud's popular medieval sibling is 3km inland. The typically Provençal hill-top village is most notable for the ruins of its **Château du Grimaud**, originally built in the 11th century and fortified four centuries later. The ruins, which can be freely strolled, are spectacularly lit in early October during the Festival Européen de Show Laser – a three-day laser festival born in 2002.

Lower down the village, local lore comes to life in Grimaud's small but interesting **Musée des Arts et Traditions Populaires** *(☎ 04 94 43 39 29; route Nationale; admission free; open 2.30pm-6pm Tues-Sat)*. Find out more with a guided tour of the village (1¼ hours) departing from place de l'Église at 10.30am every Thursday, or a self-guided thematic stroll. Ask at the **tourist office** *(☎ 04 94 43 26 98, fax 04 94 43 32 40; W www.grimaud-provence.com; 1 blvd des Aliziers;*

open 9am-12.30pm & 2.30pm-6.30pm Mon-Sat) for its brochure outlining four short village walks.

South of the village, along the D61 towards St-Tropez, the fruity aroma of local wine can be enjoyed at **Les Vignerons de Grimaud** *(☎ 04 94 43 20 14; 36 ave des Oliviers; open 8.30am-12.30pm & 2pm-6.15pm Mon-Sat)*, the local wine cooperative where you can stock up on Côtes de Provence wine for as little as €1.85 a litre (1L of non-AOC table wine costs €1.20!).

There are eight to 10 direct daily buses from St-Tropez to Grimaud or Port Grimaud (€3.20, 20 minutes) and a few to/from St-Raphaël (€7.50, 55 minutes).

Northern Var

The northern half of the Var department – generally understood to be everything north of the dusty, noisy A8 *autoroute* – is a vastly different kettle of fish to its coastal counterpart. Here, in this surprisingly rural hinterland, hill-top villages drowse in peace beneath the midday sun to create a happy illusion of an unspoilt Provence from a bygone era.

The largest town in this lovely neck of the woods is dull Draguignan, home to the French army whose military base occupies the vast **Plateau de Canjuers**. This plateau sprawls for some 30km north to the foot of the Gorges du Verdon (see the Haute-Provence chapter). The greener area east of Draguignan, known as Pays Dracénois, is pierced by the hill-top village of **Fayence**. Black truffles, terracotta tiles and ceramics are the mainstay industries of the rural populace west of Draguignan. Regional wines can be tried and tasted in and around medieval Les Arcs-sur-Argens, to the south.

DRAGUIGNAN

postcode 83300 • pop 34,814 • elevation 187m

A sign at the entrance to Draguignan, 40km north of St-Tropez, welcomes visitors to France's 'Capital d'Artillerie' (artillery capital), where an artillery school has been based since 1976. The **Musée de l'Artillerie** *(Artillery Museum; ☎ 04 98 10 83 85; admission free; quartier Bonaparte; open 9am-noon & 1.30pm-5.50pm Sun-Wed)* is in the school.

In Draguignan's American cemetery, a monument pays homage to the heavy combat that occurred around Draguignan during WWII – 9000 American and British soldiers were dropped here by parachute on 15 August 1944.

Traditional Provençal costumes, musical instruments and other ethnographic finds are displayed in the **Musée des Traditions Provençales** *(Museum of Provençal Traditions; ☎ 04 94 47 05 72; 15 rue Roumanille; open 9am-noon & 2pm-6pm Tues-Sat, 2pm-6pm Sun)*. In the tiny, last patch of Draguignan's old town, the 18m **tour d'horloge** (clock tower), topped with an ornate campanile, is worth a visit.

The **tourist office** *(☎ 04 98 10 51 05, fax 04 98 10 51 10; W www.ot-draguignan.fr; 2 blvd Lazare Carnot)* has details on accommodation; the most atmospheric places to stay are around Draguignan (see the next section).

Camping de la Foux *(☎ 04 94 68 18 27; quartier de la Foux; camping for adult/tent & car €4/4; open Apr-Oct)*, 3km southeast of the town centre along a quiet country lane, also rents bungalows and caravans.

Getting There & Around

From the **bus station** *(☎ 04 94 68 15 34; blvd des Martyrs de la Résistance)*, **Estérel Cars** *(☎ 04 94 52 00 50)* runs 16 daily buses to/from St-Raphaël (€5.40, 1¼ hours). There are less frequent services to Grasse, Marseilles and Toulon. Draguignan is also served by regular daily buses to/from Les Arcs-sur-Argens, where the closest train station is.

Pick up a pair of wheels to explore the Pays Dracénois (see the next section) from **Holiday Bikes** *(☎ 04 98 10 63 08; route de Draguignan)*. A mountain bike/50cc scooter/125cc motorbike will cost about €12/38/60 per day.

AROUND DRAGUIGNAN

Pays Dracénois

From Draguignan head east along the D562, then follow the D225 and D25 north to **Callas** (pop 1400). The wheel still turns at the **Moulin de Callas** *(☎ 04 94 39 03 20; open 10am-noon & 3pm-7pm Mon-Sat)*, an oil mill dating from 1928 at the southern foot of the village. Buy olive oil here from €13 a litre. Climb up to the heart of the village for a stunning panorama of the red-rock Massif de l'Estérel.

Bargemon (pop 1228), 6km north, has plenty of medieval streets to stroll. Its small **tourist office** *(☎/fax 04 94 47 81 73; ave Pasteur; open 9am-1pm & 4pm-6pm daily June–mid-Sept, 9am-noon daily mid-Sept–Apr)* has information on the entire area. From here, you can continue east towards medieval **Fayence** (pop 3502, elevation 350m), a pretty stepping stone between Pays Dracénois and the Cannes area, in the hills about 25km east of Draguignan. Its **tourist office** *(☎ 04 94 76 20 08; place Léon Roux)* has details on available accommodation.

Alternatively, a westbound journey takes you into the Haut-Var.

Haut-Var

West of Draguignan rises Haut-Var (literally 'high Var'), the northernmost part of the Var department, best known for its black truffles that are snouted out of its rich earth, November to March.

A trio of relatively unexplored villages – **Châteaudouble** (pop 390) in the rocky Gorges de Châteaudouble, 15km north along the D955; **Ampus** (pop 710, elevation 600m), 10km west via the narrow D51; and **Tourtour** (pop 470, elevation 650m), 8km west again – make for an exceptionally fine gastronomic tour, be it with four or two wheels.

In Châteaudouble, sample and buy freshly ripened *chèvre* (goat cheese) at the **Bastide de Fonteve** *(☎ 04 94 70 90 00; open 10am-noon & 3pm-6pm Mon-Sat Apr-Sept)*, a goat farm at the junction of the D955 and perilously narrow D51, which leads into the actual village. Guided farm visits cost €7. In the village itself, **Restaurant du Château** *(☎ 04 94 70 90 05; place Vieille; B&B €55, lunch/dinner menu €34/42)*, in the former village chateau, offers some fine rustic dining and a couple of *chambres d'hôtes* guaranteed to charm your socks off. Tables must be reserved in advance.

Tourtour really titillates the taste buds. In its restored 17th-century **Moulin à Huile** *(Oil Mill; ☎ 04 94 70 54 74)*, one of three to originally grace the village, you can watch olives being pressed from around 15 December after the harvest. Each year, the mill presses between 18,000kg and 25,000kg of olives, producing 4000L to 5000L of oil. You can also buy olive oil here. At other times, the vaulted stone building hosts art exhibitions. Guided tours of the mill and village (€1.60; by appointment only) are run by the **tourist office** *(☎ 04 94 70 59 47; montée de St-Dénis)*.

Le Relais de St-Denis *(☎ 04 94 70 54 06; place des Ormeaux; menus from €19)* and **Les Girandoles** *(☎ 04 94 70 54 29, menus €20 & €30)*, at the entrance to the village, are two highly recommended places to eat in Tourtour. Both are rustic, cook up wholly regional products and burst with character.

In the truffle season (November to March), an abundance of these deceptively ugly nuggets of black fungus can be viewed in all their unattractiveness at the Thursday morning **truffle market**, held on the central square in **Aups** (pop 1796), 10km northwest of Tourtour. Truffle hunts and demonstrations of pig-snouting techniques lure a crowd to the otherwise unremarkable village, on the fourth Sunday in January when Aups throws its Journée de la Truffe (Day of the Truffle).

Some 9km south of Aups along the wiggly D31 is **Salernes** (pop 3343) where handmade terracotta tiles, known as *terres cuites* (literally 'baked earth'), have been manufactured since the 18th century. Ask at the **tourist office** *(☎ 04 94 70 69 02, fax 04 94 70 73 34; W www.terresdesalernes.asso.fr; place Gabriel Péri; open 9.30am-12.30pm & 2.30pm-6.30pm Tues-Sat)* for a copy of the free *Artisans Terres de Salernes* guide which includes a list of 20 Salernais potters and tile-makers who open their workshop doors to visitors; many close in August. The tourist office also has information on walking and mountain-biking trails around Salernes; hire wheels for €15 a day from **Papou Cycles & Chasse** *(☎ 04 94 67 59 29; 2 rue Édouard Basset)*.

Cotignac (pop 2040), 11km southwest of Salernes, with its lively summertime Friday morning market (8am to 1pm Friday, June to September), and hill-top **Entrecasteaux** (pop 868), with its 17th-century chateau 9km east, are other pretty Varois villages worth a mooch. Between June and September **Château de Bernes** *(☎ 04 94 60 43 53; e info@chateauberne.com; chemin de Berne)*, a wine-growing estate 2km north of Lorgues, offers wine tasting, hosts craft fairs and organises enjoyable 'jazz picnics' (€13/25 for one/three concerts).

Lorgues (pop 7687, elevation 200m) is the chosen base of well-known Provençal chef Bruno, who runs his self-named restaurant, **Chez Bruno** *(☎ 04 94 85 93 93; 2350 route des Arcs; menus €52 & €100)*, in a country house amid vineyards, a couple of kilometres east of Lorgues centre on the D562 towards Les Arcs. Cooking with black truffles – predictably, given his geographic location – is Bruno's claim to fame.

Le Thoronet & La Celle

From **Cotignac** (elevation 230m), the picturesque D13 snakes though Carcès and around **Lac de Carcès**. At the lake's southern end, continue 4km east to the Romanesque Abbaye de Thoronet, the third in a trio of great abbeys built by the Cistercian order in Provence in the 12th and 13th centuries.

Abbaye de Thoronet *(☎ 04 94 60 43 90; adult/under 18 €5.50/free; open 9am-7pm Mon-Sat, 9am-noon & 2pm-7pm Sun Apr-Sept, 10am-1pm & 2pm-5pm Oct-Mar)*, built between 1160 and 1190, housed some 20 monks and several dozen lay brothers by the early 13th century. By 1790 just a handful of elderly monks remained. The church, the monks' cells and cloisters were all built with dry stone. The chapter house, where the monks met each morning to discuss community problems, is noticeably more ornate than the rest of the austere abbey, because it was the only secular room, where prayers were never held. Early Gothic influences are evident in the pointed arches, which rest on two columns. Musical soirees are held in summer.

About 15km southwest of Thoronet is **Abbaye de la Celle** *(☎ 04 94 59 10 05; adult/student €3/2)*, a 12th-century Benedictine abbey in the tiny village of La Celle, 2km south of Brignoles. It was a women's convent from 1225 until its eventual closure in 1657. The church continues to serve the village community today and the abbey cloister can be visited. The adjoining convent houses the **Maison des Vins Coteaux Varois** *(☎ 04 94 69 33 18; ⓔ cotvarois@aol.com)*, where you can taste and buy Coteaux Varois AOC wines.

Hostellerie de l'Abbaye de la Celle *(☎ 04 98 05 14 14, fax 04 98 05 14 15; Ⓦ www.abbaye-celle.com; doubles from €190)* is a fabulous four-star hotel and restaurant run by top French chefs Bruno and Alain Ducasse. It has 11 country-style rooms; the Cedar Tree room has a bathtub with legs and dashing Salernes tiles on the bathroom walls.

LES ARCS-SUR-ARGENS

postcode 83460 • pop 5515 • elevation 80m

The two draws to Les Arcs, 11km south of Draguignan and 28km from the coast, are its perfectly restored old town perched on a hillock and its House of Wines, where you can buy, taste and learn about Côtes de Provence wines.

The **tourist office** *(☎/fax 04 94 73 37 30; Ⓦ www.lesarcs.com; place Général de Gaulle; open 9am-noon & 2pm-6pm or 7pm daily)*, at the foot of the medieval village, rents bicycles (€12.20 per day). The 11th-century castle that crowns it shelters the luxury hotel, **Le Logis du Guetteur** *(☎ 04 94 99 51 10, fax 04 94 99 51 29; place du Château; doubles from €104)*.

Wine Tasting

The **Maison des Vins Côtes de Provence** *(House of Wines ☎ 04 94 99 50 20; Ⓦ www.caveaucp.fr; open 10am-1pm & 1.30pm-6pm or 7pm daily)*, 2.5km south of the village on the westbound N7, is the obvious place to start. Sixteen different Côtes de Provence wines are available for tasting each week (look for the list that tells you the ideal dish to eat with each wine, be it steamed fish with bananas or blood sausage and apple) and 700-odd different wines are for sale. Bottles are sold at producers' prices and cost from €3.80. Yet more wining (and dining) can be done at **Le Bacchus Gourmand** *(☎ 04 94 47 48 47; menu €33.50)*, the upmarket restaurant inside the House of Wines.

A prestigious *cru classé* wine, produced since the 14th century, can be tasted (and bought) at **Château Ste-Roseline** *(☎ 04 94 99 50 30; Ⓦ www.sainte-roseline.com; open 9am-6pm Mon-Fri)*, beautifully placed among vineyards 4.5km east of Les Arcs-sur-Argens on the D91 towards La Motte. A 1975 mosaic by Marc Chagall illuminates the estate's 13th-century Romanesque **Chapelle de Ste-Roseline**, home to the corpse of Saint Roseline since her death in 1329. Roseline was born at the chateau in Les Arcs in 1263 and became a Carthusian nun, much against her father's will, in 1288. She experienced numerous visions during her lifetime and was said to be able to curtail demons. Upon her death, her eyes were taken out and separately preserved. Chapelle de Ste-Roseline hosts piano recitals and musical concerts in July and August; tickets cost €20 to €31 (€50 including dinner).

A farther 3km east along the D91 (across the N555) is **La Motte**, the first village in

Provence to be liberated after the August 1944 Allied landings. For the ultimate Provençal feast, head east out of La Motte along the D47 to **Domaine de la Maurette** *(☎ 04 94 45 92 82; route de Callas; menus from €15)*, on the intersection of the D47 and the D25. On this wine estate, you can taste and buy wine, and dine in its *ferme auberge*, a roadside inn where the atmosphere of chattering people dining on wholesome, home-made food is nothing short of electric.

Getting There & Away

Les Arcs-sur-Argens train station is 2km south of the tourist office off ave Jean Jaurès. Exit the train station, turn left, then turn right (north) at the end of the street onto ave Jean Jaurès, from where it is a straight 2km walk to place de Général de Gaulle.

Les Arcs is on the rail line between St-Raphaël and Toulon and is well served by coastal trains to Nice (€11.30, 1½ hours) and Marseilles (€18.10, 1¼ hours). Les Arcs also serves as the train station for Draguignan. **Les Rapides Varois** *(☎ 04 94 47 05 05)* runs buses every 30 minutes between Les Arcs train station and Draguignan.

Massif des Maures

Much of the heavily forested Massif des Maures ('maouro' in Provençal means 'dark') is inaccessible by car, but there are five roads you can take through the hills. The lowest, straightest, southernmost road (N98) cuts through vineyards and cork oak tree plantations, from St-Tropez to Bormes-les-Mimosas and on to Hyères. The parallel D14 runs through Collobrières, the largest town in the massif, known for its chestnut produce. This road is particularly popular with cyclists and is graced with good panoramas.

The mountainous, hairpin-laced D39, which leads north from the D14 just east of Collobrières, snakes between **La Sauvette** (779m) and **Notre Dame des Anges** (780m), the massif's highest peaks. The Massif des Maures, not surprisingly, offers superb walking and cycling opportunities too. The GR9 penetrates the massif at its northern edge, near **Carnoules** (pop 2622), and wends its way past Notre Dame des Anges (topped by a small chapel) and La Sauvette to the unspoilt village of La Garde Freinet, a perfect getaway spot. From here it runs south to Port Grimaud on the coast. From Collobrières, the southbound GR90 – which cuts straight through the village – loops 12km east to an isolated Carthusian monastery. Northbound, it hooks up with the GR9 at Notre Dame des Anges.

COLLOBRIÈRES

postcode 83610 • pop 1710 • elevation 150m

If you like chestnuts, then Collobrières – a village renowned for its chestnut puree and *marrons glacés* (candied chestnuts) – is for you. It lies 24km west of Grimaud and is the self-proclaimed 'capital' of the Maures. In summer, slabs of cork and homemade chestnut puree are sold on the square in front of the tourist office. Market day is Thursday (July and August) and Sunday (year round).

Across the 12th-century bridge, the **Confiserie Azuréenne** *(☎ 04 94 48 07 20)* sells a nutty array of products. Sample *glaces aux marrons glacés* (sweet chestnut ice cream), *crème de marrons* (chestnut cream), *marrons au sirop* (chestnuts in syrup), or a shot of *liqueur de châtaignes* (chestnut liqueur). Opposite the shop is a small **Musée de la Fabrique** *(admission free; open 9.30am-1pm & 2pm-7pm or 8pm)* that explains the art of making *marrons glacé*.

Collobrières marks its annual Grande Fête des Fontaines in August by cooking up a monstrous-sized *aïoli*. It celebrates a Fête de la Châtaigne (Chestnut Festival) on the last three Sundays in October, and its Fête de la Transhumance in April.

Almost 12,000 hectares of protected forest surround the town.

Information

The **tourist office** *(☎ 04 94 48 08 00, fax 04 94 48 04 10; www.collotour.com; blvd Charles Caminat; open 10am-12.30pm & 3pm-6.30pm Mon-Sat July & Aug, 10am-noon & 2pm-6pm Tues-Sat Sept-June)* takes accommodation bookings and has details on joining in the October chestnut harvest and participating in guided forest walks (€7) organised by the Office National des Forêts (ONF). Three short walking trails – including a 200m trail to a *châtaigneraie* (chestnut grove) – are mapped out on the noticeboard in front of the tourist office.

Village des Tortues

About 20km north of Collobrières on the northern tip of the massif is a tortoise village, where one of France's rarest and most endangered species can be viewed in close quarters. The Hermann tortoise *(Testudo hermanni)*, once common along the Mediterranean coastal strip, is today found only in the Massif des Maures and Corsica. Forest fires in 1990 destroyed 250,000 hectares of forest in the massif, reducing the tortoise population further still.

The Station d'Observation et de Protection des Tortues des Maures (SOPTOM; Maures Tortoise Observation and Protection Station) was set up in 1985 by French writer and film-maker Bernaud Devaux and an English biologist to ensure the Hermann's survival. Since 1988 some 8000 tortoises have been returned to the wild.

A well-documented trail (captions in English) leads visitors around the centre, from the quarantine quarter and reproduction enclosures to the tropical conservatory, egg hatcheries (home to pregnant females from mid-May to the end of June), and nurseries, where the young tortoises (a delicacy for preying magpies, rats, foxes and wild boars) spend the first three of their 60 to 100 years. The tortoise mating season runs from March to May and August to September. From November through to early March, they hibernate. In the tortoise clinic, wounded tortoises – usually wild ones kept as domestic pets – are treated. Dog bites and lawnmower injuries are the most common wounds. Following their rehabilitation in the centre, most are repatriated into the Maures forest.

The **Village des Tortues** *(☎ 04 94 78 26 41; W www.tortues.com; adult/3-16 yrs (8/5; open 9am-7pm daily Mar-Nov)*, about 6km east of Gonfaron, is only accessible by private transport.

Places to Stay & Eat

Collobrières offers reasonably priced accommodation and a rash of farmhouses that turn home-grown produce into memorable *tables d'hôtes*.

Hôtel-Restaurant des Maures *(☎ 04 94 48 07 10, fax 04 94 48 02 73; 19 blvd Lazare Carnot; doubles €19, half-/full board per person €23/31)* has basic rooms in the centre of Collobrières. Its restaurant is on a terrace above the river. Taste chestnut ice cream in its downstairs bar for €3 a bowl.

Bastide de la Cabrière *(☎ 04 94 48 04 31, fax 04 94 48 09 90; e loic.de.saleneuve@libertysurf.fr; route de Gonfaron; doubles €60-105)*, a *chambre d'hôte* with delicious home-grown meals (€34), is 6km north of town along the relentlessly winding D39.

Chèvrerie du Peigros *(☎ 04 94 48 03 83; e fermedepeigros@free.fr; Col de Babaou)* is a farm restaurant, 1.8km along a gravel track, signposted from the top of the Babaou mountain pass. Goats and chestnuts are the mainstay of its menu which always includes farm-killed goat or poultry (depending on the season), *chèvres* and dessert (sometimes farm-made chestnut ice cream). Credit cards and cheques are not accepted.

CHARTREUSE DE LA VERNE

Majestic, 12th- to 13th-century **Monastère de la Verne** *(☎ 04 94 43 45 51; adult/8-14 yrs €5/3; open 11am-5pm or 6pm Wed-Mon)* is in a forest, 12km southeast of Collobrières. The monastery was founded in 1190 by the bishop of Toulon for the Carthusian monks (of the Chartreuse order) who settled here from 1170. Huguenots destroyed most of the original charterhouse in 1577.

The solitary complex, under restoration since the 1960s, is home to 15 Carthusian nuns today. One of the old monks' cells has been fully restored, complete with the small garden and covered corridor, where the monk would pray as he paced its length. A 70m-long cloister, bakery and mill can be visited. Various **walking trails** lead from the monastery into its forested surroundings.

Smoking and revealing clothes are forbidden in the monastery. From Collobrières, follow route de Grimaud (D14) east for 6km, then turn right (south) onto the narrow D214. Follow this road for a farther 6km to the monastery; the final section of the single-track road is unpaved.

LA GARDE FREINET

postcode 83310 • pop 1656 • elevation 365m

This village is a delight to explore in late summer when its streets are quiet. A fantastic panorama of red rooftops can be viewed from the **ruins of Fort Freinet** (450m). The fort was built in the 13th century but abandoned 200 years later when the villagers moved down to the plateau. Below the ruins is a large stone cross where pilgrims pay their respects on 1 May each year. The cross and fort are a 20-minute uphill walk from the village centre (signposted from place Neuve).

La Garde Freinet celebrates its traditional Fête de la Transhumance, marking the seasonal moving of the flocks, in mid-June and hosts a Fête de la Châtaigne (Chestnut Fair) in mid-October. Markets fill the old town squares on Wednesday and Sunday morning. Village traditions and customs unfold in the adjoining **Conservatoire du Patrimoine et du Traditions du Freinet** *(☎ 04 94 43 67 41; 1 place Neuve; adult/under 12 €1.50/free; open 10am-noon & 3pm-6pm Tues-Sat)*.

The next-door **tourist office** *(☎ 04 94 43 67 41, fax 04 94 43 08 69; ⓔ ot_lgf@club-internet.fr; 1 place Neuve; open 10am-12.30pm & 3pm-6pm Mon-Sat year round, plus 10am-12.30pm Sun Easter-Oct)* has details on walking, wine tasting and *chambres d'hôtes* in the massif.

Hôtel La Claire Fontaine *(☎ 04 94 43 63 76, fax 04 94 43 60 36; place Vieille; doubles €31, with shower €39)*, one of a trio of hotels in the village, is La Garde Freinet's cheapest place to stay.

Auberge La Sarrazine *(☎ 04 94 55 59 60; route Nationale; menu €28)* is a rustic spot to sample Provençal fare in front of an open fire (winter) or on a flowery patio (summer).

COGOLIN & LA MÔLE

Industrious Cogolin (pop 9181, elevation 13m), 15km south of La Garde Freinet, is known for its wooden pipes, cork products and carpets, the latter being woven in the village since the 1920s when Armenian refugees settled here. Several pipe-makers welcome visitors on ave Georges Clémenceau, including Monsieur Courrieu at **Les Pipes de Cogolin** *(☎ 04 94 54 63 82; 42 & 48 ave Georges Clémenceau)*. The **tourist office** *(☎ 04 94 55 01 50, fax 04 94 55 01 11; ⓦ www.cogolin-provence.com; place de la République)* has a complete lists of artisans and also arranges visits.

Provence's earliest screen hero, Jules Auguste César Muraire (1883–1946), known to the world as Raimu (see Cinema in the Facts about Provence chapter), is honoured at the **Espace Raimu** *(☎ 04 94 54 18 00; 18 ave Georges Clémenceau; adult/11-18 yrs €3.05/1.75; open 10am-noon & 3pm-6pm daily)*, a museum set up by the comic actor's granddaughter.

Cogolin's culinary delight is the *tarte Tropézienne*, created in 1955 at the Micka patisserie **La Tarte Tropézienne** *(☎ 04 94 54 42 59; 2 rue Beausoleil; ⓦ www.tarte-tropezienne.com)*. Cogolin's sandy beach and pleasure port is 5km northeast.

Equally inviting to the tastebuds is neighbouring La Môle (pop 803), 9km southwest along the vineyard-laden N98. The village is known for the nut and olive breads that come from its bakery and for the culinary delights served beneath a blue canopy at the **Auberge de La Môle** *(☎ 04 94 49 57 01; place de l'Église; menus €25 & €50)*, a former petrol station complete with old pump stuck on 333. Credit cards are not accepted. Sample local wine here or at one of the many **chateaux** along the westbound N98.

From La Môle, narrow route du Canadel (D27) dives to the coast. The one blemish in an otherwise mesmerising landscape is **Pachacaïd** *(☎ 04 94 55 70 80, fax 04 94 49 59 26; ⓦ www.pachacaid.com; route de Canadel)*, a camp site where you can rent a four-person mobile home (from €230/730 per week in low/high season) or splash around in the **Niagara Parc Nautique** *(Niagara Water Park; adult/5-12 yrs €9.50/7 June & Sept, €11/9 July & Aug; open 10.30am-7pm daily June-Sept)*, a giant water park.

Bicycles can be hired in Cogolin from **Cycles Évasion** *(☎ 04 94 54 71 13; 61 ave Georges Clémenceau)* for about €12/74 per day/week.

FORÊT DU DOM & BORMES-LES-MIMOSAS

Vineyards melt into a rich patchwork of cork oak, pine and chestnut trees as the N98 continues its path west into the Forêt du Dom, 12km west of La Môle.

From the top of the **Col de Gratteloup** (199m), the steep D41 climbs north over the **Col de Babaou** (415m) towards Collobrières. This road is a popular cycling route. Southbound, the D41 wiggles its way across the **Col de Caguo-Ven** (237m), from where there are good views of Bormes-les-Mimosas (pop 6399, elevation 180m). This attractive 12th-century village is famous for its great diversity of flora.

For a pleasant 1½-hour guided **stroll** *(adult/under 12 €5/free)*, get in touch with the **tourist office** *(☎ 04 94 01 38 38, fax 04 94 01 38 39; W www.bormeslesmimosas.com; 1 place Gambetta; open 9am-12.30pm & 3pm-6.30pm daily Apr-Sept, Mon-Sat only Oct-Mar)*. It also takes bookings for 2½-hour **nature walks** (adult/under 12 €7/free; once weekly April to October) led by forest wardens in the Forêt du Dom.

CORNICHE DES MAURES

From La Môle, the breathtaking 267m **Col de Canadel** (the D27) offers unbeatable views of the Massif des Maures, the coastline and its offshore islands before plummeting to the Corniche des Maures, a 26km coastal road (D559) that stretches southwest from La Croix-Valmer to Le Lavandou. Down here, the coast is trimmed with sandy beaches ideal for swimming, sunbathing and windsurfing.

In **Cavalaire-sur-Mer**, you'll find the largest **tourist office** *(☎ 04 94 01 92 10, fax 04 94 05 49 89; promenade de la Mer; open 9am-7pm daily mid-June–mid-Sept, 9am-12.30pm & 2pm-6pm Mon-Fri, 9am-12.30pm Sat mid-Sept–mid-June)* on the Corniche des Maures. In season, boats sail from this busy seaside resort to St-Tropez and the Îles d'Hyères – see those sections for details.

Continuing west, seaside resorts include the tiny hamlets of **Le Rayol**, **Pramousquier**, **Cavalière** and **Aiguebelle**. With the exception of busy **Plage de Cavalière** – packed with watersports activities and families – the beaches along this stretch are quiet, sandy and usually tucked in pretty coves. Tiny **Plage du Royal** and **Plage de l'Escale**, either side of fabulous four-star **Le Bailli de Suffren Hôtel** *(☎ 04 98 04 47 00, fax 04 98 04 47 99; W www.lebaillidesuffren.com; ave des Américains; doubles low/mid/high season from €145/206/267)* in Le Rayol, are particularly enchanting. Both are backed by pine trees and have a restaurant on the sand.

In Aiguebelle, **Les Roches** *(☎ 04 94 71 05 07, fax 04 94 71 08 40; W www.hotellesroches.com; 1 ave des Trois Dauphins; doubles mid/high season from €240/350, half-board for two people high season from €514)* is the stuff of dreams. Humphrey Bogart, Jean Cocteau and Winston Churchill all stayed at this fabulous four-star hotel and restaurant, perched on a cliff looking out to sea.

From Le Rayol, a narrow road runs south towards beautiful **Domaine du Rayol** *(☎ 04 98 04 44 00; e info@domaineduroyal.org; ave des Belges; adult/8-16 yrs €6.50/3.50; open 9.30am-12.30pm & 3pm-7pm July & Aug, 9.30am-12.30pm & 2.30pm-6.30pm Feb-June & Sept-Nov)*. The fabulous 20-hectare garden dates from 1910 when a Parisian banker built himself a seaside villa here. In summer, you can snorkel along the underwater **Sentier Marin** *(Marine Trail; adult/8-16 yrs €13/10; open Mon-Fri & Sun July & Aug)*; the price includes wet suit, flippers and snorkels and advance bookings are essential. In July and August, the estate hosts open-air musical soirees (adult/ to 16 years €21/15) at 9pm; again, book in advance to ensure a place.

From Cavalière, a silky smooth cycling track wends its way 4.5km west along the coast to **St-Clair**, the easternmost suburb of Le Lavandou.

LE LAVANDOU

postcode 83980 • pop 5508

Once a fishing village, Le Lavandou (from the Provençal 'Lou Lavandou', meaning 'washhouse') is a popular resort town, thanks to its 12km sandy beach, good-value accommodation and its proximity to the idyllic Îles d'Hyères.

The southwestern end of the resort is dominated by concrete blocks. The Vieille Ville (old town) at its northeastern end is beautifully intact. Here, the *pétanque* pitch beneath trees on quai Gabriel Péri buzzes with activity. The dramatist Bertolt Brecht and composer Kurt Weill wrote parts of *The Threepenny Opera* while they were holidaying here in 1928.

Le Lavandou sits northeast of **Cap de Brégançon**, a rocky cape embraced by a beautiful sandy beach in **Cabasson**, on its western side, and crowned with the 16th- to 18th-century **Fort de Brégançon**. Since 1968 the heavily guarded fortress (good views from Cabasson beach) has served as the summer residence for the president of France.

Orientation & Information

Quai Gabriel Péri and its continuation, quai Baptistin Pins, runs northeast along the beachfront. The port (Gare Maritime), quai des Îles d'Or, sits at its easternmost end, opposite the old town.

The bus station is nothing more than a shelter either side of the D559. From the station, walk one block south then turn left (east) onto ave des Martyrs de la Résistance to get to the centre. Its continuation, ave du Général de Gaulle, traverses the old town.

The **tourist office** *(☎ 04 94 00 40 50, fax 04 94 00 40 59; 🅦 www.lelavandou.com; quai Gabriel Péri; open 9am-noon & 3pm-6pm daily)* is opposite the port.

Boat Excursions

Vedettes Îles d'Or et Le Corsaire *(☎ 04 94 71 01 02; 🅦 www.vedettesilesdor.fr; 15 quai Gabriel Péri)* runs boats to the Îles d'Hyères. There are sailings six times daily to/from Île du Levant (adult/four to 12 years €20/15 return, 30 minutes) in July and August, four or five daily April to June and September, and twice daily the rest of the year. Boats to/from Port-Cros (€20/15, 40 minutes) sail eight times daily in July and August, four or five times daily April to June and September, and twice daily the rest of the year. If you are visiting both islands, buy a combined ticket for €40/28. Porquerolles (€26/18, 55 minutes) is served by one return boat daily in July and August, and one a day Wednesday and Saturday April to June and September; out of season, tickets must be reserved in advance.

April to September, the same company also runs boat trips to/from St-Tropez (€38/28, two hours); boats only sail on Tuesday and places must be booked in advance. Coastal excursions in a glass-bottomed boat (€13/9) depart every 40 minutes between 9am and 4.40pm daily all summer.

All boats depart from Le Lavandou's **port** *(quai des Îles d'Or)*. Tickets are sold at the ticket office 30 minutes before departure.

Places to Stay

The tourist office has a list of camp sites nearby; some are clustered along route Benat, 2km south in the suburb of La Favière.

Hôtel l'Oustaou *(☎ 04 94 71 12 18, fax 04 94 15 08 25; 20 ave du Général de Gaulle; doubles with shower low/mid/high season €30/39/41, with shower & toilet €38/45/48, with shower & toilet & terrace or sea view €40/47/51, triples with shower & toilet €50/60/64)* has a handful of four- and five-person rooms too.

Auberge Provençale *(☎ 04 94 71 00 44, fax 04 94 15 02 25; 🅔 provencale.auberge@wanadoo.fr; 11 rue Patron Ravello; doubles with washbasin €38, with shower €46, with shower & toilet €53.50)*, on a busy pedestrian street, offers good-value, one-star rooms.

Hôtel de l'Îlot Fleuri *(☎ 04 94 71 14 82, fax 04 94 15 03 46; rue Cazin; doubles with shower & toilet €52, with balcony & sea or garden view €64)* – the Flowery Islet – has leaf-topped balconies out the back. To snag a balcony, ask for a 1st-floor room.

Hôtel Le Rabelais *(☎ 04 94 71 00 56, fax 04 94 71 82 55; 🅔 hotel.lerabelais@wanadoo.fr; 2 rue Rabelais; doubles with/without sea view from €62/51, with balcony €68)* is a rambling building overlooking the port on quai Baptistin Pins. Its pretty-in-pink facade shields a flowery garden.

Places to Eat

The old town overflows with some great terrace restaurants.

Chez Mimi *(☎ 04 94 71 00 85; blvd de Lattre de Tassigny)*, overlooking the *pétanque* pitch from its portside perch, is an ideal spot to breakfast in the early morning sun from 7am (6.30am in July and August) or sip an aperitif early evening.

La Pignato *(☎ 04 94 71 13 02; rue de L'Église; menus €15 & €18.50)* specialises in *cuisine Provençale*. Try anchovy toasts followed by rabbit in mustard sauce.

La Favouille *(☎ 04 94 71 34 29; cnr ave Patron Ravello & Abbé Helin; menus €16 & €22)*, occupying a small square, is equally satisfying. Service is impeccable. Note the sloping tables!

La Marmite de Pêcheur *(☎ 04 94 01 34 34; 16 rue Patron Ravello; menus €16-46)* brews *bourride* (fish soup) and highly satisfying, seafood-encrusted paella. On Tuesday and Friday it cooks up a giant *aïoli Provençal complet*.

Self-caterers can shop at the **Shopi Supermarché** *(14 ave des Martyrs de la Résistance)*.

Getting There & Away

Le Lavandou is on the main bus route (up to seven buses daily) between St-Tropez (€9, one hour) and Toulon (€7, 1¼ hours). Buses follow the coastal road, stopping en route in Le Rayol, Le Lavandou, Bormes-les-Mimosas, La Londe and Hyères.

Getting Around

Hire wheels from **Holiday Bikes** *(☎ 04 94 15 19 99; ave Vincent Auriol)* or **Planète Glisse** *(☎ 04 94 71 16 50; 15 ave des Ilaires)*. Daily rates for rollerblades/mountain bikes/50cc scooters kick off at €7/20/50. At the port,

Star Bike *(☎ 04 94 01 03 82; quai Baptistin Pins)* rents road bikes with/without gears for €10/7 a day.

The Islands

The alluring Îles d'Hyères are also known as the Îles d'Or (Islands of Gold). According to legend, the islands in this archipelago were created from beautiful princesses who, upon being chased by pirates while swimming, were turned by the gods into golden islands.

Porquerolles, 7km long and 3km wide, is the westernmost and largest. Port-Cros – the middle island – is a national park; while its eastern sister, Île du Levant, is a nudist colony. Wild camping is forbidden throughout the archipelago.

Rather less magical are the Îles du Fun, the overdeveloped islands of Bendor and Embiez, farther west off Toulon's shores.

ÎLE DE PORT-CROS

postcode 83400 • pop 30

Created in 1963 to protect at least one small part of the Côte d'Azur's natural beauty from overdevelopment, **Parc National de Port-Cros** is France's smallest national park. It encompasses the 675 hectares of the island of Port-Cros and an 1800-hectare zone of water around it. Until the end of the 19th century, the islanders' vineyards and olive groves ensured their self-sufficiency. Today, tourism is their sustenance.

The island can be visited all year, but walkers – of which 220,000 descend on Port-Cros annually – must stick to the marked paths. Fishing, fires, camping, dogs, motorised vehicles and bicycles are not allowed. Smoking is forbidden outside the portside village.

Port-Cros, the smallest of the Îles d'Hyères, is primarily a marine reserve but is also known for its rich variety of insects, butterflies and birds. Keeping the water around it clean (compared with the rest of the coast) is one of the national reserve's big problems.

An **underwater trail** *(sentier sous-marin)*, marked off the island's northern shore, allows snorkellers to discover some of the park's marine flora and fauna, which include 500 algae species and 180 types of fish. Miniscule **Îlot de la Gabinière**, an islet off Port-Cros' southern shore, is popular with experienced divers. **CIP Lavandou** *(☎ 04 94 71 54 57; W www.cip-lavandou.com*, a diving school in Le Lavandou, arranges dives. One/two-island dives cost around €28/51.

Parc National de Port-Cros also manages neighbouring **Île de Bagaud** (40 hectares), the fourth of the Îles d'Hyères due west of Port-Cros. The densely vegetated island is used for scientific research and is off-limits to tourists.

Orientation & Information

Boats dock at the port in the village on the island's northwestern shores.

The **Maison du Parc** *(☎ 04 94 01 40 72; open 10am-noon & 2pm-6pm May-Oct, for 30 mins after boats dock Nov-Apr)*, at the port, has information on walking, diving and snorkelling.

Things to See & Do

From the portside post office, a track leads inland, from where 30km of marked footpaths crisscross the island. Fifteenth-century **Fort du Moulin** is the starting point for a circular, 1½-hour **botany trail** *(sentier des plantes)* to **Plage de la Palud**; it returns along an inland route. The beach itself, on the island's northern shores, is a 30-minute walk from the fort, from where snorkellers can follow a 30-minute **underwater trail** (open mid-June to mid-September); the Maison du Parc has details.

The botany trail also takes in imposing 16th-century **Fort de L'Estissac** *(admission free; open 10am-12.30pm & 2pm-5.30pm July & Aug, 10am-noon & 2pm-4.30pm June & Sept)*, host to exhibitions in summer. Climb the tower for a panoramic view of Port-Cros and its neighbouring islands.

A more demanding **crests trail** *(sentier des crêtes*; three hours) explores the southwestern corner of the island, and the slightly easier **Port-Man trail** *(sentier de Port-Man*; four hours) takes walkers to Port-Cros' northeastern tip.

Places to Stay & Eat

Accommodation is limited and needs to be booked months in advance. At the port there is a handful of self-catering studios to rent in the **Maison du Port**; the neighbouring Maison du Parc (see Information earlier) has details.

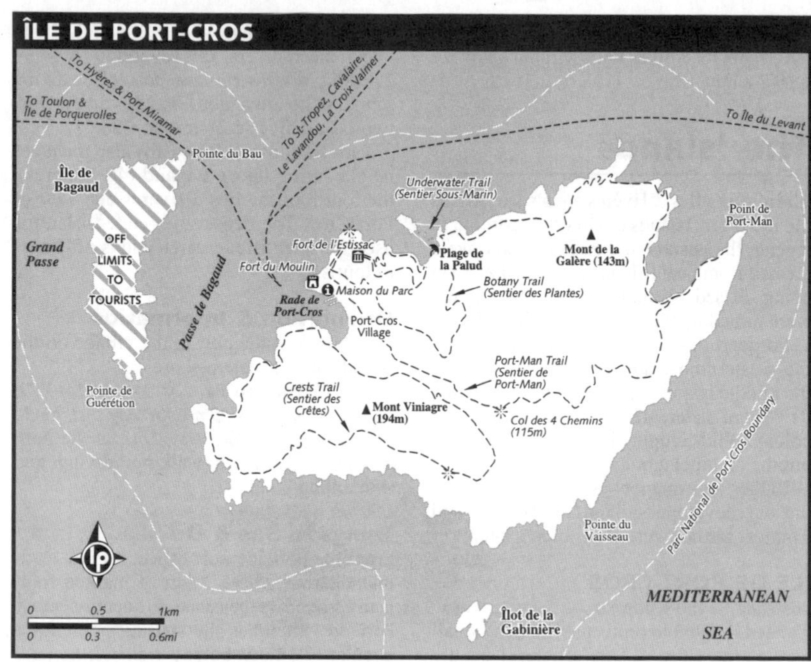

Hostellerie Provençale *(☎ 04 94 05 90 43, fax 04 94 05 92 90; doubles per person with half-board low/high season €70/75)*, on the opposite side of the port to Maison du Port, has five comfortable doubles with shower and toilet.

Le Manoir *(☎ 04 94 05 90 52, fax 04 94 05 90 89; open Apr-Oct)*, an atmospheric 23-room manor, is the exclusive option.

Five restaurants offering sea-inspired cuisine surround the port.

Getting There & Away

Le Lavandou (see Boat Excursions in that section) is the main stepping stone to Port-Cros. There are also frequent boats year round from Hyères.

Seasonal boats sail several times weekly from Toulon and St-Tropez (June to September) and Port Miramar, La Croix-Valmer and Cavalaire-sur-Mer (July and August).

ÎLE DU LEVANT

postcode 83400 • pop 186

Nowhere is the quest for natural beauty more explicit than on oddball Île du Levant, a narrow 8km strip of an island, of which 90% is a military camp and strictly off- limits. The remaining pocket of **Héliopolis**, on the island's northeastern tip, has been a nudist colony since the 1930s. Its tiny population increases 10-fold in summer when the village is overrun with bathers baring all.

Boats arrive at and depart from **Port de L'Ayguade**. A small **tourist information hut** *(☎ 04 94 05 93 52)* operates here in summer. The central square, place du Village, is 1km uphill along route de L'Ayguade, the street running along Héliopolis' southern boundary. The post office, cafés and hotels are clustered around this square. The island's only camp site, **Le Colombéro** *(☎ 04 94 05 90 29; route de l'Ayguade; camping per person €7)* is 150m from the port.

The eastern part of the colony is covered by the **Domaine des Arbousiers**, a nature reservation with rare island plants such as the *Eryngium tricuspidatum* (a type of thistle). A nature trail leads from place du Village, east into the protected area. Contact the tourist office for information on guided tours.

Baring all is not obligatory – except on sandy **Plage Les Grottes**, the main nudist beach east of Port de L'Ayguade. From the port, walk in the direction of Plage de Sable Levant along **sentier Georges Rousseau**, a rocky coastal path. Bold signs reading *'Nudisme Intégral Obligatoire'* mark the moment you are obliged to strip.

Getting There & Away

Île du Levant is 10 minutes by boat from Port-Cros. There are regular boats year round from Le Lavandou and Hyères (see those sections), and in July and August from Port Miramar (La Londe), La Croix-Valmer and Cavalaire-sur-Mer.

ÎLE DE PORQUEROLLES

postcode 83400 • pop 350

Despite being the most developed of the Îles d'Hyères, Porquerolles is home to a wide variety of indigenous and tropical flora, including the requien larkspur, which grows nowhere else in the world. In winter, blossoming mimosas bring a splash of colour to the green island. April and May are the best months to spot some of its 114 bird species. The monk seal, which used to be a regular visitor to Porquerolles, is rarely seen around its shores today.

Most of the island is protected by the Parc National de Port-Cros, which manages 1000 of its 1254 richly vegetated hectares. Exploring by foot or by bike is as good a reason as any to visit. Avoid July and August when the happy owners of Porquerolles' numerous *résidences secondaires* return to the island, increasing the population six-fold. Smoking is forbidden outside the village.

Orientation & Information

Boats dock at the port on the island's northern coast. Walk 200m to the tourist office at the end of the jetty, then bear right along rue de la Ferme to place d'Armes, the central village square.

The **tourist office** *(☎ 04 94 58 33 76, fax 04 94 58 36 39; Ⓦ www.porquerolles.com; open 9am-5.30pm daily Apr-Nov, 9am-1pm Fri-Wed Dec-Mar)* sells island maps (€0.50) showing the *pistes cyclables* (cycling paths) and *sentiers pédestres* (footpaths), and the plastic *Guide Sous-Marin des Espèces Méditerranéenes*, designed to help snorkellers identify underwater flora (€12.20).

Société Marseillaise de Crédit *(3 rue de la Ferme)* has an ATM and currency exchange. The **post office** *(open 9am-noon & 1pm-4pm Mon-Fri, 9am-11.30am Sat)* is adjacent to Église Ste-Anne on place d'Armes.

Things to See & Do

Central **place d'Armes** is dominated by a giant, tree-shaded *pétanque* pitch. In summer, music concerts are held in **Église Ste-Anne**, on the south of the square. Festivities fill both the church and the square on 25 July, when islanders celebrate their patron saint's day.

From place d'Armes, head south along chemin Ste-Agathe to the 16th-century **Fort Ste-Agathe** *(☎ 04 94 12 30 40; adult/12-18 yrs/5-12 yrs €4/3/2; open 10am-12.30pm & 1.30pm-5.30pm daily May-Sept)*, built in 1518 and the only one of Porquerolles' fortifications open to visitors. Much of it dates from between 1812 and 1814 when Napoleon had the fort rebuilt after its plundering and destruction by the British in 1739. The fort hosts summer exhibitions. An awesome island panorama is visible from the tower.

From place d'Armes, walk or cycle south along rue de la Ferme and turn right at the crossroads. The Hameau Agricole, home to the **Conservatoire Botanique National Méditerranéen** *(☎ 04 94 12 30 40; admission free; open 9.30am-12.30pm & 1.30pm-5pm May-Sept)* is 700m along this trail. Inside the laboratories a well-documented history of the island flora is presented. A botanical trail leads visitors through gardens featuring plants typical to the island: 20 types of almond trees, 150 fig types, 83 lauriers rose types, and numerous olive trees.

The island's 82m-tall **lighthouse** *(admission free; open 11am-12.30pm & 2pm-4pm daily)*, built in 1837 to tip the island's southernmost cape, is 2km farther along rue de la Ferme. In summer the keeper allows visitors to climb to the top of his tower, which offers a stunning panorama on clear days. A military semaphore (142m) northeast of here marks the highest point of the island; it cannot be visited.

Porquerolles' **vineyards**, covering 110 hectares in the western part of the island, are tended by three wine producers. Each offers *dégustation* (wine-tasting) sessions of their predominantly rosé wines; the tourist office has a list.

Beaches

Porquerolles' northern coast is laced with beautiful sandy beaches, including **Plage de**

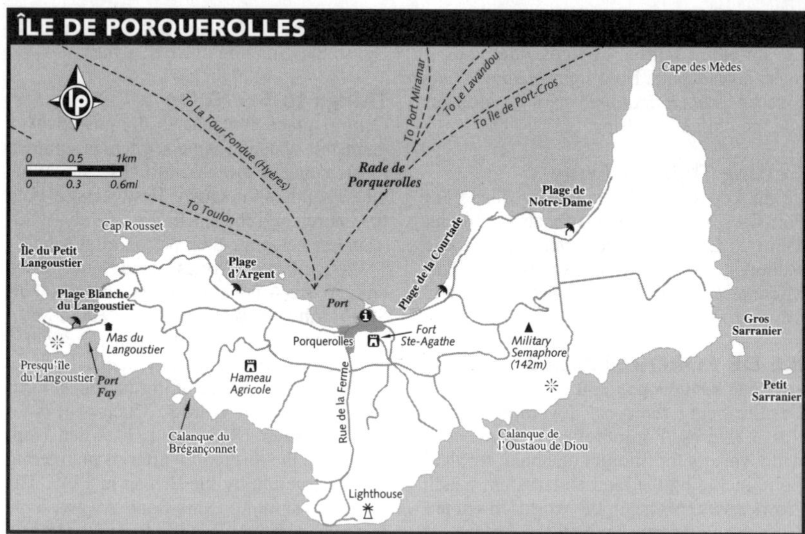

la Courtade, signposted 800m east from the port (follow the track uphill behind the tourist office). **Plage de Notre-Dame**, Porquerolles' largest and most beautiful beach, is 2.5km farther east along the same track. **Plage d'Argent**, 2km west of the village, is popular with families because of its beachside café-restaurant and lifeguards in summer. It's also the shortest walk from the port; follow rue de la Ferme, then turn right and follow the signs.

More secluded is **Plage Blanche du Langoustier**, a former lobster farm 4.5km from the village on the northern shores of the Presqu'île du Langoustier. It is called 'white' beach in contrast to the black sand that darkens the peninsula's southern shores around Port Fay – the legacy of a 19th- century soda-processing plant, which produced potash and soda from sulphuric acid and sea salt between 1828 and 1876.

Cliffs line the island's more dangerous southern coast where swimming and diving is restricted to **Calanque du Bréganҫonnet** to the east and **Calanque de l'Oustaou de Diou** to the west. Both are accessible by bicycle or foot. **Porquerolles Plongée** *(☎ 04 98 04 62 22; Ⓦ www.porquerolles-plongee.com)*, at the port, organises diving courses and expeditions here; count on paying €43/38 for a first-time/night dive, including equipment hire.

Places to Stay & Eat

Porquerolles is expensive. It has no camp site and wild camping is forbidden. The tourist office has a list of self-catering apartments to rent on a weekly basis. Hotels generally only accept guests on a half-board basis in July and August.

Relais de la Poste *(☎ 04 94 04 62 62, fax 04 94 58 33 57; Ⓔ relaispost@aol.com; place d'Armes; doubles with shower & toilet from €75)* is cranky – but cheap. It has bikes to rent for €19 a day.

Hôtel Ste-Anne *(☎ 04 94 04 63 00, fax 04 94 58 32 92; Ⓔ steanne.porquerolles@wanadoo.fr; place d'Armes; singles/doubles/triples €92/107/130, half-board high season singles/doubles/triples €115/153/190)* lends boules to guests keen to have a spin on the *pétanque* pitch in front.

Auberge des Glycines *(☎ 04 94 58 30 36, fax 04 94 58 35 22; Ⓔ auberge.glycines@wanadoo.fr; place d'Armes; 11 doubles with breakfast low/mid/high season €89/149/229, half-board per person low/mid/high season €59/99/139)* is an absolutely charming place with comfortable rooms and a garden. Its **restaurant** is rated highly and specialises in *cuisine Porquerollaise* – lots of fish dishes.

Mas du Langoustier *(☎ 04 94 58 30 09, fax 04 94 58 36 02; Ⓦ www.langoustier.com; doubles with half-board per person low/high*

LEANNE LOGAN

The quayside at St-Tropez – the tiny village is still a lure to artists and the wealthy

DAN HERRICK

One of the traditional houses found in St-Tropez

DAVID TOMLINSON

A brightly coloured *chapelle*, St-Tropez

NEIL SETCHFIELD

View over the port in Monte Carlo, Monaco

season €165/175), one of Europe's hip hotels built in 1931, has its own vineyards and offers stunning views from its seaside perch on the island's southwestern tip. Its starred restaurant – exclusively for guests – is simply divine, darling.

Place d'Armes is armed with fruit stalls, a **delicatessen** and **bakery**, enabling you to build that perfect picnic, and there's a small **supermarket** at the port.

Getting There & Away

Regular boats operated by Transport Littoral Varois (TLV) link La Tour Fondue near Hyères (see Boat Excursions under Hyères later) with Porquerolles year round. June to September, there is one boat daily to/from Toulon; four weekly boats to/from St-Tropez; and one a day from Wednesday to Saturday (daily in July and August) to/from Le Lavandou (see Boat Excursions in those sections).

June to September, **SNRTM** *(☎ 04 94 05 21 14)* operates two or three boats daily from Port Miramar, south of La Londe, to Porquerolles (adult/four to 10 years €19/12.50 return). The same company operates boats from La Croix-Valmer and Cavalaire-sur-Mer in July and August.

Getting Around

Two options: feet or wheels (motorised tourist vehicles are forbidden). There are no fewer than nine bicycle-rental outlets in the village, including **La Meduse** *(☎ 04 94 58 34 27; open 7am-6pm or 7pm daily Mar-Sept)* and **Chez Nanard** *(☎ 04 94 58 34 89; open 7am-6pm or 7pm daily Mar-Sept)* at the port. Both charge €12.50/9 per day for an adult/child's bike. Energetic parents can hire covered buggies *(remorques)* to pedal kids around the island for €12.50 per day. In the village, **Le Cycle Porquerollais** *(☎ 04 94 58 30 32; 1 rue de la Ferme)* has all types of two-wheel contraptions, including tandems that cost €18.50/27.50 per half-/full day.

Taxi The luggage-laden can hail an **electric taxi** *(☎ 06 81 67 77 12)* to bear the load between port and hotel.

Boat Opposite the tourist office at the port, **Locamarine 75** *(☎ 04 94 58 35 84, 04 94 58 31 19)* rents speedboats (6cv without a licence) for €70/85 per half-/full day for up to five people.

Yellow Pélican Taxi Line *(☎ 04 94 58 31 19, 06 09 52 31 19)* operates a 24-hour boat taxi service.

ÎLE DE BENDOR

The pinprick island of Bendor lies 300m offshore from Bandol, 19km east of Toulon. The 7-hectare rocky islet was a place of exile during the 17th century, and then uninhabited until 1951. Paul Ricard, best known for his pastis production, bought the isle and transformed it into one big leisure centre. Larger-than-life Ricard creations dominating the island include the **Espace Culturel Paul Ricard** *(☎ 04 94 29 44 34)*, where art exhibitions are held; a **Palais des Congrès** (Congress Centre); and the **Exposition Universelle des Vins et Spiritueux** *(admission free; 10am-noon & 2pm-6pm Tues-Sun)* which unravels the history and production of wine and spirits

Getting There & Away

Boats to Île de Bendor depart from Bandol (see that section under Towards Marseilles later in this chapter) every half-hour (less in winter) between 7am and 2am year round. Journey time is seven minutes.

ÎLES DES EMBIEZ

Bendor's big sister, the Embiez archipelago, is less than 1km off the Presqu'île du Cap Sicié, between Sanary-sur-Mer and Toulon.

The largest of the islet cluster, officially Île de la Tour Fondue but better known as Îles des Embiez, is also home to the **Institut Océanographique Paul Ricard** *(☎ 04 94 34 02 49; adult/4-11 yrs €4/2; open 10am-12.30pm & 1.30pm-6.30pm July & Aug, to 5.30pm Sept-June, closed Sat morning Sept-Apr)*, in an old fort. Over 100 Mediterranean species can be viewed in its 27 sea-water aquariums and marine museum.

The rest of Ricard's 95-hectare island, purchased in 1958, is occupied by a vast **pleasure port**, patches of pine forest, *maquis* scrub and vineyards, apartment blocks and a couple of expensive hotels.

Getting There & Away

Boats to the island leave year round from the small port at **Le Brusc** (adult/three to 10 years €7/4 return), a beach resort adjoining Six-Fours-les-Plages, 5km south of Sanary-sur-Mer. In summer, boats run about every 40 minutes, less frequently the rest of the year.

June and September, there are also boats to the island from Bandol (€7/4 return) and Sanary-sur-Mer (see that section later).

Toulon & Around

Relatively unspoilt coastline becomes increasingly urban as you head west to Toulon and Marseilles. A final pocket of blue and green surrounds **La Londe** (pop 8840), midway (10km) between Le Lavandou and Hyères. Olive groves, vineyards and flower gardens are but some of the pretty scapes you can explore on foot, organised by the **tourist office** *(☎ 04 94 01 53 10, fax 04 94 01 53 19; Ⓦ www.ot-lalondemaures.fr; ave Albert Roux)*. Two kilometres east, 450-odd species of tropical birds fly around the **Jardin d'Oiseaux Tropicaux** *(☎ 04 94 35 02 15; route de Valcros; adult/3-12 yrs €7/5; open 9am-7pm daily June-Sept, 2pm-6pm daily Oct & Feb-May)*, signposted off the N98.

Port Mirmar, 3km south, is a landing stage for seasonal boats to/from Porquerolles and Port-Cros (see those sections). From the small port, follow signs to **L'Argentière** and farther east to Fort de Brégançon – the scenic lane, dubbed the **Route des Vins de la Londe** (the wine trail of La Londe), goes past dozens of chateaux to taste and buy wine.

HYÈRES

postcode 83400 • pop 51,417

Hyères, with its age-old palm trees, retains a charm of its own. It was settled by Greeks from Marseilles in 350BC, Tolstoy spent time here in the 1860s and Robert Louis Stevenson worked on *Kidnapped* (1886) while he lived in Hyères.

La Capte, 4km south of Hyères centre, comprises two narrow sand bars supporting salt pans (Les Salins des Presquiers) and a lake (Étang des Presquiers). Pink flamingos add a splash of colour to the otherwise barren landscape. The spectacular, western sand bar – the route du Sel (Salt Road) – is only accessible in summer. Buses use the eastern bar road (D42), the northern section of which is lined with a silky-smooth, two-lane cycling track that runs for 2km from the beach resort of **L'Ayguade** to the roundabout in front of Toulon-Hyères airport.

At the foot of La Capte sits beach-lined **Presqu'île de Giens**. French poet and 1960 Nobel Literature prize winner, St-John Perse (1887–1975), is buried in the tiny cemetery off route Madrague, on the peninsula's northwestern shores.

Orientation

Hyères' medieval Vieille Ville (old town) is perched on a hillside north of the new town. The nearest beach is La Capte. The pleasure port, Port d'Hyères, from where boats to Le Levant and Port-Cros depart, is on La Capte's eastern shore. Boats to Porquerolles depart from La Tour Fondue – the port on the southeastern corner of Presqu'île de Giens.

The train station, place de l'Europe, is 1.5km south of the old town centre. Walk northeast from the station on ave Edith Cavelland to place du 11 Novembre, then north along palm tree-lined ave Gambetta, the main street in the new town. Buses to the centre depart from rue de la Gare, opposite the train station. Buses to Port d'Hyères and La Tour Fondue leave from the place de l'Europe, immediately in front of the station.

Information

The **tourist office** *(☎ 04 94 01 84 50, fax 04 94 01 84 51; Ⓦ www.ot-hyeres.fr; 3 ave Ambroise Thomas; open 9am-6pm Mon-Fri, 10am-4pm Sat)* takes accommodation bookings for the Hyères region and arranges guided tours.

The **post office** *(ave Joseph Clotis; open 8.30am-5.55pm Mon-Fri, to 4.55pm Wed, 8.30am-11.55am Sat)* is next to the town hall. Internet access at **Cyber L'Arène** *(rue Pierre Moulis; open 10am-10pm daily)* costs €2.30 per 30 minutes. Near the bus station, the **Maison de l'Internet** *(☎ 04 94 65 92 82; ⓔ maison.internet@voila.fr; 18 ave de Bélgique; open 9.30am-12.30pm & 1.30pm-6pm Mon-Sat)* charges €6 an hour.

Walking Tour

A Saturday morning market fills **place Georges Clémenceau** with a wonderful jumble of second-hand furniture, floor tiles, shoes, handbags, marmalade spiced with lavender and the like. Thirteenth-century **Porte Massillon**, on the western side of the square, is the main entrance to the Vieille Ville. Walk west along cobbled rue Massillon to beautifully arcaded **rue des Porches**.

North of the market square stands 13th-century **Église St-Louis**, a fine example of

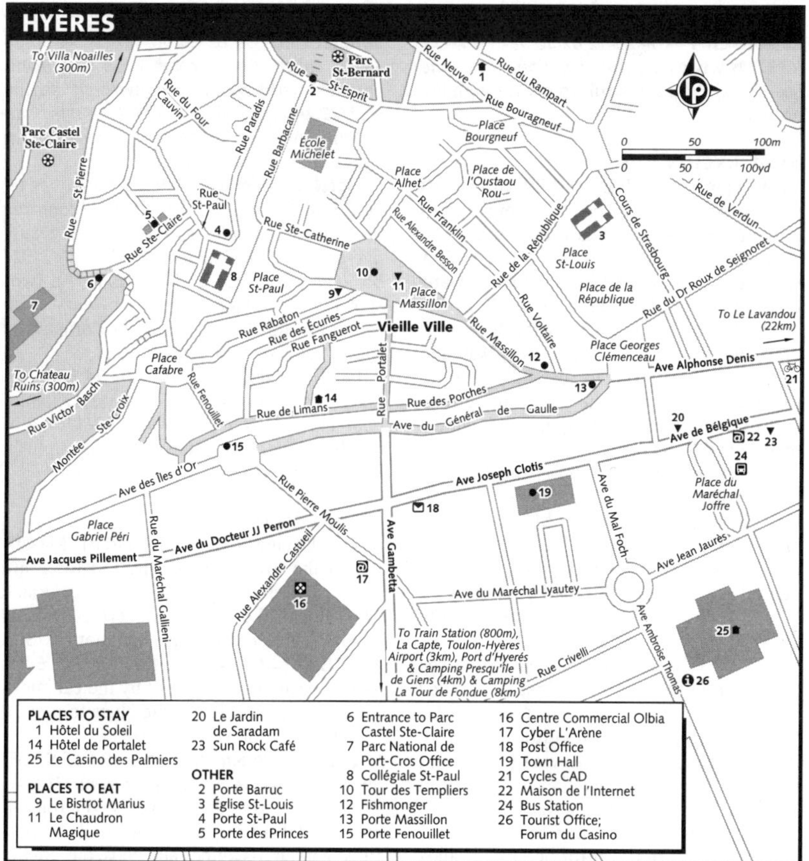

sober, Romanesque-style architecture. Weave your way uphill to rue Bourgneuf, then walk west along its continuation, rue St-Esprit, to the limestone arch of **Porte Barruc**. From here, steps pass an iron gate to the rambling hillside grove of the **Parc St-Bernard**. Remnants of the 12th-century defensive city wall and **Château St-Bernard** are visible.

Below the walls stands the imposing **Villa Noailles**, designed by Robert Mallet-Stevens in 1923 for Vicomte Charles de Noailles, a devoted patron of modern art. The architect's mission: to build a winter residence 'interesting to inhabit'. The result: a cubist maze of concrete and glass, set within a Mediterranean park designed by Noailles and featuring a cubist garden designed by Gabriel Guevrekian in 1925. The villa, host to temporary contemporary design exhibitions, is currently closed for renovation. Check at the tourist office if it is open.

Heading back downhill along rue Barbacane, you come to 12th-century **Porte St-Paul**, the first city gate to be built. It frames the **Collégiale St-Paul**, comprising two churches dating from the 12th and 14th centuries joined together perpendicularly. The Gothic section houses a vast collection of predominantly 18th-century, ex-votive paintings. From the church terrace, a panorama of old and new Hyères unfolds.

West of Porte St-Paul, rue St-Paul and rue Ste-Claire lead to the **Parc Castel Ste-Claire**, a 17th-century convent converted into a private residence. The American writer Edith Wharton lived here from 1927. Today it houses the headquarters of the **Parc National de Port-Cros** *(☎ 04 94 12 82 30, fax 04 94 12 82 31; 🅦 www.portcrosparcnational.fr; 50 rue Ste-Claire)*. You can stroll freely through the grounds.

Boat Excursions

Boats, operated by **Transport Littoral Varois** *(TLV; 🅦 www.tlv-tvm.com)* sail from Hyères to the three Îles d'Hyères year round.

Boats to Porquerolles (adult/under four €14/free return) depart from the **Gare Maritime de La Tour Fondue** *(☎ 04 94 58 21 81)* on the Presqu'île de Giens, with departures every 30 minutes or so between 7.30am and 6.30 or 7pm daily, May to September, and six to 10 daily the rest of the year. Sailing time is 20 minutes; transporting an adult/child's bicycle is €11/8.50.

In July and August, two-island tours of Porquerolles and Port-Cros (using the regular TLV boats) are available Monday to Friday (adult/under four €24/free return). You can also sail from La Tour Fondue to Porquerolles in a **glass-bottomed boat** *(☎ 04 94 58 95 14)*; there are two to four sailings daily (€16.50/free).

Boats to Île du Levant and Port-Cros leave Hyères from **Port d'Hyères** *(also called Port de la Gavine; ☎ 04 94 57 44 07)* on La Capte. There is one return sailing daily from Port d' Hyères to Île du Levant (1½ hours) in April, June and September, two daily in July and August, and four a week October to March. Boats stop at Port-Cros (one hour) en route. A return ticket for one/two islands costs €20/23 (under 4s free).

Motorists must pay €3/6 per half-/full day to park at either port.

Places to Stay

Camping There are no less than nine sites on Presqu'île de Giens, including:

Camping La Presqu'île de Giens *(☎ 04 94 58 22 86, fax 04 94 58 11 63; 🅦 www.camping-giens.com; 153 rouet de la Madrague; camping for 2 people with tent & car low/high season €12/16, 4-person mobile homes low/mid/high season €190/320/410 per week; open mid-Mar–mid-Oct)* is a well-equipped site with dozens of facilities. Its smaller sister site, **Camping La Tour de Fondue**, spitting distance – almost – from the Gare Maritime de la Tour de Fondue, charges the same rates.

Hotels At the bottom of the hill, **Hôtel de Portalet** *(☎ 04 94 65 39 40, fax 04 94 35 86 33; 🅔 chbenit@oreka.com; 4 rue de Limans; doubles with washbasin low/high season €31/39, with shower & toilet €42/49)* is comfortably snug. Rooms are large, airy and have appealing age-old furnishings.

Hôtel du Soleil *(☎ 04 94 65 16 26, fax 04 94 35 46 00; 🅦 www.hoteldusoleil.com; rue du Rampart; singles/doubles/triples/quads/five-person rooms low season €28/34/42/52/55, high season €39/52/62/73/79)*, a two-star, ivy-clad place at the top of very steep (read: not for the unfit) rue du Rampart, is Medieval Hyères' loveliest hotel.

Le Casino des Palmiers *(☎ 04 94 12 80 80, fax 04 94 12 80 94; 1 rue Ambroise Thomas; doubles low/high season from €90/110)*, top-notch in style, languishes in the city's plush, glass-topped casino.

Places to Eat

Rue de Limans, rue Portalet and rue Massillon in the lower part of the old town are lined with touristy places to eat. Place Massillon is likewise one big terrace restaurant in summer. Near the bus station, **Sun Rock Café** *(☎ 04 94 65 02 48; 22 ave de Bélgique)* – easily distinguished by the car sticking out of its facade – is the place to rock to live music while you eat.

Le Jardin de Saradam *(☎ 04 94 65 97 53; 35 ave de Bélgique; lunch/dinner menu €12.50/15.50, tajines from €13)* serves Mediterranean and oriental cuisine in a beautiful, flowerpot-filled garden. Its tajines and couscous are the best in town.

Le Bistrot Marius *(☎ 04 94 35 88 38; 1 place Massillon; menus €15, €22.50 & €30)* is reputed to serve some of the best fodder on this busy old-town square. Fish dishes are the house speciality.

Le Chaudron Magique *(☎ 04 94 35 38 45; 8 place Massillon)* invites you to lunch on a hearty plate of *aïoli Provençal complet* (a boiled egg, boiled potatoes, a mound of boiled vegetables, shellfish and a bowl of garlicky aïoli) or a well-grilled fish of the day (€16).

Picnics can be built from produce sold at the Saturday morning **fruit and vegetable market**. In the old town there are a couple of fabulous **fishmongers** *(rue Massillon; open mornings only)* where you buy the catch of the day. Delicious biscuits and bread are baked several times daily at **La Tarte Tropézienne** *(53 ave Gambetta)*.

Getting There & Away

Air Towards La Capte, **Toulon-Hyères airport** *(Aéroport de Toulon-Hyères; ☎ 04 94 00 83 83)* is 3km south of Hyères centre.

Bus From the **bus station** *(place du Maréchal Joffre)*, **Sodetrav** *(☎ 04 94 12 55 12)* operates at least seven buses daily to/from Toulon *(€5.80, 40 minutes)*, Le Lavandou (€5.80, 30 minutes) and St-Tropez (€13.20, 1¼ hours). Nice-Toulon buses run by **Phocéens Cars** *(☎ 04 93 85 66 61)* stop in Hyères.

Train From the Hyères **train station** *(place de l'Europe)*, there are numerous local trains to/from Toulon (€3.40, 20 minutes). The Marseilles–Hyères train (€11.20, 1¼ hours, four daily) stops at Cassis, La Ciotat, Bandol, Ollioules-Sanary and Toulon.

Getting Around

To/From the Airport Sodetrav runs a regular shuttle bus from Toulon-Hyères airport to Hyères bus station (€4.40, 10 minutes). During the summer there are also regular daily services from the airport to Toulon and St-Tropez; buses coincide with flight arrivals/departures.

Bus Buses link Hyères bus station with the train station (€1.20, five minutes), Port d'Hyères (€1.20, 15 minutes), La Capte (€2.40, 20 minutes), Giens (€2.90, 30 minutes) and La Tour Fondue (€2.90, 35 minutes). Buses run every 30 minutes between 6.25am and 10pm.

For Port d'Hyères (boats to Îles du Levant and Port-Cros), get off at Le Port stop, ave de la Meditérranée. For Tour Fondue (boats to Porquerolles), get off at the Tour Fondue stop.

Bicycle & Rollerblade You can rent mountain bikes at **Cycles CAD** *(☎ 04 94 65 07 69; 50 ave Alphonse Denis)* for €11/19/61 per day/weekend/week.

Hyères Roller Attitude *(☎ 04 94 00 68 74; ⓔ hyeres-roller-attitude@wanadoo.fr; 3579 route de l'Almanare)*, on the road out of the town is the place to hire tandems (€28 a day) and mountain bikes (€14), as well as rollerblades (€14).

CAP DE CARQUEIRANNE

Pretty little Cap de Carqueiranne is a pocket of coastal green, immediately west of Hyères.

Romantic images are conjured up by the remnants of a sea port founded by the Greeks in the 4th century BC at the **Site Archaéologique d'Olbia** *(☎ 04 94 57 98 28; adult/under 18 €4/free; open 9.30am-12.30pm & 2.30pm-7pm daily Apr & June-Sept)*, an archaeological site in L'Almanarre, a southern suburb of Hyères at the Presqu'île de Giens' northwesternmost tip.

From uninteresting **Carqueiranne** (pop 8560), 4km west along the D559, a confusing maze of lanes crosses the partly forested cape. The coastal path that wends its way around it is a particularly scenic means of exploring; as are the underwater snorkelling expeditions organised on Wednesday (€7, 1½ hours) in July and August by the tourist office in **Le Pradet** *(☎ 04 94 21 71 69, fax 04 94 08 56 96; ⓔ offtourismepradet@yahoo.fr; place du Général de Gaulle; open 9.30am-1pm & 3.30pm-7pm Mon-Sat, 9.30am-1pm Sun)*. Snorkelling and dives are also organised by the **Centre de Plongée** *(☎ 04 94 08 38 09)*, based at Port des Oursinières, a delightful little harbour on the cape's southwestern shore.

In La Garonne, the **Musée de la Mine** *(☎ 04 94 08 32 46; ⓔ mcg@fm.fr; chemin du Bau Rouge; adult/under 12 €6.20/3.10; open 2pm-5.30pm daily July, Aug & school holidays, 2pm-5pm Wed, Sat & Sun rest of year)*, with its distinctive red-brick chimneys, is a disused copper mine where the cape's mining tradition is delved into underground.

An indisputable highlight of Cap de Carqueiranne is lunch overlooking the sea at **L'Oursinade** *(☎ 04 94 21 77 06; L'Oursinières; menu €30)*. Tucked away on a cliff in L'Oursinières (by car follow the signs), this hidden spot only serves seafood and is famed for its fabulous Toulonnais *bouillabaisse* (€38; order 48 hours in advance), which has potatoes in it as well as a shoal of fish.

Local bus No 9 links Toulon with L'Oursinières (€1.10, hourly 6.45am to 6pm). There is also a two-way cycling track between Toulon and the cape.

TOULON

postcode 83000 • pop 160,639

Originally a Roman colony, Toulon only became part of France in 1481; the city grew in importance after Henri IV established an arsenal here. In the 17th century the port was enlarged by Vauban. The young Napoleon Bonaparte first made a name for himself in 1793 during a siege in which the English, who had taken over Toulon, were expelled.

As in any large port, there's a lively quarter, near the water, with heaps of bars, where locals and sailors spill out every door. A hectic flea market fills place du Théâtre on Friday. Women travelling on their own should avoid some of the old city streets at night, particularly around rue Chevalier Paul and the western end of rue Pierre Sémard.

Toulon's funniest contemporary product is the great Provençal actor Raimu (see the Facts about Provence chapter). A statue of the lovable comic stands tall in the old town on place des Trois Dauphins.

Orientation

Toulon is built around a *rade*, a sheltered bay lined with quays. To the west is the naval base and east the ferry terminal, where boats set sail for Corsica. The city is at its liveliest along quai de la Sinse and quai Constradt – from where ferries depart for the Îles d'Hyères – and in the old city. Northwest of the old city is the train station.

Separating the old city from the northern section is a multilane, multinamed thoroughfare (ave du Maréchal Leclerc and blvd de Strasbourg as it runs through the centre).

Information

The **tourist office** *(☎ 04 94 18 53 00, fax 04 94 18 53 09; W www.toulontourisme.com; place Raimu; open 9am-6pm Mon & Wed-Sat, 10am-6pm Tues, 10am-noon Sun)* runs guided thematic city tours (adult/12 to 18 years €3/1.50) and nature walks twice a week.

Commercial banks line blvd de Strasbourg and the **post office** *(rue Dr Jean Bertholet; open 8am-6.30pm Mon-Fri, to 6pm Tues, 8am-noon Sat)* has Cyberposte. **Cybercafé AVE** *(☎ 04 94 93 43 31; 5 place Puget; W www.a-v-e.net; open 9am-9.30pm)* is a popular bar run by the gay association AVE.

Travel agency **Voyages Wasteels** *(☎ 08 25 88 70 61, fax 04 94 91 92 60; e toulontoesca@wasteels.fr; 3 blvd Pierre Tosca)* faces the train station.

Musée de Toulon

Toulon Museum *(☎ 04 94 36 81 00; 113 ave du Maréchal Leclerc)*, in a Renaissance-style building, houses an unexceptional **Musée d'Art** *(Art Museum; admission free; open 1pm-6.30pm daily)* and a moth-eaten **Musée d'Histoire Naturelle** *(Natural History Museum; admission free; open 9.30am-noon & 2pm-6pm Mon-Fri, 1pm-6pm Sat & Sun)*.

Tour Royale & Musée de la Marine

The sturdy Royal Tower *(☎ 04 94 02 17 99; place Monsenergue; open 10am-noon & 1pm-6pm daily Apr–mid-Sept, 10am-noon & 2pm-6pm Wed-Mon mid-Sept–Mar)* on the Pointe de la Mître in the suburb of Le Mourillon, just south of Toulon centre and the ferry terminal, was constructed under Louis XII at the start of the 16th century. The tower has served as a prison in the past. Views of the bay, Toulon and Mont Faron, from the top of the tower are quite breathtaking.

The Marine Museum *(☎ 04 94 02 02 01; place Monsenergue; adult/under 18 €4.60/free)* is in Toulon's lovely 18th-century arsenal building. This sea-faring museum is open the same hours as the Royal Tower and tickets include admission to both.

Mont Faron

Overlooking the old city from the northern side is Mont Faron (580m), from where you can see Toulon's port in its true magnificence. Not far from the hill's summit rises the **Mémorial du Débarquement** *(☎ 04 94 88 08 09; adult/8-16 yrs €3.80/1.55; open 9.45am-12.45pm & 1.45pm-6.30pm daily July-Sept, to 6pm Tues-Sun May & June, to 5.30pm Oct-Apr)*, which commemorates the Allied landings that took place along the coast here in August 1944. Historical displays and a film form part of this fascinating museum.

A **cable car** *(téléphérique; ☎ 04 94 92 68 25; adult/4-19 yrs €5.80/4; open 9am-noon & 2pm-6pm Tues-Sun, closed windy days)* climbs the mountain from blvd Amiral Vence. Those who are visiting **Zoo du Mont Faron** *(☎ 04 94 88 07 89; adult/4-10 yrs €7/5; open 10am-6.30pm daily, closed rainy days)* can buy a combination zoo/cable-car ticket for €9.50/5.50.

To get to the cable car, take bus No 40 from place de la Liberté to the *téléphérique* stop. The tourist office has mountains of information on walking and mountain-bike trails on Mont Faron.

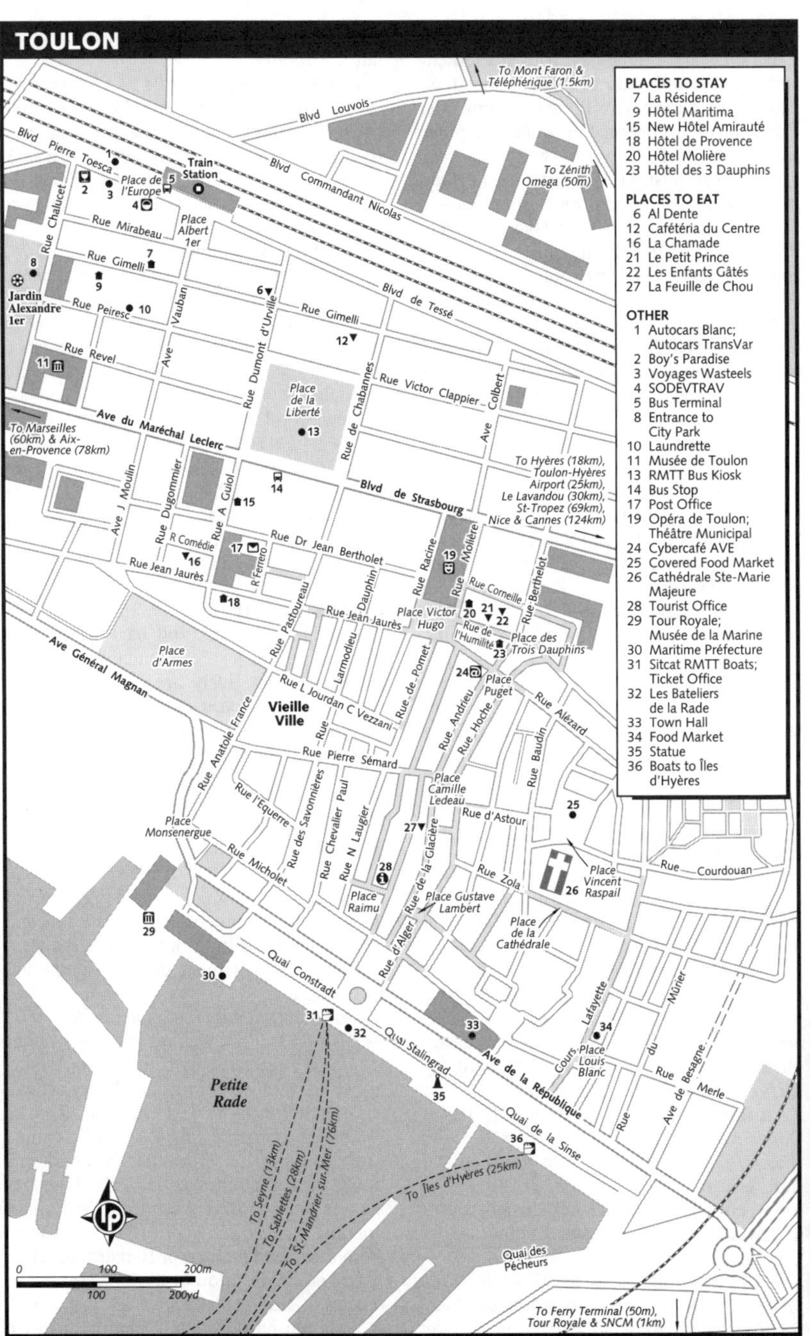
TOULON
PLACES TO STAY
7 La Résidence
9 Hôtel Maritima
15 New Hôtel Amirauté
18 Hôtel de Provence
20 Hôtel Molière
23 Hôtel des 3 Dauphins
PLACES TO EAT
6 Al Dente
12 Cafétéria du Centre
16 La Chamade
21 Le Petit Prince
22 Les Enfants Gâtés
27 La Feuille de Chou
OTHER
1 Autocars Blanc; Autocars TransVar
2 Boy's Paradise
3 Voyages Wasteels
4 SODEVTRAV
5 Bus Terminal
8 Entrance to City Park
10 Laundrette
11 Musée de Toulon
13 RMTT Bus Kiosk
14 Bus Stop
17 Post Office
19 Opéra de Toulon; Théâtre Municipal
24 Cybercafé AVE
25 Covered Food Market
26 Cathédrale Ste-Marie Majeure
28 Tourist Office
29 Tour Royale; Musée de la Marine
30 Maritime Préfecture
31 Sitcat RMTT Boats; Ticket Office
32 Les Bateliers de la Rade
33 Town Hall
34 Food Market
35 Statue
36 Boats to Îles d'Hyères
To Mont Faron & Téléphérique (1.5km)
To Zénith Omega (50m)
To Marseilles (60km) & Aix-en-Provence (78km)
To Hyères (18km), Toulon-Hyères Airport (25km), Le Lavandou (30km), St-Tropez (69km), Nice & Cannes (124km)
To Ferry Terminal (50m), Tour Royale & SNCM (1km)
To Seyne (13km)
To Sablettes (28km)
To St-Mandrier-sur-Mer (76km)
To Îles d'Hyères (25km)
Train Station
Blvd Louvois
Blvd Pierre Toesca
Blvd Commandant Nicolas
Place de l'Europe
Place Albert 1er
Rue Chalucet
Rue Mirabeau
Rue Gimelli
Rue Peiresc
Rue Revel
Jardin Alexandre 1er
Ave Vauban
Rue Dumont d'Urville
Blvd de Tessé
Rue Victor Clappier
Ave Colbert
Place de la Liberté
Rue de Chabannes
Ave du Maréchal Leclerc
Blvd de Strasbourg
Ave J Moulin
Rue Dugommier
Rue A Guiol
R Comédie
Rue Jean Jaurès
R Ferrero
Rue Dr Jean Bertholet
Rue Dauphin
Rue Racine
Rue Molière
Rue Corneille
Rue Berthelot
Place Victor Hugo
Rue de l'Humilité
Place des Trois Dauphins
Place Puget
Rue Alézard
Ave Général Magnan
Place d'Armes
Rue Pastoureau
Rue Larmodieu
Rue L Jourdan C Vezzani
Rue de Pomet
Rue Andrieu
Rue Hoche
Rue Baudin
Vieille Ville
Rue Anatole France
Rue Pierre Sémard
Place Camille Ledeau
Rue d'Astour
Rue l'Equerre
Place Monsenergue
Rue Micholet
Rue des Savonnières
Rue Chevalier Paul
Rue N Laugier
Rue de la Glacière
Place Raimu
Place Gustave Lambert
Rue d'Alger
Rue Zola
Place Vincent Raspail
Place de la Cathédrale
Rue Courdouan
Quai Constradt
Quai Stalingrad
Ave de la République
Cours Lafayette
Place Louis Blanc
Rue du Mûrier
Rue du Merle
Ave de Besagne
Quai de la Sinse
Petite Rade
Quai des Pêcheurs
0
100
200m
100
200yd

Boat Excursions

Excursions around the bay, with a commentary (French only) on the events that took place here during WWII, leave from quai Cronstadt or its continuation, quai de la Sinse *(adult/4-10 yrs €8/5; one hour)*.

June to August, **Les Bateliers de la Rade** *(☎ 04 94 46 24 65; quai de la Sinse)* runs a daily boat excursion to Îles d'Hyères (€18 to Porquerolles; €28 to Porquerolles, Port-Cros and Le Levant). The trip to only Porquerolles takes one hour. It's another 40 minutes to Port-Cros, from where it is 20 minutes to Île du Levant. **SNRTM** *(☎ 04 94 62 41 14; 1247 route du Faron)*, with an office at the port, is another company that runs seasonal boats to the Îles d'Hyères.

Sitcat boats *(☎ 04 94 46 35 46)* run by RMTT, the local transport company, link quai Cronstadt with the towns on the peninsula across the harbour, including La Seyne, St-Mandrier-sur-Mer and Sablettes. Tickets for the 20-minute journey cost €1.30 at the portside **ticket office** *(open 7.30am-12.30pm & 1.15pm-6.15pm Mon-Sat)* and €1.60 aboard. Boats run from around 6am to 8pm.

Special Events

For nearly 50 years, Toulon has held an **International Festival of Music** (mainly classical) in various locations around town, including the Théâtre Municipal on place Victor Hugo, from June to early July.

Places to Stay

There are plenty of cheap options in the old city, though some (particularly those at the western end of rue Jean Jaurès) are rumoured to double as brothels.

Hôtel Molière *(☎ 04 94 92 78 35, fax 04 94 62 85 82; 12 rue Molière; singles/doubles with washbasin from €14/19, with shower €20/25, with shower & toilet €30/36)* is a one-star place next to the opera. Use of the hallway shower costs €2.29.

La Résidence *(☎ 04 94 92 92 81; 18 rue Gimelli; doubles with washbasin €20, with shower/toilet & TV €34)*, near the train station, is a two-star pad with an impressive lobby, complete with an enormous gilt mirror and worn Oriental carpets. Rooms are far from grand, but not bad for the price.

Hôtel Maritima *(☎ 04 94 92 39 33; 9 rue Gimelli; singles/doubles with washbasin €22/23.50, doubles with shower/shower & toilet €29/33)* has equally simple – dare one say tatty? – rooms.

Hôtel de Provence *(☎ 04 94 93 19 00; 53 rue Jean Jaurès; singles/doubles with washbasin €21.50/23, doubles/quads with shower €32/35.50, doubles/quads with shower & toilet €36/39)* is dirt-cheap and often full, despite its somewhat shady location near several sex shops.

Hôtel des 3 Dauphins *(☎ 04 94 92 65 79, fax 04 94 92 55 96; 9 place des Trois Dauphins; doubles with washbasin/shower/shower & toilet €29/35/39)*, peering down on Raimu in the old town, has been recently refurbished and is as smart as you get for a one-star joint in Toulon.

New Hôtel Amirauté *(☎ 04 94 22 19 67, fax 04 94 09 34 72; ⓔ toulonamiraute@new-hotel.com; 4 rue A Guiol; singles/doubles low season €58/63, high season €61/66)* is a middle-of-the-road, could-be-anywhere-in-the-world type of place where you can happily forget you are in Toulon.

Places to Eat

Restaurants, terraces and bars with occasional live music are abundant along the quays. Another lively area is place Victor Hugo and neighbouring place Puget. Cheaper fare can be found in the dilapidated streets around rue Chevalier Paul.

Caféteria du Centre *(☎ 04 94 92 68 57; 27-29 rue Gimelli; menu €6.50)* serves cheap three-course *menu* at a price that can't be argued with.

Al Dente *(☎ 04 94 93 02 50; 15 rue Gimelli; menus €9.80 & €17.60)*, named in honour of the way pasta should be cooked, is a cool and elegant tummy-filling option near the train station. It serves meat dishes, salads and fresh pasta.

Les Enfants Gâtés *(The Spoilt Children; ☎ 04 94 09 14 67; 7 rue Corneille; starters/mains €8/15)* is a refreshingly contemporary literary café, run by a young and cheery crowd.

Le Petit Prince *(☎ 04 94 93 03 45; 10 rue de l'Humilité; starters/mains €6.50/15)*, named after Antoine de St-Exupéry's children's book, serves quintessential French dishes such as steak cooked in salt from the Camargue and *magret de canard* (the breast meat from a fattened mallard or Barbary duck).

La Feuille de Chou *(☎ 04 94 62 09 26; 15 rue de la Glacière; plat du jour €9, menu €17)* is a simple but absolutely charming bistro complete with a peaceful terrace on olive tree-bespeckled place Eugène Baboulene. Don't miss the framed beer mat collection.

La Chamade *(☎ 04 94 92 28 58; 25 rue Comédie; 2-course/3-course menu €20/31)* is an upmarket restaurant where you can dine on temptations such as *foie gras* pan-fried in three types of vinegar, roasted pigeon or chocolate soup with caramelised fruits and hot pistachio gateau. Reservations are definitely required.

Buy food outside at Toulon's open-air **food market** *(cours Lafayette; open Tues-Sun)* or inside at its covered **food market** *(place Vincent Raspail; open Tues-Sun)*.

Entertainment

Boy's Paradise *(☎ 04 94 09 35 90; 1 blvd Pierre Toesca)* opens its doors to a gay crowd at 11pm or midnight, depending on the day. The hefty €11 admission fee includes a drink.

Operas and ballets take to the stage at the **Opéra de Toulon** *(☎ 04 94 93 03 76; e operadetoulon@wanadoo.fr; blvd de Strasbourg)*. Tickets cost anything from €14 to €50.

Toulon's prime venue for rock, pop and other big-band concerts is **Zénith Omega** *(☎ 04 94 22 66 77; e zenith.omega@wanadoo.fr; blvd du Commandant Nicolas)*.

Getting There & Away

Air Twenty-five kilometres east of the city is **Toulon-Hyères airport** *(Aéroport de Toulon-Hyères; ☎ 04 94 00 83 83)*.

Bus From the Toulon **bus terminal** *(place de l'Europe)*, to the right as you exit the train station, **Sodetrav** *(☎ 04 94 28 93 40; 4 blvd Pierre Toesca)* operates buses along the coast; **Autocars Blanc** *(☎ 04 94 69 08 28; blvd Pierre Toesca)* and **Autocars TransVar** *(☎ 04 94 09 15 49; blvd Pierre Toesca)* run buses inland.

Bus No 103 to Hyères (€6.75, 40 minutes, seven daily) continues east along the coast, stopping at Le Lavandou (€7, 1¼ hours) and other towns, before arriving in St-Tropez (€15.90, 2¼ hours, seven daily).

Phocéens Cars *(☎ 04 93 85 66 61)* operates up to six buses daily to/from Nice (€22, 2½ hours, six daily Monday to Saturday), via Hyères and Cannes.

Train From the **train station** *(place de l'Europe)* there are frequent connections to numerous coastal cities, including Marseilles (€9.30, one hour), St-Raphaël (€12.20, 50 minutes), Cannes (€15.60, 1¼ hours), Nice (€18.50), Antibes (€16.70, 1½ hours), 1½ hours), Monaco (€20.20, 2¼ hours) and Menton (€20.50, 2½ hours).

Boat Ferries to Corsica and Sardinia are run by **SNCM** *(☎ 08 91 70 18 01; 49 ave de l'Infanterie de Marine)*, with an office opposite the ferry terminal. See the Getting There & Away chapter.

For information about boats to the Îles d'Hyères see Boat Excursions earlier.

Getting Around

To/From the Airport There are shuttle buses run by **Sodetrav** *(☎ 04 94 12 55 00)* from Toulon-Hyères airport to Toulon train station (€9.50, 35 minutes), via Hyères (€4.30, 10 minutes). Buses coincide with flight arrivals/departures. Tickets are sold on the bus.

Bus Local buses are run by **RMTT** *(☎ 04 94 03 87 03; w www.rmtt.fr)*, which has an **information kiosk** *(place de la Liberté; open 7.30am-noon & 1.30pm-6.30pm Mon-Fri)* at the main local bus hub. A single ticket/10-ticket carnet costs €1.30/8.30. Buses run until around 8pm. Sunday service is limited.

TOWARDS MARSEILLES

Heading towards Marseilles from Toulon, there are a couple of spots worth a stop. Sanary-sur-Mer is as serene as its name suggests; Bandol is best known for its wines; while inland, the Circuit du Castellet is strictly for wannabe racers.

Sanary-sur-Mer

postcode 83110 • pop 17,177

This quiet seaside resort, 15km west of Toulon, was home to novelist Aldous Huxley (1894–1963) in the early 1930s, his biographer Sybille Bedford in the late 1930s, and to a host of German refugees very soon after. Thomas Mann and his brother, Heinrich, sought refuge here, as did the German painter Feuchtwanger.

Sanary's sandy beaches are packed in summer. From its small but busy port, **Croix du Sud III** *(☎ 04 94 07 69 89, 06 09 87 47 97; 5 place du Coquillon; w www.croixdusud.com)* runs boat excursions west towards Cassis and its *calanques* (literally 'rocky inlets'; €20/16 for eight/five *calanques*), and around the Baies du Soleil (adult/three to 10 years €10/5). Boats to the Île des Embiez (€7/4) depart once daily, Saturday and Sunday, May to September.

Inland, **Ollioules** (pop 12,336), 14km north, is known for its cut-flower market and October Fête de l'Olivier (olive tree-festival). The **tourist office** *(☎ 04 94 74 01 04, fax 04 94 74 58 04; 🅆 www.sanarysurmer.com; Les Jardins de la Ville)* has details on both.

In Sanary, **Hôtel de la Tour** *(☎ 04 94 74 10 10, fax 04 94 74 69 49; 🄴 la.tour.sanary@wanadoo.fr; quai du Général de Gaulle; doubles with breakfast from €71)*, wrapped around a 12th-century tower – hence its name – is a particularly welcoming spot.

Bandol

postcode 83150 • pop 7975

In the 1900s Bandol, 8km west of Sanary, was a refuge for ailing foreigners such as novelists DH Lawrence and Katherine Mansfield. Today it is better known for its viticulture, an industry that is far from ailing. The terraced vineyards stretching for about 15km inland from the coast (as far north as St-Anne du Castellet) are managed by 50 wine producers who have sold their wine under their own coveted AOC since 1941. For a list of wine cellars where you can taste their wine, contact the **tourist office** *(☎ 04 94 29 41 35; fax 04 94 32 50 39; 🅆 www.bandol.fr; allées Vivien; open 9am-7pm Mon-Sat June-Aug, 9am-noon & 2pm-6pm Mon-Fri, 9am-noon Sat Sept-Apr)*. Wine growers celebrate the year's new wine production each year in early December with a Fête du Millesime.

From Bandol port, **Atlantide I** *(☎ 04 94 32 51 41, 04 94 29 13 13; 🅆 www.atlantide1.com; quai d'Honneur)* runs boat excursions, June to September, to Île des Embiez (adult/four to 12 years €7/4), Île de Porquerolles (€31/16) and around the *calanques* (€14/19/23 for six/10/12 *calanques*). You can also sail around the port in a **glass-bottomed boat** (☎ 04 94 29 74 45; adult/three to 10 years €10/5; 35 minutes). Boats sail year round to Île de Bendor (see that section earlier).

Les Lecques

The seaside resort of Les Lecques, 17km west of Bandol, is unstartling beyond the startling remnants of two Roman villas displayed in the **Musèe de Tauroentum** *(☎ 04 94 26 30 46; 131 route de la Madrague; adult/7-13 yrs €3/1; open 3pm-7pm Wed-Mon June-Sept, 2pm-5pm Sat & Sun Oct-June)*. The museum is arranged around three restored mosaics dating from around AD 1. Archaeologists believe that the Roman town after which the museum is named would have stood somewhere between here and **St-Cyr-sur-Mer**, 2km inland. For more information contact the tourist office *(☎ 04 94 26 73 73, fax 04 94 26 73 74; 🅆 www.stcyrsurmer.com; place de l'Appel du 18 Juin; open 9am-7pm Mon-Sat, 10am-1pm & 4pm-7pm Sun July & Aug, 9am-6pm Mon-Sat Sept & June, 9am-6pm Mon-Fri, 9am-noon & 2pm-6pm Sat Oct-May)* in Les Lecques.

Circuit du Castellet

The calm and tranquillity that caresses the northern realms of the Bandol vineyards around the perched village of **Le Castellet** (pop 3839, elevation 252m) is smashed with racy aplomb at the Circuit du Castellet, a motor sports race track built by industrialist Paul Ricard in 1970 and sold to Formula One racing magnate Bernie Ecclestone in 1999. See Spectator Sports in the Facts for the Visitor chapter for more racy details.

Monaco

postcode 98000 • pop 30,000

The tiny Principality of Monaco has been under the rule of the Grimaldi family for most of the period since 1297. It is a sovereign state, whose territory, surrounded by France, covers just 1.95 sq km.

Since 1949 Monaco has been ruled by Prince Rainier III, whose sweeping constitutional powers make him much more then a mere figurehead. Dubbed the 'builder prince', Rainier expanded the size of his principality by 20% in the late 1960s wit reclaimed land (to create the industrial quarter of Fontvieille); and in 2002 pledged to make it grow another 17% with his ambitious port-expansion project (see the boxed text 'Think Big' later in this chapter).

For decades, the family has been featured on the front pages of tabloids. However, since the death of the much-loved Princess Grace (best remembered from her Hollywood days as the actress Grace Kelly) in 1982, the media has concentrated on the far-from-fairytale love lives of the couple's two daughters, Caroline and Stephanie, and their son, Albert.

Glamorous Monte Carlo – Monaco's capital – is famed for its casino and its role as host to the annual Formula One (F1) Monaco Grand Prix, which sees drivers tear round a track that winds through the town and around the port. Unsurpassable views of the race, the principality and its legendary skyscraper skyline can be had from Monaco's Musée Océanographique's terrace or the Trophée d'Auguste in La Turbie, France (see that section in the Nice to Menton chapter).

Citizens of Monaco – Monégasques – of whom there are only about 5070, do not pay any taxes. They have their own flag (red and white), national anthem and national holiday (19 November), country telephone code (377) and traditional dialect, Monégasque – broadly speaking, a mixture of French and Italian – which is taught in schools alongside French, Monaco's official language. Many of the street signs are bilingual. The official religion is Roman Catholicism. There are no border formalities upon entering Monaco from France. The principality was admitted to the UN as a full member in 1993.

Highlights

- Watch the changing of the guard at the Palais du Prince
- Discover the underwater world at the Musée Océanographique
- Window-shop or shop till you drop in Monte Carlo
- Enjoy a night at the opera or a flutter at Monte Carlo Casino
- Dine à la Ducasse (one of France's most famous chefs) at Bar & Bœuf, then dance like a star at Jimmy'z
- Take a sunny seaside stroll to Cap d'Ail

By law, it is forbidden to walk around town barechested, barefooted or bikini-clad.

HISTORY

Monoïkos (Monaco) was settled by the Greeks in the 4th century and later by the Romans. In 1297, François Grimaldi entered Monaco disguised as a monk and seized the fortress, marking the start of Grimaldi rule. In 1346 the family purchased Menton and Roquebrune to add to its territory.

Monégasque independence was first recognised in 1489 by Charles VIII, king of France. Monaco came under Spanish protectorship from 1525 until 1641, when the French drove out the Spanish and established their own alliance with the principality

MONACO

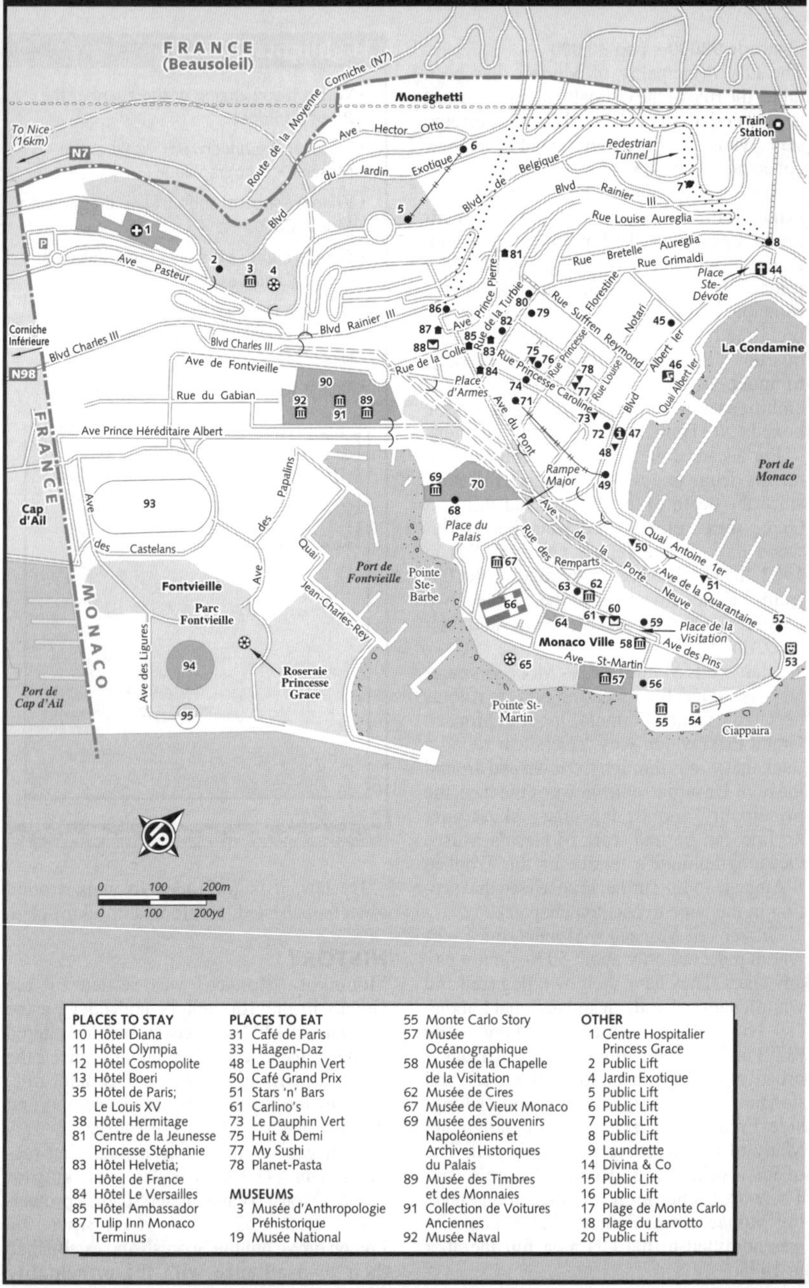

PLACES TO STAY
10 Hôtel Diana
11 Hôtel Olympia
12 Hôtel Cosmopolite
13 Hôtel Boeri
35 Hôtel de Paris; Le Louis XV
38 Hôtel Hermitage
81 Centre de la Jeunesse Princesse Stéphanie
83 Hôtel Helvetia; Hôtel de France
84 Hôtel Le Versailles
85 Hôtel Ambassador
87 Tulip Inn Monaco Terminus

PLACES TO EAT
31 Café de Paris
33 Häagen-Daz
48 Le Dauphin Vert
50 Café Grand Prix
51 Stars 'n' Bars
61 Carlino's
73 Le Dauphin Vert
75 Huit & Demi
77 My Sushi
78 Planet-Pasta

MUSEUMS
3 Musée d'Anthropologie Préhistorique
19 Musée National
55 Monte Carlo Story
57 Musée Océanographique
58 Musée de la Chapelle de la Visitation
62 Musée de Cires
67 Musée de Vieux Monaco
69 Musée des Souvenirs Napoléoniens et Archives Historiques du Palais
89 Musée des Timbres et des Monnaies
91 Collection de Voitures Anciennes
92 Musée Naval

OTHER
1 Centre Hospitalier Princess Grace
2 Public Lift
4 Jardin Exotique
5 Public Lift
6 Public Lift
7 Public Lift
8 Public Lift
9 Laundrette
14 Divina & Co
15 Public Lift
16 Public Lift
17 Plage de Monte Carlo
18 Plage du Larvotto
20 Public Lift

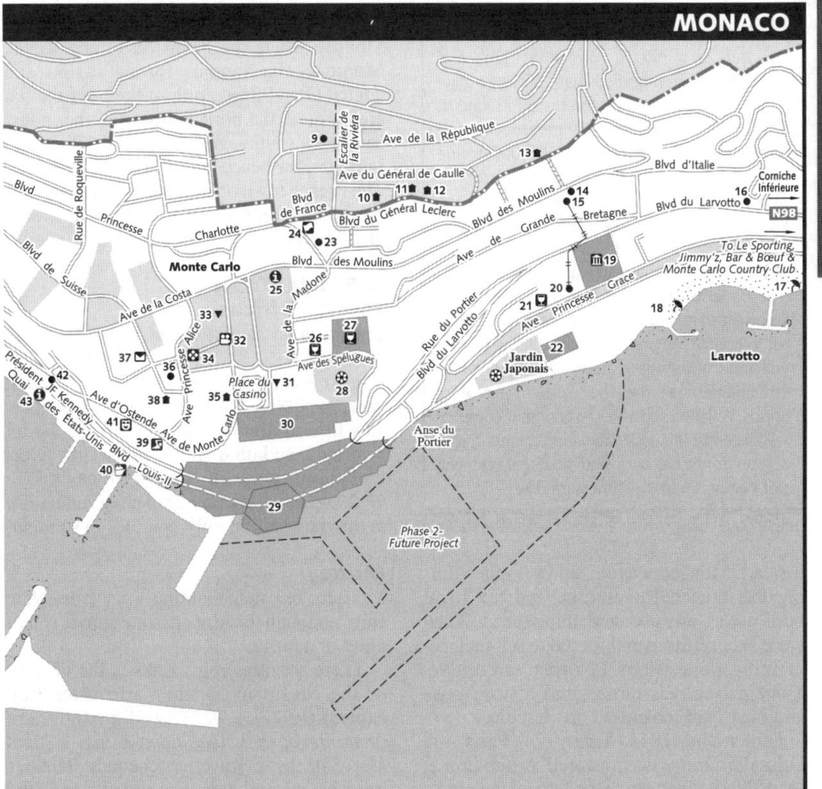

21 Sass Café
22 Salles des Princes; Zebra Square; Grimaldi Forum
23 American Express
24 UK Consulate
25 National Tourist Office
26 The Living Room
27 Tiffany's; FNAC; Centre Commercial Le Métropole; Bice
28 Jardins du Casino
29 Auditorium Rainier III; Centre de Congrès Auditorium
30 Monte Carlo Casino; Salle Garnier
32 Cinéma Le Sporting
34 Entrance to Galerie du Sporting
36 Square Beaumarchais
37 Post Office
39 Les Thermes Marins
40 Compagnie de Navigation et de Tourisme
41 Théâtre Princesse Grace
42 Compagnie des Autobus de Monaco
43 Tourist Office Kiosk
44 Église Ste-Dévote
45 Casino Supermarket
46 Stade Nautique Rainier III
47 Tourist Office Kiosk
49 Public Lift
52 Yacht Club de Monaco
53 Théâtre du Fort Antoine
54 Parking des Pêcheurs
56 Escalator to Monte Carlo Story
59 Ministère d'État
60 Post Office
63 Princess Grace Irish Library
64 Town Hall
65 Jardins St-Martin
66 Cathédrale de Monaco
68 State Apartments
70 Palais du Prince
71 Public Lift
72 Le Khédive
74 MBK
76 Scruples
79 ASM Monaco Pro Shop
80 Boutique Formule 1
82 Galerie Riccadonna
86 Entrance to Train Station
88 Post Office
90 Centre Commercial de Fontvieille
93 Stade Louis II
94 Espace Fontvieille
95 Heliport de Monaco

Think Big

Nowhere is miniscule Monaco's 'think big' attitude better embodied than in its new dike – the world's largest and the first of its kind to float as it does. Twenty-eight metres wide and 352m long, the enormous 163,000-tonne hulk took 700 Spanish workers three years to build. From Spain it was towed to Monaco where it arrived in August 2002.

The fancy, state-of-the-art breakwater is part of an ambitious project to place Port de la Condamine (also called Port Hercules) among the world's leading cruise-ship harbours. The dike – set to double the port's capacity once in place – will float alongside a new 10,000-sq-metre embankment at the foot of Fort Antoine. Shops, galleries and an entertainment complex will decorate the pedestrian embankment, and a four-storey car park and boat garages will slot neatly inside the 19m-high dike.

instead. Monaco was seized by France during the French Revolution, and the royal family was arrested and imprisoned. They were later released and forced to sell their remaining possessions in order to survive. Their palace was turned into a warehouse and their land renamed Fort Hercule.

Under the 1814 Treaty of Paris the Grimaldi family was restored to the throne. In 1860 Monégasque independence was recognised for a second time by France and consolidated a year later when Monaco relinquished all claims over its former territories of Menton and Roquebrune, which it had lost in 1848. A customs and monetary union agreement was signed with France in 1865, sealing future cooperation between the two countries.

Monaco's absolute monarchy was replaced in 1911 by a constitution, reformed by Prince Rainier III in 1962. The ruling prince is assisted by a national council comprising 18 democratically elected members. Only Monégasques aged 21 or over can vote in council elections, which are held every five years; Monégasque nationality is only granted to people born in Monaco or of Monégasque parentage.

ORIENTATION

Monaco consists of five principal areas: Monaco Ville, a 60m-high outcrop of rock 800m long on the southern side of the Port de Monaco where the Palais du Prince stands; Monte Carlo, famous for its casino and annual Grand Prix, north of the port; the flat area around the port; Fontvieille, the industrial area southwest of Monaco Ville; and Larvotto, the beach area east of Monte Carlo. The French town of Beausoleil is three streets up the hill from Monte Carlo, while Moneghetti borders Cap d'Ail's western fringe.

INFORMATION

Tourist Offices

The **national tourist office** *(☎ 377-92 16 61 16, fax 377-92 16 60 00; W www.monaco-tourisme.com; 2a blvd des Moulins; open 9am-7pm Mon-Sat, 10am-noon Sun)* operates **information kiosks** next to the Jardin Exotique, and on quai des États-Unis overlooking the port. The **tourist office** *(☎ 377-97 70 45 28; open 8am-8pm daily June-Sept)* at the train station only operates in summer.

Money

Monaco, like neighbouring France, uses the euro, although the Monégasque euro is something of a rarity.

There are numerous banks in the vicinity of the casino in Monte Carlo. **American Express** *(☎ 377-97 70 77 59; 35 blvd Princesse Charlotte; open 9.30am-noon & 2pm-5.30pm Mon-Sat)* cashes travellers cheques. **Barclays Bank** has several branches dotted around the principality, including a **branch** *(17 Blvd Albert 1er)* with a 24-hour currency-exchange machine outside.

Post

Monégasque stamps are only valid for letters sent within Monaco (use a French stamp to send a postcard). Postal rates are the same as those in France. Contrary to France's yellow post boxes, Monaco's are red.

The **post office** *(1 ave Henri Dunant; open 8am-7pm Mon-Fri, 8am-noon Sat)* is in Monte Carlo, inside Palais de la Scala.

Telephone

Telephone numbers in Monaco only have eight digits and no area code. Calls between Monaco and the rest of France are treated as international calls. When calling Monaco from the rest of France or abroad, dial ☎ 00 followed by Monaco's country code, 377. To call France from Monaco, dial ☎ 00 and

France's country code, 33. This applies even if you are only making a call from the eastern side of blvd de France (in Monaco) to its western side (in France)!

Monaco's public telephones accept Monégasque or French phonecards.

Email & Internet Access

The cybercorner at **Stars 'n' Bars** (see Places to Eat later) charges €6 for 30 minutes' Web access.

Bookshops

Scruples *(☎ 93 50 43 52; 9 rue Princesse Caroline; open 9am-noon & 2.30pm-7pm Mon-Sat)* is Monaco's English-language bookshop.

An unsurpassable choice of English- and other foreign-language newspapers and magazines are sold at **Le Khédive** *(☎ 93 90 29 33; 9 blvd Albert 1er; open 6.30am-8pm daily)*, a newsagent and tobacconist overlooking the port on the corner of rue Princesse Caroline.

Libraries

There is the **Princess Grace Irish Library** *(☎ 93 50 12 25; e pglib@monaco.mc; 9 rue Princesse Marie de Lorraine; open 9am-6.30pm Mon-Fri)*. Grace Kelly's grandparents hailed from Drimurla in county Mayo, Ireland, a remote spot visited by Kelly and Rainier in 1961.

Radio

French- and Italian-language Radio Monte Carlo (RMC) transmits from antennas on the Plateau de Fontbonne and the Col de la Madone and attracts a nationwide audience (0.9 million listeners). It can be picked up in Monaco on 98.8MHz FM and Internet relay can be found at w www.radiomontecarlo.net.

The English-language Monte Carlo-based Riviera Radio can be reached in Monaco on 106.3MHz FM or at w www.rivieraradio.mc.

Laundry

In Beausoleil, try the **laundrette** *(1 Escalier de la Riviéra; open 7am-9pm)* for your washing.

MONACO VILLE

Poetically named Le Rocher (The Rock) to reflect its geographical location atop a rock, Monaco Ville is home to the state's most alluring sights. It is connected to the port area of La Condamine by the steep Rampe Major, a red-brick pedestrian ramp built in the 16th century to link the palace and port.

Musée Océanographique & Around

Monaco's world-renowned Oceanographic Museum *(☎ 93 15 36 00; e rela@oceano.org; ave St-Martin; adult/6-18 yrs €11/6; open 9am-8pm daily Apr-Sept, 10am-6pm daily Oct-Mar)* was founded in 1910 by Prince Albert I (1848–1922), who set up an oceanographic institute for marine science here in 1906. Today, it houses 90 tanks and 4500 fish (450 different species) in an underground aquarium through which 250,000L of fresh sea water are pumped daily, a zoological hall dominated by a 20m-long whale skeleton, and a 7.5m-long glass tank through which visitors can view a coral reef at close quarters. The museum's ornate interior – which features fanciful seabird-shaped chandeliers, monumental staircases, mosaic floors, and oak door frames carved into marine-inspired shapes such as the effigy of Neptune – is like no other.

The escalator in front of the Musée Océanographique leads to the tacky **Monte Carlo Story** *(☎ 93 25 32 33; e mcstory@cyber-monaco.mc; adult/student/6-14 yrs €6.50/5/3; open 11am-5pm or 6pm daily Mar-Oct, 2pm-5pm daily Nov-Feb)*, a 30-minute film recalling the history of the Grimaldi dynasty.

Reclining gracefully beside both museums are the coastal, statue-studded **Jardins St-Martin** *(free; open 7am-6pm Oct-Mar, to 8pm Apr-Sept)*, perfect for a post-museum stroll.

Directly opposite the entrance to the Musée Oceanographique is the stop for the **Azur Express** *(☎ 92 05 64 38; ave St-Martin; adult/under 5 €6/free)*, a tourist train that offers 35-minute city tours with English commentary. Bus Nos 1 and 2, from place d'Armes, also stop here.

Palais du Prince

The **changing of the guard** at the Prince's Palace *(☎ 93 25 18 31; place du Palais)* takes place daily, at the southern end of rue des Remparts, at precisely 11.55am. The guards of the Compagnie des Carabiniers du Prince (Prince's Military Police), who carry out their state duties in smart dress uniform (white in summer, black in winter), appear resigned to the comic-opera nature of their duties. Equally comic are the acrobatic antics among the huge crowd that gathers to watch the whole affair. If the Grimaldi standard is

The Grimaldi Dynasty

The House of Grimaldi has ruled 'The Rock' with a golden fist since 1297, when François Grimaldi, disguised as a monk, sneaked through the city gates and claimed it as his own. The dynasty almost died in 1731 when Antoine I (Louis I Grimaldi's son) failed to produce a male heir. His daughter stepped in as queen, retaining her Grimaldi name. She died a few months later, following which her husband became Prince of Monaco ensuring the dynasty's survival.

Two centuries on, pioneering Prince Charles III (1818–89) gave the poverty-stricken state independence, followed in 1865 by the casino and its accompanying million-dollar fortune. His successor, the seafaring Prince Albert I (1848–1922), preferred marine biology to money-making playgrounds and devoted his life to oceanographic research. In 1873 he sailed around the Mediterranean and the Atlantic to the Azores in a 200-tonne sailing ship.

The reigning monarch, Rainier III (born 1923) succeeded his grandfather Prince Louis II (1870–1949) to the throne in 1949. Monaco's longest-ruling monarch won the heart of a nation with his fairy-tale marriage to Grace Kelly in 1956. The legendary Philadelphia-born actress had made 11 films in the 1950s, including Hitchcock's *Dial M for Murder* (1954), *Rear Window* (1954) and *To Catch a Thief* (1955), in which she starred as the quintessential cool blonde on the coast. The movie took Kelly to Cannes, then to the Monégasque palace to attend a *Paris Match* photo shoot with Rainier. One year later Monaco's prince charming wed Hollywood's movie queen. The princess made no more films and devoted herself to new duties as Princess of Monaco. She died in a car crash in 1982.

The love lives of the couple's three children – Caroline, Albert and Stephanie, born 1957, 1958 and 1965 respectively – take centre stage today. Princess Caroline was widowed in 1990 when her

flying from the top of the palace tower, it means Prince Rainier is at home.

The palace, with its Renaissance facade, was built on the site of a 13th-century Genoese fortress, later fortified by Vauban. A tour of the **state apartments** *(adult/8-14 yrs €6/3; open 9.30am-6.20pm daily June-Sept, 10am-5pm daily Oct)* allows visitors a glimpse of its interior grandeur. Guided tours (35 to 40 minutes) in English leave every 15 or 20 minutes; be prepared to queue for up to 45 minutes in July and August to get in.

The palace's southern wing houses the **Musée des Souvenirs Napoléoniens et Archives Historiques du Palais** *(Museum of Napoleonic Souvenirs & the Palace's Historic Archives; adult/8-14 yrs €4/2; open 9.30am-6.30pm daily June-Sept; 10am-5pm daily Oct; 10.30am-12.30pm & 2pm-5pm daily Dec-May)*. Displays include some of Napoleon's personal effects (handkerchiefs, a sock etc) and a fascinating collection of the bric-a-brac (medals, coins, uniforms, swords) collected by princely dynasties over the centuries.

A ticket for both the apartments and the museum costs €8/4.

Cathédrale de Monaco

The unspectacular 1875 Romanesque-Byzantine cathedral *(4 rue Colonel)* has one draw: the grave of legendary Hollywood star Grace Patricia Kelly (1929–82). Her plain, modest tombstone is on the western side of the cathedral choir. It is inscribed with the Latin words *Gratia Patricia Principis Rainerii III* and is heavily adorned with flowers. The remains of other members of the royal family, buried in the church crypt since 1885, today rest behind Princess Grace's grave.

From September to June, Sunday Mass at 10.30am is sung by **Les Petits Chanteurs de Monaco** *(☎ 93 15 80 88)*, Monaco's boys' choir. From July to September, Sunday Mass is celebrated in English at 12.15pm. Organ recitals are at held 5pm July to September.

Other Museums

Life-sized wax figures capture 24 snapshots from the history of the Grimaldi dynasty in the **Musée de Cire** *(Wax Museum; ☎ 93 30 39 05; 27 rue Basse; adult/8-14 yrs €3.80/2; open 9.30am-6pm daily Feb-Sept, 11am-5pm daily Oct-Jan)*.

Nineteenth-century art is displayed in a 17th-century Baroque chapel at the enchanting **Musée de la Chapelle de la Visitation** *(☎ 93 50 07 00; place de la Visitation; adult/6-14 yrs €3/1.50; open 10am-4pm Tues-Sun)*.

MONTE CARLO

In the 1850s, Monaco was the poorest state in Europe. Its luck changed with the opening of

The Grimaldi Dynasty

second husband (her marriage to the first was annulled), and father of her three children, was killed in a speedboat accident. In 1999, on her 42nd birthday, she wed Prince Ernst of Hanover, a cousin to Britain's Queen Elizabeth. Eight lone guests attended the civil ceremony, which took place secretly.

All eyes were on the heir to the throne, 44-year-old Albert in early 2003, as the tabloid media geared up for the confirmed bachelor to announce his rumoured engagement to 25-year-old American pole-vaulter girlfriend, Alicia Warlick – much to the elation of his father no doubt, who has made it clear that he will not relinquish the Monégasque throne until his son has wed. The press reckon Albert will propose on his 45th birthday in March.

The youngest of the trio, Princess Stephanie, wed her bodyguard in 1995, but she divorced him a year later after photographs of him frolicking by a pool with a Belgian stripper were published in Italian magazines. In July 1998, she gave birth to baby Camille Grimaldi, her third child (father unnamed). During the 1980s and early 1990s the entrepreneurial princess launched her own swimwear label – ironically called Pool Position – and released three albums and a flurry of pop singles, including *Ouragan* (Hurricane), *How can it be?* and *I am waiting for you.*

The *Bal de la Rose* (Rose Ball in May), the *Bal de l'Été* (Summer Ball) organised for Europe's jet-setting upper crust, the fundraising *Gala de la Croix Rouge* (Red Cross Ball) and the Gala Ball, hosted by the charitable Princess Grace Foundation, are Monaco's key society events of the year. They afford a rare fairy-tale glimpse of the House of Grimaldi in the spotlight of the world. Tickets cost around €1000.

Monte Carlo Casino – Europe's first – in 1865. The rather dull-sounding Plateau des Spélugues on which it stood was renamed Monte Carlo (the translation of 'Mont Charles' after Charles III) in 1866, and within months it ranked as one of Europe's most glamorous playgrounds.

Monte Carlo's alluring face is captured in a series of black-and-white photographs posted behind glass on information boards in the floral gardens on place du Casino. The series, entitled **Monte Carlo Célébrissime**, features shots of Monte Carlo's celebrated guests from 1900 to the present day: Puccino (1903), Anna Pavlova (1909), Frank Sinatra and Roger Moore (1980), Michael Jackson (1996), Laetitia Casta (1999)...

The colourful geometric mosaic, *Hexa Grace* (1975), which adorns the roof of the Centre de Congrès Auditorium, is a Vasarely creation – best viewed from the skies. From Monte Carlo a **coastal path** (two to three hours) leads to Roquebrune-Cap Martin.

Casino de Monte Carlo

The drama of watching people risk all (or shedloads of money at least) in Monte Carlo's spectacularly ornate casino *(☎ 92 96 20 00; Ⓦ www.casino-monte-carlo.com; place du Casino)* makes visiting the gaming rooms worth the stiff admission fees. These are €10/22/42/57 per day/week/month/season for the **Salon Ordinaire** *(open from noon)*, which has European roulette and trente et quarante, and €20 a day for the **Salons Privés** *(open from 4pm)*, which offer baccarat, chemin de fer, craps and English roulette.

To enter the casino, you must be aged at least 21. Short shorts (but not short skirts) are forbidden in the Salon Ordinaire. A jacket and tie are required to enter the Salons Privés. The one-armed bandits and other cheap-thrill devices (open from 2pm), to the right as you enter the casino, do not command an entrance fee or dress code.

Jardin Japonais & Grimaldi Forum

Sandwiched between the built-up quarters of Monte Carlo, Larvotto and the Mediterranean, this Japanese garden *(ave Princesse Grace; open 9am-dusk daily)* is intended as a piece of paradise. It was blessed by a Shinto high priest; quiet contemplation and meditation is encouraged in the Zen garden.

Exit the garden through its eastern gate to get to the Grimaldi Forum *(☎ 99 99 30 00; Ⓦ www.grimaldiforum.mc; 10 ave Princesse Grace)*, Monaco's congress and conference centre that hosts occasional contemporary art exhibitions – always eclectic and well worth seeing. All the more astonishing is the

Loser Risks All

The beautiful *belle époque* decor of Monte Carlo Casino – Europe's oldest – is as extravagant as those who play in it. It went up in several phases, the earliest being the Salon de l'Europe, built in 1865 and splendidly lit with eight bohemian crystal chandeliers from 1898. Each weighs 150kg. The second phase saw French architect Charles Garnier, who'd just completed Paris' opera house, move to Monte Carlo to create the luxurious fresco-adorned Salle Garnier in 1878. The atrium – the main entrance hall with its 28 marble columns and flurry of gamblers and voyeurs – opened the same year. The third part, the Salle Empire, was completed in 1910.

Monte Carlo Casino remains in the hands of its founding owners, the Société des Bains de Mer (SBM; Sea Bathing Society) established by French entrepreneur François Blanc in 1863. Original shareholders included Monaco's Prince Charles III who held a 10% stake. Indeed, the state remains the leading shareholder today. In 1875, when the then-future Edward VII and Queen Alexandra visited, around 150,000 players per day were frequenting the casino. Shotgun suicides, hot on the heels of a heavy loss at the gaming tables, were common well into the 1920s. When Charles Deville Wells broke the bank in 1891 – the first and last to do so – gaming tables were draped in black for three days.

Despite an initial drop in revenue in 1933 following the legalisation of the roulette wheel in neighbouring France, Monte Carlo Casino continues to rake it in. The SBM is Monaco's largest corporation, owning all the principality's upmarket hotels and restaurants. Income from gambling accounts for around 4% of Monaco's total state revenue, although it used to account for most of the government's budget.

gigantic glass edifice itself, two-thirds of which is submerged below the sea.

Musée National

In a sumptuous Garnier-designed villa, Monaco's National Museum *(☎ 93 30 91 26; 17 ave Princesse Grace; adult/6-14 yrs €5/3.50; open 10am-6.30pm Easter-Sept, 10am-12.15pm & 2.30pm-6.30pm rest of year)* contains a fascinating collection of 18th- and 19th-century dolls and mechanical toys made in Paris. Around 250 figurines nestle in the 18th-century crib, which originated in Naples.

FONTVIEILLE

Adjoining Cap d'Ail in neighbouring France, Fontvieille – built on reclaimed land from the sea between 1966 and 1973 – covers the southernmost part of Monaco. From here a 3.5km-long **coastal path** leads southwest to Cap d'Ail. The lush gardens of **Parc Fontvieille** are equally pleasant for a summer stroll; over 4000 rose bushes and a small swan-clad lake adorn the **Roseraie Princesse Grace** (Princess Grace Rose Garden), planted in her memory in 1984. Contemporary sculptures – including *Le Poing* (The Fist) by César and *Cavalleria Eroica* by Arman – line the length of the park's **Chemin des Sculptures**. Museum-wise, Fontvieille is Monaco's collector's corner.

Collection de Voitures Anciennes

Over 100 vehicles are on display in this classic-car museum housing the private collection of Rainier III. Highlights include the Rolls Royce Silver Cloud that was given by local shopkeepers to Prince Rainier to mark his marriage to Grace Kelly in 1956, and a black London cab (Austin 1952) fitted out especially for the Hollywood actress. The first F1 racing car to win the Monaco Grand Prix – the Bugatti 1929 – can also be seen.

Monaco's Collection of Classic Cars *(☎ 92 05 28 56; esplanade Rainier III; adult/8-14 yrs €6/3; open 10am-6pm daily)* is inside the Centre Commercial de Fontvieille.

Musée Naval

An impressive collection of model ships constructed by Grimaldi princes is displayed in Monaco's Naval Museum *(☎ 92 05 28 48; adult/8-14 yrs €4/2.50; open 10am-6pm daily)*, inside the Centre Commercial de Fontvieille. The oldest ship in the 200-odd-piece collection was stuck together by Albert I in 1874. Other pieces include an imperial gondola built in 15 days for Napoleon to admire; the *Fiorentino Emigrato* sailing ship built in the 17th century; a miniature of the *Missouri*, where the armistice with Japan was signed in 1945; and a 5m-long model of the US aircraft carrier *Nimitz*.

Musée des Timbres et des Monnaies

Prince Rainier also has a stamp and coin collection, displayed in the Museum of Stamps & Coins *(☎ 93 15 41 50; adult/12-14 yrs €3/1.50; open 10am-5pm or 6pm daily)* in the Centre Commercial de Fontvieille. Monégasque stamps dating from 1885 and numismatic wonders from 1640 on are exhibited. Admission includes a Monégasque stamp.

MONEGHETTI

The steep slopes of the Moneghetti district, immediately north of Fontvieille, are home to the wonderful **Jardin Exotique** *(Exotic Garden; ☎ 93 15 29 80; e jardin-exotique@monte-carlo.mc; 62 blvd du Jardin Exotique; adult/6-18 yrs €6.40/3.20; open 9am-7pm mid-May–mid-Sept, 9am-6pm or dusk rest of year)*. The exotic garden boasts some 7000 varieties of cacti and succulents from all over the world – including a 100-year-old South American cacti and 10m-tall African candelabras.

The spectacular view alone is worth at least half the admission fee, which also gets you into the onsite **Musée d'Anthropologie Préhistorique** *(Museum of Prehistoric Anthropology; ☎ 93 15 80 06)* and includes a guided tour (30 minutes) of the **Grottes de l'Observatoire**. These prehistoric Observatory Caves comprise a fantastical network of stalactite and stalagmite caves 279 steps down the hillside. Prehistoric rock scratchings found here are among the oldest of their kind in the world.

From the tourist office, take bus No 2 to the Jardin Exotique terminus.

ACTIVITIES

Boats & Beaches

Boats and water dominate the central quarter of La Condamine, namely the **Port de Monaco** where palatial pleasure crafts of all shapes and sizes are moored. At the eastern end of quai Antoine 1er is the exclusive members-only **Yacht Club de Monaco** *(☎ 93 10 63 00, fax 93 50 80 88; w www.yacht-club-monaco.mc; 16 quai Antoine 1er)*.

Lesser mortals can sail the waters in a glass-bottomed catamaran operated by the **Compagnie de Navigation et de Tourisme** *(☎ 92 16 15 15; w www.aquavision-monaco.com; quai des États-Unis)*, at the eastern end of the quay. Boat excursions (55 minutes) depart several times daily from May to September. Tickets are €11/8 per adult/3 to 18 years.

The nearest beaches, **Plage du Larvotto** and **Plage de Monte Carlo**, are a couple of kilometres east of Monte Carlo in Larvotto. Both beaches – fine shingle – have private, paying sections where you can hire cushioned sun-loungers and parasols. One section of Plage du Larvotto, **Handiplage**, is kitted out for disabled travellers. Take bus No 4 from the train station or bus No 6 from the port to Le Sporting stop.

Pools & Baths

The pool to swim in and be seen is the **Stade Nautique Rainier III** *(☎ 93 30 64 83; quai Albert 1er; adult/over-60/3-11 yrs €2.50/2.20; open 9am-8pm May-June, Sept & Oct, 9am-8pm daily July & Aug)*, the Olympic-sized outdoor pool at the port. You can also hire a nice comfortable mattress and/or parasol (each €3.50).

The prestigious **Les Thermes Marins** *(☎ 92 16 49 46; e thermes@sbm.mc; 2 ave de Monte Carlo)* has a heated sea-water pool and solarium and offers a variety of spa treatments. Six-day slimming, stress, well-being and cellulite-attack packages start at €2955/1125 with/without accommodation.

SPECIAL EVENTS

The **Fête de la Ste-Dévote** on 27 January celebrates the feast day of Monaco's patron saint, Sainte Dévote, whose corpse was flung in a boat and left to drift at sea after her death at the hands of a Roman general in Corsica. Thanks to a dove who blew the boat in the right direction, Dévote's corpse landed on the shores of Monaco in AD 312. Each year, a traditional Mass is celebrated in Monégasque in the **Église Ste-Dévote** *(☎ 93 50 52 60; place Ste-Dévote)*. In the evening a torch-lit procession, blessing and symbolic burning of a boat take place in front of the church.

Dancers in traditional Monégasque folk costume – long, frilly, full skirts and featuring lots of red and white in patterned garments – dance around a big bonfire on place du Palais on 23 June, the eve of St John's Day. Early August brings a glittering International Fireworks Festival to the port area, while a carnival spirit fills the streets with the **Fête Nationale Monégasque** – Monaco's National Holiday – on 19 November.

Shopping Spree

For shopaholics wanting to indulge their desires, Monte Carlo is the place.

Kick-start your shopping spree on the western side of place du Casino, where you can swirl through **Cartier**, **Chanel**, **Céline** and **Sonia Rykiel** in one fell swoop. Don't miss shoe god **Salvatore Ferragamo** or Italian fashion house **Prada** inside Hôtel Hermitage. Duck through **Galerie du Sporting** – a covered shopping arcade linking place du Casino with ave Princesse Alice – if you're seeking wine, antiques or antique wine. **Sotheby's** auction house is here, as is a clutch of antique galleries and **L'Œnothèque**, a lavish wine and champagne cellar that oenophiles will adore.

Yves St-Laurent, **Christian-Dior**, luxury-leather designer **Louis Vuitton** and Swiss watch-maker **Piaget** stand in temptation's way on ave des Beaux-Arts, the street skirting the southeastern side of Galerie du Sporting. Back on place du Casino, whirl past Hôtel de Paris and downhill along ave de Monte Carlo, a short but chic street laden with **Gucci**, **Valentino**, **Hermès, Lalique** and **Prada**. **Kenzo** brings a splash of colour to the Centre Commercial Le Métropole, an indoor shopping centre opposite the Jardins du Casino.

Having exhausted Monte Carlo, shoppers with money to blow can try their luck on rue Grimaldi in La Condamine. **Galerie Riccadonna** at No 7 sells fabulously funky, one-off pieces of designer furniture. **Boutique Formule 1** at No 15 – a boutique dedicated to motor-racing's glamorous side – stocks watches, cigarette lighters, toilet seats etc by Porsche Design and Ferrari; the official T-shirt can be bought at **L@ Boutique**, the official Automobile Club de Monaco's boutique at No 46. **L'Abondance: La Maison du Whisky** at 11 bis sells, predictably so, whisky. Gourmands seeking further titillation should try up-market *épicerie* (grocery store) **Caves & Gourmandises** *(☎ 97 70 54 94; 25 blvd Albert 1er)*.

In Larvotto, socialites flutter along blvd des Moulins and ave Princesse Grace. **Divina & Co** *(36 blvd des Moulins)* sells rings as big as gobstoppers, see-through handbags and a fantastic array of other fantasy gems, costume jewellery and accessories. **Hugo Boss** struts his stuff at No 39 on the same street, and *haute-couture* **Loris Azzaro** stands tall at No 19. **DKNY** and **Adonis** – a boutique crammed with **Klein**, **Joseph**, **Gaultier** and **Galliano** labels and British designer **Karen Millen** – gaze out to sea at 39 ave Princesse Grace. Adonis also sells traditional national costumes. If you can't afford the real thing, go second-hand – **Le Dressing** *(2 rue des Orangers)* specialises in second-hand and *couture et création*.

Essential reading for committed shoppers and fashion aficionados is the 150-odd-page *Monaco Shopping* guide, published annually and available for free at the tourist office.

PLACES TO STAY

Bar one hostel, cheap accommodation is practically nonexistent in Monaco – some 75% of hotel rooms sport four stars. Rates rocket out of control at Easter, New Year and during the Grand Prix when many hotels demand a minimum three-night stay.

PLACES TO STAY – BUDGET & MID-RANGE

Hostels

Centre de la Jeunesse Princesse Stéphanie *(☎ 93 50 83 20, fax 93 25 29 82; W www.youthhostel.asso.mc; 24 ave Prince Pierre; bed in 8- or 12-/4-bed dorm €14/16; open 7am-1am daily)*, 200m up the hill from the train station, only accepts travellers aged 16 to 31. The cost of a dorm bed includes breakfast, shower and sheets. Between September and June, hostel accommodation is only in rooms with four beds. Reception is in the block behind the pink building visible on ave Prince Pierre; continue uphill past the pink facade then bear right down the steps.

Monaco

Hôtel Cosmopolite *(☎ 93 30 16 95, fax 93 30 23 05; e hotel-cosmopolite@monte-carlo.mc; 4 rue de la Turbie; singles/doubles with washbasin from €33/40, with shower €45/52)* is a clean and pleasant, family-run place with 24 rooms; seven have showers. Breakfast at €6 is cheap.

Hôtel de France *(☎ 93 30 24 64, fax 92 16 13 34; e hotel-france@monte-carlo.com; 6 rue de la Turbie; singles/doubles with bathroom €67/85)*, a renovated pad with comfortable rooms, is a cut above the Cosmopolite's rooms. Rates include breakfast.

Hôtel Le Versailles *(☎ 93 50 79 34, fax 93 25 53 64; e hotelversailles@monte-carlo.mc; 4-6 ave Prince Pierre; singles/doubles from*

€60/70), powerfully air-conditioned, offers good-value rooms.

Hôtel Helvetia *(☎ 93 20 21 71, fax 92 16 70 51; ⓔ hotel-helvetia@monte-carlo.mc; 1 bis rue Grimaldi; singles/doubles/triples €68/78/92)*, with a handy dual entrance, charges 15% less for its 25 rooms during the low season (November to March).

Tulip Inn Monaco Terminus *(☎ 92 05 63 00, fax 92 05 20 10; 9 ave Prince Pierre; singles/doubles/triples/quads low season €90/125/164/201, high season €120/155/193/231)*, part of the Tulip Inn international hotel chain, touts elegant rooms opposite the entrance to the train station. Breakfast is included in the price.

Beausoleil

Blvd du Général Leclerc is the street to head for in Beausoleil (France) – the even-numbered side of blvd du Général Leclerc is in Monaco and is called blvd de France. Remember to call the country code for France when dialling these numbers from the train station in Monaco.

Hôtel Diana *(☎ 04 93 78 47 58, fax 04 93 41 88 94; ⓔ hotel.diana.beausoleil.monte-carlo@wanadoo.fr; 17 blvd du Général Leclerc; doubles with washbasin & bidet €29, singles/doubles with shower €32/46, with shower & toilet €42.50/53.50)* is a pleasant enough, if unmomentous, place to stay. Use of the communal bathroom costs a pricey €8 a throw.

Hôtel Cosmopolite *(☎ 04 93 78 36 00, fax 04 93 41 84 22; 19 blvd du Général Leclerc; singles/doubles €51/54)*, no relation to the hotel of the same name in La Condamine, has rooms kitted out with shower, TV, telephone, air-con and hair dryer.

Hôtel Olympia *(☎ 04 93 78 12 70, fax 04 93 41 85 04; ⓔ hotel_olympia@yahoo.fr; 17 bis blvd du Général Leclerc; singles/doubles with shower & toilet from €75/85)* is a 32-room place sandwiched between Hôtel Diana and Hôtel Cosmopolite.

Hôtel Boeri *(☎ 04 93 78 38 10, fax 04 93 41 90 95; 29 blvd du Général Leclerc; singles/doubles from €34/43)*, an appealing 30-room option, has flower-adorned balconies and a giant palm tree out front.

PLACES TO STAY – TOP END

Hôtel Ambassador *(☎ 97 97 96 96, fax 97 97 96 99; ⓦ www.Ambassadormonaco.com; 10 ave Prince Pierre; singles/doubles/triples low season €110/134/159, high season €137/168/198)*, with three stars, is known for its graceful interior and Liberty-style restaurant that cooks up tasty Italian cuisine. Prices include breakfast.

Hôtel de Paris *(☎ 92 16 30 00, fax 92 16 38 49; ⓔ hp@sbm.mc; place du Casino; doubles from €385)* is Monaco's world- famous pad. The magnificent hotel – Monte Carlo's first – is where writer Colette spent the last years of her life. It was built between 1859 and 1864 and hosts a gastronomic temple (see Louis XV in Places to Eat following).

Hôtel Hermitage *(☎ 92 16 40 00, fax 93 16 38 52; ⓔ hh@sbm.mc; square Beaumarchais; doubles in low/high/very high season €340/415/460)*, a four-star place, has a luxurious *belle époque* ambience, Italian-inspired facade and a pink-marbled restaurant.

PLACES TO EAT

Restaurants

Brasseries that don't break the bank abound on the pedestrianised rue Princesse Caroline.

Le Dauphin Vert *(☎ 93 30 86 30; 20 rue Princesse Caroline; mains €15)*, a notable standout, cooks up fish, seafood and meat, as well as fancier dishes *pour les fines bouches* (for finer palates).

Huit & Demi *(☎ 93 50 97 02; rue Princesse Caroline; pizza €9-12, pasta €10-13, meat dishes €17-22)* is a chic, clean-cut place with an industrial interior and fabulous pavement terrace that fills pedestrianised rue Langlé. The fare is Italian and delicious – the mixed seafood grill is especially scrummy.

Planet-Pasta *(☎ 93 50 80 14; 6 rue Imberty; pasta €10)*, overlooking a beautiful little green square, dishes up filling bowls of fusilli, spaghetti, penne, fagiolini et al to a hungry lunchtime crowd.

My Sushi *(☎ 97 70 67 67; 2 rue des Orangers)*, next door, is a striking minimalist affair. Raw cuttlefish, octopus and eel are among the fishy morsels to be found stuffed inside this sushi house's delicious maki and temaki.

Stars 'n' Bars *(☎ 93 50 95 95; 6 quai Antoine 1er; meals €15)* is an American bar and restaurant that sports one of Monaco's sexiest portside terraces. Dishes of American-sized portions are served in the restaurant all day from 11am to midnight; it has a nightclub too.

Bice *(☎ 93 25 20 30; 17 ave des Spélugues; pasta €15-19, meat & fish dishes €24-28)* tempts a discerning set with its highly original and delectable menu. Dishes are designer sized and strictly Italian in flavour.

Bar & Bœuf *(☎ 92 16 36 36; e b.b@sbm.mc; 26 ave Princesse Grace; full meal around €150; open evenings only)* has a minimalist wood and glass interior designed by Philippe Starck and a stylish crowd of exquisitely dressed beautiful people. A venture of French chef Alain Ducasse at Le Sporting, the Bar & Bœuf specialises in just that – sea-perch *(bar)* and beef *(bœuf)*.

Louis XV *(☎ 92 16 30 01; place du Casino; menus from €90)*, also run by Ducasse, is inside Hôtel de Paris; some say it's the best restaurant on the Riviera. The wine list alone offers a heady choice of some 250,000 bottles of wine (many priceless) stashed in a cellar carved from rock.

Cafés & Fast Food

Snack-attack places are plentiful around the port. Pizza slices to munch on the move are sold at the Pizza System counter in the **Casino supermarket** *(17 blvd Albert 1er; open 8.30am-8pm Mon-Sat)*.

Häagen-Daz *(place du Casino)* has a great little ice-cream outlet and *salon de thé* in a pavilion in the public gardens in front of the casino, and another inside the Galerie du Sporting on place du Casino. One/two scoops cost €2.30/3.70.

Café de Paris *(☎ 92 16 21 24; place du Casino; starters/mains €12/25)*, a historic café in business since 1882, is the place to people-watch in Monte Carlo. Here, on its legendary – and today sprawling – terrace, you pay €20 for a humble cod steak.

Café Grand Prix *(☎ 93 25 56 90; e reservation@cafegrandprix.com; 1 quai Antoine 1er)*, with a sister café in London, is a portside pad that throbs with drivers' girlfriends, support teams etc during the Grand Prix.

Carlino's *(☎ 97 97 88 88; place de la Visitation; breakfast €6.40)*, a sweet-toothed delight, specialises in chocolates. Sample its naughty creations in the tearoom or opt for a cocktail or cuppa tea (there are dozens of different types to choose from) instead.

ENTERTAINMENT

To find out what's on, turn to *l'essentiel*, a weekly entertainment listings magazine covering Monaco (free at the tourist office) or look online at W www.monaco-spectacle.com; the latter accepts Internet bookings for many cultural events. Alternatively, head for the individual box offices of the venues listed in this section or **FNAC** *(☎ 93 10 81 81; 17 ave des Spélugues; open 10am-7.30pm or 8pm Mon-Sat)*, inside the Centre Commercial Le Métropole, which also sells tickets.

Le Sporting *(☎ 92 16 36 36; 26 ave Princesse Grace)* is Monaco's prime pop concert venue. Cabaret shows are also held here. Tickets, costing €48/80 with a drink/dinner for concerts and €40/80 for cabarets, are sold at the Café de Paris (see Places to Eat earlier) and FNAC.

Bars & Nightclubs

Sass Café *(☎ 93 25 52 00; 11 ave Princesse Grace)*, more chic than chic, is where Monaco's jet set jives to live jazz.

Patio Latino *(☎ 92 05 67 37; 42 quai Jean-Charles Rey)*, hipper than hip, is young, fun and has tasty tapas dishes to boot. Kick off your evening like a Monégasque socialite.

Zebra Square *(☎ 99 99 25 50; 10 ave Princesse Grace)*, on the top floor of the Grimaldi Forum, is Monaco's other trendy drink 'n' dine hang-out. Take one look at its stunning terrace and you'll see why.

The Living Room *(☎ 93 50 80 31; 7 ave des Spélugues)* is a hybrid piano bar-disco, adjoining another nightclub. Ring the bell to enter.

Tiffany's *(☎ 93 50 53 13; 3 ave des Spélugues)*, adjoining the Metropole shopping centre, is a popular mainstream disco.

Jimmy'z *(☎ 92 16 36 36; 26 ave Princesse Grace)*, inside Le Sporting complex, is Monaco's most famous nightclub, complete with Cuban smoking room and lots of celebrities.

Cinemas

Cinéma Le Sporting *(French number ☎ 08 36 68 00 72; W www.cinemasporting.com; place du Casino; tickets €9, student & under 18 €5.50)* shows original-language films (usually English) daily.

Theatre

The interior of the **Théâtre Princesse Grace** *(☎ 93 25 32 27; 12 ave d'Ostende)* was designed by Grace Kelly.

The charming **Théâtre du Fort Antoine** *(☎ 93 15 80 00; ave de la Quarantaine)*, an open-air theatre in an early-18th-century fortress, remains closed until works on a sea wall below are complete. Plays and musical concerts are usually staged here in July and August.

Ballet, Opera & Classical Music

Performances by the Monte Carlo Philharmonic Orchestra (1863) are held in the **Auditorium Rainier III** inside the **Centre de Congrès Auditorium** *(☎ 93 10 85 00; W www.opmc.mc; blvd Louis II)*. Tickets cost €15 to €50. In July and August its venue shifts to the star-topped **Cour d'Honneur** (Courtyard of Honour) at the Palais du Prince. Tickets (€18 to €75), sold at the **Atrium du Casino** *(☎ 92 16 22 99; place du Casino; open 10am-5.30pm Tues-Sun)*, inside the casino, are like gold dust.

Both the ballet and orchestra also perform in the **Salles des Princes** at the **Grimaldi Forum** *(☎ 99 99 30 00; W www.grimaldiforum.mc; 10 ave Princesse Grace)* – see the Jardin Japonais & Grimaldi Forum section earlier in this chapter.

The **Salle Garnier** (1892), adjoining Monte Carlo Casino, is the permanent home of the Monte Carlo opera and ballet companies. It will remain closed for renovation until 2005.

A jacket and tie for men is obligatory at all performances.

SPECTATOR SPORTS

The sporting calendar kicks off with the legendary Monte Carlo Rally in January. The four-day event is a series of timed stages, with the rally starting and finishing at the Port de Monaco, and ripping through Haute-Provence in between. The traditional night stage and the concentration run where drivers set off from various European cities to meet in Monte Carlo – as did Disney's Herbie (the VW Beetle) on screen in the 1970s – were scrapped in 1997. More information is on the Web at W www.acm.mc.

The Monte Carlo International Tennis Championships, held at the **Monte Carlo Country Club** *(French number ☎ 04 93 41 30 15; ave Princesse Grace)*, open the hard-court season in April.

Football team AS Monaco can be seen in action on its home ground, the **Stade Louis II** *(Louis II Stadium; ☎ 92 05 40 11; 7 ave des Castelans)* in Fontvieille. The **ticket office** *(☎ 92 05 74 73; open 9am-7pm daily)* is inside the stadium. Guided tours in English (45 minutes) of the stadium depart twice daily on Monday, Tuesday, Thursday and Friday; they cost €4/2 per adult/under-12.

In town, the AS Monaco boutique, **ASM Monaco Pro Shop** *(☎ 97 77 74 74; 16 rue Grimaldi)* sells all the red-and-white gear, from shorts and shirts to ashtrays and champagne flutes.

GETTING THERE & AWAY

Air

Héli Air Monaco *(☎ 92 05 00 50; W www.heliairmonaco.com)*, **Héli Inter Riviera** *(☎ 97 77 84 84)* and **MonacAir** *(☎ 97 97 39 00)*, all based at **Héliport de Monaco** *(☎ 92 05 00 10; ave des Ligures)*, can twirl you anywhere along the coast for a not-so-small fee, including to/from Nice airport (see the Getting Around chapter).

Bus

Nice-based **Rapides Côte d'Azur** *(☎ 04 93 85 64 44; W www.rca.tm.fr)* operates daily buses from Monaco to Nice-Côte d'Azur airport (€13.90 one-way, 45 minutes). In Monaco, buses use the stop in front of the national tourist office. Bus times coincide with flight arrivals and departures.

Train

Monaco train station is at the northern end of blvd Rainier III; enter the station on ave Prince Pierre or via the public lift linking place Ste-Dévote with blvd de Bélgique.

Trains to/from Monaco are run by France's SNCF and taking the train along this coast is highly recommended – the sea and the mountains provide a magnificent sight. There are frequent trains east to Menton (€1.70, 10 minutes) and the first town across the border in Italy, Ventimiglia (Vintimille in French; €3, 25 minutes). For trains to Nice (€3, 20 minutes) and onward connections to other towns, see the Nice Getting There & Away section in the Nice to Menton chapter.

Car & Motorcycle

If you are driving out of Monaco, either east towards Italy or west to Nice, and you want to go via the A8, you need to join the Corniche Moyenne (N7). For Italy, look for

The Formula One Grand Prix

The Grand Prix Automobile de Monaco – which dates from 1911 – is the world's most glamorous race. It screams round the streets each year in May, lapping a 3.328km circuit highly revered in the racing world for its narrow, unrelenting *virages* (bends) and awkward chicanes.

Few succeed in completing the required 78 laps of the course, which takes drivers from the port, through a right-hand bend and uphill along ave d'Ostende to place du Casino, where the track bombs downhill around a hairpin and two sharp rights into the tunnel and back to the port along ave Président JF Kennedy and quai Albert 1er. Michael Schumacher smashed all records in 2001 when he screeched past the finishing line in his Ferrari in just 1h47'22"56.1 beating the previous record that he himself had set in 1999 (along with the fastest lap speed – 147.772km/h – yet to be beaten).

The race is watched by 150,000 spectators from stands around the port and on place du Casino. The cheapest spot is ave de la Porte Neuve. The wealthy survey the spectacle from Hôtel Hermitage or from a yacht deck in the harbour. The Grimaldis watch the start and finish from the royal box at the port, retiring in between for a champagne brunch at an undisclosed address overlooking the circuit. Mechanics, girlfriends, driver-support teams and so on hobnob at Stars 'n' Bars and Café Grand Prix (see Places to Eat earlier in this chapter), both near the paddock area on quai Antoine 1er.

Time trials and various races, including the Grand Prix de Monaco 3000, take place during the three days leading up to the Formula One Grand Prix, which is always held on Sunday afternoon. Tickets for all races, including the Grand Prix, are available from the **Automobile Club de Monaco** *(☎ 93 15 26 00, fax 92 25 80 08; W www.acm.mc; 23 blvd Albert 1er)*. Tickets range from *€50 to €420, and* go on sale in January and are snapped up in hours.

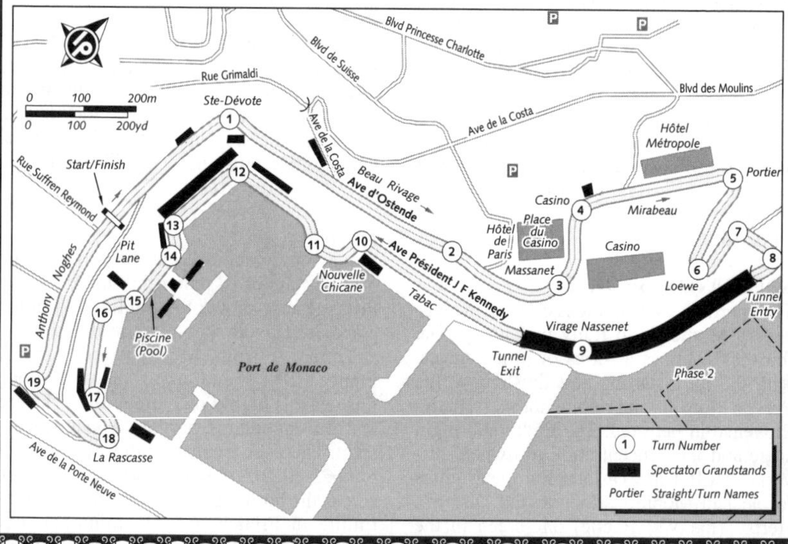

signs indicating Gênes (Genoa in English; Genova in Italian). Blvd du Jardin Exotique leads to the N7 in the direction of Nice.

GETTING AROUND

Public lifts – marked on the free (and only) maps of Monaco distributed by the tourist office – run up and down the hillside. Most operate 24 hours; some run from 6am to midnight or 1am.

Bus

Monaco's urban bus system has six lines. Line No 2 links Monaco Ville with Monte Carlo and then loops back to the Jardin Exotique. Line No 4 links the train station with the tourist office, the casino and Larvotto beach. A one-way ticket/one-day pass costs €1.30/3.30. Alternatively, buy a four-/eight-ride magnetic card (€3.30/5.25) from the bus driver or from vending machines at most bus stops. An eight-ride card taking in Monaco and Beausoleil costs €5.80. Buses run from 7am or 7.30am to 9pm.

The local bus company, **Compagnie des Autobus de Monaco** *(CAM; ☎ 97 70 22 22; Ⓦ www.cam.mc; 3 ave Président JF Kennedy; open 8.30am-noon & 2pm-6pm Mon-Thur, 8.30am-noon & 2pm-5pm Fri)* has its office on the port's northern side.

Taxi

To order a taxi call ☎ 93 15 01 01.

Bicycle

MBK *(☎ 93 50 10 80; 7 rue de Millo; open 8am-noon & 2pm-7pm Mon-Fri, 8am-noon Sat)* rents road/mountain bikes from €8/12 per day, as well as 50cc/80cc scooters that cost from €25/35 per 24 hours.

Language

Arming yourself with some French will broaden your travel experience, endear you to the locals and, in rural Haute-Provence (where tourism hasn't yet developed enough to persuade people in service industries to speak English), ensure a smooth ride around the region. On the coast, practically everyone you are likely to meet speaks basic English (and, in many cases, a rash of other European languages).

Standard French is taught and spoken in Provence. However, travellers accustomed to schoolbook French, or the unaccented, strait-laced French spoken in cities and larger towns, will find the lyrical, flamboyant French spoken in Provence's rural heart (and by most in Marseilles) absolutely incomprehensible. Here, words caressed by the heavy southern accent end with a flourish: vowels are sung; the traditional rolling 'r' is turned into a mighty long trill. So *douze* (the number 12) becomes 'douz-eh' with an emphasised 'e', and *pain* (bread) becomes 'peng'. Take time to tune in and you'll quickly pick up the beat.

PROVENÇAL

Despite the bilingual signs that greet tourists when they enter most towns and villages, the region's mother tongue – Provençal – is scarcely heard on the street or in the home. Just a handful of older people in rural Provence (Prouvènço) keep alive the rich lyrics and poetic language of their ancestors.

Provençal (*prouvençau* in Provençal) is a dialect of *langue d'oc* (Occitan), the traditional language of southern France. Its grammar is closer to Catalan and Spanish than to French. In the grand age of courtly love between the 12th and 14th centuries, Provençal was the literary language of France and northern Spain and even used as far afield as Italy. Medieval troubadours and poets created melodies and elegant poems motivated by the ideal of courtly love, and Provençal blossomed.

The 19th century witnessed a revival of Provençal after its rapid displacement by *langue d'oïl*, the language of northern France that originated from the vernacular Latin spoken by the Gallo-Romans and which gave birth to modern French (*francés* in Provençal). The revival was spearheaded by Frédéric Mistral (1830–1914), a poet from Vaucluse, whose works in Provençal landed him the Nobel Prize for Literature in 1904.

Mistral was the backbone of Félibrige, a literary society created in 1854 to safeguard Provençal literature, culture and identity. A wealth of literature in Provençal was published by Félibrige, which, from its contemporary base at Aix-Marseilles University (☎ 04 42 26 23 41, fax 04 42 27 52 89, ⓔ info@felibrige.com), Parc Jourdan, 8bis ave Jules Ferry, 13100 Aix-en-Provence, remains as vocal today as it was in years past. It has a website at Ⓦ www.felibrige.com.

FRENCH

While the French rightly or wrongly have a reputation for assuming that all human beings should speak French – until WWI it was the international language of culture and diplomacy – you'll find that any attempt to communicate in French will be much appreciated. Your best bet is always to approach people politely in French, even if the only sentence you know is *Pardon, madame/monsieur/mademoiselle, parlez-vous anglais?* (Excuse me, madam/sir/miss, do you speak English?).

Some basic French words and phrases are listed below. For a more comprehensive guide to the French language, get hold of Lonely Planet's *French phrasebook*.

Grammar

An important distinction is made in French between *tu* and *vous*, which both mean 'you'. *Tu* is only used when addressing people you know well, children or animals. When addressing an adult who is not a personal friend, *vous* should be used unless the person invites you to use *tu*. In general, younger people insist less on this distinction, and you may find that they use *tu* from the beginning of an acquaintance.

All nouns in French are either masculine or feminine and adjectives reflect the gender of the noun they modify. The feminine form of many nouns and adjectives is indicated by a silent **e** added to the masculine form, as in *ami* and *amie*, the masculine and feminine for 'friend'. In the following phrases we have indicated these forms where necessary, the masculine first, separated from the feminine by a slash. The masculine/feminine status of a noun will often be indicated by its preceding article, eg, *le/la* (the), *un/une* (a), *du/de la* (some); or a possessive adjective, eg, *mon/ma* (my), *ton/ta* (your), *son/sa* (his/her). With French, unlike English, the possessive adjective agrees in number and gender with the thing possessed, not the possessor, eg, *sa mère* (his or her mother).

Pronunciation

Most letters in French are pronounced more or less the same as their English equivalents. A few which may cause confusion are:

j as the 's' in 'leisure', eg, *jour* (day)

c before **e** and **i**, as the 's' in 'sit'; before **a**, **o** and **u** it's pronounced as English 'k'. When undescored with a 'cedilla' (ç) it's always pronounced as the 's' in 'sit'.

French has a number of sounds that are difficult for Anglophones to produce. These include:

- The distinction between the 'u' sound (as in *tu*) and 'oo' sound (as in *tout*). For both sounds, the lips are rounded and projected forward, but for the 'u' the tongue is towards the front of the mouth, its tip against the lower front teeth, whereas for the 'oo' the tongue is towards the back of the mouth, its tip behind the gums of the lower front teeth.
- The nasal vowels. With nasal vowels the breath escapes partly through the nose and partly through the mouth. These sounds occur where a syllable ends in a single **n** or **m**; the **n** or **m** is silent but indicates the nasalisation of the preceding vowel.
- The **r.** The standard **r** of Parisian French is produced by moving the bulk of the tongue backwards to constrict the air flow in the pharynx while the tip of the tongue rests behind the lower front teeth.

USEFUL WORDS

Basics

Yes.	*Oui.*
No.	*Non.*
Maybe.	*Peut-être.*
Please.	*S'il vous plaît.*
Thank you.	*Merci.*
You're welcome.	*Je vous en prie.*
Excuse me.	*Excusez-moi.*
Sorry/Forgive me.	*Pardon.*

Greetings & Civilities

Hello/Good day.	*Bonjour.*
Hello. (informal)	*Salut.*
Good evening.	*Bonsoir.*
Good night.	*Bonne nuit.*
Goodbye.	*Au revoir.*
How are you?	*Comment allez-vous?* (polite) *Comment vas-tu?/ Comment ça va?* (informal)
Fine, thanks.	*Bien, merci.*
What's your name?	*Comment vous appelez-vous?*
My name is ...	*Je m'appelle ...*
I'm pleased to meet you.	*Enchanté* (m)/ *Enchantée* (f).
How old are you?	*Quel âge avez-vous?*
I'm ... years old.	*J'ai ... ans.*
Do you like ...?	*Aimez-vous ...?*
Where are you from?	*De quel pays êtes-vous?*
I'm from ...	*Je viens ...*
Australia	*d'Australie*
Canada	*du Canada*
England	*d'Angleterre*
Germany	*d'Allemagne*
Ireland	*d'Irlande*
New Zealand	*de Nouvelle Zélande*
Scotland	*d'Écosse*
the USA	*des États-Unis*
Wales	*du Pays de Galle*

Language Difficulties

I understand.	*Je comprends.*
I don't understand.	*Je ne comprends pas.*
Do you speak English?	*Parlez-vous anglais?*
Could you please write it down?	*Est-ce que vous pouvez l'écrire?*

Getting Around

I want to go to ...	*Je voudrais aller à ...*
I'd like to book a seat to ...	*Je voudrais réserver une place pour ...*

What time does the ... leave/arrive?	*À quelle heure part/arrive ...?*
aeroplane	*l'avion*
bus (city)	*l'autobus*
bus (intercity)	*l'autocar*
ferry	*le ferry(-boat)*
train	*le train*
tram	*le tramway*

Where is (the) ...?	*Où est ...?*
bus stop?	*l'arrêt d'autobus*
metro station	*la station de métro*
train station	*la gare*
tram stop	*l'arrêt de tramway*
ticket office	*le guichet*

I'd like a ... ticket.	*Je voudrais un billet ...*
one-way	*aller-simple*
return	*aller-retour*
1st-class	*de première classe*
2nd-class	*de deuxième classe*

How long does the trip take?	*Combien de temps dure le trajet?*

The train is ...	*Le train est ...*
delayed	*en retard*
on time	*à l'heure*
early	*en avance*

Do I need to ...?	*Est-ce que je dois ...?*
change trains	*changer de train*
change platform	*changer de quai*

left-luggage locker	*consigne automatique*
platform	*quai*
timetable	*horaire*

I'd like to hire ...	*Je voudrais louer ...*
a bicycle	*un vélo*
a car	*une voiture*
a guide	*un guide*

Around Town

I'm looking for ...	*Je cherche ...*
a bank/ exchange office	*une banque/ un bureau de change*
the city centre	*le centre-ville*
the ... embassy	*l'ambassade de ...*
the hospital	*l'hôpital*
my hotel	*mon hôtel*
the market	*le marché*
the police	*la police*
the post office	*le bureau de poste/ la poste*
a public phone	*une cabine téléphonique*
a public toilet	*les toilettes*
the tourist office	*l'office de tourisme/ le syndicat d'initiative*

Signs

Entrée	**Entrance**
Sortie	**Exit**
Ouvert	**Open**
Fermé	**Closed**
Chambres Libres	**Rooms Available**
Complet	**No Vacancies**
Renseignements	**Information**
Interdit	**Prohibited**
(Commissariat de) Police	**Police Station**
Toilettes, WC	**Toilets**
Hommes	**Men**
Femmes	**Women**

Where is ...?	*Où est ...?*
the beach	*la plage*
the bridge	*le pont*
the castle/mansion	*le château*
the cathedral	*la cathédrale*
the church	*l'église*
the island	*l'île*
the lake	*le lac*
the central square	*la place centrale*
the mosque	*la mosquée*
the old city/town	*la vieille ville*
the palace	*le palais*
the quay/bank	*le quai/la rive*
the ruins	*les ruines*
the sea	*la mer*
the square	*la place*
the tower	*la tour*

What time does it open/close?	*Quelle est l'heure d'ouverture/ de fermeture?*
I'd like to make a telephone call.	*Je voudrais téléphoner.*

I'd like to change ...	*Je voudrais changer ...*
some money	*de l'argent*
travellers cheques	*chèques de voyage*

Directions

How do I get to ...?	*Comment dois-je faire pour arriver à ...?*

Is it near/far?	*Est-ce près/loin?*
Can you show me on the map/ city map?	*Est-ce que vous pouvez me le montrer sur la carte/le plan?*
Go straight ahead.	*Continuez tout droit.*
Turn left.	*Tournez à gauche.*
Turn right.	*Tournez à droite.*
at the traffic lights	*aux feux*
at the next corner	*au prochain coin*
behind	*derrière*
in front of	*devant*
opposite	*en face de*
north	*nord*
south	*sud*
east	*est*
west	*ouest*

Accommodation

I'm looking for ...	*Je cherche ...*
the youth hostel	*l'auberge de jeunesse*
the campground	*le camping*
a hotel	*un hôtel*
Where can I find a cheap hotel?	*Où est-ce que je peux trouver un hôtel bon marché?*
What's the address?	*Quelle est l'adresse?*
Could you write it down, please?	*Est-ce vous pourriez l'écrire, s'il vous plaît?*
Do you have any rooms available?	*Est-ce que vous avez des chambres libres?*
I'd like to book ...	*Je voudrais réserver ...*
a bed	*un lit*
a single room	*une chambre simple*
a double room	*une chambre double*
a room with a shower and toilet	*une chambre avec douche et WC*
I'd like to stay in a dormitory.	*Je voudrais coucher dans un dortoir.*
How much is it ...?	*Quel est le prix ...?*
per night	*par nuit*
per person	*par personne*
Is breakfast included?	*Est-ce que le petit déjeuner est compris?*
May I see the room?	*Est-ce que je peux voir la chambre?*
Where is ...?	*Où est ...?*
the bathroom	*la salle de bains*
the shower	*la douche*
Where is the toilet?	*Où sont les toilettes?*
I'm going to stay ...	*Je resterai ...*
one day	*un jour*
a week	*une semaine*

Health

I'm sick.	*Je suis malade.*
I need a doctor.	*Il me faut un médecin.*
Where is the hospital?	*Où est l'hôpital?*
I have diarrhoea.	*J'ai la diarrhée.*
I'm pregnant.	*Je suis enceinte.*
I'm ...	*Je suis ...*
diabetic	*diabétique*
epileptic	*épileptique*
asthmatic	*asthmatique*
anaemic	*anémique*
I'm allergic ...	*Je suis allergique ...*
to antibiotics	*aux antibiotiques*
to penicillin	*à la pénicilline*
antiseptic	*l'antiseptique*
aspirin	*l'aspirine*
condoms	*les préservatifs*
contraceptive	*un contraceptif*
medicine	*le médicament*
nausea	*la nausée*
painkillers	*des analgésiques*
sunblock cream	*la crème solaire haute protection*
tampons	*les tampons hygiéniques*

Time & Dates

What time is it?	*Quelle heure est-il?*
It's (two) o'clock.	*Il est (deux) heures.*
When?	*Quand?*
today	*aujourd'hui*
tonight	*ce soir*
tomorrow	*demain*
day after tomorrow	*après-demain*
yesterday	*hier*
all day	*toute la journée*
in the morning	*du matin*
in the afternoon	*de l'après-midi*
in the evening	*du soir*

Emergencies

Help!	*Au secours!*
Fire!	*Au feu!*
Call a doctor!	*Appelez un médecin!*
Call the police!	*Appelez la police!*
Leave me alone!	*Fichez-moi la paix!*
I've been robbed.	*On m'a volé.*
I've been raped!	*On m'a violée!*
I'm lost.	*Je me suis égaré/égarée.* (m/f)

Monday	*lundi*
Tuesday	*mardi*
Wednesday	*mercredi*
Thursday	*jeudi*
Friday	*vendredi*
Saturday	*samedi*
Sunday	*dimanche*

January	*janvier*
February	*février*
March	*mars*
April	*avril*
May	*mai*
June	*juin*
July	*juillet*
August	*août*
September	*septembre*
October	*octobre*
November	*novembre*
December	*décembre*

Numbers

1	*un*
2	*deux*
3	*trois*
4	*quatre*
5	*cinq*
6	*six*
7	*sept*
8	*huit*
9	*neuf*
10	*dix*
11	*onze*
12	*douze*
13	*treize*
14	*quatorze*
15	*quinze*
16	*seize*
17	*dix-sept*
18	*dix-huit*
19	*dix-neuf*
20	*vingt*
21	*vingt-et-un*
22	*vingt-deux*
23	*vingt trois*
30	*trente*
40	*quarante*
50	*cinquante*
60	*soixante*
70	*soixante-dix*
80	*quatre-vingts*
90	*quatre-vingts-dix*
100	*cent*
1000	*mille*
2000	*deux mille*

one million *un million*

FOOD GLOSSARY

Appetisers

anchoïade – anchovy puree laced with garlic and olive oil
assiette Anglaise – plate of cold mixed meats and sausages
assiette de crudités – plate of raw vegetables with dressings
banon à la Feuille – goat's cheese dipped in eau-de-vie and wrapped in a chestnut leaf
brandade de morue – mix of crushed salted cod, olive oil and garlic
brebis – sheep's milk dairy product
fromage de chèvre – goat's cheese (also called *brousse*)
pissala – Niçois paste mixed from pureed anchovies
pissaladière – anchovy, onion and black olive 'pizza' from Nice
tapenade – sharp, black olive-based dip
tomme Arlesienne – moulded goat's cheese from Arles

Soups

bourride – fish soup; often eaten as a main course
bouillon – broth or stock
croûtons – fried or roasted bread cubes, sprinkled on top of soups
potage – thick soup made with pureed vegetables
soupe au pistou – vegetable soup made with basil and garlic
soupe de poisson – fish soup

Meat, Chicken & Poultry

agneau – lamb
aiguillette – thin slice of duck fillet

alouettes sans têtes – meat slices wrapped around a stuffing; literally 'headless larks'
bœuf – beef
bœuf haché – minced beef
brochette – kebab
canard – duck
cervelle – brains
chapon – capon
charcuterie – cooked or prepared meats
cheval – horse meat
chèvre – goat
chevreau – kid (baby goat)
chevreuil – venison
cuisses de grenouilles – frogs' legs
entrecôte – rib steak
daube de bœuf à la Provençale – beef stew
épaule d'agneau – shoulder of lamb
escargot – snail
estouffade de bœuf – Carmargais beef stew with tomatoes and olive
faisan – pheasant
faux-filet – sirloin steak
filet – tenderloin
foie – liver
foie gras de canard – duck liver paté
gibier – game
gigot d'agneau – leg of lamb
jambon – ham
lapin – rabbit
lard – bacon
lardon – pieces of chopped bacon
lièvre – hare
mouton – mutton
pieds de porc – pig trotters
pieds et paquets – sheep tripe; literally 'feet and packages'
pigeon aux gousses d'ail – pigeon cooked with garlic cloves
pigeonneau – squab (young pigeon)
pintade – guinea fowl
poulet – chicken
rognons – kidneys
sanglier – wild boar
saucisson – large sausage
saucisson d'Arles – sausage made from pork, beef, wine and spice
saucisson fumé – smoked sausage
taureau de Camargue – Camargais beef
tournedos – thick slices of fillet steak
tripes – tripe
veau – veal
viande – meat
volaille – poultry

Fish & Seafood

aïoli Provençale complet – shellfish, vegetables, boiled egg and aïoli
anchois – anchovy
anguille – eel
brème – bream
brochet – pike
cabillaud – fresh cod
calmar – squid
carrelet – plaice
chaudrée – fish stew
colin – hake
coquillage – shellfish
coquille St-Jacques – scallop
crabe – crab
crevette grise – shrimp
crevette rose – prawn
écrevisse – small, freshwater crayfish
fruits de mer – seafood
gambas – king prawns
goujon – gudgeon (small freshwater fish)
hareng – herring
homard – lobster
huître – oyster
langouste – crayfish
langoustine – very small salt-water 'lobster'
lotte – monkfish
loup – sea bass
maquereau – mackerel
merlan – whiting
morue – dried, salted cod
morue pochée – poached cod
moules – mussels
oursin – sea urchin
paella – rice dish with saffron, vegetables and shellfish
palourde – clam
poisson – fish
poulpe – octopus
raie – ray
rascasse – spiny scorpion fish
rouget – red mullet
St-Pierre – a flat fish used in bouillabaisse
saumon – salmon
seiche – cuttlefish
sole – sole
stockfish (*estocaficada* in Niçois) – dried salt fish soaked in water for four to five days, stewed for two hours with onion, tomato and white wine, then laced with anchovies and black olives.
thon – tuna
truite – trout

Vegetables, Herbs & Spices

ail – garlic
aneth – dill

anis – aniseed
artichaut – artichoke
asperge – asparagus
aubergine – aubergine (eggplant)
avocat – avocado
barbouillade – stuffed or stewed aubergine
basilic – basil
betterave – beetroot
blette de Nice – white beet
cannelle – cinnamon
carotte – carrot
céleri – celery
cèpe – cepe (boletus mushroom)
champignon – mushroom
chou – cabbage
citrouille – pumpkin
concombre – cucumber
cornichon – gherkin (pickle)
courgette – courgette (zucchini)
échalotte – shallot
endive frisée – chicory
épice – spice
épinards – spinach
estragon – tarragon
fenouil – fennel
fève – broad bean
fleur de courgette – courgette flower
genièvre – juniper
gingembre – ginger
haricots – beans
haricots blancs – white beans
haricots rouge – kidney beans
haricots verts – French (string) beans
herbe – herb
laitue – lettuce
légume – vegetable
légumes farcis – stuffed vegetables
lentilles – lentils
maïs – sweetcorn
marjolaine – sweet marjoram
menthe – mint
mesclun – Niçois mix of lettuce
navet – turnip
oignon – onion
origan – oregano
oseille – sorrel
panais – parsnip
persil – parsley
petit pois – pea
poireau – leek
poivron – green pepper
pomme de terre – potato
ratatouille – casserole of aubergines, tomatoes, peppers and garlic
riz – rice
riz de Camargue – Camargais rice
romarin – rosemary
salade Niçoise – green salad featuring tuna, egg and anchovy
sarrasin – buckwheat
sarriette – savory
seigle – rye
thym – thyme
tian – vegetable and rice gratin served in a dish called a 'tian'
tomate – tomato
tourta de bléa – Niçois white beetroot and pine kernel pie
truffe – black truffle

Sauces & Accompaniments

aïoli – garlicky sauce to accompany bouillabaisse
béchamel – basic white sauce
huile d'olive – olive oil
mornay – cheese sauce
moutarde – mustard
pistou – pesto (pounded mix of basil, hard cheese, olive oil and garlic)
Provençale – tomato, garlic, herb and olive oil dressing or sauce
rouille – aïoli-based sauce spiced with chilli pepper; served with bourride
tartare – mayonnaise with herbs
vinaigrette – salad dressing made with oil, vinegar, mustard and garlic

Fruit & Nuts

abricot – apricot
agrumes – citrus fruits
amande – almond
ananas – pineapple
banane – banana
blonde de Nice – variety of orange
cassis – blackcurrant
cerise – cherry
citron – lemon
datte – date
figue – fig
fraise – strawberry
framboise – raspberry
fruits confits – candied fruits
fruits glazée – glazed fruits
grenade – pomegranate
groseille – redcurrant or gooseberry
mangu – mango
marron – chestnut
melon – melon
melon canteloup – type of Cavaillon melon
mirabelle – type of plum

myrtille – bilberry (blueberry)
noisette – hazelnut
noix de cajou – cashew
pamplemousse – grapefruit
pastèque – watermelon
pêche – peach
pignon – pine kernel
pistache – pistachio
poire – pear
pomme – apple
prune – plum
pruneau – prune
raisin – grape

Desserts & Sweets

bergamotes – orange-flavoured confectionary
berlingots – hard caramel originating in Carpentras
calisson – almond-based sweet from Aix-en-Provence
crème caramel – caramel custard
crêpe – thin pancake
crêpes suzettes – orange-flavoured crepes flambéed in liqueur
dragée – sugared almond
éclair – pastry filled with cream
flan – egg-custard dessert
gâteau – cake
gelée – jelly
glace – ice cream
île flottante – cooked egg white, floating on a creamy sauce; literally 'floating island'
macarons – macaroons (sweet biscuit made of ground almonds, sugar and egg whites)
tarte – tart (pie)
tarte aux pommes – apple tart
tarte Tropézienne – cream sandwich cake from St-Tropez
yaourt – yogurt

Breads & Biscuits

brioche – sweet soft bread
chichi freggi – sugar-coated doughnuts from around Marseilles
fougasse – elongated Niçois bread stuffed with olives, chopped bacon *(lardons)* or anchovies *(anchois)*
fougassette – brioche perfumed with orange flower
galette – wholemeal or buckwheat pancake; also a type of biscuit
gâteaux secs aux amandes – crisp almond biscuits
michettes – Niçois bread stuffed with cheese, olives, anchovies and onions
navettes – canoe-shaped, orange-blossom-flavoured biscuits from Marseilles
pain à l'ail – garlic bread
pain au son – bran bread
pain aux noix – walnut bread
pain aux oignons – onion bread
pain aux olives – olive bread
pain aux raisins – sultana bread
pain aux roquefort – blue-cheese bread
pain complet – wholemeal bread
pain de mie – sandwich loaf
pain des Alpes – white crusty bread sold by weight (kg) rather than in loaves
pain de seigle – rye bread
pain de seigle aux raisins – rye bread with sultanas
pan bagnat – Niçois bread soaked in olive oil and filled with anchovy, olives, green pepper
panisses – chickpea flour patties from in and around Marseilles
sablé – shortbread biscuit
socca – Niçois chickpea flour & olive oil pancake

Basics

beurre – butter
chocolat – chocolate
confiture – jam
crème fraîche – unsweetened cream
farine – flour
lait – milk
miel – honey
œufs – eggs
poivre – pepper
sel – salt
sucre – sugar
vinaigre – vinegar

DRINKS

eau	water
eau minérale	natural mineral water
eau gazeuse	sparkling mineral water
café	coffee
thé	tea
lait	milk
au lait	with milk
avec sucre	with sugar
jus d'orange	orange juice
bière	beer
vin rouge/blanc	red/white wine

Glossary

Word gender is indicated as (m) masculine, (f) feminine.

abbaye (f) – abbey
accueil (m) – reception
aire naturelle (f) – farm camp site
aire naturiste (f) – nudist camp
anse (f) – cove
appellation d'origine contrôlée (AOC) – wines that have met stringent government regulations governing where, how and under what conditions the grapes are grown and the wines fermented and bottled
arène (f) – amphitheatre
arrondissement (m) – one of several districts into which large cities, such as Marseilles, are split
atelier (m) – artisan's workshop
auberge (f) – inn
auberge de jeunesse (f) – youth hostel
autoroute (f) – motorway, highway

barrage (m) – dam
bastide (f) – country house
belvédère (m) – viewpoint
billetterie (f) – ticket office or counter
borie (f) – primitive dwelling, built from dry limestone around 3500 BC
boucherie (f) – meat shop, butcher's
boulangerie (f) – bread shop, bakery
bureau de location (m) – ticket office

calanque (f) – rocky inlet
cave (f) – wine or cheese cellar
centre (de) hospitalier (m) – hospital
chambre d'hôte (f) – bed and breakfast accommodation, in a private home
charcuterie (f) – pork butcher's shop and delicatessen
château (m) – castle or stately home
chèvre (m) – goat
col (m) – mountain pass
comité départemental du tourisme (m) – departmental tourist office
commissariat de police (m) – police station
conseil général (m) – general council
corniche (f) – coastal or cliff road
corrida (f) – bullfight
cour (f) – courtyard
cour d'honneur (f) – courtyard of honour
course Camarguaise (f) – Camargue-style bullfight
crèche vivante (f) – nativity scene with real people; literally 'living crib'
cueillette des olives (f) – olive harvest

défense forestière contre l'incendie (DFCI) – fire road (public access forbidden)
défilé (m) – procession or cortege
dégustation (f) – the fine art of tasting wine, cheese, olive oil or seafood
département (m) – administrative area (department)
digue (f) – dike
distributeur automatique de billets or **point d'argent** (m) – ATM, cashpoint
douane (f) – customs

eau potable (f) – drinking water
embarcadère (m) – pier or jetty
épicerie (f) – grocery shop
escalier (m) – stairs or staircase
étang (m) – lagoon, pond or lake

faïence (f) – earthenware
farandole (f) – a Provençal dance dating to the Middle Ages, particularly popular in Arles today
féria (f) – bullfighting festival
ferme auberge (f) – family-run inn that is attached to a farm or chateau; farmhouse restaurant
fermeture hebdomadaire (f) – weekly closure
fête (f) – party or festival
flamant rose (m) – pink flamingo
formule (f) – fixed main course plus starter or dessert
fromagerie (f) – cheese shop

galets (m) – large smooth stones covering Châteauneuf du Pape vineyards
gardian (m) – Camargue horseman
gare (f) – train station
gare maritime (m) – ferry terminal
gare routière (m) – bus station; sometimes called *gare d'autobus*
garrigue (f) – ground cover of aromatic plants; see also *maquis*
gitan (m) – Roma; gypsy
gîte d'étape (m) – hikers accommodation; it is often found in the mountains or in rural areas
gîte rural (m) – country cottage

golfe (m) – gulf
grand cru (m) – wine of recognised superior quality; literally 'great growth'
grotte (f) – cave

hôtel de ville (m) – town hall
hôtel particulier (m) – private mansion

jardin (botanique) (m) – (botanic) garden
jetée (f) – pier
jour férié (m) – public holiday
joute Provençale (f) – nautical jousting tournament

lacet (m) – hairpin bend
lavoir (m) – communal wash house
location du vélo (f) – bicycle rental

mairie (f) – town hall
maison de la France (f) – French tourist office abroad
maison de la presse (f) – newsagent
manade (f) – herds of bulls or horses
maquis (m) – aromatic Provençal scrub, see also *garrigue*; name given to the French Resistance movement
marais (m) – marsh or swamp
marais salant (m) – salt pan
marché aux puces (m) – flea market
marché couvert (m) – covered market
marché paysan (m) – farmers market
marché Provençal (m) – open air market
mas (m) – Provençal farmhouse
menu (m) – meal at a fixed price with two or more courses
mistral (m) – incessant north wind
monastère (m) – monastery
Monégasque – native of Monaco
moulin à huile/à vent (m) – oil/windmill

négociant (m) – a wine merchant
novillada (f) – fight between baby bulls, lcss than four years old

œuvre (f) – work of art or literature
office du tourisme, office de tourisme (m) – tourist office (run by some unit of local government)
orangerie (f) – orangery; greenhouse where originally oranges were grown
oursin (m) – sea urchin

papeterie (f) – stationery shop
parapente (f) – paragliding
parc national (m) – national park
parc naturel régional (m) – regional nature park
pâtisserie (f) – cake and pastry shop
pavillon (m) – pavilion or lodge
pétanque (f) – a Provençal game, not unlike lawn bowls
phare (m) – lighthouse
pic (m) – mountain peak
pichet (m) – jug (of wine)
pied noir (m) – Algerian-born citizen
pique nique (m) – picnic
place (f) – square
plage (f) – beach
planche à voile (f) – surfboard
platane (m) – plane tree
plat du jour (m) – dish of the day
plongée (f) – dive
plongée baptême (f) – baptism dive
point de vue (m) – viewpoint
pont (m) – bridge
port de plaisance (m) – marina or harbour for pleasure boats
porte (f) – gate or door, old-town entrance
préfecture (f) – main town of a *département*
préfet (m) – prefect; regional representative of national government, based in a *préfecture*
presqu'île (f) – peninsula
prieuré (m) – priory
producteur (f) – a wine producer or grower, also known as a *vigneron*
produits du terroir (m) – local food products
promenade à cheval (f) – horse riding
propriété privée (f) – private property

rade (f) – gulf or harbour
ravin (m) – gully or ravine
refuge (m) – hikers shelter (mountain hut)
région (m) – administrative region
rive droite (f) – right bank of river
rive gauche (f) – left bank of river
robe (f) – a wine's colour
rollers (m) – rollerblades
route forestière (f) – forest road

salin (m) – salt marsh
santon (m) – traditional Provençal figurine
saut à l'élastique (m) – bungee jump
savon (f) – soap
savonnerie (f) – soap factory
sentier (m) – trail, footpath
sentier balisé (m) – marked walking path
sentier de grande randonnée (m) – long-distance path with alphanumeric name beginning with 'GR'
sentier littoral (m) – coastal path

sentier sous-marin (m) – underwater trail
site d'escalade (m) – climbing site
ski nautique (m) – water-skiing
spectacle (m) – show, performance
stade (m) – stadium
sur rendez-vous (SRV) – by appointment only
syndicat d'initiative (m) – tourist office (run by an organisation of local merchants)

tabac (m) – tobacconist (also sells newspapers, bus tickets, *télécartes* etc)
table d'orientation (f) – viewpoint sign
taureau (m) – bull
taxe de séjour (f) – tourist tax imposed by local authorities on visitors
télécabine (m) – cable car or gondola
télécarte (f) – phonecard
téléférique (m) – cableway
télésiège/téléski (m) – chair lift/drag lift
théâtre antique (m) – Roman theatre
tour (f) – tower
trottinette (f) – microscooter

vendange (f) – grape harvest
vendangeur (m) – grape picker
vieille ville (f) – old town
vieux port (m) – old port
vigneron (m) – wine grower
vin de garde (m) – a wine best drunk after several years in storage
vin de pays (m) – literally 'country wine'
visa de long séjour (m) – long-stay visa
VTT (m) – *vélo tout terrain*; mountain bike

LONELY PLANET

You already know that Lonely Planet produces more than this one guidebook, but you might not be aware of the other products we have on this region. Here is a selection of titles that you may want to check out as well:

Paris Condensed
ISBN 1 86450 366 1
US$11.99 • UK£5.99

France
ISBN 1 74059 291 3
US$24.99 • UK£14.99

French Phrasebook
ISBN 1 86450 152 9
US$7.99 • UK£3.99

Southwest France
ISBN 1 86450 382 3
US$17.99 • UK£11.99

Paris
ISBN 1 74059 306 5
US$15.99 • UK£9.99

World Food France
ISBN 1 86450 021 2
US$12.99 • UK£7.99

Western Europe
ISBN 1 74059 313 8
US$27.99 • UK£16.99

Brittany
ISBN 1 86450 312 2
US$15.99 • UK£9.99

Normandy
ISBN 1 86450 098 0
US$15.99 • UK£9.99

Mediterranean Europe
ISBN 1 74059 302 2
US$27.99 • UK£16.99

Cycling France
ISBN 1 86450 036 0
US$19.99 • UK£12.99

Walking in France
ISBN 0 86442 601 1
US$19.99 • UK£12.99

Available wherever books are sold

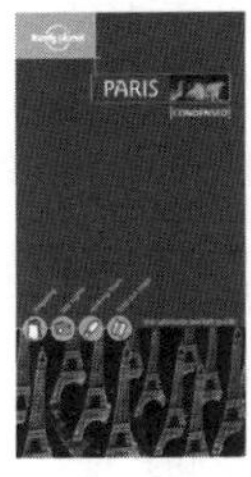

Index

Text

Bold indicates maps.

Bold indicates maps.

Bold indicates maps.

Boxed Text

MAP LEGEND

CITY ROUTES

Freeway — Freeway
Highway — Primary Road
Road — Secondary Road
Street — Street
Lane — Lane
On/Off Ramp
Unsealed Road
One Way Street
Pedestrian Street
Stepped Street
Tunnel
Footbridge

REGIONAL ROUTES

Tollway, Freeway
Primary Road
Secondary Road
Minor Road

BOUNDARIES

International
State
Disputed
Fortified Wall

TRANSPORT ROUTES & STATIONS

Train
Underground Train
Metro
Tramway
Funicular Railway
Ferry
Walking Trail
Walking Tour
Path
Pier or Jetty

HYDROGRAPHY

River, Creek
Canal
Lake
Dry Lake; Salt Lake
Spring; Rapids
Waterfalls

AREA FEATURES

Building
Park, Gardens
Market
Sports Ground
Beach
Cemetery
Forest
Plaza

POPULATION SYMBOLS

Paris — National Capital
Marseille — State Capital
Fréjus — City
La Napoule — Town
Anthéor — Village
Urban Area

MAP SYMBOLS

Place to Stay
Place to Eat
Point of Interest

Airport
Bank
Border Crossing
Bus Station
Castle, Chateau
Cathedral, Church
Cinema
Embassy, Consulate
Fountain
Hospital
Internet Cafe
Mounment
Museum
Police Station
Post Office
Pub or Bar
Ruins
Shopping Centre
Ski Field
Stately Home
Swimming Pool
Synagogue
Taxi Rank
Telephone
Theatre
Tourist Information
Vineyard
Zoo

Note: not all symbols displayed above appear in this book

LONELY PLANET OFFICES

Australia
Locked Bag 1, Footscray, Victoria 3011
☎ 03 8379 8000 fax 03 8379 8111
email: talk2us@lonelyplanet.com.au

USA
150 Linden St, Oakland, CA 94607
☎ 510 893 8555 TOLL FREE: 800 275 8555
fax 510 893 8572
email: info@lonelyplanet.com

UK
10a Spring Place, London NW5 3BH
☎ 020 7428 4800 fax 020 7428 4828
email: go@lonelyplanet.co.uk

France
1 rue du Dahomey, 75011 Paris
☎ 01 55 25 33 00 fax 01 55 25 33 01
email: bip@lonelyplanet.fr
www.lonelyplanet.fr

World Wide Web: www.lonelyplanet.com *or* AOL keyword: lp
Lonely Planet Images: www.lonelyplanetimages.com